Information Technology Strategy and Management: Best Practices

Eng K. Chew
University of Technology, Sydney, Australia

Petter Gottschalk
Norwegian School of Management, Norway

Information Science REFERENCE

INFORMATION SCIENCE REFERENCE

Hershey · New York

Director of Editorial Content:	Kristin Klinger
Assistant Development Editor:	Becca Beistline
Director of Production:	Jennifer Neidig
Managing Editor:	Jamie Snavely
Assistant Managing Editor:	Carole Coulson
Typesetter:	Carole Coulson
Copy Editor:	April Schmidt
Cover Design:	Lisa Tosheff
Printed at:	Yurchak Printing Inc.

Published in the United States of America by
Information Science Reference (an imprint of IGI Global)
701 E. Chocolate Avenue, Suite 200
Hershey PA 17033
Tel: 717-533-8845
Fax: 717-533-8661
E-mail: cust@igi-global.com
Web site: http://www.igi-global.com/reference

and in the United Kingdom by
Information Science Reference (an imprint of IGI Global)
3 Henrietta Street
Covent Garden
London WC2E 8LU
Tel: 44 20 7240 0856
Fax: 44 20 7379 0609
Web site: http://www.eurospanbookstore.com

Library of Congress Cataloging-in-Publication Data

Information technology strategy and management : best practices / Eng K Chew and Petter Gottschalk, editors.

p. cm.

Includes bibliographical references and index.

Summary: "This book explains the principles and methodologies for crafting and executing a successful business-aligned IT strategy - an integrated end-to-end process from business strategy to value delivery"--Provided by publisher.

ISBN 978-1-59904-802-4 (hardcover) -- ISBN 978-1-59904-805-5 (ebook)

1. Information technology--Management. 2. Strategic planning--Data processing. 3. Management information systems. I. Chew, Eng K. II. Gottschalk, Petter, 1950-

HD30.2.I5295 2009

004.068'4--dc22

2008023191

British Cataloguing in Publication Data
A Cataloguing in Publication record for this book is available from the British Library.

Table of Contents

Foreword

I write this foreword from an IT management practitioner's personal perspective. As the CIO of a commercial bank operating in a highly competitive marketplace, I find it difficult to stop thinking of better ways by which IT can innovate to help transform the bank's business and move on to the next level of success. As in other business enterprises, IT has always been playing a pivotal role in the banking industry. It is hard to imagine, for instance, how a bank would be able to continue to operate if the core banking system or the trading platform ceased to function, even for a short span of time. Moreover, banks must understand the market and its customers intimately in order to devise and introduce innovative products and services to retain existing and acquire new customers, particularly in retail banking. The critical dependency of banking business on IT, as in many other businesses, requires both business and IT managers to have a shared understanding of how IT enables the business to compete. Business must not take IT for granted to assume that any new business initiative will be delivered by IT (as if by natural order of things) with very little business involvement. Similarly, IT managers must not think IT is the savior of business and has the mandate to unitarily introduce new technological capabilities ahead of business needs or, even worse, devoid of business reality. Otherwise, a disastrous situation could arise where business and IT are disjointed and IT would in fact be destroying, instead of creating, business value. From my experience, to differentiate an enterprise, IT organizations must understand and think like business, and business must understand how IT can create value. These important practices and their underlying theories are well explained in this book, which I find very useful and refreshing.

In my organization, the technology and operation planning and support functions that I manage report directly into the President and CEO. As a member of the Executive, Management, and Operations Committees, as well as the chairperson of IT Committees, I am in a position to contribute directly in business decision making process at the highest level. Experience has taught me that, in nearly all cases, business is not about technology; it is about using technology to create value. Technology is nothing but a means to achieve the desired business goals, as so clearly explained and exemplified with real-life cases in this book. The best way to address the business–IT alignment is to treat it as a fundamental business operating principle, for instance by building IT teams along business lines, by sending IT managers to relevant business training programs, and by fostering close partnerships among them down to a personal level. Over time, the user community will develop an appreciation of IT capabilities and challenges, while IT people will garner a good understanding of the business priorities and issues. A simple but effective measurement of how well the two have worked as a team, in my view, is not just how often they come together for meetings, but more so for social gatherings. In our bank, there is a deep, shared business–IT understanding of how IT makes the competitive difference. Business and IT working in unison as a "single entity," from strategy creation to execution, has been central to our success. This is the gist of the practice of business–IT alignment, as so elegantly described in the book.

However, business realities and hence priorities are changing quickly, and the marketplace has become exceedingly competitive and unforgiving. In response, the organization as a whole and its IT group in particular has to continuously evolve to be more agile and robust. Given the always limited budget and hence resources available, it is crucial that both business and IT management stay focused on the company's key value propositions and build its core competencies around them. This rigorous strategic management practice is instrumental to effective IT strategy creation and execution. The book explains step-by-step and illustrates with a practical case example very clearly what business and IT managers must do to achieve effective strategic management. Business agility and cost optimization can also be achieved through a creative sourcing strategy, which combines a judicious mix of internal and external (outsourcing) resources to implement a business goal. This book gives an in-depth treatment of the theories and practices of outsourcing, which will help firms *"to assess what to outsource and how to succeed in an outsourcing arrangement."*

Many of the products we sell in banks, such as FX-Linked Deposits or Tax Loans, are highly market sensitive or have a very short lifespan. So time-to-market or time-to-value is extremely important. Not only must we nurture a culture of innovation with the attendant "high-speed" innovation process, but also have a strong knowledge management/sharing discipline to enable innovation. A product has to be built right the first time and there is no room for errors. To this end, the book provides an insightful analysis of business innovation principles and processes as well as the knowledge management capabilities that a firm must have to facilitate innovation. The book also offers insights on the principles and practices of enterprise architecture, IT investment, and IT governance, for example, using IT Portfolio Management as a tool to ensure IT organizations *"do the right thing"* and using architecture governance to ensure IT projects *"do the thing right."* If these practices are not properly understood and managed well, IT could become a show-stopper in enterprise transformation and growth, rather than a change agent and innovation driver. The book makes it abundantly clear the critical role the CIO plays in leading business innovation and IT governance practice—a finding that resonates with my personal experience.

While a considerable amount of research and publication has gone into the practice of business and IT alignment and, in a broader context, the IT strategy and management practices in recent years, there are few that can provide a comprehensive, holistic, and structured presentation of the related concepts, theories, methodologies, and approaches, and even less that can offer best practice guidelines on their implementations. This book is written by two former CIOs and current university professors. I have come to know personally one of the two authors, Professor Chew, as a seasoned professional-cum-academic, who has a unique blend and a distinguished record of industry experience and academic qualification. As such I believe he and his co-author, Professor Gottschalk, are best placed to provide IT practitioners with practical advice and guidance on the subject. I find this book as enlightening as it is rewarding to read, for it is not only structured to step through the most important issues and challenges we face every day, but also grounded its advice in practical solutions and real-world examples. I therefore recommend highly the book to both IT management practitioners and students alike. I will keep it close at hand. I hope its readers do as well.

Michael K. M. Leung
Senior Vice President & Chief Information Officer
China Construction Bank (Asia)
Hong Kong

Michael Leung *was appointed senior vice president and chief information officer of Bank of America (Asia) in March 2000.*[1] *In this capacity, he manages the bank's IT function in its entirety, including business systems design and development, project management, as well as production systems support and data center operations. In addition, Mr. Leung is also in charge of operations planning, product services, and corporate administration departments of the bank. Mr. Leung has over 25 years' local and international experience in information technology, specializing in the banking and finance industry. Before joining Bank of America (Asia), he was a senior manager at Standard Chartered Bank, overseeing service delivery systems as well as acquisition and merger activities for its consumer banking division in the Asia Pacific region. Previously, Mr. Leung was the head of the Business Research and Development Department at the Development Bank of Singapore, responsible for developing new business models and distribution channels for retail banking products and services. Prior to his banking assignments, Mr. Leung was a managing consultant at IBM Consulting Group and Price Waterhouse Management Consulting Services in Hong Kong and Australia. Immediately after his postgraduate study in Holland, Mr. Leung spent many years with the Dutch Philips Telecommunications and Data Systems, involved in the development and presales support of banking terminals and transactions processing systems. Mr. Leung holds a Master in Engineering from The Netherlands Universities Foundation and a Bachelor of Science from the Chinese University of Hong Kong. In his over two decades of career, Mr. Leung has attended executive training at London Business School, MIT Sloan School of Management, an honor diploma from Graduate School of Retail Bank Management of University of Virginia, among others. He is a fellow of the Hong Kong Computer Society and member of several professional bodies, and a seasoned speaker on a range of business and IT topics in regional conferences.*

ENDNOTE

1 The Bank is now renamed as China Construction Bank (Asia) following a strategic partnership arrangement with Bank of America and China Construction Bank.

Preface

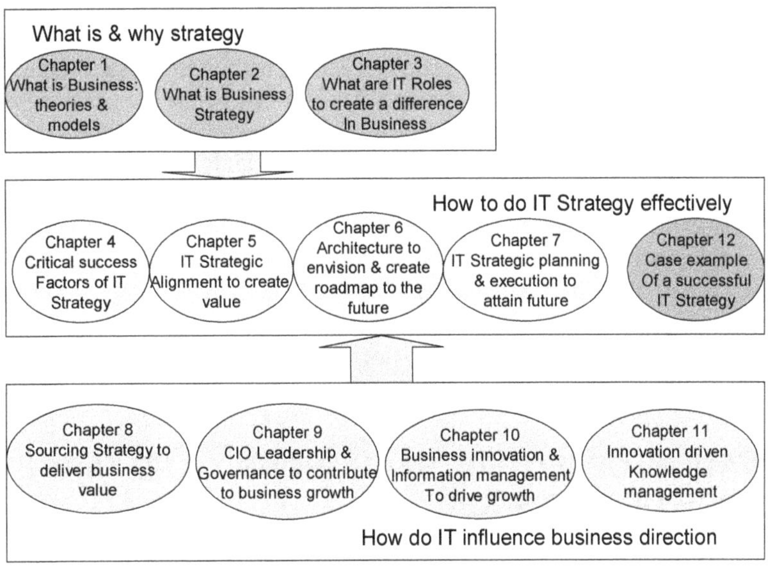

Organization of the Book

A METHOD TO SUCCESSFUL IT STRATEGY CREATION AND IMPLEMENTATION

Information technology is a means to the business end. IT is a tool designed to perform a business task within an overall business context. Thus, IT creates value only when it meets the business needs. A successful IT strategy must, therefore, align with the business, fully, from strategy setting, planning to detailed programs execution and delivery. The goal of IT strategy is to help business create and implement the unique competitive position to deliver value to customers and the firm. An effective IT strategy therefore starts with an in-depth understanding of the firm's business, mission, vision, strategic goals, and positioning in the competitive market environment. It must analyze the firm's business model, value configuration, and core business processes required for differentiation. Naturally, IT organizations should also possess in-depth knowledge of the ways in which IT can add value to the firm's business. From these insights the business-aligned IT strategy is developed, together with the requisite future target enterprise and technology architectures. The target enterprise architecture encapsulates the strategic direction and vision espoused by business and IT strategies. Architecture gap between the current and the target architectures defines the macrolevel business and information systems capabilities gap that needs to be closed in order to sustain the firm's competitive positioning for growth. The enterprise architecture thus serves as an important strategic planning tool. It plots the logical steps over a period necessary to evolve the current architecture and business environment towards the business vision. Enterprise architecture identifies the requisite strategic business programs which are prioritized and selected for implementation using IT program/project portfolio management principles, in line with business strategy and priorities. An end-to-end business–IT alignment from strategy to implementation and benefits realization is validated using a requirements traceability method. The IT strategy must also define the requisite core competency and sourcing strategies, as well as the organizational model and culture for successful execution. It incorporates and applies the IT governance as part of corporate governance for business programs prioritization and for governing disciplined programs execution to deliver the planned business outcomes. IT organizations are increasingly being expected by business to not only provide excellent service delivery but also contribute to business innovation. Indeed, business is beginning to look to chief information officers as a new source of business model innovation. Underpinning innovation is knowledge. IT strategy must therefore also encompass the need for innovation and knowledge management. IT strategy best practice is integral to IT management best practice. It requires leadership and strong disciplines in integrative and holistic management of business, people, process, and systems.

MOTIVATION, OBJECTIVE, BACKGROUND, AND TARGET AUDIENCE OF THIS BOOK

Information technology strategy is clearly a critical business discipline, which ensures IT delivers value to business. A well-crafted and executed IT strategy will deliver not only effective business operations but also competitively differentiated, innovative products, and services for the firm. Yet many business and government enterprises have found their IT organizations are, due to poor strategy and execution, either, misaligned with the business strategies or, even worse, so dysfunctional that business value is actually destroyed instead of being added by IT. With business investing close to $800 billion in IT in 2002 in United States alone (Jeffery & Leliveld, 2004), successful IT strategy and execution is undoubtedly crucial for firms aiming to achieve superior business performance.

The objective of this book is to explain the principles and methodologies for crafting and executing a successful business-aligned IT strategy, an integrated end-to-end process from business strategy to value delivery. A case example is provided to illustrate the key IT strategy and management concepts. It describes the strong disciplines required in integrative and holistic management of business, people, process, and systems for IT strategy and management best practice.

This is a practice-based textbook, derived from over 10 years of practical business experience in the subject area. To infuse academic rigor, we incorporate contemporary management and information system theories and research literature to help structure and explain the fundamentals of IT strategy and management practices. IT strategy is a business management discipline. The book is therefore business-oriented. It describes information technology strategy and management best practices from the business standpoint—step-by-step from basic models of firms to strategy management practices to business innovation practices.

The book has evolved from a current IT strategy course given to Master of Business (IT Management) program at University of Technology Sydney, where the enrolled students are mostly professional IT and business managers. It has also evolved from IT management courses taught at Fudan University (Shanghai), Nanyang University (Singapore), Norwegian School of Management (Norway), and Arab Academy (Egypt). The book will therefore be useful to all business and IT schools where MIS courses are taught, particularly to the graduate students. In addition, practicing business and IT managers responsible for their firms' IT services, from all industries, will find this book useful in their work.

Students and practitioners of IT management need to acquire a broad and deep body of knowledge to be proficient in IT strategy and management practices. The book provides the requisite body of knowledge. It is condensed below to give the readers a preview of the overarching concepts, principles, theories, methods, and the interrelationships of IT management practices that they need to master to become an effective IT manager and leader.

Body of Knowledge for Successful IT Strategy

Strategy is about creating a competitively differentiated position to win customers in the marketplace. Firms leverage their resources and the ways they conduct business (activity system or business model) to create the differentiated position (Porter, 1985; Priem & Butler, 2001). Two complementary theories of firm are commonly used to study business strategy: resource-based theory and activity-based theory.

Resource-based theory stipulates that the firm's performance and strategic advantage is differentiated by the internal resources and capabilities it possesses, rather than the external opportunities and threats dictated by the industry conditions (Barney, 2001; Hitt et al., 2001; Loewendahl, 2000; Priem & Butler, 2001). The theory holds that, in order to generate a sustainable competitive advantage, the firm's resources must provide economic value and must be unique, inimitable, nonsubstitutable, and not readily obtainable in factor markets. Thus, IT resources that are inimitable and valuable can be rent yielding. In particular, it is the unique combination of sophisticated IT infrastructure and skilled human resources (core competences) of the enterprise creating the differentiated customer value that is inimitable and valuable (Ravichandran & Lertwongsatien, 2005).

Activity-based theory of firm conceives the firm as a bundle of activities, as distinct from a bundle of resources in the resource-based theory (Sheehan, 2002). The activity-based model studies the firm's production function in value creation, transforming inputs to end products. It focuses on the flows of resources (but not the differences in stocks of resources) through a system of activities in creating economic value. From the activity-based theory, firms can configure its activities to create value, known as value configuration. Understanding the properties of value configuration is important as IT is inherently suitable as an aid to automation, coordination, and control of the activities within the configuration. Three types of value configuration can be used to model the firm: value chain (Porter, 1985), value shop, and value network (Stabell & Fjeldstad, 1998). Value chain is a firm that has a series or chain of primary activities comprising inbound logistics, production, outbound logistics, marketing and sales, and service. Economic value is created via efficient production of goods and services through this chain (Porter, 1985). This primary chain of activities is supported by secondary activities comprising infrastructure, human resources, technology development, and procurement. While value chain is modeled after manufacturing-based firms (fixed set of activities to produce standard products), it is less suited to modeling knowledge-intensive service firms (variable set of activities to produce customized solutions). This type of firms can be modeled by value shop (Stabell & Fjeldstad, 1998). Value shop is a firm that creates value by solving unique problems for customers and clients. In the value shop, activities are scheduled and resources are applied in a fashion that is dimensioned and appropriate to the needs of the client's problem. A value shop is characterized by five primary activities: problem finding and acquisition (by working with the client), problem solving, choice, execution, and control and evaluation (of how well the solution solves the problem). Control and evaluation feeds back to the problem finding in two ways: (a) solution is inadequate and problem-solving phase restarts anew, (b) solution is successful and the client may extend the problem scope and a new problem-solving phase starts. A value network is a firm that creates value by connecting clients and customers that are, or want to be, dependent on each other (Stabell & Fjeldstad, 1998). These companies distribute information, money, products, and services. While activities in both value chain and value shop are done sequentially, activities in value networks occur in parallel. The value is enhanced by "network effect"—the more the number and combination of customers and access points in the network, the more valuable the network is to the customers. The value network (firm) admits customers that complement each other, and establishes, monitors, and terminates direct and indirect relationships between customers. Examples of value network firms include telecommunication companies and financial institutions. Value networks perform three activities: (a) development of customer network through marketing and recruiting of new customers, (b) development of new services and improvement of existing services, and (c) development of infrastructure so that customer services can be provided more efficiently and effectively.

A related concept to value configuration is the business model of firm, which is also closely related the firm's business strategy. Business models explain how firms work; they identify who the customers are and define how the pieces of a business fit together as a system to create value to the customers at appropriate price so profit can be made (Magretta, 2002). Business model can be viewed as comprising three components: the offering, the unique configuration of activities and organization, and the (particularly rare and inimitable) resources. IT can be designed to contribute to the uniqueness of each of these three components (Hedman & Kalling, 2002). Business models consist of nine basic building blocks; they get implemented by translating the model into concrete elements such as a business structure (organizational model), business processes (workflow), and infrastructure and systems (Osterwalder & Pigneur, 2005). Business models are subject to change. Firms use the basic constructs of business models to analyze the impact of external forces to define how their business models (and thus IT environments) should change to sustain their competitive advantages. Four business model change approaches (realization, extension, renewal, and journey) can be adopted, depending on the firm's business strategy (Linder & Cantrell, 2000). Business models were popularized by the dot.com era. Numerous IT-enabled e-business models have been proposed, based on the firms' specific e-strategies. The basic principles of business model, which aims to profit from delivering highly valuable differentiated services to customers, must be adhered to by e-business models. It requires development of a sound e-strategy focused on value delivery to the customers. E-business can be classified into eight atomic e-business models (Weill & Vitale, 2002). These e-business models explain the roles, relationships among the firms' consumers, allies, suppliers, and identifies the major flows of products, information, and money, together with the price and benefits to the participants. The Hayes and Finnegan (2005) framework (encompassing economic control, supply chain integration, functional integration, innovation, and sourcing) can be used for determining a firm's appropriate e-business model.

Business-aligned IT strategy is developed in accordance with Porter's (1985) business strategy principles. Business strategy with a clear goal and a "continuity of direction" must be first defined. The strategy must have a unique value proposition supported by a distinctive value configuration. The strategy must also define how all the elements (resources and activities) of what the firm does fit together and reinforce each other. This usually involves making trade-offs. Corporate strategy shapes business and IT strategies, so different corporate roles must be understood. Firm uses strategic management discipline to formulate its strategic position, make strategic choices for the future, turn the strategy into action, and realize the benefits (Johnson & Scholes, 2002). Translating strategy into actions require strategic planning skills. Strategic planning is the process of deciding on the projects/programs that the organization will undertake and the appropriate amount of resources that will be allocated to each program over the next several years. Strategic planning practice performance can be measured from the perspectives of cost leadership, differentiation, focus, and intensity (Nayyar, 1993). Formal systematic strategic planning process has been found to be beneficial and it defines the key elements of strategic plan (Grant, 2003).

Resource-based strategy leverages the firm's unique resources and capabilities as a platform across many markets and products (Barney, 2001). Activity-based strategy allows the firm to gain a profitable position by configuring its activities using activity-based drivers such as scale, a unique configuration which is difficult for rivals to copy. In comparing the two strategies, resources are similar to drivers and capabilities to activities (Sheehan, 2002).

IT strategy and management must conform to the prevailing business/IT ethics. Business ethics can be studied via stakeholder theory, which is a theory of organizational management and ethics. Indeed all theories of strategic management have some moral content, though it is often implicit. Moral content in this case means that the subject matter of the theories are inherently moral topics (i.e., they are not amoral). Stakeholder theory is distinct because it addresses morals and values explicitly as a central feature of managing organizations. The ends of cooperative activity and the means of achieving these ends are critically examined in stakeholder theory in a way that they are not in many theories of strategic management (Phillips et al., 2003). Use of stakeholder theory in IT strategy research is a still subject for further study. In an IT strategy context, a stakeholder theory approach will describe the relationship as a nexus of cooperative and competitive interests possessing intrinsic value. IT strategy should ensure the design and use of information technology to be transparent and open to ongoing scrutiny by stakeholders such that the values of ethics are upheld, always. This is assured through diligent application of IT governance by business enterprises.

Competitive business strategy formulation requires competitive strategic analysis. Eight popular methods of strategy analysis are available: SWOT analysis, X-model, business direction, market strategy, competitive forces, product portfolio analysis, environmental analysis, and knowledge analysis. From analysis of each method, a strategic change can be determined and the corresponding IT system can be identified.

Internet technology will enable the reconfiguration of existing industries that had been constrained by high costs for communicating, gathering information, or accomplishing transactions. Internet-driven business strategy, known as e-strategy, has created successful new-generation companies such as eBay, Google, Amazon, and Yahoo. Differentiation is more sustainable than cost leadership strategy for e-business firms. In particular, an e-strategy will be able to achieve superior, sustainable performance through an "integrated strategy" discipline which strives to achieve *both* cost leadership and differentiation strategic positioning (Kim et al., 2004). E-strategy is also being adopted by traditional companies, such as GE and News Limited. E-strategy is developed through gaining insights on 10 fundamental properties of Internet, which include (Afuah & Tucci, 2003): mediating technology, universality, network externalities, distribution channel, time moderator, information asymmetry shrinker, infinite virtual capacity, low cost standard, creative destroyer, and transaction cost reducer. In-depth understanding of Internet capabilities in reshaping business models will give IT managers ability to influence business strategy to take advantage of, and incorporate, Internet into the business and IT strategies to keep firms competitive, adaptive, and responsive to changing market and external environments.

Alignment between business strategy and IT strategy is widely believed to improve business performance (Sabherwal & Chan, 2001). Elemental IT strategy comprises the business strategic direction and strategy outline, the enterprise architecture and attendant applications and technology infrastructure platforms, the requisite resources and capabilities (competence), and the organization model and management control (governance). Strategic management must be cognizant of the tightly coupled interrelationship between task, technology, structure, and people, which must be managed holistically to ensure strategic fit (Gottschalk, 2005).

Moreover, IT managers must anlyze and understand how IT can add value to firms organizationally. There are nine available models:

- **Model 1:** Benefits analysis identifies IT contributions to: rationalization benefits (personnel cost savings); control benefits (decision support); organizational benefits (team effectiveness and agility); and market benefits (revenue improvement).
- **Model 2:** Stages of IT organizational growth analysis identify the growing maturity of the firm's use of IT over the years, from data processing (for efficiency) to management information system (for effectiveness) to strategic information system (for competitiveness). Alternatively, the Nolan (1979) model of IT maturity growth can be used, which comprises: stage 1 – initiation (functional cost reduction), stage 2 – contagion (raid increase in all application areas), stage 3 – control (upgrade documentation, simplifying existing applications), stage 4 – integration (restructuring existing applications in a systems architecture), stage 5 – data (restructuring existing applications in a data architecture), stage 6 – architecture (application integration supporting information flows), stage 7 – (interorganizational) integration (intra and interorganizational communication), stage 8 – growth (systems connecting business with vendors and customers), stage 9 – reaction (extended infrastructure to support tailor-made applications).
- **Model 3:** Analysis of IT usage in management activities in a hierarchy of operational, tactical, and strategic management to identify the IT contributions.
- **Model 4:** Analysis of IT in business processes – business processes are activities organized, coordinated, resourced, and focused to produce goods and services of value to receivers and customers. They may appear in an intra or interorganization context.

IT adds value by automating and simplifying workflow for the repetitive manual processes.

- **Model 5:** Analysis of IT support for value configuration – IT value add is similar to Method 4, and other benefits are described in Chapter 1.
- **Method 6:** Analysis of IT value add via the King and Teo (1997) model of strategic integration – IT role in firm increases nonstrategic to competitively strategic as the firm matures from stage 1 – administrative integration (separate business and IT strategic planning) to stage 4 – full integration (joint development of business and IT strategies – dynamic strategic alignment). IT role can be analyzed in detail using ten benchmarks including, for example, role of IT function, primary role of IT executives, and performance criteria for the IT function.
- **Method 7:** Analysis of IT support for knowledge management – IT support is analyzed by a matrix of tasks (distribute knowledge, share knowledge, capture knowledge, and apply knowledge) and levels (end-user tools, who knows what, what they know, and what they think).
- **Model 8:** Analysis of IT support in e-business maturity growth – this analysis uses the Earl's six-stage e-business maturity model to show the increasing sophistication of IT and value add as the firm matures from stage 1 – external communication, through internal communication, e-commerce, e-business, e-enterprise to stage 6 – transformation.
- **Model 9:** Analysis of IT-enabled business transformation – as the name implies IT plays a critical role in this model. IT role and business influence increases as the firm evolves from level 1 – information technology efficiency, through information systems integration, business process change to level 4 – business design change.

Strategic alignment of IT to business is both a top management concern and also an important attribute of effective CIOs. A successful IT strategy must align with the business, fully, from strategy setting, planning to detailed programs execution, and delivery. The King and Teo (1997) model of strategic integration and the Luftman et al. (2004) strategic alignment model have been used in the end-to-end analysis. A fundamental principle common to all the critical success factors is "business and IT acting as one." This requires each IT task to be aligned with and justified by the business function it is designed to contribute, by which the business value is assessed. A basic requirement for success is that IT must be regarded as being part of the business, devoid of the us vs. them chasm (separating IT from the business) found in most traditional organizations where IT is viewed as a subservient role performing basically a back office function. This means the IT organization must, at a minimum, be at the sequential integration stage (2) of the King and Teo (1997) model. At this level, IT strategy and resources support and align with the business strategy, and IT executive proactively validates with the business executive to ensure the IT strategy does align with and implement the business strategy. Business and IT act as one behaviorally and organizationally via IT governance. IT governance ensures IT is "doing the right thing" to assure strategic alignment, "doing the thing right" to assure architecture compliance, and "getting it done well and realizing the benefits" to assure program portfolio management compliance (ITGI, 2006). The Y model for strategic management (Gottschalk, 2006) and the principles of corporate strategy can be used to analyze strategic planning alignment.

The Y model analyzes the gap between the desired and current business situation to identify the needs for change. The strategic plan is developed and implemented to fulfill the needs. The business and IT strategic plans comprise four key deliverables: enterprise architecture, portfolio management and program plans, core competencies, and sourcing strategy. Two critical disciplines for strategic program delivery are program portfolio management and program management. The former prioritizes and selects programs for implementation based on risk/return profiles and alignment with business strategy. The latter focuses on diligent, disciplined execution of the selected programs to budget and plan. Business benefits realization must be monitored against business (case) plan following completion of program implementation, using post implementation review process. With IT and business acting as one, IT strategy will be successful when business and IT alignment is validated in each phase of the end-to-end strategic management life cycle, namely:

- Direction setting – IT strategy is defined in line with and documented as part of the corporate strategy;
- Planning – the IT strategic plans clearly correspond to the respective business strategic plans and the business outcomes expcted of the IT plans are clearly described and justified in the business plans;
- Execution – each of the business programs constructed from the business and IT plans will have a business owner supported by a professional IT program manager responsible for on time and on budget delivery of the program, with the program outcomes (functionalities and benefits) clearly specified in business terms as targeted in the business plan;
- Outcomes – upon successful delivery of the program, each program is audited at selected milestones to ensure the intended business objectives and benefits are consistently delivered in accordance with the program's business case.

The critical organizational requirement of business and IT acting as one is founded on the rigor and discipline of IT governance.

IT managers need to recognize several critical conditions or factors for strategic alignment success, namely: shared method for business and IT strategic planning, process for stakeholder participation (shared domain knowledge between business and IT), and program management implementation to deliver stated benefits, top management involvement and support, clear business direction, business before technology, and communication and coordination (Earl, 1993; Reich et al., 2000). Strategic alignment has two dimensions: strategic fit of internal intangible assets with externally customer-focused strategy and functional integration between business and IT domains (Henderson & Venkatraman, 1993). Strategic alignment is a process of continuous adaptation due to changing external market and technology environments. A nonlinear adaptation using complex theory model is necessary to account for the co-evolution (Benbya & McKelvery, 2006). IT strategic alignment with a cost-reduction strategy is more able to deliver immediate tangible benefits to firms than a revenue-growth strategy; and profitability is shown to be higher when both business and IT strategies are rated high (Oh & Pinsonneault, 2007). An organization's strategic alignment maturity can be assessed by six criteria (Luftman et al., 2004): communication, competency/value measurement, governance, partnership, scope and architecture, and skills. The model is useful for assessing strategic alignment in each of the abovementioned four phases of strategic management life cycle.

The successful execution of IT strategy, both the implementation of the resulting strategic programs and the support and maintenance of the evolving enterprise IT environment, depends on IT strategic resources, especially IT people. Moreover, business performance and differentiation is determined by the firm's ability to configure internal and external strategic resources and capabilities, including IT resources and capabilities. According to resource-based theory of firm, unique combination of IT resources by themselves, or more likely, with other enterprise resources, which create significant value and are costly to imitate, will offer firm sustainable competitive advantage. In particular, six attributes of IT resources must be managed effectively in order to obtain competitive advantage: valuable, rare, exploitable, inimitable, nonsubstitutable, combinable, and immobile. Further, embedding IT within areas of the firm's core competency makes IT assets inimitable (Richardson & Lertwongsatien, 2005). This is explained by the difficulty for rivals to create similar bundles of complementary IT and organizational assets and, at the same time, understand the contributions of IT assets to firm performance.

Global companies and globalization of IT services require effective global IT management practice. Global IT management needs to balance the business needs of global (corporate) and local (business unit) organizations. This can be achieved by coordinating global IT functions (strategy, architecture, standards, and control) with local IT functions (local planning, integration of new applications, and operating the infrastructure and applications) in line with corporate strategy (Barton, 2003). Group CIO and IT leadership team need to effectively manage the natural tension arisen from three forces shaping global IT management: pooling of IT services, (selective) outsourcing of services, and dispersion of IT roles to business (Barton, 2003). The critical success factor is an effective IT governance to ensure business-IT alignment globally and locally.

Kaplan and Norton's (2004) strategy map accounts for Henderson and Venkatraman's (1993) strategic fit and functional integration dimensions in a series of cause–effect traceable relationships. Strategy map is an instructive tool for demonstrating strategic alignment.

Case examples of IT strategy development and implementation experiences of two Australian companies, a leading bank (CIO, 2003), and a leading retailer (Australian IT, 2005–2008), have been used to exemplify a practical application of basic concepts of business–IT alignment and the four-stage IT strategy management process. The retailer example highlights the business outcomes of a strategy-execution journey (reported over three-year duration) of IT-enabled strategic business transformation, which results in contribution of multibillion dollars of IT business value to the company's bottom line and gives it the distinct competitive advantage.

Enterprise architecture is a critical management tool for linking business and IT strategies to their disciplined execution (James et al., 2005). Enterprise architecture encapsulates the essence of business and IT strategies (Ross–Weill–Robertson, 2006). It provides structure, discipline, and a platform for articulating the firm's strategic imperatives in an integrative and holistic manner, functionally analogous to the working of a real-life enterprise. By adopting standardized terminology and definitions, business and IT stakeholders will be able to agree on the purpose, scope, content, and shape of the architecture. Thus, enterprise architecture serves as an integrator and translator of critical business and IT concepts by which business and IT stakeholders can assure strategic alignment across multiple perspectives. Much work has been expended on the principles and methods for developing business-aligned enterprise architecture to guide the development of IT solutions to implement the business strategy (Zachman, Spewak, TOGAF, Ross-Weill-Robertson, Gartner, RM-ODP, POSIX, OMG, eTOM). Enterprise architecture essentially is a formal description of the enterprise business context, including the business strategy, and the supporting information system architecture which aligns with the business context. It comprises of four interrelated viewpoints, each representing the perspective of a type of enterprise stakeholders, namely: business architecture, information architecture, application architecture, and technology architecture. Business architecture defines the firm's overarching business strategy, business model, organizational model, and underpinning core business processes. Information (or data) architecture defines the information value-chain model and information (data) entities which support the business functions defined in the business architecture (Spewak, 1992). Application architecture defines the business functional systems of the enterprise; they interact with each other in accordance with the predefined business processes (business architecture) consuming and producing business information elements defined by the information architecture (Spewak, 1992). Technology architecture defines the infrastructure platforms and distribution which support the applications, data, and business functions of the respective application, information, and business architectures (Spewak, 1992; TOGAF, 2007).

Enterprise architecture provides an integrative insight on the enterprise strategy, its environmental (market and technology) trends, the target future business state, and the principles and guidance to get there. It defines the firm's target future state architecture model for the business and information systems. It prescribes the principles of architecture solution design of information systems to ensure compliance with business strategic requirements and systems operational integrity requirements such as scalable performance, agility to adapt to business change, security, and manageability. The gap of current and target architecture defines the scope of business and systems changes required and the migration steps over a period to achieve the business strategy and vision. The gap is translated into an integrated IT strategic plan (road map) of business programs. Implementation of the IT strategic roadmap allows enterprise to close the gap and attain the target future business state. Enterprise architecture guides the development and implementation of these programs, in line with the business priorities, to ensure reliable delivery of the desired business outcomes stipulated in the business/IT strategy. Architecture governance as part of IT governance ensures architecture solutions for system development will comply with the enterprise architecture principles and guidance. Architecture governance ensures ("IT do the right thing" so that) business solutions will not only deliver the expected value (as stipulated in the business case), but also ensure they will integrate into the target enterprise system designed to give the firm the competitive advantage. Enterprise architecture, therefore, is a critical business tool for managing and implementing business changes, attaining business agility and strategic alignment.

Strategic planning and program implementation is performed systematically and diligently via the traditional Y model, specifically the stages 4 (seek for alternative actions), 5 (select actions and make an action plan), 6 (implement plan and describe results), and 7 (evaluate results). However, apart from disciplined program management, success also depends on skillful management of potential barriers to implementation. An important issue relates to human factor of change management. First, there is the need for business and IT professionals acting as one to ensure strategic alignment. Then, there is the human nature to resist change across both IT and business/user communities. Strategy implementation must manage the human factor, including engagement, consultation, communication, education, training, and commitment, as a key project deliverable from strategy creation to benefits realization.

An alternative, advanced, strategic planning practice is via enterprise architecture. The business and systems (architecture) gap needs to be decomposed into logical work packages for staged implementation as part of strategy execution (Spewak, 1992). Execution is the most critical part of strategic management; only by diligent and disciplined execution will the value of strategy be materialized. The architecture gap analysis offers systemic and integrative assessment of the business—business operating model, value configuration, core business processes, domain by domain from customer front-end to back-end supply chain and partners network, together with systems architectural changes—required to realize the business strategy. Gap analysis is performed on every viewpoint of the enterpise architecture. The scope and extent of architecture change required constitutes the overall scope of the strategic programs that need to be defined and developed to deliver the objectives of the business strategy. These programs will be prioritized by IT governance using IT portfolio management principles. Their implementations in time sequence will define the migration path of the current enterprise architecture towards the target future state architecture. The critical success factors for enterprise architecture and strategic planning are: executive management commitment and strong project leadership skills (Spewak, 1992). A key benefit of architecture approach is that the architecture solution design for each strategic program will be guided by the enterprise architecture principles and architecture direction. This is what the IT Governance Institute calls "doing the thing right" governace (ITGI, 2006).

The architecture-driven strategic plan will guide which projects to select, which to continue, and which to decommission. Selection implies judicious resource allocation including technology assets, business processes, human resources and competencies, and potentially customer and partner resources. Program/project selection requires financial investment, thus judicious consideration of risk/return and cost of each IT program/project proposal. The process for selecting the "right" IT projects to invest in is called IT portfolio management (ITPM). It unites business and IT executives to work together to make the "right" strategic decision. Thus ITPM provides a sound business communication tool for business and IT executives to jointly manage the execution of the mutually aligned business and IT strategies. It focuses on more on value maximization and cost optimization, rather than solely on cost reduction (Cameron, 2006; Jeffery & Leliveld, 2004; Luftman et al., 2004; Weill & Aral, 2006). IT portfolio is a categorized set of assets (the outputs) and investments (the inputs). A three-category approach is commonly used: operate the business, grow the business, and transform the business (Cameron, 2006). Another well known approach categorizes IT investment portfolio into four classes (Weill & Aral, 2006): *Infrastructure* asset provides shared services to be used by multiple applications to allow for future business growth as well as cost reduction through standardization, rationalization, and consolidation. *Transactional* asset is for efficiency improvement and cost reduction through automation of repetitive business processes. *Informational* asset is for business intelligence, accounting, reporting, strategic decision support, compliance, and communication. *Strategic* asset is for developing new products and services or business processes to enter new markets and gain strategic competitive advantage. Typical IT portfolio mix ranges for an average firm are: operate-the-business (50–80%), grow-the-business (10–35%), transform-the-business (0–25%) (Cameron, 2006). Alternatively, the average portfolio mix could be: 46% infrastructure, 26% transactional, 17% informational, and 11% on strategic applications (Weill & Aral, 2006). The optimal portfolio mix varies according to the firm's value discipline strategy: product leadership, customer intimacy, or operational excellence (Marchand et al., 2001).

Despite the critical importance of ITPM to business value creation, Jeffery and Leliveld (2004) found in a survey of 130 Fortune 1000 CIOs in 2003 that only 89% were aware of ITPM, and 65% believed ITPM produces business value. The reason for this patchy ITPM performance is due to the CIOs' different levels of ITPM practice maturity. For example, 4.5% of the respondents are at the lowest—*ad hoc*—level of maturity; 24.5% at the second—*defined*—level of maturity; 54% at the third—*managed*—level; and 17% at the most mature—*synchronous*—level (Jeffery & Leliveld, 2004). Some of the barriers to ITPM success are the same as poor strategic alignment skills, such as difficulty of quantifying business value, poor communication between IT and business, IT staff's lack of business skills, and business executives' lack of understanding of and low respect for IT. A sensible solution to the barriers could be *staged implementation* with a clear *roadmap* for capability upgrade, supported by extensive training and education programs. Most importantly IT organizations should involve (engage) and inform business people continuously, from the beginning (Jeffery & Leliveld, 2004). To maximize IT value, firm needs to define, under IT governance, its target future IT portfolio mix; to understand its IT asset class performance and benchmarks; to re-weigh and balance, transparently, the portfolio for strategic alignment and risk-return profile; to incorporate the IT portfolio approach into the IT governance framework; and to learn from post-implementation reviews and formal training (Weill & Aral, 2006). ITPM is an advanced management practice, typically taken by firms with higher maturity in IT management practice. Its adoption by firms is recommended to maximize business return on IT investments. To put IT portfolio management into practice firms require three key components: ITPM framework and standardized process; tools for "what-if" analysis of IT project portfolio; and a common business taxonomy for communication and governance[1] (Maizlish & Handler, 2005).

Strategic alignment of IT resources is achieved through CIO aligning IT strategy and the requisite resources to (particularly the core competencies of) business strategy. CIO and IT become enablers of corporate and business strategies when IT resources become a corporate strategic resource. Attainment and sustenance of this status requires ongoing proactive business engagement supported by disciplined application of human resource management best practice. This practice is also illustrated by the case example of a leading Asia Pacific regional corporation CLP Group's IT strategy formulation and execution, described in detail at the end of the book—specifically, the formulation and execution CLP's IT organization capital strategy.

IT sourcing is concerned with judicious deployment of internal and external IT resources to fulfill business objectives. IT managers must analyze the sourcing opportunities (Lacity & Willcocks, 1998) and threats (Barthelemy, 2003b) from the ways in which the IT functions are organized (Agarwal & Sambamurty, 2002) and define up-front the desirable performance objectives (Domberger et al, 2000). Sourcing strategy is produced as a result of analysis of business strategy (and, where available, past experience) and attendant requirements for strategic resources. Sourcing strategy serves as the logic underlying the firm's outsourcing decisions – such as degree of integration (selective or comprehensive outsourcing), allocation of control (fees for service or partnership), or contract performance periods. Outsourcing success can be measured by: strategic competence, cost efficiency and technology catalysis (Lee et al 2004). Empirical evidence shows that carefully crafted IT sourcing strategies result in more successful IT outsourcing and increase the overall performance of the firm (Barthélemy, 2003a). Outsourcing success can be measured from business and user perspective (Lee & Kim, 1999). The former is motivated by the promise of strategic, economic and technological benefits, while the latter is by the quality of offered services.

Underpinning the move toward outsourcing has been a confluence of structural and theoretical changes in the nature of business and organizations dating back approximately two decades. Theorists have suggested that the changing nature of competition has resulted from two factors: (a) globalization of commerce engendering worldwide competition, and (b) technology developments that have changed basic business processes related to time and distance. Globalization and technology have placed enormous pressure on firms to cut costs and improve efficiency in the interests of self-preservation (Clott, 2004).

Kaiser and Hawk (2004) argue that there is currently an evolution of offshore software development from outsourcing to cosourcing. Five recommendations are obtained, from the experience of a financial institution, for others on structuring offshore outsourcing relationships: (1) understand where cosourcing is applicable, (2) define and develop the appropriate in-house IT competencies, (3) build trust but avoid building a binding relationship, (4) foster mutual understanding of ethnic and corporate cultures, and (5) map out a progression to cosourcing.

More and more firms are adopting a new practice known as transformational outsourcing to facilitate rapid organizational change, launch new strategies and to reshape company boundaries – a form of business model innovation (Linder & Cantrell 2000). While this requires senior executive leadership, dramatic organizational performance improvements have been reported by many firms. To help firms assess what to outsource and how to succeed in an outsourcing arrangement, eleven theories concerned with outsourcing can be used (Gottschalk and Solli-Sæther 2006). The theories are: core competencies, resource-based, transactional cost, contractual, neoclassical economic, partnership and alliance, relational exchange, and agency. In developing sourcing strategies, IT managers can leverage from the experiences of several alternatives for sourcing strategies reported by Schniederjans et al (2004), Lacity & Willcocks (2000b), Lacity et al (1996), Laudon & Laudon (2005), and Barthelemy & Geyer (2004), and from the case studies performed by Gottschalk & Solli-Sæther (2006).

Judicious resource allocation to strategic programs and initiatives is the key to successful strategy execution. A sound IT governance lead by a disciplined Chief Information Officer (CIO) is a necessary condition for successful IT strategy execution. IT governance defines the firm's decision rights and accountability framework to encourage the desirable behaviors in the management and use of IT (Weill and Ross 2004). Distinct from IT management which focuses on effective management of IT operations to deliver quality IT services, IT governance focuses on performing and transforming IT to meet present and future demands of the business and external customers (Grembergen et al 2004). IT governance includes enterprise architecture governance and IT portfolio management governance and outsourcing governance. Research has shown that IT governance has enabled top-performing firms to generate superior returns on their IT investments (Weill and Ross 2004). Outsourcing governance model consists of four elements: contracts, principles, resources, and activities. Governance issues for each element evolve with outsourcing lifecycle which comprises three stages: formation, operation and outcome – for instance, contracts are concerned with transactions at the formation stage but evolve to relationships and partnerships at the outcome stage. The eleven outsourcing theories can also help both the client company and the outsource vendor analyze how to be successful in the relationship (Gottschalk and Solli-Sæther 2006). IT governance demands strong IT leadership to ensure success. From IT governance standpoint, CIO plays an astute resource allocator and entrepreneurial roles (Useem and Harder 2000). Both roles require strong understanding of business and competitive markets to excel. Strong leadership also renders governance process more efficient and effective. From outsourcing standpoint, CIO needs to be skilled in strategic thinking, deal making, partnership governing and managing change (Useem and Harder 2000). In hyper-competitive markets, the 'new' CIO must excel in both business and technology capabilities, as well as being organizationally (some says politically) savvy. These capabilities allow the CIO to lead IT organizations towards high level of maturity in all core practices: business/IT strategic alignment, strategic integration, enterprise architecture, IT portfolio management, service management, knowledge management and business innovation. When IT organization becomes a highly recognized key contributor to business success, CIO's leadership standing will be such that business will be seeking his/her input for future growth strategy (Broadbent and Kitzis 2005). Influencing, shaping business expectations, conceiving and implementing business model innovation may become the new CIO's core focus. It may even pave the way for possible growth into becoming a future CEO!

Business innovation is an increasingly important discipline in which the CIO must become skillful. To contribute to company growth, CIOs must be skillful in product, service and process innovation. To help transform the business, CIOs must be capable of conceiving business concept/model innovation (Hamel 2000, IBM 2006) through creative use of disruptive technologies. IT organizations must be capable of investing resources in a portfolio of incremental innovations (product and service improvement) for incremental revenue growth, and higher risk radical or disruptive innovations (business model transformation) for dramatic profit growth. IT organizations must grasp the characteristics and scale of innovation. To become an innovator, IT must first win business trust and respect by becoming an excellent IT service provider with high quality and reliable service 7x24x365. Then, IT must improve its maturity to level 5 of IT-enabled transformation – business direction change (Venkatraman 1994). At this level, IT must have simultaneously attained level 5 of strategic alignment process – optimized process (Luftman et al 2004), where strategic integration is norm (King and Teo 1997), and level 4 of IT portfolio management – synchronized process (Jeffery and Leliveld 2004). At this level, too, IT and the firm must possess all three information capabilities of information behaviors and values, information management practice, and information technology practice (Marchand et al 2001); and, more importantly, be able to concurrently manage their interactions. For example, at this level of maturity, firm's knowledge workers will be proactive in sensing dynamic external market and technology environmental changes, and taking timely action on the new 'intelligence' to create an innovative response – be it a new product idea or strategy repositioning – which will strengthen the firm's competitive position. IT will add value in three ways: provide the IT infrastructure to streamline the innovation process (with environmental sensors, collaborative and knowledge management tools, and customer feedback loop), provide the IT solution for new product idea, and create the innovative idea as a result of detection of emerging market or technology environmental changes. This is the ultimate level of IT management excellence. To prepare for the journey of business innovation excellence, IT organizations must understand the conditions for and drivers of innovation, and investigate the issues surrounding innovation process, infrastructure and management measurement. An organization's innovation capability is shaped by the leadership agenda (Barsh et al 2007). CIOs must lead by example, and actively create and sustain an innovative IT climate (Watts & Henderson 2006) and the associated culture that encourages and promotes innovation across the whole IT organization.

A firm's innovation capabilities are underpinned by its knowledge and knowledge management capabilities – that is "ability to absorb and put to use new knowledge" (Adams et al, 2006). Knowledge management contributes to value creation by enhancing: intellectual asset management, operational efficiency, customer and competitor intelligence, continuous improvement, organizational learning, product and service innovation and time to market (Metaxiotis and Psarras 2006). To leverage knowledge management for business innovation, IT leaders must understand the basic principles, theories and practices of knowledge management. Extending resource-based theory of firm to knowledge-based, the success of firms is not only based on the economics of the contracts it implements, but also on its heterogeneous stocks and flows of knowledge (Grover and Davenport 2001). Companies having superior knowledge are able to coordinate and combine their traditional resources and capabilities in new and distinctive ways, providing more value to their customers than can their competitors (Zack 1999). Knowledge, especially context-specific, tacit knowledge embedded in complex organizational routines and developed from experience, tends to be unique and difficult to imitate (Zack 1999). To gain a knowledge-based strategic advantage, firms need to understand the characteristics of knowledge. Knowledge is information combined with experience, context, interpretation, reflection, intuition and creativity. There are three categories of knowledge, with increasing level of sophistication: core (to stay in business), advanced (to remain competitively viable) and innovative (to lead entire industry) knowledge (Zack 1999). This strategic knowledge framework helps firms conduct strategic knowledge gap analysis to define their business and knowledge strategies. Knowledge management is a discipline focused on systematic and innovative methods, practices, and tools for managing the generation, acquisition, exchange, protection, distribution, and utilization of knowledge, intellectual capital and intangible assets (Montana 2000). There are three schools of knowledge management: the economic school, the organizational school, and the strategic school (Earl 2001). The economic school has a focus of income, where the aim is to exploit knowledge assets (i.e. incremental innovation). The organizational school has a focus of networks, where the aim is knowledge pooling (e.g. Socialization, Externalization, Combination, Internalization SECI process). The strategic school has a focus of competitive advantage, where the aim is to identify, exploit and explore knowledge capabilities (as the essence of the firm's strategy). Firms may choose a combination of principles from these schools to guide their knowledge management strategies. Commonly, from IT-enabling perspective, firms adopt a dual codification (automation) and personalization (people network) strategy, with one being more dominant than the other (typically 80/20 ratio) (Hansen et al 1999). Three variant strategies are identified for three different types of businesses: stock strategy for efficiency-driven business, flow strategy for experience-driven business, and growth strategy for expert-driven business (Hansen et al 1999). A Chief Knowledge Officer (CKO) is often appointed to lead corporate-wide knowledge management initiative in the organization. The CKO role is an important one for both operational and symbolic reasons (Grover & Davenport 2001). CKO is responsible for knowledge-based innovations in the firm. CKO evangelizes the business value of knowledge management to get the whole organization embrace sound knowledge management practice both operationally and behaviorally. CKO leads the development and implementation the organization's knowledge management strategy (to close the strategic knowledge gap) in line with business strategy. CKO needs to be an intrapreneur (Antoncic & Hisrich 2001), skilful in knowledge design (Davonport & Prusak 1998, Earl & Scott 1999) and knowledge architecture (Applehans et al. (1999).

Eleven distinct IT requirements of knowledge management emerge: interaction between information and knowledge; interaction between tacit and explicit knowledge; knowledge management strategy; combination of SECI process; explicit transfer of common knowledge;

link knowledge to uses; treat knowledge as an intellectual asset in the economic school; treat knowledge as mutual resource in the organizational school, treat knowledge as a strategy in the strategy school; value configuration determines knowledge needs in primary activities; and, incentive alignment (Alavi and Leidner 2001, Hansen et al 1999, Ba et al 2001).

The source of strategic advantage lies with the application of knowledge. IT can enhance the speed of knowledge integration and application by codifying and automating organizational routines. Workflow automation and rule based expert systems are example applications. IT can also facilitate each of the four knowledge processes of creation, storage and retrieval, transfer and application (Alavi and Leidner 2001). In short, IT can improve knowledge management to support business innovation for competitive advantage.

A case example of CLP Group, Hong Kong illustrates the enormous business value and competitive advantage that companies can expect to gain from meticulous formulation and execution of the business-aligned IT strategy. CLP's strategic alignment process adheres to the business and IT strategy concepts and principles and IT management best practices described in above. Using the Kaplan & Norton (2004) strategy map technique, the case example shows that CLP's IT strategy is aligned to the business strategy through three core strategic themes: regulatory and corporate governance compliance (part of CLP brand strategy), customer service differentiation, and IT organization capital alignment to contribute to business growth.

In summary, IT strategy and management best practices will not only deliver superior IT service performance to achieve operational excellence, but also business innovation to realize customer intimacy and product leadership strategies for long term growths. This requires CIO and IT organizations to have deep business knowledge, and to diligently plan, develop and manage their core competencies to attain, and with an organizational culture to match, over a period, a high level of maturity in a range of practices: service management, strategic alignment, enterprise architecture, IT portfolio management, IT governance, program management, outsourcing, IT-enabled business transformation, knowledge management and business innovation. Above all, CIOs need to create an innovative IT climate and trusting culture to help shape the business direction and contribute to business growth.

OVERVIEW OF CHAPTERS

The book is organized into three logical groups as shown in the figure below. Chapters I, II, and III form the group addressing "what is and why strategy." This group is targeted at students of IT strategy and management practices. IT practitioners may be able to skip it without loss of continuity.

Chapters IV, V, VI, VII, and XII form the group addressing "how to do IT strategy effectively." They form the basic and necessary knowledge base for successful IT strategy. In particular, Chapter XII is a case example of a successful IT strategy in practice. Both IT management practitioners and students are recommended to read these chapters.

Chapters VIII, IX, X, and XI form the group addressing "how do IT organizations influence business direction." This knowledge is required to help IT managers influence business direction and contribute to business growth. Both IT management practitioners and students are recommended to read these chapters. Overview of the chapters is as follows.

Chapter I introduces and explains the theories, basic principles, business models, and value configurations of firms with a view to identifying ways in which IT could play a role and make a difference to firm's performance. A complementary set of theories pertaining to IT strategy are the resource-based theory and activity-based theory of firm.

Chapter II explains the principles of business and corporate strategy, strategic management, strategic planning, and the methods for strategy analysis.

Chapter III reviews the issue of alignment between business and IT strategies, and describes nine organizational analyses of how IT can add value to business

Chapter IV examines the critical success factors of IT strategy, holistically, across four phases of the strategic management life cycle from strategy formulation to planning to execution and to value delivery and monitoring end-to-end. It stipulates that IT and business must act as one in producing the corresponding business and IT strategy deliverables in each of these phases.

Strategic alignment, defined as the alignment of IT to business strategy, is the cornerstone of an effective IT strategy. Chapter V discusses in detail the principles of strategic alignment. It describes a method for achieving strategic alignment in each of four phases of IT strategy identified in Chapter IV. Two case examples (a bank and a retailer) companies are used to help illustrate the practical application of the strategy concepts.

A critical management tool for linking business and IT strategies to their disciplined execution is enterprise architecture. Enterprise architecture assures business and IT strategic alignment across all perspectives of business, information, application, and technology. Chapter VI reviews the principles and various well-known models of enterprise architecture. Enterprise architecture defines the firm's target future state architecture of the business and associated information systems as defined by its business/IT strategy. It identifies the gap of current architecture and prescribes the architecture principles for guiding the firm in migrating (strategy implementation/execution) towards that target future state, stage by stage.

The decomposition of the architecture gap into work packages for staged implementation is part of strategy execution. Chapter VII focuses on strategy execution, the most critical part of strategy management as the promised value of strategy can only be realized via diligent and disciplined execution. It reviews the basic models and practices of strategic program and portfolio planning and management. The portfolio of programs (each comprising projects of similar strategic theme) constitutes the evolutionary logical stages that the firm will invest in, at a desired risk/return ratio defined by portfolio and IT governance, to deliver the maximum business value while migrating towards the target enterprise architecture.

Business performance and differentiation is determined by the firm's ability to configure internal and external strategic resources and capabilities, including IT resources and capabilities. Chapter VIII reviews strategic IT resources and how they can be aligned to the organization's strategy and improve firm performance. In particular it discusses the transformational power and theories of sourcing strategy which allow firms to combine internal and external (outsourced) resources to obtain sustainable strategic advantage.

Judicious resource allocation to strategic programs and initiatives is the key to successful strategy execution. A sound IT governance lead by a disciplined chief information officer (CIO) is a necessary condition for successful IT strategy execution. This is the focus of Chapter IX. It describes the basic principles of IT governance, linking it to architecture and portfolio governance described in previous chapters and demonstrating its application to governing outsourcing relationships. It describes the CIO leadership behaviors required to lead and govern a modern business-savvy and mature IT organization.

Chapter X reviews an increasingly important discipline in which the CIO must become skillful—business innovation. To contribute to company growth, CIOs must be skillful in product, service, and process innovation. To help transform the business, CIOs must be capable of conceiving business concept/model innovation through creative use of disruptive technologies. This chapter reviews how information and IT management practices can contribute to business innovation.

A firm's innovation capabilities are underpinned by its knowledge and knowledge management capabilities, that is, "ability to absorb and put to use new knowledge." Chapter XI reviews innovation-driven knowledge management practices. It reviews the characteristics of knowledge as a strategic resource and its relationship to strategy. The chapter describes in detail the various approaches to knowledge management and knowledge management strategy for value creation. It concludes by relating IT to supporting knowledge management to cover the full spectrum of IT management practices expected in running modern enterprises.

The book concludes by describing a case example of the business-aligned IT strategy of CLP Group, Hong Kong in Chapter XII. The case example illustrates a successful practical application of IT strategy principles and concepts, specifically strategy maps principles, described in previous chapters. Success is measured by the business value CLP has accrued through meticulous formulation and execution of its business-aligned IT strategy. It can therefore be used as a guiding example of "how to effectively develop and execute a business-aligned IT strategy."

ENDNOTE

1 IT portfolio management governance is a subset of IT governance. Maizlish and Handler (Chapter 3, 2005) regard people and governance as the most important success factor of IT portfolio management best practice. They recommend (p91) adopting the CoBIT (Control Objectives for Information and Related Technology) framework for managing and controlling IT risks in line with business risks and objectives.

Acknowledgment

This book was written when one of the authors, Professor Eng Chew, held the UTS-Gartner Chair of Business and IT Strategy (2005–2008) teaching IT strategy and conducting IT management research in the Faculty of Information Technology, University of Technology Sydney (UTS). Professor Chew expresses his deep gratitude to Gartner's sponsorship and professional support during this period, which has allowed him to work with many leading Gartner research analysts and Gartner clients. He also thanks Gartner for permission to use Gartner material on Gartner Enterprise Architecture in the book.

Professor Chew also thanks UTS for the employment opportunity to transition from industry to academia allowing him to bring his experience to the classroom. Thanks also go to his graduate students (professionals from industry) in IT strategy over the last three years, who have indirectly contributed to the book through their many work-related insightful questions during class. It has been a most stimulating and rewarding experience.

Professor Chew is grateful to many practicing CIOs for their helpful discussions, many of whom have also come to give guest lectures to his class at UTS. In particular, he wants to thank Mr. Joe Locandro, Director, Group Information Technology, CLP Group, Hong Kong, and CLP Group for permission to use CLP IT strategy as a case example for the book. In particular, heartfelt appreciation is due to Mr. Locandro for the numerous hours of interviews and discussions; Chapter 12 owes a lot to Mr. Locandro's work. Sincere thanks also go to Mr. Michael Leung, Senior Vice President and CIO, China Construction Bank (Asia), Hong Kong, for agreeing to author the Foreword and for sharing his inner thoughts on IT management and leadership practices.

Thanks also are due to Norwegian School of Management, Oslo, for hosting Professor Chew's visit in 2007 to work on the book with Professor Petter Gottschalk. UTS research seed grant which supported this project is also gratefully acknowledged.

Last but not least, Professor Chew expresses his deepest thanks to his wife Jan, son Eugene, and daughter Elaine for their encouragement and understanding, particularly Jan for her patience and constant support without which the book would not have been possible.

Eng K. Chew
Professor of Business & IT Strategy
Faculty of Engineering and Information Technology
University of Technology Sydney
August 2008

Chapter I
Theories and Models of Business Firms

INTRODUCTION

A general understanding of business firms is required in order to be able to develop business and IT strategies. This chapter will present the resource-based theory of the firm, the activity-based theory of the firm, and the firm in terms of its value configuration, business model, and e-business models. These theories and models describe conceptually how the firm is constructed and resourced in delivering uniquely differentiated customer value in sustainable ways. It highlights the ways in which IT is used in the process of value and revenue creation for the firm using the chosen value configuration. It also classifies the ways in which Internet-based business strategy, known as *e-strategy*, may be represented as e-business models. The purpose of IT strategy, which is the core subject of this book, is about analyzing the business vision, mission, and strategy and defining the value configuration (business process or business model) and the attendant IT architectural model from which the requisite IT infrastructure to support or enable the firm's business operating model is designed and implemented. It is hoped that by illustrating to the readers the varying contexts in which IT can add value to the business in each of the value configurations or e-business models, the integral nature of the ways that IT has embedded in our business today can be better appreciated.

An understanding of firm theories and value configurations is important to later discussions of the topics in the book. The resource-based theory is applied to understand resources needed for e-business, sourcing, and governance. An important resource is knowledge in terms of know-what, know-how, and know-why. Knowledge management theory and principles and their relevance to business innovation will be discussed in Chapter XI of the book.

RESOURCE-BASED THEORY OF THE FIRM

According to the resource-based theory of the firm, performance differences across firms can be attributed to the variance in the firms' resources and capabilities. Resources that are valuable, unique, and difficult to imitate can provide the basis for firms' competitive advantages. In turn, these competitive advantages produce positive returns. According to Hitt, Bierman, Shimizu, and Kochhar (2001), most of the few empirical tests of the resource-based theory that have been conducted have supported positive, direct effects of resources. An important and often critical resource is information systems/information technology (IS/IT) applications in the firm.

The essence of the resource-based theory of the firm lies in its emphasis on the internal resources available to the firm, rather than on the external opportunities and threats dictated by industry conditions. Firms are considered to be highly heterogeneous, and the bundles of resources available to each firm are different. This is both because firms have different initial resource endowments and because managerial decisions affect resource accumulation and the direction of firm growth as well as resource utilization (Loewendahl, 2000).

The resource-based theory of the firm holds that, in order to generate sustainable competitive advantage, a resource must provide economic value and must be presently scarce, difficult to imitate, nonsubstitutable, and not readily obtainable in factor markets. This theory rests on two key points: first, that resources are the determinants of firm performance and, second, that resources must be rare, valuable, difficult to imitate, and nonsubstitutable by other rare resources. When the latter occurs, a competitive advantage has been created (Priem & Butler, 2001).

Resources can simultaneously be characterized as valuable, rare, nonsubstitutable, and inimitable. To the extent that an organization's physical assets, infrastructure, and workforce satisfy these criteria, they qualify as resources. A firm's performance depends fundamentally on its ability to have a distinctive, sustainable competitive advantage, which derives from the possession of firm-specific resources (Priem & Butler, 2001).

The resource-based theory is a useful perspective in strategic management. Research on the competitive implications of such firm resources as knowledge, learning, culture, teamwork, and human capital, was given a significant boost by resource-based theory. This theory indicates it is these kinds of resources that are most likely to be sources of sustainable competitive advantage for firms (Barney, 2001). We will return to discussion of knowledge management and business innovation in Chapter XI.

Firms' resource endowments, particularly intangible resources, are difficult to change except over the long term. For example, although human resources may be mobile to some extent, capabilities may not be valuable for all firms or even for their competitors. Some capabilities are based on firm-specific knowledge, and others are valuable when integrated with additional individual capabilities and specific firm resources. Therefore, intangible resources are more likely than tangible resources to produce a competitive advantage. In particular, intangible firm-specific resources such as knowledge allow firms to add value to incoming factors of production (Hitt et al., 2001).

Resource-based theory attributes advantage in an industry to a firm's control over bundles of unique material, human, organizational, and locational resources and skills that enable unique value-creating strategies. A firm's resources are said to be a source of competitive advantage to the degree that they are scarce, specialized, appropriable, valuable, rare, and difficult to imitate or substitute.

A special branch of resource-based theory is resource-advantage theory. Resource-advantage theory is a moderately socialized and embedded theory of competition that draws on and is applied by several disciplines, including economics, management, and marketing. The theory recognizes social structures and social relations that affect competition and therefore financial performance. It is a general theory of competition that describes the process of competition. Competition is a process, not a result. At its core, resource-advantage theory combines heterogeneous demand theory with the resource-based theory of the firm (Hunt & Arnett, 2003).

Wade and Hulland (2004) presented a typology of IT resources, where the IT resources held by a firm can be sorted into three types of processes: *inside-out, outside-in, and spanning.* Inside-out resources are deployed from inside the firm in response to market requirements and opportunities and tend to be internally focused. *Inside-out resources* include *IS infrastructure, IS technical skills, IS development,* and *cost effective IS operations.* In contrast, outside-in resources are externally oriented, placing an emphasis on anticipated market requirements, creating durable customer relationships, and understanding competitors. *Outside-in resources* include *external relationship management* representing the firm's ability to manage linkages between the IT function and stakeholders outside the firm, and *market responsiveness* representing the firm's ability to sense external market changes and respond flexibly and speedily. Finally, spanning resources involve both internal and external analysis, are needed to integrate the firm's inside-out and outside-in resources. *Spanning resources* include *IS business partnerships* and *IS planning* and *change management.*

From a resource-based perspective, Ravichandran and Lertwongsatien (2005) argue that IS resources that are inimitable and valuable can be rent yielding. Technology assets such as networks and databases are unlikely to be rent yielding, since they could be easily procured in factor markets. However, combining hardware and software assets to create a flexible and sophisticated IT infrastructure can be non-imitable because creating such an infrastructure requires carefully melding technology components to fit firm needs and priorities. In addition to sophisticated IT infrastructure, skilled human resources, relationships between the IS department and user departments, and IS managerial knowledge are valuable resources that are posited to be rent yielding. It is the unique *combination* of sophisticated IT infrastructure and skilled human resources (core competences) of the enterprise creating the differentiated customer value that is particularly imitable and valuable.

We will return to the topic of resources when we discuss IT strategic resource mobilization in line with business strategic direction in Chapter VIII.

ACTIVITY-BASED THEORY OF THE FIRM

The resource-based theory of the firm grew out of efforts to explain the growth of firms. Although its origins lay primarily in economics, researchers in strategy have developed the resource-based theory. The main attraction of the resource-based theory is that it focuses on explaining why firms are different and its effect on profitability. The main tenets of the resource-based theory are that firms differ in their resource endowments that these differences are persistent, and that firm-level performance differentials can be explained by analyzing a firm's resource position. Differences in resources are seen to lead to non-replicable efficiency rents.

Sheehan (2002) discussed comparing and contrasting the resource-based theory with the activity-based theory, and his discussion hold that the activity-based theory conceives the firm as a bundle of activities, while the resource-based theory conceives the firm as a bundle of resources. The resource-based theory focuses on explaining why firms create more value than others by examining differences in resource stocks. However, the resource-based theory places little or no emphasis on resource flows. The role of the production function in transforming inputs into end products (other than having the latent ability to transform) is underconceptualized in the resource-based theory. On the other hand, the activity-based theory focuses on flows of resources in activities. It emphasizes the impact of the firm's production function on creating value, while placing little attention on differences in stocks of resources. It is implicitly assumed that all necessary inputs (resources) can be acquired from the market. From the activity-based theory, we can study the ways a firm may be able to configure its activities to create value from the perspectives of a value chain (Porter, 1985), value shop, and value network (Stabell & Fjeldstad, 1998).

VALUE CONFIGURATION OF THE FIRM

To comprehend the value that information technology provides to organizations, we must first understand the way a particular organization conducts business and how information systems affect the performance of various component activities within the organization. Understanding how firms differ is a central challenge for both theory and practice of management. For a long time, Porter's (1985) value chain was the only value configuration known to managers. Stabell and Fjeldstad (1998) have identified two alternative value configurations. A value shop schedules activities and applies resources in a fashion that is dimensioned and appropriate to the needs of the client's problem, while a value chain performs a fixed set of activities that enables it to produce a standard product in large numbers. Examples of value shops are professional service firms, as found in medicine, law, architecture, and engineering. A value network links clients or customers who are or wish to be interdependent. Examples of value networks are telephone companies, retail banks, and insurance companies.

A value configuration describes how value is created in a company for its customers. A value configuration shows how the most important business processes function to create value for customers. A value configuration represents the way a particular organization conducts business.

THE FIRM AS A VALUE CHAIN

The best-known value configuration is the value chain (Porter, 1985). In the value chain, value is created through efficient production of goods and services based on a variety of resources. The company is perceived as a series or chain of activities. Primary activities

Figure 1.1. Examples of IS/IT in the value chain

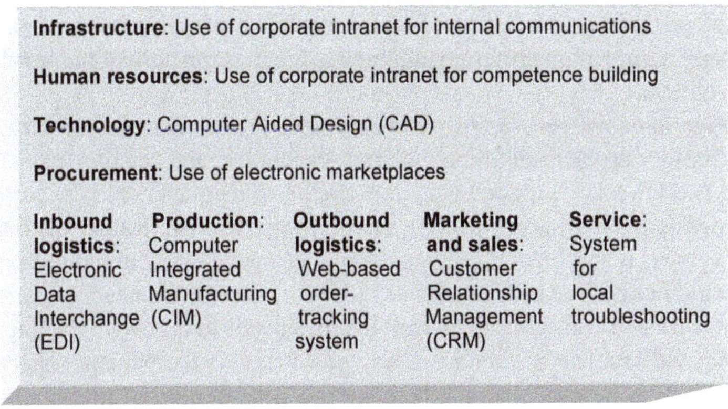

in the value chain include inbound logistics, production, outbound logistics, marketing and sales, and service. Support activities include infrastructure, human resources, technology development, and procurement. Attention is on performing these activities in the chain in efficient and effective ways. In Figure 1.1, examples of IS/IT are assigned to primary and support activities. This figure can be used to describe the current IS/IT situation in the organization as it illustrates the extent of coverage of IS/IT for each activity.

THE FIRM AS A VALUE SHOP

Value cannot only be created in value chains. Value can also be created in two alternative value configurations: value shop and value network (Stabell & Fjeldstad, 1998). In the value shop, activities are scheduled and resources are applied in a fashion that is dimensioned and appropriate to the needs of the client's problem, while a value chain performs a fixed set of activities that enables it to produce a standard product in large numbers. The value shop is a company that creates value by solving unique problems for customers and clients. Knowledge is the most important resource, and reputation is critical to firm success.

While typical examples of value chains are manufacturing industries such as paper and car production, typical examples of value shops are law firms and medical hospitals. Often, such companies are called professional service firms or knowledge-intensive service firms. Like the medical hospital as a way to practice medicine, the law firm provides a standard format for delivering complex legal services. Many features of its style—specialization, teamwork, continuous monitoring on behalf of clients (patients), and representation in many forums—have been emulated in other vehicles for delivering professional services (Galanter & Palay, 1991).

Knowledge-intensive service firms are typical value shops. Sheehan (2002) defines knowledge-intensive service firms as entities that sell problem-solving services, where the solution chosen by the expert is based on real-time feedback from the client. Clients retain knowledge intensive service firms to reduce their uncertainty. Clients hire knowledge-intensive service firms precisely because the client believes the firm knows something that the client does not and believes it is necessary to solve the problems.

While expertise plays a role in all firms, its role is distinctive in knowledge-intensive service firms. Expert, often professional, knowledge is at the core of the service provided by the type of firm.

Knowledge-intensive service firms not only sell a problem-solving service, but equally a problem-finding, problem-defining, solution-execution, and monitoring service. Problem finding is often a key for acquiring new clients. Once the client is acquired and their problem is defined, not all problems will be solved by the firm. Rather the firm may only clarify that there is no problem (i.e., the patient does not have a heart condition) or that the problem should be referred to another specialist (i.e., the patient needs a heart specialist). If a problem is treated within the firm, then the firm needs to follow up the implementation to assure that the problem in fact has been solved (i.e., is the patient's heart now working properly?). This follows from the fact that there is often uncertainty in both problem diagnosis and problem resolution.

Sheehan (2002) has created a typology of knowledge-intensive service firms consisting of the following three types. First, knowledge-intensive search firms search for opportunities. The amount of value they create depends on the size of the finding or discovery, where size is measured by quality rather than quantity. Examples of search firms include petroleum and mineral exploration, drug discovery in the pharmaceutical industry, and research in the biotechnology industry. Second, knowledge-intensive diagnosis firms create value by clarifying problems. Once the problem has been identified, the suggested remedy usually follows directly. Examples of diagnosis firms include doctors, surgeons, psychotherapists, veterinarians, lawyers, auditors and tax accountants, and software support. Finally, knowledge-intensive design firms create value by conceiving new ways of constructing material or intangible artifacts. Examples of design firms include architecture, advertising, research and development, engineering design, and strategy consulting.

Knowledge-intensive service firms create value through problem acquisition and definition, alternative generation and selection, implementation of an alternative, and follow-up to see if the solution selected resolves the problem. To reflect this process, Stabell and Fjeldstad (1998) have outlined the value configuration of a value shop.

A value shop is characterized by five primary activities: problem finding and acquisition, problem solving, choice, execution, and control and evaluation, as illustrated in Figure 1.2. Problem finding and acquisition involves working with the customer to determine the exact nature of the problem or need. It involves deciding on the overall plan of approaching the problem. Problem solving is the actual generation of ideas and action (or treatment) plans.

Choice represents the decision of choosing between alternatives. While the least important primary activity of the value shop in terms of time and effort, it is also the most important in terms of customer value. Execution represents communicating, organizing, and implementing the decision, or performing the treatment. Control and evaluation activities involve monitoring and measurement of how well the solution solved the original problem or met the original need.

This may feed back into the first activity, problem finding and acquisition, for two reasons. First, if the proposed solution is inadequate or did not work, it feeds back into learning why it was inadequate and begins the problem-solving phase anew. Second, if the problem solution was successful, the firm might enlarge the scope of the problem-solving

Figure 1.2. Examples of IS/IT in the value shop

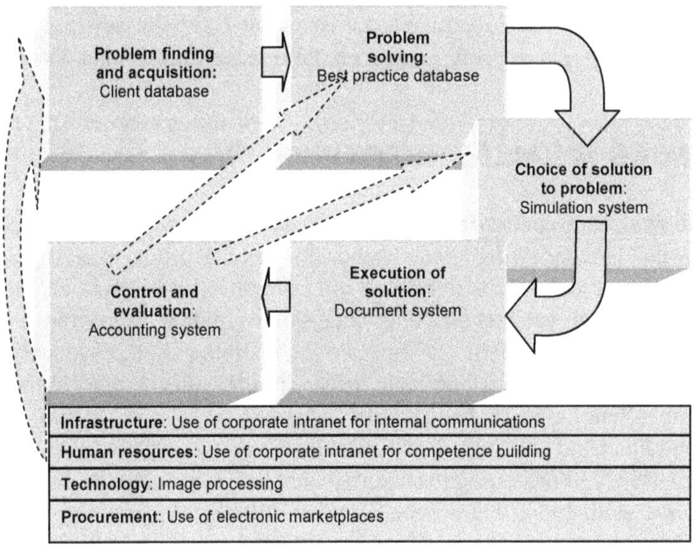

Figure 1.3. Examples of IS/IT in the value shop

Activities	Tasks	IS/IT
Problem finding and acquisition	Register client information	Financial system
	Register case information	Case database
Problem solving	Do case analysis	Case-based reasoning
	Do reference search	Library search engine
Choice	Evaluate alternatives	Case-based reasoning
	Make recommendation to client	Office systems
Execution	Participate at meetings	Office systems
	Revise recommendation	Office systems
Control and evaluation	Register recommendation	Case database
	Check client satisfaction	Financial system

process to solve a bigger problem related to or dependent upon the first problem being solved (Afuah & Tucci, 2003).

Figure 1.2 can be used to identify current IS/IT in the organization. We let a law firm serve as the example in Figure 1.3. Within each of the five activities, there are many tasks in a law firm. For each task, there may be IS/IT support. For example, problem solving may consist of the two tasks of case analysis and reference search. Lawyers will be eager to discuss the case and to search more information on similar cases. A system for case-based reasoning may be installed, where the current case can be compared to similar cases handled by the law firm. Also, intelligent search engines with thesaurus may be available in the law firm to find relevant information on the Internet and in legal databases.

THE FIRM AS A VALUE NETWORK

The third and final value configuration is the value network. A value network is a company that creates value by connecting clients and customers that are, or want to be, dependent on each other. These companies distribute information, money, products, and services. While activities in both value chains and value shops are done sequentially, activities in value networks occur in parallel. The number and combination of customers and access points in the network are important value drivers in the value network. More customers and more connections create higher value to customers.

Stabell and Fjeldstad (1998) suggest that managing a value network can be compared to managing a club. The mediating firm admits members that complement each other, and in some cases exclude those that do not. The firm establishes, monitors, and terminates direct or indirect relationships among members. Supplier–customer relationships may exist between the members of the club, but to the mediating firm, they are all customers.

Examples of value networks include telecommunication companies, financial institutions such as banks and insurance companies, and stockbrokers. Value networks perform three activities (see Figure 1.4):

- Development of customer network through marketing and recruiting of new customers, to enable increased value for both existing customers and new customers.
- Development of new services and improvement in existing services.

Figure 1.4. Examples of IS/IT in the value network

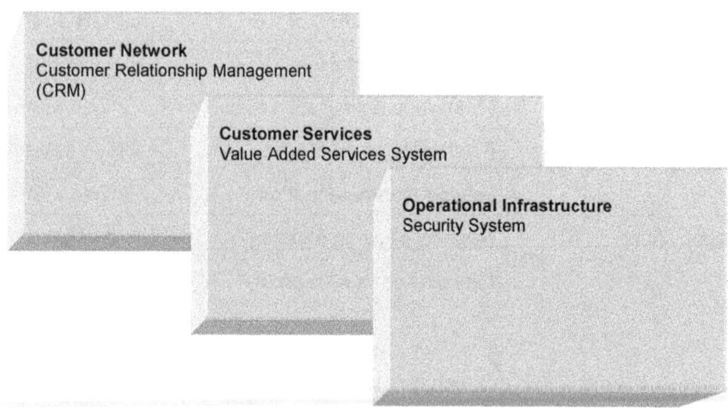

Infrastructure: Use of corporate intranet for internal communications
Human resources: use of corporate intranet for competence building
Technology: Network efficiency monitoring system
Procurement: Use of electronic marketplaces

- Development of infrastructure so that customer services can be provided more efficiently and effectively.

The current IS/IT situation in a value network will mainly be described through the infrastructure that typically will consist of information technology. In addition, many of the new services may be information systems that will be used by customers in their communication and business transactions with other customers. The knowledge component will mainly be found in the services of a value network, as information systems are made available to customers to exchange relevant information.

COMPARISON OF VALUE CONFIGURATIONS

Value chain, value shop, and value network are alternative value configurations that impact the use of information technology in the company as illustrated in Figure 1.5. While the role of IT is to make production more efficient in a value chain, IT creates added value in the value shop, while IT in the form of infrastructure is the main value in the value network. Some companies have more than one value configuration, but most companies have one dominating configuration.

In the long term, business organizations can choose to change their value configurations. A bank, for example, can be a value shop when it focuses on converting inputs to outputs. The value resides in the output and once it has the output, it can remove the production organization. This removal does not impact on the value of the output. The value shop is a solution provider. It solves problems. The input is a problem. The output is a solution to the problem. A bank that does this would view itself as a financial advisor that also has the ability to provide the money. But what it would do is identify client problems, address those problems, select a solution together with the client, and help to implement it. It would have stringent quality controls. As part of its offering, it would probably supply the client with some cash as a loan or accept some of the client's cash for investment (Chatzkel, 2002).

Or, the bank can be a value network, which is basically the logic of the marketplace. The bank would define its role as a conduit between people that do not have money and those people that do have money. What the bank does is to arrange the flow of cash between them. The bank will attract people with money to make deposits and investments. The bank will also attract people without money to make loans. As a value network, the

Figure 1.5. Characteristics of value configurations

Characteristics	**Value Chain**	**Value Shop**	**Value Network**
Value creation	Transformation of input to output	Solving clients and customers problems	Connecting clients and customers to each other
Work form	Sequential production	Integrated and cyclical problem solving	Monitored and simultaneous connections
Information systems	Making production more efficient	Adding value to the knowledge work	Main value by use of IT infrastructure
Example	Paper factory	Law firm	Telecom company

bank will connect people with opposite financial needs. The network consists of people with different financial needs. Over time, persons in the network may change status from money needer to money provider and vice versa (Chatzkel, 2002).

Both as a value shop and as a value network, the business organization can be identified as a bank. But it would have completely different consequences for what it will focus on doing well, what it will focus on doing itself, versus what it would not want to do itself. This provides a kind of strategic systems logic. It asks, "Which strategic system in terms of value configuration are we going to operate in?" Choosing an appropriate value configuration is a long-term decision with long-term consequences.

In practice, the firm must choose not only the appropriate value configuration to operate its business with but also the unique resources it must possess to perform the value configuration to create differentiated customer value in a sustainable and inimitable way. *Business models* are often used to define the firm's unique value configuration, resources, and value propositions. With the emergence of the ubiquitous Internet capable of economically and flexibly linking customers to suppliers and between suppliers and partners anywhere globally come the proliferation of e-business models used by many firms both large and small. The Internet-driven business strategy, from which e-business models are conceived, is known as e-strategy. While these e-business models owe their existence to and cannot function without information technology, they can be studied conceptually from a business standpoint. Indeed, all successfully implemented e-business models are resulted from well thought through business proposition which clearly defines how revenues can be generated and profits made from the business model conceived by the firm. A sound understanding of the principles of e-business model is also important from a business and IT strategic management standpoint.

BUSINESS MODEL OF THE FIRM

Business model is a conceptualization of the firm's value proposition for its stakeholders and the unique ways the firms create and deliver value to customers (Seddon, Lewis, Freeman, & Shanks, 2004). Thompson and Strickland (2003) regard a firm's business model as "management's plan to make money in a particular business," and is therefore closely related to the firm's strategy. They argue (p. 3) that business model is concerned with the revenue–cost–profit economics of the firm's strategy—it determines "whether the revenues and costs flowing from the strategy demonstrate business viability." According to Magretta (2002), business models explain how firms work—they identify who the customers are and define the economic logic of delivering value to the customers at appropriate cost so profit can be made. Business models describe how the pieces of a business fit together as a system to create value to the customers. Thus, to be viable as a business, firms are built on sound business models. Business model is often used to define the firm's unique value configuration, resources, and value propositions. According to Linder and Cantrell (2000), business model is the firm's core logic for creating value and making money. It highlights the unique activities and approaches that allow the firm to deliver differentiated products and services to attract customers, employees, and shareholders to sustain a profitable business. They identify many business model components that can be configured to make up a distinctive business model, such as pricing model, revenue model, channel, commerce process model, Internet-enabled commercial relationship model, organizational model, and value proposition model. Magretta (2002) asserts that business model is not strategy because business model does not address *competition* which is core to strategy. Seddon et al. (2004) support the view that business models do not consider the firm's competitive positioning. They further argue that, in terms of Porter's (1996) definition of strategy, a business model can be defined as an abstraction of "some aspects of a firm's strategy." Seddon et al. (2004) thus think a business model potentially may apply to many firms.

Hedman and Kalling (2002, p. 113) define business model as comprising six causally related components, starting at the product market level: (1) customers, (2) competitors, (3) the "offering" to the customer—that is, the firm's value proposition, (4) the firm's "internal activities and organization" to create the value, (5) the firm's resources (both tangible physical resources and intangible human and organizational resources) required to perform the requisite activities, and (6) the factor markets and production inputs which supply the "raw materials" to constitute the requisite resources. Basically, the business model can be viewed as comprising three components: the offering, the unique configuration of activities and organization, and the (particularly rare and inimitable) resources. IT can be designed to contribute to the uniqueness of each of these three components (Hedman & Kalling, 2002).

Osterwalder and Pigneur (2005) propose that the business model concept can be understood by the following.

A business model is a conceptual tool containing a set of objects, concepts and their relationships with the objective to express the business logic of a specific firm. In particular, the model makes explicit the specific concepts and relationships that elegantly describe and represent what value is delivered to the customers and how is it done and with which financial consequences.

Osterwalder and Pigneur (2005) further define the terminology or ontology for defining business models. They classify business model definitions in three different categories that can be (but not necessarily have to be) linked hierarchically to one another as follows:

1. The top level describes the business model concept as an abstract overarching concept that can be used to describe all real world businesses. It is the metamodel. It identifies what elements belong in a business model—what a business does for a living.
2. The second level describes taxonomy of types which group resembling business models into a type. It describes a number of different abstract types of business models, each describing a set of businesses with common characteristics. This level represents the sub-metamodels, identifying the common characteristics among business models.
3. The last level describes instances of the business model types. Each instance is a company specific real-world view of business models, such as Dell, Amazon, or eBay.

Osterwalder and Pigneur (2005) call the top two levels the conceptual levels of business model, and the third level the instance levels. They also distinguish a business model from a business process model. The former is about the firm's logic for creating and commercializing value—it includes financial and economic dimensions. The latter is about how a business case is implemented in processes—it is centered on activity model alone. Osterwalder and Pigneur (2005) also support the above Magretta (2002) view of business model and strategy. They further assert that business model can only be successful through diligent execution and management. Business model gets implemented by translating the model into concrete elements such as a business structure (organizational model), business processes (workflow), and infrastructure and systems. The implementation of the business model must be financed either internally or in addition through external funding such as venture capital. Thus, the successful realization of the business model of a firm depends on three interlinked elements: business strategy, business organization, and IT systems. These elements are subject to constant external pressures such as customer demand, competitive forces, local and social environmental changes, as well as technological change. To create sustainable value, in the face of these forces, business models (and their implementation) must adapt with change. Thus, business model evolves with time, and the firm must determine the best course of actions to remain competitive to win and retain customers.

Linder and Cantrell (2000) propose that firms use the basic constructs of a business model to analyze the impact of the external forces to define how the business model should change. The Linder and Cantrell (2000) business model constructs consist of the strategic questions—the answers to these questions constitute the change logic for the business model:

- How do we get and keep customers? What is our distinctive value proposition to each constituency?
  - Who are our customers and what are their needs?
  - What do we offer them? Products, services, experiences?
  - How do we reach them?
  - How do we price our offering?
- How do we deliver distinctively?
  - How do we execute?
  - What are our distinctive capabilities?
- How is our financial structure distinctive?

The answers to these questions have direct implications on the firm's revenue, cost, and asset differentiation.

Linder and Cantrell (2000) define four types of business model change strategies:

- **Realization model:** Firms use the realization model to maximize returns from their existing business model operating logic. They leverage their business model by enhancing some part of their operating logic to grow revenue and profit. An example of realization model is where a traditional bank adds Internet banking to provide convenience to their customers and at the same time extend their reach.
- **Renewal model:** Firms use the renewal model to continuously improve their products and services platforms, brand value propositions, cost structure, technology base, and capabilities to respond to increasing competition. They may even introduce disruptive products to vastly enhance their competitive positioning. Renewal models are commonly used by innovative firms to stay ahead of the price/value curve.
- **Extension model:** Firms use the extension model to expand their business to new markets, new lines of businesses, or new geography. It does not replace the existing business model but adds significantly to it with new capabilities and operating logic.

For example, BP Amoco extends their gas and oil vertically integrated business to include retail stores at its gas stations.

- **Journey model:** Firms use the journey model to totally revamp their business models and adopt a new operating logic. For example, a firm may change its business model from a local domestic niche player to become a higher value global player. More dramatically, albeit gradually, a firm may change its business from one industry to another. For example, Nokia changes from rubber and paper business to telecommunications business.

In summary, realization model does not change the firm's business model. It leverages its core to maximize profit. Renewal and extension models can change the firm's business model to some extent. However, the journey model does change the firm's business model completely. To remain agile, firms must acquire competencies to manage business model change (which includes IT system changes) in response to, or better in anticipation of, business and technological environmental changes.

Osterwalder and Pigneur (2005) define business model as follows:

A business model is a conceptual tool that contains a set of elements and their relationships which can be configured to express the business logic of a specific firm. The business model describes the value offered to the different segments of customers, and the architecture of the firm and its network of partners for creating, marketing and delivering this value and relationship capital to generate profitable and sustainable revenue streams.

They identify nine basic business model building blocks that can be used to construct a business model based on this definition. The building blocks are structured as follows:

Product

- **Value proposition:** Define the firm's bundle of products or services

Customer Interface

- **Target customer:** Describes the segments of customers targeted by the firm to offer value to
- **Distribution channel:** Describes the various means the firm uses to reach its customers
- **Relationship:** Explains the relationships (links) the firm has with its different customer segments

Infrastructure Management

- **Value configuration:** Describes the arrangement of activities and resources
- **Core competency:** Outlines the competencies required to execute the firm's business model
- **Partner network:** Describes the network of cooperative agreements with other companies necessary to efficiently offer and commercialize value

Financial Aspects

- **Cost structure:** Defines the cost base of the firm as a result of deploying the business model
- **Revenue model:** Defines the revenue streams of the business model to sustain the firm's profitability

An example of business model configuration using these building blocks is described in Hamel (2000). We will return to this topic in Chapter X to discuss business concept innovation as a "revolutionary" way (Hamel, 2000) of maximizing a firm's profit. More commonly, since the arrival of the Internet in commerce business models, derived from the firm's Internet-driven business strategy called e-strategy (Plant, 2000), have been applied to modeling the various innovative ways that e-business may help firms make money.

E-BUSINESS MODELS

A business model can be defined as the method by which a firm builds and uses its resources to offer its customers better value than its competitors and to take money doing so. A business model details how a firm makes money now and how it plans to do so in the long run. The model is what enables a firm to have a sustainable competitive advantage, to perform better than its rivals in the long term. A business model can be conceptualized as a system that is made up of components, linkages between the components, and dynamics.

With the advent of Internet technologies, many "pure play" Internet-based business strategies and associated e-business models have emerged and become a major force in global business. Examples of "pure play" Internet-based businesses are Yahoo, eBay, Google, and Amazon. At the same time, existing traditional enterprises, such as GE and government agencies, have also proactively incorporated Internet-based strategy in reshaping their enterprise strategies and their business models—using the above Linder and Cantrell (2000) renewal or extension model change strategies. The Internet-driven business strategy is commonly known as e-commerce or e-business strategy, and sometimes also called e-strategy (Plant, 2000, chap. 4). E-commerce, e-business strategy, or e-strategy is enabled by Internet IT strategy. The business models for implementing e-strategy are called e-business models.

Afuah and Tucci (2003) postulate that an e-business model must address eight factors in order to make money: (1) customer value—a distinctive offering or low cost value proposition, (2) scope—which customer segment and what products and services, (3) the price of the offering, (4) the sources of the revenue, (5) the system of interconnected and interdependent activities, which create the customer value, (6) implementation—what resources are needed, such as people, organizations, and systems, and how they are aligned with the business strategy, (7) capabilities—what skills are needed, and (8) sustainability—the uniqueness and inimitability of the business model. Weill and Vitale (2001) define an e-business model as a description of the roles and relationships among a firm's consumers, customers, allies, and suppliers that identifies the major flows of product, information, and money, and the major benefits to participants. Amit and Zott (2001) define e-business model as consisting of three components: (1) content—the exchanged goods and information and the resources required to facilitate the exchange, (2) structure—the linkage between transaction stakeholders, and (3) governance of transactions—the control of the flows of goods, information, and resources and the form of legal association.

There are many different ways to describe and classify e-business models. Weill and Vitale (2001) proposed that there are a finite number of *atomic e-business models*, each of which captures a different way to conduct e-business. Firms can combine atomic e-business models as building blocks to create tailored e-business models and initiatives, using their competencies as their guide. In particular, Weill and Vitale (2002) identified eight atomic e-business models, each of which describes the essence of conducting business electronically: (i) direct to customer, (ii) full-service provider, (iii) whole of enterprise, (iv) intermediary, (v) shared infrastructure, (vi) virtual community, (vii) value net integrator, and (vii) content provider. Weill and Vitale (2002) identified knowledge management system as the most critical service of IT infrastructure services needed for each e-business model. Knowledge management system is required by the content providers, for example, Amazon, of the e-business models to create and provides content (information, products, or services) in digital form to customers.

In e-business, IT is the enabling or transforming agent of the new ways the firm can offer its services to the customers creatively, conveniently, and cost-effectively, which places power in the hands of the customers. We review Weill and Vitale's (2001) eight atomic e-business models, from the standpoints of operating model, IT infrastructure, revenue source, and critical success factors:

1. **Direct to customer.** The distinguishing characteristic of this model is that buyer and seller communicate directly, rather than through an intermediary. The seller may be a retailer, a wholesaler, or a manufacturer. The customer may be an individual or a business. Examples of the direct-to-customer model are Dell Computer Corporation (www.dell.com) and Gap, Inc. (www.gap.com).

- *Infrastructure.* The direct-to-customer model requires extensive electronic connection with the customer, including online payment systems. Many direct-to-customer implementations include an extranet to allow customized Web pages for major business-to-business (B2B) customers. Operating a direct-to-customer e-business requires significant investment in the equivalent of the store: the Web site. Direct-to-customer businesses spend millions of dollars developing easy-to-navigate and easy-to-use Web sites with the goal of improving the B2B or business-to-consumer (B2C) shopping experience online. Lands' End (www.landsend.com) has devised a feature by which women can build and store a three-dimensional model of themselves to "try on" clothes electronically.

  In their field research, Weill and Vitale (2001) found that firms with e-business initiatives containing the direct-to-customer e-business model needed and were investing more heavily in three areas of infrastructure services: application infrastructure, communications, and IT management.

  Direct-to-customer firms particularly needed payment transaction processing to process online customer payments, enterprisewide resource planning (ERP) to process customer transactions, workflow infrastructure to optimize business process performance, communication network services linking all points in the enterprise to each other and the outside world (often using TCP/IP protocol), the installation and maintenance of workstations and local area networks supporting the large number of people required to operate a direct-to-customer model, and service-level agreements between the business and the IT group or outsourcer to ensure, monitor, and improve the systems necessary for the model.

- *Sources of Revenue.* The main source of revenue in the direct-to-customer model is usually direct sales to customers. Supplemental revenues come from advertising, the sale of customer information, and product placement fees.
- *Critical Success Factors.* Critical success factors are the things a firm must do well to flourish. The following list shows the critical success factors for the direct-to-customer model: create and maintain customer awareness, in order to build a critical mass of users to cover the fixed cost of building an electronic presence; reduce customer acquisition costs; strive to own the customer relationship and understand individual customer needs; increase repeat purchases and average transaction size; provide fast and efficient transaction processing, fulfillment, and payment; ensure adequate security for the organization and its customers; and provide interfaces that combine ease of use with richness of experience, integrating multiple channels.

2. **Full-service provider.** A firm using the full-service provider model provides total coverage of customer needs in a particular domain, consolidated via a single point of contact. The domain could be any major area of customer needs requiring multiple products and services, for example, financial services, health care, or industrial chemicals. The full-service provider adds value by providing a full range of products, sourced both internally and externally, and consolidated them using the channel chosen by the customer. Examples of the full-service provider are the Prudential Advisor (www.prusec.com) and GE Supply Company (www.gesupply.com).

- *Infrastructure.* Virtually all businesses aspire to get 100% of their customers' business, or at least to get as much of that business as they can profitably handle. Yet the number of full-service providers remains small. Part of the reason for this is required infrastructure. The missing piece of infrastructure in many businesses is often a database containing information about the customer and the products that the customer owns. Without owning these data, a provider does not own the customer relationship, and therefore some of the customer's transactions are likely to take place directly with other providers. All of the important interactions with customers occurring across any channel or business unit must be recorded in the firmwide customer database. Weill and Vitale (2001) identified in their field research databases and data warehouses as some of the most important infrastructure services associated with the full-service provider model. Other important infrastructure services included the following: the ability to evaluate proposals for new information systems initiatives to coordinate IT investments across a multibusiness-unit firm with the goal of a single point of contact for the customer; centralized management of IT infrastructure capacity to integrate across multiple business units within the firm and third-party providers, the full-service provider model is not readily workable if each business unit optimizes its own IT needs; installation and maintenance of workstations and local area networks to operate the online business linking all the business units and third-party providers; electronic support for groups to coordinate the cross-functional teams required to implement this model; and the identification and testing of new technologies to find cost-effective ways to deliver this complex business model to the customer across multiple channels.
- *Sources of Revenue.* A full-service provider gains revenues from selling its own products and those of others, and possibly also from annual membership fees, man-

agement fees, transaction fees, commissions on third-party products, advertising or listing fees from third-party providers, and fees for selling aggregated data about customers.

- *Critical Success Factors.* One important critical success factor is the brand, credibility, and trust necessary for a customer to look to the firm for its complete needs in an area. Another is owning the customer relationship in one domain and integrating and consolidating the offering of many third parties into a single channel or multiple channels. A third factor is owning more of the customer data in the relevant domain than any other player. A final factor is enforcement of policies to protect the interests of internal and external suppliers, as well as customers.

3. **Whole of enterprise.** The single point of contact for the e-business customer is the essence of the whole-of-enterprise atomic business model. Although many of this model's breakthrough innovations have occurred in public-sector organizations, the model is applicable in both the for-profit and the public sectors. An example of this model is the Australian state of Victoria with its Business Channel (www.business.channel.vic.gov.au) and Health Channel (www.betterhealth.vic.gov.au).

- *Infrastructure.* For the whole-of-enterprise model, infrastructure needs to link the different systems in the various business units and provide a firm wide perspective for management. The field research by Weill and Vitale (2001) revealed that the following infrastructure services are the most important for implementing this model: centralized management of infrastructure capacity to facilitate integration and capture economies of scale; identification and testing of new technologies to find new ways to integrate the often different systems in many business units into a single point of customer contact; management of key data independent of applications and the creation of a centralized repository for firmwide information; electronic means of summarizing data from different applications and platforms to manage the complexity arising from a single point of contact for multiple business units; development of an ERP service to process the transactions instigated by customers interacting with several different business units, often requiring consolidating or linking several ERPs in the firm; payment transaction processing, either on a firmwide basis or by linking several systems across the business units; large-scale data-processing facilities to process transactions from multiple business units, often centralized to achieve economies of scale; and integrated mobile computing applications, which provide another channel to the customer.
- *Sources of Revenue.* In the for-profit sector, revenues are generated by provision of goods and services to the customer by the business units. There may also be the opportunity to charge an annual service or membership fee for this level of service. In the government sector, the motivation is usually twofold: improved service and reduced cost. Service to the community is improved through continuous, round-the-clock operation and faster service times. Sharing more infrastructure and eliminating the need to perform the same transaction in multiple agencies can potentially reduce government costs.
- *Critical Success Factors.* The following list details the critical success factors for the whole-of-enterprise model: changing customer behavior to make use of the new model, as opposed to the customer continuing to interact directly with individual units; reducing costs in the individual business units as the direct demands on them fall, and managing the transfer pricing issues that will inevitably arise; altering the

perspective of the business units to take an enterprisewide view, which includes broad product awareness, training, and cross-selling; in the integrated implementation, reengineering the business processes to link into life events at the front end and existing legacy processes and systems at the back end; and finding compelling and practical life events that customers can use as triggers to access the enterprise.

4. **Intermediaries,** such as portals, agents, auctions, aggregators, and other intermediaries. E-business is often promoted as an ideal way for sellers and buyers to interact directly, shortening old-economy value chains by disintermediating some of their members. Yet some of the most popular sites on the Internet, both for consumers and for business users, are in fact intermediaries—sites that stand between the buyer and the seller. The services of intermediaries include search (to locate providers of products and services), specification (to identify important product attributes), price (to establish the price, including optional extras such as warranties), sale (to complete the sales transaction, including payment and settlement), fulfillment (to fulfill the purchase by delivering the product or service), surveillance (to conduct surveillance of the activities of buyers and sellers in order to report aggregate activity and prices and to inform and regulate the market), and enforcement (to enforce proper conduct by buyers and sellers). Examples of intermediaries are electronic malls, shopping agents, specialty auctions, electronic markets, electronic auctions, and portals.

- *Infrastructure.* Intermediaries generate value by concentrating information and bringing together buyers and sellers, operating entirely in space and thus relying on IT as the primary infrastructure. Weill and Vitale (2001) found in their field interviews that the most important infrastructure services for firms pursuing the intermediary atomic business model are the following: knowledge management, including knowledge databases and contact databases that enable the codification and sharing of knowledge in this highly information-intensive business; enforcing Internet and e-mail policies to ensure proper and consistent use of electronic channels to buyers, sellers, and intermediaries; workstation networks to support the products and services of this all-electronic business model; centralized management of e-business applications, ensuring consistency and integration across product offerings; information systems planning to identify the most effective uses of IT in the business; and information systems project management to ensure that business value is achieved from IT investments.
- *Sources of Revenue.* An intermediary may earn revenues from buyers, sellers, or both. Sellers may pay a listing fee, a transaction fee, a sales commission, or some combination. Similarly, buyers may pay a subscription fee, a success fee, or a sales commission.
- *Critical Success Factors.* The chief requirement for survival as an intermediary is sufficient volume of usage to cover the fixed costs of establishing the business and the required infrastructure. Attracting and retaining a critical mass of customers is therefore the primary critical success factor. Another important critical success factor is building up infrastructure just quickly enough to meet demand as it increases.

5. **Shared infrastructure.** The firm provides infrastructure shared by its owners. Other suppliers, who are users of the shared infrastructure, but not owners, can also be included. Customers who access the shared infrastructure directly are given a choice of suppliers and value propositions. The owner and the non-owner suppliers are generally represented objectively. In some situations, goods or services flow directly

from the shared infrastructure to the customer. In other situations, a message is sent by the shared infrastructure to the supplier, who then completes the transaction by providing the goods or services to the customer.

An example illustrating the features of the shared-infrastructure business model is the system from 2000 by America's largest automakers, some of their dealers, and IBM, Motorola, and Intel. The initiative was named Covisint (collaboration vision integrity). General Motors, Ford, and DaimlerChrysler see stronger potential benefits from cooperating on supply-chain logistics than from competing.

- *Infrastructure.* The shared-infrastructure business model requires competitors to cooperate by sharing IT infrastructure and information. This level of cooperation requires agreement on high-level IT architectures as well as operational standards for applications, data communications, and technology. Effective implementation of the shared-infrastructure model also requires enforcement of these standards, and most shared-infrastructure models have a joint committee to set and enforce standards. Another role of these committees is to implement the policies of the shared infrastructure about what information, if any, is shared and what information is confidential to partner firms. Weill and Vitale (2001) found in their field research that the most important infrastructure services required by firms implementing the shared-infrastructure atomic business model all concerned architectures and standards: specification and enforcement of high-level architectures for data, technology, applications, communications, and work that are agreed to by alliance partners; and specification and enforcement of detailed standards for the high-level architectures.
- *Sources of Revenue.* Revenues can be generated both from membership fees and from transaction fees. The alliance may be run on a nonprofit basis or on a profit-making basis. Not-for-profit shared infrastructures are typically open to all eligible organizations and distribute any excess revenues back to their members. The for-profit models are typically owned by a subset of the firms in a given segment, which split up any profits among themselves.
- *Critical Success Factors.* Critical success factors for the shared-infrastructure model include the following: no dominant partner that gains more than any other partner; an unbiased channel and objective presentation of product and service information; critical mass of both alliance partners and customers; management of conflict among the ongoing e-business initiatives of the alliance partners; compilation and delivery of accurate and timely statements of the services and benefits provided to each member of the alliance; and interoperability of systems.

6. **Virtual community.** Virtual communities deserve our attention, and not only because they are the clearest, and perhaps the last surviving embodiment of the original intent of the Internet. By using IT to leverage the fundamental human desire for communication with peers, virtual communities can create significant value for their owners as well as for their members. Once established, a virtual community is less susceptible to competition by imitation than any of the other atomic business models. In this business model, the firm of interest—the sponsor of the virtual community—sits in the center, positioned between members of the community and suppliers. Fundamental to the success of this model is that members are able, and in fact are encouraged, to communicate with one another directly. Communication between members may be via e-mail, bulletin boards, online chat, Web-based conferencing, or other computer-based media, and it is the distinguishing feature of this model. Examples of this model

are Parent Soup (www.parentsoup.com), a virtual community for parents, and Motley Fool (www.motleyfool.com), a virtual community of investors.

- *Infrastructure.* Virtual communities depend on IT to exist. In particular, the creation and continual enhancement of an Internet site is essential if a virtual community is to survive. Many virtual-community sites include not just static content and links, but also tools of interest to potential members. Weill and Vitale (2001) found in their field research the infrastructure services most important for the virtual-community business model: training in the use of IT for members of the community; application service provision (ASP) to provide specialized systems virtual communities need such as bulletin boards, email, and ISP access; IT research and development, including infrastructure services for identifying and testing new technologies and for evaluating proposals for new information systems initiatives; information systems planning to identify and prioritize potential investments in IT in this completely online business; and installation and maintenance of workstations and local area networks to support the electronic world of the virtual community.
- *Sources of Revenue.* A sponsoring firm can gain revenue from membership fees, direct sales of goods and services, advertising, click-throughs, and sales commissions. A firm sponsoring a virtual community as an adjunct to its other activities may receive no direct revenue at all from the virtual community. Rather, the firm receives less tangible benefits, such as customer loyalty and increased knowledge about its customer base.
- *Critical Success Factors.* The critical success factors for a virtual community include finding and retaining a critical mass of members; building and maintaining loyalty with an appropriate mix of content and features; maintaining privacy and security for member information; balancing commercial potential and members' interests; leveraging member profile information with advertisers and merchants; and engendering a feeling of trust in the community by its members.

7. **Value net integrator.** Traditionally, most firms operate simultaneously in two worlds: the physical and the virtual. In the physical world, goods and services are created in a series of value-adding activities connecting the supply side (suppliers, procurement, and logistics) with the demand side (customers, marketing, and shipping). In the virtual world, information about the members of the physical value chain are gathered, synthesized, and distributed along the virtual value chain. E-business provides the opportunity to separate the physical and virtual value chains. Value net integrators take advantage of that split and attempt to control the virtual value chain in their industries by gathering, synthesizing, and distributing information. Value net integrators add value by improving the effectiveness of the value chain by coordinating information. A pure value net integrator operates exclusively in the virtual value chain, owning a few physical assets. To achieve the gathering, synthesizing, and distributing of information, the value net integrator receives and sends information to all other players in the model. The value net integrator coordinates product flows form suppliers to allies and customers. The product flows from the suppliers to customers may be direct or via allies. In some cases, the value net integrator may sell information or other products to the customer. The value net integrator always strives to own the customer relationship with the other participants in the model, thus knowing more about their operations than any other player. Examples of value net integrators are Seven-Eleven Japan and Cisco Systems (www.cisco.com).

- *Infrastructure.* The value net integrator succeeds in its role by gathering, synthesizing, and distributing information. Thus, for a value net integrator, data and electronic connectivity with allies and other players are very important assets. Field research carried out by Weill and Vitale (2001) suggests that the most important infrastructure services required for a value net integrator include middleware, linking systems on different platforms across the many players in the value net; a centralized data warehouse that collects and summarizes key information for analysis from decentralized databases held by several players across the value net; specification and enforcement of high-level architectures and detailed standards for data, technology, applications, and communications to link together different technology platforms owned by different firms; call centers to provide advice and guidance for partners and allies in getting the most value from the information provided by the value net generator; and high-capacity communications network service to support the high volumes of information flowing across the value net.
- *Sources of Revenue.* In this model, revenues are generally earned by fees or margins on the physical goods that pass through the industry value net. By using information about consumers, the value net integrator is able to increase prices by meeting consumer demand. By using information about suppliers, the value net integrator reduces costs by cutting inventories and lead times.
- *Critical Success Factors.* The critical success factors for the value net integrator atomic business model are reducing ownership of physical assets while retaining ownership of data; owning or having access to the complete industry virtual value chain; establishing a trusted brand recognized at all places in the value chain; operating in markets where information can add significant value, such as those that are complex, fragmented, regulated, multilayered, inefficient, and large with many sources of information; presenting the information to customers, allies, partners, and suppliers in clear and innovative ways that provide value; and helping other value chain participants capitalize on the information provided by the value net integrator.

8. **Content provider.** Like many terms associated with e-business, *content provider* has different meanings to different people. We define content provider as a firm that creates and provides content (information, products, or services) in digital form to customers via third parties. The physical-world analogy of a content provider is a journalist, recording artist, or stock analyst. Digital products such as software, electronic travel guides, and digital music and video are examples of content. A virtual-world example of a content provider is weather forecasters such as Storm Weather Center (www.storm.no).

- *Infrastructure.* Content providers must excel at tailoring and manipulating their core content to meet the specific needs of customers. Content providers must categorize and store their content in well-indexed modules so it can be combined and customized to meet customer needs via a wide variety of channels. Customers and transactions tend to be relatively few, at least compared with the number of end consumers and their transactions. Often complex and unique IT infrastructures are needed to support the particular needs of the specialized professionals employed by the content provider. Field research by Weill and Vitale (2001) identified the most important infrastructure services: multimedia storage farms or storage area network infrastructures to deal with large amounts of information; a strong focus on architecture, including setting and enforcing standards particularly for work; detailed data architectures to structure, specify, link manipulate, and manage the core intellectual property; workstation network infrastructures to enable the fundamentally online business of a content provider; and a common systems development environment to provide compatible and integrated systems, ensuring the systems can provide content across multiple channels to their customers.

- *Sources of Revenue.* The primary source of revenue for a content provider is fees from its third parties or allies. These fees may be based on a fixed price per month or year, or on the number of times the third party's own customers access the content. In some situations, the fees paid are lower for content branded by the provider and higher for unbranded content, which then appears to the customer to have been generated by the third party itself.
- *Critical Success Factors.* To succeed, a content provider must provide reliable, timely content in the right format and at the right price. The critical success factors for this model include branding (the value of content is due in part to reputation), recognized as best in class (the business of content provision will be global and competitive), and network (establishing and maintaining a network of third parties through which content is distributed.

One way of comparing these e-business models is to analyze to what extent each model creates integration with customers and to what extent each model creates integration with partners. As illustrated in Figure 1.7, the business direct-to-customer model creates mainly integration with customers, while shared infrastructure creates mainly integration with partners.

APPROPRIATE E-BUSINESS MODELS FOR E-STRATEGIES

Despite works by Weill and Vitale (2002) and others, how an e-business model must be defined and specified is largely an open issue. Business decision makers tend to use the notion in a highly informal way, and usually there is a big gap between the business view and that of IT developers.

The electronic business landscape is confusing for many new entrants, and many of them face the paradox that hesitation would run the risk of being left behind, but rushing in and making an incorrect choice regarding electronic business initiatives could have dire consequences for organizations. According to Hayes and Finnegan (2005), Internet-only or "dot.com" models have proven particularly vulnerable. For example, the dot.com implosion of Spring 2000 led to a large number of high-profile collapses including boo, ClickMango, and eToys. "Clicks and mortar" strategies have also met with mixed success, for example, Wall Street Journal Interactive and Fyffes' World-of-Fruit.

The basic principles of business model which aims to profit from delivering highly valuable differentiated services to customers, as described above, must be adhered to by e-business models. It requires development of a sound e-strategy focused on value delivery to the customers. Kim, Nam, and Stimpert (2004) argue that an e-strategy will be able to achieve superior, sustainable performance through an "integrated strategy" discipline (when compared with *either* differentiation *or* cost leadership), which strives to achieve *both* cost leadership and differentiation strategic positioning. We will return to e-strategy in Chapter II.

The Internet age has produced many Internet business models. For example, Afuah and Tucci (2003) distinguish between nine: brokerage model, advertising model, infomediary model, merchant model, manufacturing model, affiliate model, community model, subscription model, and utility model. An Internet business model—sometimes labeled *b-Web*—is a business on the Internet that represents a distinct system of suppliers, distributors, commerce service providers, infrastructure providers, and customers that use the Internet for their primary business communication and transactions.

Another classification of Internet business models is presented by Laudon and Laudon (2005):

- **Virtual storefront:** Sells physical products directly to consumers or to individual businesses (Amazon.com, EPM.com)
- **Information broker:** Provides product, pricing, and availability information to individuals and businesses. Generates revenue from advertising or from directing buyers to sellers (Edmunds.com, Kbb.com, Insweb.com, IndustralMall.com)
- **Transaction broker:** Saves users money and time by processing online sales transactions, generating a fee each time a transaction occurs; also provides information on rates and terms (E*TRADE.com, Expedia.com)
- **Online marketplace:** Provides a digital environment where buyers and sellers can meet, search for products, display products, and establish prices for those products (eBay.com, Priceline.com, ChemConnect.com, Pantellos.com)
- **Content provider:** Creates revenue by providing digital content, such as digital news, music, photos, or video, over the Web (WSJ.com, CNN.com, TheStreet.com, Gettyimages.com, MP3.com)
- **Online service provider:** Provides online service for individuals and businesses. Generates revenue from subscription or transaction fees, from advertising, or from collecting marketing information from users (@Backup.com, Xdrive.com, Emploease.com, Salesforce.com)
- **Virtual community:** Provides online meeting place where people with similar interests can communicate and find useful information (Motocross.com, iVillage.com, Sailnet.com)
- **Portal:** Provides initial point of entry to the Web along with specialized content and other services (Yahoo.com, MSN.com, StarMedia.com)

Hayes and Finnegan (2005) present several classifications of e-business models. One classification includes e-shop, e-mall, e-procurement, third-party marketplace, e-auction, virtual community, collaboration platform, value chain service provider, value chain integration, information brokerage, and trust services. Another classification includes aggregation, agora/open market, alliance, and value chain. The next classification includes catalogue hubs, other hubs, yield managers, exchanges, forward aggregator, and reverse aggregator. A final classification consists of a long list, including click and mortar merchant model, virtual merchant, catalogue merchant, virtual mall, intermediary, distributor, manufacturer model, buy/sell fulfillment, market exchange, bounty broker, auction broker, reverse auction, vertical Web community, specialized portal, knowledge networks, open source model, content services, trust services, and transaction broker.

Electronic business poses significant challenges for organizations as it affects both how organizations relate to external parties (customers, suppliers, partners, competitors, and markets) and how they operate internally in managing activities, processes, and systems. Porter (2001) argues that the companies that succeed with e-business will be those that use the Internet in conjunction with their traditional business models and activities.

Hayes and Finnegan (2005) argue that business models are possibly the most discussed, yet least understood area of electronic business. They refer the point that consultants, executives, researchers, and journalists have abusively used the phrase business model but have rarely given a precise definition of what they exactly meant by using it, and that this has lead to the loss of credibility of the concept.

A business model can be understood as a blend of three streams: value, revenue, and logistics. The value stream is concerned with the value proposition for buyers, sellers, and market makers. The revenue stream identifies how the organizations will earn revenue, and the logistics stream involves detailing how supply chain issues will affect the organizations involved (Hayes & Finnegan, 2005).

A business model can also be understood as an architecture for product, service, and information flows, incorporating a description of the sources of revenue, the actors involved, their roles, and the benefits to them. An electronic business model is comprised of components, linkages, and dynamics. Components are factors such as customer scope, product (goods and services) scope, customer value, pricing, revenue sources, connected activities, implementation, capabilities of the firm, and sustainability. Linkages exist when one activity affects another in terms of cost-effectiveness, and trade-offs and optimization are sought to find the right blend to achieve competitive advantage. The dynamics represent how a firm reacts to or initiates change to attain a new competitive advantage, or to sustain an existing one, to have sustainable competitive advantage and to perform better than its rivals in the long term (Hayes & Finnegan, 2005).

While the atomic business models by Weill and Vitale (2002) were distinguished along dimensions such as infrastructure, sources of revenue and critical success factors, we can think of other criteria to classify e-business model. For example, three major areas that impact the sustainability and growth of an e-business are revenue streams, value streams, and logistical streams. These three elements are interrelated with changes in any one impacting on the other. Furthermore, e-business models can be classified in terms of integration with customers vs. integration with partners, as illustrated in Figure 1.7. Understanding the fundamental characteristics of these e-business models is necessary in order for an enterprise to be able to develop an appropriate e-strategy in support of, or integrated with, its business strategy.

At the moment, there is no single, comprehensive, and cogent taxonomy of the Web business models. Businesses face questions as to what their appropriate business model is. This is made more difficult when we consider that companies in the same industry often pursue different Internet business models. For example, companies in the automobile industry have industry consortia models such as shared infrastructure, while others have virtual community models.

As a result, determining and employing an appropriate Internet business model has become a major business issue. The problem is that there is no well-developed or complete framework to aid the decision of choosing a model.

In addition to outlining the components of a business model, some authors offer a set of business model representation tools. Weill and Vitale (2001) have developed a formalism to assist analyzing e-business initiatives, which they call e-business model schematic. The schematic is a pictorial representation, aiming to highlight a business model's important

Figure 1.7. E-business models integration with customers and partners (Weill & Vitale, 2001)

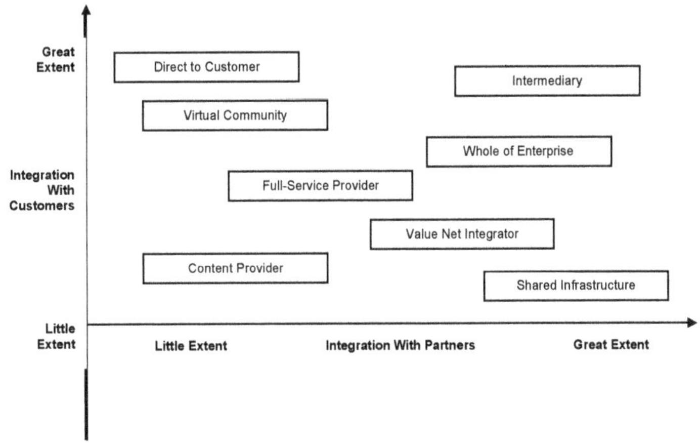

elements. This includes characteristics of the firm of interest, its suppliers and allies, the major flows of product, information and money, and finally the revenues and other benefits each participant receives.

In determining an appropriate e-business model, several criteria can be used, such as:

- **Involved parties,** such as business-to-business, business-to-consumer, and/or consumer-to-consumer.
- **Revenue sources,** such as transaction fee, product price, and/or exposure fee.
- **Value configuration,** such as value chain, value shop, and/or value network.
- **Integration** with customers and/or partners.
- **Relationships,** such as one-to-many, many-to-many, and/or many-to-one.
- **Knowledge,** such as know-how, know-what, and know-why.

Unfortunately, e-business models still fall under open and weak theory domains. An open domain is one that cannot be realistically modeled. A weak theory domain is a domain in which relationships between important concepts are uncertain. General knowledge in such domains is theoretically uncertain, incomplete, and subject to changes. Methods that rely on deductive proofs are not readily applicable. Concepts and statements in Internet business models are more or less plausible, stronger, or weaker supported, rather than true or false.

Fortunately, new research on e-business models is emerging. For example, Hayes and Finnegan (2005) present different approaches to understanding e-business models. One approach is e-business model *ontology*, which can be defined as a rigorous definition of the e-business issues and their interdependencies in a company's business model. The e-business model ontology focuses on four aspects of the organization, product innovation, infrastructure management, customer relationship, and financials.

Dimensions of product innovation are target customer segment, value proposition, and capabilities. Dimensions of customer relationship are information strategy, feel and serve, and trust and loyalty. Dimensions of infrastructure management are resources, activity configuration, and partner network, while dimensions of financials are revenue model, cost structure, and profit/loss.

Architectures for business models can be identified through the deconstruction and reconstruction of the value configuration. Value configuration elements are identified as well as the possible ways that information can be integrated in the value configuration and between the respective value configurations of the parties that are interacting.

As we have seen, decision makers are faced with an enormous range of electronic business models from which to choose. The process of fully researching each of these models can prove daunting. Such research is a feature of what has been termed the intelligence phase of decision making. This phase is important as options excluded at this stage do not get considered at a later stage. Hayes and Finnegan (2005) developed a framework for use at the intelligence phase to exclude models that are incompatible with prevailing organizational and supply chain characteristics.

The framework assesses the following characteristics: economic control, supply chain integration, functional integration, innovation, and input sourcing:

- **Economic control** refers to the degree to which a market is hierarchical or self-organizing. This characteristic can be measured in terms of the extent of regulatory bodies, government policy, customers, asset specificity, switching costs, proprietary products, capital requirements, and access to necessary inputs for new entrants in this industry.
- **Supply chain integration** is considered to be a measure of the degree to which the business functions and processes of an organization are integrated with those of their supply chain partners. This characteristic can be measured in terms of shipping scheduling, transportation management, tax reporting, negotiating customer credit terms, negotiating supplier credit terms, determining freight charges and terms, resource planning, and inventory control.
- **Functional integration** refers to the degree to which multiple functions are integrated in a business model. In order to measure the degree to which functions within an organization are integrated, a scale that considers a detailed list of processes can be applied. Examples of process integrations are purchase order processing with servicing functions, shipping scheduling with manufacturing, transportation management with financial functions, tax reporting with financial functions, negotiating customer credit terms with distribution, and negotiating supplier credit terms with distribution.
- **Innovation** is the degree of innovation of an e-business model, which can be defined as the extent to which processes can be performed via the Internet that were not previously possible. Innovation can be divided into internal and external components based on the firm's ability (internal) to innovate or assimilate innovations within the innovative environment of the industrial sector (external).
- **Sourcing** refers to the way in which inputs are sourced by the organization, either systematically from a long-term supplier or through spot markets. The issue of sourcing raw materials is more straightforward as manufacturing and operating inputs are either sourced systematically or on spot markets.

Hayes and Finnegan (2005) believe that their framework has the potential to help decision makers by providing a method of excluding from consideration those electronic business models that are unsuitable given prevailing organizational and environmental characteristics. Business models are excluded based on scale ratings for items measuring economic control, supply chain integration, functional integration, innovation, and sourcing. For each scale, the decision-maker needs to determine the number of attributes that are applicable to their organization.

SUMMARY

Strategy is about creating a competitively differentiated position to win customers in the marketplace. Firms leverage their resources and the ways they conduct business (activity system or business model) to create the differentiated position (Porter, 1985; Priem & Butler, 2001). Two complementary theories of firm are commonly used to study business strategy: resource-based theory and activity-based theory.

Resource-based theory stipulates that the firm's performance and strategic advantage are differentiated by the internal resources and capabilities it possesses, rather than the external opportunities and threats dictated by the industry conditions (Barney, 2001; Hitt et al., 2001; Loewendahl, 2000; Priem & Butler, 2001). The theory holds that, in order to generate a sustainable competitive advantage, the firm's resources must provide economic value and must be unique, inimitable, nonsubstitutable, and not readily obtainable in factor markets. Thus, IT resources that are inimitable and valuable can be rent yielding. In particular, it is the unique combination of sophisticated IT infrastructure and skilled human resources (core competences) of the enterprise creating the differentiated customer value that is imitable and valuable (Ravichandran & Lertwongsatien, 2005).

Activity-based theory of firm conceives the firm as a bundle of activities—as distinct from a bundle of resources in the resource-based theory (Sheehan, 2002). The activity-based model studies the firm's production function in value creation—transforming inputs to end products. It focuses on the flows of resources (but not the differences in stocks of resources) through a system of activities in creating economic value. From the activity-based theory, firms can configure its activities to create value, known as value configuration. Understanding the properties of value configuration is important as IT is inherently suitable as an aid to automation, coordination, and control of the activities within the configuration. Three types of value configuration can be used to model the firm: value chain (Porter, 1985), value shop, and value network (Stabell & Fjeldstad, 1998). Value chain is a firm that has a series or chain of primary activities comprising inbound logistics, production, outbound logistics, marketing and sales, and service. Economic value is created via efficient production of goods and services through this chain (Porter, 1985). This primary chain of activities is supported by secondary activities comprising infrastructure, human resources, technology development, and procurement. While value chain is modeled after manufacturing-based firms (fixed set of activities to produce standard products), it is less suited to modeling knowledge-intensive service firms (variable set of activities to produce customized solutions). This type of firms can be modeled by value shop (Stabell & Fjeldstad, 1998). Value shop is a firm that creates value by solving unique problems for customers and clients. In the value shop, activities are scheduled and resources are applied in a fashion that is dimensioned and appropriate to the needs of the client's problem. A value shop is characterized by five primary activities: problem finding and acquisition (by working with the client), problem solving, choice, execution, and control and evaluation (of how well the solution solves the problem). Control and evaluation feeds back to the problem finding in two ways: (a) solution is inadequate and problem-solving phase restarts anew, or (b) solution is successful and the client may extend the problem scope and a new problem-solving phase starts. A value network is a firm that creates value by connecting clients and customers that are, or want to be, dependent on each other (Stabell & Fjeldstad, 1998). These companies distribute information, money, products, and services. While activities in both value chain and value shop are done sequentially, activities in value networks occur in parallel. The value is enhanced by "network effect"—the more there are the number and combination of customers and access points in the network, the more valuable the network is to the customers. The value network (firm) admits customers that complement each other, and establishes, monitors, and terminates direct and indirect relationships between customers. Examples of value network firms include telecommunication companies and financial institutions. Value networks perform three activities: (a) development of customer network through marketing and recruiting of new customers, (b) development of new services and improvement of existing services, and (c) development of infrastructure so that customer services can be provided more efficiently and effectively.

A related concept to value configuration is the business model of firm, which is also closely related the firm's business strategy. Business models explain how firms work—they identify who the customers are and define how the pieces of a business fit together as a system to create value to the customers at appropriate price so profit can be made (Magretta, 2002). Business model can be viewed as comprising three components: the offering, the unique configuration of activities and organization, and the (particularly rare and inimitable) resources. IT can be designed to contribute to the uniqueness of each of these three components (Hedman & Kalling, 2002). Business models consist of nine basic building blocks; they get implemented by translating the model into concrete elements such as a business structure (organizational model), business processes (workflow), and infrastructure and systems (Osterwalder & Pigneur, 2005). Business models are subject to change. Firms use the basic constructs of business models to analyze the impact of external forces to define how their business models (and thus IT environments) should change to sustain their competitive advantages. Four business model change approaches (realization, extension, renewal, and journey) can be adopted, depending on the firm's business strategy (Linder & Cantrell, 2000). Business models were popularized by the dot.com era. Numerous IT-enabled e-business models have been proposed, based on the firms' specific e-strategies. The basic principles of business model, which aims to profit from delivering highly valuable differentiated services to customers, must be adhered to by e-business models. It requires development of a sound e-strategy focused on value delivery to the customers. E-business can be classified into eight atomic e-business models (Weill & Vitale, 2002). These e-business models explain the roles, relationships among the firms' consumers, allies, suppliers, and identifies the major flows of products, information, and money, together with the price and benefits to the participants. The Hayes and Finnegan (2005) framework (encompassing economic control, supply chain integration, functional integration, innovation, and sourcing) can be used for determining a firm's appropriate e-business model.

REFERENCES

Afuah, A., & Tucci, C. L. (2003). *Internet business models and strategies* (2nd ed.). New York: McGraw-Hill.

Amit, R., & Zott, C. (2001). Value creation in e-business. *Strategic Management Journal, 22*(6-7), 493–520.

Barney, J. B. (2001). Is the resource-based "view" a useful perspective for strategic management research? Yes. *Academy of Management Review, 26*(1), 41–56.

Chatzkel, J. (2002). A conversation with Göran Roos. *Journal of Intellectual Capital, 3*(2), 96–117.

Galanter, M., & Palay, T. (1991). *Tournament of lawyers: The transformation of the big law firms.* Chicago: The University of Chicago Press.

Hayes, J., & Finnegan, P. (2005). Assessing the potential of e-business models: Towards a framework for assisting decision-makers. *European Journal of Operational Research, 160*, 365–379.

Hedman, J., & Kalling, T. (2002). *IT and business models: Concepts and theories.* Forfattarna och Liber AB.

Hitt, M. A., Bierman, L., Shimizu, K., & Kochhar, R. (2001). Direct and moderating effects of human capital on strategy and performance in professional service firms: A resource-based perspective. *Academy of Management Journal, 44*(1), 13–28.

Hunt, S. D., & Arnett, D. B. (2003, Winter). Resource-advantage theory and embeddedness: explaining r-a theory's explanatory success. *Journal of Marketing Theory and Practice*, pp. 1–17.

Kim, E., Nam, D., & Stimpert, J. L. (2004). The applicability of Porter's generic strategies in the Digital Age: Assumptions, conjectures, and suggestions. *Journal of Management, 30*(5), 569–589.

Laudon, K. C., & Laudon, J. P. (2005). *Essentials of management information systems: Managing the digital firm* (6th ed.). Upper Saddle River, NJ: Pearson Education.

Linder, J. C., & Cantrell, S. (2000, May). Changing business models: Surveying the landscape. *Research and Insights.* Institute for High Performance Business, Accenture. Retrieved August 11, 2008, from http://www.accenture.com/Global/Research_and_Insights/Institute_For_High_Performance_Business/By_Subject/Strategy/BeInternet.htm

Loewendahl, B. R. (2000). *Strategic management of professional service firms* (2nd ed.). Copenhagen, Denmark: Copenhagen Business School Press.

Osterwalder, A., & Pigneur, Y. (2005). Clarifying business models: Origins, present, and future of the concept. *Communications of the Association for Information Systems, 16*, 1–25.

Magretta, J. (2002, May). Why business models matter. *Harvard Business Review*, pp. 3–8.

Plant, R. (2000). *eCommerce: Formulation of strategy.* Prentice Hall PTR.

Porter, M. E. (1985). *Competitive strategy.* New York: The Free Press.

Porter, M. E. (1996, June). What is strategy? *Harvard Business Review*, pp. 61–78.

Porter, M. E. (2001, March). Strategy and the Internet. *Harvard Business Review*, pp. 63–78.

Priem, R. L., & Butler, J. E. (2001). Is the resource-based "view" a useful perspective for strategic management research? *Academy of Management Review, 26*(1), 22–40.

Ravichandran, T., & Lertwongsatien, C. (2005). Effect of information systems resources and capabilities on firm performance: A resource-based perspective. *Journal of Management Information Systems, 21*(4), 237–276.

Robson, W. (1997). *Strategic management and information systems* (2nd ed.). London: Prentice Hall.

Seddon, P. B., Lewis, G. P., Freeman, P., & Shanks, G. (2004). The case for viewing business models as abstractions of strategy. *Communications of the Association for Information Systems, 13*, 427–442.

Sheehan, N. T. (2002, April). *Reputation as a driver in knowledge-intensive service firms* (Series of Dissertations). Sandvika, Norway: Norwegian School of Management.

Stabell, C. B., & Fjeldstad, Ø. D. (1998). Configuring value for competitive advantage: On chains, shops, and networks. *Strategic Management Journal, 19*, 413–437.

Thompson, A. A., & Strickland, A. J., III (2003). *Strategic management concepts and cases* (13th ed.). McGraw-Hill, Irwin.

Wade, M., & Hulland, J. (2004). The resource-based view and information systems research: Review, extension, and suggestions for future research. *MIS Quarterly, 28*(1), 107–142.

Weill, P., & Vitale, M. R. (2001). *Place to space: Migrating to eBusiness models.* Boston: Harvard Business School Press.

Weill, P., & Vitale, M. R. (2002). What IT infrastructure capabilities are needed to implement e-business models? *MIS Quarterly Executive, 1*(1), 17–34.

Chapter II
Strategic Management Principles

INTRODUCTION

Building on the understanding of the theories and models of firms, this chapter reviews the basic principles of strategic management of business enterprises. First, the basic principles of business strategy are explained. Only through in-depth understanding and diligent application of these principles will business executives be able to make strategic choices and craft an appropriate business strategy and the corresponding value configuration, business model, or e-business model for the firm.

Second, the role of corporate strategy and its relationships with business unit strategies are discussed. The discipline of strategic management is introduced together with the principles of strategy maps—a model which is explained and illustrated by case example of its application by a leading corporation in more detail in Chapter V as part of a strategic alignment discussion.

Third, the principles of strategic planning and the measurement of competitive strategy are described. These tasks ensure a corporate/business strategy is rigorously planned, resourced, and diligently executed to deliver the requisite strategic goals.

Following on from the resource-based and activity-based theories of firms discussed in Chapter I, this chapter describes the corresponding resource-based and activity-based strategies. In addition, with the increasing importance of corporate governance comes the need to ensure due consideration is given to ethics in information technology deployment. Theories for ethics in IT and their incorporation in IT strategy are still emerging. The basic issues for IT strategy developmental consideration are reviewed.

Fourth, to help managers develop sound business strategies for their firms, the chapter describes nine basic methods for business strategy analysis. From this analysis, firms will be able to analyze the needs for change from comparing the current state to the future target state of the business envisioned by the resultant business strategy.

Finally, to ensure firms will be able to leverage the strategic advantage that Internet technology may able to offer, this chapter continues from Chapter I's discussion of e-business models to explain the basic properties of e-strategies.

BASIC PRINCIPLES OF STRATEGY

Strategy is not about finding the universally best way of competing, nor is it an effort to be all things to every customer. Strategy is about defining a way of competing that delivers unique value in a particular set of uses or for a particular set of customers (Porter, 1985). Indeed, as Thompson and Strickland (2003, p. 3) postulate, "a company's strategy is the game plan management is using to stake out a market position, conduct its operation, attract and please customers, compete successfully, and achieve organizational objectives." To establish and maintain a distinctive strategic positioning, Porter (2001) stipulates that a company needs to follow six fundamental principles:

- It must start with the *right goal*: superior long-term return on investment. Only by grounding strategy in sustained profitability will real economic value be generated. Economic value is created when customers are willing to pay a price for a product or service that exceeds the cost of producing it.
- A company's strategy must enable it to deliver a *value proposition*, or set of benefits, different from those that competitors offer.
- Strategy needs to be reflected in a *distinctive value configuration.* To establish a sustainable competitive advantage, a company must perform different activities than rivals or perform similar activities in different ways.
- Robust strategies involve *trade-offs.* A company must abandon or forego some product features, services, or activities in order to be unique at others.
- Strategy defines how all the elements of what a company does *fit* together. A strategy involves making choices throughout the value configuration that are independent; all a company's activities must be mutually reinforcing.
- Strategy involves *continuity* of direction. A company must define a distinctive value proposition that it will stand for, even if that means foregoing certain opportunities.

Thus, the value configuration or e-business model (described in Chapter I) that the firm will choose can only be determined after the firm has decided on its strategic goal and the distinct value proposition that it intends to deliver to win the target markets it wishes to serve and make profit from. The unique value configuration and strategic resources required to deliver that distinct value proposition are designed as part of the strategy creation process. Only then will it make sense to define the IT strategy, which specified the IT applications and infrastructure required to implement the value configuration and support and integrate the various strategic resources required to deliver the distinct value proposition. This will ensure that the IT strategy is aligned with the business strategy—a practice which is called *strategic alignment* and the central theme of this book. This practice is described in Chapter V.

Strategy is both a plan for the future and a pattern from the past; it is the match an organization makes between its internal resources and skills (sometimes collectively called competencies) and the opportunities and risks created by its external environments. Strategy is the long-term direction of an organization. Strategy is a course of action for achieving an organization's purpose. Strategy is the direction and scope of an organization over the long term, which achieves advantage for the organization through its configuration of resources within a changing environment and to fulfill stakeholder expectations (Johnson & Scholes, 2002).

Strategy as a plan is a direction, a guide or course of action into the future, a path to get from here to there. Strategy as a pattern is a consistency in behavior over time. Strategy as a position is the determination of particular products in particular markets. Strategy as perspective is an organization's way of doing things (Mintzberg, 1994).

Necessary elements of a *business strategy* include mission, vision, objectives, market strategy, knowledge strategy, and our general approach to the use of information, information systems, and information technology.

Mission describes the reason for firm existence. For example, the reason for law firm existence is client's needs for legal advice. The mission addresses the organization's basic question of "What business are we in?"' This single essential sentence should include no quantification, but must unambiguously state the purpose of the organization and should just as carefully define what the organization does not do. The mission is an unambiguous statement of what the organization does and its long-term overall purpose. Its primary role is to set a direction for everyone to follow. It may be short, succinct, and inspirational, or contain broad philosophical statements that tie an organization to certain activities and to economic, social, ethical, or political ends. Values are also frequently stated alongside the mission. Three differing examples of missions are: To help people move from one place to another; to provide medical treatment to sick people; and to enable electronic communication between people.

Vision describes what the firm wants to achieve. For example, the law firm wants to become the leading law firm in Norway. The vision represents the view that senior managers have for the future of the organization, so it is what they want it to become. This view gives a way to judge the appropriateness of all potential activities that the organization might engage in. The vision gives a picture, frequently covering many aspects that everyone can identify with, of what the business will be in the future, and how it will operate. It exists to bring objectives to life and to give the whole organization a destination that it can visualize so that every stakeholder has a shared picture of the future aim.

Objectives describe where the business is heading. For example, the law firm can choose to merge with another law firm to become the leading law firm in Norway. Objectives are the set of major achievements that will accomplish the vision. These are usually small in number but embody the most important aspects of the vision such as financial returns, customer service, manufacturing excellence, staff morale, and social and environmental obligations.

Market strategy describes market segments and products. For example, the law firm can focus on corporate clients in the area of tax law.

Figure 2.1. Corporate strategy above other levels (Johnson & Scholes, 2002)

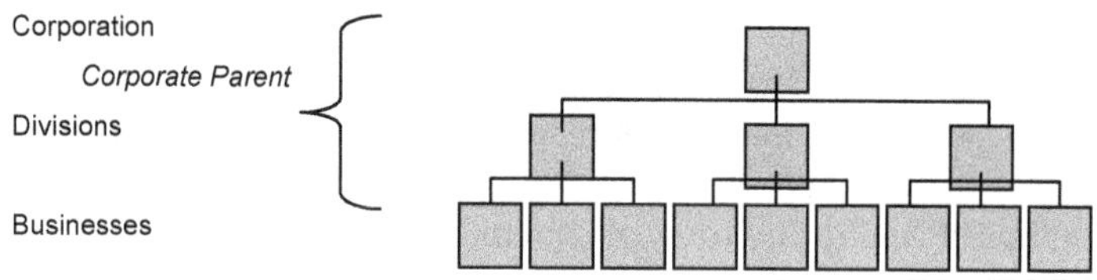

CORPORATE STRATEGY

Corporate strategy is concerned with the strategic decisions at the corporate level of organizations, decisions which may affect many business units. Managers at this level are acting on behalf of shareholders, or other stakeholders, to provide services and, quite possibly, strategic guidance to business units that seek to generate value by interacting with customers. In these circumstances, a key question is to what extent and how the corporate level might add value to what the businesses do or in the least how they might avoid destroying value (Johnson & Scholes, 2002).

A multibusiness company structure may consist of a number of business units grouped within divisions and a corporate center or head office providing, perhaps, legal services, financial services, and the staff of the chief executive. There are different views as to what is meant by corporate strategy and what represents corporate as distinct from business-level strategy. Johnson and Scholes (2002) argue that anything above the business unit level represents corporate activity.

The levels of management above that of business units are often referred to as the corporate parent (Figure 2.1). So, for example, the divisions within a corporation, which look after several businesses act in a corporate parenting role. The corporate parenting role can be as (Johnson & Scholes, 2002):

- **The portfolio manager.** A corporate parent acting as an agent on behalf of financial markets and shareholders with a view to enhancing the value attained from the various businesses in a more efficient or effective way than financial markets could. Their role is to identify and acquire undervalued assets or businesses and improve them.
- **The restructurer.** A corporate parent identifying restructuring opportunities in businesses and having the skills to intervene to transform performance in those businesses. They may well hold a diverse range of businesses within their portfolio. However, they do have a limited role at the business-unit level, which is to identify ways in which businesses can be turned around or fitness improved and to manage the restructuring period.
- **The synergy manager.** Synergy is often seen as the main reason for the existence of the corporate parent. Potentially, synergy can occur in situations where two or more activities or processes complement each other, to the extent that their combined effect is greater than the sum of the parts. In terms of corporate strategy, the logic is that value can be enhanced across business units. This can be done in a number of

ways: activities might be shared, and there may exist common skills or competences across businesses.

- **The parental developer.** A corporate parent seeks to employ its own competences as a parent to add value to its businesses. Here, the issue is not so much about how it can help create or develop benefits across business units or transference between business units, as in the case of managing synergy. Rather, parental developers have to enhance the potential of business units.

From a strategic planning perspective, corporate strategy will depend on the main role of the corporate parent. The portfolio manager is not directly intervening in the strategies of business units. Rather, they are setting financial targets, making central evaluations about the well-being and future prospects of such businesses, and investing or divesting accordingly. The restructurer is directly intervening in business units, as it is likely that the business restructuring opportunities that will be sought will be those that match the skills of the corporate center. The synergy manager will initiate activities and develop resources that are shared across business units. Managers in the businesses have to be prepared to cooperate in such transference and sharing (Johnson & Scholes, 2002).

Finally, the parental developer has to enhance the potential of business units in various ways. Suppose, for example, it has a great deal of experience in globalizing domestically based businesses; a valuable brand that may enhance the performance or image of a business; or perhaps specialist skills in financial management, brand marketing, or research and development. If such parenting competences exist, corporate managers then need to identify a parenting opportunity—a business or businesses not fulfilling their potential but where improvement could be made by the application of the competences of the parent (Johnson & Scholes, 2002).

STRATEGIC MANAGEMENT

Strategy without actions has no value to the company. To realize the future that the strategy aims to effect, the company must "manage" the strategy from formulation to implementation and benefits realization. This discipline is called *strategic management,* which includes understanding the strategic position of an organization, strategic choices for the future, and *turning strategy into action.* Understanding the strategic position is concerned with impact on strategy of the external environment, internal resources and competences, and the expectations and influence of stakeholders. Strategic choices involve understanding the underlying bases for future strategy at both the corporate and business unit levels and the options for developing strategy in terms of both the directions in which strategy might move and the methods of development. Translating strategy into action is concerned with ensuring that strategies are working in practice. A strategy is not just a good idea, a statement, or a plan. It is only meaningful when it is actually being carried out (Johnson & Scholes, 2002). The discipline of developing the strategy into a series of action plans is called *strategic planning.* Strategic planning is a subset of the strategic management discipline. It focuses on prioritizing resources to the selected action plans, and coordinating and controlling the activities to ensure the envisioned future will be created. This is described in detail in the next section.

Thompson and Strickland (2003, p. 6) stipulate that strategic management is a combined process of strategy making and strategy implementation, which comprises five interrelated managerial tasks:

1. Develop strategic vision and business mission—set the long-term direction and define what the company is trying to become so as "to infuse the organization with a sense of purposeful action."
2. Set objectives—translate the strategic vision into a set of (measurable) business outcomes that the company must accomplish.
3. Craft a strategy to achieve the objectives—the game plan to realize the business outcomes.
4. Implement and execute the chosen strategy efficiently and effectively to realize the desired business outcomes.
5. Evaluating performance, monitoring new developments (such as external market, industry, regulatory, and technology developments), and initiating corrective adjustments in vision, strategic objectives, strategy, or execution, as required, as a result of the actual experience, changing conditions, new ideas, and new opportunities.

As these tasks are interrelated, they need not be done sequentially. Strategic management is an ongoing process—not a start-stop event (Thompson & Strickland, 2003). Strategy and its implementation will adapt with performance experience and internal and external business environmental changes.

Generally, there are some characteristics of strategic decisions that are usually associated with the word *strategy* (Johnson & Scholes, 2002):

- Strategy is likely to be concerned with long-term direction of an organization.
- Strategic decisions are normally about trying to achieve some advantage for the organization over competition.
- Strategic decisions are likely to be concerned with the scope of an organization's activities.
- Strategy can be seen as the matching of the resources and activities of an organization to the environment in which it operates.
- Strategy can also be seen as building on or expanding an organization's resources and competences to create opportunities or to capitalize on them.
- Strategies may require major resource changes for an organization.
- Strategic decisions are likely to affect operational decisions.
- The strategy of an organization is affected not only by environmental forces and resource availability but also by the values and expectations of those who have power in and around the organization.

The notion of *strategic fit* is developing strategy by identifying opportunities in the business environment and adapting resources and competences so as to take advantage of these. The correct *positioning* of the organization is important, for example, in terms of the extent to which it meets clearly identified market needs. *Strategic position* is concerned with impact on strategy of the external environment, internal resources and competences, and the expectations and influence of stakeholders (Johnson & Scholes, 2002).

Strategy development is linked to strategic planning procedures. They represent the design approach to managing strategy, which views strategy development as the deliberate positioning of the organization through a rational, analytic, structured, and directive process. *Strategy as design* is an important strategy lens. Alternative and supplementing lenses are strategy as experience and strategy as ideas. *Strategy as experience* suggests that strategies develop in an adaptive fashion and change gradually. Strategy is here understood in terms of continuity; once an organization has adopted a particular strategy, it tends to develop from and within that strategy, rather than fundamentally changing direction. *Strategy as ideas* sees strategy as the emergence of order and innovation from the variety and diversity that exists in and around an organization. New ideas, and therefore innovation, may come from anywhere in an organization or from stimuli in the world around it (Johnson & Scholes, 2002).

Strategy development and strategy formation is also concerned with concepts such as strategic leadership, organizational politics, strategic incrementalism, the learning organization, imposed strategy, and multiple processes of strategy development. A *strategic leader* is an individual upon whom strategy development and change are seen to be dependent. Managers often suggest that the strategy being followed by the organization is really the outcome of *organizational politics* in terms of the bargaining and power politics that go on between important executives. Managers may have a view of where they want the organization to be in years to come and try to move towards this position incrementally, where *strategic incrementalism* can be thought of as the deliberate development of strategy by learning through doing over time. The concept of the *learning organization* and strategy as a learning process implies continual regeneration of strategy from the variety of knowledge, experience, and skills of individuals with a culture, which encourages mutual questioning and challenge around a shared purpose or vision. Forces or agencies external to the organization may cause *imposed strategy* that the organization has to follow. Different lenses and different strategy development processes may cause *multiple processes of strategy development*, since there is no right way in which strategies are developed (Johnson & Scholes, 2002).

At the beginning of this chapter, strategy is defined as a course of action for achieving an organization's purpose. Where managers have a clear understanding of their organization's purpose, this can provide strong guidance during processes of strategic thinking, strategy formation, and strategic change. The *organizational purpose* can function as a fundamental principle, against which strategic options can be evaluated. Organizational purpose can be defined as the reason for which an organization exists. The broader set of fundamental principles giving direction to strategic decision making, of which organizational purpose is the central element, is referred to as the *corporate mission*. The corporate mission may have elements such as organizational beliefs, organizational values, and business definition (Wit & Meyer, 2004).

Some authors distinguish between deliberate strategy and emergent strategy as two alternative processes of strategy formulation. According to Christensen and Raynor (2003), *deliberate strategy*—such as strategic planning—is the appropriate tool for organizing action if three conditions are met. First, the strategy must encompass and address correctly all of the important details required to succeed, and those responsible for implementation must understand each important detail in management's deliberate strategy. Second, if the organization is to take collective action, the strategy needs to make as much sense to all employees as they view the world from their own context as it does to top management, so that they will all act appropriately and consistent. Finally, the collective intentions must be realized with little unanticipated influence from outside political, technological, and market forces.

Emergent strategy bubbles up from within the organization and is the cumulative effect of day-to-day prioritization and investment decisions made by middle managers, engineers, salespeople, and financial staff. These tend to be tactical, day-to-day operating decisions that are made by people who are not in a visionary, futuristic, or strategic state of mind (Christensen & Raynor, 2003). Emergent strategy is also often the result of the dynamically readjusted strategy in response to external changing competitive market forces and conditions (Marchand, Kettinger, & Rollins, 2001).

Some authors distinguish between intended strategy and realized strategy. *Intended strategy* is an expression of desired strategic direction deliberately formulated and planned by managers. *Realized strategy* is the strategy actually being followed by an organization in practice. *Strategic drift* occurs when an organization's strategy gradually moves away from relevance to the forces at work in its environment (Johnson & Scholes, 2002).

As we will see throughout this book, strategic alignment is the key to successful strategic management. Strategic alignment calls for methods for analysis, choice, and implementation. A general method is available in terms of *strategy maps* as defined by Kaplan and Norton (2004), which represent interesting perspectives on strategy development and strategy formation. Strategy maps are used to describe how the organization creates value, and they were developed for the balanced scorecard. The strategy map is based on several principles:

- **Strategy balances contradictory forces.** Investing in intangible assets for long-term revenue growth usually conflicts with cutting costs for short-term financial performance.
- **Strategy is based on a differentiated customer value proposition.** Satisfying customers is the source of sustainable value creation.
- **Value is created through internal business processes.** The financial and customer perspectives in strategy maps and balanced scorecards describe the outcomes, that is, what the organization hopes to achieve.
- **Strategy consists of simultaneous, complementary themes.** Operations management, customer management, innovation, regulations, and societal expectations deliver benefits at different points in time.
- **Strategic alignment determines the value of intangible assets.** Human capital, information capital, and organization capital are intangible assets.

We will return to strategy maps in Chapter V. Understanding the strategic position of an organization and considering the strategic choices open to it are of little value unless the strategies managers wish to follow can be turned into organizational action. Strategies cannot take effect until they take shape in action. Such action takes form in the day-to-day processes and relationships that exist in organizations; and these need to be managed desirably in line with the intended strategy (Johnson & Scholes, 2002). The critical first step of turning strategy into action is called strategic planning.

STRATEGIC PLANNING

Translating strategies into action is no simple task. First, it is important to organize for success by introducing appropriate structure, processes, relationships, and boundaries. Second, it is important to enable success by managing people, managing information, managing finance, managing technology, and integrating resources. Finally, strategic change has to be managed by diagnosing the change situation, applying relevant styles and roles, and implementing levers for managing strategic change, such as organizational routines and symbolic processes (Johnson & Scholes, 2002).

The design school of strategic planning is built on the belief that strategy formation is a process of conception—the use of a few basic ideas to design strategy. Of these, the most essential is that of congruence, or fit, between external and organizational factors. A number of premises underlie the design school (Mintzberg, 1994):

1. Strategy formation should be a controlled, conscious process of thought.
2. Responsibility for the process must rest with the chief executive officer; that person is *the* strategist.
3. The model of strategy formation must be kept simple and informal.
4. Strategies should be unique: the best ones result from a process of creative design.
5. Strategies must come out of the design process fully developed.
6. The strategies should be made explicit and, if possible, articulated, which means they have to be kept simple.
7. Finally, once these unique, full-blown, explicit, and simple strategies are fully formulated, they must then be implemented.

Numerous researchers and executives advocate strategic planning. They argue that an explicit planning process rather than haphazard guesswork results in the collection and interpretation of data critical to creating and maintaining organization–environment alignment. They argue that planning generally produces better alignment and financial results than does trial-and-error learning (Miller & Cardinal, 1994).

Despite the intuitive appeal of these arguments, several researchers have countered that explicit strategic planning is dysfunctional or, at best, irrelevant. One of the most widely circulated criticisms is that planning yields too much rigidity. Proponents of the rigidity hypothesis maintain that a plan channels attention and behavior to an unacceptable degree, driving out important innovations that are not part of the plan. Given that the future parameters of even relatively stable industries are difficult to predict, these theoreticians consider any reduction in creative thinking and action dysfunctional (Miller & Cardinal, 1994).

Miller and Cardinal (1994) developed a model that might explain the inconsistent planning–performance findings reported in previous research. Results from the model suggest that strategic planning positively influences firm performance. Researchers who have concluded that planning does not generally benefit performance appear to have been incorrect.

Strategic planning procedures represent the design approach to managing strategy. Such procedures may take the form of highly systematized, step by step, chronological procedures involving many different parts of the organization.

Some of the key concepts in strategic planning are future thinking, controlling the future, decision making, integrated decision making, and a formalized procedure to produce an articulated result in the form of an integrated process of decisions. *Strategic planning is the process of deciding on the projects that the organization will undertake and the approximate amount of resources that will be allocated to each program over the next several years.*

Planning represents the extent to which decision makers look into the future and use formal planning methodologies. Planning is something we do in advance of taking action; it is anticipatory decision making. We make decisions before action is required. The focus of planning revolves around objectives, which are the heart of a strategic plan (Mintzberg, 1994).

The whole purpose of strategizing is to give organizations direction, instead of letting them drift. Organizations cannot act rationally without intentions; if you do not know where you are going, any behavior is fine. By first setting a goal and then choosing a strategy to get there, organizations can get organized. A structure can be chosen, tasks can be assigned, responsibilities can be divided, budgets can be allotted, and targets can be set. Not unimportantly, a control system can be created to measure results in comparison to the plan so that corrective action can be taken (Wit & Meyer, 2004).

Another advantage of the planning approach to strategy formation is that it allows for the formalization and differentiation of strategy tasks. Because of its highly structured and sequential nature, strategic planning lends itself well to formalization. The steps of the strategic planning approach can be captured in planning procedures to enhance and organize the strategy formation process. In such planning procedures, not all elements of strategy formation need to be carried out by one and the same person but can be divided among a number of people. The most important division of labor is often between those formulating the plans and those implementing them (Wit & Meyer, 2004).

We will return to strategic planning in Chapter IV to address its critical success factor.

MEASUREMENT OF COMPETITIVE STRATEGY

The measurement of competitive strategy is an important issue in strategic management. Porter (1985) first defined three generic competitive strategies: cost leadership, differentiation, and focus. Attempts to measure these strategies seek to capture differences in the extent to which firms emphasize various competitive dimensions. Competitive strategy is traditionally measured at the business level. Yet businesses often consist of product portfolios in which a different competitive strategy is used for each product. Thus, business-level measures may not be good indicators of product-level competitive strategy. Further, business-level analyses have found combined cost-leadership and differentiation strategies. But if competitive strategies are formulated at the product level, it is unclear whether combined strategies exist at that level.

Nayyar (1993) examined these issues. He found that business-level measures are not good indicators of product-level competitive strategies. He also found no evidence supporting the existence of combined competitive strategies at the product level. He found that cost-leadership and differentiation are mutually exclusive at the product level. They do not appear to be two dimensions of any strategy. Previously used business-level measures tend to identify combined competitive strategies, a result that may reflect the existence of product portfolios, rather than combined competitive strategies.

These findings suggest a need for a reexamination of the concept of competitive strategies. It appears that firms use competitive strategies for products and then construct product portfolios to obtain overall cost, differentiation, and preemption advantages. Within any industry, different firms may construct different product portfolios.

In his measurement of competitive strategy, Nayyar (1993) used the following competitive dimensions associated with a cost-leadership strategy: operating efficiency, cost control, pricing below competitors, managing raw materials cost and availability, trade sales promotion, manufacturing process improvements and innovation, and product cost reduction. The following competitive dimensions were associated with a differentiation strategy: new product development, extensive customer service, building and maintaining brand equity, marketing innovation, influence over distribution channels, targeting high-priced segment(s), advertising, building and maintaining the firm's reputation, providing product(s) with many features, and premium product quality. The following competitive dimensions were associated with a focus strategy: serving special market segment(s) and manufacturing and selling customized products.

Instead of measuring competitive strategy in terms of alternative strategies, Julien and Ramangalahy (2003) measured competitive strategy in terms of intensity. The more competitive a strategy is, the more intense is the competitive strategy. The intensity was measured in terms of marketing differentiation, segmentation differentiation, innovation differentiation, and products service. Marketing differentiation is based on competitive pricing, brand development, control over distribution, advertising, and innovation in terms of marketing techniques. Segmentation differentiation relies on the ability to offer specialized products to specific customer groups. Innovation differentiation is based on the ability to offer new and technologically superior products. Product service is based on the quality of the products and services provided by customers.

Competitive strategy must drive other strategies in the firm such as knowledge strategy. Executives must be able to articulate why customers buy a company's products or services rather than those of its competitors. What value do customers expect from the company? How does knowledge that resides in the company add value for customers? Assuming the competitive strategy is clear, managers will want to consider three more questions that can help them choose a primary knowledge management strategy (Hansen, Nohria, & Tierny, 1999):

- *Do you offer standardized or customized products?* Companies that follow a standardized product strategy sell products that do not vary much, if at all. A knowledge management strategy based on reuse fits companies that are creating standardized products.
- *Do you have a mature or innovative product?* A business strategy based on mature products typically benefits most from a reuse of existing knowledge.
- *Do your people rely on explicit or tacit knowledge to solve problems?* Explicit knowledge is knowledge that can be codified, such as simple software code and market data.

Strategic planning in a turbulent environment is challenging. The challenge of making strategy when the future is unknowable encourages reconsideration of both the process of strategy formulation and the nature of organizational strategy. Attempts to reconcile systematic strategic planning with turbulent, unpredictable business environments included the following (Grant, 2003):

- *Scenario planning.* Multiple scenario planning seeks not to predict the future but to envisage alternative views of the future in the form of distinct configurations of key environmental variables. Abandoning single-point forecasts in favor of alternative futures implies foresaking single-point plans in favor of strategy alternatives, emphasizing strategic flexibility that creates option values.
- *Strategic intent and the role of vision.* If uncertainty precludes planning in any detailed sense, then strategy is primarily concerned with establishing broad parameters for the development of the enterprise with regard to domain selection and domain navigation. Uncertainty requires that strategy is concerned less with specific actions and the more with establishing clarity of direction within which short-term flexibility can be reconciled with overall coordination of strategic decisions.
- *Strategic innovation.* If established companies are to prosper and survive, new external environments require new strategies. Strategic planning may be a source of institutional inertia rather than innovation. Yet, systematic approaches to strategy can be encouraging to managers to explore alternatives beyond the scope of their prior experiences. Strategic inertia may be more to do with the planners than of planning.
- *Complexity and self-organization.* Often faced with a constantly changing fitness landscape, maximizing survival implies constant exploration, parallel exploration efforts by different organizational members, and the combination of incremental steps. A key feature of strategic processes is the presence of semistructures that create plans, standards, and responsibilities for certain activities, while allowing freedom elsewhere. One application of the semistructure concept to strategy formulation concerns the use of simple rules that permit adaptation while establishing bounds that can prevent companies from falling off the edge of chaos.

Hopkins and Hopkins (1997) investigated relationships among managerial, environmental, and organizational factors, strategic planning intensity, and financial performance in U.S. banks. The results suggested that the intensity with which banks engage in the strategic planning process has a direct positive effect on banks' financial performance and mediates the effects of managerial and organizational factors on banks' performance. Results also indicated a reciprocal relationship between strategic planning intensity and performance. That is, strategic planning intensity causes better performance, and, in turn, better performance causes greater strategic planning intensity.

Strategic planning takes many different forms in different organizations. However, Boyd and Reuning-Elliotts' (1998) study of strategic planning provide strong support for the measurement properties of the strategic planning construct. In particular, the study results indicate that strategic planning is a construct that can be reliably measured through seven indicators: mission statement, trend analysis, competitor analysis, long-term goals, annual goals, short-term action plans, and ongoing evaluation. This evidence is important because previous researchers rarely tested for dimensionality of the planning construct, nor did most studies report tests of the reliability of their measures.

A small entrepreneurial startup may operate without any explicit strategy. The firm's strategy is likely to exist only in the head of the founder and, apart from being articulated through verbal communication with employees, suppliers, and other interested parties, may have been made explicit only when a business plan was required by outside investors. Most corporations with an established management structure tend to have some form of strategic planning process, though in small single-business companies, the strategy process may be highly informal with no regular cycle and may result in little documentation. Most larger companies, especially those with multiple businesses, have more systematic strategic planning processes, the outcome of which is a documented plan that integrates the business plans of the individual divisions (Grant, 2003).

Whether formal or informal, systematic or ad hoc, documented or not, the strategy formulation process is an important vehicle for achieving coordination within a company. The strategy process occupies multiple roles within the firm. It is in part a coordination device encouraging consistency between the decisions being made at different levels and in different parts of the organization. And it is in part a mechanism for driving performance by establishing consensus around ambitious long-term targets and by inspiring organizational members through creating vision and a sense of mission. In these roles, the strategy process can be important in achieving both coordination and cooperation (Grant, 2003).

The system through which strategy is formulated varies considerably from company to company. Even after the entrepreneurial startup has grown into a large company, strategy making may remain the preserve of the chief executive. Medium-sized single-business companies typically have simple strategic planning processes where functional managers provide key inputs such as financial projections and market analysis, but the key elements of strategy—goals, new business developments, capital investment, and key competitive initiatives—are decided by the chief executive (Grant, 2003).

The more systematized strategic planning processes typical of large companies with separate divisions or business units traditionally follow an annual cycle. Strategic plans tend to be for three to five years and combine top-down initiatives (indications of performance expectations and identification of key strategic initiatives) and bottom-up business plans (proposed strategies and financial forecasts for individual divisions and business units). After discussion between the corporate level and the individual businesses, the business plans are amended and agreed and integrated into an overall corporate plan that is presented to and agreed by the board of directors (Grant, 2003).

The resulting strategic plan typically comprises the following elements (Grant, 2003):

- A statement of the goals the company seeks to achieve over the planning period with regard to both financial targets and strategic goals.
- A set of assumptions or forecasts about key developments in the external environment to which the company must respond.
- A qualitative statement of how the shape of the business will be changing in relation to geographical and segment emphasis, and the basis on which the company will be establishing and extending its competitive advantage.
- Specific action steps with regard to decisions and projects, supported by a set of mileposts stating what is to be achieved by specific dates.
- A set of financial projections, including a capital expenditure budget and outline operating budgets.

Although directed toward making decisions that are documented in written strategic plans, the important elements of strategic planning form the strategy process: the dialog through which knowledge is shared and ideas communicated, the establishment of consensus, and the commitment to action and results (Grant, 2003).

RESOURCE-BASED STRATEGY

Strategic management models traditionally have defined the firm's strategy in terms of its product/market positioning—the products it makes and the markets its serves. The resource-based approach suggests, however, that firms should position themselves strategically based on their unique, valuable, and inimitable resources and capabilities rather than the products and services derived from those capabilities. Resources and capabilities can be thought of as a platform from which the firm derives various products for various markets. Leveraging resources and capabilities across many markets and products, rather than targeting specific products for specific markets, becomes the strategic driver. While products and markets may come and go, resources and capabilities are more enduring.

According to Hitt, Bierman, Shimizu, and Kochhar (2001), scholars argue that resources form the basis of firm strategies and are critical in the implementation of those strategies as well. Therefore, firm resources and strategy seem to interact to produce positive returns. Firms employ both tangible resources (such as buildings and financial resources) and intangible resources (like human capital and brand equity) in the development and implementation of strategy. Outside of natural resource monopolies, intangible resources are more likely to produce a competitive advantage because they are often rare and socially complex, thereby making them difficult to imitate.

According to Barney (2001), resource-based theory includes a very simple view about how resources are connected to the strategies a firm pursues. It is almost as though once a firm becomes aware of the valuable, rare, costly to imitate, and nonsubstitutable resources it controls, the actions the firm should take to exploit these resources will be self-evident. That may be true some of the time. For example, if a firm possesses valuable, rare, costly to imitate, and nonsubstitutable economies of scale, learning curve economies, access to low-cost factors of production, and technological resources, it seems clear that the firm should pursue a cost leadership strategy.

However, it will often be the case that the link between resources and the strategy of a firm is not being so obvious. Resource-based strategy has to determine when, where, and how resources may be useful. Such strategy is not obvious, since a firm's resources may be consistent with several different strategies, all with the ability to create the same level of competitive advantage. In this situation, how should a firm decide which of these several different strategies it should pursue? According to Barney (2001), this and other questions presented by Priem and Butler (2001) concerning the resource-based theory of the firm indicate that the theory is still a theory in many respects, and that more conceptual and empirical research has to be conducted to make the theory more useful to business executives who develop resource-based strategies for their firms.

Resource-based strategy is concerned with the mobilization of resources. Since perceived resources merely represent potential sources of value-creation, they need to be mobilized to create value. Conversely, for a specific resource to have value, it has to increase or otherwise facilitate value-creation. The activity whereby tangible and intangible resources are recognized, combined, and turned into activities with the aim of creating value is the process here called resource mobilization. The term *resource mobilization* is appropriate, as it incorporates the activity-creation based on both individual and organizational resources, as well as tangibles and intangibles. According to Haanaes (1997), alternative terms such as resource allocation, resource leveraging, or resource deployment are appropriate when describing the value-creation based on tangible resources, but less so for intangibles. For example, a competence cannot be allocated, as the person controlling it has full discretion over it. Moreover, the competence can be used in different ways. An engineer can choose to work for a different organization and to work with varying enthusiasm. Also, the same engineer can choose not to utilize his or her competence at all. The term resource mobilization is thus meant to cover the value-creation based on all types of resources, and it recognizes that all activity creation has a human aspect.

In strategic management and organization theory, the importance for the firm of reducing uncertainty and its dependence on key resources that it cannot fully control has received much attention. If a large part of the resource accumulation takes place in terms of increased competences that key professionals could easily use for the benefit of other employers, the firm needs to set priorities in terms of linking these individually controlled resources to the firm. Loewendahl (2000) suggests three alternative strategies. The simplest strategy, which may be acceptable to some firms, involves minimizing the dependence on individual professionals and their personal competence. In this sense, the firm chooses to avoid the dependence on individual tangibles. A second strategy is that of linking the professionals more tightly to the firm and reducing the probability of losing them. The third alternative strategy involves increasing the organizationally controlled competence resources without reducing the individually controlled resources. Such a strategy leads to a reduction in the relative impact of individual professionals on total performance without reducing the absolute value of their contributions. Firms that have been able to develop a high degree of organizationally controlled resources, including relational resources that are linked to the firm rather than to individual employees, are likely to be less concerned about the exit and entry of individual professionals and more concerned about the development and maintenance of their organizational resource base.

According to Maister (1993), there is a natural, but regrettable, tendency for professional firms, in their strategy development process, to focus on new things: What new markets does the firm want to enter? What new clients does the firm want to target? What new services does the firm want to offer? This focus on new services and new markets is too often a cop-out. A new specialty (or a new office location) may or may not make sense for the firm, but it rarely does much (if anything) to affect the profitability or competitiveness of the vast bulk of the firm's existing practices.

On the other hand, an improvement in competitiveness in the firm's core businesses will have a much higher return on investment since the firm can capitalize on it by applying it to a larger volume of business. Enhancing the competitiveness of the existing practice will require changes in the behavior of employees. It implies new methods of operating, new skill development, and new accountabilities. Possible strategies for being more valuable to clients can be found in answers to the following questions (Maister, 1993):

- Can we develop an innovative approach to *hiring* so that we can be more valuable to clients by achieving a higher caliber of staff than the competition?

- Can we *train* our people better than the competition in a variety of technical and counseling skills so that they will be more valuable on the marketplace than their counterparts at other firms?
- Can we develop innovative *methodologies* for handling our matters (or engagements, transactions, or projects) so that our delivery of services becomes more thorough and efficient?
- Can we develop systematic ways of helping, encouraging, and ensuring that our people are skilled at client *counseling* in addition to being top suppliers?
- Can we become better than our competition at accumulating, disseminating, and building our firmwide expertise and experience, so that each professional becomes more valuable in the marketplace by being *empowered* with a greater breadth and depth of experience?
- Can we organize and *specialize* our people in innovative ways so that they become particularly skilled and valuable to the market because of their focus on a particular market segment's needs?
- Can we become more valuable to our clients by being more systematic and diligent about *listening* to the market: collecting, analyzing, and absorbing the details of their business than does our competition?
- Can we become more valuable to our clients by investing in research and *development* on issues of particular interest to them?

In resource-based strategy, there has to be consistency between resources and business. The logic behind this requirement is that the resources should create a competitive advantage in the business in which the firm competes. To meet this requirement, corporate resources can be evaluated against key success factors in each business. When doing so, it is important to keep in mind that in order to justify retaining a business, or entering a business, the resources should convey a substantial advantage. Merely having pedestrian resources that could be applied in an industry is seldom sufficient to justify entry or maintain presence in an attractive industry (Collis & Montgomery, 1997).

Moreover, managers must remember that, regardless of the advantage of a particular corporate resource appears to yield, the firm must also compete on all the other resources that are required to produce and deliver the product or service in each business. One great resource does not ensure a successful competitive position, particularly if a firm is disadvantaged on other resource dimensions (Collis & Montgomery, 1997).

ACTIVITY-BASED STRATEGY

The goal of strategy formulation in the resource-based theory is to identify and increase those resources that allow a firm to gain and sustain superior rents. Firms owning strategic resources are predicted to earn superior rents, while firms possessing no or few strategic resources are thought to earn industry average rents or below average rents. The goal of strategy formulation in the activity-based theory is to identify and explore *drivers* that allow a firm to gain and sustain superior rents. *Drivers* are a central concept in the activity-based theory. To be considered drivers, firm level factors must meet three criteria: they are structural factors at the level of activities, they are more or less controllable by management, and they impact the cost and/or differentiation position of the firm. The definition of drivers is primarily based on what drivers do. Drivers are abstract, relative, and relational properties of activities. For example, scale of an activity is a driver, as the size of the activity relative to competitors may represent a competitive advantage.

The analytical focus of the resource-based theory is potentially narrower than that of the activity-based theory. While the activity-based theory takes the firm's entire activity set as its unit of analysis, the resource-based theory focuses on individual resources or bundles of resources. Having a narrower focus means that the resource-based theory may not take into account the negative impact of resources, how a resource's value may change as the environment changes, or the role of noncore resources in achieving competitive advantage.

The activity-based and resource-based theories are similar as they both attempt to explain how firms attain superior positions through factors that increase firm differentiation or lower firm cost. While drivers and resources share a common goal of achieving and sustaining superior positions, the manner by which they are seen to reach a profitable position is different. With the resource-based theory, it is the possession or control of strategic resources that allow a firm to gain a profitable position. On the other hand, drivers within the activity-based theory are not unique to the firm. They are generic structural factors available to all firms in the industry in the sense that they are conceptualized as properties of the firm's activities. *A firm gains a profitable position by configuring its activities using drivers. It is this position that a firm may own but only if it is difficult for rivals to copy the firm's configuration.*

The sustainability of superior positions created by configuring drivers or owning resources is based on barriers to imitation. The sustainability of competitive advantage as per the activity-based theory is through barriers to imitation at the activity level. If the firm has a competitive advantage, as long as competitors are unable to copy the way activities are performed and configured through the drivers, the firm should be able to achieve above-average earnings over an extended period. The sustainability of superior profitability in the resource-based theory is through barriers to imitation of resources and immobility of resources. If resources are easily copied or substituted, then the sustainability of the position is suspect.

Sheehan (2002) concludes his discussion by finding similarities between the resource-based theory and the activity-based theory. Resources in the resource-based theory are similar to drivers in the activity-based theory, as both are based on earning efficiency rents. Furthermore, capabilities in the resource-based theory are similar to activities in the activity-based theory, as both imply action.

ETHICS IN IT

Schultz (2006, p. 2) argues: "Nowadays, 'ethics' seems to be an *inclusive* term for concerns referred to by 'morality', 'value', and 'justice'...and it is also concerned with the value or goodness of things and situations and with the justness of institutions (both formal and informal)."

Stakeholder theory is a theory of organizational management and ethics. Indeed all theories of strategic management have some moral content, though it is often implicit. Moral content in this case means that the subject matter of the theories are inherently moral topics (i.e., they are not amoral). Stakeholder theory is distinct because it addresses morals and values explicitly as a central feature of managing organizations. The ends of cooperative activity and the means of achieving these ends are critically examined in stakeholder theory in a way that they are not in many theories of strategic management (Phillips, Freeman, & Wicks, 2003).

As far as we know, there is no comprehensive use of stakeholder theory in IT strategy research. Although Lacity and Willcocks (2000) have used the term in identifying four distinct customer stakeholders and three distinct supplier stakeholders, their research has not gotten any further on this path. In an IT strategy context, a stakeholder theory approach will describe the relationship as a nexus of cooperative and competitive interests possessing intrinsic value.

The term *stakeholder* is a powerful one. This is due, to a significant degree, to its conceptual breadth. The term means many different things to many different people and hence evokes praise and scorn from a wide variety of scholars and practitioners of myriad academic disciplines and backgrounds. Such breadth of interpretation, though one of stakeholder theory's greatest strengths, is also one of its most prominent theoretical liabilities as a topic of reasoned discourse. Much of the power of stakeholder theory is a direct result of the fact that, when used unreflectively, its managerial prescriptions and implications are merely limitless. When discussed in instrumental variation (i.e., that managers should attend to stakeholders as a means to achieving other organizational goals such as profit or shareholder wealth maximization), stakeholder theory stands virtually unopposed (Phillips et al., 2003).

Ethics in information technology is an emerging research field. Schultz (2006, p. 5) identifies four basic features of information technology that could create new ethical issues: (1) *speed* of information technology; (2) unlimited size of information *storage* capacity; (3) *availability* of information at any location (connectivity); and (4) easy *reproduction* of digital information. Earlier research (Salehnia, 2002) has addressed ethical issues related to these basic features such as Internet privacy, digital contract laws, copyright, piracy, and other security issues. Schultz (2006) has analyzed, among other things, the ethical issues of offshoring from both the perspectives of the source and destination countries. A recent article (Intorna, 2007) addressing the question of morality of technology, published in the specialist journal *Ethics and Information Technology*, exemplifies the kinds of ethical issues that IT strategy must address. Intorna (2007) argues that it is important to make the ethics (politics) of information technology visible via (a) disclosive ethical archaeology—to subject technology sites to ongoing disclosive scrutiny, (b) transparent design—to open up design and development (and implementation) activity to multiple stakeolders for ongoing scrutiny and debate, (c) engaging and multistable[1] design—to prevent the user of technology design from becoming unwittingly enrolled into political programs not of their choosing, and (d) materializing morality—technology is transparent and open to ongoing scrutiny.

Ethics of information technology is a corporate governance issue managed through IT governance (Raghupathi, 2007). IT ethical issues within organizations arise from the relation between IT professionals and non-IT personnel, known as *users* (Schultz, 2006, p. 34). Standards and policies are usually specified by organizations to ensure ethical conduct is conformed by IT professionals and the user community as part of IT governance. The contemporary ethics issues currently being addressed by IT governance include codes of ethics, for example, ACM Code of Ethics (Schultz, 2006, p. 48); Web/e-mail policy; data protection and privacy; integration of customer relationship, supplier management, and compliance with privacy laws; and compliance with corporate governance (such as the

Sarbanes-Oxley Act) and USA Patriot Act (Raghupathi, 2007). IT governance as an IT management practice is discussed in detail in Chapter IX.

BUSINESS STRATEGY ANALYSIS

Before we can define the desired business situation and craft the appropriate business strategy, we must analyze the current business situation. There are many business analysis techniques for strategy development. Some are general, while others are more specific. General analysis techniques include SWOT analysis and the X model. Specific analysis techniques include business direction (mission, vision, objectives), market strategy, value system, competitive forces, and product life cycle. We will review the following methods:

I. **SWOT analysis.** SWOT analysis is an analytical tool for assessing the present and future situation focusing on strengths (S), weaknesses (W), opportunities (O), and threats (T). The whole company may be the object of analysis, but also a department in a company or a project in a company may be the study object.

II. **X model.** The X model is a tool for description and analysis of both the current and a desired situation. It is a method for assessing the situation within a company, a project, or a department. The situation consists of a time period in which work is done. In the beginning of the time period, there are both factual and personal inputs, and at the end of the period, there are both factual and personal outputs.

III. **Business direction.** Important business concepts are mission, vision, and objectives. What are the business outcomes that the strategy must achieve?

IV. **Market strategy.** The market strategy shows our position and ambition in the marketplace. We can either have the same product as our competitors, or we can have a different product. If we have the same product as everyone else, it has to be sold at the same price as all the others (as in a vegetable market or through the Internet). It is not possible for an Internet bookstore to sell at a higher price than others, when there is perfect information, and information searching is associated with no costs. This is called the law of indifference. In order to survive, the company must have a cost advantage that will give higher profits and result in higher earnings for the owners. If we are selling a product that our customers perceive to be different from our competitors' product, then we have differentiation. A service may in its basic form be the same for all companies, like an airline travel, in the sense that all airlines are supposed to bring you safely to your destination. The product is differentiated by supplementary services.

V. **Competitive forces.** The basis of this method is that a company exists within an industry, and to succeed, it must effectively deal with the competitive forces that exist within the particular industry. For example, the forces in an emerging industry such as mobile communication are considerably different from those of established industries such as financial services. The company interacts with its customers, suppliers, and competitors. In addition, there are potential new entrants into the particular competitive marketplace and potential substitute products and services. To survive and succeed in this environment, it is important to understand these interactions and the implications in terms of what opportunities or competitive advantage can occur.

VI. **Product portfolio analysis.** There are a number of approaches that aim to relate the competitive position of an organization to the maturity of its product. The models assume there is a basic S-shaped curve description to the growth phenomenon of products. Four stages in the life cycle of any product can be identified as introduction, growth, maturity, and decline. When we look at the life cycle of all products in the firm, we can apply product portfolio analysis. This method shows the relationship between a product's current or future revenue potential and the appropriate management stance. The two by two matrix names the products in order to chart symptoms into a diagnosis so that effective management behavior can be adopted. The matrix classifies products according to the present market share and the future growth of that market. A successful product that lasts from emergent to mature market goes around the matrix. This strategy is simply to milk the cows, divest the dogs, invest in the stars, and examine the wild cats.

VII. **Environmental analysis.** Environmental analysis is concerned with the external corporate environment. An analysis of the environment is important because it increases the quality of the strategic decision making by considering a range of the relevant features. The organization identifies threats and opportunities facing it, and those factors that might assist in achieving objectives and those that might act as a barrier. The strategy of the organization should be directed at exploiting the environmental opportunities and blocking environmental threats in a way that is consistent with internal capabilities. This is a matter of environmental fit that allows the organization to maximize its competitive position. An external analysis can investigate politics, the economy, the society, and the technology. This is sometimes called PEST analysis. If we include the study of legal and environmental matters, we call it PESTLE. The analytical work that has to be done in the company when doing environmental analysis is concerned with questions such as: What are the implications of the trends (changes in the environment)? What can the company do in order to meet the opportunities and threats that follow?

VIII. **Knowledge analysis.** Distinctions can be made between core knowledge, advanced knowledge, and innovative knowledge. While core knowledge is required to stay in business, advanced knowledge makes the firm competitively visible, and innovative knowledge allows the firm to lead its entire industry. The knowledge map can be applied to identify firm position compared with competitors' knowledge levels.

In the following sections, we describe each method in detail. All methods are generally used by enterprises with varying degree of details in crafting the appropriate business strategy to achieve the enterprise vision and strategic objectives.

Method I: SWOT Analysis

SWOT analysis is an analytical tool for assessing the present and future situation focusing on strengths, weaknesses, opportunities, and threats. The whole company may be the object of analysis, but also a department in a company or a project in a company may be the study object. As illustrated in Figure 2.2, strengths and weaknesses are concerned with the internal situation, while opportunities and threats are concerned with the external situation.

The main advantage of this technique is its readiness for application. The main disadvantage is that it will represent subjective views. Furthermore, management has to be

Figure 2.2. Example of SWOT analysis

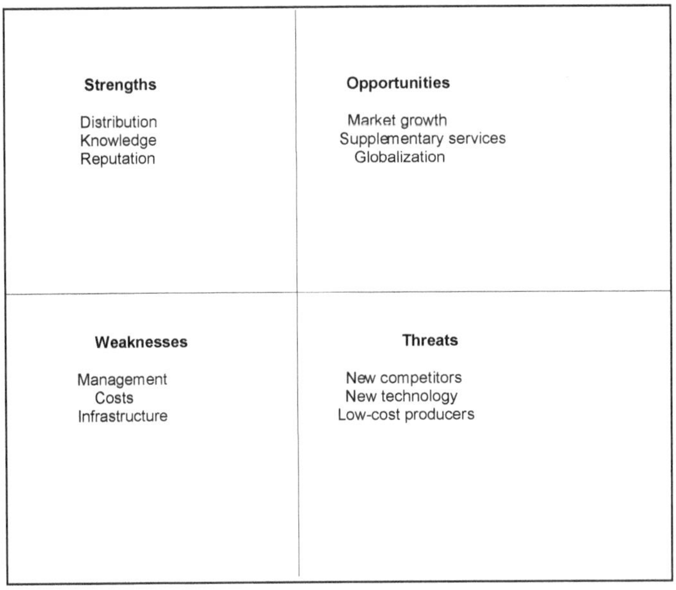

aware of employee expectations if employees are invited to contribute in a SWOT analysis, as they will expect something to happen after the analysis is completed.

The SWOT model reveals the needs for changes in business. The company has to change in order to take advantage of tomorrow's opportunities and to avoid future threats. The company does also need to change to utilize strengths and to avoid weaknesses. For example, the company in Figure 2.2 could:

- Seek more benefits from distribution, knowledge, and reputation
- Improve management, reduce costs, and improve infrastructure
- Find ways of participating in the market growth
- Develop supplementary services
- Expand market activities worldwide
- Develop entry barriers for competitors
- Learn and introduce new technology
- Cut costs where there are low-cost producers

Method II: X Model

The X model is a tool for description and analysis of both the current and a desired situation. It is a method for assessing the situation within a company, a project, or a department. The situation consists of a time period in which work is done. In the beginning of the time period, there are both factual and personal inputs, and at the end of the period, there are both factual and personal outputs, as illustrated in Figure 2.3.

Figure 2.3. The X model in a time perspective

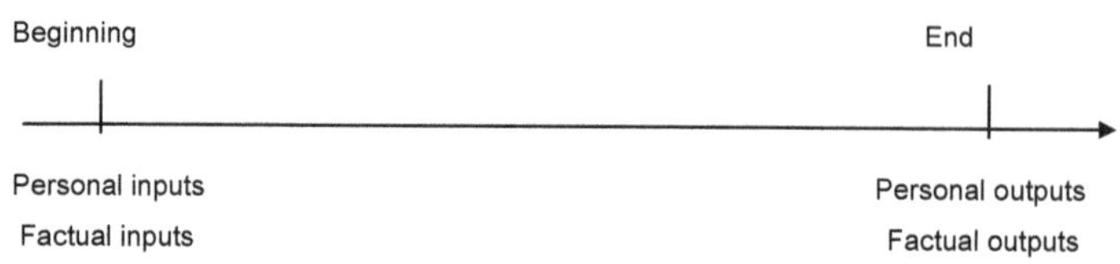

Figure 2.4. Inputs and outputs of the X model

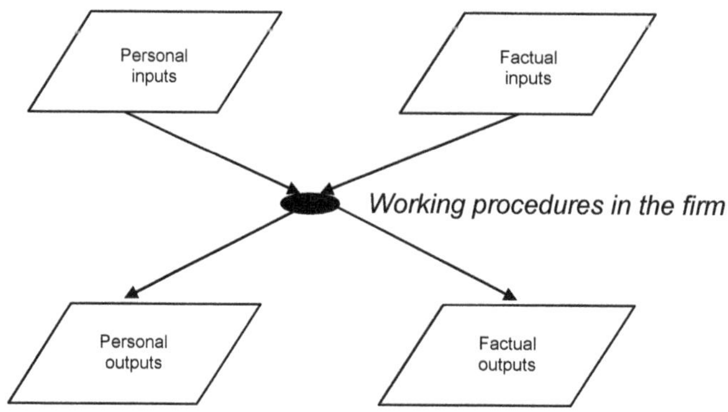

This technique is called the X model because of the visual image we see illustrated in Figure 2.4. It uses the same description technique as the Y model, where a rectangle represents an information set and a dot represents an information process.

The personal inputs consist of people with knowledge, experience, attitudes, needs, and ambitions. The factual inputs consist of tasks, objectives, plans, procedures, and resources. The working manners and procedures consist of working styles, cooperation, and communication. Personal outputs consist of people with new knowledge, new experience, new attitudes, new needs, and new ambitions. Similarly, factual outputs consist of executed tasks, objectives achieved or not, plans implemented or not, new procedures installed, and used resources.

The main advantage of the X model is its very compressed description; a description of a comprehensive situation is condensed onto a page. Thereby, it gives a very good overview of what has happened or will happen. Another advantage is that the model focuses both on factual and personal inputs, thereby providing a good starting point for business analysis. An example of a knowledge management project will illustrate the X model in Figure 2.5.

We see in this example that the expected outcome is reduced motivation. Reasons for this may be too much work close to milestones as well as medium quality communication. Probably, we may be able to achieve improved motivation if these two factors are changed as illustrated in Figure 2.6. The working manner is determined by the factual and personal inputs. The reason for too much work close to milestones might be that there is too short a time allocated to the work. We would also like to change the inputs, but that might not always be possible as they are given or determined by others.

Figure 2.5. The X model applied to a project in the company

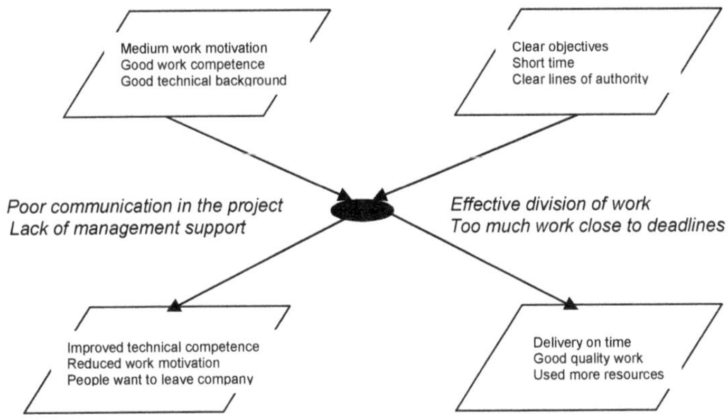

Figure 2.6. Example of causal analysis in the X model

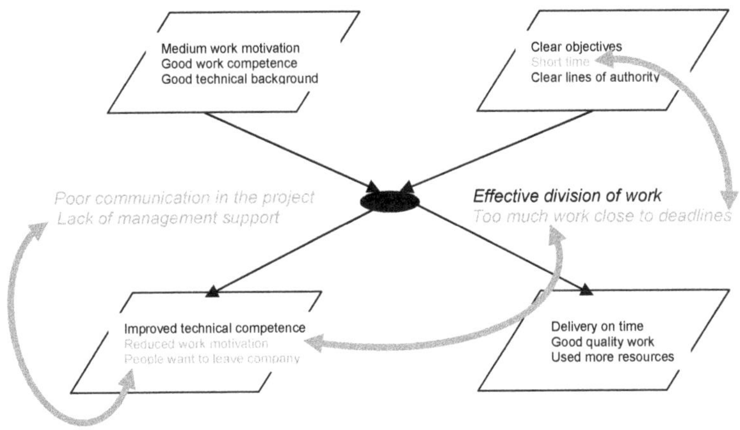

When we have described the current situation and working manners, we can explain why personal and factual outputs become what they do. The next step is to describe the desired situation. It is easy to say what we would like the desired situation to be. Then we can go backwards in the X model to revise personal and factual inputs as well as working procedures.

Method III: Business Direction

Important business concepts are mission, vision, and objectives. A *mission* is an unambiguous statement of what the company does and its long-term, overall purpose. It indicates what kind of business the company is in and which markets it serves. For example a telecom corporation such as Telenor in Norway is in the business of providing connections, while a power corporation such as Statnett is in the business of providing energy. The mission of a law firm is to provide legal advice. The mission describes a justification for firm existence; it states the purpose of the organization. The mission answers the question: What business are we in?

A *vision* is a statement of what the business will be in the future (three to five years) and how the company will operate. It indicates how good the company wants to be. Given the mission that describes the justification for existence, the vision is to describe what ambitions the firm has for the future. For example, the vision of Telenor may be to develop from a local operator in Norway to a global player in the telecommunications market. For Statnett, the vision might be to expand into other energy sources besides hydroelectric power. For a law firm, the vision might be to become the leader in business law. The vision represents the view that senior management has for the future of the organization; it is what they want it to become or achieve. The vision answers the question: What do we want to achieve in this business?

Objectives are short-term (such as annual) and interim (such as 2–3 years) targets that management is setting to take the company toward its vision. Objectives are quantified targets, such as financial returns, customer service, manufacturing performance, staff morale, and social and environmental contributions. For example, the objective of Telenor may be to double its income from foreign business by a certain date. For Statnett, it may be to have a fraction of its business in nonhydropower. For a law firm, an objective might be to recruit all the best business lawyers. Objectives define the desired future positions of the organization; they are specific and tangible measures of future targets. Objectives answer the question: What should be our future positions in this business?

The Norwegian School of Management BI (NSM) will serve as an example. The mission of NSM is teaching business administration and management and doing research. Its vision is to be one of the leading research-based business schools in Europe and an attractive workplace for leading faculty members within important management areas such as marketing, finance, and technology. Objectives include the number of doctoral students and the amount of research funding in the next one, two, and three years.

Method IV: Market Strategy

The market strategy shows our position and ambition in the marketplace. Figure 2.7 provides an illustration of generic market strategies. We can either have the same product as our competitors, or we can have a different product. If we have the same product as everyone else, it has to be sold at the same price as all the others (as in a vegetable market or through the Internet). It is not possible for an Internet bookstore to sell at a higher price than others when there is perfect information and information searching is associated with no costs. This is called the law of indifference. In order to survive, the company must have a cost advantage that will give higher profits and result in higher earnings for the owners.

If we are selling a product that our customers perceive to be different from our competitors' product, then we have differentiation. A service may in its basic form be the same for all companies, like an airline travel, in the sense that all airlines are supposed to bring you safely to your destination. The product is differentiated by supplementary services. For example, some airlines give you the option of booking certain seats in advance; some airlines have frequent flyer programs, while others have better meals.

The two generic market strategies are concerned with cost leadership or differentiation. In Figure 2.8, required skills and resources as well as organizational requirements are listed for the two strategies.

Figure 2.7. Generic market strategies

	Same product	Different product
Broad market scope (all markets)	Overall cost leadership	Differentiation
Narrow market scope (selected markets)	Cost based focus	Differentiation based focus

Figure 2.8. Characteristics of generic market strategies

Generic strategy	Required skills and resources	Organizational requirements
Cost leadership	• Frequent investments and easy access to capital • Process skills • Intensive supervision of labor	• Tight cost control; frequent, detailed control reports • Structured organization and responsibilities • Incentives based on meeting quantitative targets
Differentiation	• Strong on marketing and creativity • Product skills • Strong capability in basic research • Corporate reputation for quality or technological leadership • Strong cooperation with distribution channels	• Strong coordination in research and development (R&D), product development, and marketing • Market based incentives • Ability to attract highly skilled labor and creative people • Looser, more trusting organizational relationships

Cost leadership means the organization aims to be the lowest-cost producer in the marketplace. The organization enjoys above-average performance by minimizing costs. The product or service offered must be comparable in quality to those offered by others in the industry in order that customers perceive its relative value. Typically, there is only one cost leader. If more than one organization seek advantage with this strategy, a price war ensues, which eventually may drive the organization with the higher cost structure out of the marketplace.

Differentiation means the organization qualifies its products or service in a way that allows it to appear unique in the marketplace. The organization has identified which qualitative dimensions are most important to its customers, and it has found ways to add value along one or more of those dimensions. In order for this strategy to work, the price charged customers by the differentiator must seem fair relative to the price charged by competitors. Typically, multiple firms in any given market will employ this strategy (Pearlson, 2001).

Method V: Competitive Forces

The basis of this method is that a company exists within an industry, and to succeed, it must effectively deal with the competitive forces that exist within the particular industry. For example, the forces in an emerging industry such as mobile communication are considerably different from those of established industries such as financial services.

The company interacts with its customers, suppliers, and competitors. In addition, there are potential new entrants into the particular competitive marketplace and potential substitute products and services. To survive and succeed in this environment, it is important to understand these interactions and the implications in terms of what opportunities or competitive advantage can occur. Figure 2.9 illustrates the competitive forces model (Porter, 1985).

At any one time, one or more of the forces may be exerting particular pressure on the competing company. The competitive forces method models the competitive world in which any organization exists and the forces that play upon it. The current competitive position of any organization will be the net force of these five aggregated. In order to understand the strength of any one of these forces, an understanding must be built up of the contributory factors to its power. Theoretically, there are a large number of these, but for any given organization, many of them will not be relevant (Robson, 1997):

- **Rivalry among existing competitors.** This rivalry can range from intense in a cut-throat industry to mild in an affluent one. When rivalry is high, profits tend to be low. Industries that are static or in decline will have more intense rivalry than those that are rapidly growing. When there are high fixed costs or high storage costs, then the volume of sales must be maintained, so rivalry heightens. Rivalry is more intense when there is overcapacity caused by demand fluctuations or production constraints. Where there is no brand loyalty, that is, no differentiation, then demand depends on price, and when switching costs are small, this is very elastic, so rivalry will be heated. If there are lots of organizations of a similar size in the same pool,

Figure 2.9. Porter's (2001) competitive forces model

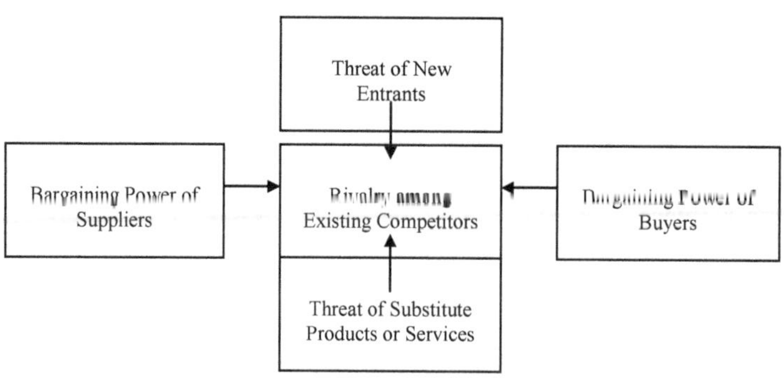

then rivalry will be intense. If leaving the industry will cost a lot either physically or emotionally, then the rivalry will tend to be intense.

- **Threat of new entrants.** The height of the barriers against this threat and the determination to get over them defines the industry's profitability. Government policy can represent such a barrier when a license to operate is required or strict safety rules have to be applied. The threat of reactions to a new entrant acts as a barrier, since dealing with aggressive countermoves needs strong capabilities and significant advantages. For example, Color Air was a new entrant that was met by aggressive countermoves by existing airlines in Norway. After having lost five hundred million Norwegian kroner, Color Air gave up. If existing firms have lower costs than new entrants can have, then this absolute cost advantage is a very high barrier. A new entrant must establish access to distribution channels so the difficulties of access act as a barrier to entry. If buyers would have to face extra costs to change suppliers, or have a reluctance to do so, this acts as an entry barrier. If economies of scale are an important pricing factor, then new entrants either need large markets straightaway or must face higher costs. The degree of product differentiation and brand loyalty is directly related to the height of the entry barrier. Some industries involve major startup costs, and obviously in them, the barriers to entry are very high.
- **Threat of substitute products or services.** When this threat is high, then the profit margin is low, as customers more readily change when prices are high. If a similar product or service is available at the same, or lower, price, then the threat is high. If potential substitutes are more expensive, or inferior, then the threats are low. Switching costs for customers determine the threat of substitutes as well as determine the height of the entry barrier. If no extra costs are incurred, then change is likely. Apathetic or satisfied buyers are not likely to change; militant or dissatisfied ones are. Generally, the more significant the purchase is to the customer, the higher is their propensity to switch.
- **Bargaining power of buyers.** This primarily depends on their price sensitivity and their bargaining leverage. The bargaining power of buyers depends on the purchaser's relative cost importance. A number of things can reduce price sensitivity: brand loyalty and differentiation, impacts of the product on their product, and customer's own profitability. The bargaining power of buyers depends on buyer concentration and volume, buyer switching costs, buyer information, threat of backward vertical integration by buyers, and existence of substitutes.
- **Bargaining power of suppliers.** This is the differentiation of the inputs and matters when the organization's process needs a rare commodity. When switching costs of changing to an alternative supplier are high, then suppliers are relatively powerful since the organization would face significant costs if it were to leave them. When substitute suppliers are available, the power of the supplier is reduced. The higher supplier concentration, the higher supplier power is. If the supplier has to achieve high volume sales, then they hold less bargaining power. Supplier power is low when the costs of goods provided are high relative to the purchasing industry's total costs. Supplier power is higher when their product is significant to the buyer organization's chances of product differentiation. When suppliers will find it easy to forward integrate into the purchaser's industry, then they have high bargaining power.

To produce a model of the competitive forces playing upon an organization requires detailed research into its industry, but it then allows the net power of the five forces as well as extreme single powers to be judged in order to concentrate attention on those most significant.

Method VI: Product Portfolio Analysis

There are a number of approaches that aim to relate the competitive position of an organization to the maturity of its product. The models assume there is a basic S-shaped curve description to the growth phenomenon of products. Four stages in the *life cycle* of any product can be identified as illustrated in Figure 2.10:

- **Introduction.** The product is new, and there is an initial stage of experimentation and gradual acceptance. IS/IT can support product specification, customer requirements, process design, market research and forecasting, logistics planning, and cost estimation.
- **Growth.** There is a rapid increase in sales. IS/IT can support product enhancement, customer service, capacity development and utilization, new distribution channels, monitoring price margins, service from suppliers, promotion to expand customer base, and identifying competitors' position.
- **Maturity.** Sales remain high, but there is no further increase. IS/IT can support product variations, customer segmentation, product cost reduction, costing and sourcing of components, inventory control, pricing flexibility, analysis of contribution, and targeting specific competitors.
- **Decline.** Competition, product displacement, or other factors cause a decline in sales. IS/IT can support reduced inventory levels, sales forecasting, subcontracting, release of capacity for other uses, rationalization of distribution channels, and reduction in administrative costs.

When we look at the life cycle of all products in the firm, we can apply product portfolio analysis. This method shows the relationship between a product's current or future revenue

Figure 2.10. Product life cycle

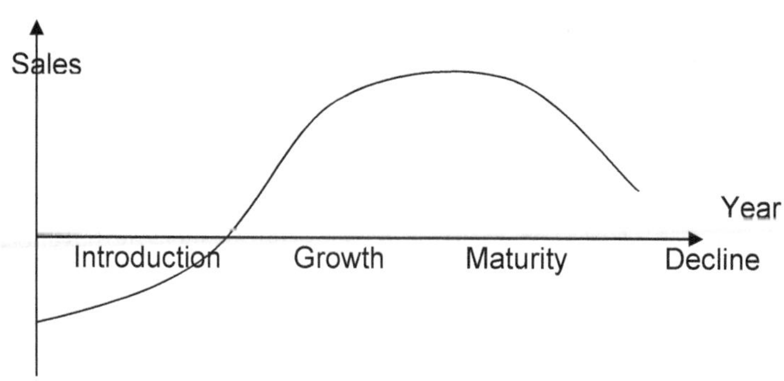

Figure 2.11. Product portfolio analysis (Robson, 1997)

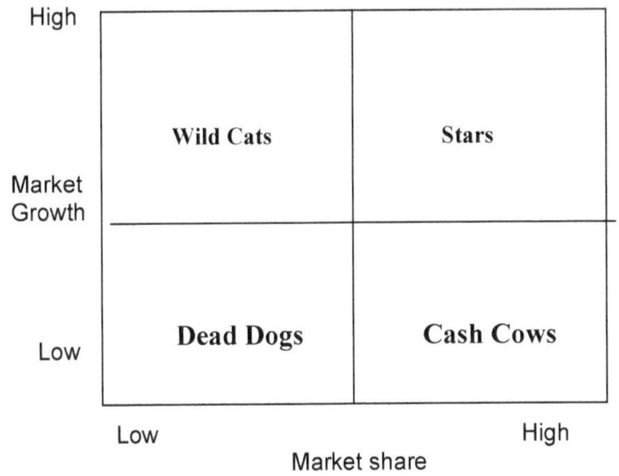

potential and the appropriate management stance as illustrated in Figure 2.11. The two by two matrix names the products in order to chart symptoms into a diagnosis so that effective management behavior can be adopted. The matrix classifies products according to the present market share and the future growth of that market. A successful product that lasts from emergent to mature market goes clockwise around the matrix.

The matrix segments summarize the expected profit and cash flow and also recommends an outline strategy to follow. This strategy is simply to milk the cows, divest the dogs, invest in the stars, and examine the wild cats (Robson, 1997):

- **Cash cows.** Products in this segment are those that are the current high-income earners for the organization. They are expected to provide the major part of current profits and form the major source of funding for future developments. Cash cows are relatively short-term, so they are not expected to provide significant future revenues. Management will try to increase profitability by milking more intensively and by extending the lifetime. IS/IT will tend to focus on control of the business environment rather than innovation—to defend the current position.
- **Stars.** Products in this segment are the ones that provide significant revenue now and are expected to continue to do so in the future. In this segment, the organization will wish to seek opportunities to increase profits and extend the life of the product. IS/IT will tend to focus on the customer—identifying customers and their requirements to achieve a better understanding of demand than actual and potential competitors.
- **Dead dogs.** Products in this segment provide little or no contribution to profits today, and it is not expected that this situation will change. Such products should be removed. IS/IT will tend to focus on reducing costs and securing customers.
- **Wild cats.** Products in this segment are those that the organization is currently prepared to continue, although they make little or no contribution to revenue now, they are expected to in the future. These are usually young products and are probably still being developed. Investments should be made cautiously in this segment since the risks associated with it are higher than with others. Wild cats are potential rising

stars. The organization will seek ways to ensure that products quickly mature into highly profitable stars. IS/IT will tend to focus on innovative product and process improvements.

Product portfolio analysis is an important tool for innovation management. Companies will strive to invent new products before the existing ones decline. Innovations will be either incremental improvements on existing products to increase their customer values and extend their commercial lifespan, or disruptive or radical new products which are markedly different from the existing products and have great potential to become star products. New products tend to start their life as a promising wild cat, which through marketing excellence and/or further product improvement, could potentially transition into a star. Agile enterprises are responsive to competitive market changes and able to quickly introduce new products to capitalize on the market opportunities. Agile enterprises are therefore more able to rapidly increase their new product revenues over old products over a 2–3 year time frame. Agile enterprises sustain their competitive advantage through constant product innovation in synchrony with market changes. We will return to the topic of product innovation in Chapter X.

Method VII: Environmental Analysis

Environmental analysis is concerned with the external corporate environment. An analysis of the environment is important because it increases the quality of the strategic decision making by considering a range of the relevant features. The organization identifies threats and opportunities facing it, and those factors that might assist in achieving objectives and

Figure 2.12. External factors for environmental analysis

External Factor	Examples of Trends	Implications for Company
Politics	Less trade barriers	Global competition
Economy	Deregulation	Global competition
	Larger, freer markets	Alliances and partnerships
Society	Increasing number of older people	New services and products
	Growing unemployment	Market decrease
	More knowledge	Changing customer needs
Technology	IT can support knowledge work	Technology to achieve benefits
	New communications networks	Technology to become global
Legal issues	Privacy legislation	Data security
	Electronic signature	Paperless trading
Ecology	Green movements	Reusable resources
	Terrorism	Contingent plans

those that might act as barriers. The strategy of the organization should be directed at exploiting the environmental opportunities and blocking environmental threats in a way that is consistent with internal capabilities. This is a matter of environmental fit that allows the organization to maximize its competitive position.

An external analysis can investigate politics, the economy, the society, and the technology. This is sometimes called PEST analysis. If we include the study of legal and environmental matters, we call it PESTLE. In Figure 2.12, some examples of external factors are listed with their implications for the company. The analytical work that has to be done in the company when doing environmental analysis is concerned with questions such as: What are the implications of the trends (changes in the environment)? What can the company do in order to meet the opportunities and threats that follow?

The success of an environmental analysis is largely dependent on the characteristics of the environment: its complexity—that is, how many variables are in the environment, the rate of change, and the amount (and cost) of available information about it. Environmental analysis considers the external situation within which the organization exists. It is important to audit the environmental influences, assess the nature of the environment to judge whether it is simple or complex, identify the key environmental forces, and identify the key opportunities and threats to be handled by the company (Robson, 1997).

Environmental analysis is an important competence for innovation. Environmental changes are often the source of inspiration for generating new ideas for innovation. Enterprises must be very well in-tune with the environment to sustain their competitive advantages. Otherwise, they may rapidly become industry laggards, rendering the products and services less appealing or less effective in the emergent environment. Chapter X will address the issues of business innovation and environmental analysis in more detail.

Method VIII: Knowledge Analysis

Distinctions can be made between core knowledge, advanced knowledge, and innovative knowledge. While core knowledge is required to stay in business, advanced knowledge makes the firm competitively visible, and innovative knowledge allows the firm to lead its entire

Figure 2.13. Knowledge map for external analysis (Tiwana, 2000)

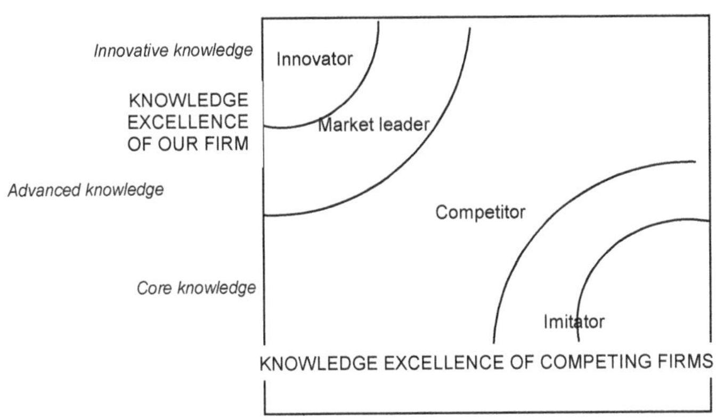

Figure 2.14. Identifying knowledge gap in internal analysis (Tiwana, 2000)

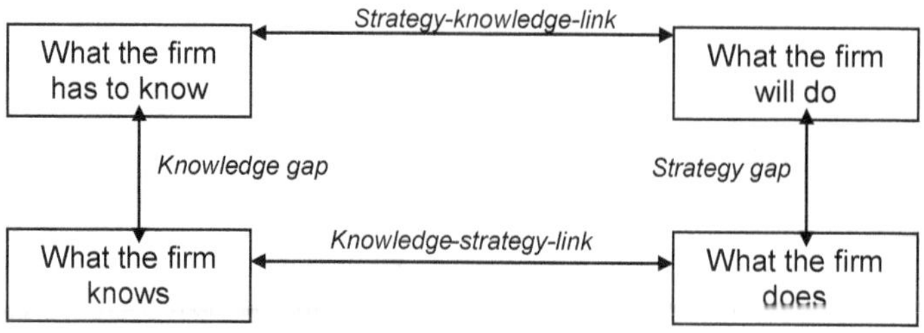

industry. The knowledge map in Figure 2.13 can be applied to identify firm position. The map illustrates firm knowledge levels compared with competitors' knowledge levels.

While the knowledge map represents an external analysis of the firm's current knowledge situation, the knowledge gap in Figure 2.14 represents an internal analysis of the firm's current knowledge situation. The knowledge gap is dependent on business strategy. What the company does is different from what the company will do, creating a strategy gap. What the company knows is different from what the company has to know, creating a knowledge gap. Two important links emerge: the strategy-knowledge link and the knowledge-strategy link (Tiwana, 2000).

ANALYZING NEEDS FOR CHANGE: THE STRATEGY

After descriptions of the current situation and the desired situation, the needs for change can be identified. The gap between desired and current situation is called needs for change. In Figure 2.15, all business analysis methods presented earlier are listed, and examples of desired and current situation are presented. Needed changes are exemplified, and potential IS/IT are suggested. We see many changes needed, and IS/IT solutions include executive information system (EIS), project management system (PMS), research library system (RLS), customer relationship management (CRM), enterprise resources planning (ERP), electronic marketplaces (EMS), and knowledge management system (KMS). Many of these systems will rely on Internet technology. For example, EIS, PMS, and KMS will use both intranet and extranet as well as the Internet.

The same kind of analysis should be done for the current and desired IS/IT situation as illustrated in Figure 2.14. Again, we see IS/IT solutions include customer relationship management (CRM), knowledge management system (KMS), and executive information system (EIS). The column "change needed" in both Figures 2.15 and 2.16 represent answers to the what question, while the column "IS/IT potential" suggests answers to the how question.

One of the elements of the IS/IT strategy is identification of future applications. In order to discuss this subject, we have to familiarize ourselves with what kinds of application software a company might have and how applications are developed or acquired.

A company seldom starts from scratch. There are already computers, terminals, printers, operating systems, application software, databases, and communication networks in the firm. This implies that potential IS/IT as listed in Figures 2.15 and 2.16 have to be considered in view of existing infrastructure, architecture, and applications.

Furthermore, at this stage, needs for change have to be prioritized. This implies that not all needs can get attention and not all potential IS/IT can be implemented.

Analyzing needs for change, identifying potential IS/IT, comparing with current IS/IT in the company, and then prioritizing needs for change should result in proposals for new IS/IT in the organization. For example, our company may prioritize extending product lives, sharing and developing advanced and innovative knowledge, improving internal and external communication, improving support for knowledge workers, improving human resources management, improving problem solving, and coding information from knowledge sources. If such needs for change have priority, then a knowledge management system (KMS) should be implemented in the organization.

Figure 2.15. Identification of potential IS/IT based on needs for business change

Business Analysis	**Desired Situation**	**Current Situation**	**Change Needed**	**IS/IT Potential**
SWOT analysis	Strong management	Weak management	Strengthen management	Executive Information System (EIS)
X model	Even distribution of work	Too much work close to milestones	Improve work scheduling	Project Management System (PMS)
Business direction	Research-based business school	Education-based business school	Strengthen research	Research Library System (RLS)
Market strategy	Strong differentiation	Weak differentiation	Add services to base product	Customer Relationship Management (CRM)
Competitive forces	High entry barriers for new entrants	Low entry barriers for new entrants	Achieve economies of scale	Enterprise Resources Planning (ERP)
Product portfolio analysis	Many stars	Many cash cows	Extend life of products	Knowledge Management System (KMS)
Environmental analysis	Reach young people	Customers are old people	Apply new technology-based market channels	Electronic Market Places (EMP)
Knowledge analysis	Market leader	Imitator	Share and develop advanced and innovative knowledge	Knowledge Management System (KMS)

Figure 2.16. Identification of potential IS/IT based on needs for technology change

IS/IT Analysis	Desired Situation	Current Situation	Change Needed	IS/IT Potential
Benefits of IS/IT	Market benefits	Rationalization benefits	Achieve competitive advantage	Customer Relationship Management (CRM)
Stages of IS/IT growth	Growth stage	Architecture stage	Improve internal and external communication	Knowledge Management System (KMS)
IS/IT in management activities	Knowledge management	Administrative and support functions	Improve support for knowledge workers	Knowledge Management System (KMS)
IS/IT in business processes	Excellent human resources management	Poor human resources management	Improve human resources management	Knowledge Management System (KMS)
IS/IT support for value configuration	Excellent problem solving in value shop	Poor problem solving in value shop	Improve problem solving	Knowledge Management System (KMS)
Strategic integration	Reciprocal integration	Administrative integration	Top management participation	Executive Information System (EIS)
IS/IT support for knowledge management	What they know stage	End user tools stage	Coding information from knowledge sources	Knowledge Management System (KMS)
IS/IT in e-business	E-business stage	Internal communication stage	Business process reengineering and design	New IS/IT infrastructure

E-STRATEGY

The Internet is an extremely important new technology, and it is no surprise that it has received so much attention from entrepreneurs, executives, investors, and business observers. Caught up in the general fervor, many have assumed that the Internet changes everything, rendering all the old rules about companies and competition obsolete. According to Porter (2001), that may be a natural reaction, but it is a dangerous one. It has led many companies, dot-coms, and incumbent alike to make bad decisions—decisions that have eroded the attractiveness of their industries and undermined their own competitive advantage. The time has come to make a clearer view of the Internet.

The Internet provides a global infrastructure that enables compression of time and space, integrated supply chains, mass customization, and navigational ability. The impact of the Internet can be described as breaking down traditional trade-offs between richness of interaction possible with a customer and the number of customers a business can access or products it can offer. Internet-based businesses can compete on huge selections of products as they are not constrained by physical stores. Also, richer interaction (e.g., check order status, seek online advice) and customized relationships with large numbers of customers at incremental costs are increasingly feasible with the economics of information (Grover & Saeed, 2004).

Internet technology provides better opportunities for companies to establish distinctive strategic positioning than did previous generations of information technology. The Internet's greatest impact has been to enable the reconfiguration of existing industries that had been constrained by high costs for communicating, gathering information, or accomplishing transactions. For example, the Internet tends to dampen the bargaining power of channels to providing companies with new, more direct avenues to customers (Porter, 2001).

Kim, Nam, and Stimpert (2004) find that Porter's generic strategies of differentiation and cost leadership will still be applicable to e-business firms in a broad sense. However, they argue that a strategy of focus will be less viable in e-business than traditional business contexts. They argue that differentiation is more sustainable than cost leadership strategy for e-business firms. In particular, Kim et al. (2004) argue that an e-strategy will be able to achieve superior, sustainable performance through an "integrated strategy"[2] discipline (when compared with *either* differentiation *or* cost leadership), which strives to achieve *both* cost leadership and differentiation strategic positioning. Kim et al. (2004) also suggest that "clicks-and-bricks firms will enjoy superior performance relative to their pure play counter-parts *only* when their online and offline operations are aligned and tightly integrated."

The Internet has many properties, but 10 of them stand out (Afuah & Tucci, 2003):

- **Mediating technology.** The Internet is a mediating technology that interconnects parties that are independent or want to be. The interconnection can be business-to-business (B2B), business-to-consumer (B2C), consumer-to-consumer (C2C), or consumer-to-business (C2B). It can also be within a firm or any other organization, in which case it is called an intranet.
- **Universality.** Universality of the Internet refers to the Internet's ability to both enlarge and shrink the world. It enlarges the world because anyone anywhere in the world can potentially make his or her products available to anyone anywhere else in the world. It shrinks the world in that distance is reduced on electronic highways.
- **Network externalities.** A technology or product exhibits network externalities when it becomes more valuable to users as more people take advantage of it. A classic example is the telephone, where the value for each subscriber increases with number of subscribers. The more people that are connected to a network within the Internet, the more valuable the network is.
- **Distribution channel.** The Internet acts as a distribution channel for products that are largely information bits, such as software, music, video, news, and tickets. There is a replacement effect if the Internet is used to serve the same customers serviced by the old distribution channel without bringing in new customers. There is an extension effect if the Internet is used by more people and for new services.
- **Time moderator.** The fifth property of the Internet is time moderation or its ability to shrink and enlarge time. It shrinks time for customers who want information on products when regular stores are closed. It enlarges time when related work can be done at different points in time.

- **Information asymmetry shrinker.** An information asymmetry exists when one party to a transaction has information that another party does not—information that is important to the transaction. The Web reduces such information asymmetries, as the other party can find the same information on the Web.
- **Infinite virtual capacity.** Access to the Internet is perceived as unlimited; you do not have to wait on hold or in a long line. For example, virtual communities like chat houses have infinite capacity for members who can talk anytime of the day for as long as they want.
- **Low cost standard.** Firms could not exploit the properties of the Internet if they did not adopt it. For two reasons, adoption has been easy. First and most important, the Internet and the Web are standards open to everyone everywhere and are very easy to use. Second, the cost of the Internet is a lot lower than that of earlier means of electronic communications.
- **Creative destroyer.** These properties of the Internet have enabled it to usher in a wave of creative destruction in many industries. Newspapers, for example, offer their readers material on their Web sites. The Internet is a low cost standard printing press of sorts and a distribution network with unlimited capacity that reaches more people than any newspaper could ever hope to reach. This tears down a large part of the barriers to entry that exist in the newspaper business.
- **Transaction cost reducer.** The Internet also reduces transaction costs for many industries—thanks in part to the universality, distribution channel, low cost standard, and information asymmetry reduction properties. Transaction costs are the costs of searching for sellers and buyers; collecting information on products; negotiating, writing, monitoring, and enforcing contracts; and the costs of transportation associated with buying and selling.

However, as supply chains are becoming more dispersed and global in their orientation, and thereby have given rise to the problem of coordinating flow of information and materials across organizations that are linked together, transaction costs will rise (Grover & Malhotra, 2003).

The Internet provides a global infrastructure that enables compression of time and space, integrated supply chains, mass customization, and navigational ability. The impact of the Internet can be described as breaking down traditional trade-offs between richness of interaction possible with a customer and the number of customers a business can access or products it can offer. Internet-based businesses can compete on huge selections of products, as they are not constrained by physical stores. Also, richer interaction (e.g., check order status, seek online advice) and customized relationships with large numbers of customers at incremental costs are increasingly feasible with the economics of information (Grover & Saeed, 2004).

The digital transformation of traditional businesses is occurring (Andal, Cartwright, & Yip, 2003). New information technologies, such as broadband networks, mobile communications, and the Internet, have well-known but often unrealized potential to transform businesses and industries. The key to success is knowing how and when to apply technologies. Companies should look at 10 specific drivers to help determine their best strategy.

From a study of large corporations in North America and Europe, Andal et al. (2003) identified the different drivers that determine the competitive advantage of deploying new information technology. Each of the drivers is very specific to how new IT can be applied in a particular industry. They are not general factors, such as the overall cost of a technology. And they are different from the critical success factors that affect the implementation of information technology and that are mostly specific to a company, as opposed to being characteristic of an industry. There are a total of 10 drivers to help determine an appropriate enterprise e-strategy:

1. **Electronic deliverability.** Some products have a large component that can be delivered electronically. Airline companies, for instance, enable customers to book reservations online, after which the confirmations and tickets can be delivered efficiently through e-mail.
2. **Information intensity.** Nearly all products and services have some information content, but the amount varies dramatically. Cars come with volumes of operating instructions, for instance.
3. **Customizability.** New information technology allows many companies to tailor an overall offering to the specific needs and preferences of individual customers. In the past, newspapers were a one-size-fits-all product. Today, online editions can be customized to include just the news and information that a particular subscriber is likely to want.
4. **Aggregation effects.** Products and services differ in the way they can be aggregated or combined. Thanks to new information technology, institutions can offer customers bundled services.
5. **Search costs.** Before the advent of Internet companies such as Amazon.com, finding an out-of-print book could require considerable time and effort. Now, the Web provides people with vast amounts of information, regardless of their location or time zone, lowering the search costs for finding exactly the product or service they want.
6. **Real-time interface.** A real-time interface is necessary for companies and customers dealing with important information that changes suddenly and unpredictably. A good example is online trading, in which rapid fluctuations in the stock market can be devastating for those who lack instantaneous access to that information.
7. **Contracting risk.** Buying new books online has little contracting risk for customers. Prices are relatively low, and specifying the exact titles is straightforward. Buying cars online is a completely different matter. Prices are substantially higher.
8. **Network effects.** In many industries, the utility of a good or service increases with the number of people who are using it (or one that is compatible). A key benefit of using Microsoft Office, for instance, is that the suite of programs is ubiquitous in the business world, enabling people to share Word, PowerPoint, and Excel documents easily.
9. **Standardization benefits.** New information technology enabled companies to synchronize and standardize certain processes, resulting in greater efficiency in business-to-business transactions as well as increased convenience for customers.
10. **Missing competencies.** New information technology can facilitate company alliances in which partners use each other to fill in missing competencies.

These 10 drivers can be classified into three types of drivers. The first four drivers are inherent characteristics of product or service, drivers 5–7 are concerned with interactions between company and its customers, while the last three are concerned with interactions between company and its partners and competitors.

The 10 drivers determine what type of mediation approach is most likely to succeed in particular industries. For each of three defined strategies, a couple of drivers are dominant, several are ancillary, and others have little consequence. The three strategies, classic disintermediation, remediation, and network-based mediation, are explained in terms of drivers by Andal et al. (2003) as follows:

A. Classic disintermediation is cutting away layers of middlemen, such as distributors, that separate the company from its customers. Disintermediation is the elimination of traditional intermediaries, be they retail stores, direct mail operations, or 800-number-style telephone support operations. With market-facing systems, the selling of products directly to consumers and businesses has become a powerful force in many industries. This strategy is affected mainly by the drivers that pertain to the inherent characteristics of a product or service. Specifically, electronic deliverability is a major factor. That is, why use a distributor when a product or service can be delivered electronically to the customer? Information intensity is another dominant driver. Before new information technology, products or services with high information intensity often needed intermediaries, such as an insurance agent, to explain a complex policy. Now, a sophisticated Web site can perform much of that functionality. Less powerful drivers of disintermediation include customizability, search costs, real-time interface, and low contracting risk. An industry that benefits from technology that provides a real-time interface, for instance, will favor disintermediation in order to eliminate the time lag caused by middlemen.

B. Remediation is introducing and embracing middlemen. Historically, whenever transportation and communications infrastructures have markedly improved, industry value chains have tended to lengthen, with products and services becoming increasingly specialized. This has led many to suggest that the Web will also create whole new classes of intermediaries: market-facing enterprises whose primary presence is on the Web and who will provide portals that allow online users to access producers of goods and services. Remediation is affected mainly by two drivers: aggregation effects and high contracting risk. When there are benefits to combining products or services, companies can use technology to work more closely with their middlemen partners, building strong, ongoing relationships. Some insurance companies, for example, now provide potential customers with online estimates of different policies through the Web site of the Automobile Association of America (www.aaa.com). High contracting risks also encourage companies to use technology to establish closer—and more secure—relationships. Ford, for instance, relies on the Web-based applications of middleman Vastera Inc., a Viriginia-based firm, to handle import and export processes, customs clearance, trade regulation compliance, and cost calculations for shipments to Mexico and Canada. Other drivers of remediation are customizability (if the middleman can contribute to the customization process rather than get in its way), real-time interface (if the interface is between the middleman and either the producer or customer—and not between the producer and customer, which would instead encourage disintermediation), and missing competencies. High search costs tend to favor disintermediation instead of remediation.

C. *Network-based mediation* is building strategic alliances and partnerships with new and existing players in a tangle of complex relationships. This mediation is affected mainly by drivers that pertain to a company's interactions with its partners and competitors. Specifically, network effects and standardization benefits are clearly important reasons for industry players to work more closely together. Other drivers include high search costs (which favor the use of a network for locating products and information), the need for a real-time interface (which encourages partners to build a system that enables them to deal with each other in real time), and missing competencies (which encourage companies, even competitors, to partner with one another to fill those gaps).

These Internet-enabled business transformative drivers can be selected using Porter's strategy principles to create an appropriate e-strategy that fits the purpose of the firm.

SUMMARY

Business-aligned IT strategy is developed in accordance with Porter's (1985) business strategy principles. Business strategy with a clear goal and a "continuity of direction" must first be defined. The strategy must have a unique value proposition supported by a distinctive value configuration. The strategy must also define how all the elements (resources and activities) of what the firm does fit together and reinforce each other. This usually involves making trade-offs. Corporate strategy shapes business and IT strategies, so different corporate roles must be understood. The firm uses strategic management discipline to formulate its strategic position, make strategic choices for the future, turn the strategy into action, and realize the benefits (Johnson & Scholes, 2002). Translating strategy into actions requires strategic planning skills. Strategic planning is the process of deciding on the projects/programs that the organization will undertake and the appropriate amount of resources that will be allocated to each program over the next several years. Strategic planning practice performance can be measured from the perspectives of cost leadership, differentiation, focus, and intensity (Nayyar 1993). Formal systematic strategic planning process has been found to be beneficial, and the key elements of strategic plan are described (Grant, 2003).

Resource-based strategy leverages the firm's unique resources and capabilities as a platform across many markets and products (Barney, 2001). Activity-based strategy allows the firm to gain a profitable position by configuring its activities using activity-based drivers such as scale—a unique configuration which is difficult for rivals to copy. In comparing the two strategies, resources are similar to drivers and capabilities to activities (Sheehan, 2002).

Business ethics can be studied via stakeholder theory, which is a theory of organizational management and ethics. Indeed all theories of strategic management have some moral content, though it is often implicit. Moral content in this case means that the subject matter of the theories are inherently moral topics (i.e., they are not amoral). Stakeholder theory is distinct because it addresses morals and values explicitly as a central feature of managing organizations. The ends of cooperative activity and the means of achieving these ends are critically examined in stakeholder theory in a way that they are not in many theories of strategic management (Phillips et al., 2003). Use of stakeholder theory in IT strategy research is a still subject for further study. In an IT strategy context, a stakeholder theory approach will describe the relationship as a nexus of cooperative and competitive interests possessing intrinsic value. IT strategy should ensure the design and use of information technology to be transparent and open to ongoing scrutiny by stakeholders such that the values of ethics are upheld, always. This is assured through diligent application of IT governance (which is described in Chapter IX) by business enterprises.

Competitive business strategy formulation requires competitive strategic analysis. Eight popular methods of strategy analysis are available: SWOT analysis, X-model, business direction, market strategy, competitive forces, product portfolio analysis, environmental analysis, and knowledge analysis. From analysis of each method, a strategic change can be determined and the corresponding IT system can be identified.

Internet technology will enable the reconfiguration of existing industries that had been constrained by high costs for communicating, gathering information, or accomplishing transactions. Internet-driven business strategy, known as e-strategy, has created successful new-generation companies such as e-Bay, Google, Amazon, and Yahoo. Differentiation is more sustainable than cost leadership strategy for e-business firms. In particular, an e-strategy will be able to achieve superior, sustainable performance through an "integrated strategy" discipline (when compared with *either* differentiation *or* cost leadership), which strives to achieve *both* cost leadership and differentiation strategic positioning (Kim et al., 2004). E-strategy is also being adopted by traditional companies such as GE and News Limited. E-strategy is developed through gaining insights on 10 fundamental properties of the Internet, which include (Afuah & Tucci, 2003): mediating technology, universality, network externalities, distribution channel, time moderator, information asymmetry shrinker, infinite virtual capacity, low cost standard, creative destroyer, and transaction cost reducer. In-depth understanding of Internet capabilities in reshaping business models will give IT managers the ability to influence business strategy to take advantage of, and incorporate, Internet into the business and IT strategies to keep firms competitive, adaptive, and responsive to changing market and external environments.

REFERENCES

Afuah, A., & Tucci, C. L. (2003). *Internet business models and strategies* (2nd ed.). New York: McGraw-Hill.

Andal, A., Cartwright, P. A., & Yip, G. S. (2003, Summer). The digital transformation of traditional businesses. *MIT Sloan Management Review*, pp. 34-41.

Barney, J. B. (2001). Is the resource-based "view" a useful perspective for strategic management research? Yes. *Academy of Management Review, 26*(1), 41-56.

Boyd, B. K., & Reuning-Elliott, E. (1998). A measurement model of strategic planning. *Strategic Management Journal, 19*, 181-192.

Christensen, C. M., & Raynor, M. E. (2003). *The innovator's solution.* Boston: Harvard Business School Press.

Collis, D. J., & Montgomery, C. A. (1997). *Corporate strategy: Resources and the scope of the firm.* Chicago: Irwin, McGraw-Hill.

Grant, R. M. (2003). Strategic planning in a turbulent environment: Evidence from the oil majors. *Strategic Management Journal, 24*, 491-517.

Grover, V., & Malhotra, M. K. (2003). Transaction cost framework in operations and supply chain management research: Theory and measurement. *Journal of Operations Management, 21*, 457-473.

Grover, V., & Saeed, K. A. (2004). Strategic orientation and performance of Internet-based businesses. *Information Systems Journal, 14*, 23-42.

Haanaes, K. B. (1997). *Managing resource mobilization: Case studies of Dynal, Fiat Auto Poland and Alcatel Tecom Norway* (Ph.D. series 9.97). Copenhagen Business School, Copenhagen, Denmark.

Hansen, M. T., Nohria, N., & Tierny, T. (1999, March-April). What's your strategy for managing knowledge? *Harvard Business Review*, pp. 106-116.

Hitt, M. A., Bierman, L., Shimizu, K., & Kochhar, R. (2001). Direct and moderating effects of human capital on strategy and performance in professional service firms: A resource-based perspective. *Academy of Management Journal, 44*(1), 13-28.

Hopkins, W. E., & Hopkins, S. A. (1997). Strategic planning: Financial performance relationships in banks: A causal examination. *Strategic Management Journal, 18*(8), 635-652.

Introna, L. D. (2007). Maintaining the reversibility of foldings: Making the ethics (politics) of information technology visible. *Ethics and Information Technology, 9*, 11-25.

Johnson, G., & Scholes, K. (2002). *Exploring corporate strategy.* Harlow, Essex, UK: Pearson Education, Prentice Hall.

Julien, P. A., & Ramangalahy, C. (2003, Spring). Competitive strategy and performance of exporting SMEs: An empirical investigation of the impact of their export information search and competencies. *Entrepreneurship Theory and Practice*, pp. 227-245.

Kaplan, R. S., & Norton, D. P. (2004). *Strategy maps: Converting intangible assets into tangible outcomes.* Harvard Business School Press.

Kim, E., Nam, D., & Stimpert, J. L. (2004). The applicability of Porter's generic strategies in the Digital Age: Assumptions, conjectures, and suggestions. *Journal of Management, 30*(5), 569-589.

Lacity, M. C., & Willcocks, L. P. (2000). Relationships in IT outsourcing: A stakeholder perspective. In R. W. Zmud (Ed.), *Framing the domains of IT management: Projecting the future through the past* (pp. 355-384). Cincinnati, OH: Pinnaflex Educational Resources.

Loewendahl, B. R. (2000). *Strategic management of professional service firms* (2nd ed.). Copenhagen, Denmark: Copenhagen Business School Press.

Maister, D. H. (1993). *Managing the professional service firm.* New York: Free Press.

Marchand, D. A., Kettinger, W. J., & Rollins, J. D. (2001). *Making the invisible visible: How companies win the right information, people and IT.* John Wiley & Son.

Miller, C. C., & Cardinal, L. B. (1994). Strategic planning and firm performance: A synthesis of more than two decades of research. *Academy of Management Journal, 37*(6), 1649-1665.

Mintzberg, H. (1994). *The rise and fall of strategic planning.* New York: The Free Press.

Nayyar, P. R. (1993). On the measurement of competitive strategy: Evidence from a large multiproduct U.S. firm. *Academy of Management Journal, 36*(6), 1652-1669.

Pearlson, K. E. (2001). *Managing and using information systems: A strategic approach.* London: Wiley & Sons.

Phillips, R., Freeman, R. E., & Wicks, A. C. (2003). What stakeholder theory is not. *Business Ethics Quarterly, 13*(4), 479-502.

Priem, R. L., & Butler, J. E. (2001). Is the resource-based "view" a useful perspective for strategic management research? *Academy of Management Review, 26*(1), 22-40.

Porter, M. E. (1985). *Competitive strategy.* New York: The Free Press.

Porter, M. E. (2001, March). Strategy and the Internet. *Harvard Business Review*, pp. 63-78.

Raghupathi, W. (2007, August). Corporate governance of IT: A framework for development. *Communications of the ACM, 50*(8).

Robson, W. (1997). *Strategic management and information systems* (2nd ed.). London: Prentice Hall.

Salehnia, A. (2002). *Ethical issues of information systems.* Hershey, PA: IRM Press.

Schultz, R. (2006). *Contemporary issues in ethics and information technology.* Hershey, PA: IRM Press.

Thompson, A. A., & Strickland, A. J., III. (2003). *Strategic management concepts and cases* (13th ed.). McGraw-Hill, Irwin.

Tiwana, A. (2000). *The knowledge management toolkit: Practical techniques for building a knowledge management system.* New York: Prentice Hall.

Wit, B. D., & Meyer, R. (2004). *Strategy: Process, content, context* (3rd ed.). London: Thomson Learning.

ENDNOTES

1. Introna (2007, p. 23) refers to multistability as "technologies which afford multiple interpretations—and ways of doing—to the users. This means that the users can interpret and use these artifacts in multiple ways that encourage active engagement with the artifact, as in the case of a manual camera." He argues that "the higher the level of engagement the less likely it will be for the user to become unwittingly enrolled into political programs not of their choosing."
2. Kim et al (2004) argue that this is in contrast to Porter's stuck in the middle conundrum, without clear strategic focus, in traditional business contexts.

Chapter III
Strategic Alignment, IT Value, and Organizational Analysis

INTRODUCTION

Over the last several decades, strategy researchers have devoted attention to the question of how corporate elites (i.e., corporate executives and directors) affect corporate strategy. The CEO as a person in position shapes the scope of the firm, while the CIO as a person in another position shapes the scope of IT in the firm. Jensen and Zajac (2004) proposed and tested the notion that while differences in individual characteristics of corporate elites may imply different preferences for particular corporate strategies such as diversification and acquisitions, these basic preferences, when situated in different agency contexts (e.g., CIO, CEO) generate very different strategic outcomes.

Strategy can simply be defined as principles, a broad based formula, to be applied in order to achieve a purpose. These principles are general guidelines guiding the daily work to reach business goals. Strategy is the pattern of resource allocation decisions made throughout the organization. These encapsulate both desired goals and beliefs about what are acceptable and, most critically, unacceptable means for achieving them.

While the business strategy is the broadest pattern of resource allocation decisions, more specific decisions are related to information systems and information technology. How should IS/IT resources be allocated within business organizations? How can business ensure the IS/IT resources will deliver the desired business value? Hann and Weber (1996) see IS/IT strategic planning as a set of activities directed toward achieving the following objectives:

1. Recognizing organizational opportunities and problems where IS/IT might be applied successfully
2. Identifying the resources needed to allow IS/IT to be applied successfully to these opportunities and problems
3. Developing strategies and procedures to allow IS/IT to be applied successfully to these opportunities and problems
4. Establishing a basis for monitoring and bonding IT managers, so their actions are more likely to be congruent with the goals of their superiors
5. Resolving how the gains and losses from unforeseen circumstances will be distributed among senior management and the IT manager
6. Determining the level of decision rights to be delegated to the IT manager.

Empirical studies of information systems/information technology planning practices in organizations indicate that wide variations exist. Hann and Weber (1996) found that organizations differ in terms of how much IS/IT planning they do, the planning methodologies they use, the personnel involved in planning, the strength of the linkage between IS/IT plans and corporate plans, the focus of IS/IT plans (e.g., strategic systems vs. resource needs), and the way in which IS/IT plans are implemented.

In this chapter, we will review the principles of strategic alignment and discuss in detail the various methods for IT value and organizational maturity analysis.

STRATEGIC ALIGNMENT

Alignment between business strategy and IT strategy is widely believed to improve business performance (Sabherwal & Chan, 2001). Therefore, strategic alignment is both a top management concern and also an important characteristic of the attributes of effective CIOs. While the business strategy is the broadest pattern of resource allocation decisions, more specific decisions are related to information systems and technology platforms. IS must be seen both in a business and a technology context. IS is in the middle because IS supports the business while using technology platforms.

Business strategy is concerned with achieving the mission, vision, and objectives of a company, while IS strategy is concerned with use of IS applications, and technology strategy is concerned with the technical infrastructure—both in line with the business strategy. A company has typically several IS applications. The connection between them is also of great interest, as interdependencies should prevent applications from being separate islands. Furthermore, the arrows in the illustration in Figure 3.1 are of importance. Arrows from business strategy to IS strategy and from IS to technology strategy represent the alignment perspective, and they illustrate the *what* before *how*. Arrows from technology to IS strategy and from IS to business strategy represent the extension from *what* to *how* to *what*. This is the impact perspective, representing the potential impacts of modern information technology on future business options.

As described in Chapter II, necessary elements of a *business strategy* include mission, vision, objectives, market strategy, the unique value propositions, and value configuration to achieve the mission, vision, and objectives. It should also include the corresponding

Figure 3.1. Relationships between strategies at three levels

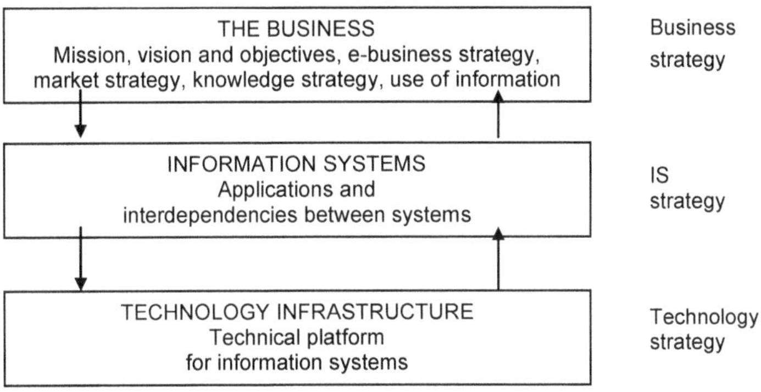

IS/IT strategy, which encompasses knowledge strategy, and our general approach to the use of information, information systems and technology platforms.

Cassidy (2006) opines that true strategic alignment is achieved when IS/IT strategy is developed concurrently with business strategy, instead of sequentially so that it is possible for IT to enable business strategy. It means IS/IT strategy forms part of the business strategy, in an integrated sense. This close coupling of business and IS/IT strategy will ensure that all IS/IT activities will provide optimal support for the business goals, objectives, and initiatives.

Necessary elements of an *IS strategy* include future IS/IT applications, future competence of human resources (IS/IT professionals), and future IS/IT organizational structure, and control of the IS/IT function. An important application area is knowledge management systems (KMSs). The future applications are planned according to priorities, how they are to be developed or acquired (make or buy), how they meet user requirements, and how security is achieved. The future competence is planned by types of resources needed, motivation, and skills needed (managers, users, IS/IT professionals), salaries, and other benefits. The future IS/IT organization defines tasks, roles, management, and possibly outsourcing.

Necessary elements of a technology *strategy* include selection of IT hardware, basic software, and networks, as well as how these components should interact as a technological platform, and how required security level is maintained. The technology platform consists of hardware, systems software, networks and communications, standards, and support from selected vendors.

An *IS/IT strategy* is a combined strategy including business context, the IS in a narrow sense, and the technological platform. Necessary elements of an IS/IT strategy include business direction and strategy (mission, vision, objectives, knowledge strategy), applications (knowledge management systems), people (future competence of human resources), organization (future organization and control of IT function), and technology platform (future technical infrastructure). Hence, IS/IT is quite a broad term. The term is broad to take care of all connections and interdependencies in a strategy, as changes in one element will have effect on all other elements, as illustrated in Figure 3.2.

For example, for an enterprise with customer intimacy value discipline (Cassidy, 2006; Tracey & Wiersema, 1995), the business strategy will be highly focused on customer ex-

Figure 3.2. IS/IT strategy elements and interdependencies

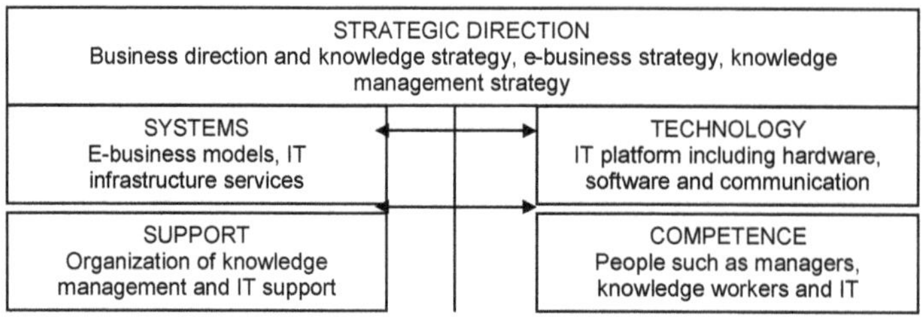

perience and customer satisfaction will be a key measure of success. By extension, the IT strategy must therefore be driven by customer needs and must provide excellent support for customer relationship management (Cassidy, 2006). From these strategies, the technology requirements are derived which will include high priority focus on customer relationship management, order management, shipping, and marketing to ensure superior customer experience (as articulated by the value proposition stipulated in the business strategy) is maintained. Customer intimacy will also demand a customer database that provides a "single source of truth" so that personalized service can be offered to the customer. Often this will be supported by an Internet channel or interface for customer support and customer survey. To align with the business strategy, IT organization will often be decentralized and organized by customer segments (Cassidy, 2006). Business analysts (to support customer requirements analysis) will be an important IT role. Similarly, the IT processes will also be customer-focused. Service level management process, customer satisfaction management process, and customer requirements analysis process will be core IT processes in alignment with the business strategy. Finally, IT metrics will be tied to customer satisfaction metrics (Cassidy, 2006). In short, IT is fully aligned to the business strategy from all aspects of IT strategy, technology, organization, processes, and metrics.

The same thinking is represented in a famous model called Leavitt's diamond (Gottschalk, 2005). Everything is connected, and changes in one element affect all the others as illustrated in Figure 3.3. Tasks are performed using systems; structure is important for support functions; and people represent the competence. The diamond can only create change in desired strategic business direction if all interdependencies between elements are taken care of over time.

Figure 3.3. Leavitt's diamond of elements and interrelationships

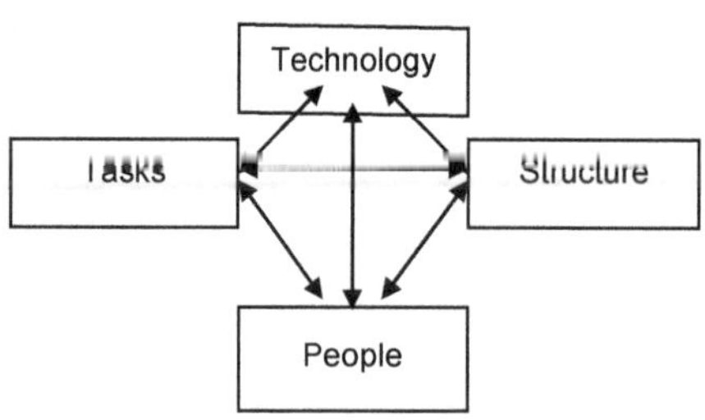

Most large companies in the United States and Europe have long struggled with the need for tighter relationships between IT and business management. This perennial management problem is echoed once again in a study of how French CEOs and CIOs view the performance of information systems within their organizations. Insights from the study suggest that CEOs are growing keener to find a solution and that both CIOs and the leaders of business units may soon be held more accountable for business ownership of IT (Monnoyer, 2003).

In the survey, CEOs say that IT is not meeting their (admittedly high) performance expectations, particularly in providing systems and tools to support managerial decision making and in gaining the scale advantages of deploying common systems and processes across business units. CEOs attribute the gap between expected and actual performance mainly to the insufficient involvement of business units in IT projects to the weak oversight and management of these projects and to IT's inadequate understanding of their business requirements (Monnoyer, 2003). The IS organizational performance gaps observed in many enterprises are the result of poor strategic alignment between business and IS. Improving strategic alignment and IS organization performance is the purpose of IS/IT strategy practice. We now describe the methods and principles.

IT VALUE AND ORGANIZATIONAL ANALYSIS

First, we have to understand in what ways and for what value is the company using IS/IT. IS/IT is said to add value to the enterprise when its implementation delivers the expected business benefits in line with the articulated business strategy. Many approaches can help us gain an understanding of the current IS/IT value in companies. We will look at some of them:

I. **Benefits of IS/IT.** IS/IT is applied in business organizations to achieve benefits. We can study current IS/IT in the organization to understand what benefits have been achieved so far. Here we can determine what main benefit categories are currently the case. We will make distinctions between rationalization, control, organizational, and market benefits.

II. **Stages of IS/IT growth.** IS/IT in business organizations change over time. New hardware and software, new areas of applications, and new IS/IT support functions emerge. Most business organizations develop through stages over time. Here we can determine at what stage the business organization is for the time being. We will make distinctions between a total of nine stages. These nine stages are classified into three eras: data processing, information systems, and information networks.

III. **IS/IT in management activities.** Management activities can be studied in a hierarchical perspective of operational, tactical, and strategic management. Current IS/IT in the organizations can be assigned to these levels to determine the extent of support at each level.

IV. **IS/IT in business processes.** In a company, many business processes take place at the same time. Some of the processes may rely heavily on IS/IT, while others are mainly manual at the current point in time.

V. **IS/IT support for value configuration.** We make distinctions between value chain, value shop, and value network. In each of these value configurations, IS/IT can support activities. The current IS/IT situation is described by identifying activities in the value configuration depending on the extent of technology support.

VI. **Strategic integration.** Business strategy and IT strategy have for a long time suffered from lack of coordination and integration in many organizations. Here we measure the current IS/IT situation by use of 10 integration mechanisms to determine integration stage in an organization.

VII. **IS/IT support for knowledge management.** We have introduced four ambition levels for knowledge management, so here we can determine at what level a business organization is.

VIII. **IS/IT in e-business.** For most firms, becoming an e-business is an evolutionary journey. We introduce six stages to describe the evolving e-business: external communications, internal communications, e-commerce, e-business, e-enterprise, and transformation.

IX. **IS/IT enabled business transformation.** IT-enabled transformation can include business direction change, but more often we find examples at lower levels, such as business design change and business process change.

The description of the current situation of IT value added in the company assumes that we have been able to define borders for our study. Borders exist for both breadth and depth. Breadth is a question of whether the whole company or only one division should be studied. Depth is a question of whether all aspects such as technology, marketing, management, and finance should be included in the study. We recommend both extensive breadth and thorough depth to ensure that a wide range of alternative solutions and alternative actions can be identified in later stages of the Y model. In the case of breadth, this may imply that both suppliers and customers are included because there may be electronic marketplaces used by our suppliers and customers. In the case of depth, this may imply that analysis of top management is included because management competence in the area of IS/IT can influence both management attitudes and ambitions concerning future applications of IS/IT.

Description of the current IS/IT value should focus on issues of importance in technology and knowledge management. Less emphasis should be put on technology itself, such as drawings of company networks and servers. Technology management is focused on the management of information technology, while knowledge management is focused on knowledge strategy and knowledge management systems.

Method I: Benefits of IS/IT

The main reason for using IS/IT in organizations is the achievement of benefits. There are several kinds of benefits: rationalization benefits, control benefits, organizational benefits, and market benefits. These benefits are at different levels and have different implications. Rationalization benefits are found at the operational level and imply cost reductions. Control benefits are at the operational management level and imply both cost reductions and increased revenues. Organizational benefits are found at middle management and top management levels and imply both cost reductions and increased revenues. Market benefits are found externally and imply increased revenues. Each benefit category can be described as follows:

- **Rationalization benefits** occur when IS/IT is taking the place of people through automation. Person-years may be saved when replacing people with IS/IT. Personnel costs drop while IS/IT costs rise. Benefits are the net difference. A necessary requirement for achieving this kind of benefit is that there are other tasks for the people released of their duties, or that people can be dismissed from their jobs if it is socially acceptable in the corporate culture. Rationalization benefits were the typical justification of early investments, even if they created unemployment. For example, when lawyers revise a document, they no longer get a printout on paper to correct and get typed by secretaries. Instead, lawyers correct their own documents on the screen.
- **Control benefits** occur when employees are able to make better and different decisions and actions than they would have done without the information. For example, when secretaries make appointments for lawyers, information on client profitability and importance can make them schedule more meetings in the law office, thereby reducing travel time for lawyers.
- **Organizational benefits** occur when IS/IT opens up for organizational structures (more decentralization, flatter), which create higher motivation, better work from the employees, and better economic results. Some tasks in the organization were previously worked on sequentially, while IS/IT today enables parallel work. For example, an updated document can be accessed by lawyers at different locations at the same time.
- **Market benefits** occur when the IS/IT provides the business with competitive advantages leading to more sales and higher profits. Information systems can make the company look distinctly different from its competitors. The Internet has created new opportunities for e-commerce and e-business. For example, online legal services can generate an additional revenue source for law firms.

This analysis of current IS/IT benefits will provide information on the current IS/IT situation. If most benefits are found within rationalization and control, then there has been a cost control approach to IS/IT applications in the organization. If most benefits are found within organizational and market effects, then there has been a revenue increase approach to IS/IT applications in the organization.

IS/IT in knowledge management can create some or all of four kinds of benefits. Although the typical expectation will be concerned with organizational benefits and market benefits, efficient and effective use of IS/IT in knowledge management will also create rationalization benefits and control benefits.

A new IS/IT may cause some or all of four kinds of benefits. The challenge when deciding to make an IS/IT is to identify and quantify the benefits in monetary terms. Companies with little experience using IS/IT will look for mainly rationalization benefits, while more experienced companies will look for control and organizational benefits. The most experienced companies will look for market benefits.

What kind of benefits the company has utilized in the present IS/IT will tell us the current situation of the company when it comes to the use of IS/IT. For example, we may find a distribution of benefits as illustrated in Figure 3.4. A possible interpretation of this distribution is that the company has been good at exploring rationalization and control benefits, but not so good at achieving market benefits and organizational benefits.

Figure 3.4. Example of IS/IT benefits distribution

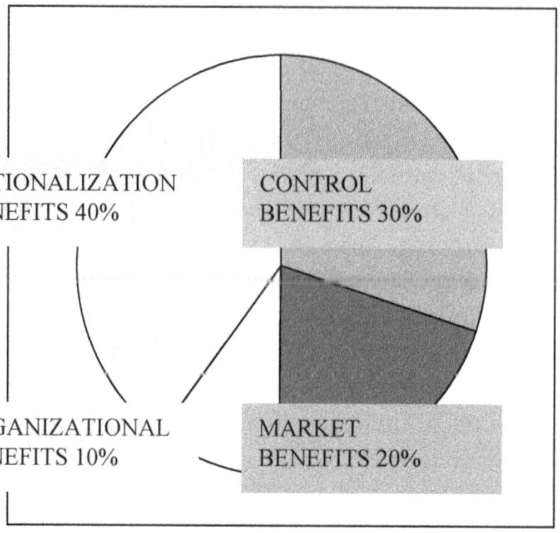

Method II: Stages of IS/IT Growth

Over time, business organizations have developed and advanced in their use of IT. In the beginning, there was data processing (DP) and data processing systems. Then there were management information systems (MIS) and strategic information systems (SIS). Organizations in the DP era will improve operational efficiency by automating information-based processes. Organizations in the MIS era will improve management effectiveness by satisfying their information requirements. Organizations in the SIS era will improve competitiveness by changing the nature or conduct of business.

This is sometimes called the EEC model, where organizations move from concerns about efficiency (E) to effectiveness (E) and finally to competitiveness (C). In the DP era, efficiency is about doing things right. In the MIS era, effectiveness is about doing the right things. In the SIS era, competitiveness is about gaining competitive advantage in the marketplace. Based on the EEC model, we now have a method of distinguishing between three eras of IS/IT growth to describe the current IS/IT situation in a company:

- **Era 1.** Data processing to achieve efficiency. Here focus is on *data*, where humans have to interpret data to make information out of it.
- **Era 2.** Management information systems to achieve effectiveness. Here focus is on *information*, where access to information is achieved.
- **Era 3.** Strategic information systems to achieve competitiveness. Here focus is on *knowledge*, where information is organized to support knowledge work.

The EEC model is only one of many stages of IS/IT growth models. Nolan (1979) introduced a model with six stages, which later has been expanded to nine stages. It has been suggested as a theory of IS/IT development over time in organizations. *Nolan's model* focuses on the level of IS/IT expenditures as illustrated in Figure 3.5.

Figure 3.5. Nolan's (1979) six stage model of IS/IT evolution in organizations

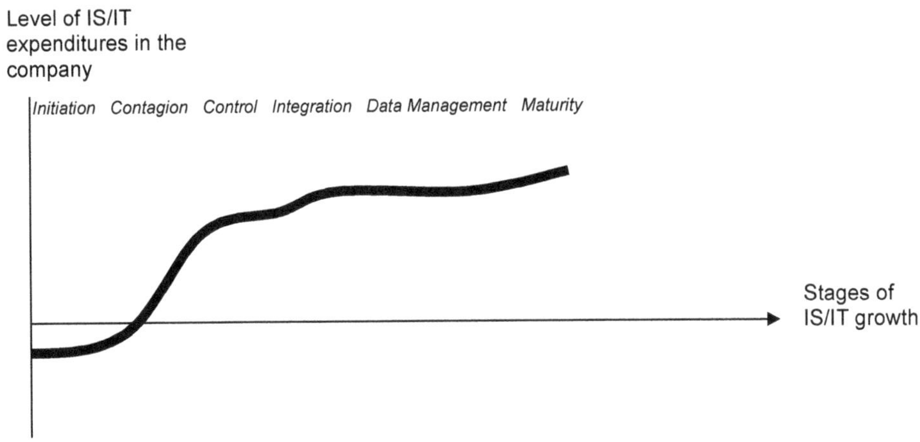

Nolan's model suggests that organizations slowly start out in the initiation stage. Then a period of rapid spreading of IT use takes place in the contagion stage. After a while, the need for control emerges. Control is followed by integration of different technological solutions. The data management enables a development without rising IS/IT expenditures. Then constant growth will take place as the stage of maturity is reached.

To understand the current IS/IT situation in a specific business organization, IS/IT expenditures can be mapped over time. Hopefully, there are historical accounting figures available at least for the last decade to draw the curve and to judge what stage in the curve the business is at right now. We can get more help to identify the appropriate stage by looking at specific characteristics of each stage as described in the following.

The stage of IS/IT maturity of an organization is not only indicated by the level of IS/IT expenditures. We can also look at the application portfolio, the IS/IT organization, the IS/IT planning and control, and the user awareness to estimate stage of growth of an organization. For example, an organization in the initiation stage will have an application portfolio of functional cost-reduction applications, while an organization in the maturity stage will have an application portfolio of applications integrated to handled information flows as illustrated in Figure 3.6.

Figure 3.6 can be compared with Leavitt's diamond introduced earlier. Leavitt's diamond argues that everything is connected, requiring changes in tasks (applications), people, structure (organization), and technology to move from one stage to the next. We see from the figure that application portfolio (tasks), IS/IT organization, and user influence (people), as well as IS/IT planning (organization) all change from one stage to the next. Each stage represents the technology level itself.

Nolan's stages of growth were introduced three decades ago. Several revisions have been done to the model. In the 1990s, three more stages were added to the model to cover recent developments in IS/IT in companies. These stages are labeled functional integration, tailored growth, and rapid reaction as illustrated in Figures 3.7 and 3.8.

Figure 3.6. Characteristics of stages in Nolan's (1979) model

Growth Characteristics	Stage 1 Initiation	Stage 2 Contagion	Stage 3 Control	Stage 4 Integration	Stage 5 Data	Stage 6 Maturity
Application portfolio	Functional cost-reduction applications	Rapid increase in all application areas	Upgrade documentation, simplifying existing applications	Restructuring existing applications in a systems architecture	Restructuring existing applications in a data architecture	Application integration supporting information flows
IS/IT organization	Specialization for technological learning	User-oriented computer programmers	Middle management	Establish IS/IT support function and user accounts	Establish data administration function	Establish IS/IT resource management function
IS/IT planning	No planning, operational managers taking initiatives on an individual basis	No planning, operational managers and IT experts taking initiatives on an individual basis	Formal planning and control procedures for IS/IT	Focused planning concerned with integration of information systems	Focused planning concerned with integration of databases	Strategic IS/IT planning
User influence	No influence, trained to use technology	No influence, trained to use technology	Some influence concerned with efficient use of technology	Some influence concerned with control of IS/IT costs	Some influence concerned with data flows in systems	Significant influence concerned with effective use of technology

Figure 3.7. Extended Nolan's (1979) six stage model to nine stages of IS/IT evolution in organizations

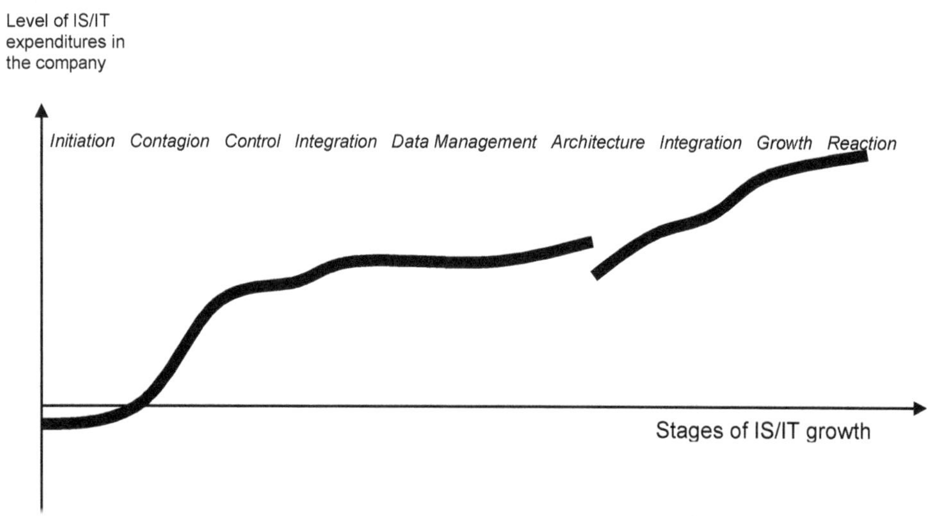

Figure 3.8. Characteristics of revised and extended Nolan (1979) model

Growth Characteristics	Stage 4 Integration	Stage 5 Data	Stage 6 Architecture	Stage 7 Integration	Stage 8 Growth	Stage 9 Reaction
Application portfolio	Restructuring existing applications in a systems architecture	Restructuring existing applications in a data architecture	Application integration supporting information flows	Intra- and interorganizational communication	Systems connecting business with vendors and customers	Extended infrastructure to support tailor-made applications
IS/IT organization	Establish IS/IT support function and user accounts	Establish data administration function	Establish IS/IT resource management function	Central IS/IT coordination and local helpdesks	IS/IT operations outsourcing and ASP	Network of system owners
IS/IT planning	Focused planning concerned with integration of information systems	Focused planning concerned with integration of databases	Strategic IS/IT planning	Focused strategic IS/IT planning such as standardization and open systems	Focused strategic IS/IT planning such as e-business strategy	Focused strategic IS/IT planning such as infrastructure strategy
User influence	Some influence concerned with control of IS/IT costs	Some influence concerned with data flows in systems	Significant influence concerned with effective use of technology	Significant influence as project managers	Significant influence as system owners	Significant influence as strategic partners
Knowledge management	End-user tools for knowledge workers	End-user tools for knowledge workers	End-user tools for knowledge workers	Information about knowledge sources	Information from knowledge sources	Information processing as knowledge work

Figure 3.9. Example of current IS/IT stage of growth in an organization (Nolan, 1979)

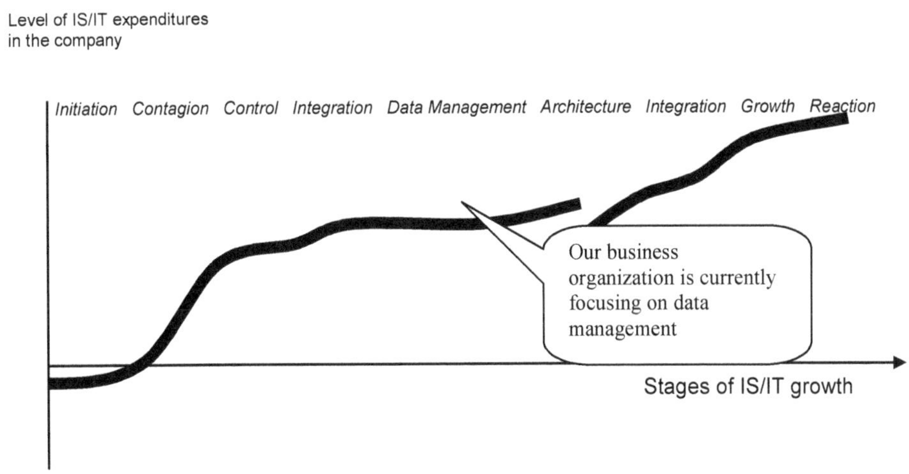

Figure 3.10. Comparative maturity of IS/IT in various geographic regions (Gottschalk & Khandelwal, 2002)

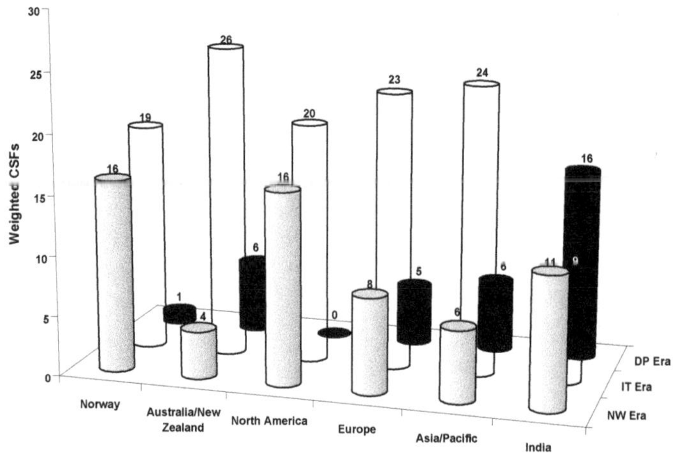

To describe the current IS/IT value-added situation in a business organization using the method of stages of growth, we can circle our finding as illustrated in Figure 3.9. Assuming that our business organization is at stage 5, concentrating on data management, we can indicate that the next natural step in the future will be to work on architecture.

The nine stages can be divided into three eras; each era consists of three stages. The first era is called data processing (DP) era, the second is information technology (IT) era, while the third is network (NW) era.

In a study conducted by Gottschalk and Khandelwal (2002), the extent to which business organizations were in these areas was measured. The approach was through identification of critical success factors (CSF). As illustrated in Figure 3.10, Norwegian business organizations have left the DP era. Half of them are now in the IT era, while the other half are in the NW area.

Method III: IS/IT in Management Activities

Management activities can be studied in a hierarchical perspective as illustrated in Figure 3.11. This is an old, famous representation of the company. The company is a pyramid with different layers of functions. When assessing the current situation, the challenge is to find where IS/IT supports functions in the pyramid. Different kinds of IS/IT support different aspects of the business. The different IS/IT are related to the pyramid. An IS/IT may cover several functions in the pyramid.

In Figures 3.12 to 3.14, we see how the five levels in the pyramid may have support from IS/IT. In the Figure 3.12, strategic control is concerned with products, markets, and objectives. The main purpose of IS in this function is control by providing information for decision making. In the Figure 3.13, we see characteristics of IS depending on level

Figure 3.11. Management activities in a hierarchical perspective

Figure 3.12. Purpose of IS/IT applications

Tasks	Kind of Problems	Purpose of IS
Strategic control	What kind of business? Which products? Which markets? How reach objectives?	Control benefits Market benefits
Tactical control	Given business, what kinds of resources are needed and how are they best developed?	Control benefits Organizational benefits
Knowledge management	Given business, what kind of knowledge is needed in knowledge work?	Organizational benefits Market benefits
Operational control	Given business, what kind of resources, how are they utilized?	Control benefits Rationalization benefits
Administrative support functions	How to do these functions in the best way?	Rationalization benefits Control benefits
Operations	How to make the products in the best way?	Rationalization benefits Control benefits

in the pyramid. While an IS for strategic control has very few users, an IS for operations has very many users. In Figure 3.14, only three of the levels in the pyramid are illustrated. We see that while strategic control is based on external information, operational control is based on internal information. Both strategic and operational control use information independent of the context in which it was previously used.

We will use the Norwegian School of Management BI (NSM) to illustrate this approach. NSM is in the business of economic and administrative education, undergraduate and

Figure 3.13. Information processing of IS/IT applications

Type of IS	Users	User requirements	Information processing
IS for strategic control	Very few	Unstable, nonrepetitive, and unpredictable	Aggregation and combination of large volumes of data from many sources
IS for tactical control	Not so many, but in different departments	Unstable, repetitive, and predictable	Calculations to determine performance
IS for knowledge management	All knowledge workers and managers who provide input and receive output from knowledge work	Unstable, nonrepetitive, and predictable	Communication and combination of information
IS for operational control	Many in different departments	Stable, repetitive, and unpredictable	Optimization of performance
IS for administrative support functions	Few when administrative support functions centralized, more if decentralized	Stable, nonrepetitive, and predictable	Combination of information
IS for operations	Many in different departments, also customers and suppliers	Stable, repetitive, and predictable	Transactions to be handled efficiently

graduate, and extended management education, as well as classroom teaching and distant learning. Products include bachelor, master, and doctoral degrees as well as different kinds of diplomas. The market is mainly Norway with some activities abroad. An example of a management problem at the strategic level might be: Should NSM start IT education and offer a Master of Science in Technology and Knowledge Management? We might wonder what kind of IS/IT would help at this strategic control level. Management would need an IS/IT, which provides information about educational needs of society and what competitors are doing and intend to do. At the tactical control level, resource issues arise: Teachers, administrative staff, school buildings, computers, and classroom equipment. The management problem at the tactical level might be: How do we combine our resources? Here management needs an IS/IT that provides information that can enable trade-offs between different kinds of resources.

At the knowledge management level, information needs arise: the knowledge workers (e.g., professors) need to make existing knowledge explicit and to acquire and develop new knowledge through research. The knowledge management problem might be: How do we organize knowledge creation, sharing, and distribution in new educational programs? At the operational control level, the problem is to allocate teachers to courses, classrooms, and hours. Do we have IS/IT for this purpose? Finally, for operational functions: Do we use computers in our teaching?

Figure 3.14. IS for strategic control, knowledge management, and operational control

Information Characteristics	Strategic control	Knowledge management	Operational control
Sources of information?	External	Internal and external	Internal
Which time period?	Future (forecasts, plans)	Past (history)	Past (history)
Degree of detail?	Low degree	Low and high	High degree
How frequent?	Infrequent	Frequent	Frequent
Is it correct?	No, based on judgment	Yes, based on experience	Yes, based on actual data
Information context?	Context independent	Context dependent	Context independent

Here we have illustrated how we can describe the IS/IT situation in the company by identifying IS/IT in management activities. We can describe the situation by documenting at what hierarchical levels there is IS/IT support currently and the extent of this support as illustrated in the example in Figure 3.15. According to this example, current IS/IT provide strong support for administrative support functions as well as operational control. Operations do also rely heavily on IS/IT. The top three layers have only marginal support from IS/IT.

Method IV: IS/IT in Business Processes

Information systems in an organization have three purposes:

- **Management purpose:** To make information available that can be used in planning and decision making.
- **Communication purpose:** To create contact and dialogue between various parts of the organization and between the organization and its environment.
- **Learning purpose:** To develop knowledge about the company, its operations, and its environment.

Management, communication, and learning purposes are tightly linked to tasks in the company. Persons in the company perform tasks in business processes. A business process can be defined as a structured and organized collection of activities and duties that exist to produce a result in the form of goods or services for an internal receiver in the company or an external customer in the marketplace. A business process has a beginning and an end, uses one or more resources, and creates a result of value for the receiver in the organization or the customer in the marketplace. Activities in the business process are primarily important to the extent that they contribute to complete the process, that is, that the business process delivers expected results in the form of goods or services. Typical examples of business processes include mortgage application handling in a bank, order

Figure 3.15. Example of current IS/IT situation based on a hierarchical perspective

Figure 3.16. The business process of customer complaint handling

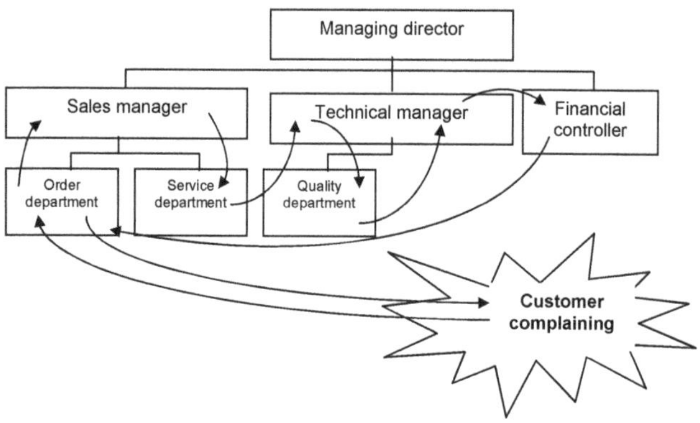

execution in a net shop, product development in the manufacturing industry, and client problem solving in a law firm.

In a company, many business processes take place at the same time. These processes are often dependent on each other, as they produce goods and services through process interactions. The company also interacts with its environment. The environment includes everything and everyone influencing the company, such as competitors, suppliers, customers, authorities, and interest groups.

Business processes are concerned with how work is organized, coordinated, staffed, and focused to produce goods and services of value to receivers and customers. Business processes are workflows in the form of materials and information. Hence, business processes are collections of activities. Furthermore, business processes are the very special way the company has chosen to coordinate work and knowledge, and the way management chooses to coordinate all production of goods and services. For example, all companies have a workflow to handle customer complaints. This workflow will be organized differently in different companies.

Figure 3.17. Business processes with different knowledge intensity and IS/IT support

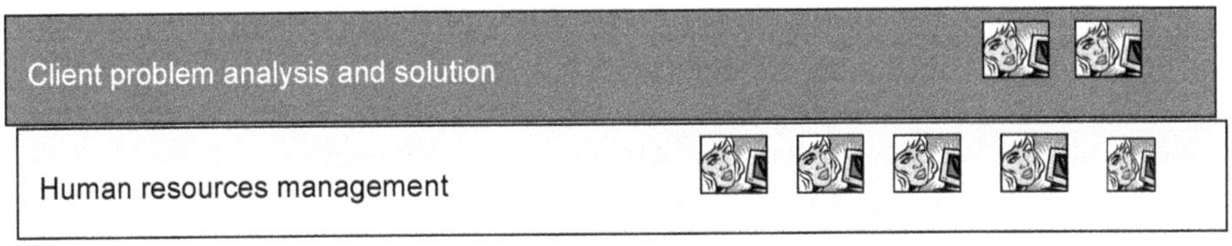

Today, executives are interested in identifying and improving business processes. This interest has emerged as executives realize that company success is dependent on the ability to deliver products at low prices, with high quality and professional service to customers. This interest has also emerged as more and more business processes have important interactions with the environment, such as supply and delivery business conducted over the Internet.

Business processes do normally cross departmental borders. A business process can involve sales department, technical department, and service department. Business processes may involve several levels in the hierarchy. Figure 3.16 illustrates an example of a customer complaint handling process. The customer is dissatisfied with a PC ordered over the Internet and returns the PC. The order department gets a notice and informs the sales manager. The service department receives the PC and sends it to the technical manager. Then the PC moves on to the product control department, which concludes that the PC is defective and that the customer should be offered the opportunity to get it repaired for free. However, the customer had asked for the money back, so the matter is forwarded to the financial controller who decides that the customer may choose between repair and money return. The financial controller informs the service department of this decision, and the service department sends an e-mail to the customer.

IS/IT supports business processes. Information-intensive business processes will typically find intensive support by information systems. Business processes that were manual and inefficient may have been restructured and activities in the processes may have been automated using information technology.

The current IS/IT situation in the company can be described by linking applications of information technology to businesses processes. Sometimes a company has defined a few core business processes, and the description can then focus on the extent to which IS/IT support these core business processes.

In knowledge management, our focus is on knowledge in business processes. We want to identify and describe how knowledge workers participate and contribute in business processes, and how IS/IT support their work. Figure 3.17 may illustrate this point. This is an example where we have identified two core business processes of client problem analysis and solution and human resources management in a consulting firm. While the first process involves heavy knowledge work as indicated with the dark color, human resources management is just as much an administrative task. On the other hand, the current situation in the organization is such that human resources management receives more support from IS/IT than does the business process of client problem analysis and solutions.

Method V: IS/IT Support for Value Configuration

The most important business processes are often found in the company's value configuration. A value configuration describes how value is created in a company for its customers. A value configuration shows how the most important business processes function to create value for customers. A value configuration represents the way a particular organization conducts business. The best-known value configuration is the value chain.

In the *value chain*, value is created through efficient production of goods and services based on a variety of resources. The company is perceived as a series or chain of activities. Primary activities in the value chain include inbound logistics, production, outbound logistics, marketing and sales, and service. Support activities include infrastructure, human resources, technology development, and procurement.

Value can not only be created in value chains. Value can also be created in two alternative value configurations: value shop and value network (Stabell & Fjeldstad, 1998). In the *value shop*, activities are scheduled and resources are applied in a fashion that is dimensioned and appropriate to the needs of the client's problem, while a value chain performs a fixed set of activities that enables it to produce a standard product in large numbers. The value shop is a company that creates value by solving unique problems for customers and clients. Knowledge is the most important resource, and reputation is critical to firm success.

The third and final value configuration is the value network. A value network is a company that creates value by connecting clients and customers that are, or want to be, dependent on each other. These companies distribute information, money, products, and services.

IS/IT will add value to value configuration in ways that are similar to business processes, since the configuration constitutes the core business processes that exhibit service characteristics that are unique to the firm. Other examples of IT/IS support to value configuration are shown in several diagrams in Chapter I. These value configurations were thoroughly presented in Chapter I.

Method VI: Strategic Integration

The current state of IS/IT value in a company can be measured through the extent of integration between business strategy and IS/IT strategy. King and Teo (1997) have defined four stages of integration. The lower the degree of integration, the lower or less strategic (or more commoditized) is the value of IS/IT to the company. The first is separate planning with administrative integration. The second is one-way linked planning with sequential integration, while the third is two-way linked planning with reciprocal integration. The fourth stage is integrated planning with full integration. The four stage model can also be used assessing the maturity of the IS organization. IS organization will evolve from a lower stage to the next higher one after it gains proficiency in the lower stage.

The four stages of integration can be described in terms of *benchmark variables* as shown in Figure 3.18. Benchmark variables indicate the theoretical characteristics at each stage of integration. For example, firms at Stage 1 can theoretically be expected to conform to values of benchmark variables listed under Stage 1. However, this does not mean that it is not possible for firms at Stage 1 to have values of benchmark variables applicable to other stages.

Each of the 10 benchmark variables can be explained more in detail as follows:

Figure 3.18. Stages of integration between business strategy and IS/IT strategy (King & Teo, 1997)

BENCHMARK VARIABLES	**Stage 1 Administrative Integration**	**Stage 2 Sequential Integration**	**Stage 3 Reciprocal Integration**	**Stage 4 Full Integration**
Purpose of integration	Administrative and nonstrategic	Support business strategy	Support and influence business strategy	Joint development of business and IS strategies
Role of the IS function	Technically oriented and nonstrategic	Resource to support business strategy	Resource to support and influence business strategy	Critical to long-term survival of organization
Primary role of the IS executive	Functional administrator responsible for back room support	IS expert who formulates IS/IT strategy to implement business strategy	IS expert who provides valuable inputs during strategy formulation and implementation	Formal and integral member of top management who is involved in many business matters
Performance criteria for the IS function	Operational efficiency and cost minimization	Contribution to business strategy implementation	Quality of IS inputs into business strategy formulation and implementation	Long-term impact on organization
Triggers for developing IS applications	Need to automate administrative work processes	Business goals considered first	Business goals and IS capabilities considered jointly	IS applications are critical to success of business strategy
Top management participation in IS/IT planning	Seldom	Infrequent	Frequent	Almost always
User participation in IS/IT planning	Seldom	Infrequent	Frequent	Almost always
IS executive participation in business planning	Seldom	Infrequent	Frequent	Almost always
Assessment of new technologies	Seldom	Infrequent	Frequent	Almost always
Status of IS executive (Number of levels below the CEO)	Four or more	Three	Two	One

1. **Purpose of integration.** At Stage 1, integration focuses primarily on the support of administrative work processes. This gradually changes as the IS function begins to support business strategy (Stage 2) or influence business strategy (Stage 3). At Stage 4, there is joint strategy development for both business and IS strategies.
2. **Role of the IS function.** The general transition from being technically oriented to business oriented is a trend for most IS functions. At Stage 1, the IS function is viewed as being primarily technically oriented. Gradually, this role changes when the IS function is used as a resource to support the implementation (Stage 2) and formulation (Stage 3) of business strategies. At Stage 4, the IS function is viewed as critical to the long-term success of the organization. This variable contributes to the quantification of the IT value to the business.
3. **Primary role of the IS executive.** There seems to be a general decrease in the size of the central IS function. This may have resulted in a shift in the responsibilities of the IS function from systems design to systems integration, and from the role of a developer to that of an advisor. Due to increasing decentralization, the IS function may assume a staff role similar to a federal government in coordinating dispersed IS resources. The skill requirements of the senior executive have also changed over the years with increasing emphasis on both knowledge about changing technology and knowledge about the business. In addition, significant political and communication skills are required. The role of the IS executive gradually changes from being a functional administrator responsible for providing back room support (Stage 1) to being an IS expert who formulates IS strategy to implement business objectives (Stage 2). As the firm begins to apply IT for strategic purposes, the role of the IS executive becomes more important. He or she begins to play a major role in facilitating and influencing the development and implementation of IS applications to achieve business objectives (Stage 3). Finally, in Stage 4, the IS executive becomes a formal and integral member of the top management team and provides significant inputs in both IS and non-IS related matters.
4. **Performance criteria for the IS function.** As the IS function matures, the performance criteria for the IS function change from a structured focus on operational efficiency to a more unstructured concern for the impact of IS on strategic direction. It follows that the early performance criteria (Stage 1) for the IS function are primarily concerned with operational efficiency and cost minimization. When the IS function begins to play a more strategic role, the emphasis gradually shifts to effective strategy implementation (Stage 2) and then to the quality of IS inputs into business strategy formulation and implementation (Stage 3). Ultimately, the performance criteria for the IS function should be its long-term impact on the organization (Stage 4). Related to the role of IS, this variable will similarly contribute to the quantification of the value of IT to the business. The IT value moves from a commodity value of Stage 1 focused on cost efficiency to a transformative value of Stage 4 which is unique to the firm and will give the firm a sustainable competitive advantage.
5. **Triggers for developing IS applications.** Initially, the triggers for the development of new IS applications are opportunities for achieving greater efficiencies through process automation. As IS applications begin to be increasingly used to support business strategies, business goals become trigger mechanisms in deciding appropriate IS applications to be developed (Stage 2). At Stage 3, the joint consideration of business goals and IS capabilities becomes important as the firm attempts to develop

systems for sustainable competitive advantage. Finally, in Stage 4, IS applications are developed because they are critical to the success of the firm's strategy and the creation of business value. This variable also contributes to determining the value of IT to the business. Typically, it contributes to the growth of the business, so the IT value is measurable by the new revenue opportunities that the IS applications will enable.

6. **Top management participation in IS/IT planning.** Traditionally, as in Stage 1, top management had not paid great attention to the IS function because it was an overhead function that generated only cost. At Stage 2, greater top management participation in IS/IT planning begins when IS strategies come to be used to support business strategies. The realization that strategic IS/IT planning can also influence business strategy motivates top management to participate more actively in this kind of strategy work (Stage 3). Finally, in Stage 4, when the IS function becomes critical for the survival of the organization, top management and the senior IS executive jointly formulate business and IS plans.
7. **User participation in IS/IT planning.** Before the availability of end-user computing, user management was generally not significantly involved (Stage 1). However, as end-user systems and tools begin to dominate individual work, and the IS function begins to influence functional units in terms of its effects on business strategies, participation of users becomes more important in order to fully exploit the potential of information technology. User participation gradually increases through the stages, until at Stage 4, users participate extensively in IS/IT planning.
8. **IS executive participation in business planning.** The other side of business management participation in IS/IT planning is having IS executives participate in business planning. The traditional role of the IS function in providing administrative support does not require the senior IS executive to participate in business planning (Stage 1). The senior IS executive reacts to business plans and does not have any influence on their formulation. At Stage 2, the senior IS executive participation is initiated. As the IS function becomes more important in achievement of business objectives, it becomes necessary to include more frequent participation of the senior IS executive in business planning because the traditional participants are relatively unfamiliar with the potential of information technology (Stage 3). With greater participation, the senior IS executive becomes more informed about business objectives and is better able to provide higher quality inputs into the planning process. At Stage 4, the senior IS executive becomes an integral member of the top management team and participates extensively in both business planning and IS/IT planning.
9. **Assessment of new technologies.** During IS/IT planning, new technologies, which can impact the firm, are usually assessed. The level of sophistication involved in assessing new technologies is the basis for this ninth benchmark variable. In the early stages of IS/IT planning (Stages 1 and 2), assessment of the impact of new technologies, if any, is usually done rather informally and infrequently. At Stage 3, the need for formal and frequent procedures for assessing new technologies becomes apparent as the IS function begins to play a more important role in business planning. At Stage 4, assessment of the impact of new technologies becomes an integral part of business planning and IS/IT planning.
10. **Status of IS executive.** The responsibilities of the IS function have changed over the years due to technological and conceptual changes that made information technology

more important to organizations. IS line responsibilities are being rapidly distributed in many organizations as the IS function begins to take on more staff responsibilities. With these changing responsibilities of the IS function, the status of the senior IS executive is likely to become higher. The position of the senior IS executive—in terms of the number of levels below the CEO—can serve as an indication of the importance of the IS function to the firm's strategy.

Method VII: IS/IT Support for Knowledge Management

Information technology can be applied at four different levels to support knowledge management in an organization. At the first level, end-user tools are made available to knowledge workers. At the second level, information on who knows what is made available electronically. At the third level, some information representing knowledge is stored and made available electronically. At the fourth level, information systems capable of simulating human thinking are applied in the organization. These four levels are illustrated in Figure 3.19, where they are combined with knowledge management tasks. The entries in the figure only serve as examples of current systems.

The four different levels of support for knowledge management in an organization are described in Chapter XI. The levels are discussed in the context of the stages of growth model for knowledge management technology.

Figure 3.19. Examples of IS/IT at different knowledge management levels

LEVELS TASKS	I END USER TOOLS	II WHO KNOWS WHAT	III WHAT THEY KNOW	IV WHAT THEY THINK
Distribute Knowledge	Word Processing Desktop Publishing Web Publishing Electronic Calendars Presentations	Word Processing Desktop Publishing Web Publishing Electronic Calendars Presentations	Word Processing Desktop Publishing Web Publishing Electronic Calendars Presentations	Word Processing Desktop Publishing Web Publishing Electronic Calendars Presentations
Share Knowledge		Groupware Intranets Networks E-mail	Groupware Intranets Networks E-mail	Groupware Intranets Networks E-mail
Capture Knowledge			Databases Data Warehouses	Databases Data Warehouses
Apply Knowledge				Expert systems Case-based reasoning

Method VIII: IS/IT in E-Business

For most firms, becoming an e-business is an evolutionary development (Porter, 2001). Earl (2000) has described the typical six-stage journey that corporations are likely to experience. The six stages are not necessarily definitive periods of evolution, as companies may have activities at several neighboring stages at the same time. The six stages are illustrated in Figure 3.20.

Each of the six stages of evolving the e-business as illustrated in Figure 3.20 can be described as follows (Earl, 2000):

1. **External communication.** It was more than a decade ago that most corporations wanted a home page on the Internet for the first time. The realization that the Internet was a potential communications channel to external stakeholders, such as investors, analysts, customers, potential recruits, and suppliers, was matched by the recognition that the Web provided an interesting and not too difficult means of designing and publishing corporate public relations material.
   The vision behind creating such Web sites rarely extends beyond external corporate communications. Perhaps the only interactive aspect is a provision for e-mailed questions to corporate departments from external stakeholders.
2. **Internal communication.** Intranets, using the Internet and Web techniques, are introduced at this stage to raise the information and communication capacity of the organization. An integrated, familiar front end to frequently used internal applications does appeal to end users. Knowledge management applications have evolved from this stage. And sometimes having internal access to the same information that is provided externally is well received.

Figure 3.20. Stages of e-business maturity (Earl, 2000)

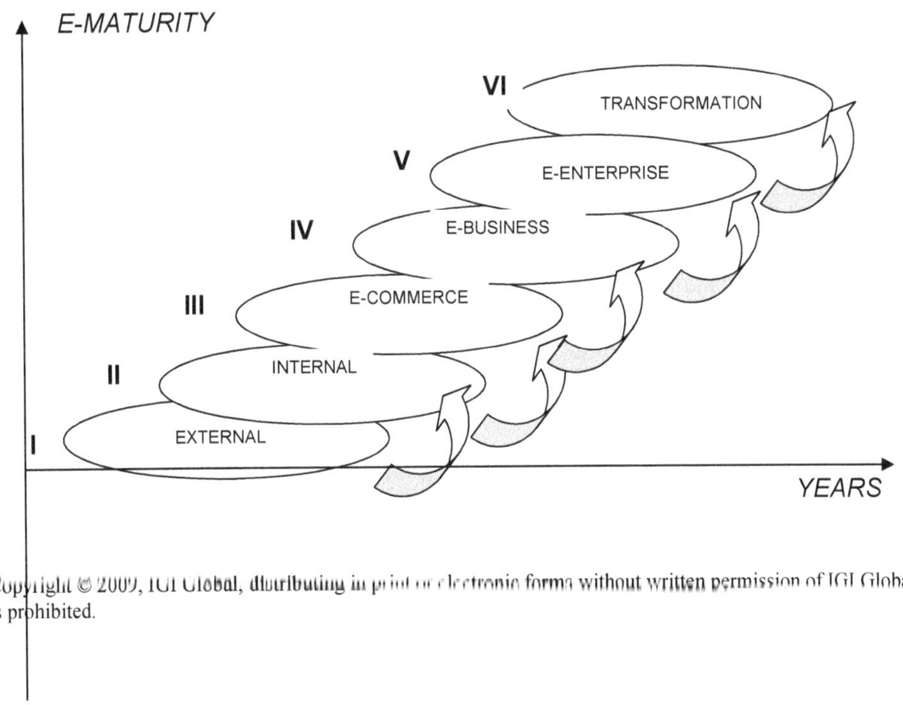

Information technology is applied to design consistent and user-friendly front ends to e-mail, groupware, administrative support systems, and other systems used by most people in the organization.

3. **E-Commerce.** Buying and selling on the Internet take place at this stage. Electronic channels and services are promoted to complement traditional forms of distribution. In the case of startups, customers are identified and attracted by using the Web and other advertising channels.

   At this stage, organizations struggle with questions such as: What and how do we tell customers and suppliers that they can trade with us online? What pricing policies do we adopt and how do they relate to pricing in our traditional channels? Which products and services are suited to electronic market trading? What IS/IT applications and functions are needed to support e-commerce?

4. **E-business.** Many companies discover a critical lesson at the e-commerce stage. Building an online channel on top of inadequate or inefficient business processes achieves only one thing: it broadcasts and magnifies the fact that the company's back office systems or operational processes are really bad. So this fourth stage is about reengineering and redesigning business processes to match customers' expectations.

   Customers already recognize the signs of business processes that are not synchronized with the demands and expectations of e-commerce: goods that do not arrive on time; e-mailed requests that do not receive response; clumsy handling of returns; inability to track order status; network access that breaks down; and telephone requests where persons answering the phone have no idea what you are talking about.

   Most firms learn the hard way and treat Stage 3 as inevitable, evolutionary, experiential learning. Then they accept the costs of Stage 4, where reengineering of business processes and redesign of architecture and infrastructure of their technology base have to be implemented. The lesson at Stage 4 is that high-performance processes are needed to stay in e-business.

5. **E-Enterprise.** Web-enabled online business puts new pressures on management processes. Decision making occurs increasingly on the network, rather than in meeting rooms. Transactions can be monitored and analyzed in real time. Information can be collected online. New ways of representing and analyzing these data are being developed. We are witnessing new ways of communicating across the enterprise using wireless and mobile technologies.

   Wireless and mobile technologies are about to change Internet business. This is being driven by customer demand for wireless devices and the desire to be connected to information and services available through the Internet from anywhere and at any time. Similarly, company employees see no reason anymore for showing up in the office at eight o'clock and leave again at five. As a result, telecommunications, the Internet, and mobile computing are merging their technologies to form the basis for mobile work and management.

   In Stage 5, decision making is becoming entrepreneurial and about communicating decisions across the enterprise. This stage is the dawn of cybernetic models of management where traditional top managers find the time to leave the company. The critical success factor is to recruit, develop, and empower people who have the skills to use information and act on it.

6. **Transformation.** The company has successfully made the journey of e-business. The challenges of the previous stages have been met, and the new business and management solutions required for the e-enterprise are embedded. In many ways, this is the goal. However, we know that nothing stabilize, market forces and emerging technologies drive continuous change.

Method IX: IS/IT-Enabled Business Transformation

The role of IS/IT in shaping business operations is a distinctive one. IS/IT has become a fundamental enabler in creating and maintaining flexible business activities. Using a framework that breaks IS/IT-enabled business transformation into five levels, Venkatraman (1994) provides a description of each level's characteristics and offers guidelines for deriving maximal benefits. He suggests that each organization first determines the level at which the benefits are in line with the costs or efforts of the needed changes and then proceeds to higher levels as the demands of competition and the need to deliver greater value to the customer increases as illustrated in Figure 3.21.

Level One: Information Technology Efficiency. The first level is the basic one for leveraging IS/IT functionality within a business through localized exploitation. The expression "localized exploitation" is chosen to indicate that, in many cases, decisions to deploy isolated systems (e.g., a customer order-entry system, inventory control system, internal electronic mail system) are decentralized to the appropriate functional, operational managers. Typically, managers initiate and deploy these systems to respond to operational problems or challenges. This level one is best viewed as the deployment of standard IS/IT applications with minimal changes to the business processes.

Figure 3.21. Level of IT-enabled transformation as identity of current IS/IT situation (Venkatraman, 1994)

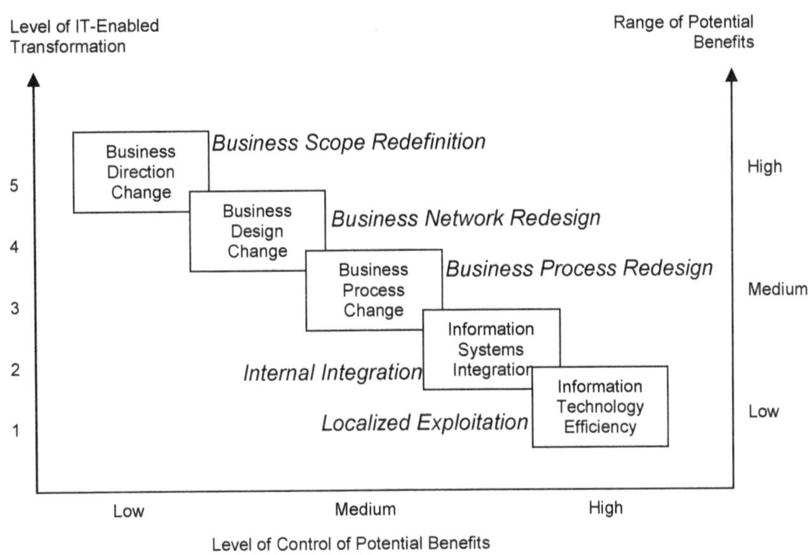

This underutilizes IS/IT's potential capabilities and fails to provide organizations with as many possible advantages if the company attempted to change the business processes to leverage the technical functionality. The main weakness is that competitors can easily imitate standard technical applications with minimal changes to the underlying business processes to neutralize sources of strategic advantage.

Level Two: Information Systems Integration. The second level is a logical extension of the first, reflecting a more systematic attempt to leverage IS/IT capabilities throughout the entire business process. This level involves two types of internal systems integration: technical interconnectivity (dealing with the interconnectivity and interoperability of the different systems and applications throughout a common IT platform) and business process interdependence (dealing with the interdependence of organizational roles and responsibilities across distinct functional lines). Neither type alone is sufficient. Often, firms allocate more attention to technical interconnectivity than to business process interdependence. Efforts at technical interconnectivity have been enhanced by significant developments in connectivity capabilities during the past decade such as increased availability of integrated technological solutions and favorable cost-performance trends.

Efforts at business process interdependence should first emphasize the view that the firm should develop its own vision for internal integration after assessing the benefits of integrating current businesses processes. If a company deems the current processes to be effective, then it is important to articulate the specific objectives of internal integration: for instance, some firms may seek to create cross-functional, horizontal business processes that are parallel to the traditional organization. Alternatively, the logic for internal integration may reflect a transition toward fundamentally redesigning the business processes over a period of time.

Efforts at business processes interdependence should then emphasize the need to ensure that marketplace considerations guide internal integration efforts. Simply fine-tuning existing outmoded processes through current technological capabilities does not create the required organizational capabilities.

Level Three: Business Process Change. The third level reflects a strong view that the benefits from IS/IT functionality are not fully realized if superimposed on the current business processes—however integrated they might be. This is because the current business processes subscribe to a set of organizational principles that responded to the industrial revolution. Organizational concepts such as centralization vs. decentralization, span of control, line vs. staff, functional specialization, authority-responsibility balance, and administrative mechanisms for coordination and control are all derived from the general principles. Although these concepts are still valid, IS/IT functionality can significantly alter some of these old principles. Some modes of organizing may be rendered relatively inefficient. In the opinion of professionals and academics, the new logic of organization should be predicated on current and emerging IS/IT capabilities. IS/IT functionality should not be simply overlaid on existing business processes but should be used as a lever for designing the new organization and associated business processes.

Three critical questions for exploiting IS/IT-related benefits at the level of business proccss redesign are: (i) what is the rationale for the current organizational design? (what are its strengths and limitations?), (ii) what significant changes in business processes are occurring in the marketplace? (what are the likely impacts?), (iii) what are the costs of continuing with the status quo? (when should we redesign the business process? what should be our pace of redesign?).

A company should initiate business process redesign after ascertaining the significant changes in its key competitors' business processes, especially those of new entrants, so that it can formulate appropriate responses beforehand.

Benefits from business process redesign are limited in scope if the processes are not extended outside the focal organizational boundary to identify options for redesigning relationships with the other organizations that participate in ultimately delivering value to the customer.

Level Four: Business Design Change. The three levels discussed thus far have focused on IS/IT-enabled business transformation within a single organization. These levels—either implicitly or explicitly—assumed that the boundary of the focal organization is fixed or given. Even when there are interconnections with external businesses—such as suppliers, buyers, and other intermediaries—the distribution of business activities across the different firms is not altered. In contrast, this level represents the redesign of the nature of exchange among multiple participants in a business network through effective deployment of IS/IT capabilities.

If this is the current IS/IT level in the company, then we should see evidence of a strategic logic influencing related participants in the business network to provide products and services in the marketplace, exploiting IS/IT functionality for learning from the extended network as well as for coordination and control. We should further see evidence of elimination of activities where our organization may not have the required level of competence, streamlining business scope to remain flexible as well as responsive to fast-changing and diverse customer needs, and ability to exploit sources of competence in the larger business network (beyond what is available in our organization).

Level Five: Business Direction Change. Strategy analysis typically starts with the mission and vision. When the mission describes the business we are in, then the vision describes what we want to achieve in that business. At the fifth level, IS/IT will play a role in influencing mission and vision.

If this is the current IS/IT level in the company, then we should see evidence of a business scope redefinition that is enabled and facilitated by IS/IT functionality. We should see evidence of opportunities and actions to take advantage of IS/IT capabilities to create a more flexible and effective business entity. We should see substitution of interfirm business relationships as an effective alternative to vertical integration.

SUMMARY

Alignment between business strategy and IT strategy is widely believed to improve business performance (Sabherwal & Chan, 2001). Business–IT alignment is optimal when IT strategy is integrated with and forms part of business strategy (Cassidy, 2006). Elemental IT strategy comprises the business strategic direction and strategy outline, the enterprise architecture, and attendant applications and technology infrastructure platforms, the requisite resources and capabilities (competence), and the organization model and management control (governance). Strategic management must be cognizant of the tightly coupled interrelationship between task, technology, structure, and people, which must be managed holistically to ensure strategic fit (Gottschalk, 2005).

Moreover, IT managers must analyze and understand how IT can add value to firms, organizationally. There are nine available methods for IT value-added analysis:

- **Method 1:** Benefits analysis identifies IT contributions to: rationalization benefits (personnel cost savings); control benefits (decision support); organizational benefits (team effectiveness and agility); and market benefits (revenue improvement).
- **Method 2:** Stages of IT organizational growth analysis identifies the growing maturity of the firm's use of IT over the years—from data processing (for efficiency) to management information system (for effectiveness) to strategic information system (for competitiveness).
- **Method 3:** Analysis of IT usage in management activities in a hierarchy of operational, tactical, and strategic management to identify the IT contributions.
- **Method 4:** Analysis of IT in business processes—business processes are activities organized, coordinated, resourced, and focused to produce goods and services of value to receivers and customers.
- **Method 5:** Analysis of IT support for value configuration—IT value added is similar to Method 4.
- **Method 6:** Analysis of IT value added via the King and Teo (1997) model of strategic integration—IT role in firm increases from nonstrategic to competitively strategic as the firm matures from Stage 1—administrative integration (separate business and IT strategic planning) to stage 4—full integration (joint development of business and IT strategies—dynamic strategic alignment).
- **Method 7:** Analysis of IT support for knowledge management—IT support is analyzed by a matrix of tasks (distribute knowledge, share knowledge, capture knowledge, and apply knowledge) and levels (end-user tools, who knows what, what they know, and what they think).
- **Method 8:** Analysis of IT support in e-business maturity growth—this analysis uses Earl's six-stage e-business maturity model to show the increasing sophistication of IT and value added as the firm matures from Stage 1—external communication, through internal communication, e-commerce, e-business, e-enterprise to Stage 6—transformation.
- **Method 9:** Analysis of e-strategy and IT-enabled business transformation—as the name implies, IT plays a critical role in this model. IT role and business influence increases as the firm evolves from Level 1—information technology efficiency through information systems integration and business process change to Level 4—business design change.

REFERENCES

Cassidy, A. (2006). *Information systems strategic planning* (2nd ed.). Auerbach Publications.

Earl, M. J. (2000). Evolving the e-business. *Business Strategy Review, 11*(2), 33-38.

Gottschalk, P. (2005). *Strategic knowledge management technology.* Hershey, PA: Idea Group Publishing.

Gottschalk, P., & Khandelwal, V. K. (2002). Global comparison of stages of growth based on critical success factors. *Journal of Global Information Management, 10*(2), 42-51.

Hann, J., & Weber, R. (1996). Information systems planning: A model and empirical tests. *Management Science, 42*(7), 1043-1064.

Jensen, M., & Zajac, E. J. (2004). Corporate elites and corporate strategy: How demographic preferences and structural position shape the scope of the firm. *Strategic Management Journal, 25*, 507-524.

King, W. R., & Teo, T. S. H. (1997). Integration between business planning and information systems planning: Validating a stage hypothesis. *Decision Sciences, 28*(2), 279-308.

Monnoyer, E. (2003). What CEOs really think about IT. *McKinsey Quarterly, 3*, 80-82.

Nolan, R. L. (1979, March-April). Managing the crises in data processing. *Harvard Business Review*, pp. 115-126.

Porter, M. E. (2001, March). Strategy and the Internet. *Harvard Business Review*, pp. 63-78.

Sabherwal, R., & Chan, Y. E. (2001). Alignment between business and IS strategies: A study of prospectors, analyzers, and defenders. *Information Systems Research, 12*(1), 11-33.

Stabell, C. B., & Fjeldstad, Ø. D. (1998). Configuring value for competitive advantage: On chains, shops, and networks. *Strategic Management Journal, 19*, 413-437.

Treacy, M., & Wiersema, F. (1995). *The discipline of market leaders.* Cambridge, MA: Perseus Books.

Venkatraman, N. V. (1994, Winter). IT-enabled business transformation: From automation to business scope redefinition. *Sloan Management Review*, pp. 74-86.

Chapter IV
Critical Success Factors of IT Strategy

INTRODUCTION

As discussed in Chapter III, a successful IT strategy must align with the business, fully at every stage of the end-to-end strategic management process, from strategy setting and planning to detailed program execution and delivery. Most publications (Luftman & McLean, 2004) on business–IT alignment to date have been centered on one dimension of the alignment issues, for example, on strategic planning or organizational issues. In this chapter, we discuss the critical success factors of IT strategy holistically across four dimensions of the strategic management process from strategy formulation to planning to execution and to value delivery monitoring end-to-end because IT leaders have to manage alignment in all four dimensions in order to maximize the strategic value of information technology deployment.

The most basic requirement for the success is that IT must be regarded as being part of the business, devoid of the "us" vs. "them" chasm (separating IT from the business) found in most traditional organizations where IT is viewed as a subservient role performing basically a "back office" function.

This critical organizational culture requirement of "IT and business acting as one" is founded on the rigor and discipline of IT governance. IT governance is integral to corporate governance, subject to periodic governance compliance audit by is chapter will briefly describe this function as it applies to the end-to-end process of IT strategy. A more complete treatment will be covered in Chapter IX.

IT AND BUSINESS AS ONE

IT is recognized as a critical business discipline because it is central to all business activities of modern enterprises in the creation of customer value. To create business value from IT, business needs to understand the role IT plays, not only in supporting the running of the business in such back-office functions as human resources (HR), finance, and inventory control but, more importantly, the special and competitively differentiated ways that IT plays in delivering products and services to the firm's end customers. The integral role that IT has enmeshed into all business functions today means that IT has become a central nervous system of the business. In particular, information *is* the bloodstream of business that flows through all business functions (processes) supported by the IT nervous system. Business value is created by each business function or process through dynamic consumption (processing) of input information and creation of new output information, which in turn will be "consumed" by another business function (process) as defined by the value configuration of the business (see Chapter 1)—information acting much like the bloodstream that flows through the human organs to make the human body (the firm) alive and productive. Thus, to be able to achieve a sustainable competitive advantage position in its chosen industry, the firm must treat IT and its management as a critical business discipline. IT and business must act as one integral *organism* much like *yin and yang* which complements each other to get the right balance to achieve the competitive advantage. Smaczny (2001), in his argument for IT being part of business strategy, refers to this tight integration of IT with business as *fusion.*

The *fundamental principle* of all the critical success factors of IT strategy is therefore IT and business *acting as one.* This requires each IT task to be *aligned* with and *"justified"* by the business function it is designed to contribute, for and based on which its business value is *measured.* This means the IS/IT strategy, organization, processes, infrastructure, applications, projects, budget, and metrics should all verify their alignment to the business goals, objectives, and strategies (Cassidy, 2006). The issue of business–IT alignment has been studied for over 10 years (Avison, Jones, Powell, & Wilson, 2004; Luftman & Papp, 1995). It is commonly reported in the literature (Avison et al., 2004) that alignment will allow enterprise to achieve competitive advantage through IT, achieve maximum return on IT investment, and provide direction and flexibility to respond to new business opportunities.

IT and business acting as one is easier said than done, however. In reality, not many enterprises have yet fully mastered the practice of the fundamental principle of IT and business acting as one. This is because of the bad old tradition of IT in the past (and even today for some enterprises) working (either being treated or wanted to be treated) as the *back-office techie guys* who seemed to do as they were told (or requested) by the business without having any concern for the end customers or indeed the business purpose of the tasks requested. In the past, IT saw themselves as the technical guys who would do whatever technical task is requested of them by the business. There was no need to understand the business, let alone the business strategy or points of differentiation. The "us-versus-them" working relationship or company culture has permeated between IT and business in most enterprises in the past, and indeed even today.

While this scenario may be an extreme example for today's enterprises, it is nonetheless still a common issue for most enterprises today that some degree of misalignment still exists between business and IT. The varying degrees of organizational misalignment and functional disconnect between business and IT have been the key inhibitor of value creation by IT in all enterprises, past and present. Despite rigorous and diligent attempts by researchers and practitioners alike, in the past 20 years, various recent surveys (Luftman & McLean, 2004) have shown that business–IT alignment remains a strategically critical priority for business and IT leaders to manage and achieve.

King and Teo (1997) investigate the degree of alignment and integration between business strategy and IS/IT strategy in enterprises. King and Teo (1997) find that companies go through four stages of strategic integration with increasing degree of integration as the company becomes excellent (mature) in exploiting and managing IT for business differentiation. The first stage is separate planning with administrative integration. The second is one-way linked planning with sequential integration, while the third is two-way linked planning with reciprocal integration. The fourth stage is fully integrated business and IT planning—the most mature level of business and IT acting as one.

There are many factors affecting the ability of business and IT acting as one. The combination of these factors defines the level at which business and IT are acting as one in strategy formulation, planning, and execution. King and Teo (1997) identify 10 factors affecting business–IT partnership in business–IT strategic management. They call these factors *benchmark variables.* The four stages of integration can be described in terms of benchmark variables as shown in Figure 4.1. Benchmark variables indicate the theoretical characteristics at each stage of integration. For example, firms at Stage 1 can theoretically be expected to conform to values of benchmark variables listed under Stage 1. However, this does not mean that it is not possible for firms at Stage 1 to have values of benchmark variables applicable to other stages.

Each of the 10 benchmark variables can be explained more in detail as follows (King & Teo, 1997):

1. **Purpose of integration.** At Stage 1, integration focuses primarily on the support of administrative work processes. IT is still a commodity service and not critical for business strategy. This gradually changes as the IS function begins to support business strategy (Stage 2) or influence business strategy (Stage 3). At Stage 4, there is joint strategy development for both business and IS strategies—at which business and IS truly acting as one with strategic influences going both directions.
2. **Role of the IS function.** The general transition from being technically oriented to business oriented is a trend for most IS functions. At Stage 1, the IS function is viewed as being primarily technically oriented. Gradually, this role changes when the IS function is used as a resource to support the implementation (Stage 2) and formulation (Stage 3) of business strategies. At Stage 4, the IS function is viewed as critical to the long-term success of the organization. To be able to act as one with the business, IS acts and thinks like a business with strong business skills. Similarly, business becomes very IT savvy.
3. **Primary role of the IS executive.** There seems to be a general decrease in the size of the central IS function. This may have resulted in a shift in the responsibilities of the IS function from systems design to systems integration, and from the role of a developer to that of an advisor. Due to increasing decentralization, the IS function may assume a staff role similar to a federal government in coordinating dispersed IS resources. The skill requirements of the senior executive have also changed over the years with increasing emphasis on both knowledge about changing technology

Figure 4.1. Stages of integration between business strategy and IS/IT strategy (King & Teo, 1997)

Benchmark Variables	Stage 1 Administrative Integration	Stage 2 Sequential Integration	Stage 3 Reciprocal Integration	Stage 4 Full Integration
Purpose of integration	Administrative and nonstrategic	Support business strategy	Support and influence business strategy	Joint development of business and IS strategies
Role of the IS function	Technically oriented and nonstrategic	Resource to support business strategy	Resource to support and influence business strategy	Critical to long-term survival of organization
Primary role of the IS executive	Functional administrator responsible for back room support	IS expert who formulates IS/IT strategy to implement business strategy	IS expert who provides valuable inputs during strategy formulation and implementation	Formal and integral member of top management who is involved in many business matters
Performance criteria for the IS function	Operational efficiency and cost minimization	Contribution to business strategy implementation	Quality of IS inputs into business strategy formulation and implementation	Long-term impact on organization
Triggers for developing IS applications	Need to automate administrative work processes	Business goals considered first	Business goals and IS capabilities considered jointly	IS applications are critical to success of business strategy
Top management participation in IS/IT planning	Seldom	Infrequent	Frequent	Almost always
User participation in IS/IT planning	Seldom	Infrequent	Frequent	Almost always
IS executive participation in business planning	Seldom	Infrequent	Frequent	Almost always
Assessment of new technologies	Seldom	Infrequent	Frequent	Almost always
Status of IS executive (Number of levels below the CEO)	Four or more	Three	Two	One

and knowledge about the business. In addition, significant political and communication skills are required. The role of the IS executive gradually changes from being a functional administrator responsible for providing back room support (Stage 1), to being an IS expert who formulates IS strategy to implement business objectives (Stage 2). As the firm begins to apply IT for strategic purposes, the role of the IS executive becomes more important. He or she begins to play a major role in facilitating and influencing the development and implementation of IS applications to achieve business objectives (Stage 3). Finally, in Stage 4, the IS executive becomes a formal and integral member of the top management team and provides significant inputs in both IS and non-IS related matters.

4. **Performance criteria for the IS function.** As the IS function matures, the performance criteria for the IS function change from a structured focus on operational efficiency to a more unstructured concern for the impact of IS on strategic direction. It follows that the early performance criteria (Stage 1) for the IS function are primarily concerned with operational efficiency and cost minimization. When the IS function begins to play a more strategic role, the emphasis gradually shifts to effective strategy implementation (Stage 2), and then to the quality of IS inputs into business strategy formulation and implementation (Stage 3). Ultimately, the performance criteria for the IS function should be its long-term impact on the organization (Stage 4)—IS becoming a business transformer to create a sustainable strategic advantage.
5. **Triggers for developing IS applications.** Initially, the triggers for the development of new IS applications are opportunities for achieving greater efficiencies through process automation. As IS applications begin to be increasingly used to support business strategies, business goals become trigger mechanisms in deciding appropriate IS applications to be developed (Stage 2). At Stage 3, the joint consideration of business goals and IS capabilities becomes important as the firm attempts to develop systems for sustainable competitive advantage. Finally, in Stage 4, IS applications are developed because they are critical to the success of the firm's strategy and the creation of business value.
6. **Top management participation in IS/IT planning.** Traditionally, as in Stage 1, top management had not paid great attention to the IS function because it was an overhead function that generated only cost. At Stage 2, greater top management participation in IS/IT planning begins when IS strategies come to be used to support business strategies. The realization that strategic IS/IT planning can also influence business strategy motivates top management to participate more actively in this kind of strategy work (Stage 3). Finally, in Stage 4, when the IS function becomes critical for the survival or sustainable strategic advantage of the organization, top management and the senior IS executive jointly formulate business and IS plans—business and IT truly acting as one.
7. **User participation in IS/IT planning.** Before the availability of end-user computing, user management was generally not significantly involved (Stage 1). However, as end-user systems and tools begin to dominate individual work, and the IS function begins to influence functional units in terms of its effects on business strategies, participation of users becomes more important in order to fully exploit the potential of information technology. User participation gradually increases through the stages, until at Stage 4, users participate extensively in IS/IT planning.

8. **IS executive participation in business planning.** The other side of business management participation in IS/IT planning is having IS executives participate in business planning. The traditional role of the IS function in providing administrative support does not require the senior IS executive to participate in business planning (Stage 1). The senior IS executive reacts to business plans and does not have any influence on their formulation. At Stage 2, the senior IS executive participation is initiated. As the IS function becomes more important in achievement of business objectives, it becomes necessary to include more frequent participation of the senior IS executive in business planning because the traditional participants are relatively unfamiliar with the potential of information technology (Stage 3). With greater participation, the senior IS executive becomes more informed about business objectives and is better able to provide higher quality inputs into the planning process. At Stage 4, the senior IS executive becomes an integral member of the top management team and participates extensively in both business planning and IS/IT planning.
9. **Assessment of new technologies.** During IS/IT planning, new technologies, which can impact on the firm, are usually assessed. The level of sophistication involved in assessing new technologies is the basis for this ninth benchmark variable. In the early stages of IS/IT planning (Stages 1 and 2), assessment of the impact of new technologies, if any, is usually done rather informally and infrequently. At Stage 3, the need for formal and frequent procedures for assessing new technologies becomes apparent as the IS function begins to play a more important role in business planning. At Stage 4, assessment of the impact of new technologies becomes an integral part of business planning and IS/IT planning. The business and IT executives are constantly seeking out potential disruptive technologies to transform the business.
10. **Status of IS executive.** The responsibilities of the IS function have changed over the years due to technological and conceptual changes that made information technology more important to organizations. IS line responsibilities are being rapidly distributed in many organizations as the IS function begins to take on more staff responsibilities. With these changing responsibilities of the IS function, the status of the senior IS executive is likely to become higher. The position of the senior IS executive—in terms of the number of levels below the CEO—can serve as an indication of the importance of the IS function to the firm's strategy.

So what must business and IT do to act as one—resonating harmonically even in the event of changing business environment? In addition to the mutual understanding of business and IT roles and capabilities in customer value creation described above, two more ingredients are required:

- Behavioral
- Organizational

ACTING AS ONE BEHAVIORALLY

The behavioral component deals with establishment of strong relationship and trust between business and IT. This component requires IT to work proactively to engage the business. It requires strong leadership and communications skills, as well as business skills. IT is a means to a business end. IT executives must therefore have a deep understanding of their company business and master the art of business communication. All IT activities and service performance levels must be explained in terms of business context. For instance, instead of saying IT has improved the order management process by implementing a business process management platform using the state of the art service oriented architecture, we say that the order management process has been redesigned with in-built flexibility for ease of adaptation for future business change and has reduced the order-to-cash from x days to y hours. This business context communication will improve the business understanding of IT role, and indeed IT value to business.

Most importantly, however, trust and respect from business is earned by IT through diligent hard work and consistent successful delivery of commitments made to the business. It is through results and sharing of success and failure that a relationship between IT and business is founded and sustained. This depends on IT organization's strategy execution skills and the model for IT delivery accountability adopted by the enterprise. This is the core of the next ingredient—organizational process. As King and Teo (1997) have shown, the company can attain full business–IT integration stage by stage as IS value to business improves (as defined by the benchmark variables) with continuous successful service delivery in each stage of the evolution.

ACTING AS ONE ORGANIZATIONALLY

The organizational process deals with the mutually dependent nature of business and IT accountabilities in setting strategic direction and planning for, and execution and value-delivery of IT-dependent business programs (and projects). This is known as IT governance, part of corporate governance. Detailed treatment of IT governance will be covered in Chapter 9. Here we discuss briefly to highlight its importance in ensuring business and IT acting as one.

IT governance consists of the leadership and organizational structures and processes that ensure that the organization's IT sustains and extends the organization's strategy and objectives (Grembergen et al., 2004).

IT governance matters because it influences the benefits received from IT investments. Through a combination of practices (such as redesigning business processes and well-designed governance mechanisms) and appropriately matched IT investments, top-performing enterprises generate superior returns on their IT investments (Weill & Ross, 2004).

IT governance can be defined as specifying decision rights and accountability framework to encourage desirable behavior in the use of IT (Weill & Ross, 2004). This is the definition we will use here.

Other definitions are for example: (i) IT governance is the structures and processes that ensure that IT supports the organization's mission. The purpose is to align IT with the enterprise, maximize the benefits of IT, use IT resources responsibly, and manage IT risks, (ii) A structure of relationships and processes to direct and control the enterprise in order to achieve the enterprise's goals by adding value while balancing risk vs. return over IT and its processes; (iii) IT governance is the responsibility of the board of directors and executive management. It is an integral part of enterprise governance and consists of the leadership and organizational structures and processes that ensure that the organization's IT sustains and extends the organization's strategies and objectives; and (iv) IT governance

Figure 4.2. The "four are's" of IT governance (IT Governance Institute, 2006)

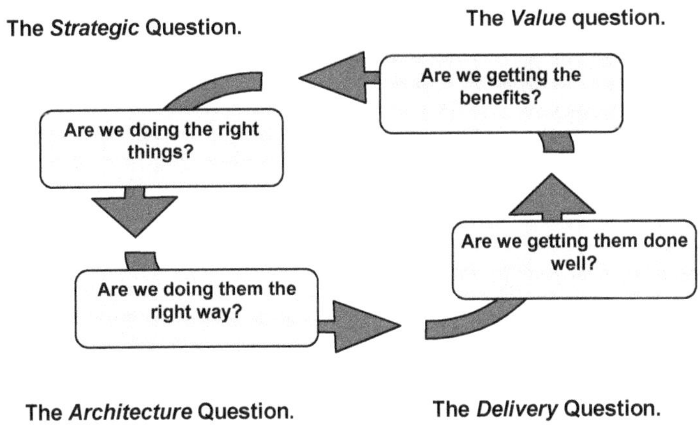

is the system by which an organization's IT portfolio is directed and controlled. IT Governance describes (a) the distribution of decision-making rights and responsibilities among different stakeholders in the organization, and (b) the rules and procedures for making and monitoring decisions on strategic IT concerns (Peterson, 2004).

The central tenet of IT governance is the transparency in the decision processes of business investment in IT from the strategic decision to invest (doing the *right thing*) in a business program at the start of the process, right through to delivering the desired benefits at the end of the business program. This is illustrated by the "four are's" (see Figure 4.2 below) of the IT Governance Institute's Val IT Framework (ITGI, 2006). Business and IT must work in unison in addressing each of the four questions of the IT strategy process in Figure 4.1 (ITGI, 2006):

- The strategic question (Are we doing the right things?) deals with the alignment of IT direction and strategic plan with the business direction and strategic plan. It seeks to ensure that the proposed IT investment resulting from the IT strategy is: (a) consistent with the firm's business principles, (b) contributing to the firm's strategic objectives, (c) providing optimal value, at affordable cost, at an acceptable level of risk.
- The architecture and delivery questions deal with the execution of the IT plan. The architecture (more detail in Chapter VI) question seeks to ensure that the IT investment is: (a) in line with the enterprise architecture, (b) consistent with the firm's architecture principles, and (c) contributing to the population of the firm's architecture. The delivery question seeks to ensure that IT organization has: (a) effective and disciplined management, delivery, and change management processes; and (b) competent and available technical and business resources to deliver the required capabilities and the organizational changes required to leverage the capabilities.
- The value question deals with the outcomes of the business program execution. It seeks to ensure that both business and IT have: (a) a clear and shared understanding

of the expected benefits, (b) clear accountability for realizing the benefits, (c) relevant metrics, and (d) an effective benefits realization process.

Therefore, IT strategy will be successful when IT and business acting as one across the complete life cycle of the IT strategy process. The next section will give an overview of the critical success factors.

OVERVIEW OF THE CRITICAL SUCCESS FACTORS

IT strategy will be successful when IT and business acting as one across the complete life cycle of the IT strategy process, and business and IT alignment is validated in each step of the end-to-end strategy process (as shown in Figure 4.3):

1. **Strategy direction setting:** IT strategy is defined in line with and documented as part of the enterprise strategy
2. **Strategic planning:** The IT strategic plans clearly correspond to the respective business strategic plans and the business outcomes the IT plans must deliver are clearly described and justified in the business plans
3. **Strategy execution:** The business programs constructed from the business and IT plans will have a business owner supported by a professional IT program manager responsible for on time and on budget delivery of the program
4. **Business outcome monitoring:** Upon successful delivery of the program, each program is audited at selected milestones to ensure the intended business objectives and benefits are consistently delivered

Cassidy (2006) proposes a similar approach to ensuring alignment between business and IT plan. Cassidy (2006, p. 9) models the strategic planning process as a linear sequence comprising: direction setting, industry analysis, situation analysis, success criteria, plans, and financial model. Cassidy (2006) argues business and IT must be shown to be aligned at each stage of this sequence, as shown in Table 4.1.

Figure 4.3. End-to-end business–IT alignment

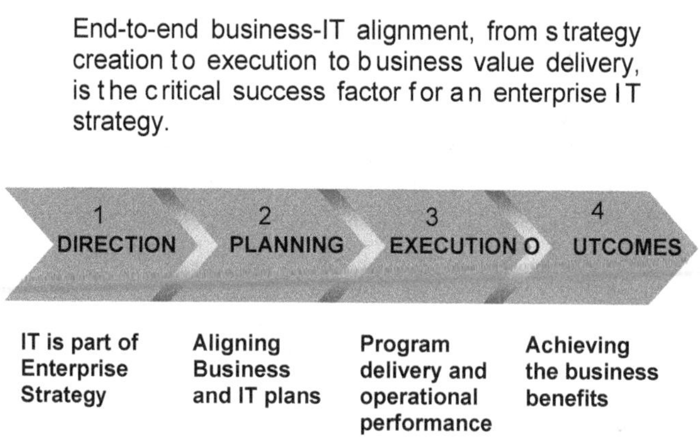

Table 4.1. Business and IT plan alignment (adapted from Cassidy, 2006)

Strategic planning stage	Business plan components	IT plan components
Direction setting	Business mission, vision, values, priorities	Drives IT vision, mission, objectives, and strategies
Industry analysis	Industry structure, markets, relationships, finances	Identifies future IT requirements, competitive advantages for IT
Situation analysis	Business strengths, weaknesses, opportunities, threats	Impacts ability to execute projects, identifies potential IT projects, impacts IT strengths, weaknesses, opportunities, and threats
Success criteria	Business requirements, success factors, operating vision, key metrics	Drives IT metrics, identifies requirements
Plans	Business objectives and strategies	Identifies IT projects and priorities
Financial model	Finances	Provides IT budget and project targets

Through the strategic planning alignment, it makes the process of transforming IT capabilities to match the required future business capabilities systematic and methodical. It facilitates traceability of strategic requirements. CIO will be able to identify specific IT weaknesses and declare the action required to convert the weakness to a strength. For example, if IT organization is seen as "High cost and lack value," IT plan will explicitly state the initiative required to change from the old state to the new state of "IT costs matching value provided" (Cassidy, 2006). Cassidy (2006) argues that a cause-effect map of business strategy to IT strategy and IT metrics can be derived, as illustrated in Table 4.2.

A useful end-to-end strategy model called the Y model is described by Gottschalk (2006). A graphical representation of the Y model is shown in Figure 4.4. It is called the Y model as it looks like the letter Y. The model consists of seven stages covering analysis, choice, and implementation. The stages are as follows (Gottschalk, 2006):

1. **Describe current situation.** The current IS/IT situation in the business can be described using several methods. The benefits method identifies benefits from use of IS/IT in the business. Distinctions are made between rationalization benefits, control benefits, organizational benefits, and market benefits. Other methods include the three-era model, management activities, and stages of growth.
2. **Describe desired situation.** The desired business situation can be described using several methods. Examples of methods are value configuration, competitive strategy, management strategy, business process redesign, knowledge management, the Internet and electronic business, and information technology benefits (Gottschalk, 2006).
3. **Analyze and prioritize needs for change.** After descriptions of the current situation and the desired situation, the needs for change can be identified; this stage defines the desired strategy. The gap between desired and current situation is called needs for change. Analysis is to provide details on needs, what change is needed, and how

Table 4.2. Causal mapping of IT strategy to business strategy (adapted from Cassidy, 2006)

Business Strategy	IT Strategy	IT Metrics
Low cost producer (Operational excellence strategy)	Low cost technology	Total costs (business and IT)
High customer satisfaction (Customer intimacy strategy)	Customer access	Customer satisfaction survey
High quality product (Product leadership strategy)	Quality modules, metrics	Number of incident reports
Quick time to market (Product leadership strategy)	Flexible systems	Mean time to implement changes

Figure 4.4. The Y model for IS/IT strategy work (Gottschalk, 2006)

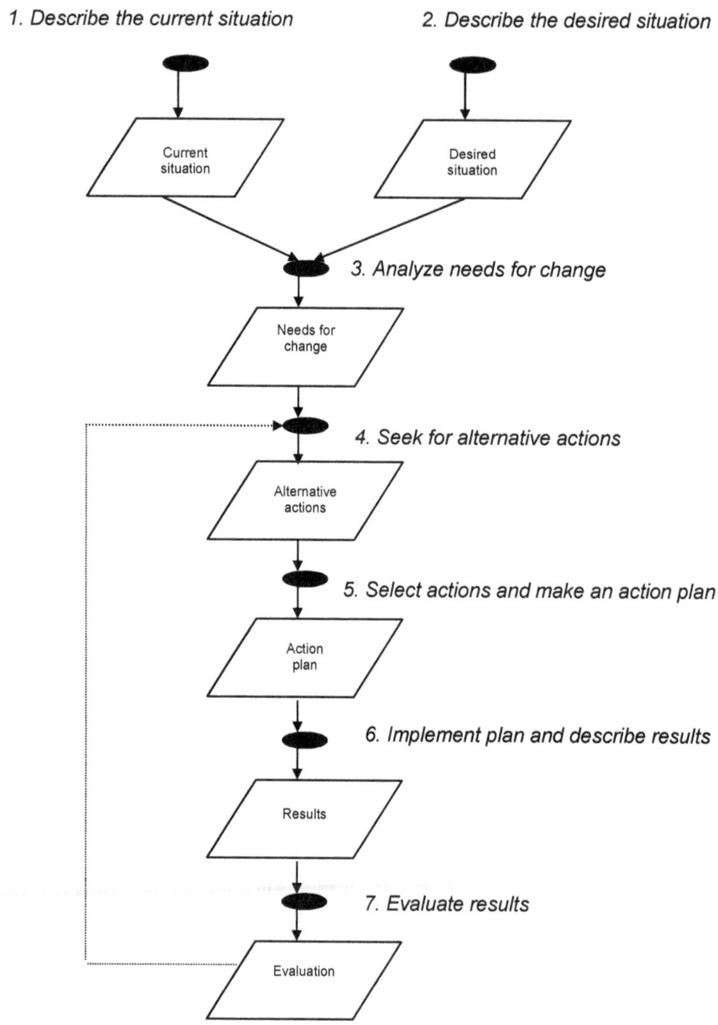

changes can take place. *What*-analysis will create an understanding of vision and goals, knowledge strategy, market strategy, and corporate problems and opportunities. *How*-analysis will create an understanding of technology trends and applications. These analyses should result in proposals for new IS/IT in the organization. This stage will define the degree of business–IT strategic alignment.

4. **Seek for alternative actions.** When needs for change have been identified and proposals for filling gaps have been developed, alternative actions for improving the current situation can be developed. New IS/IT can be developed, acquired, and implemented in alternative ways. For example, an information system can be developed in-house by company staff, it can be purchased as a standard application from a vendor, or it can be leased from an application systems provider (ASP). This stage will define the strategic architecture which includes both strategic high level solution options and sourcing options or strategy. Business and IT alignment is ensured by describing the solution options in business terms and business and IT making joint decision in selecting the strategically optimal solution options.
5. **Select actions and make an action plan.** When needs for change and alternative actions have been identified, several choices have to be made and documented in an action plan. Important issues here include development process, user involvement, time frame and financial budget for IS/IT projects. This is the strategic planning stage which delineates the project plans for all selected actions in a time sequence in line with agreed business priorities (defined by the business–IT aligned strategies). Business and IT alignment is assured by the target IT outcomes (business benefits of the projects) directly traceable to the desired business outcomes in line with the target dates stipulated by the business operating plan. Business value accounting of IT projects under the guidance of IT governance.
6. **Implement plan and describe results.** This is the stage of action. Technical equipment such as servers, PCs, printers, and cables are installed. Operating systems are installed. Application packages, software programs, programming tools, end-user tools, and database systems are installed. Development projects are organized. Management and user training takes place. Document results over time. This is the strategy execution stage. Standard program and project management disciplines apply. As in Stage 5, the project by project business benefits of IT projects are aligned with the corresponding desired business outcomes stipulated in the strategic plan above.
7. **Evaluate results.** Implementation results are compared with needs for change. It is determined to what extent gaps between desired and current situation have been closed. This is the beginning of the IS/IT strategy revision process, where a new process through the Y model takes place. Typically, a new IS/IT strategy process should take place every other year in business organizations. This is the business outcome monitoring phase. The aim is to ensure that the approved business plan for each project is duly achieved such that the desired return on investment (and other similar business metrics for project success) can be confirmed.

Stages 1 to 3 cover *analysis*, 4 and 5 cover *choice*, and 6 and 7 cover *implementation*. In some strategy models, stage 2 is listed as the first stage. It is recommended to do stage 1 before stage 2. It is easier to describe the ideal situation when you know the current situation. If you start out with stage 2, it often feels difficult and abstract to describe what you would like to achieve. Having done stage 1 first makes the work more relevant. Stage 3 is a so-called gap analysis, looking at the difference between the desired and actual situation. This stage also includes prioritizing. Stage 4 is a creative session as it calls for ideas and proposals for alternative actions. Stages 5 and 6 are typical planning stages. The final stage 7 is important because we can learn from performing an evaluation. There is one feedback arrow, from stage 7 to stage 4, to compare the evaluation with the desired situation.

STRATEGY DIRECTION SETTING ALIGNMENT

Corporate strategy is concerned with the strategic decisions at the corporate level of organizations; decisions which may affect many business units. Managers at this level are acting on behalf of shareholders, or other stakeholders, to provide services and, quite possibly, strategic guidance to business units which, themselves, seek to generate value by interacting with customers. In these circumstances a key question is to what extent and how might the corporate level add value to what the businesses do; or at the least how it might avoid destroying value (Johnson & Scholes, 2002). Furthermore, how will IT strategy align with the corporate strategy? What process must be instituted by the enterprise to assure the strategy direction alignment between the corporate, business units, and IT? We address these issues in this section.

A multibusiness company structure may consist of a number of business units grouped within divisions and a corporate center or head office providing, perhaps, legal services, financial services, and the staff of the chief executive. There are different views as to what is meant by corporate strategy and what represents corporate at distinct from business-level strategy. Johnson and Scholes (2002) argue that anything above the business unit level represents corporate activity. The levels of management above that of business units are often referred to as the corporate parent. So, for example, the divisions within a corporation, which look after several businesses act in a corporate parenting role. The corporate parenting role can be as (Johnson & Scholes, 2002):

- **The portfolio manager.** A corporate parent acting as an agent on behalf of financial markets and shareholders with a view to enhancing the value attained from the various businesses in a more efficient or effective way than financial markets could. Their role is to identify and acquire undervalued assets or businesses and improve them.
- **The restructurer.** A corporate parent identifying restructuring opportunities in businesses and having the skills to intervene to transform performance in those businesses. They may well hold a diverse range of businesses within their portfolio. However, they do have a limited role at the business-unit level, which is to identify ways in which businesses can be turned around or fitness improved and to manage the restructuring period.
- **The synergy manager.** Synergy is often seen as the main reason for the existence of the corporate parent. Potentially, synergy can occur in situations where two or more activities or processes complement each other, to the extent that their combined effect is greater than the sum of the parts. In terms of corporate strategy, the logic is that value can be enhanced across business units. This can be done in a number of ways: activities might be shared, and there may exist common skills or competences across businesses.

- **The parental developer.** A corporate parent seeks to employ its own competences as a parent to add value to its businesses. Here, the issue is not so much about how it can help create or develop benefits across business units or transference between business units, as in the case of managing synergy. Rather, parental developers have to enhance the potential of business units.

Corporate strategy will depend on the main role of the corporate parent. The portfolio manager is not directly intervening in the strategies of business units. Rather, they are setting financial targets, making central evaluations about the well-being and future prospects of such businesses and investing or divesting accordingly. The restructurer is directly intervening in business units, as it is likely that the business restructuring opportunities that will be sought, will be those that match the skills of the corporate center. The synergy manager will initiate activities and develop resources that are shared across business units. Managers in the businesses have to be prepared to cooperate in such transference and sharing (Johnson & Scholes, 2002).

Finally, the parental developer has to enhance the potential of business units in various ways. Suppose, for example, it has a great deal of experience in globalizing domestically based businesses; a valuable brand that may enhance the performance of image of a business; or perhaps specialist skills in financial management, brand marketing, or research and development. If such parenting competences exist, corporate managers then need to identify a parenting opportunity—a business or businesses which are not fulfilling their potential but where improvement could be made by the application of the competences of the parent (Johnson & Scholes, 2002).

IT strategy for such a complex corporate–business hierarchical organization must be developed through tight and disciplined coordination between the corporate or group CIO and the business unit CIOs. The group CIO must be aligned with the group CEO and the individual business unit heads in terms of business understanding and corporate strategy direction, irrespective of which of the above operating models the corporate parent chooses to play. Further, the business unit BU) CIOs[1] must stay aligned with the BU CEO and the emergent BU strategies, whose alignment with the corporate strategy is being managed by the BU CEO. The disciplined coordination of BU CIOs and the group CIO is a critical success factor for achieving a business-aligned IT strategy. Care must be taken by the BU CIOs to ensure their business and IT strategies for the individual BUs must reflect the BU value creation model desired by the corporate parenting role chosen by the enterprise. A significantly critical success factor is the leadership behavioral skills as well as the business skills of the group and BU CIOs which underpin the constant dialogues and debates between senior leadership teams in driving maximum value from the portfolio of businesses. It is through these skills that business–IT alignment across both corporate and individual BU's will become manageable and assured.

Companies that depend on IT to achieve differentiation should aim to achieve full strategic integration, as defined in King and Teo's (1997) study. At this level, business and IT heads will be able to collaborate as a unified team in defining the corporate and IT strategic direction. As a result, the IT strategy will be defined in line with and documented as part of the corporate strategy. Corporate strategy is the responsibility of the enterprise's executive management team, led by the CEO. To be effective in acting as one with the business, the CIO must be a member of the executive management team. The CIO must also have a deep knowledge of the business and will be able to act as a business executive. Accession to the executive management team by the CIO is earned through consistent successful delivery of business commitments made by the CIO. The CIO is the custodian of technology capabilities that have the potential to reshape the business model of the enterprise. Therefore, the CIO is responsible for contributing to the corporate strategy setting by finding new angles where the enterprise may be able to exploit current and future technologies to create sustainable competitive differentiation to the enterprise's value propositions. In this role, the CIO must seek to transform IT from being simply a necessary means to support the business to being a critical weapon for the enterprise's distinctive value offerings to the customers. For example, IT may have been successful in sustaining the enterprise's Operational Excellence strategy through business process redesign and process automation, while at the same would find some new product innovations through clever exploitation of an emerging disruptive technology to distinctly transform the enterprise's product offering into an industry leadership position. In this case, IT has become a core competence for the enterprise's growth strategy. In both cases of necessity and differentiation, though, the CIO must exert influence on the executive management team to win buy-in on new (technology exploitation) strategic business ideas through leadership behavioral excellence. The buy-in ensures unison in business and IT strategic directions. Broadbent (2005) calls this new CIO role in contributing to shaping corporate direction as managing demand, as distinct from the traditional CIO role of managing supply where the CIO reactively responds to the corporate strategy to determine the appropriate IT strategy and required IT resource (supply) allocation to execute on the corporate strategy.

STRATEGIC PLANNING ALIGNMENT

Alignment between IT strategy and business strategy is important, and distinctions are often made between administrative, sequential, reciprocal, and full integration (King & Teo, 1997). Administrative integration is separate planning; sequential integration is one-way linked planning; reciprocal is two-way linked planning; and full integration is simultaneous planning. Results from a survey of large law firms in Norway indicate that 27% of the law firms had administrative integration, 54% had sequential integration, 9% had reciprocal integration, and 9% had full integration (Gottschalk, 2006). Irrespective of the planning integration method adopted by the enterprise, the end-goal of strategic planning alignment is for business and IT to validate (and jointly approve) the IT strategic plans clearly correspond to the respective business strategic plans and the business outcomes the IT plans must deliver are clearly described and justified in the business plans. This process answers the IT governance question of "Are we doing the right things?" While business leaders are responsible for the business strategic plans, the CIO is responsible for the IT strategic plan and its alignment with the business strategic plans.

Strategic planning procedures represent the design approach to managing strategy. Such procedures may take the form of highly systematized, step by step, chronological procedures involving many different parts of the organization. For example, the annual strategic planning cycle in a company may follow a procedure like this:

1. *May.* Broad strategic direction.
2. *June.* Review of current strategy.
3. *August.* Goals for business units.

4. *September.* Strategies for business units.
5. *October.* Board meeting to agree strategic plan.
6. *November.* Board meeting to agree operational plan and budget.

Some of the key concepts in strategic planning are future thinking, controlling the future, decision making, integrated decision making, and a formalized procedure to produce an articulated result in the form of an integrated process of decisions. *Strategic planning is the process of deciding on the projects that the organization will undertake and the approximate amount of resources that will be allocated to each program over the next several years.*

Planning represents the extent to which decision makers look into the future and use formal planning methodologies. Planning is something we do in advance of taking action; it is anticipatory decision making. We make decisions before action is required. The focus of planning revolves around objectives, which are the heart of a strategic plan. Strategic planning is a formalized process. It allows organizations to coordinate their activities taking into account the future they wish to create, and thereby control their evolutionary path towards the intended destiny (Mintzberg, 1994). According to Mintzberg (1994), strategic planning has the following characteristics:

- **Planning is future thinking.** It is forward looking, taking the future into account. Planning is action laid out in advance.
- **Planning is controlling the future.** It is not just thinking about it but achieving it and enacting it. Planning is the design of a desired future and of effective ways of bringing it about. It is to create controlled change in the environment.
- **Planning is decision making.** Planning is the conscious determination of courses of action designed to accomplish purposes. Planning are those activities concerned specifically with determining in advance what actions and/or human and physical resources are required to reach a goal. It includes identifying alternatives, analyzing each one, and selecting the best ones.
- **Planning is integrated decision making.** It means fitting together ongoing activities into a meaningful whole. Planning implies getting somewhat more organized; it means making a feasible commitment around which already available courses of action get organized. This definition may seem close to the preceding one. But because it is concerned not so much with the making of decisions as with the conscious attempt to integrate different ones, it is fundamentally different and begins to identify a position for planning.
- **Planning is a formalized procedure to produce an articulated result, in the form of an integrated system of decisions.** What captures the notion of planning above all—most clearly distinguishes its literature and differentiates its practice from other processes—is its emphasis on formalization, the systemization of the phenomenon to which planning is meant to apply. Planning is a set of concepts, procedures, and tests. Formalization here means three things: (a) to decompose, (b) to articulate, and (c) to rationalize the process by which decisions are made and integrated in organizations.

Strategic planning does not attempt to make future decisions, as decisions can be made only in the present. Planning requires that choices be made among possible events in the future, but decisions made in their light can be made only in the present. Once made, these decisions may have long-term, irrevocable consequences. Strategic planning has many benefits for an organization (Johnson & Scholes, 2002, p. 61):

- It can provide a structured means of *analysis and thinking* about complex strategic problems, at its best requiring managers to *question and challenge* the received wisdom they take for granted.
- It can encourage a *longer term view* of strategy than might otherwise occur. Planning horizons vary, of course. In a fast-moving consumer goods company, 3–5 year plans may be appropriate. In companies which have to take very long-term views on capital investment, such as those in the oil industry, planning horizons can be as long as 14 years (in Exxon) or 20 years (in Shell).
- It can be used as a means of *control* by regularly reviewing performance and progress against agreed objectives or previously agreed strategic direction.
- It can be a useful means of *coordination*, for example, by bringing together the various business unit strategies within an overall corporate strategy, or ensuring that resources within a business are coordinated to put strategy into effect.
- Strategic planning may also help to *communicate* intended strategy.
- It can be used as a way of involving people in strategy development, therefore perhaps helping to create *ownership* of the strategy.
- Planning systems may provide a sense of security and logic for the organization and, in particular, management who believe they *should* be proactively determining the future strategy and exercising control over the destiny of the organization.

In the strategic planning perspective on strategy formation, strategies are intentionally designed, much as an engineer designs a bridge. Building a bridge requires a long formulation phase, including extensive analysis of the situation, the drawing up of a number of rough designs, evaluation of these alternatives, choice of a preferred design, and further detailing in the form of a blueprint. Only after the design phase has been completed do the construction companies take over and build according to plan. Characteristic of such a planning approach to producing bridges and strategies is that the entire process can be disassembled into a number of distinct steps that need to be carried out in a sequential and orderly way. Only by going through these steps in a conscious and structured manner will the best results be obtained (Wit & Meyer, 2004).

In many large companies, the managers proposing the plans are also the ones implementing them, but deciding on the plans is passed up to a higher level. Often other tasks are spun off as well, or shared with others, such as diagnosis (strategy department or external consultants), implementation (staff departments), and evaluation (corporate planner and controller). Such task differentiation and specialization can lead to better use of management talent, much as the division of labor has improved the field of production. At the same, having a formalized procedure allows for sufficient coordination and mutual adjustment, to ensure that all specialized elements are integrated back into a consistent organization-wide strategy (Wit & Meyer, 2004).

An important advantage of strategic planning is that it encourages long-term thinking and commitment. Strategic planning directs attention to the future. Managers making strategic plans have to take a more long-term view and are stimulated to prepare for, or even create, the future. Instead of just focusing on small steps, planning challenges managers to define a desirable future and to work towards it. Instead of wavering and opportunism, strategic planning commits the organization to a course of action and allows for investments to be made at the present that may only pay off in the long run (Wit & Meyer, 2004).

With the corporate strategy defined, the individual business units will develop their respective business plans to collectively execute on the corporate strategy. It is important to note the distinction of strategy and strategic planning. The former articulates the strategic position the company intends to achieve, while the latter defines the action plans to achieve that strategic position. Strategic planning is about creating the "game plan" for executing the strategy. It makes a decision about the amount of resources to invest and the commercial return expected by a target date, which is often set or influenced by the business' desire to be the first to market. The business strategic plans will include specific business initiatives to achieve both the growth and productivity improvement goals. Similarly, IT will develop its business plan in synchrony with the individual business unit plans. In particular, it will articulate the parts of the IT strategic plan which will be shared among all business units to deliver the articulated shared corporate goal, and those parts that are directly linked to the individual business unit business plans. In all cases, however, the expected business outcomes to be delivered by the IT strategic plan must be clearly stated and linked to the corporate and business unit business plans. The explicit linkages will ensure plan, execution, and outcome alignment. The business and IT strategic plans must articulate clear directions on the following:

- Portfolio management—business program priorities (sequencing) and trade-offs
- Core competences required for competitive differentiation
- Sourcing strategy (which we refer to as the people or capability architecture to mirror the enterprise architecture strategic decision) for flexible and agile resource allocation
- Enterprise architecture to articulate the target business model architecture and the underpinning process, information, application, and infrastructure architectures

Alignment with the business strategic plan is further assured by formal approval of the IT strategic plan by the IT steering committee with business unit leaders and CIO as members and CIO as chair. As per the IT governance, the IT strategic plan approval is subject to assuring that all the stated business objectives of the corporate strategy and business plans have been accounted for in the IT strategic plan.

Strategic planning takes many different forms in different organizations. How will the consolidated IT strategic plan stay aligned with the business strategic plans? We address this issue in this section.

Boyd and Reuning-Elliotts (1998) study of strategic planning indicates that strategic planning is a construct that can be reliably measured through seven indicators: mission statement, trend analysis, competitor analysis, long-term goals, annual goals, short-term action plans, and ongoing evaluation.

A small, entrepreneurial startup may operate without any explicit strategy. The firm's strategy is likely to exist only in the head of the founder, and apart from being articulated through verbal communication with employees, suppliers, and other interested parties, may have been made explicit only when a business plan was required by outside investors. Most corporations with an established management structure tend to have some form of strategic planning process, though in small, single-business companies the strategy process may be highly informal, with no regular cycle and may result in little documentation. Most larger companies, especially those with multiple businesses, have more systematic strategic planning processes, the outcome of which is a documented plan that integrates the business plans of the individual divisions (Grant, 2003).

Whether formal or informal, systematic or ad hoc, documented or not, the strategy formulation process is an important vehicle for achieving coordination within a company. The strategy process occupies multiple roles within the firm. It is in part a coordination device encouraging consistency between the decisions being made at different levels and in different parts of the organization. And it is in part a mechanism for driving performance by establishing consensus around ambitious long-term targets and by inspiring organizational members through creating vision and a sense of mission. In these roles, the strategy process can be important in achieving both coordination and cooperation (Grant, 2003).

The system through which strategy is formulated varies considerably from company to company. Even after the entrepreneurial startup has grown into a large company, strategy making may remain the preserve of the chief executive. Medium-sized, single-business companies typically have simple strategic planning processes where functional managers provide key inputs such as financial projections and market analysis, but the key elements of strategy—goals, new business developments, capital investment, and key competitive initiatives—are decided by the chief executive (Grant, 2003).

The more systematized strategic planning processes typical of large companies with separate divisions or business units traditionally follow an annual cycle. Strategic plans tend to be for three to five years and combine top-down initiatives (indications of performance expectations and identification of key strategic initiatives) and bottom-up business plans (proposed strategies and financial forecasts for individual divisions and business units). After discussion between the corporate level and the individual businesses, the business plans are amended and agreed and integrated into an overall corporate plan that is presented to and agreed by the board of directors (Grant, 2003).

Extending from the business–IT strategy alignment process, the group CIO and BU CIO's construct the consolidated IT strategic plan by participating in partnership with the business in the crafting of the BU strategic plans and analyzing the likely impacts to the IT environment (current and future) of the proposed business programs. The impact analysis yields the requisite IT strategic plan to form part of the overall integrated enterprise strategic business plan (roll-up of the individual BU strategic plans). Where IT were successful in influencing the strategic direction of the enterprise through, for example, adopting a new disruptive technology-based business model, the IT impacts naturally would have been well understood.

The resulting strategic plan typically comprises the following elements (Grant, 2003):

- A statement of the goals the company seeks to achieve over the planning period with regard to both financial targets and strategic goals.
- A set of assumptions or forecasts about key developments in the external environment to which the company must respond.
- A qualitative statement of how the shape of the business will be changing in relation to geographical and segment emphasis, and the basis on which the company will be establishing and extending its competitive advantage.

- Specific action steps with regard to decisions and projects, supported by a set of mileposts stating what is to be achieved by specific dates.
- A set of financial projections, including a capital expenditure budget and outline operating budgets.

Although directed toward making decisions that are documented in written strategic plans, the important elements of strategic planning form the strategy process: the dialog through which knowledge is shared and ideas communicated the establishment of consensus, and the commitment to action and results (Grant, 2003).

The correspondent IT strategic plan will articulate the technology and system architecture directions which will align with the action steps (business initiatives and projects) prescribed with the targeted business outcomes. In particular it will spell out how IT will contribute to the reshaping of the business (model). Apart from the itemized project plan line items locked in synch with the itemized business program plan, the IT strategic plan will include a clear articulation of the new enterprise architecture that will result from the implementation of these business programs. Put another way, the enterprise architecture will define the strategic blueprint for the evolution of the information systems in delivering the desired business capabilities defined in the business program plans. The enterprise architecture will also prescribe a set of design principles to guide the solution design of the individual business programs. Adherence with these design principles will ensure system flexibility, scalability for future growth, as well as minimal total cost of ownership of the target information systems. It answers the IT governance question of: "Are we doing it right?" More detailed treatment of the enterprise architecture will be provided in Chapter VI.

STRATEGY EXECUTION ALIGNMENT

Stages 6 and 7 of the Y model address strategy implementation. While Stage 6 is concerned with implementing the plan and describing results, Stage 7 is concerned with evaluating results.

The creation of IS/IT strategy has become a major challenge to business executives and IS/IT executives in recent years. Investments in information technology have been large, and many failed investments reflect this challenge. The impact of IT on organizational performance has grown in strategic importance, and thus the significance of failed IT investments is even greater. Information processing and information technology are becoming critical to many business and government operations, and the technology itself is changing at a rapid rate. New information technology will continue to transform organizations, and changes in how industry participants use IT can alter established relationships in an industry. Strategic IS/IT planning can play a critical role in helping organizations increase efficiency, effectiveness, and competitiveness. Although organizations use different methods in their analysis of current and desired situations, the resulting plans are to be implemented.

The importance of the implementation of strategic IS/IT plans is illustrated by the significant attention paid to it in recent years. Studies show that implementation is important for four reasons. First, the failure to carry out the strategic IS/IT plan can cause lost opportunities, duplicated efforts, incompatible systems, and wasted resources. Second, the extent to which strategic IS/IT planning meets its objectives is determined by implementation. Third, the lack of implementation leaves firms dissatisfied with and reluctant to continue their strategic planning. Fourth, the lack of implementation creates problems establishing and maintaining priorities in future strategic IS/IT planning.

IS/IT strategy implementation can be defined as the process of completing the projects for application of information technology to assist an organization in realizing its goals. However, implementing an IS/IT strategy is not simply the act of implementing many projects and individual. Execution – the business programs constructed from the business and IT plans will have a business owner supported by a professional IT program manager responsible for on time and on budget delivery of the program, with the program outcomes (functionalities and benefits) clearly specified in business terms as targeted in the business plan. The success of an IT strategy depends critically on the ability of the business and IT team in executing the strategic plan. Execution excellence depends on both (a) the ability to position the business program in question holistically in the context of the overall business and corporate plans, and (b) the laser sharp focus of the program team in addressing the details of the business program within the life cycle of program execution.

The holistic view will articulate the business rationale of the program and its relative priority in the context of the overall corporate strategy, the specific business goals and outcomes it aims to deliver, and its relationships and interdependencies, if any, with the other business programs encompassed in the corporate business plans. The holistic strategy execution is aided by the discipline of portfolio management. The IT steering team, on behalf of the executive management team, will treat all the proposed business programs conceived by the business plans as a portfolio of investments (risks vs. returns) with varying degrees of short- and long-term business value return. The portfolio management discipline will ensure the resource allocation strategy (investment decision criteria) will deliver a balance of short- and long-term productivity and growth results to give the enterprise a sustainable competitive advantage. The proposed portfolio (by IT steering team) for each financial year will need to be presented and approved by the executive management team to ensure alignment with the corporate strategy and overall business plans.

The program execution focus is achieved by disciplined application of program and project management practice. The business is accountable for the business requirements of the program—its accuracy and clarity. Business and IT alignment is achieved by IT capturing and documenting the business requirements by close engagement with the business owner of the program. The critical success factor is the IT analyst's in-depth understanding and knowledge of the business. This business knowledge allows the IT analyst to probe and "pressure-test" the vision and outcome expectations of the business owner by challenging the owner to justify each feature and operational requirement of the program in the context of realizing the corporate strategy for differentiation—both in terms of the product or service capabilities to be offered to the customers and expected customer experience from using the product or service. Time and time again, we have found that program failures have been caused by program requirements being either ambiguous, over ambitious, or lacking of alignment with the corporate strategy. The combination of the business owner's knowledge of corporate strategy (best assured by bottom-up contribution through business unit executive to shaping the corporate strategy) plus the IT analyst's in-depth understanding of the business and the IT environment will be a critical success factor for program execution excellence. Another critical success factor is the business and IT team working in unison in managing change requests during the execution and process and work practice change at the conclusion of the program management life cycle.

Table 4.3. IT Governance Institute definitions (ITGI, 2006)

Value	The end business outcome(s) expected from an IT-enabled business investment where such outcomes may be financial, nonfinancial, or a combination of the two.
Project	A structured set of activities concerned with delivering to the enterprise a defined capability (that is necessary but not sufficient to achieve a required business outcome) based on an agreed schedule and budget.
Program	A structured group of *interdependent* projects that are both necessary and sufficient to achieve the business outcome and deliver value. These projects could include, but are not limited to, changes to the nature of business, business processes, the work performed by people, as well as the competencies required to carry out the work, enabling technology and organizational structure.
Portfolio	A grouping of programs, projects, services, or assets selected, managed, and monitored to *optimize* business return.

Program execution will be in accordance with the portfolio management priority decision. It will implement the sourcing strategy articulated by the IT strategic plan. Its solution design for each program will adhere to the enterprise architecture design principles and deliver the targeted new component (or parts thereof) of the enterprise architecture.

Strategy execution is concerned with the professional discipline of project management, program management, and portfolio management with business and IT acting as one in taking responsibility for successful delivery of IT value. Table 4.3 summarizes the IT Governance Institute's definitions for IT value, project, program, and portfolio based on the Val IT Framework (ITGI, 2006).

According to the Project Management Institute (PMI 2003), enterprises need to practice *organizational project management (OMP)* discipline which is the *systematic* management of projects, programs, and portfolios in alignment with the achievement of strategic goals. PMI (2003) asserts that there is a close correlation between the enterprise's organizational project management capability and its effectiveness in implementing enterprise strategy. PMI (2003) has defined OMP3 as the standard for organizational project management practice. OMP3 also provides a framework for assessing an enterprise's organizational project management maturity, which indirect measures the enterprise's capability in effective strategy execution or implementation. In other words, OMP3 consists of three parts: (1) knowledge—define the OMP standards and how to use it; (2) assessment—define the methodology for assessing an enterprise's OMP maturity; and (3) improvement—define guidelines for developing the capabilities towards achieving best practices.

PMI (2003) defines a *project* as a temporary endeavor undertaken to create a unique product, service, or result. According to PMI (2003), the concept of projects is a natural means for organizations to manage the many dimensions of any initiative in an orderly and repeatable manner to achieve the strategic objectives. Thus, projects help organizations deliver desired strategic changes in a changing world (PMI, 2003, p. 4).

In most organizations, however, multiple projects may interact to collectively produce the desired business outcomes. Thus, it is common to group a cluster of related projects with interdependencies into a *program* so that the projects can be managed in a coordinated way to obtain benefits and control not available from managing them individually (PMI, 2003). Thus, program management is a key strategy execution discipline that ensures that the business benefits, time, and resources are optimized to achieve the program strategic goals across a set of projects comprising the program. Program management provides the flexibility required to identify, define, and manage a set of interrelated projects as a single unit, called program, to achieve greater synergistic benefits and align with the broader strategic objectives. Program management function includes program planning (in line with strategic plan), coordination of project delivery, change and risk management, active and open communications to various stakeholders, measurement of program results, and business–IT collaboration (especially important for decisions affecting business architecture and processes). Most major program initiatives may extend across functional and business unit lines. This means that program managers need expertise in the business as well as IT functions. They also need "soft skills" to bring stakeholders to consensus on the program plan, proposed solution, resource allocation, and risk and change management required to bring the program to completion and deliver the business outcomes stipulated by the business strategy.

Similarly, PMI (2003) defines a *portfolio* as a collection of projects and/or programs, which may not necessarily be related or interdependent, and other work grouped together to facilitate effective management of that work to meet strategic objectives. Portfolio management plays a complementary role to program management. In a portfolio, projects must be prioritized based on a set of agreed-on value-versus-risk criteria. The variables that affect decisions about the contents of the portfolio need to be continuously monitored and communicated. Its explicit goal is to enable the organization to effectively prioritize trade-off and sequence projects and programs competing for the same limited resources. Business and IT together determine the priorities and trade-offs under portfolio management discipline, based on business priorities and sourcing strategy defined by business and IT strategic plans. They also decide on the project definition and optimization objective and the associated resource allocation strategies for program management. The portfolio management function includes the processes, governance, and tools required to plan, create, assess, balance, and communicate the execution of an IT project or program portfolio (sometimes called the investment portfolio).

MONITORING BUSINESS OUTCOMES AGAINST STRATEGIC OBJECTIVES

Business outcomes are *the fruits of the end-to-end alignment* of business and IT strategies. Thus, the IT governance process mandates that the business outcomes must be monitored following the production roll-out of the business program. This is Stage 7 of the Y model. In practice, upon successful delivery of the program, each program must be audited at selected milestones to ensure the intended business objectives and benefits are consistently delivered in accordance with the program's business case. Too often, program management practice prematurely ends when the program is completed and put into production for the business owner. For the IT strategy to be deemed successful, the final step of business outcomes monitoring must be performed. While IT takes responsibility for bringing the program in on time, on budget, and according to plan, it is the business owner's accountability to ensuring the operational program delivers its intended business outcomes, in terms of customer value propositions and, most importantly, the commercial returns accrued by the successful operation of the program. IT must assist business in monitoring the service level performance of the program, particularly the part that impacts customer experience. Further, IT must be ready in assisting the business to fine tune the program systems, as required, to achieve the business outcomes anticipated by the program's business plan. This complementary nature of business–IT cooperation to drive the program to achieve its business plan is another critical success factor of IT strategy.

Business outcomes are the fruits of end-to-end alignment of business and IT. They are the determinants of whether the corporate and business competitive strategies are successful or not. It is therefore of paramount importance that business outcomes are rigorously monitored and concerted efforts be expended, based on monitored results, by both business and IT to re-adapt the business environment to improve the business performance such that the intended business outcomes and thus strategic goals are achieved. Carried out as part of IT and corporate governance due diligence, all program outcomes must be monitored to ensure compliance with approved business cases (budget and business benefits). According to the IT Governance Institute's Val IT Framework (ITGI, 2006), the business goal of realizing optimal value from IT-enabled business investments, at an affordable cost with an acceptable level of risk, is guided by a set of principles (known as Val IT principles) applied in *value management* processes that are measured by key outcome and performance metrics. The Val IT principles (ITGI, 2006) are:

- IT-enabled investments will be managed as a portfolio of investments;
- IT-enabled investments will include the full scope of activities that are required to achieve business value;
- IT-enabled investments will be managed through their full economic cycle;
- Value delivery practices will recognize that there are different categories of investments that will be evaluated and managed differently;
- Value delivery practices will define and monitor key metrics and will respond quickly to any changes or deviations;
- Value delivery practices will engage all stakeholders and assign appropriate accountability for the delivery of capabilities and the realization of benefits;
- Value delivery practices will be continually monitored, evaluated, and improved.

The ITGI (2006) value management processes for optimizing the value of IT-enabled investments consist of:

- Value governance process – it establishes the governance, monitoring, and control framework, provides strategic directions for the investments, and defines the investment characteristics.
- Portfolio management process – it establishes and manages resource profiles, defines investment thresholds, evaluates and prioritizes new investments, manages the overall portfolio, and monitors and reports on portfolio performance.
- Investment management process – it identifies business requirements, develops a clear understanding of candidate investment programs, analyzes the alternatives, defines the program and documents a detailed business case, including the business benefit details, assigns clear accountability and ownership, manages the program through its full economic life cycle, and monitors and reports on program performance. The latter focuses on actively managing the realization of benefits from the programs from

"concept to cash" by monitoring the business outcome against the business case of the programs.

Business outcome monitoring (BOM) is the *commercial* part of post-implementation review (PIR). Different from the traditional PIR, which tends to be a once off activity at the conclusion of a program delivery, BOM will occur at the predefined milestones of the operational life of the program. These milestones should be selected at the time the business case for the program is produced. This is because they are the signposts of the expected commercial success of the program—be it productivity improvement of revenue growth being the expected business outcomes. Thus, BOM starts its life at the initiation of the program—the business case being developed by the appointed program manager with the approval of the business program owner. Its success therefore depends critically on the rigor and soundness of the business case (not overly optimistic with the expected business benefits). Conversely, BOM cannot be conducted with due diligence if a business case was not produced for the business program in the first place —which in itself is a major violation of IT governance.

In reality, however, BOM and its parent process PIR is not commonly conducted by most enterprises. There are many reasons for this failure. One reason is because the expected outcome from PIR, or postproject review, is not clear (Apfel, Smith, Hotle, Duggan, Light, & Landry, 2007). So the first task is, as part of IT governance, for the enterprise's IT steering team (and executive management team) to clearly state the objectives of PIR and BOM. Put simply, PIR and BOM are intended to evaluate if the program has effectively and efficiently met business case expectations. In particular, they aim to answer three key questions:

- What has the organization learned from this program implementation to improve the program and portfolio management processes for subsequent programs?
- Has the program met the first milestone and will it meet the future milestones of its business case expectations?
- What remedial actions, if any, are required for the reviewed program, and by when?

Apfel et al. (2007) have found that PIR is most successful for organizations which encourage learning and lack a "blame" culture. The spirit of PIR and BOM is to learn, continuously improve, and achieve the enterprise's stated strategic goals. Thus, the process should avoid the "blame" game in order to encourage an open and collaborative mode of process review and improvement. For organizations that have any degree of "blame" orientation, an enterprise-wide top-down driven "cultural change" program should be introduced with ample time for training and education of key personnel involved in the process of business program execution from both the business and IT organizations. Often, a pilot with some early adopters (enthusiasts) would be helpful to "test" the process and "show" the way for the wider populace. To increase the chance of success, the change management program is recommended as a prerequisite for introducing the PIR as an IT governance tool.

Who should conduct the PIR and BOM? From our own practice experience, it should be a senior person with business credibility (political clout) and sound knowledge of program management and business case processes. Often, it could be a senior manager from the program management office or equivalent organization in the enterprise.

Apfel et al. (2007) have identified four key measures of success for postproject evaluations:

- **Overall business success:** Has the program met the business expectations it was originally chartered with?
- **Governance and chartering success:** Has the governance process been effective, and has the program charter been effectively used to manage the assumptions and business expectations in controlling the program?
- **Project execution success:** Has the program been delivered within budget, time, quality, and the specified functionality?
- **Client satisfaction success:** Have all the end-user requirements been met?

Apfel et al. (2007) argue that postproject evaluations are an important part of improving the program and portfolio management capabilities of an organization.

RECOMMENDATIONS

From the above analysis, we provide a list of recommendations for practitioners to assure business and IT acting as one in each stage of the end-to-end business/IT strategy process. They are as follows:

Strategy Direction Setting

- Win trust and respect from business by consistently delivering commitments (value) made to business;
- Earn a seat at the executive management committee where corporate strategy is defined
- Master the business of the enterprise and run IT as a business (a value center, not a cost center)
- Take accountability for technology leadership with a passion for achieving business differentiation through creative uses of current or emerging disruptive technologies
- Transition IT from a reactive to proactive business value contributor, when focus is shifted from managing supply to managing demand
- Use balanced scorecard to communicate IT value in terms of business value
- Use corporate and IT governance to formally "validate" the continuous alignment of IT strategy with the business strategy as business changes to keep in-step with the competitive market changes

Strategic Planning

- Use business strategic plans to define the requisite business programs and expected new business capabilities for growth and productivity improvements
- Use the selected business programs as requirements to identify the corresponding IT programs and the intended business outcomes to be achieved

- Apply financially rigorous business case methodology to justify the priority of each business program which includes the corresponding IT programs or projects and the anticipated business benefits (or outcomes)
- Agree with business on the core IT competencies required to make the enterprise competitive and differentiated now and most importantly in the future
- Use the IT governance process to achieve enterprise-wide agreement on the requisite sourcing strategy to achieve item 11
- Business and IT to jointly practice the discipline of program and portfolio management to define the optimal investment portfolio and program sequencing to deliver the maximum strategic value envisioned by the corporate strategy

Strategy Execution

- Business and IT execute approved program plan with laser sharp focus on risk management and business outcome delivery with strong commercial acumen

Business Outcome Monitoring

- Each program is sponsored by a business executive (owner) who "owns" the business case justified for the program and approved by the IT steering in accordance with IT governance rules
- The business owner and sponsor of the business program is accountable for enforcing the post-implementation review and ongoing monitoring of the business benefits to confirm achievement of business objectives, or where a gap exists between actual and expected benefits, to take corrective business actions to ensure the business objectives are met.

SUMMARY

Alignment between business strategy and IT strategy is widely believed to improve business performance (Sabherwal & Chan, 2001). Therefore, strategic alignment is both a top management concern and also an important attribute of effective CIOs. A successful IT strategy must align with the business, fully, from strategy setting and planning to detailed program execution and delivery. King and Teo's (1997) model of strategic integration and Luftman and McLean (2004) strategic alignment model have been used in the end-to-end analysis. A fundamental principle common to all the critical success factors is "business and IT acting as one." This requires each IT task to be aligned with and justified by the business function it is designed to contribute, by which the business value is assessed. A basic requirement for success is that IT must be regarded as being part of the business, devoid of the "us" vs. "them" chasm (separating IT from the business) found in most traditional organizations where IT is viewed as a subservient role performing basically a "back office" function. This means the IT organization must, at a minimum, be at the sequential integration stage (2) of the King and Teo (1997) model. At this level, IT strategy and resources support and align with the business strategy, and IT executive validates with the business executive to ensure the IT strategy aligns with and implements the business strategy. Business and IT act as one behaviorally and organizationally via IT governance. IT governance ensures IT is "doing the right thing" – ensures strategic alignment, "doing the thing right" – ensures architecture compliance, "getting it done well and realizing the benefits" – ensures program portfolio management compliance (ITGI, 2006). The Y model for strategic management (Gottschalk, 2005) and the principles of corporate strategy can bc used to analyze strategic planning alignment. The Y model analyzes the gap between the desired and current business situation to identify the needs for change. The strategic plan is developed and implemented to fulfill the needs. The business and IT strategic plans comprise four key deliverables: enterprise architecture, portfolio management and program plans, core competencies, and sourcing strategy. Two critical disciplines for strategic program delivery are program portfolio management and program management. The former prioritizes and selects programs for implementation based on risk/return profiles and alignment with business strategy. The latter focuses on diligent, disciplined execution of the selected programs to budget and plan. Business benefits realization must be monitored against business (case) plan following completion of program implementation, using a post-implementation review process. With IT and business acting as one, IT strategy will be successful when business and IT alignment is validated in each phase of the end-to-end strategic management life cycle, namely:

- **Direction setting:** IT strategy is defined in line with and documented as part of the corporate strategy;
- **Planning:** The IT strategic plans clearly correspond to the respective business strategic plans and the business outcomes expcted of the IT plans are clearly described and justified in the business plans;
- **Execution:** Each of the business programs constructed from the business and IT plans will have a business owner supported by a professional IT program manager responsible for on time and on budget delivery of the program, with the program outcomes (functionalities and benefits) clearly specified in business terms as targeted in the business plan;
- **Outcomes:** Upon successful delivery of the program, each program is audited at selected milestones to ensure the intended business objectives and benefits are consistently delivered in accordance with the program's business case.

The critical organizational requirement of business and IT acting as one is founded on the rigor and discipline of IT governance.

REFERENCES

Apfel, A. L., Smith, M., Hotle, M., Duggan, J., Light, M., & Landry, S. (2007). Toolkit tutorial: Post-project evaluation process. Retrieved August 14, 2008, from http://www.*gartner.com* (ID number: G00147455).

Avison, D., Jones, J., Powell, P., & Wilson, D. (2004). Using and validating the strategic alignment model. *Journal of Strategic Information Systems, 13*, 223–246.

Boyd, B. K., & Reuning-Elliotts, E. (1998). A measurement model of strategic planning. *Strategic Management Journal, 19*, 181–192.

Broadbent, M. (2005). *The New CIO.* Boston: Harvard Business Press.

Cassidy, A. (2006). *A practical guide to information systems strategic planning* (2nd ed.). New York: Auerbach Publications.

Gottschalk, P. (2006). *E-business strategy, sourcing and governance.* Hershey, PA: Idea Group Publishing.

Grant, R. M. (2003). Strategic planning in a turbulent environment: Evidence from the oil majors. *Strategic Management Journal, 24*, 491–517.

Grembergen, W. Van, Haes, S. De, and Guldentops, E. (2004). Structure, Processes and Relational Mechanisms for IT Governance. In *"Strategies for Information Technology Governance"* by Wim Van, Grembergen, IGI 2004.

ITGI. (2006). *Enterprise value: Governance of IT investments: The Val IT framework.* Author.

Johnson, G., & Scholes, K. (2002). *Exploring corporate strategy.* Harlow, Essex, UK: Pearson Education, Prentice Hall.

King, W., R., & Teo, T. S. H. (1997). Integration between business planning and information systems planning: Validating a stage hypothesis. *Decision Sciences, 28*(2), 279–307.

Luftman, J., & McLean, E. R. (2004). Key issues for IT executives. *MIS Quarterly Executive, 3*(2), 89–104.

Luftman, J., & Papp, R. (1995). Achieving and sustaining business–IT alignment. *California Management Review, 42*(1), 109–122.

Mintzberg, H. (1994). Rounding out the manager's job. *Sloan Management Review, 36*(1), 11–26.

Project Management Institute. (2003). *Organizational Project Management Maturity Model: OMP3 Knowledge Foundation.* Pennsylvania, USA: Newtown Square.

Smaczny, T. (2001). Is an alignment between business and IT the appropriate paradigm to manage IT in today's organization? *Management Decision, 39*(10), 797–802.

Weill, P., & Ross, J. W. (2004). *IT governance.* Boston: Harvard Business School Press.

Wit, B. D., & Meyer, R. (2004). *Strategy: Process, content, context* (3rd ed.). London: Thomson Learning.

ENDNOTE

1 We assume the company has adopted a federated model for organizing the IT group, in which a business unit CIO is appointed accountable to both the BU CIO and the Group CIO who oversights and provides functional leadership to all BU CIOs. Federated model is a common model for large companies. The BU CIO is accountable to the BU CEO (and the Group CIO) for the alignment of the BU's IT services with the business unit. The BU CIO is also responsible for complying with the corporate technology standards and enterprise architecture to maximize economies of scale and scope.

Chapter V
Strategic Alignment for Business Value Creation

INTRODUCTION

Chapter IV defines the macromodel for achieving business/IT alignment. This chapter defines the detailed methodology for each step of the IT strategy process.

First, the business strategy process must be methodical and able to clearly show the linkage between corporate strategic intents and the respective specific business functional plans for realizing the intents. For example, for a specific productivity goal defined for the corporation, the respective initiatives planned for sales and marketing, and those for supply chain management must be clearly linked and explicitly correlated in a "cause-and-effect" manner. A good method invented by Norton and Kaplan called strategy map is an effective tool for this purpose.

This chapter reviews the basic principles of IT strategy. It briefly discusses various models used to analyze or describe disparate parts of strategic alignment. These strategic alignment models are contrasted with our end-to-end alignment model for defining and executing business-aligned IT strategy. It shows that our model has integrated all the individual disparate alignment elements proposed by these models. Further, it shows our model has addressed some key requirements which have either not been considered or only partially considered by some of these models. The main strengths of our model compared to previous work are twofold: (a) it addresses all alignment elements in an integrated fashion to make them meaningful and useful for practitioners; and (b) it addresses the full life cycle of strategic alignment from direction setting to strategic outcome monitoring and ongoing feedback loop for self-adjusted alignment (aided by architecture principles and IT governance).

We use the Kaplan and Norton (2004) strategy map as a basis for developing the business-aligned IT strategy. This leads us to the first stage (strategy direction) of our four stage strategic alignment model. The first step to producing the IT strategy is to have a clearly defined business strategy, which states explicitly the business directions and objectives desired. These business strategic objectives will define the new business capabilities required for competition—the operating model for the firm (Ross, Weill, & Robertson, 2006). It will articulate the strategic business information and process capabilities required. A gap analysis is defined to assess what specific information and process capabilities are lacking in the existing IT environment to meet these strategic needs. Because these capabilities are interrelated, the results of the analysis and the desired future state should be best described in terms of integrated enterprise architecture. A key strength of the methodology is the prescribed method used to explicitly trace the linkage between the source business strategic drivers and resultant IT strategic requirements. From this analysis, we can develop the IT competencies required to deliver the business strategic objectives—the IT competency or capability strategy—over the duration of the business strategy. Sourcing strategy is then developed from the IT competency strategy. It determines with the view to achieve competency flexibility and market adaptability, in line with the business strategy, what skills must be kept in-house and what are best sourced from partners, either locally or offshore. Finally, it defines the IT governance model required to guide the execution of the strategy. The execution methodology follows the end-to-end strategic management process defined in Chapter IV.

In this chapter, we will use the case examples of the business transformation strategies of a major Australian bank (Bushell, 2003) and a retailer (Mills, 2005) to illustrate an application of the end-to-end strategic alignment principles. We break down the banking example into three parts by reviewing the approach taken by the bank's CIO at each of the first three stages of our four-stage IT strategy process. And we describe IT business value delivery reported by the retailer to illustrate the last stage of IT strategy process—business outcome monitoring.

We will return to the practical application of strategy map by example in Chapter XII through a case study of the business–IT strategy alignment process and outcomes of an Asia Pacific leading electricity utility company.

STRATEGIC ALIGNMENT PRINCIPLES

Basic Elements of Strategic Alignment

IT is a means to the business end. Thus, as discussed in previous chapters, IT strategy is part of the business strategy and it focuses on the direction and the paths the IT organization, process, systems, and people must take in helping implement the business strategy. The basic principle of IT strategy is therefore very simple—every directional intent, every technical path, and every technical standard and architectural principle it prescribes, and every process model and operating guideline it recommends must be accounted for by ensuring the business outcomes they produce are in line with the business strategic objectives. Thus, as described in Chapter IV, the key to producing a high quality business-relevant IT strategy is by aligning every step of the IT strategy process with the business strategy process.

In this chapter, we describe the principles and method for producing a business-aligned IT strategy. In particular, we highlight the alignment method and process as they are the critical disciplines that practitioners must master.

Strategic business–IT alignment has been studied for over 20 years. Yet, there is a paucity of practical approach (Avison, Jones, Powell, & Wilson, 2004; Chan, 2002) to guide practitioners in developing a business-aligned IT strategy which will deliver the planned strategic business outcomes. Practical approaches are the focus of this chapter.

In Earl's (1993) study of strategic information systems planning carried out in 27 companies, he discovers that successful IS strategies and plans must satisfy the following requirements:

1. Three *necessary conditions* for success: *method or technique* for strategic planning, *process* for stakeholders (particularly line management and end users) participation, and *implementation* to deliver the stated strategic business objectives.
2. Five *critical success factors*: top management involvement, top management support, business strategy available, studying business before technology, and good IS management.

Furthermore, he finds that of the five approaches used by the 27 companies to develop IS strategy and strategic plan, the holistic *organizational* approach has the best result. This approach treats planning as "*business as usual*" in which all stakeholders are engaged (which ensures organizational wide buy-in of the strategy). The strategy creation process uses a continuous, *iterative method of learning* to "discover" how to best fit IT with business, and together as a team, they identify the pragmatic ways to execute for best outcomes. The *social behavioral* component of the process is as *critical* as having a sound practical method.

On the other hand, enterprise will experience poor business–IT alignment when business executives cannot clearly articulate their IT needs, or when IT personnel have limited understanding of business, business vision, and strategy (Chan, 2002). Lack of business alignment will reduce or even destroy IT organization's ability to deliver business value and compromise the firm's overall performance. Chan (2002) defines business–IT alignment as comprising two components: *strategic alignment*—which focuses on strategic fit between business and IT priorities and activities and *structural alignment*—which focuses on the structural fit between business and IT in the areas of organizational structure, staff reporting relationships, deployment of IT personnel, and decision-making rights.

Chan (2002, p. 100) observes that there are four preconditions for success in strategic alignment: (1) communication and understanding between line and IT executives; (2) linked business and IT missions, priorities, and strategies; (3) interconnected business and IT planning processes; (4) and line executive commitment to IT issues and initiatives.

Similarly, Chan (2002, p. 100) identifies six preconditions for success in structural alignment: (1) line personnel with appropriate IT skills and IT personnel with business skills, (2) decentralized reporting relationships and committees, (3) *informal* networks and relationships, (4) career paths and cross-functional linkages, (5) incentives and rewards, and (6) performance measurement and evaluation.

In the empirical study of eight companies in North America, Chan (2002) finds that:

- Strategic alignment theory and practice are in synch.
- Structural alignment varied by organization—there is no one right way.
- IS strategic alignment mattered more than formal IS structural alignment.
- Flexibility of IT structures was important.
- Structure is a means to an end.
- The informal organizational structure is more important to IS alignment than commonly recognized.
- Strong company culture may be a precondition to an informal structure that fosters alignment.
- Alignment of the informal structure needs more attention.

In particular, Chan (2002, p. 109) surmises from these findings that:

To improve overall IS alignment and performance, scarce management time and resources should be spent on improving the robustness of the informal organization (relationship-based structures that transcend the formal division of labor and coordination of tasks) and on aligning business units and IS strategies, but probably not on aligning formal structures.

Reich and Benbasat (2000) argue that strategic alignment may be studied from two perspectives: *process* or *outcome*. Process perspective concentrates on the planning activities and outcome perspective on the strategies produced. Further, they note that developing a business-aligned IT strategy needs to address not only the outcome (strategic plans) and the process (planning steps and activities), but also the *social* aspect concerning the *people involved* in the process. They also show that short-term alignment can be achieved through five factors:

- Shared domain knowledge between IT and the business domain (business knowledge and skills)
- Business direction
- Planning connections between IT and business
- IT implementation success (increasing business trust of IT's ability to deliver)
- Communication (particularly in business terms)

As described in Chapter IV, we too suggest that these are desirable characteristics for strategic alignment. Reich and Benbasat (2000) find that for long-term alignment, shared business domain knowledge and business direction are most critical. We argue that by our approach of end-to-end alignment from strategy direction setting right down to strategy implementation and outcome monitoring, both short- and long-term alignment can be achieved by means of an *iterative process*. The iterative development of strategic alignment is critical for managing the evolution of the business (and the attendant emergent strategy). This is because the business world is dynamic and constantly changing. The iterative alignment process manages the change and keeps IT and business in synch.

Das, Zahr, and Warkentin (1991) identify five dimensions of *alignment process*:

- **Formality:** About the structure of the planning process
- **Scope:** Assesses its comprehensiveness

Figure 5.1. Strategic alignment model (Henderson & Venkatraman, (1993)

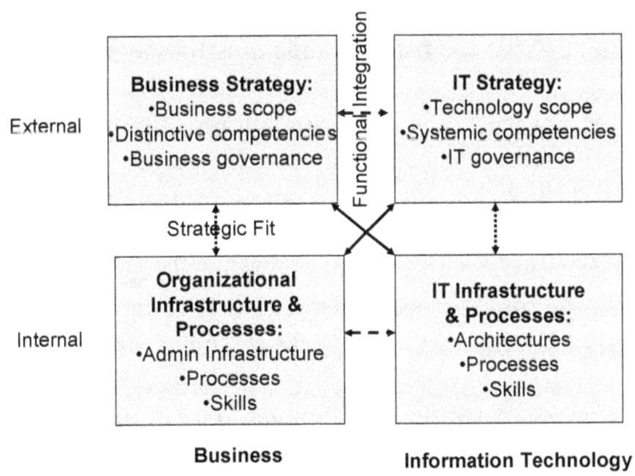

- **Participation:** Requires the involvement of managers (senior management)
- **Influences:** About the power of stakeholders
- **Coordination:** Investigates planning process corrections

Similar to our work on end-to-end alignment, Das et al. (1991) are interested in the outcome of the realized strategy rather than solely the resulting strategy itself.

Henderson and Venkatraman (1993) define the strategic alignment model (SAM) as a framework for describing and developing business-IT alignment. As shown in Figure 5.1, SAM depicts business on one side and IT on the other. Each functional area has two domains, where each of the business domains mirrors the corresponding one on the IT side. These domains are as follows:

- For business, the top level domain describes the business strategy – the *external* facing domain of the business. The business strategy domain comprises three core elements: (a) business scope—what the business strategic directions are about; (b) distinctive competencies—unique capabilities the firm with which the firm excels in serving its customers; (c) business governance—the business and regulatory rules that the firm uses to make strategic decisions.
- For IT, the mirroring top level domain describes the IT strategy—the *external* facing domain of IT. It too has three mirroring elements: (a) technology scope—the critical technologies or applications that support the business strategy initiatives; (b) systemic competencies—unique technology capabilities that help make the firm distinctive; (c) IT governance—rules that IT and business use to make decision about IT priority and investment.
- For the business, the lower level *internal* domain refers to the organizational infrastructure and processes. They are what Kaplan and Norton (2004) refer to as the intangible assets. It comprises three elements: (a) administrative infrastructure—the

organizational architecture with which the firm configures the distinctive competencies and executes the business strategy; (b) critical business processes—the most critical core processes that the firm uses to create distinctive value for its customers; (c) skills—the unique skills the firm's people must possess to execute the business strategy.

- Similarly for IT, the lower level *internal* domain refers to the IT infrastructure and processes. It comprises three elements: (a) IT architecture—the framework that logically integrates all technical artifacts of process, information, application, system, and network infrastructure, and that defines the technical standards and operating principles for guiding/governing business solution design; (b) IT processes—the internal processes used for IT service delivery (such as the one defined by ITIL[1]); (c) IT skills—the (unique) skills required to execute the IT strategy.

There are *two dimensions* of strategic alignment. The first dimension concerns the *strategic fit* (vertical alignment) of the internal domain (intangible assets) with the external domain (strategy). For instance, the organizational infrastructure and processes are designed to create a strategic fit with the business strategy on the left-hand side, and similarly are aligned to be supported by the IT strategy on the right-hand side. The second dimension concerns the alignment of IT domain (on the right) to the business domain (on the left): (a) on the corresponding external domains the IT strategy will align with business strategy—*technology transformation* or *technology-enabled competitive advantage*; and (b) on the corresponding internal domains, the IT infrastructure and processes will align with the business organization infrastructure and business processes—*strategy execution* or *service excellence*. Henderson and Venkatraman (1993) call the process of business and IT domains alignment as *functional integration*. It is the glue that allows business to differentiate its products and services. Henderson and Venkatraman (1993) further observe that "strategic alignment is *not an event* but a *process of continuous adaptation and change*."

Dynamic Nature of Strategic Alignment

Benbya and McKelvery (2006) support this dynamic nature of strategic alignment. They contend that the lack of adaptation to the constant change is the root cause of ineffective strategic alignment. They reason this is because the dynamic characteristics of strategic alignment and their management are not well understood. They state three levels of strategic alignment that need to be studied and managed:

- **Individual level:** Aligning IT infrastructure with end-user needs
- **Operational level:** Aligning business and IT departments (processes)
- **Strategic level:** Aligning business and IT strategies

At each level, business and IT elements (or variables), like living organisms in an ecosystem, co-evolve with one another as business and IT environments change. However, because each level also has dependency on the other, an elemental change in one level will have an impact on elements in the other levels. For example, when the business strategy changes at the strategic level, not only the IT strategy needs to re-adapt to align with it, but also the elements in the operational and individual levels. This means strategic alignment has multidirectional causalities within and between levels. Benbya and McKelvery (2006) propose the co-evolutions within each level and between levels need to be understood (modeled) and managed to minimize business–IT deviations.

They use co-evolutionary and complexity theories to improve strategic alignment. Benbya and McKelvery (2006) offer the following five approaches to improving adaptation efficacies:

1. **Deviation amplification:** Co-evolution leads IS alignment to positive feedback which, according to Benbya and McKelvery (2006), equates to deviation amplification. In response to a competitive environment, business champions critical IT initiatives to achieve competitive advantage. Further, business partners with IT select and deploy *adaptive infrastructure* so as to be responsive to user needs (at the individual level). This bottom-up processes of *self-organization and emergence* will create significant structures and processes suitable for greater exploitation of IT. Benbya and McKelvery (2006) call this phenomenon a *self-organizing positive feedback* to IS alignment, whereby IS and end users institute a "development spiral" (as in Boehm's 1988 spiral model of software development) in which an initial end-user conception can quickly "spiral" (iterative prototyping and user feedback to adapt to change) into a dramatic new functionality embedded into the IT infrastructure.
2. **Management by tension:** Bringing tension to bear as a means of sparking co-evolution dynamics. Benbya and McKelvery (2006) assert this dynamics will improve IS alignment at any level. For example, they claim co-evolutionary adaptation of IS alignment will result when tension is imposed by management through high management commitment and expectations of IT on one hand, and strong IT–business partnership on the other hand. Because this tension will strive to improve fitness, which they claim, as in biology, will "set off positive feedback spirals that generate spontaneous order in the form of fractal structures"—a deep simplicity in co-evolutionary adaptation.
3. **Requisite complexity:** According to Benbya and McKelvery (2006), organizations need to develop internal degrees of freedom in the form of IS and organizational abilities enabling a firm to respond to levels of external business and IS complexities that also may be changing. In this context, they claim the *least-effort* scale-free theory will apply in that: first, firms will pay for *just enough* internal capabilities to respond to external business, and second, they will only learn just the *minimum necessary* level about the external degrees of freedom. However, Benbya and McKelvery (2006) note that in reality, based on other research work, the opposite is true as firms seem to have difficulty applying least effort. This phenomenon has seriously compounded the misalignment problem.
4. **Near decomposability:** IS alignment aims to achieve *self-organized criticality* in IS application modularity. According to Benbya and McKelvery (2006), this involves balancing *numerous small* or *a few large* adjustments in near decomposability—that is, adjustment between more modules (more flexible) with more communication links (thus higher cost) and fewer modules (less flexible) and less communication links (cheaper). In other words, after a certain (optimal) critical point of decomposition, the effect of diminishing return will occur. IS alignment adaptability requires a modular architecture to manage the IS complexity. The architecture will achieve the *optimal balance* (near decomposability) of modularity-versus-cost and will create an agile IS environment to adapt with business change.

5. **Rate of genetic variance:** According to Benbya and McKelvery (2006), efficacious adaptation is enhanced by the rate of internal change. For firms, this means they need the ability to change their internal capabilities to remain competitive. This depends on the employees' ability to learn new knowledge (quickly) and the organization's ability to acquire new and (re)allocate skilled resources.[2] Thus, in addition to modularity, the effectiveness of IS alignment at all levels depends on resource availabilities and flows. With the optimum number of modules architected, each allocated with the right amount of skills and resources, IS/business co-evolutionary adaptation will be able to respond to and resolve unplanned environmental changes flexibly, speedily, and effectively.

IT Business Value Model

Melville, Kraemer, and Gurbaxani (2004) conclude from their analysis of contemporary IT business value models that "the locus of IT business value generation is the organization that invests in and deploys IT resources," which they term as the *focal firm*. They contend that external factors, such as industry competitive characteristics, trading partner resources and business processes, also play a major part in shaping the extent to which IT business value can be generated and captured. Melville et al. (2004) propose that these factors and their interplay can be understood by an integrative model of IT business value, as shown in Figure 5.2. The core of the focal firm is the IT business value generation process, which allocates judicious IT and complementary organizational resources to perform the firm's core business processes—that is, to conduct the firm's business. The strategic fit (alignment) of these resources and business processes with the enterprise strategy will ensure optimal business process performance (e.g., business operational efficiency, superior

Figure 5.2. IT business value model (Melville et al., 2004)

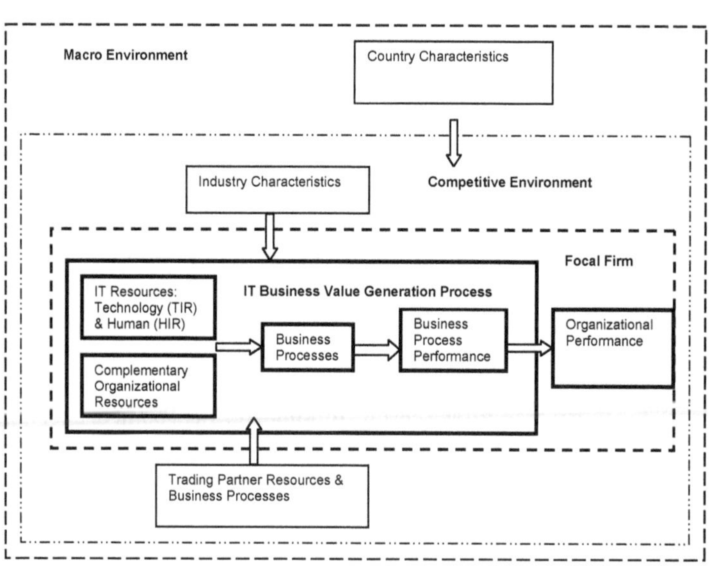

customer service experience) and thus the overall firm (organizational) performance (e.g., profitability and market share increase).

Melville et al. (2004) define technological IT resources (TIR) to comprise the IT infrastructure, the business applications that use the IT infrastructure, and human IT resources (HIR) to comprise technical and managerial skills. They define complementary organizational resources to comprise non-IT and nonhuman resources such as organizational structure, policies and rules, workplace practices, culture, and so on. These resources, together with the trading partner resources and business processes, in line with the principles of the resource-based view of the firm, impact directly the firm's performance and its strategic positioning in the competitive environment. The performance will be moderated by the industry characteristics, such as competitive and regulatory conditions, and to some extent by the country characteristics, such as the country's basic infrastructure, education, population growth rate, and culture. For example, Melville et al. (2004) conclude from analysis of the integrative IT business value model, among others, that:

- "The IT resources create economic value for a focal firm by conferring operational efficiencies that vary in magnitude and type depending upon the organizational context."
- "The greater the inimitability of rare organizational resources that are complementary to IT and lacking substitutes, the greater the degree to which the focal firm can obtain a sustained competitive advantage."
- "The greater the degree of competition in an industry, the greater the extent to which firms achieve efficiency gains via IT...[but]...the lower the extent to which firms are able to capture the benefits of efficiency gains and achieve profitability gains via IT."
- "The IT and non-IT resources and the business processes of electronically connected trading partners shape the focal form's ability to generate and capture organizational performance impact via IT."
- "Telecommunications infrastructure moderates the economic value of an inter-organizational information system to the focal firm and its trading partners...depending on the organizational and technological context."

Business Value Creation

Oh and Pinsonneault (2007) study strategic alignment and particularly the strategic value of IT resulting from business alignment from 110 firms using the contingency-based theory. The contingency-based theory argues that IT resources will create business value and improve the firm's financial performance only when they are purposely planned and used to support or execute the firm's key strategic objectives. This theory is also the basis of the *strategy map* developed by Kaplan and Norton (2004) to guide the development of a business-aligned IT strategy. Oh and Pinsonneault (2007) note that although it is well known by researchers that "alignment between business strategy and IT strategy should be conceptualized as a dynamic, fluid, and nonlinear state, the relationship between alignment and organizational performance is typically assumed to be linear."

In particular, in line with Benbya and McKelvery (2006), they note that business and technology environments are co-evolving and constantly undergoing changes making it difficult for business and IT to maintain alignment equilibrium. Furthermore, they note that small degrees of misalignment as a result of the dynamic environmental change can result in huge variations in organizational performance. Oh and Pinsonneault (2007) therefore use a nonlinear approach to investigate the dynamic and complex relationships between business strategy, IT, and business performance. They focus on how IT strategy is developed and implemented in relationship to business strategy. Specifically, they measure the degree by which the IT applications portfolio is aligned with the business objectives articulated in the firm's strategy. In other words, they assess the degree of strategic alignment and organizational performance impact by measuring the implemented IT strategy (via the portfolio of IT applications) against the stated business strategic objectives. Specifically, Oh and Pinsonneault (2007) decompose business strategic objectives into three dimensions which must be satisfied by IT applications portfolio. The three strategic (business value) objectives for IT strategy implementation used by Oh and Pinsonneault (2007) in assessing business alignment are:

- **Cost reduction or operational efficiency:** The objective is to minimize operational costs while maintaining a satisfactory level of quality of service (service level agreements with business);
- **Quality improvement:** The objective is to improve the quality of products and services (including superior design features and product capabilities) to increase product/service differentiation and customer value propositions;
- **Revenue growth:** The objective is to increase the speed of *new* product development and the ability to tailor products and services to meet customer needs, that is, the firm's innovation, to increase revenue growth.

Oh and Pinsonneault (2007) postulate two hypotheses in their strategic alignment measurement research:

Hypothesis 1: *The contingency-based perspective is a better predictor of the strategic value of IT than the resource-centered perspective.*[3]

Hypothesis 2: *In the contingency-based perspective, a non-linear model is a better predictor of the strategic value of IT than a linear model.*

They find that support for both hypotheses is strong when expense is used as a performance measure. Conversely, support for both hypotheses is weak when revenue is used as a performance measure. A practical implication of these findings is that IT alignment with a cost-reduction strategy is more able to deliver immediate tangible benefits to firms than one that aims to facilitate revenue growth. Oh and Pinsonneault (2007) argue a possible explanation for the mixed results could be that cost savings impact of IT strategy is usually more directly detectable than IT influence on macrofinancial indicators such as revenue because revenue is strongly impacted by external market and competition uncertainty. Importantly, however, Oh and Pinsonneault (2007) find that profitability is higher when both business and IT strategies are rated high than when both are rated low—signifying the importance of strategic fit between business and IT, and thus the business value of IT.

Another important implication of Oh and Pinsonneault's (2007) findings is some initial support for the nonlinear phenomenon of dynamic nature of business strategy, IT, and organizational performance. They suggest there is a need for firms to continuously refine and fine-tune their efforts to maintain an *optimal state of alignment* in which superior business performance can be attained.

Kaplan and Norton (2004) use the *strategy map* to model the Henderson and Venkatraman (1993) SAM processes of *strategic fit* and *functional integration* in a sequence of *cause–effect* relationships. We extend their work and use the same principles and define them in terms of a *business alignment traceability matrix.*

Business–IT Alignment Maturity Model

Luftman (2000) in the paper "Assessing Business–IT Alignment Maturity"[4] defines the strategic alignment maturity model, which is modeled after the Software Engineering Institute's Capability Maturity Model. Luftman claims to have tested the maturity model against 500 Fortune 1000 companies globally. So it would have significant practical value in assessing and helping companies improve their strategic alignment capability. This capability is fundamental to helping enterprises align their IT capabilities with the business to ensure IT delivers business value.

The Luftman strategic alignment maturity model defines six criteria for assessing business/IT alignment (see Figure 5.3):

Figure 5.3. Luftman's criteria for assessing business–IT strategic alignment maturity (Luftman, 2000)

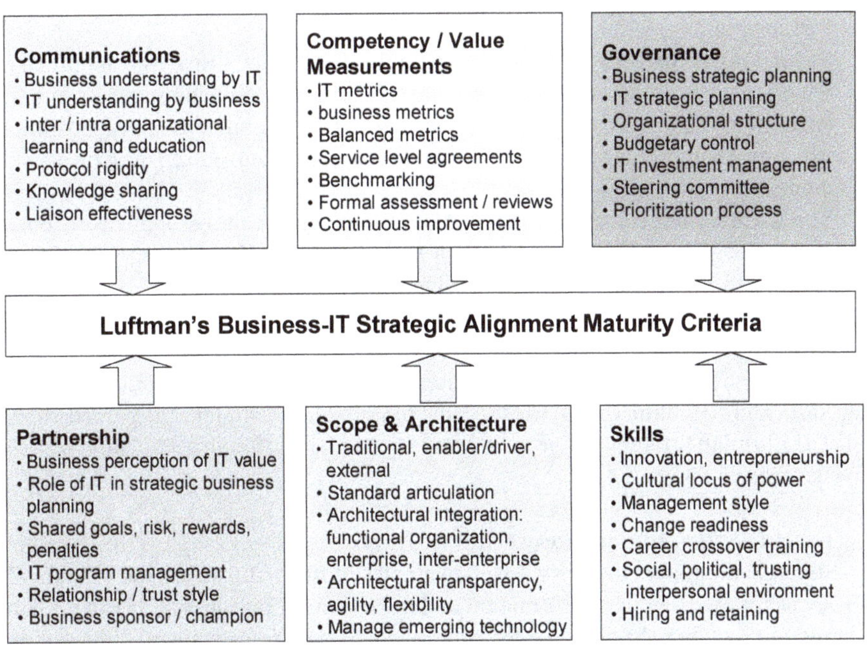

- **Communication:** Effective exchange of ideas between IT and business. This requires IT to have strong business acumen to understand the firm's business, so they can exchange ideas with business using business terms. Conversely, it also requires the business to understand the capabilities and potential that IT can bring to bear on the business capability to compete. It is only through this level of mutual understanding that it would be possible to ensure that the firm's IT (or CIO) priorities will align with the business expectations for competitive advantage.
- **Competency/value measurement:** Business-oriented IT metrics for value creation. Too often, IT is criticized for not being able to add value to business. Some may even argue that IT destroyed value. A root cause is due to IT metrics being technically oriented such that they have no apparent relevance to business. This criterion measures IT's ability to measure its output in business terms and its value added to business performance. With IT having strong business acumen, this criterion would be easier to achieve, so it relates to the communication criterion.
- **Governance:** Authority for resources, risk, conflict resolution, and responsibility for IT shared between business and IT. IT governance has been described briefly in Chapter IV and in more detail in Chapter IX.
- **Partnership:** IT/business partnership in strategy setting and execution. CIO's are increasingly being admitted to the executive committee or senior management team of the enterprise. While this admission would help with the IT/business partnership, it is not an automatic guarantee that this partnership would be high. The partnership is built on the bedrock of IT being able to deliver value to business which wins the respect and trust of the business. Similarly, it also depends on the business (including the CEO) understanding of IT and commitment to leverage advantage from IT (and share gains and risks with IT). It has been found (Gartner, 2007) that highly effective enterprises have highly effective IT organization and a highly effective CEO–CIO partnership.
- **Scope and architecture:** Technology moving from back office to front office (customer-centric) by creating a flexible infrastructure and customizable solutions to enable agile business capabilities. It measures the firm's ability to leverage technology to create a competitive advantage, and to the extent of reinventing the firm's business model for the future.
- **Skills:** Core competency management and organization culture supportive of business innovation. This refers to the skills in Henderson and Venkatraman's (1993) SAM model and the human and organizational capitals in Kaplan and Norton's (2004) strategy map.

Each of these six criteria has a set of attributes (see Figure 5.3) used by Luftman, Bullen, Liao, Nash, and Neumann (2004) to assess the organization's strategic alignment maturity level. The Luftman Strategic Alignment Maturity Model (Luftman et al., 2004) has a scale of five levels (see Figure 5.4):

- **Level 1:** *Initial/Ad Hoc Process* (little to no alignment)—Level 1 is the lowest of the strategic alignment maturity. Some examples of the maturity attributes at this level are as follows. There is little mutual understanding by business and IT of each other, and only ad hoc sharing of information and inter/intra-organizational learning. IT metrics are highly technical and not business related. There are no formal assess-

Figure 5.4. Luftman business–IT strategic alignment maturity model (Luftman et al., 2004)

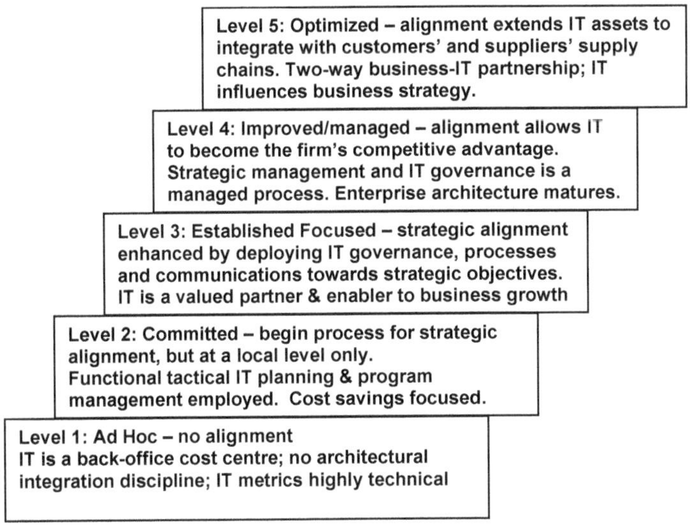

ments or reviews nor improvement processes of competency and value measurements. Business and IT strategic planning is ad hoc and uncoordinated. IT is a cost center and holds no seat at the business table. IT program management is ad hoc, and business sponsorship of programs does not exist. There is no architectural integration discipline and no programs for attracting and retaining the best talent. Culturally, innovation is not encouraged, and there tends to be a strong resistance to change.

- **Level 2:** *Committed Process*—Level 2 organizations are characterized by their commitment to begin the process for strategic alignment maturity. For example, there is now a limited mutual awareness between business and IT of each other's role, some semiformal process begins to exist for knowledge sharing. IT metrics are focused on cost savings and efficiency. Some forms of formal assessments or reviews of competency begin to exit. Functional tactical planning of IT is employed. IT program management standards now exist and business sponsorship is limited to functional organization. IT begins to be perceived as an asset by business. IT talent management is focused on technology skills. Innovation is still not widespread and depends on functional organization. Any alignment tends to exist on a local level but is not enterprise-wide.
- **Level 3:** *Established Focused Process*—At level 3 of strategic alignment maturity, firms build on their level 2 capabilities and focus on driving their governance, processes, and communications towards specific strategic business objectives. They use governance process to guide their decision making about which business processes should be invested with scarce IT resources. The decision criteria will be based on which business processes will deliver the sustainable competitive advantage expected by business strategy. The firm needs to be effective in communicating its vision and strategy to win the support from management and all employees. IT becomes a critical enabler of business and is emerging as a critical strategic asset enterprise-wide to

be managed by IT governance. Application portfolio shifts from traditional transaction-based to include information-based to support the business decision making process. Knowledge sharing is around key processes and inter/intra-organizational infrastructure is extended to key partners. IT metrics are linked to financial objectives (principally cost savings). Formal linkage between business and IT metrics is emerging, as is formal review and assessment of value and competency. IT is emerging as a valued service provider—service quality and reliability becomes dependable by business. Culturally, risk tolerant behaviors are emerging to spark some innovations. Change is being recognized as a necessity for competition. Enterprise architecture is emerging which is linked to business strategy and key business processes.

- **Level 4:** *Improved/Managed Process*—Building on level 3 capabilities, firms in level 4 of strategic alignment maturity leverage IT assets systematically enterprise-wide to gain sustainable competitive advantage. Their focus is on business process enhancement and integration, breaking down the "process silos" which isolate business units and impede collaboration. At level 4, IT is seen by the firm as a driver of business value and critical to business strategy. Understanding of business is pushed down through the IT organization. Strategic planning and governance becomes a managed process, with IT investment focused on cost effectiveness and process excellence. Business and IT metrics are closely linked and focused on end-customer values. Level 4 organizations will deploy enterprise architecture to leverage the intangible ("soft") assets (information and knowledge embedded in the firm's business processes and practices) such as those about customers, competitors, product, and employee skills, to achieve competitive differentiation.[5] Knowledge sharing is institutionalized across the enterprise. The application portfolio has further shifted toward a balance of transaction-based for cost efficiency, information-based for management decision making, and strategy-based for innovation and revenue growth. IT management style is value-based. IT is seen as innovative and a valued service provider.
- **Level 5:** *Optimized Process* (complete alignment)—Level 5 organizations extend the level 4 capabilities to leverage IT assets beyond the firm's boundary to integrate with the supply chains of the customers and the suppliers. IT becomes the heart of the business, to the extent that IT is the business (such as IT in Amazon.com). A sustained governance process ensures IT and business strategic planning is a two-way process. IT has significant business knowledge and is able to influence the business strategy. Mutual understanding between business and IT roles is pervasive throughout the organization. IT and business become close partners, able to co-evolve and adapt to each other incrementally to maintain alignment equilibrium despite market and other environmental changes. Knowledge sharing extends to "extra-enterprise" to include partners and customers. Innovation is a common practice. Talent (core differentiation competency) management is a formal process to sustain high organizational performance.

More detail on the strategic alignment maturity model and the process for improving the firm's strategic alignment maturity level can be found in Luftman et al. (2004).

Our end-to-end alignment model to be described in this chapter incorporates key elements of Earl (1993), Reich and Benbasat (2000), Das et al. (1991), Henderson and Venkatraman (1993), and Luftman (2000). Further, our model addresses the firm as a whole. It takes into account the social and human behavioral aspects as well as process and content of alignment.

The IT strategy development methodology follows the end-to-end process described in Chapter IV.

STRATEGY DIRECTION

In terms of the SAM model, this stage of our strategy alignment process is concerned with the two externally focused domains of business and IT strategies—the method and process for ensuring their alignment. The output is principally, for a *developing* CIO (in the sense that they are still establishing their credibility to win business trust and becoming a true business partner), a business-aligned IT strategy (which includes an outline of the business model or business oriented enterprise architecture). In this case, we assume that the corporate strategy has already been developed by the executive management team, and the CIO is engaged to work with the executive team to develop the corresponding IT strategy to ensure strategic alignment. This situation is quite common for many enterprises which view IT as an important support organization, but perhaps do not yet treat it on the same level as a strategic business unit.

On the other hand, for a well established (mature) CIO, with a strong partnership with the business and the ability to influence the corporate strategy, this stage of our process will also include the corporate strategy as an output. Broadbent and Kitzis (2005) refer to this as the "new" CIO capability to *proactively* (influence and) manage demand (of IT resources) from business—as distinct from the "old" traditional CIO role of *reactively* managing supply (of IT resources) in response to strategic business requirements.

There are two interrelated steps. First, enterprise strategy development is commonly led by the CEO (or corporate strategy leader as CEO delegate) and senior executives below the CEO will propose key elements of the enterprise strategy pertaining to their functional responsibilities, and develop the appropriate strategic initiatives (in consultation with the CEO) to help execute the enterprise strategy (Thompson & Strickland, 2003). Thus, the CIO on behalf of IT contributes new technology-enabled business capabilities or business models to differentiate the enterprise. The first step will be more commonly taken by a mature and well established CIO who has a strong relationship with the CEO and the business peers.

Second, led by the CIO, the IT steering team (comprising of business/line managers, IT end users, and IT leaders) on behalf of the executive committee develop and articulate (verify) explicit business/IT alignment to deliver the company's growth and operational excellence strategic objectives. It focuses on exploring how exploitation (or leveraging) of new technologies or new ways of exploiting (leveraging) existing technologies may help create a new business model which will generate a disruptive change to the competitive landscape and propel the enterprise into a new plane of profitability and growth:

- Business direction defined, and influenced by, IT direction
- New IT capabilities enable new business models that in turn influence business direction

In terms of Luftman's strategic alignment maturity model, at this stage of our process, the CIO must leverage the *communication* and *partnership* capabilities to demonstrate how the strategic IT direction will align and support the business strategy, and most importantly use the *competency/value measurements* capability to confirm the business value that the IT strategy will deliver.

Concurrently, the CIO shall use the *scope and architecture* capability to define the enterprise architecture for the agreed strategies. The business aspect of the enterprise architecture can be used as a communication tool to explain and gain consensus on the potentially new business operating model that the strategy may envision. It is also a critical tool for scoping out the strategic plan in the next stage of our process. Ross et al. (2006) call this a critical foundation for excellent strategy execution.

We define the *alignment principle,* which relates to the *scope and architecture,* to be followed for business and IT strategies as follows:

- *Business→ IT (reactive–supply management): For each business strategic intent or imperative, define the process and information capabilities (i.e., technological IT resources) and human IT resources* (Melville et al., 2004) *that the enterprise needs to implement that strategic intent* and a set of business strategy-aligned IT principles to guide the IT implementation. For example, a traditional bank wants to offer a direct online banking facility to its customers to counter the threat of ING Direct stealing its market share.

- *IT → Business (proactive–demand management): Using a combination of process and information (not technologies), define how a new business model can deliver value to the customers and the enterprise.* For example, the eBay business model of intermediation is enabled by a proprietary application and the Internet to allow buyers and sellers to trade online anywhere in the world. Ross et al. (2006) call the IT-driven business model definition a business operating model definition.

The focus of this process is to define the new business capabilities and the requisite IT capabilities to compete distinctively. The outline of the enterprise architecture described in business language will show how these capabilities will create value for customers. We illustrate these concepts using the case example of a large Australian bank's business transformation strategy below. More detail on enterprise architecture will be described in Chapter VI.

Case Example: Banking

In this example, we illustrate an approach to business–IT strategy alignment by reviewing the early journey taken by one of the leading banks in Australia, the Commonwealth Bank of Australia (CBA), in transforming the company from a product-centric to a customer-centric corporate strategy (Bushell, 2003). The publicly announced CBA (2005) business transformation goal is to achieve *customer service excellence.* The enterprise strategy is to deliver responsive, convenient, and reliable customer service by *engaged people* who are empowered, motivated, and skilled in service delivery, and *supported by simple processes,* that are fast, accurate, and efficient (CBA, 2005). This is akin to the *customer intimacy* value discipline defined by Treacy and Wiersema (1995).

To develop the CBA, IT strategy in response to the customer-centric business strategy, the CIO first clearly articulates the changing business challenges from which he then derives the IT capability implications (Bushell, 2003). In particular, the CIO establishes a high level of discipline and rigor into all aspects of IT management, using a "building block" approach to defining the business-aligned IT strategy—to ensure that business strategy is enabled by the right IT capabilities (Bushell, 2003). The three interrelated building blocks, namely IT strategy, IT management model, and IT sourcing strategy, are used to align IT organization to the business strategy. IT strategy defines how *technologies* will enable the business; IT management model defines the *organizational model* to implement the strategy; and IT sourcing strategy defines the *IT competencies* required to deliver the solutions (Bushell, 2003). According to the CIO:

They (building blocks) are largely driven by an overall framework that is all about acting in the best interests of *the group as a whole*, as well as the individual business units. It's about trying to get that enterprise view of what you're trying to achieve. (Bushell, 2003)

Business–IT strategic alignment is performed on each strategic imperative by mapping the correspondence of strategic change required in business and IT. For example, the business wants to shift from the old way of "vertically integrated business systems (business unit silos)" to the new way of "transparent business systems (holistic model of a financial services organization with a range of products and solutions)." This corresponds to the strategic shift in IT from the old way of "product oriented application across value chain" to the new way of "decoupling of front-end customer-segment oriented, back-end product oriented and separate information repository—to better manage customer relationship for the group." Similarly, moving the business focus from "proprietary customer management model" to "shared customers management model" corresponds to moving IT from "channel specific customer facing applications to integrated sales and services platform." By deriving the IT implications of the new business challenges arising from the customer-focused enterprise strategy, CBA will be able to keep business driven front-end application programs in synch with infrastructure program around data repository (Bushell, 2003). For example, as mortgage operation process becomes increasingly complex, there is a need to "eliminate paper from the process and automate the process with workflow systems as much as possible"—that is to shift from managing *stock* to managing *information* flow (Bushell, 2003). This will improve customer experience and reduce operations costs.

STRATEGIC PLANNING

Corporate and Business Strategic Planning

At this stage of the strategy development process, the enterprise will articulate the new business capabilities or the new business model that the corporate strategy seeks to deliver in order to achieve the business strategic objectives. It will also stipulate the specific business benefits expected, and in what sequence should they be delivered based on the committed business plans for the current and the new financial years. This is the initial stage of strategy execution, in which the *corporate governance* will be used to enforce *alignment and integration* of business unit plans with the corporate strategy.

In terms of the SAM model, the external domain for corporate strategy is "decompose" or "mapped" into business unit (BU) strategies by an iterative process under the jurisdiction of corporate governance to ensure strategic alignment with corporate strategy. For example, each BU will replicate the company's core *operating (or business) model* and competencies into a BU local context to ensure the stipulated customer value proposition and the desired customer experience consistent with the corporate brand will be delivered. Further, these business unit strategies are mapped to or strategically fitted with the intangible assets of business administrative infrastructure, process, and skills for at the business unit level. Once aligned, these assets are the *organisms* that will *enact* the distinctive corporate operating or business model and the attendant customer value proposition.

The business units will develop and commit to their individual business plans in line with the corporate strategy approved in the previous stage. It is the responsibility of the executive committee to ensure that these business plans individually and collectively align with and deliver the corporate strategic objectives for the new financial year, and, in the case of multiyear program, the future financial years. This process will leverage the *corporate governance* to ensure that short-term profit goals are balanced with investment for longer term growth objectives.

The group CIO and the business unit CIOs will participate with the BU heads in contributing to the development of their individual BU business plans and validate alignment with the corporate strategy. As mentioned above, in the case of the CIO with less developed partnership with the business, this process may be *lesser in contributing to* but more *in support of* the corporate and business strategic plans to ensure the strategic alignment of the corresponding corporate and BU IT strategic plans (the next stage). In this case, the CIO's focus is more on *communications capability* to gain a good understanding of what the business wants to achieve strategically and to use the IT strategy developed in the previous stage to ensure business understanding of the requisite IT capabilities *(skills capability)* that will be deployed to realize *(competency/value measurement capability)* the business strategic objectives.

IT Strategic Planning

With the CIO having contributed to or confirmed understanding of the corporate and BU strategic plans, this stage is focused on developing the requisite IT strategic plans in line with the above corporate and BU strategic plans.

This stage of our process has a multiplicity of activities that need to be coordinated to produce an integrated and implementable IT strategic plan. In this stage, the CIO and IT organization will need to leverage all six capabilities defined in the Luftman strategic alignment maturity model to gain business commitments for the resulting business-aligned IT strategic plan.

First, following on from the enterprise architecture and business operating model developed at the corporate strategy stage, this stage will add to the business aspect of the enterprise architecture with the remaining details of process, information, application, and infrastructure. It will define the target enterprise architecture which integrates process, data/information/knowledge, applications, and infrastructure (operations and security) to effect the operating/business model defined by the corporate strategy. The enterprise architecture will also define the architecture principles and standards to guide the implementation of the operating model. They include the technology platform standards to constitute the standard operating environment for the enterprise. Chapter VI will describe in detail the role of enterprise architecture in corporate and IT strategies.

Second, using the enterprise architecture as a framework and IT governance as guide, analyze the corporate/business plans to identify the portfolio of strategic IT applications required to deliver the new business capabilities (for the new operating/business model). Use portfolio and program management techniques, guided by IT governance, to aggregate synergistic projects (or work packages) into business programs which will deliver the desired new business capabilities in a time sequence consistent with the corporate/business plans. The business programs will incrementally, stage by stage, implement the target enterprise architecture for strategic differentiation. Chapter VII will discuss portfolio and program management.

Third, in terms of the SAM model, develop the IT competency (capabilities/skills) strategic plan and IT processes to achieve the strategic fit with the corporate and IT strategies.

Fourth, develop the optimal sourcing plan to realize the previously mentioned IT capability strategic plan. The sourcing plan is a resource allocation plan, and it aims to achieve *resource flexibility* by using a mixture of internal and third party contract or outsourced IT skills. The accent on resource choice and allocation is first on speed to market and maximum business value for strategic advantage, and second on cost minimization. Ravichandran and Lertwongsatien (2005) in a study of 129 firms show that effective use and allocation of IT capabilities and resources, respectively, directly impact the effective performance of business enterprise.

Aligning IT Resources to the Organization's Strategy

Strategic alignment includes enterprise-wide strategic planning, practical strategic planning, and the importance of the CIO's involvement as a full participant in the strategic planning process and strategic resource management. Once the executive team agrees on the strategic plan, it is the CIO's responsibility to see that the IT resources are aligned with those strategies. The CIO works to align resources to strategy on two levels: within the IT organization and its strategies, and those of the IT organization within the company as a whole. Once the strategic plan for the IT organization is in alignment with the overall company's strategic plan, the CIO aligns the IT resources to the IT organization's strategic plan and validates that alignment with the strategic plans of the peers and partners. Real alignment means that all local strategic plans support the achievement of company strategy. As an enabler of local and global strategy, the CIO and the IT organization figure as one of the company's primary strategic resources (Schubert, 2004).

Alignment is the capacity to demonstrate a positive relationship between information technologies and accepted measures of performance. The means by which alignment takes place is the allocation of resources. Understanding which and how many resources are needed and how much time is required to accomplish goals and meet commitments is critical to a CIO's success and to the success of the IT organization (Schubert, 2004).

When information technology human capital is a strategic resource, its effective management represents a significant organizational capability. Ferratt, Agarwal, Brown, and Moore (2005) applied configuration theory to examine organizational practices related to the management of IT human capital. Organizations manage human capital by instituting a variety of human resource and work practices. Such practices typically include activities associated with recruiting workers with desired competencies, providing training and development opportunities, designing jobs and performance appraisal processes, developing compensation systems, and the like. Collectively, this set of practices for managing workers is an organization's configuration of human resource management (HRM) practices and is a proximal determinant of significant outcomes, such as employee turnover, job performance, job satisfaction, and firm performance.

Ferratt et al. (2005) ask the question: Given the potentially bewildering variety in practices that organizations can implement, how do CIOs make strategic choices about IT HRM practices? There are at least three choices here. One theoretical perspective, the universalistic approach, argues that there is a set of HRM practices that is effective across multiple organizational contexts regardless of situational contingencies. This best practice or high performance work system approach exhorts all firms to implement specific practices for managing workers, for example, extensive training and incentive pay to realize desired outcomes. A second perspective, the contingency approach, suggests that the effects of HRM practices on outcomes are moderated by a variety of contingency variables such as firm strategy. Finally, the configuration perspective focuses attention on patterns of HRM practices that exhibit nonlinear, synergistic effects on outcomes. Configuration theories therefore focus on the identification of sets of practices, recognizing that the benefit of adopting one practice may increase with the adoption of other complementary practices.

Building on the theoretical foundation of configuration analysis and previous research in management of human capital, Ferratt et al. (2005) empirically investigated predictions about the relationship between different bundles of human resource practices and IT staff turnover rates. They developed two hypotheses regarding the relationship of IT HRM configurations to turnover. They tested these hypotheses based on a field survey of more than 100 IT organizations.

The first hypothesis suggested that organizations with a human capital focused configuration for managing IT professionals will have significantly lower IT staff turnover rates than organizations with a task focused configuration for managing IT professionals. This hypothesis was confirmed in the empirical study.

The second hypothesis suggested that firms with intermediate IT HRM configurations will have IT staff turnover rates higher than those firms with a human capital focused configuration and lower than those firms with a task focused configuration. Intermediate configurations represent strategies for IT professionals between the extremes of short-term and long-term investment strategies. This hypothesis was not confirmed in the empirical study.

Effect of IT Resources on Firm Performance

Ravichandran and Lertwongsatien (2005) drew on resource-based theory to examine how information systems resources and capabilities affect firm performance. A basic premise was that a firm's performance could be explained by how effective the firm is in using information technology to support and enhance its core competencies. It was assumed that it is the targeted use of IS assets that is likely to be rent yielding.

Ravichandran and Lertwongsatien (2005) developed the theoretical underpinnings of this premise and proposed a model that interrelates IS resources, IS capabilities, IT support for core competencies, and firm performance. The model was empirically tested using data collected from 129 firms in the United States. The results provide strong support for the research model and suggest that variation in firm performance could be explained by the extent to which IT is used to support and enhance a firm's core competencies. The results also support the proposition that an organization's ability to use IT to support its core competencies is dependent on IS functional capabilities, which, in turn, are dependent on the nature of human, technology, and relationship resources of the IS department.

Core competencies are the basis for firms to compete in the market. Core competencies can be categorized into market-access, integrity-related, and functionality-related competencies. Market-access competencies include all those that allow a firm to be in proximity to its customers, identify their needs effectively, and respond in a timely manner to shifts in customer needs and tastes. Capabilities to segment and target markets precisely and tailor offerings to match the demands of customers are examples of market-access competency. Integrity-related competencies include those that allow a firm to offer reliable products and services at competitive prices and deliver them with minimal inconvenience. Efficient manufacturing operations, streamlined supply chains, and integrated business processes are some indicators of integrity-related competencies. Finally, functionality-related competencies are those that enable a firm to offer unique products and services with distinctive customer benefits. This competency reflects strengths in product development and the innovation potential of an organization (Ravichandran & Lertwongsatien, 2005).

Firm competencies are developed over a period of time and reflect choices made by the organization about resource acquisition and deployment. All firms have limited IT resources and have to make choices about how these resources are deployed. Choices that result in embedding IT within areas of critical importance to the organization are likely to yield resource bundles that are dissimilar to those of the competitors, which in turn, can be rent yielding. Embedding IT within areas of core competence makes the IS assets inimitable by making it difficult for competitors to create similar bundles of complementary IS and organizational assets as well as understand the contributions of IS assets to firm performance. Thus, other things being equal, firms that target IS initiatives toward core competencies are likely to realize greater value from their IS assets than those that are less focused in their IT deployment (Ravichandran & Lertwongsatien, 2005).

Using IT to improve activities that are integral to a firm's core competencies results in resource bundles that are unlikely to be easily imitated by competitors. This is due to the isolating mechanisms such as causal ambiguity and resource connectedness. For example, Wal-Mart's ability to perform better than most of its competitors in the retail industry is partly due to the complementarities between its business practices and its use of IT. Despite attempts by other retailers to copy Wal-Mart's IT systems, they fail to replicate its success in reaping returns from IT investment because of difficulties in understanding how IT and business capabilities interact to affect Wal-Mart's performance (Ravichandran & Lertwongsatien, 2005).

Ravichandran and Lertwongsatien's (2005) findings about causal relationship between IS capabilities and IT support for core competencies and those between IS resources and IS functional capabilities highlight the path and time dependencies involved in using IT in pursuit of firm strategies. Organizations that have successfully used IT to gain competitive advantage have been able to do so because of a history of choices about the acquisition and deployment of IS resources.

Ravichandran and Lertwongsatien's (2005) research model is illustrated in Figure 5.5. This model can serve as a basis for IS performance evaluation. By providing empirical evidence that IT support for core competencies has a positive effect on firm performance, their study highlights that CIOs have to do more than invest in the latest technologies or

Figure 5.5. Model for effect of information systems resources on firm performance (Ravichandran & Lertwongsatien, 2005)

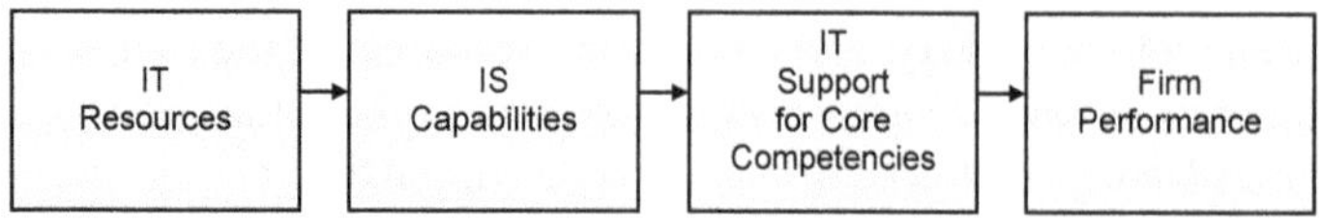

develop a strong IT department. The results indicate that CIOs have to clearly understand the strategic thrust of the organization and institute mechanisms to ensure that IS capabilities are channeled toward areas of importance to the organization. Among other things, this requires close interactions with business managers and the CEO to play an active role in IT deployment decisions.

Chapter VIII will discuss in more detail people, organization, and sourcing as a critical tool for effective execution of IT strategy.

Case Example: Banking

To develop the IT strategic plan for the execution of the CBA corporate strategy described previously, the CIO has developed the requisite enterprise architecture. According to the CIO, the enterprise architecture was developed (Bushell, 2003) by "working with the business to understand where we felt the organisation was going to be five years out, and what type of architecture would we need at an enterprise level to give the organisation the capabilities it needed." According to the CIO, enterprise architecture defines *how to simplify business processes and manage effective information flow* across the enterprise in order *to create the business capabilities required* to achieve the business strategic direction (Bushell, 2003).

The enterprise architecture encapsulates the envisioned new IT capabilities[5] required to achieve the future state of the business. It comprises three key (decoupled) elements: customer-facing (access channel) front-office, enterprise (information) management, and products and funds administration back-office (Bushell, 2003). IT systems gap analysis was then performed by comparing the target enterprise architecture with the current portfolio of systems. System gaps were identified in a number of areas such as Web-enabled front ends, integrated sales and service platforms, improved information infrastructure, common and reusable interfaces, and rationalizing of product systems (Bushell, 2003). In particular, the then information architecture was found to be inadequate to support customer relationship management (Bushell, 2003).

IT governance (including program portfolio management) process is used by CBA, involving business and IT executives, to prioritize the strategic programs and their expected business values, and the investments required to implement them.

Next, the CIO articulates the IT sourcing strategy required to implement these programs and deliver the solutions required by the business strategy. The sourcing strategy must support the bank's need for a portfolio of services that deliver flexibility, scale, and leverage new and enhanced capabilities, and value for money. It must also take into account changes in the business and technology environments, vendor capabilities, economics, and internal IT (technical and) management capabilities to support the sourcing alternatives (Bushell, 2003).

According to the CIO, the IT sourcing principles defined and practiced by the bank in the execution of the IT strategy are (Bushell, 2003):

- Manage and be responsible for IT strategy, architecture, policy, technology planning and demand forecasting
- Protect intellectual property in relation to unique group systems
- Seek to preserve architectural integrity while optimizing flexibility and the cost base
- Always seek to source and integrate the best applications development/solution delivery outcomes for the business
- Generate return to scale wherever possible
- Only outsource into competitive markets
- Do not stretch suppliers beyond their capabilities
- Do not commit to supply contracts where services and risks cannot be defined, understood, priced and monitored
- Maintain flexibility to exploit, or minimize impacts of, shifts in supply markets

STRATEGY EXECUTION

We are now at the most critical part of IT strategy—execute the strategic plan to deliver business value. It is the most critical because without execution, an IT strategy, no matter how aligned and integrated with the business, is rendered useless. All the business opportunities will be lost thus weakening the firm's competitive positioning. It has been said, and our practical experience supports it, that a less than perfect strategy with excellent execution (which meets the market window and most of customer requirements at minimal costs) delivers much more value than a perfect strategy with poor execution (which missed the market window altogether and with excessively over-run costs resulting in negative returns).

This stage of our process relies on professional portfolio, program, and project management skills from both the business and IT personnel. Again, all six capabilities of the Luftman strategic alignment maturity model are required to achieve efficient and effective strategy execution. The accountabilities of business and IT are also clearly articulated in accordance with the IT governance.

IT must excel in not only program development but also in operations and maintenance of the strategic applications delivered (put in production) by the program. The delivered program must achieve the minimum total cost of ownership (TCO), operational excellence objectives (such as business process performance expected by customers and other business-oriented IT performance metrics), and the new business capabilities (per the new operating or business model) stipulated by the IT strategic plan and the program plan. Excellent program delivery requires IT to apply consistent and diligent application and monitoring of the following practices to each program:

- Methodology and standards
- Sourcing contract management and benchmarking
- Intellectual property management
- Competency/HR development

- Risk management
- Change management (function, cost, time trade-off)
- Quality management

Chapter VII will describe the management best practice of portfolio, program, and project management discipline in detail.

Case Example: Banking

The CBA CIO says that "having a sound strategy is vitally important, but ultimately strategy is only as good as the ability to implement. Execution is everything" (Bushell, 2003).

In the CBA case, this is aided by the IT management model—the third element of the IT strategy. It defines the accountability model for managing IT and a set of principles for guiding decision making—in other words, the IT governance model. It is principally based on CoBit[6] (www.itgi.org) and ITIL (www.itgovernance.co.uk) standards, enhanced by adoption of strong IT portfolio management practice (Bushell, 2003).

The IT management model ensures an appropriate balance between business unit and enterprise outcomes. According to the CIO, it defines the HR and organizational culture strategies to execute the corporate strategy, and consists of the following elements (Bushell, 2003):

- **Principles:** For preserving architecture integrity while optimizing flexibility and the cost base.
- **Roles and responsibilities:** For IT strategy, architecture, technology planning, demand forecasting toward ensuring enterprise-level outcomes.
- **Governance:** Authority determined by policies and risk, and allow for collaboration.
- **Portfolio management approach to managing IT assets.**
- **IT community structure:** Resources and reporting aligned to the distribution of roles and responsibilities.
- **Performance measurement:** Effectiveness of IT management measured against group contribution objectives

In short, the IT management model enables the successful execution of the IT strategy. It ensures judicious resources are allocated to the high priority programs in accordance with the business strategy, and it ensures the expected IT business value is created and captured by the enterprise.

BUSINESS OUTCOME MONITORING

Too often, enterprises treat the task of program delivery ends at the completion of the program, when the desired strategic applications are successfully put into live production. However, from IT (and business) governance viewpoint, this is only the start of the business program journey in serving its business purpose of generating revenue growth or/and cost reduction. A critical last stage of our process is to monitor the operational performance of the applications (to ensure they meet the expected service level agreements) and the commercial performance of the business program (to ensure the commercial objectives of the program in terms of revenue growth, market share growth, and productivity improvement are all met at every milestone of monitor point in accordance with the business case based on which the program priority was assigned by the IT steering committee's IT governance principles). This monitoring is in addition to the often-stated but seldom done objective of post-implementation review of the delivered program. Post-implementation review is important for lessons learned so as to improve best practices for delivery of future programs. This is the accountability of IT, although it may be chaired and conducted by the business sponsor. Similarly, monitoring of the total cost of ownership at the operations and maintenance (O&M) level is IT accountability. IT must develop action plan to reduce ongoing variances in line with O&M strategy and to ensure TCO minimization is achieved.

Commercial monitoring of the program performance is the business' accountability. It could be conducted by IT or more appropriately by the finance department to ensure the business case is achieved. Where variance to business case exists, the business owner must develop action plan for performance recovery to the IT steering committee, as per the IT governance principles.

Last but not least, IT must work with business to develop an applications release plan for future application enhancement. The application release plan aims to deliver further business benefits. It will optimize the time-to-market of additional value with incremental costs to develop. It requires judicial balancing of benefits bundle with frequency of releases to meet market opportunities and cost per release.

Case Example: Retail

The practice of business outcome monitoring is exemplified by the IT business value delivered by the high-profile multiyear Australian $1 billion IT-enabled business transformation program undertaken by Australia's largest grocery retailer, Woolworths, over an 8-year period. The IT business value generated by IT and captured by business is monitored annually and reported by the CEO in periodic company briefings, as summarized below from various press reports by *The Australian IT*.[7]

Woolworths began its IT-enabled supply chain transformation program, code-named Project Refresh, in 1999 (Mills, 2005a). Project Refresh aims to deliver cost leadership to Woolworths. Woolworths chairman James Strong says information technology is central to the *company's "whole future"* and its board is closely involved in technology decisions (Mills, 2005b). The chairman added, "Well applied technology was the best form of competitive advantage" (Mills, 2005c).

By March 2005, Woolworths CEO reported that "the supply chain initiatives were well underway and "underpin our forecast cost reductions. Project Refresh had delivered cost savings amounting to 4.03 per cent of sales, a cumulative saving over the past five and half years of $3.2 billion" (Mills, 2005a). The Woolworths supply chain operational excellence is attributed to successful implementation of the twin systems: Stocksmart as the distribution center forecast-based replenishment system; and AutoStockR as the store-forecast replenishment system (Mills, 2005a). Equally important has been the cooperation of Woolworths suppliers to enable efficiency improvement across the supply chain end-to-end. The retailer aimed to introduce an improved system through which to exchange information with suppliers, which will result in an integrated collaborative planning, forecasting, and replenishment process (Mills, 2005d).

In 2005, Woolworths began phase 2 of Project Refresh, known as the Mercury Program. In this phase, the retail company planned to spend about Australian $1 billion on technology and supply chain infrastructure with an expected return of cost savings of more than Australian $6.2 billion (Mills, 2005b). According to Woolworths' chief logistics and information officer, the Mercury Program aims to make Woolworths more "store friendly." It aims to take significant costs out from the last 55 meters of the supply chain, where the CIO estimated about 55% of supply chain costs occur (Mills, 2005b). The Mercury Program invests in IT systems to give business the capability to predict, order, and control stock—by integrating the store–forecast replenishment system with the distribution center forecast-based replenishment system. It will transform the practice to more on managing information and less on managing stock—a practice which is more cost-efficient and effective operationally. According to the CIO, "technology (in Woolworths) has become very business-focused and all major IT projects are driven by a business sponsor...(and) about 75 per cent of technology spending supports the business strategy." The CIO also stressed the critical success factor of human IT resources (technical and leadership skills of IT staff). In particular, the CIO "places more emphasis on leadership strengths than technical skills, which can be learnt over time" (Mills, 2005b).

Woolworths supply chain overhaul by the Mercury Program and Project Refresh to reduce the retailer's cost of doing business has a direct impact on the company's market performance. It receives high profile attention in Woolworths' company briefings. For example, the CEO states at the 2006 Annual Report: "Technology required to support our new supply chain is critical to its success and was complex in construction" (Mills, 2006).

In 2008's half-year financial results statement to the Australian Securities Exchange, Woolworths CEO states (Mills, 2008):

Our IT platform (including AutoStockR and Stocksmart) continues to perform exceptionally well. This provides Woolworths with an enhanced ability to plan and manage volumes across the distribution and store network, providing lower costs and improved in-stock positions. We continue to refine and improve our IT capabilities, which will continue to provide further benefits.

IT-enabled supply chain transformation program roll-out thus far has been fundamental to Woolworths' competitive advantage, as reported in Mills (2007):

RETAIL giant Woolworths is extending computer and supply chain systems rolled out in its multibillion-dollar Project Refresh to its other brands, including the Big W discount chain. The extension of Woolworths' supply chain and business software into other parts of the business could enable the retailer to consolidate the technological lead it has grabbed over its chief rival, Coles.

GLOBAL IT STRATEGY AND MANAGEMENT

A global or regional corporation with business operations in multiple countries will need to develop a global or regional IT strategy. The global IT strategy and management will ensure alignment of each country's IT strategy and implementation with both the corporate and local business unit strategic objectives. This gives rise to the practice and study of global information management (GIM). GIM research investigates the development, implementation, management, and use of information systems in a global or international context (Tan, 2003). A related phenomenon is the globalization of software and business process services where corporations will be able to outsource/offshore their IT or business process services to an organization in another country with the appropriate skill set and at a much lower cost base (Aspray, Mayadas, & Vardi, 2006). CIOs must therefore possess the core competence to manage the globalization of IT services and GIM.

What is the practical approach to global IT management? How do CIOs manage and balance the diverse IT requirements of corporate and local business to deliver the optimal value for both? Barton (2003) describes a practical approach that separates the generic IT functions into global and local core functions. The global IT management functions consist of IT processes that need to be run globally: strategy, architecture, standards, and control. The local core IT functions managed by country IT managers consist of local planning, deployment (integrate new solutions), and operations (run the infrastructure and run the applications). The global IT functions influence the local functions in the following manner (Barton, 2003):

- **Global IT strategy:** It defines the agreed IT priorities in line with the business strategy and priorities, and implements the required initiatives. It has a direct impact on the new solutions to be integrated into the local IT environment (to run the local business). The relationship of corporate and business unit strategies, which applies to the global vs. local strategy contexts, has been described in detail in Chapter IV.
- **IT architecture:** It provides the flexibility to meet evolving business requirements by defining the desired IT organization model, core applications, and IT infrastructure to be implemented by local IT organizations to form an integrated global IT organization that meets both local and global (mid- and long-term) business requirements. It has a direct impact on all local IT functions (plan, build, and run IT platforms). Chapter VI will describe in more detail the enterprise architecture practice, which bridges business strategy to IT strategy and strategic plan.
- **Standards:** It manages complexity and exploits opportunities for cost savings and speed to market through economies of scale. Standards are selected for IT processes and platforms (infrastructure and applications) to be implemented by local IT organizations where they will give local business the cost and speed advantage without compromising the business flexibility required to meet some *locally unique* customer requirements. Strong IT governance process is critical to successfully manage any standards deviation requirements due to varying local business conditions. Examples of standards include ITIL standard for IT service management, enterprise resource planning (ERP) standard for business applications, and e-mail, desktop, local area network/wide area network (LAN/WAN), and database standards for back-office systems. Selecting IT platform standards from architectural consideration as a best practice is covered in Chapter VI.
- **Control:** It manages basic IT performance in terms of cost, value, and risk across all local IT organizations. The management focus is on maximizing business value while reducing IT risks and costs in each local IT organization. Local IT costs accrue in three broad areas: capital expenditure (CAPEX) of integrating new solutions to local IT environment and operating expenditure (OPEX) of running infrastructure and

applications. CAPEX will be controlled by maximizing business value and minimizing costs through effective practice of IT project portfolio management (Maizlish & Handler, 2005), program management, and project management disciplines, which will be described in detail in Chapter VII. OPEX will be controlled by operational excellence in running IT services using operations standards such as ITIL. As described in Chapter IV, control will be managed transparently, globally, and locally through IT governance (ITGI 2006). The IT application portfolio mix of the organization is determined by the evolving strategic focus of the corporation in line with the business strategy (Weill & Aral 2006). It is the product of diligent application of IT project portfolio management under IT governance (Jeffery & Leliveld, 2004).

Barton (2003) proposes that global IT management best practice is achieved through the following stakeholders:

- **Group CIO:** Accountable for the global IT management functions of strategy, architecture, standards, and control;
- **Local IT Heads:** Accountable for IT services in the local business unit in line with local business strategy and global IT strategy, architecture, standards, and control;
- **Functional Information Manager:** Accountable for IT functions of a business line function, for example, sales and marketing function, or supply chain function, or a line of business function such as retail banking or merchant banking;
- **IT Steering Committee:** Comprising business and IT leaders globally and locally who are accountable for the business and IT strategies and investment priorities;
- **IT Board:** Comprising the IT leadership team globally and locally who are accountable for the reliable, effective, and efficient operations of IT across the corporation, that is, operational excellence in IT service delivery to each business unit and the corporate parent overall.

According to Barton (2003), IT governance is lead by the group CIO and operates through IT steering committee (strategic) and IT board (operational). Barton (2003) observes that there are three forces shaping a global IT organization, which must be managed:

- **Pooled IT services:** IT functions that can be commonly applied to many local units offer the opportunity of pooling together to create economies of scale to reduce costs and increase speed to market. Examples include help desk, specialist IT services, application development, and support of a standard application platform.
- **Outsourcing:** With globalization of IT services, companies can leverage the competencies of global IT service providers by outsourcing offshore to them the commodity IT services, where they fit in with the sourcing strategy of the corporation. Some of the pooled IT services may be a commodity and therefore will be subject to offshore outsourcing consideration to leverage the even (purportedly) greater economies of scale offered by the global service providers. Some important considerations before a global offshoring decision can be made include cultural, business process, values, and security compatibility between the clients and the service providers. Chapter VIII describes outsourcing and sourcing strategy in detail.
- **Dispersion into business:** The natural tendency of the local IT head to have stronger allegiance to the local business unit head to whom local IT is directly accountable.

Depending on corporate politics and culture, some IT resources may even be dispersed to the business.

These three forces are likely to create natural tension between global and local IT management, driven by the local business unit's requirements (Barton, 2003). Group CIOs will need to draw on their corporate leadership strength and business skills to effectively manage the tension through strong relationships with the business unit heads and effective use of IT governance.

A best practice case example of a regional group IT strategy will be described in Chapter XII to illustrate the practical application of these concepts and principle.

IT STRATEGY MAP

There are many ways for aligning business and IT strategies (see, for example, survey by Oh & Pinsonneault, 2007). We find the most methodical, practical, and easy to follow one is the strategy map conceived by Kaplan and Norton (2004). The strategy map concept evolves from the balance scorecard (Kaplan & Norton, 2000), which is now in wide use by many corporations in the world. Thus, a firm's strategy map implementation and its ongoing performance monitoring can be readily integrated with the firm's balance scorecard practice. We summarize the Kaplan and Norton strategy map methodology in this section. We illustrate strategy map in action in Chapter XII by describing a case example of its application to the strategic planning and execution of a leading Asia Pacific electricity utility company's corporate and IT strategies.

The strategy map, based on balanced scorecard, is explained by the schematic causal model in Figure 5.6. Based on Kaplan and Norton's experience with over 300 organizations, in their book *Strategy Maps: Converting Intangible Assets into Tangible Outcomes* (Kaplan & Norton, 2004), they developed the following *principles*:

- **Strategy balances contradictory forces:** The need to invest in intangible assets such as human, organizational, and information capitals for long-term growth vs. the need to cut costs to increase margin and profitability in the short term. Based on industry and customer insights, the strategy map starts with the articulation of a balanced portfolio of cost-efficiency productivity and revenue growth strategic imperatives to which the business model and intangible assets will be aligned.
- **Strategy is based on differentiated customer value proposition:** The productivity and growth strategic imperatives will only be achieved by satisfying the customer needs through a differentiated customer value proposition. This is the most critical dimension of the strategy map as it must be compelling to achieve the strategic objectives, and it defines the "shape" of the enterprise (business processes and all its intangible assets) to ensure the customer value proposition will be delivered seamlessly and coherently by all elements of the enterprise in a well-orchestrated fully *aligned* way. In other words, using Porter's principle for strategy (Porter, 1985), the customer value proposition defines the "*strategic fit*" criteria for all the enterprise's business systems and intangible assets. The customer value proposition will typically be belong in one of the three generic *value disciplines* defined by Treacy and Wiersema (1995): product leadership, operational excellence, or customer intimacy.

Figure 5.6. The strategy map of an enterprise (Kaplan & Norton, 2004)

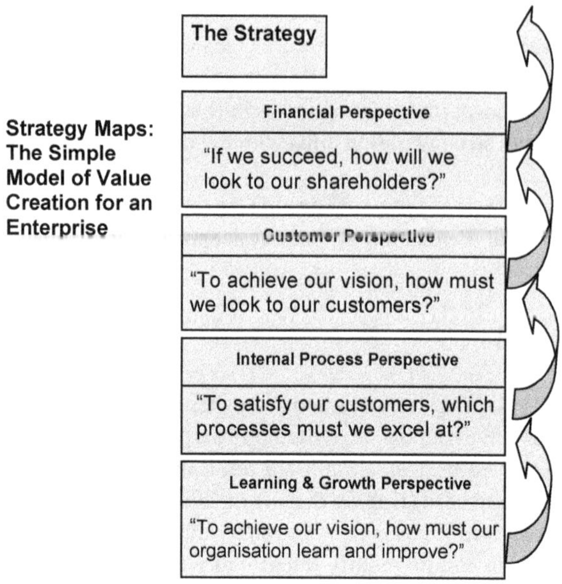

Product leadership refers to offering the customers with the market leading products. It accentuates the enterprise's strength in innovation capability—for example, iPod for Apple. Operational excellence refers to the offering of market leading cost efficiency to the customers through its simple and efficient end-to-end processes in customer service delivery. It accentuates the enterprise's strength in supply chain, logistics, and distribution channel management excellence—for example, Dell or FedEx. Customer intimacy refers to the offering of customer service excellence and achieving the market leading customer loyalty. It accentuates on the enterprise's deep knowledge of customer needs, products, and service experience and its strength in proactively anticipating and delivering the industry best customer experience—for example, Wal-Mart.

- **Value is created through internal business processes:** While the strategic objectives for productivity and growths, and the customer value proposition are the desired outcomes of the corporate strategy, it is the internal business processes that will execute the strategy to deliver these desired outcomes. Shaped by the customer value proposition, the enterprise must select which core processes it must excel in to achieve the differentiated value proposition. Corresponding to the three value disciplines of operational excellence, customer intimacy, and product leadership, there are three core internal business processes: operations management, customer management, and innovation processes, respectively. In addition, Kaplan and Norton have identified the fourth core process called regulatory and social process to manage the increasingly important regulatory and social obligations of business enterprises, for example, SOX and climate change environmental obligations.

- **Strategy consists of simultaneous complementary themes:** Reflecting the contradicting forces of productivity and growth strategies, each cluster of internal processes will have a different strategic theme with a different time horizon which must be harnessed in a balanced and complementary way to deliver the stated strategic objectives. For example, the operations management process will take a shorter time (e.g., 6–9 months) than the innovation process (2–3 years).
- **Strategic alignment determines the value of intangible assets:** The value of the intangible assets such as human, organizational, and information capitals are determined by their degree of alignment with the corporate strategy, specifically their ability in accomplishing the above simultaneous complementary themes derived from the corporate strategy. Thus, according to Kaplan and Norton, it would be logical to use the identified set of strategic themes to determine the appropriate strategic job families (human capital strategy) and strategic IT portfolio (information capital or IT strategy) and organizational change agenda (organizational capital strategy) that would align with and implement the strategic themes.

This causal mapping of the requisite strategic capabilities for the intangible assets to align with the corporate strategy through the identified strategic themes is the foundation of the strategy alignment methodology defined by the Kaplan and Norton strategy map methodology. Thus, using these principles, the strategy map is developed as a "causal map" with one "high level" perspective driving the "shape" (alignment) of the next "lower level" perspective. So the top level starts with defining the business strategic objectives—known as the financial perspective—in terms of the growth and productivity objectives. These financial performance objectives set out a balance of short-term profitability and long-term growth objectives, which must be determined from the enterprise corporate strategy through in-depth industry and market competitive analyses and customer insights. They represent the value the enterprise has committed on creating on behalf of the shareholders—the realization of which will link to the compensation potentials of the executive management team.

The strategy map then defines the unique customer value propositions with which the enterprise wishes to differentiate its products and services in order to achieve the strategic financial objectives. The map will show specifically how each value proposition may contribute to these objectives. This is called the customer perspective. The uniqueness of the customer value propositions will strongly impact the enterprise's competitive positioning in the market. It can only be defined with an in-depth understanding of both the enterprise's customers and the competitors' offerings. It should seek to not only satisfy current customer base (as part of customer retention strategy) but also the needs of the competitors' customers and new customers entering the market (customer acquisition strategy). This is an extremely critical strategy decision as it will drive the shape of the enterprise's business models in the internal process perspective as well as the enterprise resource allocation strategy for the learning and growth perspective.

Next, the internal process perspective will define the core processes that the enterprise must excel in so as to deliver the unique customer value propositions defined in the customer perspective. There are four core processes typically found in most enterprises: operation management, customer management, innovation management, and regulatory management. Each of these must be analyzed to determine the core competencies to differentiate the enterprise from its competitors.

Finally, to achieve the strategic objectives and the attendant customer and internal process perspectives, the enterprise must decide what skills and core competences it must possess and how the human capital should be organized to be effective, and what information capital is required to execute on the objectives of the customer and internal process perspectives.

Chapter XII will describe a leading Asia Pacific electricity utility company's IT strategy development as a case example to illustrate the strategy map methodology.

Corporate Strategy and the Financial Perspective

The methods for creating a corporate strategy are well described in many papers and books (Hamel & Prahabad, 1994; Porter, 1985). All these methods set out to help enterprises to *invent* the future and define and develop a new growth platform which will leverage the enterprise's competitive advantage to create a step change in the enterprise's financial performance. This requires the enterprise to be able to perform in-depth industry and market analyses and customer insights to postulate potential future industry and market scenarios and changing customer needs. Johnston and Bate (2003) call this process of inventing a new growth platform to compete for market supremacy in the future "*strategy innovation.*" According to Johnston and Bate (2003), strategy innovation is centered on:

- **Creativity:** Instead of using an analytical quantitative process based on historical data, strategy innovation uses market, and customer insights to imagine what future market scenarios are possible in order to conceive possible new business opportunities;
- **Market-centric process:** Instead of being company-internal focused, strategy innovation is market-external focused to find the business opportunities that will add value to both the customers and the company;
- **Heuristic discovery process:** As the future market dynamics are unpredictable and will evolve nonlinearly, the future business opportunities will be "discovered" through heuristic acquisition of future customer and market insights. Thus, strategy innovation relies on understanding the potential future scenarios to identify the "new values" to be created. It starts from the "future" and works "backwards" to today to determine what key milestones and resources are necessary to achieve to get "there." Strategy innovation uses what Johnston and Bate call a "future-pulled" resource allocation process.

Johnston and Bate (2003) argue that strategy innovation applies analytical quantitative process to strategic planning only after the future new business opportunities have been clearly articulated from a customer value proposition standpoint. From this point, the traditional strategic planning process will be conducted, in which the business opportunities will be evaluated commercially and prioritized. A balanced portfolio of strategic objectives comprising the longer term step-change growth objectives based on the new business opportunities and shorter term incremental growth objectives based on today's business model and opportunities. The balanced portfolio of objectives will define the financial perspective in the strategy map.

We will describe a best practice case example of a business-aligned Asia Pacific regional IT strategy in Chapter XII to illustrate how the strategy map and other strategy concepts and principles described in this chapter and the rest of the book are applied in the real world. The strategy map for the corporation will also be produced.

SUMMARY

IT managers need to recognize several critical conditions or factors for strategic alignment success, namely, shared method for business and IT strategic planning, process for stakeholder participation (shared domain knowledge between business and IT), and program management implementation to deliver stated benefits, top management involvement and support, business direction, business before technology, and communication and coordination (Earl, 1993; Reich & Benbasat, 2000). Strategic alignment has two dimensions: strategic fit of internal intangible assets with externally customer-focused strategy, and functional integration between business and IT domains (Henderson & Venkatraman, 1993). Strategic alignment is a process of continuous adaptation due to changing external market and technology environments. A nonlinear adaptation using complex theory model is necessary to account for the co-evolution (Benbya & McKelvery, 2006). IT strategic alignment with a cost-reduction strategy is more able to deliver immediate tangible benefits to firms than a revenue-growth strategy; and profitability is shown to be higher when both business and IT strategies are rated high (Oh & Pinsonneault, 2007). An organization's strategic alignment maturity can be assessed by six criteria (Luftman et al., 2004): communication, competency/value measurement, governance, partnership, scope and architecture, and skills. The model is useful for assessing strategic alignment in each of the previously mentioned four phases of the strategic management life cycle.

The successful execution of IT strategy—both the implementation of the resulting strategic programs and the support and maintenance of the evolving enterprise IT environment—depends on IT strategic resources, especially IT people. Moreover, business performance and differentiation is determined by the firm's ability to configure internal and external strategic resources and capabilities, including IT resources and capabilities. According to resource-based theory of the firm, a unique combination of IT resources by themselves, or more likely, with other enterprise resources, which create significant value and are costly to imitate, will offer firm sustainable competitive advantage. In particular, six attributes of IT resources must be managed effectively in order to obtain competitive advantage: valuable, rare, exploitable, inimitable, nonsubstitutable, combinable, and immobile. Further, embedding IT within areas of the firm's core competency makes IT assets inimitable (Richardson & Lertwongsatien, 2005). This is explained by the difficulty for rivals to create similar bundles of complementary IT and organizational assets and, at the same time, understand the contributions of IT assets to firm performance.

Global IT management needs to balance the business needs of global (corporate) and local (business unit) organizations. This can be achieved by coordinating global IT functions (strategy, architecture, standards, and control) with local IT functions (local planning, integration of new applications, and operating the infrastructure and applications) in line with corporate strategy (Barton, 2003). Group CIO and IT leadership team need to effectively manage the natural tension arisen from three forces shaping global IT management: pooling of IT services, outsourcing, and dispersion to business (Barton, 2003).

The critical success factor is an effective IT governance to ensure business–IT alignment globally and locally.

Kaplan and Norton's (2004) strategy map accounts for Henderson and Venkatraman's (1993) strategic fit and functional integration dimensions in a series of cause–effect traceable relationships. Strategy map is an instructive tool for demonstrating strategic alignment.

Case examples of IT strategy development and implementation experiences of two Australian companies, a leading bank (Bushell, 2003) and a leading retailer (Mills, 2005a–d; Woodhead, 2006–2008), have been used to exemplify a practical application of basic concepts of business–IT alignment and the four-stage IT strategy management process. The retailer example highlights the business outcomes of a strategy-execution journey (reported over 3-year duration) of IT-enabled strategic business transformation, which results in contribution of multibillion dollars of IT business value to the company's bottom line and gives it the distinct competitive advantage. A more comprehensive case study of an Asia Pacific regional corporation to illustrate the practical application of the strategy concepts and principles described in this book, especially strategy maps, will be described in Chapter XII.

REFERENCES

Aspray, W., Mayadas, F., & Vardi, M. Y. (Eds.). (2006). *Globalization and offshoring of software: A report of the ACM Job Migration Task Force.* ACM.

Avison, D., Jones, J., Powell, P., & Wilson, D. (2004). Using and validating the strategic alignment model. *Journal of Strategic Information Systems, 13*, 223-246.

Barton, R. (2003). *Global IT management: A practical approach.* Chichester, UK: John Wiley & Sons.

Benbya, H., & McKelvery, B. (2006). Using coevolutionary and complexity theories to improve IS alignment: A multi-level approach. *Journal of Information Technology,* 284-298.

Boehm, B. (1988). A spiral method of software development and enhancement. *IEEE Computer, 21*(5), 61-72.

Broadbent, M., & Kitzis, E. (2005). *The new CIO leader: Setting the agenda and delivering results.* Boston: Harvard Business School Press.

Bushell, S. (2003, April). From here to maturity. *CIO Magazine* (Australia). Retrieved August 15, 2008, from www.cio.com.au

CBA. (2005, January 26). *Commonwealth Bank Shareletter.*

Chan, Y. (2002, June). Why haven't we mastered alignment? The importance of the informal organizational structure. *MIS Quarterly Executive, 1*(2), 97-112.

Das, S., Zahr, S., & Warkentin, M. (1991). Integrating the content and process of strategic MIS planning with competitive strategy. *Decision Sciences, 22*(5), 953-984.

Earl, M. (1993, March). Experiences in strategic information systems planning. *MIS Quarterly.*

Ferratt, T. W., Agarwal, R., Brown, C. V., & Moore, J. E. (2005). IT human resource management configurations and IT turnover: Theoretical synthesis and empirical analysis. *Information Systems*

Research, 16(3), 237-255.

Gartner. (2007, January). *Creating enterprise leverage: The 2007 CIO agenda.* Gartner EXP Premier.

Hamel, G., & Prahalad, C. K. (1994, July-August). Competing for the future. *Harvard Business Review*, pp. 122-128.

Henderson, J. C., & Venkeraman, N. (1993). Strategic alignment: Leveraging information technology for transforming organizations. *IBM Systems Journal, 32*(1).

ITGI. (2006). Enterprise value: Governance of IT investments: The Val IT Framework. Author.

Jeffery, M., & Leliveld, I. (2004, Spring). Best practices in IT portfolio management. *MIT Sloan Management Review, 45*(3), 41-49.

Johnston & Bate. (2003). *The power of strategy innovation: A new way of linking creativity and strategic planning to discover great business opportunities.* AMACOM Books.

Kaplan, R. S., & Norton, D. P. (2004). *Strategy maps.* Boston: Harvard Business School Press.

Luftman, J. (2000, December). Addressing business: IT alignment maturity. *Communications of the Association for Information Systems.*

Luftman, J., Bullen, C., Liao, D., Nash, E., & Neumann, C. (2004). *Managing the information technology resource: Leadership in the Information Age* (international ed.). Pearson Education.

Maizlish, B., & Handler, R. (2005). *IT portfolio management step-by-step: Unlocking the business value of technology.* John Wiley & Sons.

McKinnon, R. (2003, April). Enabling business strategy with IT capabilities. *CIO Magazine* (Australia), pp. 42-45.

Melville, N., Kraemer, K., & Gurbaxani, V. (2004, June). Review: Information technology and organizational performance: An integrative model of IT business value. *MIS Quarterly, 28*(2), 283-322.

Mills, K. (2005a, March 1). Woolies saving on chain revamp. *The Australian.* Retrieved August 15, 2008, from www.theaustralianit.news.com.au

Mills, K. (2005b, May 10). $1 billion attack on retailer's handling costs. *The Australian.* Retrieved August 15, 2008, from www.theaustralianit.news.com.au

Mills, K. (2005c, May 5). IT beats moving stock: Woolies. *The Australian.* Retrieved August 15, 2008, from www.theaustralianit.news.com.au

Mills, K. (2005d, July 19). Woolies in no hurry on RFID. *The Australian.* Retrieved August 15, 2008, from www.theaustralianit.news.com.au

Oh, W., & Pinosonneault, A. (2007, June). On the assessment of the strategic value of information technologies: Conceptual and analytical approaches. *MIS Quaterly, 31*(2), 239-295.

Porter, M. E. (1985). *Competitive strategy.* New York: The Free Press.

Ravichandran, T., & Lertwongsatien, C. (2005). Effect of information systems resources and capabilities on firm performance: A resource-based perspective. *Journal of Management Information Systems, 21*(4), 237-276.

Reich, B., & Benbasat, I. (2000). Factor that influence the social dimension of alignment between business and IT objectives. *MIS Quarterly, 24*(1), 81-113.

Ross, J., Weill, P., & Robertson, D. (2006). *Enterprise architecture as strategy.* Harvard Business School Press.

Schubert, K. D. (2004). *CIO survival guide: The roles and responsibilities of the chief information officer.* Hoboken, NJ: John Wiley & Sons.

Tan, F. (2003). *Advanced topics in global information management* (vol. 2). Hershey, PA: Idea Group Publishing.

Thompson, A. A., & Strickland, A. J., III. (2003). *Strategic management concepts and cases* (13th ed.). McGraw-Hill, Irwin.

Treacy, M., & Wiersema, F. (1995). *The discipline of market leaders.* Cambridge, MA: Perseus Books.

Weill, P., & Aral, S. (2006, Winter). Generating premium returns on your IT investments. *MIT Sloan Management Review, 47*(2), 41-48.

Woodhead, B. (2006, August). A drop in mercury. *The Australian.* Retrieved August 15, 2008, from www.theaustralianit.news.com.au

Woodhead, B. (2007, August 28). Woolies expands Refresh. *The Australian.* Retrieved August 15, 2008, from www.theaustralianit.news.com.au

Woodhead, B. (2008, February 26). Supply chain drives Woolies. *The Australian.* Retrieved August 15, 2008, from www.theaustralianit.news.com.au

ENDNOTES

1. ITIL (IT Infrastructure Library) defines a set best practices for IT service management (www.itgovernance.co.uk). ITIL is a British standard which is being processed by the International Organization for Standardization (ISO) to become an international ISO standard.
2. We discuss in detail the role of knowledge management in a learning organization in Chapter XI of this book.
3. According to Oh and Pinsonneault (2007), the resource-based perspective argues that because IT is a strategic resource, the long-term sustainable competitive advantage of a firm can be achieved by acquiring IT resource bundles that are firm-specific, valuable, unique, inimitable, and not substitutable.
4. Jerry Luftman. Assessing business–IT alignment maturity (article 14). *Communications of AIS, 4.*
5. The new IT capabilities are derived by mapping each business strategic imperative to a corresponding new IT strategic capability. Examples of this mapping are described as an illustration in the Strategy Direction section.
6. CoBIT (control objectives for information and related technology) is a governance framework defined by the IT Governance Institute.
7. The weekly technology section of *The Australian*, a national daily newspaper in Australia.

Chapter VI
Enterprise and Technology Architectures

INTRODUCTION

The role of integrated enterprise architecture in IT strategy and strategic alignment is explained in Chapter V. This chapter describes in detail the principles and methods for developing a business-aligned enterprise architecture that will define the roadmap to attain the future state of the enterprise envisioned by the business strategy and guide the IT investment portfolio necessary for the state change.

Enterprise architecture can be understood from the terms enterprise, architecture, and architecture framework defined by the Open Group Architecture Framework (TOGAF, 2007):

Enterprise is defined as any collection of organizations that has a common set of goals and/or a single bottom line.

Architecture is defined as a formal description of an information system, organized in a way that supports reasoning about the structural properties of the system. It defines the components or building blocks that make up the overall information system and provides a plan from which products can be procured, and systems developed, that will work together to implement the overall system.

Architecture framework is a tool for assisting in the production of organization-specific architectures. An architecture framework consists of a Technical Reference Model, a method for architecture development, and a list of component standards, specifications, products, and their interrelationships, which can be used to build up architectures. Architecture framework will speed up and simplify architecture development.

Enterprise architecture is a formal description of the enterprise business context, including the business strategy and the supporting information system architecture which aligns with the business context. Enterprise architecture therefore defines a model of the fundamental technology and process structure of a business-aligned IT strategy. Enterprise architecture allows business to devise solutions to achieve cost efficiency and business innovation. It provides the strategic context for the evolution of the information system in response to changing market and business needs (TOGAF, 2007).

A generic architecture framework is needed to help firms define the firm-specific enterprise architecture. An architecture framework is critical to the definition of business and IT strategies. This is because it provides structure and discipline and provides a vehicle for communication of the strategic imperatives in an integrative and holistic manner, functionally analogous to the working of a real-life enterprise. It serves as a *translator and integrator* of critical business and IT concepts by which business and IT executives will be able to articulate the congruence of business and IT strategies[1] and how, at a high level, IT will implement that strategy. This is one of the first tasks of strategic alignment. In particular, as a communication tool, the architecture framework enables the enterprise business and IT executives to exchange their understanding of the respective strategies in a high level graphically and multidimensionally integrative way, combining business and technology concepts fundamental to defining the unique way in which the enterprise seeks to operate in the crowded marketplace. It will remove any potential misunderstanding that could occur if each executive were to simply use the one-dimensional English language descriptions of business and IT strategies. This business-IT dialog using the architecture framework will lead to an agreement on the value and benefits of the enterprise architecture (EA) because the EA is a manifestation of the business/IT strategies (eTOM, 2005; James, Handler, Lapkin, & Gall, 2005; OMG, 2003; POSIX, 2000; RM-ODP, 1997; Ross et al., 2006; Spewak, 1992; TOGAF, 2007; Zachman, 1987).

The task of specifying enterprise architecture can often be complex and confusing. This is because it must take into account a wide range of perspectives from the business consideration for customers, suppliers, partners, organizational, regulatory, and geographical requirements, on one hand, to the IT consideration for the multiplicity of rapidly evolving technology options available for the architecture solution, on the other hand. The architecture framework, which defines the representations of important business and IT terms into basic architecture concepts, is helpful in ensuring that the stakeholders have a common definition of the purpose, scope, content, and *shape* of the architecture in line with the business/IT strategies (James et al., 2005; Spewak, 1992; TOGAF, 2007). By using a common architecture framework tool, the business and IT executives together can position the business scope and technology solution options conceptually relative to one another. The framework also allows architecture complexity to be decomposed and simplified into manageable and easy-to-understand domains and perspectives (James et al., 2005; Spewak, 1992; TOGAF, 2007). Also, by using a common conceptual tool, business and IT will improve the communication competency, a key success factor of strategic alignment (Luftman, 2004). It also enforces professional discipline (in business and IT) in architecture specification and implementation as they must be done in a systematic methodical way in accordance with technically consistent sets of architecture principles and guidance.

The architecture principles will be incorporated as part of the IT governance to ensure IT projects will develop solutions in compliance with the architecture framework. Thus, EA definition and implementation will ensure the resultant information systems will deliver the expected business values articulated in the business strategy.

Today, there exist many variant, though similar and often confusing, definitions of enterprise architecture. They range from a largely technical-oriented IT architecture definition to a largely business-oriented business architecture definition. From practice experience, enterprise architecture is most practical as part of the IT systems development methodology when it contains a well-balanced definition of both the firm's business model perspective (from the standpoint of business architecture) and the corresponding technical or technology architectural perspectives that align with the business model perspective. This practice-based architecture model is covered well in the literature. This chapter reviews the basic principles of enterprise and IT architectures and describes several selected well-known architectural frameworks with the emphasis on explaining how enterprise architecture can be put into good practice.

Enterprise architecture is defined as comprising several interrelated perspectives, namely, business architecture, information architecture, application architecture, and technology (or infrastructure) architecture (James et al., 2005; RM-ODP, 1997; Spewak, 1992; TOGAF, 2007). Business architecture translates the overarching business strategy, its underlying business model, and the core business processes that underpin the business model; information architecture defines the information framework operated on by the business processes to operationalize the business architecture; application architecture defines the business functional systems of the enterprise; they interact with each other in accordance with the predefined business processes consuming and producing business information in accordance with the information architecture; and finally the technology infrastructure defines the underlying software and hardware systems through which the business applications are connected and interoperated (James et al., 2005; RM-ODP, 1997; Spewak, 1992; TOGAF, 2007).

This chapter reviews several architecture frameworks that have been used widely. As an illustration of "architecture in practice," we also describe the Gartner enterprise architecture framework (James et al., 2005) since it is commonly used by practitioners in industry.

ENTERPRISE ARCHITECTURE PRINCIPLES

The earliest significant work related to enterprise architecture is reported by Zachman (1987). With the increasing complexity of information systems deployed to support and differentiate business enterprises, Zachman (1987) calls for the need of an architecture framework to manage the complexity and prevent the business from "*dis*integrating." Zachman's focus is on information systems (IS) architecture, not business or IT strategy or strategic planning. He argues that the information system architecture is the result of business and IT strategies and strategic plan. Indeed, the IS architecture must manifest the imperatives of the business and IT strategies. In particular, Zachman (1987) states that the IS architecture framework clearly articulates *a set of perspectives* (levels of abstraction) important to the *three key* (different) *stakeholders* of the information systems: the business (system *owner*) (the business scope and business model); the system *designer* (the system model); and the system "*builder*" (the technology model)—see Figure 6.1.

Figure 6.1. Zachman framework (from www.zifa.com)

	Data	Function	Network	People	Time	Motivation
Scope	Ballpark perspective					
Business Model	Business perspective					
System Model	Designer perspective					
Technology Model	Builder perspective					
Detailed Representation						
Functioning Enterprise						

At the top level abstraction, Zachman (1987) denotes the *ballpark* perspective of the business. This perspective defines the scope and objectives of the information systems as derived from the business and IT strategies. It comprises the list of "things" critical to the business and to the operation of the business such as product, part, supplier, customer, employee, organization unit, and so forth.

At the second level, the *business* perspective defines what the business does and how it must operate to conduct the business. It reflects a model of the business or business description, how the "things" will relate to (and work with) one another to operate the business.

In the first two levels, the architecture descriptions are intentionally kept at a high level. Their main purpose is to gain a common understanding between business and IT as to the business model and strategies IS must fulfill for business success.

At the third level, the *designer* perspective focuses on the logical model (designer view) of how the information systems will support the operation of the business; it produces a design model of the information systems (or IS description), which is an approximation (subject to modeling limitations) of what the business wants. It is clearly important to validate the "*closeness*" of the approximation (or alignment). Otherwise, chaos will ensue and business "disintegration" will result.

At the fourth level, the *builder* perspective defines the technology model of how the logical design will be implemented. As Zachman calls it, the model will be subject to the "laws of nature" and "technology constraints."

The fifth level, the *out-of-context* perspective, defines the detailed technical specifications of the information systems. This is followed by the machine language representation, level 6, which defines the object code, to realize (and put into production) the end-product which is the information system.

The Zachman principles for decomposition, particularly the first *four perspectives (contextual, conceptual, logical, and physical)*, have been used as a foundation, albeit with varying interpretations, by all subsequently developed enterprise architecture frameworks. Zachman has reserved the logical and physical levels to the design and implementation phases of a system development life cycle. Thus, the bottom four levels (perspectives) of the Zachman framework could be considered to belong in the system development life cycle. The development life cycle, however, must follow and comply with the enterprise architecture framework.

In the original framework, Zachman (1987) identifies three *key dimensions* of information systems that business and IT personnel will need to define and design to enable and support the operation of the desired business model and strategy: *data, function (or process),* and *network.* To fully define and design the desired information systems, the Zachman framework applies the six levels (perspectives) on each of these three dimensions. Thus, the Zachman framework consists of a six-by-three matrix of architectural cells, each addressing a specific concern of the various stakeholders (see Figure 6.1). The process of IS architecture specification, planning, and implementation requires the enterprise architects and planner to clearly analyze and specify the intention for each of the 18 cells. However, Zachman (1987) originally only defines the architecture framework and does not prescribe the method to fill these cells. Subsequently, Zachman (1993) further extends the three dimensions (data, function, network) to add three more: people, time, and motivation (see www.zifa.com). This makes the Zachman framework extremely comprehensive with a six-by-six matrix (36 cells). To fully specify, all 36 cells may be prohibitively costly (in terms of time), thus practitioners are likely to choose to concentrate architecture and implementation efforts on those cells deemed critical to the company's business operation.

SPEWAK ENTERPRISE ARCHITECTURE PLANNING (EAP) METHODOLOGY

Spewak's book (1992) uses and complements the 1987 Zachman framework by developing the methodology for enterprise architecture planning (EAP). In particular, Spewak (1992) focuses on the top two levels of the Zachman framework. According to Spewak, the top two levels of the Zachman framework are truly concerned with what the enterprise architecture is, whereas the bottom four are more concerned with the design, development, and implementation (production) phases of the enterprise architecture planning.

The Spewak (1992) EAP methodology is for the purpose of *defining (not designing)* the enterprise architecture for the top two perspectives of business scope/objectives and business model. In short, EAP defines "*how to define enterprise architecture and plan for its implementation*" for the top two levels of the Zachman framework.

Spewak (1992) names the top two levels of the data column, *data architecture*, the function or process column, *application architecture*, and the network column, *technology architecture*. The design and implementation of these architectures occur in the bottom four levels. As in the Zachman framework, Spewak (1992) EAP is strongly *data-driven* and *business-driven.* This is because information is the basis of business operation and differentiation. Information quality (including definition standard, accuracy, accessibility, integrity, and currency) therefore is of paramount importance to business. The information model and information use by business to run the business must be defined first, derived from the business strategy, scope, and model. This means the enterprise architecture definition must follow a strict sequence of data architecture first, and then the application architecture will be defined from the data architecture and the technology architecture from the application architecture. This will ensure architecture alignment among each other and with the business—a critical requirement for strategic alignment.

Figure 6.2. Spewak EAP methodology (Spewak, 1992, p. 13)

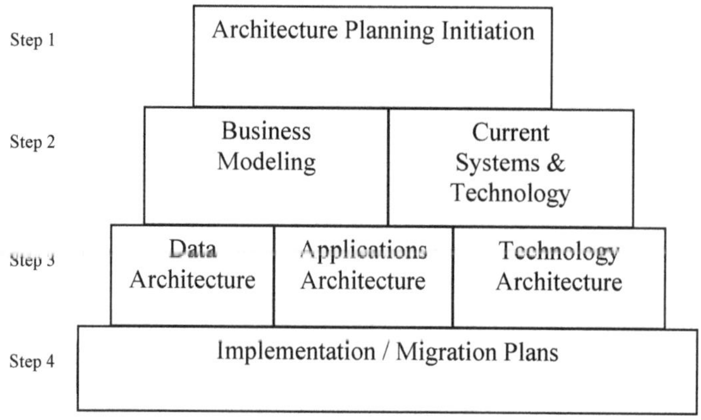

Spewak (1992) strongly believes that there are two critical success factors of enterprise architecture and strategic planning: *executive management commitment* and *strong project leadership skills.* The Spewak EAP as described in the book strongly reflects this view. The Spewak EAP is a four-step process (Figure 6.2):

- Step 1 is the architecture planning initiation phase - this is concerned with getting the management buy-in of the scope, objectives, roles and responsibilities, methodology to be adopted, project plan, and resource requirements.
- Step 2 assesses the current IS environment - this involves modeling of today's business and stock-take of current systems and technology in use within the company. Business modeling defines the organizational model and the preliminary functional business model such as the business activities, processes, and information used. The current systems and technology are a baseline inventory of IS currently in the enterprise captured in an *information resource catalog.*
- Step 3 defines the architecture vision for the future using the business vision and strategy as a basis - this consists of the *target* data architecture, application architecture, and technology architecture (in that order). Data architecture defines business entities, entity-relationship diagrams, and entity to function matrices, all of which are required to support the target business model and activities. Application architecture defines conceptual applications needed to support the business functions and information processing to make the business model effective. Technology architecture defines the distribution of the data and applications and the technology platforms (conceptual not product-specific) required to provide the technology infrastructure to run the applications to support the business operational model.
- Step 4 defines the target architecture implementation/migration plans - the implementation plan defines the sequence of applications to be implemented, the migration plan, costs and benefits, and recommendations. This is part of the general portfolio and program management discipline as governed by the IT governance (in which the architecture principles will be enforced among others). Spewak (1992) also includes the planning conclusion phase as a formal closure of the planning activities in which

a final report will document the "EAP Planning Books," including the committed funds and resources for the migration plan.

Typically, IS strategic plans once approved may undergo a transition period before the first strategic plan starts. Spewak (1992) includes a last project phase called, *Transition to Implementation*, in the EAP methodology. Moving from architecture planning (the top two levels of the Zachman framework) to design and implementation of the architectures requires transition or change management. This transition phase defines the steps and tasks that need to be done before the first strategic project kicks off, tasks including recruitment, training, policies, and standards to be followed.

In summary, Spewak (1992) EAP provides a systematic and methodical approach to defining the blueprint for data, application, and technology architectures aligned with business vision and strategy. Based on Spewak's decades of experience, EAP is very practical and extensive in prescribing the steps, tasks, and templates required to produce a sound IS enterprise architecture plan. Spewak stresses the importance of IS and business professionals doing the planning rather than getting bogged down by semantic debates of conceptual terminology or framework "contest." Architecture planning is an iterative discovery process; Spewak places high importance in pragmatism over detailed accuracy, using the 80/20 rule. Successful EAP practice requires strong people, leadership, and execution skills, as well as a culture of continuous organizational learning and improvement.

CARBONE ENTERPRISE ARCHITECTURE TOOLKIT

Carbone (2004) refers enterprise architecture as the plan for IT—"how all parts (data, functions, technology, people) of the IT infrastructure need to behave to support the enterprise needs and goals." Carbone defines the enterprise architecture toolkit comprising of three frameworks:

- **Business framework:** It provides a roadmap for collecting and analyzing enterprise business needs and goals that will drive architecture;
- **IT framework:** It provides a roadmap for creating the outputs of IT architecture and their relationships that will enable business goals;
- **Implementation framework:** It provides the best practices for implementing the architecture that supports the business goals.

According to Carbone (2004), the EA toolkit principally models the first three levels or rows (scope, business model, and system model) and addresses the data, function, network/technology, people, time, and motivation columns of the Zachman framework. The business framework is roughly aligned to Zachman's first (scope) row, and the IT architecture framework is roughly aligned with the second (business model) and third (system model) rows.

The Carbone (2004) EA toolkit adds value to the Zachman framework by defining how the three frameworks can be integrated to explicitly "link" the outputs of the three toolkit frameworks to assure alignment of the resulting IT plans to the strategic business goals and needs. From practice experience, Carbone (2004, p. 12) has distilled six key success factors for EA:

- A clear understanding of the future state vs. current state of the business;
- A clear architecture scope with *simple* and *effective* models (to maximize understanding and diligent application by stakeholders);
- A clear mapping of the architecture into a small set of well-scoped, business-oriented projects (to realize the architecture into business operations);
- Metrics (business-aligned) are defined and tracked for each project (to ensure the expected business values are delivered);
- Marketing of (the benefits) of the architecture (to maximize buy-in by all stakeholders);
- Processes (and governance) that support the architecture development and implementation (to instill professional discipline into EA practice and integrate it as part of IT and corporate governance).

Business Framework

The business framework captures and analyzes the current and future (target) states of the business. Carbone (2004) prescribes the following key indicators for analyzing the current state of a business:

- Stress points/risks - "the longer term major factors that may cause extreme change and require a proactive stance"
- Strengths and weaknesses
- Challenges (usually short-term situations to be overcome)
- Environmental factors
- Growth/cost containment opportunities

"The business target state describes the positive characteristics of the desired future state of the business." It is determined by the mission, strategy, and goals of the enterprise, on one hand, and by the "solutions" to the current state "problems" analyzed by the above key indicators, on the other (Carbone, 2004). The gap analysis between the target and current states and the business opportunities defined by the target business state will drive the definition of the toolkit's IT framework.

IT Framework

The EA toolkit IT framework is defined as a five-by-five matrix of scope of work for the enterprise architecture—five rows comprising data (about the business), function (business operation), platform (i.e., technology), and people (functional users)/process; and five columns comprising principles, models, inventory, and standards, as shown in Figure 6.3. "The framework provides a roadmap for constructing related IT infrastructure outputs based on the business target state opportunities." Each component (cell in Figure 6.3) of the IT outputs is related to one another and traceable to the target business state (Carbone, 2004).

Figure 6.3. The enterprise architecture toolkit IT framework (Carbone, 2004, p. 47)

	Principles	Models	Inventory	Standards
Data				
Function				
Platform				
People/ Process				

Principles

Carbone (2004) defines principles as "representing the abstraction of the business target state to form guidelines for IT decision making." They translate the business target statement to a statement of intent for IT. Principles are the basic tenets regarded as universally true in the company. They impose business constraints on the models and standards developed for the enterprise architecture. For example, the data principle might mandate that data be modeled as "a *single* source of truth"; the function principle might be that "functions be built or bought as *reusable* components"; the platform principle might be that "vendor *service* is as important as product capability" (p. 48).

Models

Carbone (2004) defines the architecture model as "the graphical representation of the *business view* of data, functions, technology, people, and the relationships and/or interactions between them." A model consists of a *context* and *standards* for modeling. The context defines the audience, scope, time horizon, environment,[2] and documentation requirements of the architecture model. Modeling standards are a set of ground rules to be followed (Carbone, 2004): (1) agree on a set of standard components to be included in the architecture, (2) use a standard representation scheme, (3) set a scope (of component modeling), (4) determine the level of detail (audience dependent), (5) define the state to be modeled (current, interim, or target), (6) define the environment (execution, development, or operations) to be modeled (pp. 51-82).

IT Inventory

Carbone (2004, p. 83) defines IT inventory as the listing of all the key IT resources of the organization—data, applications, platform/technology, people assets, and their key attributes. Carbone (2004) recommends applying the same ground rules for models to guiding the IT inventory documentation.

Standards

The EA toolkit framework defines standards as the last and one of the most detailed tasks for architecture development. Carbone (2004) defines a standard as the agreed-to or corporate set of key data entities, functions, technologies, or processes—their names, definition, or description (p. 91). Standards are set in accordance to the following ground rules: "(1) establish ownership, (2) define the state, (3) define the environment, and (4) define the level of detail" (p. 92).

Implementation Framework

The implementation framework is concerned with the business realization of the enterprise architecture. It consists of the following components (Carbone, 2004):

- **Projects:** Identify candidate projects from the architecture, select/prioritize key projects based on business priorities, and narrow the scope of selected projects—that is, project portfolio management (p. 107).
- **Metrics:** For assessing the effectiveness and value of architecture. From a project's perspective, it measures the business value of the project, the extent to which the project objectives are met, and the extent to which the project complies with the architecture (p. 129).
- **Buy-in:** Communications and change management plans to win active support (buy-in) and commitments from executives and stakeholders of the EA initiative.
- **Process:** Integration of the architecture process with corporate product and service development processes to ensure the architecture positively influences development. This requires: (a) sanctioned, repeatable architecture processes (and governance), (b) standardized, accessible architecture outputs, and (c) clear relationships with other IT processes (p. 149).
- **People:** Human resource policy and management plan to ensure architecture competency is developed, recognized, measured, and effectively deployed to positively add value (through effective delivery of architecture-compliant projects) to the enterprise (p. 159).

INDUSTRY AND INTERNATIONAL ARCHITECTURE FRAMEWORK STANDARDS

Several industry and international architecture framework standards have been published over the last decade or so. These include POSIX, IEEE, RM-ODP, OMG, and eTOM. While some of these standards may have begun their lives with stronger technical orientation due to the heritage of the standards bodies, they have since evolved during their development life cycle to incorporate varying degrees of business perspective. They all have relevance to enterprise architecture.

POSIX

The first technology-oriented architecture framework, POSIX was published by ISO (International Organization for Standardization) in 1996 (ISO/IEC TR14252). POSIX defines a three-level abstraction. The *conceptual* level of the architecture defines the high level functional model of the business (based on business strategy) to be supported by the systems architecture. The *logical* level defines the information and application services required to support the business functions. The *physical* level defines the implementation of the architecture by selecting specific technology products for the construction.

IEEE

In 2000, the Institute of Electrical and Electronics Engineers (IEEE) ratified the IEEE Standard 1471-2000 architecture framework standard. This framework is used for describing the architecture of software-intensive (information) systems in an enterprise. It is founded on the same basic principle of logical abstraction of the perspectives and concerns of the various stakeholders (of the enterprise information systems) into corresponding conceptual viewpoints which together constitute the IS architecture.

The Reference Model for Open Distributed Processing (RM-ODP)

RM-ODP is an ISO and ITU (International Telecommunication Union) architecture framework standard, published in 1997, for the creation of an information system architecture that supports applications distribution, networking, interoperability, and portability within an enterprise and between enterprises. RM-ODP defines the architecture of open distributed enterprise systems in terms of viewpoints or abstract conceptual views of the enterprise systems. Viewpoints enable logical separation of concerns of the stakeholders of the enterprise systems. Each viewpoint defines the concerns, or architecture requirements, of the specific stakeholder (e.g., information analyst vs. system programmer) excluding the details of the other viewpoints (of other stakeholders). Each viewpoint is a description of the different perspectives of the same thing, so while there is clear logical separation, each viewpoint description must be *consistent* with other viewpoint descriptions. RM-ODP defines five viewpoints for the specification of enterprise architecture, namely (ITU-T X.901/ISO/IEC 10746-1, 1997):

- **Enterprise viewpoint:** Enterprise viewpoint is concerned with the business activities of the enterprise system. It defines the purpose, scope, and policies of the system. Enterprise viewpoint therefore defines the context and overall environment within which the enterprise system will be built, including the constraints and obligations that must apply in all other viewpoints.
- **Information viewpoint:** Information viewpoint specifies the information that needs to be stored and processed in the system to perform the business activities. It uses schemata to specify the ways that information may be transformed in performing the business activities. The information viewpoint must conform to the policies of the enterprise viewpoint. For example, some roles, activities, and behaviors identified

in the enterprise viewpoint will have correspondences in the schema definitions in the information viewpoint.

- **Computational viewpoint:** Computational viewpoint provides a decomposition of the enterprise system into objects that interact at standard interfaces. These objects define the constructs by which the system may be partitioned for distribution. An object encapsulates data and processing, and offers interfaces for interactions with other objects. The computational viewpoint must also comply with the policies of the enterprise viewpoint.
- **Engineering viewpoint:** Engineering viewpoint is concerned with the deployment aspects of the system. Distribution mechanisms are explicitly specified in the engineering viewpoint, showing how distributed objects can interact with one another. The engineering viewpoint must also comply with the policies of the enterprise viewpoint.
- **Technology viewpoint:** Technology viewpoint details specific technologies, both hardware and software, which will be used to implement the system. As technologies change constantly, the other four viewpoints must be specified to be as independent from the technology viewpoint as possible.

A viewpoint language is used to develop each viewpoint specification. For example, an enterprise language is used to specify the enterprise viewpoint. Though viewpoints can be related to one another, they are not layered. The viewpoint specifications provide a means for system architects to handle the design complexity of distributed systems. Viewpoints allow common ODP services to be provided that make the underlying distribution networks transparent to the cooperating distributed applications. ODP functions can be designed and implemented to provide a range of transparencies as common services such as access, location, relocation, and transaction transparencies. ODP services can be accessed by any users from anywhere in the network as long as they have the interface contract published by the ODP service provider.

RM-ODP serves as a framework for developing other ODP standards. For example, X.950 ODP Trading Function, a kind of Yellow Pages service, has been standardized that records service offers and matches requests for advertised services.

The OMG Model Driven Architecture

The Object Management Group (OMG) Model Driven Architecture (MDA) aims to enable software portability, interoperability, and reusability through architectural separation of concerns (OMG, 2003). It provides an approach for, and enables tools to be provided for (OMG, 2003):

- Specifying a system independently of the platform that supports it;
- Specifying platforms—a platform (e.g., CORBA) is defined as a set of subsystems and technologies that provide a coherent set of functionality through interfaces;
- Choosing a particular platform for the system; and
- Transforming the system specification into one for a particular platform.

MDA is an approach for system development. It provides a means for using models to direct (hence the name model-driven) the software life cycle of understanding, design, construction, deployment, operation, maintenance, and modification of the software system. MDA prescribes what kinds of models to be used, how these models may be prepared, and what their relationships are. Similar to RM-ODP, MDA uses viewpoint as a technique for abstraction. MDA defined three viewpoints: a computation independent viewpoint, a platform independent viewpoint, and a platform specific viewpoint.

MDA standard specifications consist of five categories: (1) service specifications, (2) data model specifications, (3) language specifications, (4) mapping specifications, and (5) network protocol specifications.

Enhanced Telecom Operations Map (eTOM)

The eTOM business process framework (Telemanagement Forum, 2003) is a reference framework for categorizing all the business activities that a telecom service provider will use. It serves as a blueprint for standardizing and categorizing business activities (or process elements) needed to define a telecom service provider's enterprise process model —the model that specifies the service provider's requirements for the business and operations support systems. Telecom business activities are specified in the form of components of overall business processes that can be decomposed to a lower level of granularity progressively. The process components (or elements) can be positioned within a model to show organizational, functional, and other relationships. They can also be combined within process flows that define activity paths through the business. eTOM serves as a telco industry-standard reference model for specifying a service provider's internal process reengineering needs, partnerships, alliances, and general working agreements with other service providers (www.teleforum.org).

THE OPEN GROUP ENTERPRISE ARCHITECTURE FRAMEWORK

The Open Group Enterprise Architecture Framework (TOGAF) was originally designed for technology architecture (TOGAF, 2007). It traces its origin to the POSIX architecture framework, ISO/IEC TR14252 Guide to POSIX Open Systems Environment (1996). Developed by the Open Group's Architecture Forum, TOGAF is based on the U.S. Department of Defense (DoD) Technology Architecture Framework for Information Management (TAFIM), which in turn is based on the TR14252 POSIX standard. Prior to version 7, TOGAF was technically oriented. Since v.7, significant efforts have been expended to move TOGAF "up the value chain" to become business oriented to include business, information, and application architecture specifications. Current version 8.11 is well balanced in coverage which includes business, information, application, and technology viewpoints.

Like Spewak (1992), the TOGAF enterprise architecture is principally an architecture planning framework. TOGAF provides the methodology and recommends users, where appropriate, to adopt and adapt a well-known industry architecture framework to match their business requirements instead of inventing one from scratch.

According to the Open Group's Architecture Forum, the mission and purpose of TOGAF (2007) is as follows:

TOGAF is an architecture framework which includes a set of methods and tools for developing a broad range of different IT architectures. Its purpose is to enable IT users to design, evaluate, and build the right architecture for their organizations and reduce its costs of planning, designing, and implementing architectures based on open systems solutions. The key to TOGAF is the TOGAF Architecture Development Method (ADM) for defining business needs and developing an architecture that meets those needs, using elements of TOGAF and other assets available to the organization.

It is the Open Group's stated aim to make ADM an industry standard method, which is technology- and tool-independent, and can be used with other frameworks.

ADM is the core of TOGAF. It is the TOGAF method for enterprise architecture development. It integrates two other key elements of TOGAF and other publicly available architecture assets to meet the architecture needs of business and IT in the firm. The other two main parts of TOGAF are:

- **The Enterprise Continuum:** It provides the context for explaining the different types and scopes (or continuum) of the architecture artifacts and assets that exist at a given stage of architecture development or evolution. It serves as a framework for leveraging and reusing these assets, and other publicly available architecture assets, such as architecture descriptions, models, and patterns, to develop the enterprise architecture using ADM. The Enterprise Continuum in practice is the repository of the architecture assets which might be sourced externally as well as produced internally in the course of the enterprise architecture development. These assets are organized in categories in accordance with the framework defined for the repository. The purpose of the Enterprise Continuum is to maximize reuse of architecture assets to reduce the efforts and speed up the process of enterprise architecture development. The architecture development process is iterative and ongoing. The ADM will populate the Enterprise Continuum incrementally with specified architecture building blocks as the iterative process progresses.
- **The TOGAF Resource Base:** It includes a set of resources, such as guidelines, templates, and checklists, that are needed to support the ADM.

The ADM is iterative. For each iteration, the ADM defines the breadth and depth of the architecture scope and coverage, as well as the time-box allocated. It also defines the architecture assets (internal and industry) to be leveraged from the Enterprise Continuum.

The central element of the ADM is the architecture *requirements management* process. TOGAF stipulates that this process will ensure "requirements for enterprise architecture are identified, stored, and fed into and out of the relevant ADM phases." The architecture requirements management process is dynamic. It captures the initial architecture requirements and subsequent requirements changes as the architecture evolves with the business and technology trends. The ADM cycle consists of nine ADM phases (Figure 6.4):

1. **Preliminary phase:** Defines the purpose, scope, and stakeholders of the enterprise architecture and the architecture principles that will guide the architecture definition.
2. **Architecture vision phase:** Defines the key business requirements (including business principles, goals, and strategic drivers) for the architecture and constraints, and

Figure 6.4. TOGAF architecture development cycle (adapted from TOGAF, 2007, p. 20)

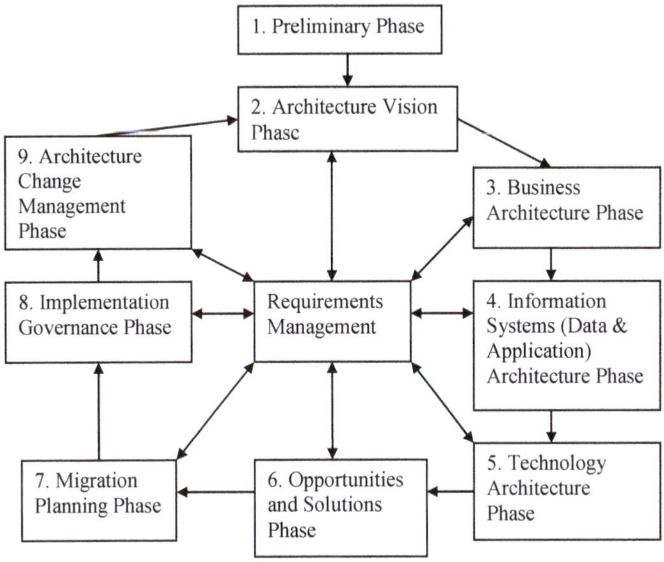

articulates the architecture vision (including business mission, vision, strategy, and goals) in response to the business requirements and constraints.

3. **Business architecture phase:** Defines the baseline business architecture, the target business architecture, and the gap analysis. The business architecture defines how the business strategy will be implemented by the business process model. Business architecture is a prerequisite knowledge for the definition of the other architecture domains (information, application, and technology).
4. **Information systems architectures phase:** Information systems architectures comprise the data and application architectures. This phase defines the baseline and target architectures for these two viewpoints to meet the business strategic requirement.
5. **Technology architecture phase:** Defines the baseline and target technology architecture to meet the business strategic requirements.
6. **Opportunities and solutions phase:** This phase evaluates and selects among the implementation options identified in the development of the various target architectures (for example, build vs. buy). It also identifies the strategic parameters for change. It partitions and sequences the top level work packages into projects or programs (including their costs/benefits and interdependencies) into timelines to be undertaken to migrate the current architecture to the target architecture.
7. **Migration planning phase:** This phase prioritizes and selects the work packages or programs and develops the migration plan for executing these work packages to attain the target architecture.
8. **Implementation governance phase:** This phase provides the architecture oversight of the migration implementation. It is part of the architecture governance process, which in turn is part of the IT governance.

9. **Architecture change management phase:** It establishes the procedures for managing change to the new architecture. Architecture change could be caused by a change in business or technology environments from the time the new architecture is defined. The change request could be a simplification change, incremental change, or re-architecting change. The former two are typically minor work requests and can be handled by change management techniques. However, re-architecting change is a major work request. It will put the architecture through the ADM cycle again starting from phase 2, the architecture vision phase.

TOGAF has defined a generic ADM to allow individual enterprises to adapt it to suit their specific purposes and needs. The adaptation required depends on the architecture maturity of the enterprise. For instance, for an enterprise without enterprise architecture, then it is prudent to start the ADM process from phase 1. On the other hand, if an enterprise architecture already exists, then the phases can be fast-tracked and their order may also be changed in order to expedite the re-architecture process in response to market changes. Further, a small to medium enterprise may wish to use a "cut-down" version of ADM to align with a lower level of architect resources available.

In summary, ADM is an architecture governance process. It ensures the correct methods are being applied in all phases of the cycle, and appropriate deliverables have been produced. Compliance with the ADM is fundamental to the governance of the architecture.

ROSS-WEILL-ROBERTSON MODEL

In their recent book, Ross et al. (2006) define enterprise architecture from a business standpoint; they regard that enterprise architecture is the business strategy. According to Ross et al., enterprise architecture is focused on describing the high-level business process and IT requirements of a company's *operating model* (business model). In particular, they define enterprise architecture as the *organizing logic* for business processes and IT infrastructure reflecting the integration and standardization requirements of the company's operating model. However, Ross et al. model the high-level abstraction only and do not deal with the details of the so-called IT architecture comprising the underlying process, information/data, application and infrastructure. In a sense, Ross et al. enterprise architecture model is very high level *integrative* overview of Spewak's (1992) and TOGAF's (2007) more detailed model comprising all the perspectives of business, process, information, applications, and infrastructure architectures on a page; it is a kind of *"Enterprise Architecture on a Page."* Its purpose is to serve as a communication and management tool for business and technology executives to ensure strategic alignment.

According to Ross et al. (2006), the first step towards defining enterprise architecture is for the executive management team to define and agree on what is the firm's operating model. They see enterprise architecture as the strategic management tool for implementing the firm's operating model. Thus to understand the Ross et al.'s model, it is necessary to first appreciate what an operating model for a firm is.

Ross et al. define an operating model as "*the necessary level of business process integration and standardization for delivering goods and services to customers.*" In essence, it is the firm's business model of how it will deliver value (for a price) to their customers—seen specifically from the business process standpoint. The operating model manifests the firm's strategy by accentuating the distinctive mechanism (process) by which the firm chooses to deliver its services to the customers. For example, eBay was conceived as an efficient, reliable, and safe online auction site for its clients. Its basic operating model is to serve as intermediary "match maker" for matching the "right" seller (merchant) of goods to the "prospective" buyers. The buyer and seller are responsible for the transaction for which eBay charges a small modest fee. This distinctive operating model is eBay's point of differentiation, and eBay strategy and enterprise architecture will focus on and accentuate this differentiating feature. The effective execution of the operating model through the enterprise architecture has allowed eBay to grow over the years to become a highly profitable corporation.

According to Ross et al. (2006), an operating model has two dimensions: business process *standardization* and *integration*. *Standardization* defines how a business process should be executed. It sets design constraints on the business process and its underlying system support which must comply with the stipulated standard. The business purpose of process standardization is to deliver companywide operating consistency, efficiency, and predictability to ensure consistently superior customer experience. While standardization improves efficiency, it can produce an undesirable side effect; it restricts local ability to innovate and adapt to the sometimes idiosyncratic requirement of local customers. *Integration* is concerned with integrating disparate core business processes and business units through *data sharing*. For example, by integrating the store's inventory level data of the front-end point-of-sales process with the supply chain process in a retail enterprise, it becomes possible for the retail to automatically replenish its shelf-space with minimal human intervention. This will improve customer service as it eliminates the "stock-out" phenomenon, which is one of the most frustrating experiences for (particularly the high value time-poor) shoppers of a fast-moving-goods retail store. *Integration* requires data standard. Enterprise integration requires enterprisewide data standards for all business and customer related information—semantically and syntactically. (This will require highly developed information architecture, to be described later.) It requires operational and data transparency through a high degree of coordination between multiple stakeholders and business owners of core processes. Where process integration is an operating model requirement, data transparency and coordination must be integral to the firm's IT (and hence process)

Figure 6.5. Four types of business operating model (adapted from Ross et al., 2006, p. 29, Figure 2-1)

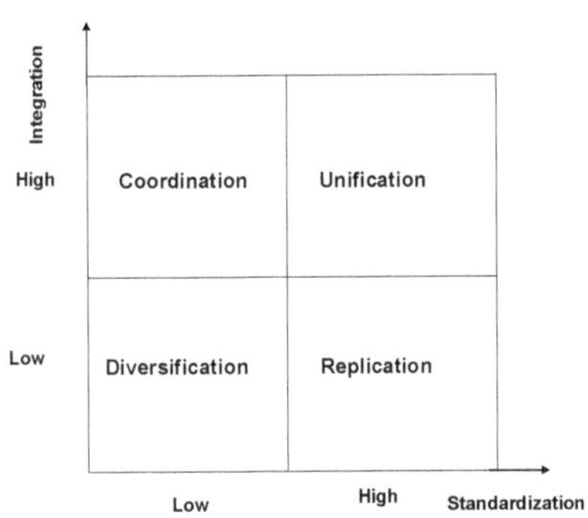

governance. These design constraints may be costly; they will ensure process efficiency and agility, which are the main reasons for a firm to emphasize this dimension.

Using business process integration[3] and business process standardization as two axes, Ross et al. (2006) define a two-by-two matrix of generic operating model characteristics found in most firms around the world. They call these four operating models as (see the four quadrants in Figure 6.5):

1. Diversification (low standardization, low integration)
2. Coordination (low standardization, high integration)
3. Replication (high standardization, low integration)
4. Unification (high standardization, high integration)

Diversification

Diversified companies typically have business units operating independently and autonomously as separate profit-and-loss "subsidiary" companies, as they seldom share common customers or suppliers. Often they have different ways of doing business. For example, GE is a diversified company with businesses in energy, heavy machinery, health care products, and television media. Diversified companies will adopt a diversified operating model as a business model, by which the corporate management will exert management control over these business units. Each business unit itself, however, may in turn determine which operating model is best suited to its business. Thus, business units will determine their own process design and IT support requirements, without central control. A possible exception might be sourcing and procurement processes where economies of scale may present as a business opportunity to gain competitive cost advantage should a common supplier, for example, advertising and marketing agency, be identified between business units.

Coordination

A coordination based operating model has a high level of integration with little requirements for standardization of processes. This model is suitable for enterprises which share common products, customers, partners, or suppliers. The process integration through data sharing aims to provide a *single source of truth*. For instance, a single view of customer will enable integrated customer service. From the integrated customer insights, it becomes easier to up- and cross-selling of products based on customer needs and preferences. Moreover, it allows end-to-end integration of front-of-house sales with back-of-house supply chain to achieve operational excellence. The process integration will improve the rate of stock-turn in the warehouse and reduce the probability of stock-outs in the stores. This model tends to be favored by firms, such as telecommunications and financial services companies, seeking to achieve a customer intimacy strategy. It requires strong coordination of data standards and process interfaces (to ensure integration) through discipline IT (and business) governance at the corporate management center. The human and organizational assets in the business units will need to align with this coordination policy, through corporatewide training and incentive systems. Ross et al. (2006) cite Merrill Lynch's Global Private Client (GPC) business unit as a good example of a coordination operating model. GPC provides a wealth management service to individuals and small businesses through tens of thousands of financial advisers around the globe. In servicing each client, a financial adviser has access to the full range of Merrill Lynch products and customer details at his/her disposal to provide tailored advice or solution to match the client's financial goal and risk profile. The product data sharing and integrated customer data view allow the financial adviser to be proactive in anticipating and servicing the client's emerging wealth management needs. It results in superior customer experience which is critical to implementing Merrill Lynch's customer retention strategy.

Replication

According to Ross et al. (2006), the replication operating model enforces highly *standardized* operational business processes but allows each business unit to run autonomously. Its strength lies in the repeatable efficient business processes that can be readily adopted (replicated) by an autonomous business unit. It favors enterprises that have business units that are fairly independent of each other in terms of customers and products but can benefit significantly from the economies of replicable efficient business processes. For these firms, having limited discretion over process design is a small price to pay for high return in efficiency offered by standardized operations. Examples are companies with franchise business model, such as McDonald. According to Ross et al. (2006), Seven-Eleven Japan and Cemex have successfully exploited this model to grow their businesses differently. Seven-Eleven Japan has successfully improved the operating model to introduce new products and services quickly. They are able to replicate the standardized business processes into new territories within Japan and grow the markets rapidly. Over three decades, Seven-Eleven Japan has reduced average stock turn in each store from over 20 days to less than 10 days, and improved operating margin per store from 20 to 30 percentage points (p. 170); Cemex has grown its company from a domestic Mexican company into the world's top three cement company through replicating its successful operating model in a series of companies they acquire or merge with over more than a decade period (p. 177).

Unification

The unification operating model has tightly integrated and highly standardized business processes. It aims to provide highly efficient (through standardized processes) and excellent (through integrated data and processes) customer service. This type of enterprise tends to have highly integrated supply chain and customer service delivery processes, and data are standardized and shared across processes and between business units. Between business units, standardized business processes (such as financial, HR, and manufacturing processes) are adopted to maximize efficiencies and economies of scale. According to Ross et al. (2006, p. 167), UPS is a good example of companies that have been successfully exploiting the unification model to consistently grow their business. This stems from UPS' ability to use integrated data and processes to better service their customers, and most importantly their ability to leverage the economies of scale while they embark on service, product, and process innovations[4] to enrich their core business. According to Ross et al., the unification operating model gives UPS the agility to expand into new markets and create new products more quickly than can their competitors.

ROSS-WEILL-ROBERTSON ENTERPRISE ARCHITECTURE

According to Ross et al. (2006), the enterprise architecture is the organizing logic for describing the process and IT integration and standardization requirements of the business operating model. It follows, thus, according to Ross et al., that there are four types of enterprise architecture that are being deployed by companies researched in their book. The enterprise architecture is constructed using what they called a *Core Diagram* (pp. 47-64), which consists of four elementary building blocks:

- The *end-to-end core processes*–such as operations management, customer management, innovation management, and regulatory and social management processes required to create value for customers (Kaplan & Norton, 2004);
- The *customer segments (or types)* to be serviced by the core processes - such as consumer or corporate customer segments;
- The *data to be shared* between processes and business units–such as customer or product data;
- The *technologies (and standards) for digitizing* the core processes and for data and process integration - such as the IT infrastructure platform or applications.

The building blocks are composed by the enterprise architect to highlight the uniqueness of the firm's operating model. So even though two enterprises adopting the same operating model may look similar in broader shape, their architecture compositions will be different. In other words, the enterprise architecture core diagram will tease out the key factors critical for the chosen business operating model to differentiate its services from the competitors (who may choose the same or a different operating model). It defines the guiding business and technical principles for integration and standardization but leaves out the details for implementation considerations at the project design architecture level. The Ross-Weill-Robertson Enterprise Architecture model is hence akin to a summarized high level diagram of the more detailed enterprise architectures, such as those of Spewak (1992) and TOGAF (2007) reviewed in this chapter.

In modeling the enterprise information systems requirements and strategic direction, the enterprise architecture must account for all the individual stakeholder viewpoints and concerns. It captures these viewpoints by various levels of abstraction. The EA framework provides a common set of semantics to ensure consistent descriptions and integration of all the diverse stakeholder requirements and strategic intents. These principles have been used by others (reviewed below) to define and describe enterprise architecture.

GARTNER ENTERPRISE ARCHITECTURE[5]

Gartner defines the process and scope of enterprise architecture as follows:

Enterprise architecture is the process of translating business vision and strategy into effective enterprise change by creating, communicating and improving the key principles and models that describe the enterprise's future state and enable its evolution. The scope of the enterprise architecture includes the people, processes, information and technology of the

Figure 6.6. Gartner enterprise architecture framework (James et al., 2005, p. 3)

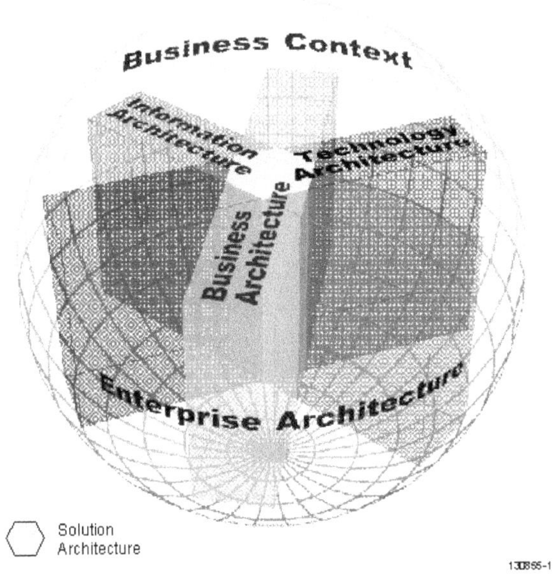

Source: Gartner (October 2005)

enterprise, and their relationships to one another and to the external environment. Enterprise architects compose holistic solutions that address the business challenges of the enterprise, and support the governance needed to implement them. (Weiss, 2006, p. 3)

The Gartner enterprise architecture framework (GEAF), Figure 6.6, describes a *business or enterprise context layer* that overlays the enterprise architecture to ensure alignment with the business strategy. The business context contains the articulation of the business strategy and its implications. It also articulates external "environmental" trends such as regulatory requirements, market trends, or technology trends that influence the enterprise architecture (James et al., 2005, p. 3).

The GEAF also describes three primary viewpoints: enterprise business architecture (EBA), enterprise information architecture (EIA) and enterprise technology architecture (ETA). Each viewpoint represents the concerns central to a specific set of stakeholders. Roughly speaking, the EBA represents the process and organizational concerns of business architects, the EIA represents the information flow and information modeling concerns of information architects, and the ETA represents the technical implementation and operational concerns of technical architects (James et al., 2005, p. 3).

To illustrate using a hypothetical Bank XYZ as an example, Lapkin and Handler (2007) have identified specific stakeholder needs that will be addressed by these primary viewpoints:

- **Business architecture viewpoint:** Addresses business functions, processes, and organizational and primary stakeholders concerns. The business architecture viewpoint addresses the following stakeholder needs:
  1. To reduce cost and/or improve regulatory compliance.
  2. To create a more agile organization that can efficiently and effectively develop and implement new services.
  3. To get the highest returns from implementing the future-state architecture.
- **Information architecture viewpoint:** Addresses information structures and assets. The information architecture viewpoint addresses the following stakeholder needs:
  1. To improve customer relationship management and develop improved systems for business intelligence and investment management.
  2. To increase margins, reduce costs, and gain maximum return on investment on service products.
  3. To ensure consistent perceptions of the bank among customers after a merger.
  4. To improve training programs to remedy the lack of a consistent, unified corporate culture.
  5. To ensure that financial and human resources are not wasted on nonvalue-added programs.
- **Technology architecture viewpoint:** Addresses technical standards for software and hardware, middleware, and infrastructure. The technology architecture viewpoint addresses the following stakeholder needs:
  1. To integrate the latest technical advances.
  2. To reduce system redundancy in the newly merged organization.
  3. To implement better technology to improve employee retention.
  4. To increase security for online services and consolidated operations.

James et al. (2005, p. 3) contend that while a well-formed enterprise architecture contains at least three viewpoints, additional viewpoints may be "extracted" and called out explicitly if there is a requirement from specific stakeholders to do so. For example, in an organization in which regulatory compliance is a critical driver for the architecture, it would be reasonable to expect the compliance components to be extracted from the business, information, and technology viewpoints to supply the chief compliance officer with a distinct compliance view of the architecture. For example, for the Bank XYZ, Lapkin and Handler (2007) have identified two additional viewpoints that address important and strategic concerns of the bank. These viewpoints are (Lapkin & Handler, 2007):

- **Security viewpoint:** Addresses security policies and access controls for the entire enterprise. The security viewpoint addresses the following stakeholder needs:
  1. To centralize management of security policies and access controls.
  2. To create an enterprise-wide security framework for enforcing compliance with all local, state, and federal information privacy and data security regulations.
  3. To manage security across all customer touch points.

Figure 6.7. Additional viewpoints for future iterations of the EA (Lapkin & Handler, 2007)

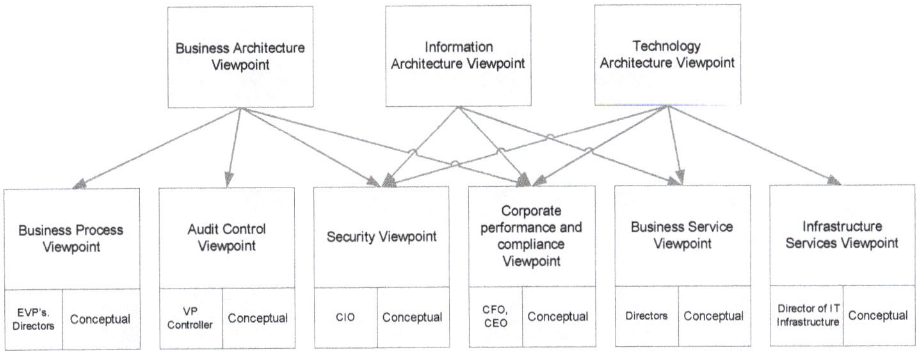

Source: Gartner (April 2007)

- **Compliance viewpoint:** Addresses compliance policies and access controls for the entire enterprise. The compliance viewpoint addresses the following stakeholder needs:
    1. To monitor and audit transactional data updates and accesses.
    2. To create an enterprisewide compliance framework for managing, monitoring, and enforcing all state and federal compliance regulations.
    3. To monitor progress on all initiatives toward meeting company goals and provide reporting on key performance metrics.

Figure 6.7 illustrates what those additional viewpoints might be, who the stakeholders are, and what level of abstraction is relevant to them. Lapkin and Handler (2007) have also illustrated which primary viewpoints contribute to each of these additional viewpoints.

Business Context

According to Weiss (2006, p. 3), the business context informs the subsequent architecture work, ensuring a focused direction of effort. EA can bridge the gap between strategic planning and implementation efforts. Bridging that gap requires a process that is holistic in its coverage and enterprisewide in scope. The EA process must cover the impact of strategic business change on more than just technology; it must also cover the impact of change on people, business processes, and information. The business context is the step in the EA process that combines the analysis of environmental trends and the business strategy and directs the EA team effort in the direction of the future state (Weiss, 2006, p. 3).

Weiss (2006, p. 3) opines that "EA is not about a master design to satisfy an aggregated set of requirements across a few projects. Rather, future-state EA is directly derived from business strategy. Projects, inspired by the business strategy, will therefore be meaningfully guided by the EA, in a manner that consistently contributes towards a common goal."

Figure 6.8. The enterprise value network anchor model (Allega, 2006, p. 5)

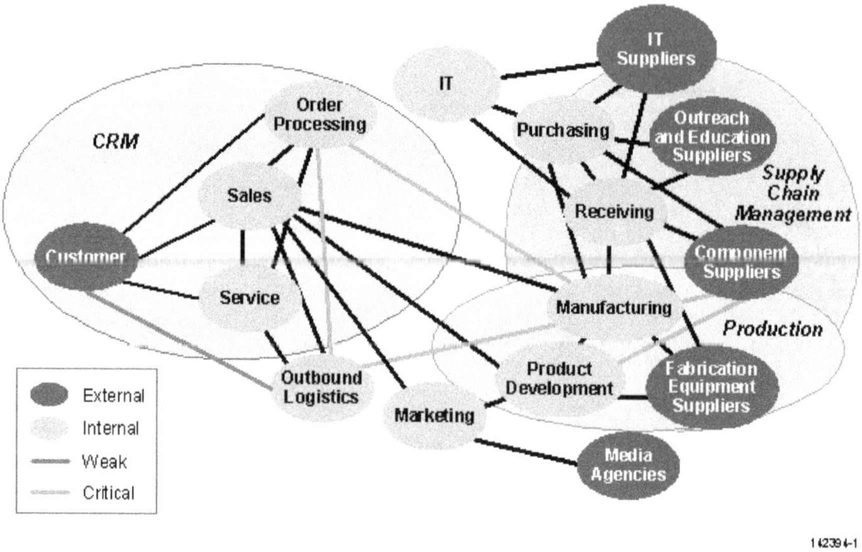

Source: Gartner (December 2006)

The analysis in the creation of the business context refines the business strategy, and creates and communicates this common goal across the enterprise. The business context consists of (Weiss, 2006, p. 4, 6, 8):

- Analysis of the business strategy
- Analysis of the environmental trends (including internal and external environmental conditions that will affect the enterprise's future state such as economic climate, customer market demand, regulation and other legalities, geography, political conditions, culture, labor, and technology)
- An anchor model defining the business (overall big picture view)

Allega (2006) argues that: "Understanding the big picture of the enterprise is a neglected yet critical element of developing EA. Although many techniques can be used to describe the view of the business, the enterprise value network (EVN) is one such model that provides business leaders with a big picture of the enterprise that they can recognize and support. In turn, this model can be used in future modelling work to support further decomposition and relationships across EA viewpoints.

The high-level anchor model, the EVN (see Figure 6.8) can be used to identify the core value-adding processes executed by the enterprise. The model must be objectively accurate but should not be a picture of the organizational chart. The purpose of developing an anchor model is to communicate the relationships between the highest-order entities inside and outside the company. The focus of EVN creation is to determine the strategic alignment with an enterprise's generic competitive strategy (such as operational excellence, customer intimacy or product leadership) for internal and external activities."

Allega (2006, p. 4) further asserts that:

The focus of this visual model is the view of the elements that helps the business operate. The resulting picture should succinctly capture the highest-level representation of the business ecosystem. Entity selections require business management to first identify key business partners and entities from the business that are most important to it (for example, generating revenue, serving clients and keeping supply costs low). The model is owned by the business and will resist attempts to use database normalization techniques.

In summary (Weiss, 2006, p. 1):

To create an effective enterprise architecture, architects, business managers and IT professionals must achieve a common and cohesive vision of the business and key business challenges, as well as the opportunities and "problem corridors" the organization expects to encounter. The business context provides this vision, which overlays the enterprise architecture and ensures its alignment with the business strategy.

Enterprise Solution Architecture

James et al. (2005, p. 4) note that:

While similar architecture viewpoints are found in a variety of frameworks, the GEAF introduces a unique and innovative concept called the Enterprise Solution Architecture Framework (ESAF). The ESAF deals directly with arguably the single most important and challenging architecture issues: combining and reconciling the loosely coupled and often conflicting viewpoints of the primary stakeholders into a unified architecture for an enterprise solution that actually solves a business problem without creating other, even larger, problems.

James et al. (2005, p. 4) assert that:

The ESAF is specifically designed to reunite the divided viewpoints of EBA, EIA and ETA. As such, it is essentially a meta-architecture or an "architecture of architectures". Whereas a specific enterprise solution architecture (ESA) is the intersection of the three primary viewpoints that forms a consistent architectural description of a specific enterprise solution, the ESAF is an architectural description of how to create such ESAs. The ESAF combines and reconciles the requirements, principles and models of intersecting stakeholder-specific viewpoints within the three primary viewpoints (see Figure 6.6) into a set of architectural descriptions that can be used to generate the entire portfolio of enterprise solutions.

The ESAF highlights specific dependencies and inconsistencies among business architecture, information architecture, technical architecture and the subsequent solution architecture at the individual project level and the enterprise level. While these dependencies can be broken, there may be negative or even detrimental consequences to ignoring them. Calling out these dependencies, however, enables enterprise architecture emergence at the project level and incremental enterprise architecture development centrally or in federated environments (James et al., 2005, p. 4).

Levels of Abstraction

As described above (Weiss, 2006, p. 3), the business context is the step in the EA process that combines the analysis of environmental trends and the business strategy and directs the EA team effort in the creation of the future state architecture. Three types of artifacts are typically used to describe the desired future state architecture (Lapkin & Handler, 2007). These are:

1. Requirements (which articulate the needs of the business).
2. Principles (which articulate the decisions of the architecture).
3. Models (which illustrate how the components of the future-state architecture interoperate to deliver business value).

Specifically, consistent levels of abstraction are defined for each architecture viewpoint. In addition to the *business context* layer, which is the highest level of abstraction, each viewpoint contains a *conceptual*, a *logical,* and an *implementation* layer of abstraction (James et al., 2005, p. 5; Lapkin & Handler, 2007, p. 6).

Different layers of abstraction are used for different purposes. For example, company leaders, who require a "big picture" view to enable effective strategic decisions, are predisposed to the business context layer. Senior management, focusing on specific concerns, but still requiring a big picture view, are apt to find great utility in the conceptual viewpoint. Operationally focused management tends to need a more operationally focused enterprise architecture perspective, represented by the logical view, to make better operational decisions. Change agents, requiring more granular details to enable change, be it process improvement or system implementation, are predisposed to the implementation view (Lapkin & Handler, 2007, p. 6).

The primary artifacts, requirements, principles, and models are developed within each viewpoint at each level of abstraction. In the technology viewpoint, for example, one might find service-level requirements at the conceptual level, defining the data throughput and storage requirements of the business. At the logical level, one might decompose these to infrastructure design requirements, which would dictate the constraints for designing infrastructure to meet specific service levels. At the implementation level, one would have specific product standards to be used in implementing infrastructure (Lapkin & Handler, 2007, p. 6).

Use of consistent levels of abstraction enforces a progressive decomposition. Since artifacts at lower levels of abstraction are demonstrably derived from the higher levels, traceability from the conceptual design of the architecture to the detailed implementation guidance is maintained (James et al., 2005, p. 5; Lapkin & Handler, 2007, p. 6).

Architecture Roadmap

According to Weiss and Robertson (2006, p. 3), enterprise architects must project the future state of the enterprise over time. This most commonly includes the future states of solutions (including applications) and infrastructure as well as changes in technology strategy. However, the future state may include information and process change strategies as well. In fact, change over time in any EA viewpoint may be represented by an *EA roadmap* deliverable. An EA roadmap is an excellent tool for communicating the stage in Gartner's EA process termed "closing the gap" between the present and future state—or indeed how the future state itself changes over time (Weiss & Robertson, 2006, p. 3).

A roadmap is a concise and commonly a graphical depiction of a planned migration toward a future state. A regular roadmap shows a car's driver the path to a location (a goal). An EA roadmap shows not just one path to a future state (or goal), but a series of incremental or intermediate steps toward that future state. The scope of a particular roadmap deliverable is usually limited to a particular domain or subset of an EA viewpoint, such as network with the technology architecture viewpoint or marketing within a business architecture viewpoint. This limited scope makes the resulting graphical view concise, usually fitting on a single slide for clarity and best communication (Weiss & Robertson, 2006, p. 3).

BUSINESS ARCHITECTURE

Spewak Business Architecture

Spewak (1992) defines the business architecture in two steps. First, he defines the preliminary business model; then through the enterprise survey, he defines the target business model. According to Spewak (1992), the business model must be a complete, comprehensive, consistent definition of the business that can be used to define the information, application, and technology architectures and implementation plans. The preliminary business model defines the brief business functions and the organization model of the business functions. The enterprise survey extends the preliminary model to complete the business model definition by formal engagement with the business (to fill in the details and validate understanding).

Spewak (1992) defines three steps to developing the preliminary business model:

1. **Define the organizational structure:** To identify the business stakeholders, and to determine the extent of data and application sharing.
2. **Define the business functions:** To define the business and the structure of the business model. Spewak (1992) recommends using the Porter value chain model for identifying each business function, its purpose, specific value added, and specific business activities for value creation, and the business unit that performs the business function. Each function in the value chain (e.g., marketing) is decomposed to the next level of granularity (usually 2 or 3 levels maximum), subfunctions (e.g., planning, research, customer acquisition, customer retention) to reflect enterprise-specific structure.
3. **Document the preliminary business model for business community's validation and correction of understanding.** The Spewak (1992) business model consists of "tables" (or diagrams) of core business functions arranged in logical activity sequence according to the value-chain model. Each function is decomposed in two or three level subfunctions and also arranged in value-added logical sequence, with each (lowest) subfunction assigned with the business units that perform the subfunction. In short, each "table" is analogous to an end-to-end process model of activities (business functions) and resources (business units), produced for each core (top level) business

function (eg marketing). The linkages between core business functions (and tables) are in accordance with the enterprise's value chain model.

According to Spewak (1992), the enterprise survey will gather the details from the business to complete the preliminary business model, following its validation feedback from the business. The functional details sought by the Spewak EAD process are:

- Information used to perform a business function
- Time the function is performed
- Location of the function
- Performance frequency of function
- Opportunities for functional improvement

In summary, the Spewak business architecture is the business model of the enterprise. It describes the high level definition of the *logical sequence (or network)* of *business functions (activities)* performed by the enterprise's *business units (resources)* together with the *information* required by each function to create value for the customers.

TOGAF Business Architecture

TOGAF business architecture addresses the concerns of the users, planners, and business managers of the information system. It focuses on the *functional aspects* of the system and provides the direction and foundation for the definition of TOGAF information, application, and technology architectures. Business architecture embodies the *enterprise mission, vision, strategy, and goals,* and thus the business requirements for the enterprise architecture. It defines the enterprise's organizational structure, business goals, and objectives for each organizational unit, business functions, and business services that each organizational unit provides to its customers (internal and external), business processes, business roles, and business data model required to achieve the enterprise mission and strategy. Business architecture describes the flow of business information between people and business processes. It clearly identifies the information requirements of each business function as to when, where, how often, and by whom the function will be performed, and what information (and where its source) is needed to perform it. It defines the architecture building blocks and the set of principles, guidelines, and constraints for modeling the architecture.

In summary, TOGAF business architecture includes the following views[6] of the information system:

- **The people view:** Human resource aspects of the system
- **The business process view:** The user processes
- **The business function view:** Functions required to support the processes
- **The usability view:** Usability aspects of the system
- **Business performance view:** The performance aspects of the system

Gartner Business Architecture

The Gartner Business Architecture is one viewpoint within the GEAF framework that provides the business view of the future state of the enterprise. A business architecture is the expression of the enterprise's key business strategies. It is derived from the business strategy through the common requirements vision process (Allega, 2006) of the business context development. It has an impact on how the business operates: "How do we change the way we do business to realize this strategy?" It defines the business design for sustainable competitive advantage and in most cases drives change on the information and technology architectures. The business architecture also needs to change as a result of a decision made in the technology or information viewpoint architectures. The relationship between the architectural viewpoints is often peer-to-peer process (Weiss, 2007, p. 3).

The business architecture includes (Rosser, 2006, p. 3):

1. The enterprise value chain (what the organization does to deliver value)
2. The major business processes that are performed to deliver the value
3. The primary business functions performed within the processes
4. The primary application systems in place

The critical process view (2) is especially valuable when looking across the functions from the viewpoint of end-to-end process. A classic illustration of an end-to-end process is "order-to-cash," which itself consists of a whole string of functional activities such as credit authorization, order entry, scheduling, delivering, and billing. This overall business perspective must remain at a high summary level until it can be determined just where opportunities for improvements may lie (Rosser, 2006, p. 3).

For the business process management (BPM) discipline, the business architecture establishes a consistent high-level view of the broader business functional environment as well as an established set of planned business functional directions, and a consistent array of principles, techniques, and building blocks to employ during design that bring familiarity, economy, support, and a planned life cycle. The enterprise payoff comes via a better productivity of the IT effort, clearer visibility for all and greater opportunity for innovation. Although the emphasis here is generally on business architecture to guide IT leverage, it can also be valuable in the creation of organization and process designs, even without formal IT systems (Rosser, 2006, p. 3).

A well-defined business architecture is a prerequisite for developing a successful enterprise architecture and defines how the business moves in response to strategic change. It also provides both the business and IT organization with a better understanding of the business designs for the future that the technology must support (Weiss, 2007, p. 2).

In most organizations, business architecture is even more than the set (four elements) defined above. Weiss (2007, p. 3) summarizes some of the elements of a business architecture that are required for a business unit manager to make decisions about a future-state business architecture to address the changes required by the business strategy. The additional elements identified include, for example, organizational structure, organizational design, geography, product lines, fiscal management, performance management, human capital management, etc. (Weiss, 2007, p. 3). These elements are quite diverse, and the impact of strategic change on these elements is often considered independently, not collaboratively. Weiss (2007) proposes leveraging the technology architectural tools and techniques such as a framework of patterns, services, domains, and components to model these diverse elements in an integrative manner. This framework allows the business architecture components to be grouped together to provide strategic change dimensions aligned with strategy execution (Weiss, 2007, p. 5).

As explained above, business context is the basis from which all Gartner viewpoint architectures are developed. Business architecture is developed from analysis of the business context[7] to create the future state and guidelines (and principles) for the value chain, the processes, the functions, and the relevant applications (at a high level) when and where they are critical for enterprise success (Rosser, 2006, p. 4).

Current State: Rosser (2006, p. 4) recommends starting the development of the business architecture from the current state,[8] as distinct from approaches for the other two viewpoints (information and technology) where it is often felt that it is better to describe the ideal future state at the outset—not hindered by what exists now… . By doing the current state of the business functions first, this tends to be more inclusive, to gain more immediate attention and to stimulate more ideas for improvement, than to start out defining the future state.

The current state of the value chain, the business processes, and the functions performed are reviewed and documented (at a high level). It is useful to add the perspective of the hierarchy of business purpose (Rosser, 2006, p. 4).

Future State: In conjunction with the larger business context, the future state business system descriptions can be generated. The future state represents a vision of where the enterprise wants to be in terms of business processes and so on, at a future date, such as two or three years into the future. Creating this series of "visions" is a critical part of the larger architecture process (Rosser, 2006, p. 4).

Principles: The same analysis can be used to generate a series of architectural principles (that is, values and beliefs based on the business strategy), which should be observed in subsequent work. Even here, the principles effort might come in a different order, starting at a high level, such as "customer service is No. 1," that may be important to resolve before the future state. This becomes a question of perspective because principles can exist at multiple levels (Rosser, 2006, p. 4). For example, one business architecture principle might be "all customer related business processes must yield superior customer experience." The architecture principles constitute a part of the IT governance. It drives the desirable IT behavior to achieve maximum business value delivery. From the principles, a set of design guidelines may be developed. For instance, to achieve the superior customer experience principle, a design guideline might be: "business data must use common data model integrated and shared across all business units."

Gap Analysis: Comparing the future state with the current state becomes a type of "gap analysis" used to determine opportunities, to decide on prioritization, and to generate a series of stages or a roadmap to be pursued. The goal is to lay out a proposed sequence and investment plan to create systems that support the business strategy in optimal fashion (the investment decisions are made by a governance body dealing with the investment strategy) (Rosser, 2006, p. 5).

Guideline: Once the future state vision and principles are in place, there is also a need for day-to-day design guidance in the form of guidelines to be employed by the business process designers that is separate from the future state vision. An example might be that "Common enterprisewide processes must be employed unless specific local requirements justify an exception—approved by the governance council." The benefit is that the entire process and system design and enhancement effort should comply with sound practices and design methods from the architecture rather than each step being taken as a single event with design on an ad hoc design approach (Rosser, 2006, p. 5).

Business Architecture Bricks

According to Weiss (2007, p. 1), business architecture is a creative process of the future-state design of the business and can consist of representations of processes, functions, geographies, and organizational structures. One of the challenges of business architecture has always been developing business architecture models that encompass more than just process. With the new wave in business process management, the challenge has become even greater. Vital for enterprise architecture success is the development of enterprise business architecture to enable the operational implementation of business strategy. To that end, Weiss (2007, p. 2) defines a basic set of business architecture bricks that can be expanded and refined to suit each organization. The basic set consists of:

1. **Subprocesses:** Activities, tasks, gateways, and events
2. **People:** Skills and roles
3. **Resources:** Assets, raw materials, and financial resources
4. **Products and services**

The creation of bricks within the business architecture enables the architects to create future-state business architectures to solve key business issues. Architects should be motivated to create artifacts that are open-ended and easily assembled to solve a problem. The business architecture bricks are the key Lego-like pieces required to complete holistic business architecture. Its application to defining the procurement business function is illustrated in Weiss (2007, p. 5).

INFORMATION ARCHITECTURE

Spewak Information Architecture

Spewak (1992) data (or information) architecture defines the major kinds of data which support the business functions defined in the business architecture. The Spewak (1992) information architecture consists of *data entities*, each of which has *attributes* and *relationships* with other data entities. In short, the Spewak (1992) data architecture defines the *data model* of the enterprise. According to Spewak (1992), *"data architecture only requires sufficient detail for planning purposes."* The details and semantics constructs are added after the architecture implementation plans have been approved by executive management. Spewak (1992) positions the information architecture to include the planner's and owner's views (top two rows) of the data column of the Zachman framework.

Spewak (1992) prescribes guidelines for defining the entities and relationships from the business architecture (business model). *Data entities* and *attributes* are derived from the business functions. Relationshps are derived from the linkages between business functions in the Spewak (1992) business architecture (model).

Spewak (1992) prescribes a methodology for step-by-step development of the enterprise data architecture (model), comprising a network of entity-relationships diagram. In particular, Spewak (1992) stipulates that the data architecture must have the following properties:

- **Understandable:** The entity definitions must be understandable by the business;
- **Complete and consistent:** All major data entities have been captured, and all definitions are consistent, not contradictory or overlapped;
- **Stable:** Data definitions are based on business model and independent of the user, time, location, and purpose of its use, flows, and the technology for its storage.

Further, Spewak (1992) prescribes a process of mapping the data entities back to the business functions to validate which entities are created, retrieved, updated and deleted by business functions. This ensures data completeness and consistency, and most importantly alignment of data and business architectures. From this process, the Spewak (1992) data architecture produces two additional deliverables:

- Entitiy-to-business function lists and matrices (mandatory–it defines data entity usage by business functions)
- Entity-to-current application lists and matrices (optional–it identifies opportunities for improvement in data storage and usage).

In summary, the Spewak (1992) information architecture comprises:

- Complete list of data entities: names and definitions
- Entity-relationship diagrams
- Entity usage (by business functions) matrices

TOGAF Data (Information) Architecture

The TOGAF data (information) architecture addresses the concerns of the database designers, administrators, and system engineers responsible for developing and integrating the various database components of the system. It contains the business data model (entities, attributes, and relationships), logical data model, data management process models, including data dissemination, life cycle, security, and model management views. It describes the data flow. It relates clearly in a matrix the data entities to the business functions in the business architecture, indicating which CRUD operations are performed by which functions. It also defines the architecture principles, guidelines, and constraints to be complied by the information architecture. It specifies the required service level agreements for the data services to be used by business functions.

Gartner Information Architecture

Information supports and reflects business activity. One need only look at the success of companies such as Wal-Mart to understand how the use of information in a competitive global environment can mean the difference between success and failure. An organization's strategic intent is reflected in its enterprise architecture (how it aligns business strategy with technology). This strategic intent is reflected in its enterprise information architecture, which identifies the information required to execute the business strategy (Handler & Newman, 2005, p. 5).

Newman (2005, p. 2) observes that:

The struggle to ensure that information is accurate, timely and consistent, and can flow seamlessly and continuously across boundaries, remains a barrier to successful business strategy execution. Current techniques for managing information at a project level, or across several projects at a time, do not satisfy strategic requirements for enterprise agility, innovation and operational excellence.

He notes further that (p. 2):

Although historically overlooked as an organizational discipline, the management of information is now paramount, as there is no end in sight to the increasing volume and velocity of various types of content. In addition, as organizations seek to achieve competitive differentiation through new sense-and-response capabilities, the demand for seamless, continuously flowing and consistent information will intensify. Moreover, the current information management challenges become exposed when migrating to service-oriented architectures (SOAs).

Instead, the answer is an organizational commitment that maximizes the quality, value, usefulness, accessibility, and security of information within and beyond the organizations (Newman, 2005, p. 2). Gartner calls this imperative "enterprise information management" (EIM). EIM is the implementation vehicle for the Gartner Enterprise Information Architecture (EIA) (Newman & Blechar, 2007).

EIA is a discipline that details the enterprise's information strategies, its extended information value chain, and its impact on enterprise technical architecture. EIA is therefore the planning and design of information in context for the enterprise—and at the enterprise level—such that it is structurally consistent with organizational principles and objectives (Handler & Newman, 2005, p. 4). EIA is a discipline for organizing and classifying information across enterprise, organization, and application boundaries so that it can be used effectively by the business. Although EIA efforts historically focused on structured data (databases and file systems), the scope has now broadened to include unstructured content (such as documents and rich media). EIA must address content convergence to solve issues of "info glut," especially on enterprisewide initiatives such as compliance and relationship management (Handler & Newman, 2005).

The EIA provides the policies, models, and rules for designing and implementing effective software and data services and databases (Blechar, 2007). EIM is defined as a program to organize, design, and safeguard all information assets, including content found in databases, data warehouses, transaction systems, documents, and digital media. EIM solves semantic inconsistencies and master data management issues, which have added significant cost and complexity to application integration and cross-functional initiatives (Newman, 2005, p. 2). EIA is a process for organizing, prioritizing, and planning information assets in support of strategic business objectives. EIA creates the blueprint to ensure information achieves organizational objectives. These blueprints (and the associated polices and procedures) are managed and implemented through an EIM program (Handler & Newman, 2005, p. 5).

As part of enterprise architecture, the information viewpoint is a bridge between the business strategy and its implementation through enterprise information management (EIM) (James, 2007, p. 2). James defines eight information architecture patterns as a starter set. Enterprise architecture patterns provide guidance on combinations of architecture elements that can be repeated in multiple implementations. The initial set of IA patterns comprises (James, 2007):

1. **Operational usage patterns:** These patterns describe the use of information to support transaction processing systems and focus on the need to provide an integrated view of information for these applications. This arises from the fragmentation of information throughout the enterprise. For example, customer information is typically stored in multiple databases with little consensus in identifiers to indicate individual instances. This limits the ability to match instances automatically. Two patterns are defined:
   a. *Operational data store (ODS):* It integrates data from various sources to address the needs of transaction processing applications. These data present the most current values. Typically, an ODS is initially populated by bulk data loads and kept current by real-time or near real-time updates. Applications do not usually update an ODP directly, but rather, access it for reference.
   b. *Master data hub:* James (2007, p. 3) defines master data management (MDM) as "the consistent set of identifiers and extended attributes that describe the core entities and groupings of the enterprises." Common MDM subjects are customer, product, and supplier.
2. **Analytical usage patterns:**
   a. *Data warehouse:* A data warehouse holds data extracted from a range of sources spanning applications, operational data stores, and external sources. It spans the entire enterprise rather than a particular group of users, specific business unit, or geography. Because the data warehouse is used for analytical processing, it contains data reflecting a specific point in time rather than the most current values.
   b. *Data mart:* A data mart holds analytical data designed to meet the needs of a specific group of users and their analytical requirements. It can be sourced directly from applications, ODS, and/or external sources, although often from the data warehouse.
3. **Publishing usage patterns:**
   a. *Content management:* It spans the information life cycle and includes acquisition, indexing, and finally archiving and retirement, as well as search, retrieval, and display through various means such as portals and other middleware.
4. **Information integration patterns:**
   a. *Metadata:* Management of metadata is the essential underpinning for the virtual integration of information.
   b. *Bulk data movement:* Movement of data is a key information integration mechanism. Bulk movement of data plays an important role in satisfying less time-sensitive requirements. It usually involves *extracting* (E) multiple records from a source and *transforming* (T) the records to resolve semantic and syntactic

differences between the source and the destination before *loading* (L) them into the destination database.

c. *Real-time or near real-time data movement:* This is used to satisfy more time-sensitive requirements.

In summary, the enterprise information architecture typically produces the following sample outputs (Newman & Blechar, 2007, p. 5):

- **Conceptual perspective:**
  a. Information principles and standards
  b. Integration policies
  c. Information flows
- **Analysis and design perspective:**
  a. Data models
  b. Object/component models
  c. Design guidelines, patterns, frameworks
- **Implementation perspective:**
  a. Data, software, and user interface services
  b. Master data stores
  c. Databases and software solutions

Enterprise Information Management

For companies to manage their information assets better, they need to clearly understand enterprise information management. Newman and Logan (2006, p. 3) defines EIM as:

an integrative discipline for structuring, describing and governing information assets, regardless of organizational and technological boundaries, to improve operational efficiency, promote transparency and enable business insight. The scope of EIM requires a level of organizational commitment to improve the accuracy, integrity, accessibility and security of information assets. The objective of EIM is to resolve semantic issues across applications and content stores. The mission of EIM is to implement the organization's enterprise information architecture.

In terms of the Gartner enterprise architecture process model, EIM picks up at the planning-and-design level (of the life cycle), and continues through the development, deployment, and optimization of solutions. EIM supports the gap-planning phase in which development activities are prioritized and sequenced based on future state business objectives. EIM's role is also to ensure that the proper governance and organizational processes for information management are followed. In addition, EIM manages the technologies required to support migration from current state to future state (Newman & Blechar, 2007, p. 2).

EIM is not achieved by technology alone. Instead, it requires a holistic approach that balances technology choices with equally important organizational, governance, process, and architecture dimensions to ensure an enterprisewide impact. EIM's vision aligns with the enterprise information architecture (EIA) vision. EIM implements EIA (Newman, 2005, p. 2).

Newman (2005, p. 3) defines the EIM framework as a set of building blocks that represent EIM's interdependent components, comprising the following:

- **Vision** - it addresses the question: What does the organization need in terms of EIM to meet its business objectives? For example, a vision for enterprise agility will require a comprehensive EIM program targeting improved sense-and-respond capabilities such as real-time information flows, semantic reconciliation, and closed-loop analytics.
- **Strategy** - it addresses the question: How can the vision of EIM be realized? EIM has a defined charter, organization, and resource plan.
- **Governance** (p. 4) - it addresses the question: What governance of information is needed, and what impact will governance have on the organization? EIM governance addresses the development, maintenance, communication, and enforcement of information management policies and procedures typically identified during the EIA initiative. It may affect traditional system development life cycle. For example, to achieve goals for information consistency, standardization, and reuse, certain activities are introduced into the development process.
- **Organization** - it addresses the question: What organizational model is required for implementing the EIM governance process, and how does this affect the current organization? It reinforces the belief that *information* in the enterprise is as important as *process* (application development) and *infrastructure* (technology) components.
- **Process** (p. 5) - it addresses the question: What processes are needed in EIM? It includes a broad spectrum of activities for implementing EIM functions and services. For example, data stewardship is a business process that addresses compliance requirements for the increased accountability and transparency of information across the organization. It requires active, ongoing cooperation between IT and business areas.
- **Reference architecture** - it addresses the question: What are the technology enablers for EIM, and how should they relate to each other? It defines the technology components for success. The purpose of reference architecture is to eliminate redundancy and reduce complexity.
- **Metrics** (p. 6) - it addresses the question: How can the success and impact of EIM be measured? It enables organizations to baseline where to start, provide a balanced method for determining and communicating progress, and evaluate the relative performance towards program objectives.

Agile Enterprise Information Architecture

Newman and Blechar (2007, p. 8) crystallize the practice of enterprise information architecture as follows:

To "manage information as an enterprise asset", organizations should start by applying the outputs from the enterprise architecture. Next, they should define the principles of the enterprise information architecture. Then, they should build the EIM vision and team, and put in place an information centric infrastructure to share and exchange all information across the enterprise.

In particular, Blechar (2007, p. 8) recommends the following 10 best practices for building an agile information architecture:

1. Make information modeling an integral part of enterprise architecture efforts.
2. Align business, information, and technical architectures.
3. Promote reuse through architectural patterns and master data management.
4. Wrap selected legacy data to improve transparency and productivity.
5. Put process-centric "data in context" rules in separate services (that is, as opposed to in stored procedures).
6. Promote understanding and reuse of information assets and metadata (that is, via a common business taxonomy and use of metadata repositories/registries).
7. Balance process-driven solutions with content-driven ones.
8. Build an EIM reference model to support business process management and service oriented architecture.
9. Build an EIM roadmap to enable the information architecture, then execute it.
10. Focus on the three types of future business improvement opportunities:
    - Business process improvement through the redesign and optimization of human-to-human processes and workflows
    - Business process agility through orchestrated workflows using coordinated process and information services
    - New composite content-driven solutions (with possibly limited, if any, process change) based on information agility and reuse

APPLICATION ARCHITECTURE

Spewak Application Architecture

According to Spewak (1992), the purpose of application architecture is to *define* the major types of applications needed to manage the data and support or enable the business functions of the enterprise. "It is *not* a *design* but a *definition* of what these applications will do to manage data and provide information to people performing the business functions." According to Spewak, it is about what the applications must do to manage data and provide information to business people—quality information at an acceptable cost—not how to do it. Spewak positions the application architecture definition as the owner's view of the process column in the Zachman framework.

According to Spewak (1992), the sources for application definition are data architecture definitions, data usage matrix, functional business model, and the information resource catalogue (of existing information systems). The objective is to identify strategic use of information and technology application for competitive business advantage. Thus the applications proposed are *conceptual,* not products. In particular, each application proposed for the (potentially many) business functions must articulate its purpose, capabilities, and the business benefits, in line with the business strategy for differentiation and/or cost efficiency. It will be assigned a unique name that fits its purpose.

As with the data architecture, Spewak (1992) prescribes the following desirable properties for the application architecture:

- **Understandable:** Application definitions (purpose, capabilities, and benefits) are understandable by everyone in the enterprise
- **Complete and consistent:** It supports most business functions and *all* data entities are being managed; and no overlap or duplications of application capabilities
- **Stable:** Each application definition is based on the business model and data architecture, and independent of users, how it works, its location, and time of operation

Similarly, Spewak (1992) methodology requires the applications defined in the architecture be mapped back to the business functions. For each application, the business functions supported are identified and tabulated. To cite a Spewak example as an illustration, the application named *Sales Lead Tracking* supports the following functions: *Handle walk-in traffic, Handle sales lead, Handle customer calls, Perform sales follow up, Close a sales, and so on.* Again, this is a sound method for confirming strategic alignment. This task produces a supplementary deliverable to the list of application definitions, comprising application-to-function cross-reference lists and matrices. A further strategic alignment task is to map the applications to the organizational units identified in the business model via business functions. This process will identify data and application sharing. In additional to facilitating the enforcement of the "single source of truth" data principle, it provides a useful tool for determining data and application ownership and accountability, a critical requirement of IT governance.

Finally, Spewak (1992) recommends performing impact analysis of the application architecture to the current environment (defined in the information resource catalog). Or, put another way, using Kaplan and Norton's (2004) term, to assess the strategic readiness of the current systems against the target architecture strategy. Others, such as Gartner, call this a gap analysis of current IS compared to the target architecture. This analysis will determine whether the existing application can be retained with minimal enhancement, partially replaced (or modified into a shared environment), or completely replaced a new application to be developed or purposed in accordance to the application architecture. This is a critical phase of architecture implementation. From IT governance perspective, it offers important facts to the executive management to assess application priority and decide the application portfolio mix that best fits the business strategy.

TOGAF Application Architecture

The TOGAF (2007) application architecture addresses the concerns of system and software engineers responsible for developing and integrating the various application software components of the system. It aims to define the kinds of application system (logical capabilities not product) necessary to process the data (defined by the data/information architecture) and support the business functions (defined by business architecture). It also defines what the application system must do with the data management and how it must present the information to the human and computer actors in the enterprise. Application architecture articulates the information processing needs of the enterprise. TOGAF (2007) defines application architecture to encompass process system, place system, time system, and people system models, together with the applications interoperability requirements. It should also provide common application services, application interoperability, application/information, and application/user locations views.

TECHNOLOGY ARCHITECTURE

Spewak Technology Architecture

According to Spewak (1992), as with the information and application architectures, the technology architecture is a *conceptual* model that defines the technology *platforms* required to provide an environment for the applications that are managing data to run the business. It defines, not designs, the platforms. Spewak maps the technology architecture to the owner's view (second row) of the network column of the Zachman framework. Spewak *distinguishes* the technology architecture from the *technology model* (fourth row) of the Zachman framework. From Spewak's viewpoint, Zachman's technology model is concerned with "physical designs, for example, for data in a DBMS, and applications in a program language, and technology with a particular equipment."

Spewak's (1992) technology architecture consists of the following deliverables:

- **Technology platform principles:** Based on analysis of technology trends of importance to the business (from insights of the business, application, and information architectures as well as the information resource catalog) and industry, the technology principles are defined for the enterprise. They will serve as the basis for technology architecture. An example might be that the service-oriented approach will be adopted for all data and application technologies.
- **Technology platforms and distribution:** Based on the above principles, the distribution strategy for applications and data (from the corresponding architectures) is determined and the target configuration of technology platforms defined (conceptually). This process creates the *technology architecture*. Spewak's technology architecture consists of three levels:
  - *User access level:* It defines the conceptual model for user access to data and applications
  - *Enterprise network level:* It defines the infrastructure that supports the distribution and running of applications and storage and management the data
  - *Business systems architecture level:* It refers to the technology for implementing and maintaining the applications and databases of the enterprise. The architecture shows the relationships of databases and applications in support of the target user access scenarios to perform the envisioned business functions as defined by the business model.

For high volume transactional business with mission critical operational requirements, Spewak also recommends evaluating the conceptual technology architecture against the business functional performance requirements. This is to ensure such critical performance requirements are factored into the architecture definition.

- Technology platform-to-application and technology platform-to-business function cross reference lists and tables - these identify the degree of dependency of an application for a technology platform and an approximate relationship of the technology platforms with the business functions and organizations that will use them. This is useful for determining service level agreements and business value of technology platforms at the implementation phase and for broader general IT governance purposes.

TOGAF Technology Architecture

TOGAF (2007) technology architecture addresses the concerns of acquirer or procurement personnel responsible for acquiring the commercial-off-the-shelf software and that of operations staff, system administrators, and system and network engineers responsible for the operations and support of the system. It defines a service-oriented technical architecture using the TOGAF (2007) foundation architecture's technical reference model. It is defined by an integration of conceptualized architecture building blocks. It also specifies the requirements traceability to validate that it aligns with and meets the business architecture requirements. The acquirer's view defines the costs and technology standards requirements that must be adhered to by the technology architecture.

Gartner Technology Architecture

Enterprise Technology Architecture Principles

Robertson (2007) explains the fundamental principles required for the development of the technology architecture:

Enterprise Technical (Technology) Architecture (ETA) modeling and design work should reflect careful integration with overall business goals, as well as adherence to particular IT drivers and specific technology guidelines and best practices. Enterprise Architecture principles are part of the guidelines to leverage—and leverage explicitly. Principles present expected behaviors that if adhered to will enable strategies to become realities. Choosing which principles are appropriate for a given organization at a lower level—for example, for standard ETA models such as technical patterns and technical services, or for particular individual infrastructure designs and implementations—should reflect the general goals of the organization at a high level. For enterprise technical architects to incorporate a principled approach to designing technology and infrastructure, key models or designs must be defined using a common, well-understood set of principles. Principles have often been part of formal EA efforts. They provide a stronger linkage between individual decisions and basic business goals that are broadly applicable and independent of the specific decision. Principles are guidelines or best practices chosen by an organization to stimulate best behavior. They may well be traced themselves (at the highest level) back to basic business requirements and strategy. Used well, key choices or decisions within a given solution should be traceable back to both the goals of the solution in particular and the principles that were applied during its creation, representing the more general goals of all IT projects or solutions of the IT organization (ITO)—or of specific constituencies in IT or even the business as a whole. For ETA or infrastructure planning, then, it is useful for this same reason to define key ETA design architecture principles (DAPs) and agree on them before completing designs or models such as technical patterns and technical services. Linking the ETA to overall EA (or IT) and business principles can help ease adoption and foster real changes in behavior [see Figure 6.9].

Figure 6.9. EA principles: Levels of inheritance and linkages to EA models (Robertson, 2007)

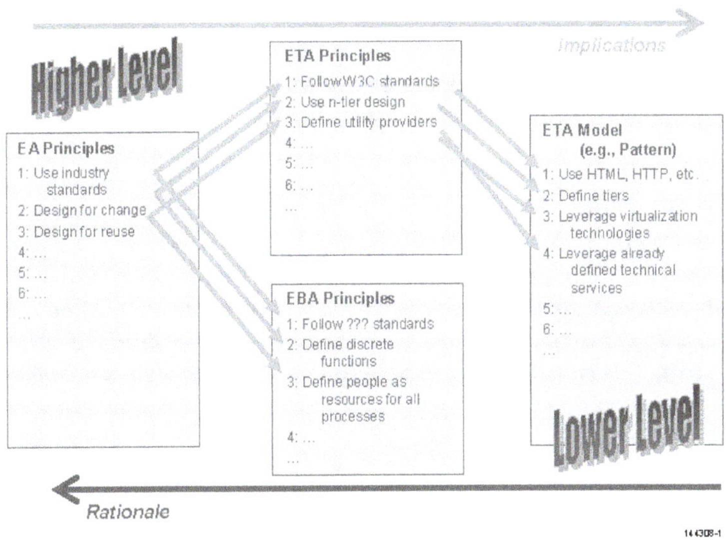

Source: Gartner (December 2007)

Table 1. Sample high-level principle (Robertson, 2007)

Principle	Description
Industry-standard design architecture principle	Technical patterns, technical services, technical components, and related product standards or other models for technology and/or infrastructure must leverage industry standards (especially Internet and Web services standards)

Source: Gartner (December 2007)

Robertson (2007) shows that: There are several levels or scopes for DAPs (Design Architecture Principles)—from the most general (common ETA DAPs), down to general for all technical patterns (technical pattern DAPs) and technical services (technical service DAPs), and even into specific designs (individual DAPs—see Figure 6.8). Implications of a principle often will apply more to an individual design (a particular technical pattern or technical service) than to the whole set of designs (the whole technical pattern portfolio)—this reality, as well as linkage back to larger-scope principles, is worth noting in the more specific designs. For example, everyone will have a high-level principle such as the one in Table 1.

Defining the enterprise technical architecture means defining requirements, principles, and models, and there are multiple models to define: technical patterns, services, domains, and components (Robertson, 2006). The goals of these architecture and infrastructure planning technology models are to reduce complexity, increase flexibility or adaptability, shorten time to market, and deliver integrated applications to the enterprise (Robertson, 2005, p. 4).

Service Oriented Models

Robertson (2005, p. 4) prescribes the use of service oriented approach to modeling the enterprise technology architecture, as follows:

To save money and yet make their infrastructures more agile, IT organizations must take a service-oriented approach to planning infrastructure. The technology viewpoint in Gartner's EA framework must catalyze planning shared infrastructure services in a more formal and consistent manner, while ensuring they are leveraged by project behavior. Together EA (specifically technical architects) and infrastructure planners must define a new kind of technology viewpoint architecture model and standard—a well-defined shared infrastructure service strategy. This planning must encompass and unify operational (often called shared infrastructure support processes, production services, or systems management services) as well as technical "services" (shared hardware and software), while reducing confusion across IT constituencies on service terminology. A formal EA approach must drive the description of the characteristics for shared infrastructure leverage. EA must lead the definition of a service-oriented shared infrastructure strategy within the technology viewpoint.

Infrastructure designs and standards must increasingly be composed of shared services rather than new equipment in a bill of materials for each new project or application (Robertson, 2005, p. 4). Furthermore, EA technology architecture teams increasingly build such services into technical pattern designs to ensure the best application leverage of these shared infrastructure services (Robertson, 2005, p. 5).

To meet the above-mentioned architecture goals of adaptability and complexity reduction, Robertson (2005) expands the service oriented modeling approach and defines a framework of patterns, services, domains, and components for the enterprise technology architecture. The Robertson (2005) framework is summarized in the following sections.

Technical Components

Robertson (2005, p. 4) defines technical components as the ETA parts. In any IT organization, the simple list of technology used (at any time) must be well-articulated and shared across planning groups, regardless of their scope. This sample list can be organized in the form of a "technical component catalog," containing descriptions and vendor examples. For each technical component, detailed technology expertise must be provided. An infrastructure professional or group should be identified as the definitive technical subject-matter expert. For any technical component, further detailed information could be provided such as rationale for key architectural or technology requirements, product requirements, product choices, or configuration details. Many architects augment this with a ranking system, designating which component choices are:

- Emerging (available for limited use in new implementations)
- Mainstream (strongly recommended for new implementations)

- Containment (installed and still requiring support)
- Retirement (installed and marked for early retirement)

Such life-cycle-stage value definitions help guide decisions governing the best choice of a technical component for a given project."

Technical Domains

Robertson (2005, p. 6) argues that given the high number of technical components that planners must choose from to assemble each application, compiling a large, undifferentiated list of items and standards is not organized enough. Moreover, certain guiding principles that go beyond the scope of any single component must be understood. Most organizations have therefore devised higher level aggregate models to better organize this morass of components. The traditional technology architecture approach organizes components into *technical domains* that are based on technology or organizational similarities. Examples include network, security, hardware/OS platform, and middleware domains. Gartner's domain architecture template delineates the following attributes for a domain (Robertson, 2005, p. 6):

- A definition of the domain architecture
- An overview describing the domain architecture
- Identification of the IT or technology trends relevant to the environment
- A description of the global design principles associated with the domain architecture
- A description of more-specific principles, trends, technologies, standards, products, and configurations for each major area included in this domain architecture
- References to other related domain architecture

Technical Patterns

Although technical domains are useful concepts for planning, they often lead to an impractical design. Properly focused architectural efforts should be unified across technical domains through requirements and enterprise-level principles, drilling down to domain-level requirements and principles based on business goals. Therefore, although technical domain models are necessary and useful, they are not sufficient by themselves. *Technology planning requires a holistic, end-to-end view.* In particular, designers (architects or engineers) must articulate models that provide a more useful expression of the goals of application and shared-service delivery. This requires a more-direct, end-to-end technical model, which maps technical components from the required technical domains. *This end-to-end model is called a "technical pattern" (or "infrastructure pattern") model* (Robertson, 2005, p. 9).

A technical pattern model is designed to serve as the standard blueprint or model for a set or class of applications that use the same—or highly similar—infrastructure designs because they have similar service-level requirements (Robertson, 2005, p. 9). Standardized "blueprints" for complete infrastructure delivery plans are (preferred because they are) more easily reused than parts-level standards by themselves. Interactions between technical components (and especially between components in different technical domains) should be defined and well-understood, particularly after a few implementations of the pattern are completed. This provides more confidence in the value of the pattern in reducing per-project implementation time (for example, because of fewer choices and less testing needed to confirm integration) (Robertson, 2005, p. 9).

The technical pattern approach pushes this grouping approach to a full, end-to-end model for a complete application (or set of similar applications). Although any given implementation will have differences, many implementations follow a sufficiently similar model that this reusable approach will work. Even in cases in which a custom design is required, it should be based on reusable components and services that relevant pattern designs use with exceptions noted (Robertson, 2005, p. 9).

One key attribute of a technical pattern (or of any standard) is the "*use case*," describing when this particular pattern should be employed (and when it should not). It should provide an easy way to pick the right pattern for the task at hand. With use cases, technical pattern attributes should include service levels, ownership, and design "freshness dating," the technical component and technical service manifest, principles involved, and sample implementations of the pattern to use as case studies (Robertson, 2005, p. 9).

The technical pattern approach models the connection of the technology viewpoint (or ETA) to the application portfolio or enterprise solution architecture constructs. Technical patterns represent the direct mapping of applications to technology or infrastructure as complete, end-to-end products. Patterns make this mapping explicit (Robertson, 2005, p. 11).

Technical patterns define repeatable, ordered sets of technical components and services that support common, repeatable requirements. Because technical patterns preselect the most appropriate technical components from the larger list of supported choices, they *reduce the complexity* of translating EA standards into project needs (Robertson, 2006).

Gartner has defined a starter kit of nine technical patterns in three main categories (Robertson, 2006):

- **"Transact" technical patterns**
  - *1-tier Transact:* It supports batch processing or online transaction processing
  - *2-tier Transact:* It defines "fat" desktop client accessing backend database server
  - *N-tier Transact:* It defines a Web browser or "thin" client access to Web presentation
- **"Publish" technical patterns**
  - *Client/server publish:* It uses a fat client and associated session-oriented protocol between the client and back-end database
  - *Web publish:* For read only access to XML, HTTP, and other structured documents
  - *Stream publish:* For real-time publishing
- **"Collaborate" technical patterns**
  - *Real-time collaborate:* As with the stream publish technical pattern, this involves bidirectional transmission of information
  - *Store and forward collaborate:* The use case for this technical pattern is the ad hoc sharing of documents

- *Structured collaborate:* This pattern implements the automated coordination of changes (for example, workflow and document management) that the store-and-forward pattern lacks.

Technical Services

Beyond providing complete, end-to-end technical patterns, another common infrastructure planning goal is defining shared technical services (or infrastructure services) with implementations to be used repeatedly by applications—and often to replace parts of some single applications with more-common approaches. This enables greater levels of physical reuse (for example, using a shared network instead of a separate one for each application or conducting a capacity analysis, rather than a purchasing exercise that documents every bill of materials), as well as easier consolidation and more-flexible sourcing strategies. Infrastructure planners and technical architects must design such shared services, which include local area networks (LANs), wide area networks (WANs), storage area networks, and server farms (Robertson, 2005, p. 13).

Service Levels or Requirements

Service levels and characteristics of the attributes of technical components, technical domains, technical patterns, and technical service designs become increasingly critical. These requirements describe the value of infrastructure to an application and thus to a business. These service levels, rather than the raw technology components, are what negotiations should focus on. Design templates should provide a place to denote service levels for a given technical service or technical pattern. For instance, conventional/operational infrastructure service-level metrics (measured, quantitative) include scalability (throughput and response time), availability, and recoverability (Robertson, 2005, p. 15).

Summary

Using a complete set of unified technology models is a critical technique for effectively managing complexity. The unification of architecture and infrastructure perspectives yields such a complete technology viewpoint framework. Beyond this set of models, the application portfolio (or ESA) with information and business viewpoints must be structured. Infrastructure planners and technical architects must remain focused on developing complete technical component, domain, pattern, and service standards and defining the appropriate ways to use them on a per-project level (Robertson, 2005, p. 19).

TOGAF ARCHITECTURE REFERENCE MODELS

There are many types of architecture reference models such as the reference model for open distributed processing (ITU/ISO RM-ODP, 1997) or model driven architecture (OMG, 2003) described above. These reference models could be candidates for the TOGAF architecture continuum. TOGAF (2007, p. 132) also defines two reference models for consideration for inclusion in a firm's enterprise continuum:

- **The TOGAF Foundation Architecture:** Comprising a *technical reference model* of generic services and functions that can serve as a platform upon which more specific architectures and architectural components can be built and a *standard information base* (of relevant specifications and standards).
- **The Integrated Information Infrastructure Reference Model:** Based on the foundation architecture, the information infrastructure reference model will enable integrated intra and interorganizational information flows to support seamless interactions between a firm and its customers, partners, and suppliers to improve the firm's strategic capabilities for customer value creation and thus competitive advantage. The integrated information infrastructure will depend on data standardization to enable end-to-end integration of partnering enterprises, which Ross et al. (2006) call process integration (described earlier in this chapter).

The reference models can be leveraged in the specification of the TOGAF technology architecture.

The inclusion of a technical reference model and its reuse for architecture specification via the enterprise continuum is formally managed under the architecture governance process.

ARCHITECTURE GOVERNANCE

The success of enterprise architecture depends critically on the practice of architecture governance. TOGAF defines architecture governance as "the practice and orientation by which enterprise architectures and other architectures are managed and controlled at an enterprise-wide level." Architecture governance is a subset of IT governance, which in turn is a subset of corporate governance (Weill & Ross, 2004). Governance is basically about ensuring that "business is conducted properly" to meet the organization's strategic objectives. It has the following characteristics (TOGAF, 2007, p. 240):

- **Discipline:** Commitment to adhere to governance procedure and processes
- **Transparency:** All decisions and actions are auditable
- **Independence:** Free of conflicts of interest
- **Accountability:** Decisions made by authorized and accountable persons
- **Responsibility:** Contracted party acting responsibly to the organization and its stakeholders
- **Fairness:** Decisions taken and processes used are fair to all parties in the organization

In the context of corporate governance and IT governance, TOGAF stipulates that architecture governance consists of the following:

- A system of controls to manage the effective introduction, implementation, and evolution of architectures within the organization
- A system to ensure architecture compliance with internal and external standards and regulatory obligations

- Processes that support effective management of the above systems within agreed parameters
- Accountability model of a clearly identified stakeholder community, both within and outside the organization

The architecture governance ensures that enterprise architecture is defined, implemented, and maintained "properly" in line with business (and IT) strategy to achieve the business and IT strategic objectives. Thus, the TOGAF architecture implementation governance phase of ADM described earlier is just one aspect of architecture governance.

TOGAF (2007, p. 243) also defines an architecture governance framework to support the architecture governance practice. The framework identifies the key processes and organization structures by which the business responsibilities associated with architecture governance can be elucidated, communicated, and managed effectively. The TOGAF architecture governance framework defines two structures for these purposes: (a) the conceptual structure which identified the key processes, architecture contents (assets), and context for governance management, and (b) organizational structure for implementing the governance process.

The framework is integral to the enterprise continuum. It manages all content pertaining to the enterprise architecture as well as to the architecture governance process itself. According to TOGAF (2007), governance processes enable the enterprise to identify, manage, audit, and disseminate all information (and decisions) related to architecture management, contracts, and implementation. They also allow all architecture assets to be monitored to ensure their currency and consistency. These processes are therefore critical to the integrity of the enterprise continuum. TOGAF (2007) defines the following architecture governance processes:

- **Policy management and take-on:** All architecture contents (assets) will undergo formal registration, validation, ratification, and publication.
- **Compliance:** Assessment of compliance against architecture standards, service level agreements, operational level agreements, and regulatory requirements.
- **Dispensation (or waiver):** Formal process for granting dispensation to noncompliant subject area such as design, operational service level, or technology standards. Dispensation is usually time-bound to allow future reassessment and realignment of the solution with enterprise architecture (or vice versa if the architecture is proved to be deficient). Effective architecture implementations should have minimal number of dispensation cases.
- **Monitoring and reporting:** Performance management to ensure the architecture implementation meets service or operational level agreements.
- **Business control:** Ensuring compliance with business policies.
- **Environment management:** It identifies all services required to ensure that the repository-based environment underpinning the governance framework is effective and efficient.

The organizational structure proposed by TOGAF (2007) architecture governance framework addresses the full life cycle of system development which ensures end-to-end architecture compliance from development to implementation to deployment of the business programs. The key organizational units defined in accordance with the architecture life cycle by the proposed structure are:

- Development phase - Architecture Board
- Implementation phase - Program Management Office
- Deployment phase - Service Management

The architecture board is a cross-organizational entity comprising representatives (executives) of key stakeholders of enterprise architecture. It is responsible for the effective management of the development, implementation, and deployment of the architecture. The architecture board is accountable to the enterprise executive management group for effective architecture governance practice within the organization. The board governs using the governance processes described above, such that architecture compliance is enforced and maintained in all three phases. Board meetings will be conducted in accordance with the COBIT[9] framework.

The program management office is responsible for managing the execution of the work packages or programs identified and segmented by enterprise architecture in accordance with the business strategy and objectives. It will implement the IT project portfolio management practice to ensure the programs will deliver maximum business value (as identified by the architecture) at a manageable risk and budget level. (More of this topic will be described in the next chapter.) Architecture compliance of solution designs is assessed against the architecture principles and models.

Service management is responsible for monitoring and assuring the operational performance of the deployed information system meets the criteria set by the service level agreements and operational level agreements.

PRACTICE EXPERIENCES

Enterprise architecture practice is a multidisciplinary practice involving both business and IT management disciplines and skills. Practice experiences of various organizations investigated and reported by a number of researchers in the literature are summarized in this section.

Richardson and Jackson (1990) describe the lessons learned from implementing a principles-based enterprise architecture for the then (1989) newly created Texaco-Saudi Arabian Oil Company joint venture organization, Star Enterprise, which inherited staff, facilities, and information resources within Texaco Inc. at the time of formation.

According to Richardson and Jackson (1990):

The environment in which Star Enterprise exists is changing at an accelerating pace. The Star Enterprise EA is a set of long-term, consensus-based criteria for evaluating and managing information technology that will persist in the face of change. It is a mechanism for identifying and resolving conflicts and building consensus on technology directions and strategies.

Richardson and Jackson argue that it is necessary for the architecture to achieve a high degree of consistency in addressing technology problems, so as to improve information flow among entities, reduce support costs for overall system, and improve portability of software from one segment to another.

The proposed star enterprise EA can be classified into four general areas: principles, inventory, models, and standards, of which principles are regarded to have most far-reaching and significant impact on the organization (Richardson & Jackson, 1990). The star enterprise EA principles were developed by senior IT management and validated in discussion with the IT steering committee. The EA principles, which guide the architectural decision making process, consist of four areas: *organization, application, data,* and *infrastructure* (Richardson & Jackson, 1990).

Some key lessons learned by Richardson and Jackson (1990) could be summarized as:

- Architectural design consistency improves overall synergy of technical support and software resource mobility throughout the information network.
- The real value EA as a means for achieving strategic company goals will often not be appreciated at the beginning but only recognized at later stages of implementation.
- Gaining consensus for the underlying architecture principles is fundamentally paramount for the success of the EA process.

Other more detailed lessons learned by Richardson and Jackson (1990) include:

- A consistent connectivity and architectural plan improves firm's operational performance.
- "The timing of small key technologies can greatly influence the success of large architectures and their related products. Attention to small details is very important to this process."
- Technology migration to the future target architecture can often be discontinuous. "Bridging these discontinuities may require a multiyear transition plan during which time the architecture will be a hybrid of each phase."
- Data integrity, security, and recovery issues are increasingly complex and require innovative architectural solutions.

The above experiences have lead Richardson and Jackson to reach three conclusions:

(1) principles-based architecture is a long term process, not a single event; (2) being consistent throughout the EA is more important than individual groups searching for local solutions; and (3) time must be spent building consensus among technical staff and communicating derived principles throughout the organization.

Matthee, Tobin, and van der Merwe (2007) investigated the state of EA practices in six South African financial services companies (of varying sizes), including the place of EA in organizational and strategic governance. From the survey, Matthee et al. (2007) found that:

1. EA's role as support for *business and IT alignment* as well as *guiding change* management is well appreciated by these firms.

2. The EA maturity level of these companies differs but is not linked to their size.
3. EA is still the responsibility of the CIO and IT managers.
4. The TOGAF and Zachman frameworks seem popular as does business process modeling technique for business modeling, and unified modeling language (UML) for application modeling. However, some companies still rely heavily on their own business and system modeling techniques.
5. "The *establishment of a comprehensive set of architectural principles* to guide, inform and support the way in which an organization fulfils its mission through the use if IT, as well as the *adoption of an architecture compliance strategy* as the two *most critical success factors* for EA."
6. Mature (successful) EA implementations have *a high level of business and technology strategy alignment* and *executive management involvement.*

The case study of the Australian Bureau of Statistics (ABS) enterprise architecture practice, by Gregor, Hart, and Martin (2007), also confirm the critical role of EA in enabling the alignment of ABS business strategy and information systems and technology (IS/IT).

Gregor et al. (2007) notes that strategic alignment has two dimensions: social and intellectual dimensions. The intellectual dimension refers to the congruence and consistency of IT and business objectives (strategies). The social dimension refers to the mutual understanding and commitments of business and IT executives to each other's mission, objectives, and plans. The ABS EA was case-studied in both dimensions.

According to Gregor et al. (2007):

the aims of the ABS architecture (which was developed internally in 1999-2001) were directly targeted at developing and maintaining alignment:

- *To ensure that the IT environment is aligned with the ABS business imperatives (its mission, objectives, and processes); and*
- *To help ABS build an IT environment that can be easily changed and extended, so as to retain its alignment with changing business imperatives*

The ABS EA is reviewed periodically (every 6-12 months) and updated when there are shifts in business products, changes in service delivery patterns, and the associated investment activities (Gregor et al., 2007). The ABS EA makes conscientious steps in demonstrating alignment by dynamically creating and maintaining business and IS/IT architecture components and structures that explicitly support each another (Gregor et al., 2007). They found that "The ABS architecture is characterized by a strong and equal focus on business operations, the deliberate inclusion of an IS/IT governance framework, the structuring and hosting of corporate information for business delivery and the efficient reuse of IS/IT components." Gregor et al. (2007) conclude that it is the combination of these social and intellectual dimensions, not by a formal EA *alone*, that will ensure strategic alignment.

Lindtrom, Johnson, Johansson, Ekstedt, and Simonsson (2006) surveyed a number of Swedish CIOs to investigate their principal concerns for the IT management and leadership role. Lindtrom et al. (2006) argue that "the CIO role is the primary stakeholder of Enterprise Architecture, so his/her need for decision support should guide Enterprise Architecture research and framework development." Thus, they investigate the extent by which two existing enterprise architectures, the Zachman framework, and the Department of Defense architecture framework, address the surveyed concerns of the CIOs. Lindtrom et al. (2006) find that the top three CIO concerns are: (1) reducing business organizational costs, (2) improving the quality of interplay between IT and business organizations, and (3) providing new computer-aided support to the business organization. Further, Lindtrom et al. (2006) find that discrepancies exist between these top three concerns and the foci of the architecture frameworks—the largest gap being the lack of decision support for issues related to the IT organization. They also find that the architecture frameworks also lack support for explicit estimation and management of costs. Lindtrom et al. (2006) suggest that this disharmony "might be remedied by the incorporation of models on IT governance, IT procurement and development processes, IT project portfolios and similar IT organizational-related issues. And, in many cases, cost information could adorn existing entities, such as functions, processes and systems."

According to Rico (2006), over 46 of the more than 100 U.S. federal agencies use enterprise architecture today, and the Zachman framework and the DoD architecture framework have large following among these agencies. The U.S. government has instituted a framework for assessing the maturity, state, status, and progress of federal EA initiatives. The framework consists of five levels: (1) creating awareness (aware of EA's importance but not applied), (2) building foundation (e.g., has allocated resources and EA metrics), (3) developing products (e.g., has an organizational policy), (4) completing products (e.g., has a maintenance policy), and (5) leveraging products (e.g., has a compliance policy). Each level is characterized by four attributes: (a) demonstration of commitment, (b) capability for commitment, (c) satisfaction of commitment, and (d) verification of commitment (Rico, 2006). Over 80% of agencies are in levels 1 and 2, and only 5% in levels 4 (4%) and 5 (1%) (Rico, 2006).

Rico (2006) derives seven principles for successful enterprise architecture practice:

1. Form a clear vision and stick to it
2. Define early measurable objectives
3. Think small, fast, and lean ("complete the EA in small, frequent and near-term increments")
4. Manage like a well-run project
5. Apply top-down systems analysis ("EA is about determining IT needs")
6. Create style guides and standards
7. Think outside of the box for tools ("choose a tool that does a few models really well rather than one that does many models very poorly")

According to Rico (2006), "The goal of EA is to improve the operational efficiency and effectiveness of organizations by aligning their strategies with their IT. Return on investment (ROI) is an excellent way to measure EA's success or failure." Thus, closely associated with the above principles for success, Rico (2006) defines additional seven principles for successful EA return on investment:

1. Use ROI as a success factor
2. Etch the desired benefits in stone
3. Establish early ROI objectives
4. Operationalize a core set of metrics

5. Continuously measure the payback
6. Use automated tools to do the work
7. Standardize ROI reporting

Finally, Shupe and Behling (2006) conclude that "successfully deploying information technology requires executive-level support, a structured decision making process, and a strategy based on an understanding of the organization's vision and its enterprise architecture."

SUMMARY

Enterprise architecture is a critical management tool for linking business and IT strategies to their disciplined execution (James et al., 2005). Enterprise architecture encapsulates the essence of business and IT strategies (Ross et al., 2006). It provides structure, discipline, and a platform for articulating the firm's strategic imperatives in an integrative and holistic manner, functionally analogous to the working of a real-life enterprise. By adopting standardized terminology and definitions business and IT stakeholders will be able to agree on the purpose, scope, content, and shape of the architecture. Thus, enterprise architecture serves as an integrator and translator of critical business and IT concepts by which business and IT stakeholders can assure strategic alignment across multiple perspectives. Much work has been expended on the principles and methods for developing business-aligned enterprise architecture to guide the development of IT solutions to implement the business strategy (Zachman, Spewak, TOGAF, Ross-Weill-Robertson, Gartner, RM-ODP, POSIX, OMG, eTOM). Enterprise architecture essentially is a formal description of the enterprise business context, including the business strategy, and the supporting information system architecture which aligns with the business context. It comprises of four interrelated viewpoints, each representing the perspective of a type of enterprise stakeholders, namely, business architecture, information architecture, application architecture, and technology architecture. Business architecture defines the firm's overarching business strategy, business model, organizational model, and underpinning core business processes. Information (or data) architecture defines the information value-chain model and information (data) entities which support the business functions defined in the business architecture (Spewak, 1992). Application architecture defines the business functional systems of the enterprise; they interact with each other in accordance with the predefined business processes (business architecture) consuming and producing business information elements defined by the information architecture (Spewak, 1992). Technology architecture defines the infrastructure platforms and distribution which support the applications, data, and business functions of the respective application, information, and business architectures (Spewak, 1992; TOGAF, 2007).

Enterprise architecture provides an integrative insight on the enterprise strategy, its environmental (market and technology) trends, the target future business state, and the principles and guidance to get there. It defines the firm's target future state architecture model for the business and information systems. It prescribes the principles of architecture solution design of information systems to ensure compliance with business strategic requirements and systems operational integrity requirements such as scalable performance, agility to adapt to business change, security, and manageability. The gap of current and target architecture defines the scope of business and systems changes required and the migration steps over a period to achieve the business strategy and vision. The gap is translated into an integrated IT strategic plan (roadmap) of business programs. Implementation of the IT strategic roadmap allows enterprise to close the gap and attain the target future business state. Enterprise architecture guides the development and implementation of these programs, in line with the business priorities, to ensure reliable delivery of the desired business outcomes stipulated in the business/IT strategy. Architecture governance as part of IT governance ensures architecture solutions for system development will comply with the EA principles and guidance. Architecture governance ensure business solutions will not only deliver the expected value (as stipulated in the business case), but also ensure they will integrate into the target enterprise system designed to give the firm the competitive advantage.

Enterprise architecture, therefore, is a critical business tool for managing and implementing business changes, and attaining business agility and strategic alignment.

REFERENCES

Allega, P. (2006, December). *Advancing the common requirements vision deliverable* (ID No. G00142394). Retrieved August 30, 2008, from www.gartner.com

Blechar, M. J. (2007, November). *Establishing an agile information architecture* (ID No. G00152365). Retrieved August 30, 2008, from www.gartner.com

Carbone, J. A. (2004). *IT architecture toolkit.* Prentice Hall PTR.

Gregor, S., Hart, D., & Martin, N. (2007). Enterprise architectures: Enablers of business strategy and IS/IT alignment in government. *Information Technology & People, 20*(2), 96-120. Retrieved August 30, 2008, from www.emeraldinsight.com/0959-3845.htm

Handler, R., & Newman, D. (2005, August). *Making a compelling case for enterprise information architecture* (ID No. G00129962). Retrieved August 30, 2008, from www.gartner.com

Handler, R., & Newman, D. (2005, September). *Use enterprise information architecture techniques to move to information management* (ID No. G00130267). Retrieved August 30, 2008, from www.gartner.com

ITU-T X.901/ISO/IEC 10746-1 (1997). The reference model for open distributed processing: Part 1. *International Telecom Union and International Organization for Standardization.*

James, G. (2007, March). *Information architecture patterns provide valuable guidance* (ID No. G00147224). Retrieved August 30, 2008, from www.gartner.com

James, G., Handler, R. A., Lapkin, A., & Gall, N. (2005, October). Gartner Enterprise Architecture Framework: Evolution 2005 (ID No. G00130855). Retrieved August 30, 2008, from www.gartner.com

Kaplan, R. S., & Norton, D. P. (2004). *Strategy map: Converting intangible assets into tangible outcomes.* Harvard Business School Press.

Lapkin, A., & Handler, R. (2007, March). Gartner Leader Toolkit: Bank XYZ Enterprise Architecture Framework. Retrieved August 30, 2008, from www.gartner.com

Lindtrom, A., Johnson, P., Johansson, E., Ekstedt, M., & Simonsson, M. (2006). A survey on CIO concerns: Do enterprise architecture frameworks support them? *Information Systems Front, 8*, 81-

89. Springer Science.

Matthee, M., Tobin, P., & van der Merwe, P. (2007). The status quo of enterprise architecture implementation in South African financial services companies. *South African Journal of Business Management, 38*(1), 11-23.

Newman, D. (2005, September). *The essential building blocks for enterprise information management* (ID No. G00130527). Retrieved August 30, 2008, from www.gartner.com

Newman, D., & Blechar, M. J. (2007, June). *Putting enterprise information management in context* (ID No. G00148273). Retrieved August 30, 2008, from www.gartner.com

Newman, D., & Logan, D. (2006, October). *Gartner definition clarifies the role of enterprise information management* (ID No. G00143330). Retrieved August 30, 2008, from www.gartner.com

OMG. (2003). *Model driven architecture.* Author.

Richardson, G., & Jackson, B. (1990, December). A principles-based enterprise architecture: Lessons from Texaco and Star Enterprise. *MIS Quarterly, 14*(4), 385-403.

Rico, D. (2006, April). A framework for measuring ROI of enterprise architecture. *Journal of Organizational and End User Computing, 18*(2), i-xii. ABI/INFORM Global.

Robertson, B. (2005, November). *Architecting the technology viewpoint requires defining a service-oriented infrastructure strategy* (ID No. G00134007). Retrieved August 30, 2008, from www.gartner.com

Robertson, B. (2005, December). *A framework of patterns, services, domains and components defines the technology viewpoint* (ID No. G00135179). Retrieved August 30, 2008, from www.gartner.com

Robertson, B. (2006, September). *Use technical patterns to speed architecture benefits* (ID No. G00143285). Retrieved August 30, 2008, from www.gartner.com

Robertson, B. (2006, December). *EA modeling made simple: ETA domain strategy example* (ID No. G00144602). Retrieved August 30, 2008, from www.gartner.com

Robertson, B. (2007, December). *Toolkit best practice: Using EA principles in enterprise technical architecture* (ID No. G00144308). Retrieved August 30, 2008, from www.gartner.com

Rosser, B. (2006). *Creating a business architecture: Where do you start?* (ID No. G00144983). Retrieved August 30, 2008, from www.gartner.com

Shupe, C., & Behling, R. (2006, July/August). Developing and implementing a strategy for technology deployment. *Information Management Journal, 40*(4), 52-57. ABI/INFORM Global.

Spewak, S. H. (1992). *Enterprise architecture planning: Developing a blueprint for data, application and technology.* QED Publishing Group.

Telemanagement Forum. (2003). *GB921: The enhanced telecom operations map eTOM.* Author.

TOGAF. (2007). *The Open Group enterprise architecture framework* (V8.1.1 enterprise ed.). The Open Group.

Weill, P., & Ross, J. (2004). *IT governance.* Harvard Business School Press.

Weiss, D. (2006, September). *Enterprise architecture framework approaches to business context* (ID No. G00141955). Retrieved August 30, 2008, from www.gartner.com

Weiss, D. (2006, October). *An enterprise architect's guide to working for the business* (ID No. G00142309). Retrieved August 30, 2008, from www.gartner.com

Weiss, D. (2006, December). *Introducing business context* (ID No. G00144386). Retrieved August 30, 2008, from www.gartner.com

Weiss, D. (2007, March). *Business architecture viewpoint: A framework ofpatterns, services, domains and components* (ID No. G00146461). Retrieved August 30, 2008, from www.gartner.com

Weiss, D. (2007, September). *The business architecture viewpoint: Defining the bricks* (ID No. G00149915). Retrieved August 30, 2008, from www.gartner.com

Weiss, D., & Robertson, B. (2006, September). *Enterprise architecture road maps: Closing the gap to the future* (ID No. G00140082). Retrieved August 30, 2008, from www.gartner.com

Zachman, J. A. (1987). A framework for information systems architecture. *IBM Systems Journal, 26*(3), 276-292.

ENDNOTES

1 To that end, enterprise architecture is a more in-depth specification of the firm's business model described in Chapter I of this book.

2 Carbone (2004) models enterprise architecture in terns of three environments: **execution environment** models the set of architecture components used to run the enterprise; **development environment** models the set of components (e.g., data stores to support billing functions) required to support the development staff (e.g., programming language compilers); and **operations environment** models the set of components (e.g., network operating system) required to monitor and manage the health of the IT infrastructure (p. 59).

3 According to Weill and Ross (2004, p. 31), the key to process integration from a technology perspective is data standardization. Thus they assert process and data standardization (or process standardization and integration) are the two defining characteristics of enterprise architecture.

4 The relationship of innovation and IT is discussed in Chapter X of this book.

5 With permission by Gartner Inc., the descriptions and figures of Gartner Enterprise Architecture and its attendant Business, Information, and Technology Architectures are composed by excerpts, selected and integrated by the author from numerous Gartner Research Notes published in 2005-2007. The source of each excerpt is referenced by the specific author name(s) of the individual Gartner Research Note from which the excerpt is extracted.

6 A view (as seen by a stakeholder) is defined by TOGAF as a representation of a whole system from the perspective of a related set of concerns. It is specific to the architecture for which it is created.

7 Specifically from the anchor model developed as part of the common requirements vision (Weiss, 2007, p. 4).

8 Opinions about the order of current state and future state evaluation, depending on viewpoint, vary considerably (Rosser, 2006, p. 4).

9 Control objectives for information and related technology is a way to implement IT governance. Details can be found at www.itgi.org.

Chapter VII
Strategic Programs: Planning and Execution

INTRODUCTION

The previous chapters describe how IT strategy and enterprise architecture can be defined in line with business strategy. The success of business and IT strategies, as explained in Chapter IV, depends on the firm's ability to translate the strategies into work packages known as strategic programs, and diligently plan, prioritize, and execute the strategic programs in a sequence that is in accordance with the business strategy and priorities. Chapter VI describes enterprise architecture as the link between business strategy and information systems planning and implementation (which, in effect, executes the strategy). The gap analysis of the current enterprise architecture in comparison with the target or future state architecture will identify the scope and extent of change required on the current architecture to transition towards the target architecture. Compared to business strategy gap analysis, architecture gap analysis offers a more granular and integrative assessment of the business and system changes required to realize the business strategy. The scope and extent of architecture change required constitutes the overall scope of the strategic programs that need to be defined and developed to deliver the objectives of the business strategy. These programs will be prioritized by IT governance using IT project portfolio management principles. Their implementations in time sequence will define the migration path of the current enterprise architecture towards the target future state architecture. This chapter explains the theory behind and the practice of strategic program planning and program management. We first describe two contrasting approaches to IT strategic planning, namely: the Cassidy model, and the Y model discussed in Chapter IV. The Cassidy

(2006) model uses the business vision to define the IT architecture direction from which the IT strategic plan is then specified including its business case justification. In terms of the Y model, strategic program planning and execution fall in stages 4, 5, 6, and 7 of the model. Discussions of the Y model and analysis of barriers to strategy implementation will give the readers a basic understanding of IT strategic planning and program execution (introductory project management practice). We conclude the chapter by describing the principles and methods for enterprise architecture-driven strategic planning as well as IT project portfolio management principles. This is a more advanced practice, typically taken by firms with higher maturity in IT management practice.

CASSIDY STRATEGIC PLANNING MODEL

Similar to the Y model, the Cassidy (2006) model for strategic planning starts with identifying the future target and current states of the enterprise, assessing the IT gap between these two states, and determining the path (roadmap) or IT strategic (program) plan to get from the current state to the future target state.

The Cassidy strategic planning model comprises four phases, as shown in Figure 7.1. The four phases start from business vision and ends with recommendations for the IT strategic program plan or roadmap for realizing the business vision.

The Cassidy model is summarized below (Cassidy, 2006):

Phase 1: Visioning (Business Focus)

Initiate and Manage the Project

This phase establishes and initiates the planning project. Like any project, it has a project plan, schedule, tasks, and deliverables. It also has a resource plan of the resources (including roles and responsibilities of business and IT personnel) expected to contribute to the formulation of the strategic plan. It also establishes the governance and communications processes for project control and status reporting, which include the formal announcement of the commencement of the project to the stakeholders.

Understand Business Situation and Vision

From business (either via business plan documentation or interview of selected executives), clarify and confirm IT understanding of business mission, vision, values, strategic goals, and priorities. This process has some resemblance to the business architecture process described in Chapter VI.

Document and Confirm the Business Analysis

Analyze the external environmental trends: what future customers (market) and suppliers and regulatory requirements are to be satisfied by the envisioned future business operating model. Analyze the strengths, weaknesses, opportunities, and threats (SWOT) of the business. How will the business vision address SWOT, and how will this business situation impact IT environment?

Figure 7.1 Cassidy (2006) Strategic Planning Model

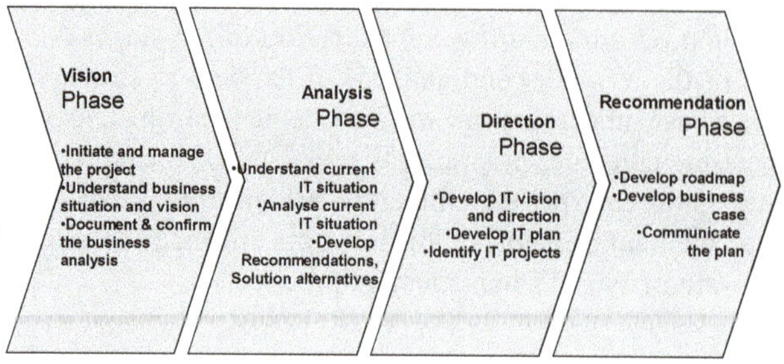

Phase 2: Analysis (of IT Environment)
Understand Current IT Situation

Review IT documents and interview/workshop IT personnel and executives to confirm current IT environment.

Analyze Current IT Situation
Analyze the IT industry and technology trends and competitor profiles. Conduct industry benchmarking of the current IT environment. Review the enterprise information needs and current data architecture, and current business process model and application portfolio. From the business vision, identify the high level functional IT requirements. Conduct IT SWOT analysis in the context of the business vision (and attendant functional IT requirements). Assess and confirm with business and IT executives the resultant IT functional or architecture gap identified.

Develop Recommendations, Solution Alternatives
Identify information and business requirements, and determine the extent by which they can be met by current business applications and infrastructure. The gaps identified will inform the business application options and infrastructure options, from which an initial set of recommendations will be formulated. From the IT organizational and process gap, the corresponding recommendations for closing these gaps will be formulated.

Phase 3: Direction (of IT)
Develop IT Vision and Direction

From the business situation and vision, the corresponding IT mission and vision is articulated. From each business goal, the corresponding IT goals and strategies, which will help achieve the business goal, are determined. IT balanced scorecard and metrics for tracking IT progress towards achieving business goal will be established.

Develop IT Plan (Architecture Direction)
Develop the IT architecture: Business application direction, information management direction, technical infrastructure direction, and, where appropriate, e-business direction. Develop the IT service architecture which includes the desired IT organizational and process models for excellent service delivery. This includes the sourcing strategy by which projects will be resourced, whether in-house or outsourced resources (or both) will be used. Develop the prioritization process (as part of IT governance). As explained in Chapter V, the above-identified IT, organizational, and sourcing gaps are, respectively, referred to by Kaplan and Norton (2004) in their business strategy map analysis as the strategic readiness of information, organizational, and human capital.

Identify IT Projects
From the IT plan, specific projects are identified for development. For each project a business case is developed which includes estimation of costs and benefits. Project prioritization is enforced with business owners and sponsors as an integral part of IT governance.

Phase 4: Recommendation
Develop Roadmap

From the IT direction, document the detailed roadmap including estimated costs, risks, concerns, readiness assessment, and organizational impact statements.

Develop Business Case
Summarize business benefits of the roadmap and the business case for executive committee approval through the IT governance process.

Communicate the Plan
Develop the communication plan for ongoing status update of the strategic plan to all stakeholders.

In summary, according to Cassidy (2006), the business-aligned IT strategic plan documentation should contain the following information to enable effective implementation to achieve the business vision:

1. Current business situation: Comprising information, direction, operating vision, and SWOT analysis
2. Business–IT link: Comprising IT implications, key business measures, key business requirements, and business process improvements
3. Current IT situation: Comprising business application, technical infrastructure, organization, processes, and budget
4. IT industry: Comprising IT industry trends, benchmark statistics, and competitive profiles
5. IT assessment: Comprising SWOT analysis, scorecard, survey results, and recommendations
6. IT high level direction: Comprising vision, mission, goals, strategies, scorecard, metrics, e-business directions, and prioritization process

7. IT direction: Comprising business application, technical infrastructure, organization, and processes
8. Implementation plan: Comprising projects, roadmap, costs, investment, organizational impact, business case, financial funding model, next steps, communication plan, and planning process
9. Appendix
10. Executive summary

Y STRATEGIC PLANNING MODEL

A strategic plan, covering strategy choice, is developed in stages 4 to 5 of the Y model. While stage 4 is concerned with seeking alternative actions, stage 5 is concerned with selecting actions and making an action plan as illustrated in Figure 7.2.

Figure 7.2. The two stages of choice

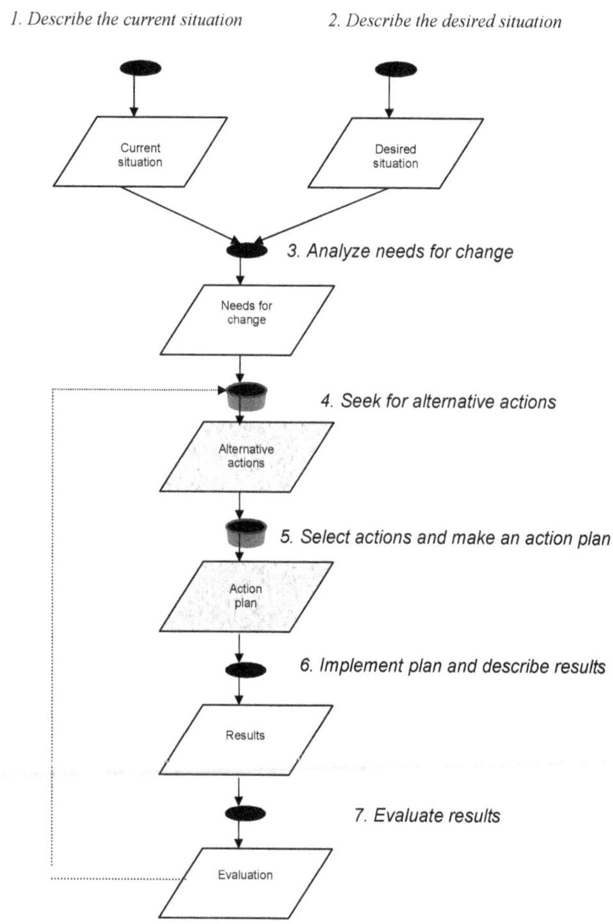

Figure 7.3. The life cycle methodology for information systems development

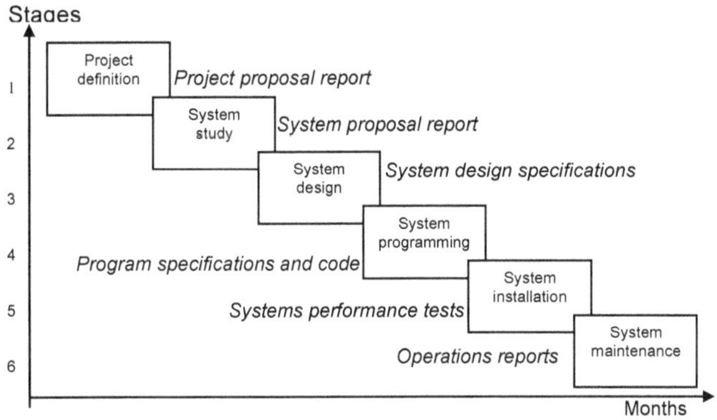

Identifying Alternative Actions

When needs for change have been identified (through architecture gap analysis) and proposals for filling gaps have been developed, alternative actions for improving the current situation can be developed. New IS/IT can be developed, acquired, and implemented in alternative ways. Several decisions have to be made when a new IS/IT is chosen. Such decisions are called systems development strategy, and they are illustrated later when we discuss IT governance as allocation of decision rights.

New IS/IT can be developed using analytical or experimental methodology. Analytical methodology implies defining the needs of users through intellectual reasoning techniques. Such techniques define stages of systems study, systems design, programming, installation, testing, implementation, and maintenance. Experimental methodology is showing the users alternative computer screens with information and asking for their opinions. This is sometimes called prototyping. Through iterations, we might improve and create even better systems. The decision here will depend on systems complexity and the available time for development.

A common analytical methodology is the systems life cycle. The *systems life cycle* partitions the systems development process into formal stages that must be completed sequentially with a formal definition of labor between end users and information systems

Figure 7.4. The prototyping methodology for systems development

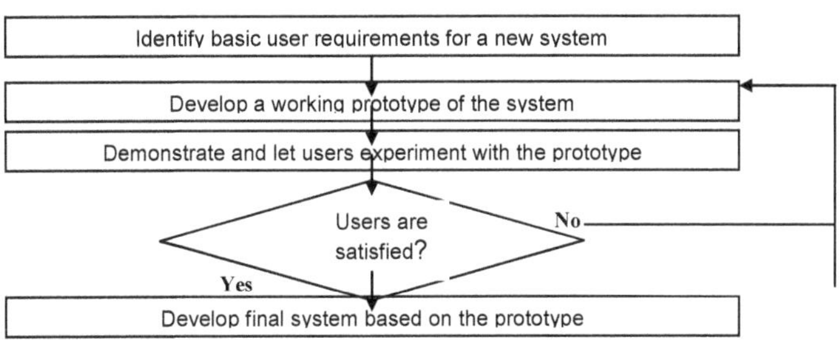

specialists. The life cycle for an information system has six stages: (1) project definition, (2) system study, (3) design, (4) programming, (5) installation, and (6) maintenance. Figure 7.3 illustrates these stages. Each stage consists of basic activities that must be performed before the next stage can begin.

The systems life cycle is useful for building large complex systems in-house that require a rigorous and formal requirements analysis, predefined specifications, and tight controls over the systems-building process. However, the systems life cycle methodology is costly, time consuming, and inflexible. Often, volumes of new documents must be produced and steps repeated if requirements and specifications need to be revised. Because of the time and cost to repeat the sequence of life cycle activities, the methodology encourages freezing of specifications early in the development process, discouraging change.

A common experimental methodology is prototyping. *Prototyping* consists of building an experimental system rapidly and inexpensively for end users to evaluate. By interacting with the prototype, users can get a better idea of their information requirements. The prototype accepted by the users will be the basis for creating the final system. The prototype is a working version of an information system or part of the system, but it is meant only to be a preliminary model. The process of building a preliminary system, trying it out, improving it, and trying it again is called an iterative process of systems development because the steps required to build a system can be repeated over and over again. In Figure 7.4, a four-step model of the prototyping process is illustrated.

Prototyping is most useful when there is some uncertainty about requirements or design solutions. Prototyping encourages end-user participation in building a system; therefore, it is more likely to produce a system that fulfills user requirements. However, rapid prototyping runs the risk of ignoring essential steps in systems development. Such ignorance may later cause rise in maintenance costs.

A systems project can either be completely expert-driven or completely user-led, or something in between. It is an important part of Scandinavian culture to have user participation. Totally user-led may be difficult, as technical problems will require the assistance of IS/IT experts. The decision here will depend on technical skills needed as well as availability of competent and motivated users. We can distinguish between the following four user participation roles:

- **Resources manager.** This is a user who has management responsibility and makes decisions concerning resources for new IS/IT, including people involved in systems development and money for procurement of equipment.
- **Solutions entrepreneur.** This is a user who has ideas about new information systems, both related to applications areas and systems design.
- **Requirements developer.** This is a user who has strong opinions about functions in a new information system.
- **System champion.** This is a user who is enthusiastic and dedicated to the successful implementation of the new system.

The result of a systems project can be a product and/or a process. Product means only the new IS/IT. Process means paying attention to the learning and increased insight gained from participating in the IS/IT development activity. The decision here will depend on systems complexity as well as company culture for learning. We can distinguish between the following four kinds of results:

- **Systems success:** The benefits from the new information system in terms of rationalization benefits, control benefits, organizational benefits, and market benefits.
- **User success:** The extent of user satisfaction with the new system.
- **Development success:** The extent to which the new IS/IT was developed on time and within budget.
- **Learning success:** The extent to which participating persons have improved their skills in IS/IT development.

Coordination of systems development can be defined along a scale. This scale runs from one-sided systems development to a balanced development of personnel, system, and organization. A completely one-sided systems development may create an efficient technological solution, but it may not work in the organization as personnel and organizational issues were not considered. The decision here will depend on company culture for linking human resources management to information technology management. We can distinguish between four alternative coordination approaches:

- **One-sided:** Attention is concentrated on the technical solution of the new IS/IT. We put all our efforts into optimizing both hardware and software by selecting machines, servers, and network, as well as database system and application software, so that the technology itself works as efficient as possible.
- **Two-sided:** Attention is expanded to users, where solutions may be tailor-made to individual users.
- **Three-sided:** Attention is further expanded to the organization, where solutions are designed in such a way that business processes are improved.
- **Four-sided:** Attention is further expanded to the environment, where solutions are designed in such a way that stakeholders may find it attractive to do business with us.

Selecting Appropriate Actions

At stage 5, we have to make final decisions concerning content of actions and development actions. For more mature IT organizations, we recommend using enterprise-architecture facilitated IT project portfolio management (ITPM) discipline to select appropriate actions (portfolio of projects) to create the strategic plan for execution. The ITPM management discipline is described in detail at the end of this chapter.

While content of actions is our final priority of needed changes, development of actions is our final systems development strategy.

In stage 3 of the Y model, we analyzed needs for change, identified potential IS/IT, compared them with current IS/IT in the company, prioritized needs for change, and proposed new IS/IT in the organization. We are going to look a little closer at the task of choosing which IS/IT to develop/acquire when discussing IT governance as allocation of decision rights in Chapter IX.

Making the Plan

The Y model focuses on the different steps in strategy work, including making an IS/IT strategy. We have discussed in-depth the analysis part of an IS/IT strategy. The analysis covered description of the current situation, description of desired situation, analysis of needs for change, and priority of needs for change. When the analysis part was complete, decisions had to be made. The choices should be made by business management, preferably by the chief executive of the organization. When all necessary decisions have been made, then the important task of implementation can start, as described in the remainder of this chapter.

The Y model outlines the working steps. Analysis and choice should result in an approved IS/IT strategy, that is, a strategy which is decided to be implemented. An approved strategy is the product of strategy work. We may distinguish between product (plan) and process (learning). The process should ideally involve all affected and give them access to all the analyses of the work and give them a possibility for voicing their opinions and listen to the viewpoints of others. In that way the process will give learning to all involved and might be a way of securing support for the strategy.

The work of developing an IS/IT strategy for the first time might be organized as a project. A project is a unique task, which can be contrasted by continuous line activities. Later on, the updating and maintenance of the strategy might be part of the responsibilities of the line organization. But even then they have to involve all the necessary parties in the work.

We might focus even more on what is involved in a process. There are three well-known stages in an organizational development process, and making an IS/IT strategy might well be looked at as organizational development. The first stage is unfreeze. Here it is important to create a climate for change, getting acceptance and readiness for change. In the analysis part it is certainly of importance to focus on the need for changes and create a common understanding of the need for changes. Such needs should be recognized by all involved. The second stage is change. In the implementation part, we have to be aware that it is a change process. Growth and changes might hurt. They can result in opposition and counter attacks. It is necessary to alter attitudes, beliefs, and values of individuals directly, or indirectly, by changing the structure, goals, or technology of the organization. The final stage is refreeze. Here the new state is institutionalized. The new situation is stabilized. Here we sum up what we have achieved and are happy about it before we start over again.

There should be some clear goals set for what we would like to achieve during the process. We want the commitment of management, and we should also use the process to educate management about benefits and risks of IS/IT. We want management to understand how IS/IT is applied, and we want to increase managers' own use of IS/IT. At the same time we want the commitment of users, and we want to educate them as well concerning the importance of IS/IT for the business. Changes in users' attitudes toward IS/IT will create commitment to strategy and implementation plans as well as better understanding of business and its dependence on IS/IT. Hopefully, the process will lead to better relationships between the IS/IT department and user departments. The close cooperation in the strategy process should lead to such a result.

At the outset there might be resistance among management against getting involved in the process, and they may oppose any new strategies for IS/IT. The problem might be that top management belongs to an older generation and are subject to a general resistance to

Figure 7.5. Strategy project organization structure

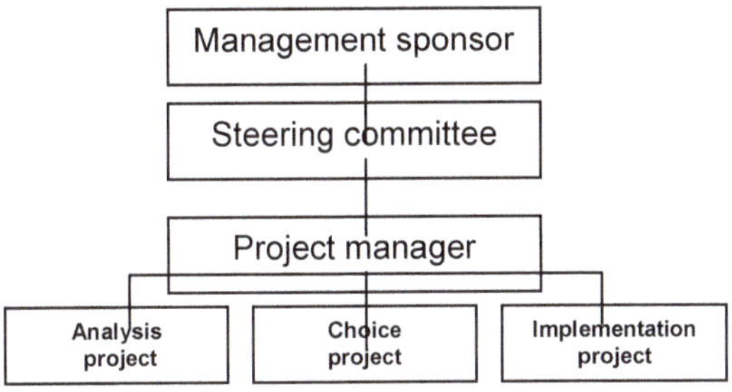

change. There may also be some specific explanations for resistance. One such explanation might be the uncertainty about benefits of IS/IT. Generally, resistance of management can be identified as:

- Ignorance of IS/IT and its potential uses and benefits
- Poor communication between the IS/IT department and the rest of the business
- General resistance to change
- Lack of focus on opportunities for competitive advantage
- Lack of instruments for decisively measuring the benefits of IS/IT.

There are several approaches to overcoming management resistance. Education or information—creating knowledge—is of importance, if it is possible to get management involved. If they do not want to listen to IS/IT people from the company, then it might be a good idea to have management meet with managers from other companies that have experienced the benefits of IS/IT themselves. All the time it is of importance to link IS/IT to business needs. It is also of importance to involve management in the decision making. A good idea might be a kind of steering committee, which should consist of all the functional managers. Functional budgets for IS/IT would make the functional managers strongly involved. Quick positive results might also convince management about the benefits of IS/IT. It is not certain that such applications are available, but in prioritizing one should look for applications that are low risk, relatively quick to acquire/develop and give good, fast results. In summary, here are some tactics for involving and influencing management:

- Educate management about use and benefits of IS/IT
- Have management meet other managers who are enthusiastic about IS/IT
- Link IS/IT to business management needs
- Form a steering committee
- Develop functional IS/IT budgets
- Rapid development of low-risk, managerially useful systems

The development of an IS/IT strategy might be organized as a project, as we discussed earlier. As illustrated in Figure 7.5, we can have a traditional organizational structure with a steering committee, project manager, and project team (consisting of both business people and IS/IT people). One special aspect is that one should look for a management sponsor, that is, a member of the top management group of the company that would like to sponsor the work. A sponsor serves as a change agent and is a strong supporter of change using IS/IT.

The management sponsor is crucial for project success. The perfect sponsor does the following tasks:

- Chairing the steering committee meetings
- Assuring top management participation and commitment, through active backing and allocation of the right resources
- Representing the interests and priorities of the business
- Heading the marketing effort—the effort of selling the project to the whole organization should not be underestimated
- Acting as the focal point for decisions about scope, priority, and conduct of project work

The steering committee is of key importance for project success. We are here focusing on what should be done by the steering committee in order to get a positive decision by top management concerning IS/IT strategy:

- Providing strategic direction and guidance on business requirements, and priorities to the project team
- Reviewing and approving plans and raising risk management issues
- Conducting checkpoint reviews and authorizing continuation of work
- Reviewing and contributing to final result, before submission to top management.

We advocate strong interaction between the steering committee and the project team. The steering committee gives its general directions at the outset and gives feedback several times on the material presented to them by the project manager.

IT Strategy Document

The IS/IT strategy document may be long or short depending on traditions and expectations in the company. In large organizations, the strategy document will typically have the following elements:

1. Introduction
   - Purpose (its use, distribution of plan)
   - Background (why and the way it was developed, participants, methods)
   - Qualifications (what is not covered)
2. Current business situation
   - Analysis of business direction, market strategy, and competitive forces
   - SWOT analysis, X model, product portfolio analysis, and environmental analysis
   - Knowledge analysis

3. Future business situation
   - Changes in business direction
   - Changes in business activities
   - Changes in knowledge management
4. Current IS/IT situation
   - Benefits, stages, management activities, strategic integration
   - Business processes, value configuration, e-business
   - IS/IT support for knowledge management
5. IS/IT vision and overall strategy
   - Important IS/IT trends
   - IS/IT vision (for the next 3–5 years)
   - Enterprise architecture encompassing the business and IT visions and principles
   - Main priorities
6. IS/IT applications
   - Needs for changes in application portfolio
   - Required development portfolio
   - Existing portfolio upgrade
   - Future potential portfolio
   - Analysis of applications and portfolios, cost-benefit analysis
   - Proposed priorities
7. IS/IT organization
   - Need for changes
   - IT Governance Model, general guidelines
8. IS/IT human resources
   1. Need for changes
   2. Capability and sourcing strategies, general guidelines
9. IT infrastructure
   - Need for changes
   - Strategy, general guidelines

One important ambition of the IS/IT strategy is to align business and IS/IT. There are both enablers and inhibitors of business–IS/IT alignment. Such enablers and inhibitors should be identified, analyzed, and solved while making the plan. Solutions should be described in the IS/IT strategy document. The two most significant enablers are often senior executive support for IS/IT and IT involved in strategy development:

1. Senior executive support for IS/IT can be documented by asking them to define and describe strategies that include the role of IS/IT. These descriptions from executives should be included in section 5 of the plan.
2. IT's participation in creating business strategy can be documented by asking the CIO to define and describe the future business situation. These descriptions from the CIO should be included in section 3 of the plan.

The senior executive support for IS/IT strategy is the effort of executives to contribute to strategy analysis, choice, and implementation. Management support includes management expectations, participation, monitoring, knowledge, time, and enthusiasm. Senior executive support is widely recognized as an important factor in the implementation of information systems and information technology strategy. Management may be hesitant to IS/IT strategy work, hence representing a problem. Some top executives may seem committed to the status quo.

Both middle management attitudes and senior management attitudes towards strategy are important influences on the extent of plan success. It may be difficult to secure top management commitment for a strategic plan with commitment defined as acceptance of plan values and willingness to exert effort on its behalf.

The planning methodology itself may require too much top management involvement. The output of planning is not necessarily in accordance with management expectations. Top management monitoring of strategy work may represent an effective planning mechanism. Management control systems may in this context provide a comprehensive mechanism for effective planning. Management monitoring and control of strategic planning may be organized through a steering committee.

Generally, senior executive support is pivotal to the adoption of innovations. CEOs in particular have a major impact on changes in their organizations. A plan must be a call for action, one that recognizes management's responsibility to fix what is broken and to harvest opportunities proactively and in real time. It is imperative that IT personnel educate their top managers and make them aware of the importance of their support in major IT initiatives. Top management support is a key recurrent factor critical for effective IS/IT strategy.

Strategy Implementation

Stages 6 and 7 cover strategy implementation in the Y model. While stage 6 is concerned with implementing the plan and describing results, stage 7 is concerned with evaluating results as illustrated in Figure 7.6.

The creation of IS/IT strategy has become a major challenge to business executives and IS/IT executives in recent years. Investments in information technology have been large, and many failed investments reflect this challenge. The impact of IT on organizational performance has grown in strategic importance, and thus the significance of failed IT investments is even greater. Information processing and information technology are becoming critical to many business and government operations, and the technology itself is changing at a rapid rate. New information technology will continue to transform organizations and changes in how industry participants use IT can alter established relationships in an industry. Strategic IS/IT planning can play a critical role in helping organizations to increase efficiency, effectiveness, and competitiveness. Although organizations use different methods in their analysis of current and desired situations, the resulting plans are to be implemented.

The importance of the implementation of strategic IS/IT plans is illustrated by the significant attention paid to it in recent years. Studies show that implementation is important for four reasons. First, the failure to carry out the strategic IS/IT plan can cause lost opportunities, duplicated efforts, incompatible systems, and wasted resources. Second, the extent to which strategic IS/IT planning meets its objectives is determined by implementation. Third, the lack of implementation leaves firms dissatisfied with and reluctant to continue their strategic planning. Fourth, the lack of implementation creates problems establishing and maintaining priorities in future strategic IS/IT planning.

Figure 7.6. The two stages of implementation

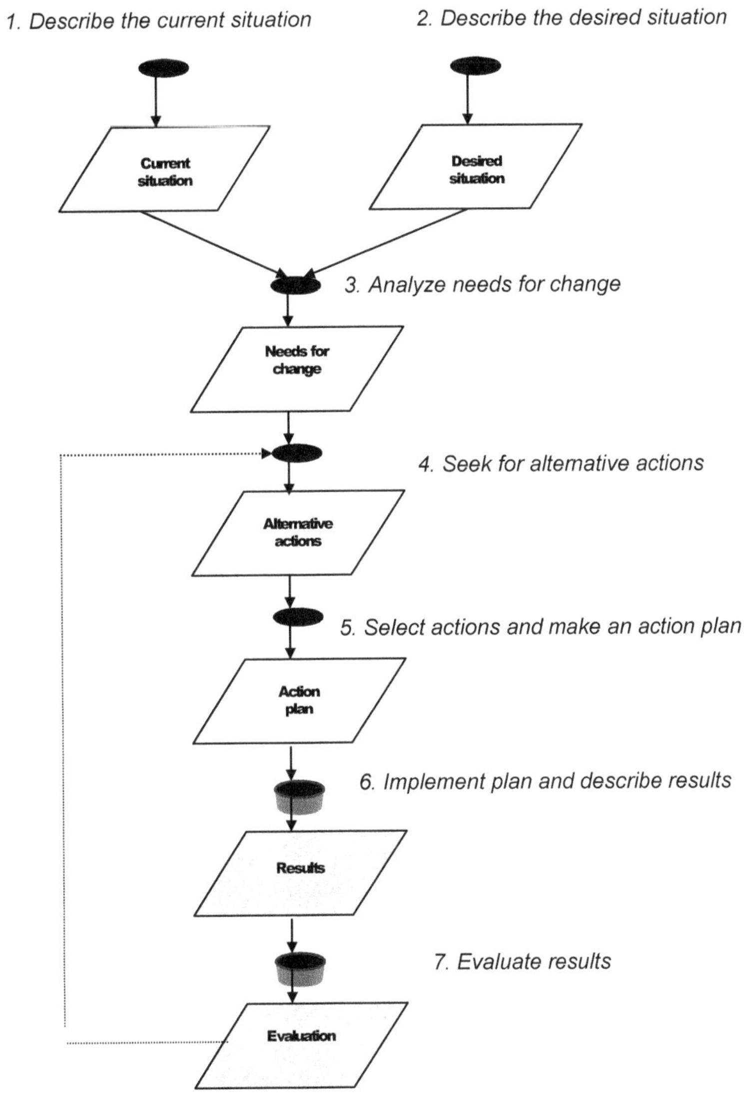

IMPLEMENTING PLAN

IS/IT strategy implementation can be defined as the process of completing the projects for application of information technology to assist an organization in realizing its goals. However, implementing an IS/IT strategy is not simply the act of implementing many projects and individual systems. Instead, implementing such a plan demands a gestalt view in the planning of individual systems. A gestalt view represents the implementation of the plan philosophy, attitudes, intentions, and ambitions associated with IS/IT use in the organization. It may include decisions about the IS organization and the implementation of IT architecture.

The term implementation is given a variety of meanings in the literature. Implementation can be described as a procedure directed by a manager to install planned change in an organization. Change is an empirical observation of difference in form, quality, or state over time in an organizational entity. Implementation can be the process of gaining targeted organizational members' appropriate and committed use of an innovation. Information technology implementation from strategic IS/IT planning is a typical innovation.

When is an IS/IT application implemented? Is it implemented when it is approved by top management as part of the IS/IT strategy? When it is installed on a company computer? When it is put into its first use? When it is widely accepted by people in the company? When it is modified as a result of use, based on both detected errors and needs for improvement? When the benefits of the IS/IT strategy are finally appearing? There is no unified answer to this question, but most scholars agree that installation of a system is too early, while benefits are too late to wait for. This is illustrated in Figure 7.7. Most scholars agree that an IS/IT application is implemented when it is used and accepted by users. So in the example in Figure 7.6, we would say that implementation occurred in 2007.

Using the gestalt view, we can say that an IS/IT strategy implementation is defined by a degree of implementation. If the complete IS/IT strategy is implemented, we can talk about 100% implementation. If nothing is implemented, we can talk about zero implementation. A strategic IS/IT plan is implemented over time, as illustrated in Figure 7.8. The process of implementation can follow different paths. In Figure 7.8, there are two examples of early and late implementation respectively, both ending at an implementation degree of 60%.

There is no optimal extent of implementation. It depends on the situation in the company over time. If the IS/IT strategy has an excellent match with desired business situation and actual business development, then more of the strategy is likely to be implemented. If the IS/IT strategy consists of a few large, focused projects that, when first started, have to be finished, then more of the strategy is likely to be implemented. If the organization has a culture of walk and talk consistency, then more of the strategy is likely to be implemented. Walk and talk consistency implies that management actually does what it says it is going to do. If the IS/IT strategy has a short time horizon, then more of the strategy is likely to be implemented. If management is able to predict the future, then more of the strategy is likely to be implemented.

While there is no optimal extent of implementation generally, we would be surprised to find everything or nothing implemented. If everything is implemented, then it creates an impression of ignoring changes over time that should influence implementation. If nothing is implemented, then it creates an impression that the organization is completely unable to create change, and there is complete inconsistency between talk and walk. An empirical study of Norwegian business organizations tells us that on average 60% of an IS/IT strategy was implemented. Whether this is good or bad is hard to tell. We may suggest a rule of thumb that two thirds should be implemented.

We have to remind ourselves that initially, at the start of implementation, the complete IS/IT strategy is to be implemented. All actions were written into the plan to be executed. Nothing was written into the plan without the intention of being executed. What we are saying about implementation extent is that environmental changes as well as internal changes over time may create a situation where some of the plan contents are not smart

Figure 7.7. Implementation of an IS/IT application

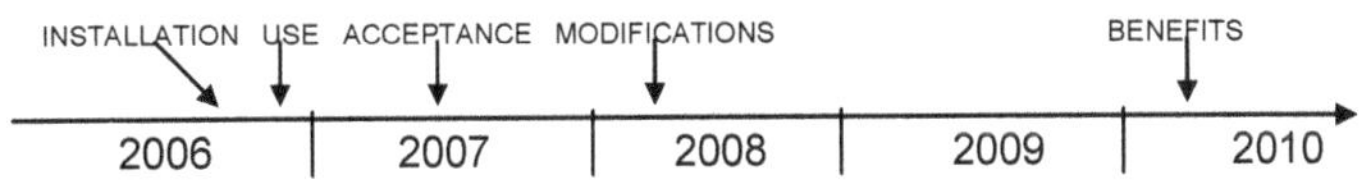

Figure 7.8. Implementation of IS/IT strategy over time

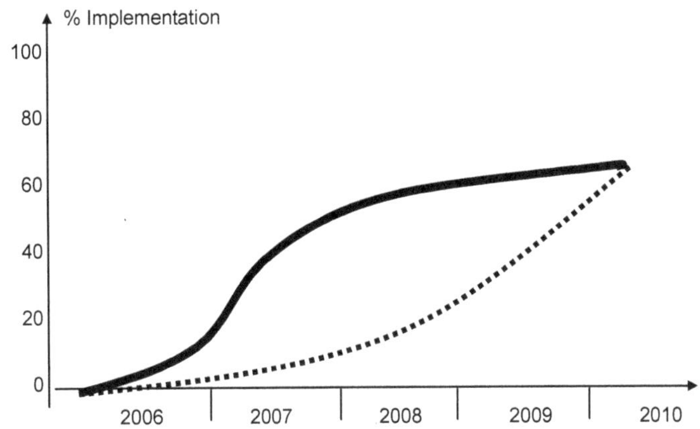

to do anymore. Such evaluation of the plan after some time, often after one or two years, may cause revision of the plan.

BARRIERS TO IMPLEMENTATION

At stage 6 in the Y model of implementing the plan, all attention should be focused on implementation of the whole plan. This is the stage of action. Technical equipment such as servers, PCs, printers, and cables are installed. Operating systems are upgraded. Application packages, software programs, programming tools, end user tools, and database systems are installed. Development projects are initiated. Management and user training takes place.

At this stage we should focus on the tackling of implementation challenges. The literature on implementation challenges is steadily growing. A series of factors influencing implementation have been identified. In the following, we will discuss some important factors for implementation of IS/IT strategy:

- Resources needed for the implementation
- User involvement during the implementation
- Solutions to potential resistance during the implementation
- Responsibility for the implementation

- Management support for the implementation
- Information technology needed for implementation

RESOURCES NEEDED FOR THE IMPLEMENTATION

One reason for the lack of implementation is that resources are not made available. The answer to the simple question "Can it be done?" is dependent on competence and resources. It is important to identify the resources and actions needed to implement new applications and development tools. Resource mobilization for implementation is an effective implementation mechanism to secure quality implementation. An important resource issue in the field of strategic IS/IT is the difficulty of recruiting IS specialists and defining their role in projects. In an IS/IT strategy written in English in a Norwegian organization, this problem was confirmed: "Technological expertise is a precondition for development and migration of new and complicated technology in the institution, but the dependence on such expertise also represents a problem to management." Some information systems professionals are systems rationalists preoccupied with new capabilities of technology, tending to ignore goal incongruence and assuming consensus on goals. Generally speaking, information systems innovations are dependent on an IS professional environment. Just as important, there is a need for those users who will champion the new systems and have the drive and vision to push the projects forward. In addition, many businesses are dependent on external expertise such as consultants for implementation. In summary, the following resources are important:

- Financial resources needed for the implementation
- Technical abilities needed for the implementation
- Human resources needed for the implementation
- Project team time needed for the implementation
- External consultants needed for the implementation
- A project champion needed for the implementation

User Involvement During the Implementation

Both resources for and extensive performance of user training are necessary to secure implementation of IS/IT strategy. Education, training, and other implementation activities are generally viewed as outside the IS role in part because formal authority for training usually is assigned elsewhere. Training may consist of both formal and informal training. Formal training can be long-term as well as short-term instruction received through seminars, classes, conventions, and private lessons, while informal training can be on-the-job training received from coworkers and supervisors as the need arises. Many training efforts are based on needs analysis, needs assessment, or performance analysis. User involvement in implementation is an effective implementation mechanism to secure quality implementation. It is usually better to use a high-involvement process that utilizes the knowledge and creativity of the people who actually do the work. Implementation represents a situation of transition in which users experience a threat to their sense of control over their work, if not direct loss of control. Interventions, which restore the users' sense of control, will reduce the threatening quality of the implementation experience and, as a result, heighten the users' satisfaction with the new systems. In this view, the active ingredient for user involvement is the perceived control. User needs are the source of benefits, which motivate the use of an information technology application, and user satisfaction increases the implementability. In summary, the following user involvement issues are important:

- Training of information systems users
- Users' understanding of systems' functional features
- Users' participation in systems projects
- Users' involvement in the operation of information systems
- Participation in the ongoing development of information systems
- Users' support for the implementation

Solutions to Potential Resistance During the Implementation

Solutions to potential resistance during the implementation are methods and processes of solving problems created by latent opposition to the implementation. Resistance involves a stubbornness in fulfilling the expectations of others. Resistance to implementation may have many facets, such as quiet ignorance, active argumentation, low priority put on implementation compared with other assignments, and so forth. Potential bases of resistance to the adoption of the plan should be identified, and the plan should define solutions needed for avoiding and/or dampening potential resistance to the necessary changes. Resistance may be caused by uncertainty, lack of competence, or commitment to the status quo. Some may find their influence threatened; others think that implementation may be harmful to the organization, and still some think that the plan should be improved before implementation. In summary, the following resistance issues are important:

- Solutions to potential resistance caused by job security
- Solutions to potential resistance caused by change of position
- Solutions to potential resistance caused by new skills requirements
- Solutions to potential resistance caused by skepticism about results
- Solutions to potential resistance caused by functional units' interests
- Solutions to potential resistance of our customers

Responsibility for the Implementation

During implementation, the frames of implementers (those responsible for the introduction of the technology to prospective users) will influence the extent of implementation. Most IS units do not have responsibility for key organizational results. Line managers are increasingly assuming responsibility for planning, building, and running information systems that affect their operation. It is important to identify the IT departments actions necessary to expedite adoption of the plan. A monitoring system to review implementation and provide feedback is an effective implementation mechanism. For each benefit desired from the implementation, specific responsibility for realizing benefits should be allocated within the business. Only when specific people are responsible for implementation actions is implementation likely to occur. Responsibility has to be defined in such detail that responsible people take expected initiatives when problems occur during implementation. It may also be valuable to consider whether the chief executive responsible for strategy is willing to accept the personal risk involved. If not, the strategy may be good but is unlikely to be implemented. Implementation participants must accept responsibility for their own behavior, including the success of the actions they take to create change. Responsibility as such may take on two forms, negative duty and positive duty. Negative responsibility implies that action be taken due to threats and is often motivated by loyalty, while positive responsibility implies that action be taken due to commitment. In summary, the following responsibility issues are important:

- Responsibility for implementation on time
- Responsibility for implementation within budget
- Responsibility for implementation with intended benefits
- Responsibility for stepwise implementation of large projects
- Responsibility for implementation of high priority projects
- Responsibility for short-term benefits from initial projects
- Personnel rewards from successful implementation

Management Support for the Implementation

Management support is widely recognized as an important factor in the implementation of information systems. Management may be hesitant to the implementation of IS/IT strategy, hence representing an implementation problem. Some top executives are in reality committed to the status quo. Both middle management attitudes and senior management attitudes toward implementation are important influences on the extent of plan implementation. It may be difficult to secure top management commitment for implementation with commitment defined as acceptance of plan values and willingness to exert effort on its behalf. The planning methodology itself may require too much top management involvement. The output of planning is not necessarily in accordance with management expectations. Top management monitoring of implementation may represent an effective implementation mechanism. Management control systems provide a comprehensive mechanism for implementing plans. Management monitoring and control of the implementation may be organized through a steering committee. Management support is pivotal to the adoption of innovations. CEOs in particular have a major impact on changes in their organizations. A plan must be a call for action, one that recognizes management's responsibility to fix what is broken proactively and in real time. It is imperative that IT personnel educate their top managers and make them aware of the importance of their support in major IT initiatives. Top management support is a key recurrent factor critical for effective implementation. In summary, the following management issues are important:

- Management expectations of the implementation
- Management participation in the implementation
- Management monitoring of the implementation
- Management knowledge about the implementation
- Management time needed for the implementation
- Management enthusiasm for the implementation

Information Technology Needed for Implementation

Information technology to be implemented is the hardware and software to be developed, acquired, installed, used, and modified. Information technology is developing rapidly, but in many organizations IT is still lagging behind users' needs. For example, artificial intelligence is still in its infancy as a technology. This implies that a firm that wants to implement knowledge management level IV may have problems finding suitable technology. It is, therefore, important that the IS/IT strategy has identified available technology. It is seldom smart to trust vendors' promises concerning future features of new technology when developing the IS/IT strategy. Instead, technological constraints should be identified and accepted. It is often emphasized that information architecture is not enough unless data access issues can be resolved. In summary, the following technology is important:

- Hardware to be implemented
- Communications technology to be implemented
- Databases to be implemented
- Applications software to be implemented
- Operating systems to be implemented
- A data infrastructure for the organization

IMPLEMENTATION PREDICTORS

Resources needed for the implementation, user involvement during the implementation, solutions to potential resistance during the implementation, responsibility for the implementation, management support for the implementation, and information technology needed for the implementation are all considered important factors for IS/IT strategy implementation. These factors were empirically evaluated first in Norway and then in Australia (Gottschalk & Khandelwal, 2002).

In additon to the six factors listed above, four more factors were added in the empirical studies: analysis of the organization, anticipated changes in the external environment, projects' relevance to the business plan, and clear presentation of implementation issues.

In Norway, two factors were significant: responsibility for the implementation and user involvement during the implementation. In Australia, one factor was significant: projects' relevance to the business plan.

The average extent of strategic IS/IT plan implementation in Australia was 3.4, while the average plan implementation in Norway was 3.3, on a scale from 1 (little extent) to 5 (great extent). These results indicate that in both Australia and Norway, roughly 60% of a strategic IS/IT plan is implemented on average.

In Australia, responding organizations had an extensive description of projects' relevance to the business plan (3.7), while they had a limited description of solutions to potential resistance (1.9). In Norway, responding organizations had an extensive description of technology to be implemented (3.6), while they had a limited description of solutions to potential resistance (2.0).

The significant predictor in Australia was projects' relevance to the business plan which had the highest overall description rating (3.7), indicating that relevance is both important and taken care of in many Australian firms. The two significant predictors in Norway were responsibility of implementation and user involvement during implementation, which had high overall description ratings of 2.7 and 3.0.

The interesting difference between Australia and Norway lies in the finding that strategic descriptions are more important for implementation in Australia, while resource descriptions are more important for implementation in Norway. Given that both have about the same extent of plan implementation, 3.4 and 3.3, there is little reason to argue that firms in one nation are more successful than firms in the other.

One emerging proposition is that smaller organizations will tend to be more dependent on resources to get a plan implemented, while larger organizations will tend to be more dependent on strategic relevance to get a plan implemented. This proposition is relevant as responding Australian firms were much larger than the Norwegian respondents were. However, no significant relationship was found between organization size and the extent of relevance description (Gottschalk & Khandelwal, 2002).

Another emerging proposition is related to cultural differences. According to the Scandinavian research on information systems development, Scandinavia has high living standards and educational levels, an advanced technology infrastructure, an open community, and key innovative leaders. This tradition seems different from research in other countries such as the UK with control structures, which may imply different strategic IS/IT plan implementation problems (Gottschalk & Khandelwal, 2002).

IT STRATEGY EVALUATION: EVALUATING THE RESULTS

At this final stage of the Y model, implementation results are compared with needs for change. It is determined to what extent gaps between desired and current situation have been closed. This is the beginning of the IS/IT strategy revision process, where a new process through the Y model takes place. Typically, a new IS/IT strategy process should take place every other year in business organizations.

Let us look at an evaluation example. We assume that the company now has implemented an e-business system or a knowledge management system (KMS). The system may have been implemented to achieve results such as:

- Both organizational and market benefits
- Move from architecture stage to integration stage
- Improved communication and combination of information
- Improved business processes
- Improved efficiency and effectiveness in value shop activities
- Reach knowledge management level III
- Enable e-business at level IV
- Develop supplementary services to take advantage of opportunities
- Improve working procedures in accordance with firm vision
- Create different product according to market strategy
- Create entry barriers according to competitive forces model
- Extend the life of products classified as stars
- Attract knowledgeable people in the labor market
- Move from imitator to competitor according to the knowledge map

As this list illustrates, there may have been a variety of reasons for implementing a knowledge management system in the organization. When we do the evaluation of results, we will evaluate to what extent such results have been achieved. But the evaluation should not be limited to such planned, positive effects of a new system. The evaluation should investigate all kinds of effects as illustrated in Figure 7.9.

All planned, positive effects listed above belong in the upper-left quadrant for planned benefits. Here we evaluate to what extent we have achieved results in accordance with the IS/IT strategy. However, we will also have achieved other benefits from systems implementation that we did not think of when the IS/IT strategy was developed. These benefits may be just as valuable as the results than we aimed for. Hence, results are both planned and unplanned results.

At the other side of Figure 7.9, there are negative effects of implementing the IS/IT strategy. Some problems were known, and these problems have been dealt with. However, we will also experience new problems from systems implementation that we did not think of when the IS/IT strategy was developed. These new problems cause an increase in negative effects from implementing the IS/IT strategy.

Evaluating results at stage 7 of the Y model implies that all effects have to be considered, both positive and negative, as well as planned and unplanned. This total picture of effects is now compared with the original needs for change from stage 3 of the Y model. Discrepancies will be identified and have several consequences:

- Learning will occur from evaluating results
- Revision of implementation approach may be needed, including systems development strategy
- Revision of the IS/IT strategy may be needed
- A new IS/IT strategy may be needed

So far, we have discussed evaluating results in terms of strategy content. We also need to evaluate results in terms of plan implementation. An important result of IS/IT strategy is the extent of plan implementation. Implementation can be operationalized in several ways:

Figure 7.9. Evaluating effects from IS/IT

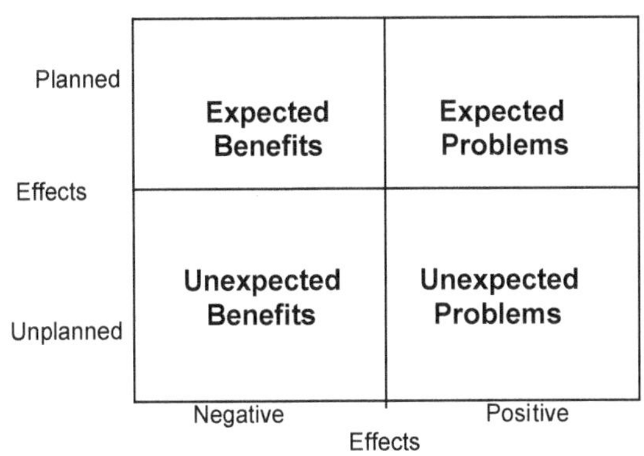

Implementation rate to date. Implementation rate to date is the extent to which projects scheduled to be implemented to date have actually been implemented to date. The number of projects in the IS/IT strategy actually implemented to date is divided by the number of projects in the IT strategy scheduled to be implemented to date. If the number of projects actually implemented is greater than the number of projects scheduled to be implemented, then the implementation rate is set to one (or hundred percent) in line with the spirit of implementation research measuring exclusively the extent to which a plan—here, scheduled projects—is implemented.

Implementation rate to end. Implementation rate to end is the extent to which projects will be implemented by the end of the implementation horizon, assuming that the implementation extent to date will continue for the remaining implementation horizon. The number of projects in the IS/IT strategy actually implemented to date is divided by the fraction of implementation horizon expired. If the implementation rate to end is greater than one (or hundred percent) in line with the spirit of implementation research measuring exclusively the extent to which a plan; planned projects are expected to be implemented.

Implementation extent. Implementation extent is the degree to which the plan has been carried out. Implementing an IS/IT strategy provides a gestalt view of the organization, whereas implementing several separate projects can be viewed in a more piece-meal manner. Gestalt thinking leads to a larger complete picture, which is often too easily ignored by looking at individual projects. The gestalt view represents the implementation of the plan philosophy, attitudes, intentions, and ambitions of the overall plan. Important dimensions of implementation extent are (i) implementation completed on time, (ii) implementation completed within budget, (iii) implementation completed as expected, (iv) implementation achieved desired results, (v) no deviations from the strategy occurred during implementation, and (vi) satisfaction with strategy implementation.

Contribution to improved organizational performance. Contribution to improved organizational performance is the extent to which the IS/IT strategy implementation has an impact on organizational performance. Evaluating organizational performance is perhaps the oldest and most commonly used form of evaluation for planning systems. The link between strategic planning and organizational performance is often elusive. While the three preceding constructs attempt to measure actual implementation, this construct attempts to measure overall effect of implementation. Objectives of IS/IT strategy implementation include improved IS performance, alignment of IS with business needs, achievement of competitive advantage from IS, achievement of top management commitment, prediction of future trends, increased user satisfaction, and improved IS function. Contribution to improved organizational performance can be measured by (i) return on investment, (ii) increased market share of goods and services, (iii) improved internal efficiency of operations, (iv) increased annual sales revenue, (v) increased customer satisfaction, and (vi) alignment of IS with business needs.

The creation of IS/IT strategy has become a major challenge to executives. Investments in IT are large, and many failed investments reflect this challenge. The impact of IT on organizational performance has growth in strategic importance, and thus the significance of failed IT investments is even greater. Information systems and information technology are critical to many business and government operations. New information technology for e-business will continue to transform organizations, and changes in how industry participants use IT is altering established relationships in an industry. Strategic information systems and information technology planning can play a critical part in helping organizations to increase efficiency, effectiveness, and competitiveness.

ENTERPRISE ARCHITECTURE DRIVEN IT STRATEGIC PLAN

Spewak (1992) describes the EAP Enterprise Architecture Planning methodology for IT strategic planning (see Chapter VI for details). This methodology has four steps: (1) architecture planning, (2) assessment of current IS environment, (3) definition of the future target enterprise (IS) architecture using the business strategy and corresponding IT strategy, and (4) target architecture implementation and migration planning. Implementation of the target architecture will deliver the desired future IS environment necessary to achieve the articulated business strategy. Thus, the EAP step 4 is about IT strategic program planning and execution, and encompasses steps 4-7 of the Y model described previously. The Open Group Architecture Framework (TOGAF, 2007) further reinforces the EAP methodology and defines an architecture governance framework (which is a subset of IT governance) by which the planning development and implementation of firm's enterprise architecture (and hence information systems) can be managed and controlled. The aim of architecture governance is to ensure the architecture is aligned with business strategy, its development and implementation has appropriate resources, and the implementation system solutions are compliant with the architecture such that the desired business outcomes (benefits) will be delivered by the implemented information systems. Thus, the end goal of enterprise architecture governance is to ensure the enterprise architecture and the corresponding systems implementation will deliver maximum business value with manageable risks. The critical success factors for enterprise architecture and strategic planning are executive management commitment and strong project leadership skills (Spewak, 1992). The rest of this chapter is focused on this strong discipline of program planning and execution.

TOGAF propose an IS organizational structure for managing architecture governance as shown in Figure 7.10.

Architecture defines the general shape of the target future information systems that will deliver the strategic outcomes envisioned by the business strategy. To realize the target future information systems and create the desired business value, a selection of IT projects must be established whose step-wise implementations in a time sequence (determined by business priorities) will deliver the target IS architecture. Potential IT projects are identified by the gap analysis of the current architecture in comparison with the target future enterprise architecture. Projects are aggregated into programs in accordance with their affinity to specific strategic themes encapsulated in the business strategy and objectives. Strategic plan defining a time sequence of the strategic programs identified is thus constructed with the guidance of the enterprise architecture and business strategy. The strategic plan defines the set of business program objectives as articulated by business and IT strategies and encapsulated in the enterprise architecture. The strategic plan will guide which projects to select, which to continue, and which to decommission. Selection implies judicious resource allocation, including technology assets, business processes, human resources, and competencies, and potentially customer and partner resources. Program/project selection

Figure 7.10. IS organizational structure for managing architecture governance (TOGAF, 2007)

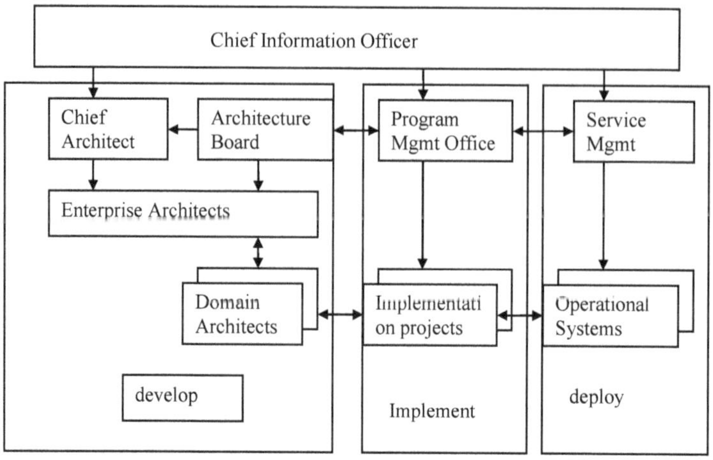

requires financial investment, thus judicious consideration of risk/return and cost of each IT program/project proposal. The process for selecting the "right" IT projects to invest in is called IT portfolio management (ITPM). It unites business and IT executives to work together to make the "right" strategic decision. Thus, ITPM provides a sound business communication tool for business and IT executives to jointly manage the execution of the mutually aligned business and IT strategies. It focuses on more on value maximization and cost optimization, rather than solely on cost reduction.

Cost optimization is managed from a total cost of ownership (TCO) perspective. TCO is the cost of developing, owning, and using IT assets over their lifetime. TCO allows firms to measure, manage, and contain IT costs while enhancing IT overall lifetime value. TCO analysis includes the following (Luftman, Bullen, Liao, Nash, & Neumann, 2004):

- Provide predictable costs and level of budgets
- Determine which IT resources can be applied to the firms core missions
- Determine current costs and services of IT operations
- Ways to increase service levels at affordable cost
- Track actual ongoing IT costs
- Find cost-effective way of improving IT expertise
- Most effective implementation of strategy to improve effective and efficient delivery of IT services

A related cost/value management discipline is called activity based management. This discipline focuses on the management of activities with the view to both maximizing the value received by the customer and the profit achieved by service provider. Based on activity based costing, activity based management includes cost driver analysis, activity analysis, and performance measurement.

The SIM (Society for Information Management) International Working Group on "Managing the IT Investment Portfolio" (2001) recommends that firms need to adopt a portfolio management process to assess and manage the firm's IT environment. This will ensure (Luftman, 2004, p. 394):

1. IT investment proposals are justified in terms of expected business outcomes (returns), efforts required, and risks involved
2. IT investments will deliver value to the firm
3. Risks associated with the investments are within the acceptable risk profile of the firm
4. IT investments are aligned with business strategy

The Best Practices Committee of the U.S. Federal CIO Council (2005, p. 239) pragmatically defines the ITPM practice as comprising five basic steps: (1) define the goals and objectives of the portfolio; (2) understand, accept, and make trade-offs in determining the investment profile of the portfolio; (3) identify, eliminate, minimize, and diversify risk to ensure the portfolio delivers optimal business value; (4) monitor the portfolio performance; and (5) achieve the desired objectives (optimal business value) of the portfolio.

Another way of looking at ITPM is through the lens of total value outcome, or TVO (Luftman, 2004). The complete TVO process combines the use of portfolio management, options, and the value management governance process to maximize the value of a portfolio of IT projects. Each project is compared with all projects from the perspective of the entire organization, business unit, and individual employee. Those that meet the overall priorities of the firm are selected. Those projects that have been selected are decomposed into manageable work packages ad implemented using an options approach. Each project will have articulated the organization, business unit, and individual value. The business members of the governance process will assess overall business change and outcomes, while IT members the IT solution (guided by enterprise architecture) necessary to drive or enable the changes. IT and business teams use this method during strategy formulation to select and allocate resources and during project execution to evaluate and monitor project progress, and after the project is deployed to assess attainment of value. TVO process ensures: (1) IT and business work together to identify and ensure value attainment—relationship essential for mature business–IT alignment; (2) IT management focus moves from being cost-centric to value-centric; (3) a portfolio of projects is evaluated and coordinated with effective IT governance process where business and IT share accountability—business actually taking "ownership" of projects. Thus, TVO will result in more effective resource allocation.

ITPM serves as a bridge from strategic planning and architecture to the practice of IT project management, which implements the selected portfolio of projects, staged in a time sequence in accordance with the priorities stipulated by business strategy. The selected projects are expected to deliver the business outcomes (value) to reflect the business strategy. They form the incremental steps or building blocks toward realizing the target future enterprise architecture. Project delivery is a project management discipline. Business value delivery is a business management process, which requires superior sales and marketing coordination to ensure the potential value of the project as articulated in the project business case is realized. The validation of the value delivered by an IT project against the business plan and business strategy is called post-implementation review/business outcome monitoring, a step often neglected by many organizations (see Chapters IV and V). Linking IT to firm performance is not feasible without completing all these steps diligently, including particularly post-implementation review. Thus, IT portfolio management must be synchronized with strategic planning and IT project management (Cameron, 2006).

Portfolio management is an investment discipline originated in financial management. Investment alternatives are assessed by their costs, returns, and risks, and decisions will be based on the financial objective. Similarly IT investment alternatives will be based on risks, returns, and costs, and decisions will be driven by business strategies. Return of a project is measured by the expected value the completed project may generate. The value includes both the tangible and intangible returns. Tangible return is financially measurable benefits such as expected cost savings and revenue enhancements that the project will deliver. Intangible return includes service quality improvement, customer satisfaction improvement, and improved speed to market. These benefits can be (sometimes indirectly) quantified and measured using nonfinancial metrics. Both financial and nonfinancial benefits are equally important in determining the value/return of a project for the purposes of IT portfolio prioritization. Traditional financial modeling methods which convert costs and benefits into offsetting streams of discounted cash flows have been used for determining project value. Net present value (NPV) and internal rate of return (IRR) are two most common models utilized in IT project portfolio management (Cameron, 2006).

IT portfolio is a categorized set of assets (the outputs) and investments (the inputs). A three-category approach is commonly used: operate the business, grow the business, and transform the business (Cameron, 2006). Operate-the-business investments are business-as-usual costs necessary to keep the business operational ("keep the light on"). They are core and nondiscretionary. Grow-the-business investments are required to improve existing or introduce new products and services to increase revenues. They may also contribute to operational excellence and process agility to allow the firm to be adaptive to business and technological changes. Transform-the-business investments are needed to create new business capabilities, such as through introduction of disruptive technologies or business model innovation, which enable the firm to change the competitive landscape to give itself unparallel advantage or to enter new markets. Transform-the-business assets will create new revenue streams and take the firm to a higher level of competitive advantage.

Another well known approach to categorizing IT portfolio is from the IT application assets perspective developed by Weill and Broadbent (1998). This approach categorizes IT investment portfolio into four classes (Weill & Aral, 2006):

- **Infrastructure:** Infrastructure investments are for the creation of shared services to be used by multiple applications, such as servers, networks, middleware, and customer databases. They commonly aim to provide a flexible base for future business expansion or long-term cost reduction through standardization and consolidation. It facilitates business integration and reduces marginal costs of business unit's IT.
- **Transactional:** Transactional investments are principally used for efficiency improvement and cost reduction through automation of repetitive business processes.
- **Informational:** Informational investments are for the creation of information base for accounting, reporting, strategic decision analysis, compliance, and communication. It improves information management, speeds up decision making processes, and improves innovation processes.
- **Strategic:** Strategic investments are used for developing new products and services or business processes to enter new markets and gain strategic competitive advantage. It improves service, product, and process innovations to give the firm better market positioning.

Typical IT portfolio mix ranges for an average firm are: operate-the-business (50–80%), grow-the-business (10–35%), transform-the-business (0–25%) (Cameron, 2006). According to Weill–Broadbent classification, the average firm in 2005 invests 46% of total budget on infrastructure, 26% on transactional, 17% on informational, and 11% on strategic applications (Weill & Aral, 2006). Investment for a single (large) project can also be classified by the Weill–Broadbent classification. For example, a multimillion-dollar project for CRM in a large U.S. firm spreads its investment into 10% infrastructure, 25% transactional, 60% informational, and 5% strategic (Weill & Aral, 2006).

Despite the critical importance of ITPM to business value creation, Jeffery and Leliveld (2004) found in a survey of 130 Fortune 1000 CIOs in 2003 that only 89% were aware of ITPM, and 65% believed ITPM produces business value. However, 41% did not have central oversight of IT budget, a basic requirement of ITPM; 47% did not track projects centrally; 46% did not document their applications and infrastructure well; 57% had no criteria for project success definition; and 68% did not follow up postproject implementations to track the project benefits against business case. Consequently, only 17% of the CIOs were able to realize the value of ITPM. The reason for this patchy ITPM performance is due to the CIOs' different levels of ITPM practice maturity. For example, 4.5% of the respondents are at the lowest (*ad hoc*) level of maturity; 24.5% at the second (*defined*) level of maturity; 54% at the third (*managed*) level; and 17% at the most mature (*synchronous*) level (Jeffery & Leliveld, 2004).

Jeffery and Leliveld (2004) define the *ad hoc level* as one where the firms make decisions about IT investments in an uncoordinated way. They define the *defined level* as one where the firms have identified and documented the key components of IT portfolios and provided costs/benefits estimates for each component. A central project management office equipped with financial and project management skills and a central database for prioritizing and overseeing the projects. The *defined level* still lacks consistency in organizationwide compliance. It also lacks linkage to budgeting cycles and benefits tracking. Most critically, it lacks the standards and consistent stakeholder behaviors to align the IT portfolio to business strategy. Jeffery and Leliveld (2004) define the *managed level* as one where a standardized ITPM process exists, which uses risks/returns and business alignment as criteria for project prioritization and selection. However, this process is conducted on an annual rather than ongoing process. They classify the firms that use evolving metrics (pertinent to the phase of the project) to measure a project's value/risk throughout its life cycle as operating at the *synchronous level*. At this level, business alignment is assured by continuous business feedback and course adjustment, and IT portfolio value is maximized by the rigorous application of the financial and management disciplines at the project and portfolio (through optimal blending of project types) levels. Jeffery and Leliveld (2004) find a clear statistical link of superior return-on-asset (ROA) performance to the synchronous level of ITPM maturity for companies with large IT investments. However, operating at the defined or managed level is not sufficient to improve ROA performance appreciably.

Some of the barriers to ITPM success are the difficulty of quantifying business value, poor communication between IT and business, IT staff's lack of business skills, and business executives' lack of understanding of and low respect for IT. To overcome these barriers, Jeffery and Leliveld (2004) recommend four approaches: (1) staged implementation of the ITPM process, for example, business unit by business unit before tackling the whole organization; (2) create a process for ITPM capability upgrade; for example, at the start or design phase, get the business buy-in on the upgrade objectives; at the diagnosis stage, define the baseline portfolio for improvement; at the opportunities phase, identify the quick-wins and emergency remediation required to improve the IT portfolio performance; at the tools stage, appropriate new tools or capabilities such as risk management skills are added to improve ITPM performance; and finally, the new capabilities are incorporated into the existing budgeting and decision-making processes of the ITPM; (3) ensuring staff members are well trained; and (4) informing and involving business people continuously from the beginning.

Weill and Aral (2006) find that companies can generate premium returns for every IT dollar invested when they possess a "mutually reinforcing set of practices and capabilities" which they call *IT savvy*. They study each company's relative IT savvy by categorizing the company's practices, processes, and capabilities for each of the four types of IT application comprised in most IT portfolios. For instance, they find that high IT savvy companies on average get $247 higher net profit the following year after $1 investment in the IT infrastructure; yet, low IT savvy companies on average yield $909 *lower* profits the next year for dollar invested on infrastructure. Indeed, high IT savvy firms get much higher returns from investments in all four types of IT applications than less IT savvy firms. It is thus important to understand the characteristics of IT savvy firms and how to extract more value from IT portfolio.

Weill and Aral (2006) find that IT savvy firms have five mutually reinforcing characteristics: three of which are concerned with practices and two are concerned with competencies. The three practices are: (1) IT for internal and external communication – high IT savvy firms have higher intensity electronic communication via media such as e-mail, intranets, and wireless devices for internal and external communications and work practices; (2) Internet use – high IT savvy firms use Internet-based architecture extensively for key functions such as sales force management, employee performance management, and training and postsales customer support; and (3) digital transactions – high IT savvy companies have a higher degree of digitization of their transactions with suppliers (supply chain management) and customers (customer interface and relationship management). The two competencies are (1) companywide IT skills – higher IT savvy firms have IT staff who are strong in both technical and business skills; and business staff who have strong IT skills and have great ability to hire skilled IT people; and (2) management involvement – higher IT savvy firms have higher degree of senior management commitments to IT projects and have higher degree of business involvement in IT decisions. In general, they find that high IT savvy firms have developed the interlocked practices with the requisite IT skills that complement the four IT asset classes. These firms have the widest spread of digitization of their business processes.

Weill and Aral (2006) recommend seven ways to extract greater value from the firm's IT portfolio:

1. From business value performance of IT portfolio in the prior three years, define (under IT governance) the target future IT portfolio profile to maximize value
2. Understand IT asset class performance and benchmarks for the firm's business
3. Understand and track (and improve) the firm's IT savvy
4. Balance, transparently, the portfolio for alignment and risk-return profile
5. Re-weight portfolios annually and whenever major changes occur
6. Incorporate the IT portfolio approach into the IT governance framework
7. Learn from post-implementation reviews and formal training

IT portfolio management has three key components (Maizlish & Handler, 2005):

1. A framework and associated standardized processes to plan, create, assess, balance, and communicate the execution of the IT portfolio;
2. Tools for "what-if" analysis of IT project portfolio information such as value, costs, risks, benefits, requirements, architecture, and alignment to business strategic objectives to facilitate IT investments ranking and prioritization;
3. A common business taxonomy for communication and governance[1] that defines the principles, policies, guidelines, criteria, accountability, decision-making authority, and control mechanisms.

According to Maizlish and Handler (2005), IT portfolio management methodology has eight steps (not necessarily in linear order):

1. **Develop an IT portfolio management game plan (p. 194):** Defines the objectives based on the baseline architecture requirements, the business capability, and IT portfolio maturity gaps, the shareholder assessment, and value/cost analysis. It also identifies the most critical success areas and the process (and metrics) for performance monitoring.
2. **Plan the IT portfolio (p. 202):** Plan the investment strategy and attendant portfolio (and subportfolio) structures in line with the business and IT strategies, using top-down and bottom-up approaches. As explained above, it categorizes the investment plan into run-the-business, grow-the-business, and transform-the-business types. A more refined and commonly used finance-based categorization is structured hierarchically: core and nondiscretionary investments are for running the business; discretionary enhancements and growth investment are for growing the business; and venture investment is for transforming the business. A common portfolio mix could be a ratio of 6/3/1 for run/grow/transform (the business) respectively.
3. **Create the IT portfolio (p. 211):** Create an inventory in a central database of all current (active) and future (proposed) IT investments (IT projects) using standardized templates and (business case) metrics, which capture the assumptions, alternatives, decision criteria, and (investment) screening process. Candidates for IT project proposals can be most readily identified from the enterprise architecture planning process described in Chapter VI. The portfolio will be classified in accordance with the taxonomy approved by the IT portfolio governance process. We return to this point later.
4. **Assess the portfolio (p. 234):** Measures the portfolio (risks/returns) performance against the objectives set in step 1, and monitors internal and external (e.g., exceeding predetermined business or IT risk level) conditions for possible trigger events for refining/changing the portfolio to achieve the target business value—akin to funds managers changing their portfolios to stay on course to achieving their portfolio financial objectives in light (or despite) of significant financial market condition changes. Example devices for "portfolio health" performance monitoring include balanced scorecard, key performance indicators, critical success factors, and service level agreements.
5. **Balance the portfolio (p. 246):** Through continuous monitoring and performance feedback (in step 4), the portfolio undergoes constant rebalancing to ensure the value

target is achieved ("portfolio equilibrium"). The activities involved are identifying the tuning options, analyzing the options to determine trade-offs, selecting and approving portfolio changes, and implementing the approved changes.

6. **Communicate the portfolio (p. 260):** Business involvement and communication is the cornerstone of IT portfolio success. Communication must be integrated with each step of the end-to-end IT portfolio management process. It maximizes the dialog between business and IT to ensure alignment and communicate clearly the need for change as well as, at project completion, the change itself.
7. **Develop and evolve the IT portfolio governance and organization (p. 266):** Governance "identifies responsibilities of individuals, specifies processes to follow, and puts down principles and policies to eliminate ambiguity." This step consists of defining the portfolio management policy, identifying and defining the process integration between portfolio management and other business processes, identifying the specific areas for governance compliance, defining the portfolio governance processes, and establishing the organizational model for supporting and sustaining the portfolio management process.
8. **Assess IT portfolio management process execution (p. 270):** Portfolio management process metrics are measured as the project portfolio evolves through its life cycle to validate performance to (intermediary) targets, and particularly at the completion of each project to ensure that the business outcomes match up with the business case objectives. The business case validation report resulting from the execution assessment is the most powerful way of communicating the business value that IT portfolio has contributed. It maximizes IT organization's credibility and reputation as a value business peer whose contribution to business strategy and execution is critical for the firm's success.

Applying the Maizlish–Handler methodology will lead to the establishment of sound ITPM practice. It will enable firms to develop a superior strategic plan with maximum business value potential at an acceptable risk profile. However, successful application of ITPM depends on existence of sound IT governance. According to Grembergen (2004), "IT governance is the system by which an organization's IT portfolio is directed and controlled. IT governance describes (a) the distribution of IT decision-making rights and responsibilities among different shareholders in the organization, and (b) the rules and procedures for making and monitoring decisions on strategic IT concerns." A corollary to this close dependency to IT governance is ITPM's dependency to management and stakeholder buy-in. Both disciplines demand that business and IT professionals behave organizationally in compliance with the governance policies. It also requires that business and IT maintain close communication and act as one team to maximize success rate.

We return to discussion of IT governance in Chapter IX.

SUMMARY

Strategic planning and program implementation is performed systematically and diligently via the traditional Y model, specifically stages 4 (seek alternative actions), 5 (select actions and make an action plan), 6 (implement plan and describe results), and 7 (evaluate results). However, apart from disciplined program management, success also depends on skillful management of potential barriers to implementation. An important issue relates to the human factor of change management. First, there is the need for business and IT professionals acting as one to ensure strategic alignment. Then, there is the human nature to resist change across both IT and business/user communities. Strategy implementation must manage the human factor, including engagement, consultation, communication, education, training, and commitment, as a key project deliverable, from strategy creation to benefits realization.

An alternative, advanced, strategic planning practice is via enterprise architecture. The business and systems (architecture) gap needs to be decomposed into logical work packages for staged implementation as part of strategy execution (Spewak, 1992). Execution is the most critical part of strategic management—only by diligent and disciplined execution will the value of strategy be materialized. The architecture gap analysis offers systemic and integrative assessment of the business—business operaing model, value configuration, core business processes, domain by domain from customer front-end to back-end supply chain and partners network, together with systems architectural changes required to realize the business strategy. Gap analysis is performed on every viewpoint of the enterpise architecture. The scope and extent of architecture change required constitutes the overall scope of the strategic programs that need to be defined and developed to deliver the objectives of the business strategy. These programs will be prioritized by IT governance using IT portfolio management principles. Their implementations in time sequence will define the migration path of the current enterprise architecture towards the target future state architecture. The critical success factors for enterprise architecture and strategic planning are executive management commitment and strong project leadership skills (Spewak, 1992). A key benefit of architecture approach is that the architecture solution design for each strategic program will be guided by the enterprise architecture principles and architecture direction. This is what the IT Governance Institute calls "doing the thing right" governace (ITGI, 2006).

The architecture-driven strategic plan will guide which projects to select, which to continue, and which to decommission. Selection implies judicious resource allocation, including technology assets, business processes, human resources, and competencies, and potentially customer and partner resources. Program/project selection requires financial investment, thus judicious consideration of risk/return and cost of each IT program/project proposal. The process for selecting the "right" IT projects to invest in is called IT portfolio management. It unites business and IT executives to work together to make the "right" strategic decision. Thus, ITPM provides a sound business communication tool for business and IT executives to jointly manage the execution of the mutually aligned business and IT strategies. It focuses more on value maximization and cost optimization, rather than solely on cost reduction (Cameron, 2006; Jeffery & Leliveld, 2004; Luftman et al., 2004; Weill & Aral, 2006). IT portfolio is a categorized set of assets (the outputs) and investments (the inputs). A three-category approach is commonly used: operate the business, grow the business, and transform the business (Cameron, 2006). Another well-known approach categorizes IT investment portfolio into four classes (Weill & Aral, 2006): *Infrastructure* asset provides shared services to be used by multiple applications to allow for future business growth as well as cost reduction through standardization, rationalization, and consolidation. *Transactional* asset is for efficiency improvement and cost reduction through automation of repetitive business processes. *Informational* asset is for business intelligence, accounting, reporting, strategic decision support, compliance, and communication. *Strategic* asset is for developing new products and services or business processes to enter new markets and gain strategic competitive advantage. Typical IT portfolio mix ranges for an average firm are operate-the-business (50–80%), grow-the-business (10–35%), and transform-the-business (0–25%) (Cameron, 2006). Alternatively, the average portfolio mix could be 46% infrastructure, 26% transactional, 17% informational, and 11% strategic applications (Weill & Aral, 2006).

Despite the critical importance of ITPM to business value creation, Jeffery and Leliveld (2004) found the ITPM performance of companies surveyed had been rather patchy due to the CIOs' different levels of ITPM practice maturity. Some of the barriers to ITPM success are the same as poor strategic alignment skills, such as difficulty of quantifying business value, poor communication between IT and business, and IT staff's lack of business skills and business executives' lack of understanding of and low respect for IT. A sensible solution to the barriers could be *staged implementation* with a clear *roadmap* for capability upgrade, supported by extensive training and education programs. Most importantly, IT organizations should involve (engage) and inform business people continuously from the beginning (Jeffery & Leliveld, 2004). To maximize IT value, the firm needs to define, under IT governance, its target future IT portfolio mix; to understand its IT asset class performance and benchmarks; to re-weigh and balance, transparently, the portfolio for strategic alignment and risk-return profile; to incorporate the IT portfolio approach into the IT governance framework; and to learn from post-implementation reviews and formal training (Weill & Aral, 2006). ITPM is an advanced management practice, typically taken by firms with higher maturity in IT management practice. We recommend its adoption by firms to maximize business return on IT investments. To put IT portfolio management into practice, firms require three key components: ITPM framework and standardized process; tools for "what-if" analysis of IT project portfolio; and a common business taxonomy for communication and governance[2] (Maizlish & Handler, 2005).

REFERENCES

Cameron, B. (2006). Chapter III: IT portfolio management: Implementing and maintaining IT strategic alignment. In B. Walters & Z. Tang (Eds.), *IT-enabled strategic management: Increasing returns for the organization*. Idea Group Publishing.

Cassidy, A. (2006). *A practical guide to information systems strategic planning* (2nd ed.). New York: Auerbach Publications.

Federal CIO Council, Best Practices Committee. (2005). Chapter 6.1: A summary of first practices and lessons learned in information technology portfolio management. In H. A. Levine (Ed.), *Project portfolio management: A practical guide to selecting projects, managing portfolios, and maximizing benefits.* San Francisco: Jossey-Bass Publication, John Wiley & Sons.

Gottschalk, P., & Khandelwal, V. K. (2002). Global comparison of stages of growth based on critical success factors. *Journal of Global Information Management, 10*(2), 42–51.

Grembergen, W. V. (2004). *Strategies for information technology governance.* Idea Group Publishing.

Jeffery, M., & Leliveld, I. (2004, Spring). Best practices in IT portfolio management. *MIT Sloan*

Management Review, 45(3), 41–49.

Kaplan, R. S., & Norton, D. P. (2004). *Strategy maps.* Boston: Harvard Business School Press.

Luftman, J., Bullen, C., Liao, D., Nash, E., & Neumann, C. (2004). *Managing the information technology resource: Leadership in the information age* (international ed.). Pearson Education.

Maizlish, B., & Handler, R. (2005). *IT portfolio management step-by-step: Unlocking the business value of technology.* John Wiley & Sons.

Spewak, S. H. (1992). *Enterprise architecture planning: Developing a blueprint for data, application and technology.* QED Publishing Group.

TOGAF. (2007). *Enterprise architecture.* Author.

Weill, P., & Aral, S. (2006, Winter). Generating premium returns on your IT investments. *MIT Sloan Management Review, 47*(2), 41–48.

Weill, P., & Broadbent, M. (1998). *Leveraging the new infrastructure: How market leaders capitalize on information technology.* Boston: Harvard Business School Press.

ENDNOTES

1 IT portfolio management governance is a subset of IT governance. Maizlish and Handler (2005, chap. 3) regard people and governance as the most important success factor of IT portfolio management best practice. They recommend (p. 91) adopting the CoBIT (Control objectives for information and related technology) framework for managing and controlling IT risks in line with business risks and objectives.

2 IT portfolio management governance is a subset of IT governance. Maizlish and Handler (Chapter 3, 2005) regard people and governance as the most important success factor of IT portfolio management best practice. They recommend (p. 91) adopting the CoBIT (control objectives for information and related technology) framework for managing and controlling IT risks in line with business risks and objectives.

Chapter VIII
Strategic IT Resources and Sourcing Strategy

INTRODUCTION

As introduced in Chapter II and Chapter V, performance differences across firms can be attributed to the variance in firms' resources and capabilities. The essence of the resource-based theory of the firm lies in its emphasis on the internal resources available to the firm, rather than on the external opportunities and threats dictated by industry conditions. A firm's resources are said to be a source of competitive advantage to the degree that they are scarce, specialized, appropriable, valuable, rare, and difficult to imitate or substitute.

A fundamental idea in resource-based theory is that a firm must continually enhance its resources and capabilities to take advantage of changing conditions. Optimal growth involves a balance between the exploitation of existing resource positions and the development of new resource positions. Thus, a firm would be expected to develop new resources after its existing resource base has been fully utilized. Building new resource positions is important if the firm is to achieve sustained growth. When unused productive resources are coupled with changing managerial knowledge, unique opportunities for growth are created (Pettus, 2001).

The term *resource* is derived from the Latin word *resurgere*, which means "to rise" and implies an aid or expedient for reaching an end. A resource implies a potential means to achieve an end, or as something that can be used to create value. The first strategy textbooks outlining a holistic perspective focused on how resources needed to be allocated or deployed to earn rents. The interest in the term was for a long time linked to the efficiency of resource allocation, but this focus has later been expanded to issues such as resource accumulation, resource stocks, and resource flows (Haanaes, 1997).

The resource-based theory prescribes that firm resources are the main driver of firm performance. The resources to conceive, choose, and implement strategies are likely to be heterogeneously distributed across firms, which in turn are posited to account for the differences in firm performance. This theory posits that firm resources are rent yielding, when they are valuable, rare, imperfectly imitable, and nonsubstitutable. Moreover, resources tend to survive competitive imitation because of isolating mechanisms such as causal ambiguity, time-compression diseconomies, embeddedness, and path dependencies (Ravichandran & Lertwongsatien, 2005).

Firms develop firm-specific resources and then renew these to respond to shifts in the business environment. Firms develop dynamic capabilities to adapt to changing environments. According to Pettus (2001), the term dynamic refers to the capacity to renew resource positions to achieve congruence with changing environmental conditions. A capability refers to the key role of strategic management in appropriately adapting, integrating, and reconfiguring internal and external organizational skills, resources, and functional capabilities to match the requirements of a changing environment.

If firms are to develop dynamic capabilities, learning is crucial. Change is costly; therefore, the ability of firms to make necessary adjustments depends upon their ability to scan the environment to evaluate markets and competitors and to quickly accomplish reconfiguration and transformation ahead of competition. However, history matters. Thus, opportunities for growth will involve dynamic capabilities closely related to existing capabilities. As such, opportunities will be most effective when they are close to previous resource use (Pettus, 2001).

According to Johnson and Scholes (2002), successful strategies are dependent on the organization having the strategic capability to perform at the level that is required for success. So the first reason an understanding of strategic capability is important is concerned with whether an organization's strategies continue to fit the environment in which the organization is operating and the opportunities and threats that exist. Many of the issues of strategy development are concerned with changing a strategic capability better to fit a changing environment. Understanding strategic capability is also important from another perspective. The organization's capability may be the leading edge of strategic developments, in the sense that new opportunities may be created by stretching and exploiting the organization's capability either in ways which competitors find difficult to match or in genuinely new directions, or both. This requires organizations to be innovative in the way they develop and exploit their capability.

In this perspective, strategic capability is about providing products or services to customers that are valued or might be valued in the future. An understanding of what customers value is the starting point. The discussion then moves to whether an organization has the resources to provide products and services that meet these customer requirements.

A resource is meant to be anything that could be thought of as a human or nonhuman strength of a given firm. More formally, a firm's resources at a given time can be defined as those (tangible and intangible) assets that are tied to the firm over a substantial period of time. Examples of resources are brand names, in-house knowledge of technology, employment of skilled personnel, trade contracts, machinery, efficient procedures, capital, and so forth. According to the economic school, resources include human capital, structural capital, relational capital, and financial capital.

Priem and Butler (2001) find it problematic that virtually anything associated with a firm can be a resource, because this notion suggests that prescriptions for dealing in certain ways with certain categories of resources might be operationally valid, whereas other categories of resources might be inherently difficult for practitioners to measure and manipulate. One example of a resource that might be difficult to measure and manipulate is tacit knowledge. Some have argued for tacit knowledge—that understanding gained from experience but that sometimes cannot be expressed to another person and is unknown to oneself—as a source of competitive advantage. Tacit knowledge in this sense is unknown to its owner until it emerges in a situation of knowledge application.

Another example is the "CEO resources." Prescriptions have been made to top managers of poorly performing firms that they are the cause of the problem and should think about voluntarily exiting the firm. This is a case where viewing CEOs as a resources would have more prescriptive implications for boards of directors than for the CEOs themselves. Similarly, viewing boards of directors as resources would have more prescriptive implications for the CEOs who appoint boards or the governments that regulate them than the boards themselves. Thus, some resources may be of less interest to strategy than others, depending in part on whether the resource can be manipulated and in part on the group—frequently CEOs—for whom prescriptions are desired. Identifying specific resources that may be particularly effective for certain actors in certain contexts might be a helpful first step in establishing boundaries for (and contributions of) the resource-based view in strategic management (Priem & Butler, 2001).

CHARACTERISTICS OF STRATEGIC RESOURCES

Barney (2002) discusses how value, rarity, nonduplication, and organization can be brought together into a single framework to understand the return potential associated with exploiting any of a firm's resources and capabilities. The framework consists of the following five steps (Barney, 2002):

1. If a resource or capability controlled by a firm is *not valuable*, that resource will not enable a firm to choose or implement strategies that exploit environmental opportunities or neutralize environmental threats. Organizing to exploit this resource will increase a firm's costs or decrease its revenues. These types of resources are weaknesses. Firms will either have to fix these weaknesses or avoid using them when choosing and implementing strategies. If firms do exploit these kinds of resources and capabilities, they can expect to put themselves at a competitive disadvantage compared to firms that either do not possess these nonvaluable resources or do not use them in conceiving and implementing strategies. Firms at a competitive disadvantage are likely to earn below-normal economic profits.
2. If a resource or capability is *valuable but not rare*, exploiting this resource in conceiving and implementing strategies will generate competitive parity and normal economic performance. Exploiting these valuable-but-not-rare resources will generally not create above-normal economic performance for a firm, but failure to exploit them can put a firm at a competitive disadvantage. In this sense, valuable-but-not-rare resources can be thought of as organizational strengths.
3. If a resource or capability is *valuable and rare but not costly to imitate (duplicate)*, exploiting this resource will generate a temporary competitive advantage for a firm and above-normal economic profits. A firm that exploits this kind of resource is, in

an important sense, gaining a first-mover advantage, because it is the first firm that is able to exploit a particular resource. However, once competing firms observe this competitive advantage, they will be able to acquire or develop the resources needed to implement this strategy through direct duplication or substitution at no cost disadvantage compared to the first-moving firm. Over time, any competitive advantage that the first mover obtained would be competed away as other firms imitate (duplicate or replicate) the resources needed to compete. However, between the time a firm gains a competitive advantage by exploiting a valuable and rare but imitable resource or capability, and the time that competitive advantage is competed away through imitation, the first-moving firm can earn above-normal economic performance. Consequently, this type of resource or capability can be thought of as an organizational strength and distinctive competence.

4. If a resource is *valuable, rare, and costly to imitate*, exploiting this resource will generate a sustained competitive advantage and above-normal economic profits. In this case, competing firms face a significant cost disadvantage in imitating a successful firm's resources and capabilities, and thus cannot imitate this firm's strategies. This advantage may reflect the unique history of the successful firm, causal ambiguity about which resources to imitate, or the socially complex nature of these resources and capabilities. In any case, attempts to compete away the advantages of firms that exploit these resources will not generate above-normal or even normal performance for imitating firms. Even if these firms are able to acquire or develop the resources and capabilities in question, the very high costs of doing so would put them at a competitive disadvantage compared to the firm that already possessed the valuable, rare, and costly to imitate resources. These kinds of resources and capabilities are organizational strengths and sustainable distinctive competencies.
5. The question of organization operates as an adjustment factor in the framework. If a firm with a resource that is *valuable, rare, and costly to imitate is disorganized*, some of its potential above-normal return could be lost. If the firm completely fails to organize itself to take advantage of this resource, it could actually lead the firm that has the potential for above-normal performance to earn normal or even below-normal performance.

Barney (2001) discusses how value and rarity of resources can be determined. *Value* is a question of conditions under which resources will and will not be valuable. Models of the competitive environment within which a firm competes can determine value. Such models fall into two large categories: (1) efforts to use structure-conduct-performance-based models to specify conditions under which different firm resources will be valuable and (2) efforts to determine the value of firm resources that apply other models derived from industrial organization models of perfect and imperfect competition.

As an example of resource value determination, Barney (2001) discusses the ability of a cost leadership strategy to generate sustained competitive advantage. Several firm attributes may be associated with cost leadership, such as volume-derived economies of scale, cumulative volume-derived learning curve economies, and policy choices. These firm attributes can be shown to generate economic value in at least some market settings. The logic used to demonstrate the value of these attributes is a market structure logic that is consistent with traditional microeconomics. After identifying the conditions under which cost leadership can generate economic value, it is possible to turn to the conditions under which cost leadership can be a source of competitive advantage (i.e., rare) and sustained competitive advantage (i.e., rare and costly to imitate).

The resource-based theory postulates that some resources will have a higher value for one firm than for other firms. The reasons why the value of resources may be firm-specific are multiple and include (Haanaes, 1997): the experience of working together as a team, the firm possessing superior knowledge about its resources, the bundling of the resources, and the existence of cospecialized or complementary assets.

The value of a given resource may change over time as the market conditions change, for example, in terms of technology, customer preferences, or industry structure. Thus, it is often argued that firms need to maintain a dynamic, as opposed to static, evaluation of the value of different resources.

Rarity is a question of how many competing firms possess a particular valuable resource. If only one competing firm possesses a particular valuable resource, then that firm can gain a competitive advantage; that is, it can improve its efficiency and effectiveness in ways that competing firms cannot. One example of this form of testable assertion is mentioned by Barney (2001). The example is concerned with organizational culture as a source of competitive advantage. If only one competing firm possesses a valuable organizational culture (where the value of that culture is determined in ways that are exogenous to the firm), then that firm can gain a competitive advantage; that is, it can improve its efficiency and effectiveness in ways that competing firms cannot. Both these assertions are testable. If a firm uniquely possesses a valuable resource and cannot improve its efficiency and effectiveness in ways that generate competitive advantages, then these assertions are contradicted. One could test these assertions by measuring the extent to which a firm uniquely possesses valuable resources, for example, valuable organizational culture, measuring the activities that different firms engage in to improve their efficiency and effectiveness, and then seeing if there are some activities a firm with the unique culture engages in to improve its effectiveness and efficiency—activities not engaged in by other competing firms.

Efficient firms can sustain their competitive advantage only if their resources can neither be extended freely nor imitated by other firms. Hence, in order for resources to have the potential to generate rents, they must be rare. Valuable, but common, resources cannot by themselves represent sources of competitive advantage because competitors can access them. Nobody needs to pay extra for obtaining a resource that is not held in limited supply.

In addition to value and rarity, inimitability has to be determined. *Inimitability* can be determined through barriers to imitation and replication. The extent of barriers and impediments against direct and indirect imitation determine the extent of inimitability. One effective barrier to imitation is that competitors fail to understand the firm's sources of advantage. The lack of understanding can be caused by tacitness, complexity, and specificity that form bases for competitive advantage (Haanaes, 1997).

Several authors have categorized resources. A common categorization is tangibles versus intangibles. Tangibles are relatively clearly defined and easy to identify. Tangible resources include plants, technology, land, geographical location, access to raw materials, capital, equipment, and legal resources. Tangible resources tend to be property based and may also include databases, licenses, patents, registered designs, and trademarks, as well as other property rights that are easily bought and sold.

Intangibles are more difficult to define and also to study empirically. Intangible resources encompass skills, knowledge, organizational capital, relationships, capabilities, and human capital, as well as brands, company and product reputation, networks, competences, perceptions of quality, and the ability to manage change. Intangible resources are generally less easy to transfer than tangible resources, as the value of an intangible resource is difficult to measure (Haanaes, 1997).

STRATEGIC IT RESOURCES

The resource-based view started to appear in IT research one decade ago. Now IT resources can be compared to one another and, perhaps more importantly, can be compared with non-IT resources. Thus, the resource-based view promotes cross-functional studies through comparisons with other firm resources.

In the beginning of resource-based studies of IT resources, IT was divided into three assets, which together with processes contribute to business value. These three IT assets were labeled human assets (e.g., technical skills, business understanding, problem-solving orientation), technology assets (e.g., physical IT assets, technical platforms, databases, architectures, standards), and relationship assets (e.g., partnerships with other divisions, client relationships, top management sponsorship, shared risk, responsibility). IT processes were defined as planning ability, cost effective operations and support, and fast delivery. This categorization was later modified to include IT infrastructure, human IT resources, and IT-enabled intangibles.

Wade and Hulland (2004) presented a typology of IT resources, where the IT resources held by a firm can be sorted into three types of processes: inside-out, outside-in, and spanning. Inside-out resources are deployed from inside the firm in response to market requirements and opportunities, and tend to be internally focused. In contrast, outside-in resources are externally oriented, placing an emphasis on anticipated market requirements, creating durable customer relationships, and understanding competitors. Finally, spanning resources, which involve both internal and external analysis, are needed to integrate the firm's inside-out and outside-in resources.

Inside-out resources include IS infrastructure, IS technical skills, IS development, and cost effective IS operations:

- **IT infrastructure.** Many components of the IT infrastructure (such as off-the-shelf computer hardware and software) convey no particular strategic benefit due to lack of rarity, ease of imitation, and ready mobility. Thus, the types of IT infrastructure of importance are either proprietary or complex and hard to imitate. Despite research attempts to focus on the non-imitable aspects of IT infrastructure, the IT infrastructure resource has generally not been found to be a source of sustained competitive advantage for firms.
- **IT technical skills.** IT technical skills are a result of the appropriate, updated technology skills, relating to both systems hardware and software that are held by the IS/IT employees of a firm. Such skills do not include only current technical knowledge, but also the ability to deploy, use, and manage that knowledge. Thus, this resource is focused on technical skills that are advanced, complex, and, therefore, difficult to imitate. Although the relative mobility of IS/IT personnel tends to be high, some IS skills cannot be easily transferred, such as corporate-level knowledge assets and technology integration skills, and, thus, these resources can become a source of sustained competitive advantage.

- **IT development.** IT development refers to the capability to develop or experiment with new technologies, as well as a general level of alertness to emerging technologies and trends that allow a firm to quickly take advantage of new advances. Thus, IT development includes capabilities associated with managing a systems development life cycle that is capable of supporting competitive advantage and should therefore lead to superior firm performance.
- **Cost effective IT operations.** This resource encompasses the ability to provide efficient and cost-effective IS operations on an ongoing basis. Firms with greater efficiency can develop a long-term competitive advantage by using this capability to reduce costs and develop a cost leadership position in their industry. In the context of IS operations, the ability to avoid large, persistent cost overruns, unnecessary downtime, and system failure is likely to be an important precursor to superior performance. Furthermore, the ability to develop and manage IT systems of appropriate quality that function effectively can be expected to have a positive impact on performance.

Outside-in resources include external relationship management and market responsiveness:

- **External relationship management.** This resource represents the firm's ability to manage linkages between the IT function and stakeholders outside the firm. It can manifest itself as an ability to work with suppliers to develop appropriate systems and infrastructure requirements for the firm, to manage relationships with outsourcing partners, or to manage customer relationships by providing solutions, support, and/or customer service. Many large IT departments rely on external partners for a significant portion of their work. The ability to work with and manage these relationships is an important organizational resource leading to competitive advantage and superior firm performance.
- **Market responsiveness.** Market responsiveness involves both the collection of information from sources external to the firm as well as the dissemination of a firm's market intelligence across departments, and the organization's response to that learning. It includes the abilities to develop and manage projects rapidly and to react quickly to changes in market conditions. A key aspect of market responsiveness is strategic flexibility, which allows the organization to undertake strategic change when necessary.

Spanning resources include IS-business partnerships and IS planning and change management:

- **IS-business partnerships.** This capability represents the processes of integration and alignment between the IS function and other functional areas or departments of the firm. The importance of IS alignment, particularly with business strategy, has been well documented. This resource has variously been referred to as synergy, assimilation, and partnerships. All of these studies recognize the importance of building relationships internally within the firm between the IS function and other areas or departments. Such relationships help to span the traditional gaps that exist between functions and departments, resulting in superior competitive position and firm performance. An element of this resource is the support for collaboration within the firm.

- **IS planning and change management.** The capability to plan, manage, and use appropriate technology architectures and standards also helps to span these gaps. Key aspects of this resource include the ability to anticipate future changes and growth, to choose platforms (including hardware, network, and software standards) that can accommodate this change, and to effectively manage the resulting technology change and growth. This resource has been defined variously in previous research as "understanding the business case," "problem solving orientation," and "capacity to manage IT change." It includes the ability of IS managers to understand how technologies can and should be used, as well as how to motivate and manage IS personnel through the change process.

From a resource-based perspective, Ravichandran and Lertwongsatien (2005) argue that IS resources that are inimitable and valuable can be rent yielding. Technology assets such as networks and databases are unlikely to be rent yielding, since they could be easily procured in factor markets. However, combining hardware and software assets to create a flexible and sophisticated IT infrastructure can be non-imitable, because creating such an infrastructure requires carefully melding technology components to fit firm needs and priorities. In addition to sophisticated IT infrastructure, skilled human resources, relationships between the IS department and user departments, and IS managerial knowledge are valuable resources that are posited to be rent yielding.

In order to explore the usefulness of the resource-based theory for IT resources, it is necessary to explicitly recognize the characteristics and attributes of resources that lead them to become strategically important. Although firms possess many resources, only a few of these have the potential to lead the firm to a position of sustained competitive advantage. What is it then that separates regular resources from those that confer a sustainable strategic benefit?

According to Wade and Hulland (2004), resource-based theorists have approached this question by identifying sets of resource attributes that might conceptually influence a firm's competitive position. Under this view, only resources exhibiting all of these attributes can lead to a sustained competitive advantage for the firm. We have already mentioned Barney's (2001) attributes of value, rareness, inimitability, nonsubstitutability, combination, and exploration.

In addition, an important seventh attribute is immobile. Once a firm establishes a competitive advantage through the strategic use of resources, competitors will likely attempt to amass comparable resources in order to share in the advantage. A primary source of resources is factor markets. If firms are able to acquire the resources necessary to imitate a rival's advantage, the rival's advantage will be short-lived. Thus, a requirement for sustained competitive advantage is that resources be imperfectly mobile or nontradable.

To govern IT resources efficiently and effectively, it is necessary to understand the strategic attributes of each resource. In Figure 8.1, the table shows an example of how strategic IT resources can be identified. The scale from 1 (little extent) to 5 (great extent) is applied.

In this example, we see that IT infrastructure is the IT resource with the greatest potential to lead to sustained competitive advantage, which would contradict that the IT infrastructure

Figure 8.1. IT resources in terms of strategic importance based on attributes

Attributes / Resources	Valuable	Rare	Exploitable	Inimitable	Non-substitutable	Combinable	Immobile	TOTAL
IT infrastructure	4	2	5	5	2	5	4	27
IT technical skills	4	2	3	3	4	4	3	23
IT development	4	3	3	3	4	3	2	22
Cost- effective IT operations	4	2	3	2	4	3	1	19

resource has generally not been found to be a source of sustained competitive advantage for firms. On the other hand, cost-effective IT operations have the least potential.

Wade and Hulland (2004) suggest that some of the resources create competitive advantage, while others sustain that advantage. A distinction is made between resources that help the firm attain a competitive advantage and those that help the firm to sustain the advantage. These two types of resource attributes can be thought of as, respectively, ex ante and ex post limits to competition.

Ex ante limits to competition suggest that prior to any firm's establishing a superior resource position, there must be limited competition for that position. If any firm wishing to do so can acquire and deploy resources to achieve the position, it cannot by definition be superior. Attributes in this category include value, rarity, and appropriateness.

Ex post limits to competition mean that subsequent to a firm's gaining a superior position and earning rents, there must be forces that limit competition for those rents. Attributes in this category include replicability, substitutability, and mobility.

Damianides (2005) applied a different approach to identify resources. He defined the following naturally grouped processes of IT resources: plan and organize, acquire and implement, deliver and support, and monitor and evaluate. He also developed an IT governance checklist, listing questions to ask to uncover IT issues, questions to ask to find out how management addresses the IT issues, and questions to self-assess IT governance practices.

Melville, Kraemer, and Gurbaxani (2004) developed an integrative model of IT business value to link information technology and organizational performance. In a resource-based perspective, they found that IT is a valuable resource, but the extent and dimensions are dependent upon internal and external factors, including complementary organizational resources of the firm and its trading partners, as well as the competitive and macro environment.

Similarly, Santhanam and Hartono (2003) applied resource-based theory to link information technology capability to firm performance. Their results indicate that firms with superior IT capability indeed exhibit superior current and sustained firm performance when compared to average industry performance, even after adjusting for effects of prior firm performance.

OUTSOURCING DEFINITIONS

If a firm does not want to use its internal resources to build or operate information systems, it can hire an external organization that specializes in providing these services to do the work. The process of turning over an organization's computer center operations, telecommunications networks, and/or applications development to external vendors is called outsourcing (Laudon & Laudon, 2005).

Loh and Venkatraman (1992a) define IT outsourcing as *the significant contribution by external vendors in the physical and/or human resources associated with the entire or specific components of the IT infrastructure in the user organization.* Vendors may contribute computer assets for the user from outside the organization. Alternatively, the ownership of certain computer assets of the user may be transferred to the vendor. Similarly, vendors may utilize their personnel to provide the required services, or the vendor may employ existing staff of the user. In their research, they attempted to explain the degree of IT outsourcing by using cost structures and economic performance. They found that the degree of IT outsourcing is positively related to both business and IT cost structures, and negatively related to IT performance. IT outsourcing was framed as a make-vs.-buy decision, where contractual modes differ in the domain of influence within the corporation (Loh & Venkatraman, 1992a, 1992b).

Lacity, Willcocks, and Feeny (1996) define outsourcing *to dismantle internal IT departments by transferring IT employees, facilities, hardware leases, and software licenses to third-party vendors.* Hirschheim and Lacity (2000) define information technology outsourcing as the practice of *transferring IT assets, leases, staff, and management responsibility for delivery of services from internal IT function to third-party vendors.*

In research by Grover, Teng, and Cheon (1998), they define outsourcing of IS functions as *the organizational decision to turn over part or all of an organization's IS functions to external service provider(s) in order for an organization to be able to achieve its goals.* This decision-making approach is interesting because it focuses on an early stage of a long process. Resource-based theory and resource-dependence theory from the field of strategic management and transaction cost theory and agency theory from economics are used in order to describe its implications for outsourcing research and practice. The definition includes decisions about how to arrange external IT services. Using several theoretical perspectives of outsourcing, they presume that organizations attempt to make these decisions in their best interests. Similarly, Grover, Cheon, and Teng (1996) define outsourcing as involving *a significant use of resources—either technological and/or human resources—external to the organizational hierarchy in the management of information technology.*

Hu, Saunders, and Gebelt (1997) define information systems outsourcing as *a business practice in which a company contracts out all or part of its information systems operations to one or more outside suppliers.* Here we find that outsourcing is a practical issue that also has a significant impact on business organization. Even though outsourcing is a business practice, for IS executives acquiring outside services is an important strategic issue confronting their organizations. Thus, their theoretical perspective is strategic decision making. In their research they have identified sources of influence in the adoption decision. One significant influence is the combined effects of external media, vendor pressure, and internal communications at the personal level among managers.

Kern and Willcocks (2002) are more process oriented in their approach, focusing on the long-term interaction. They focus on the key elements of the exchange and the relationship between different stakeholder groups. They recognize the influence of the environment and the atmosphere in which the interaction takes place. They define outsourcing as *a process whereby an organization decides to contract-out or sell the firm's IT assets, people and/or activities to a third party supplier, who in exchange provides and manages these assets and services for an agreed fee over an agreed time period.* In their process-oriented approach, they are using Håkansson's (1982) interaction model to explain the client-vendor relationship of IT outsourcing. Although Lacity and Willcocks (2000) did not explicitly provide a definition of outsourcing, it seems that they are in line with this process-oriented approach. They introduced a relationship framework that focuses on relationship stakeholders, relationship types, and six phases (scooping, evaluation, negotiation, transition, middle, and mature phase) and activities related to these phases. In this perspective, IT outsourcing is viewed as a longitudinal process involving several stakeholder groups.

Outsourcing can be defined as *turning over all or part of an organizational activity to an outside vendor* (Barthélemy, 2003b). Here outsourcing is the purchasing, from outside the organization, of IT services needed to perform business functions. According to Langfield-Smith and Smith (2003), outsourcing is *the contracting of any service or activity to a third party*. Both definitions are concerned with the interfirm relationship, and the authors pay attention to how to deal with uncertainty and risk encompassed in outsourcing. Where Barthélemy is concerned with management expertise as a predictor of success or failure, Langfield-Smith and Smith are concerned with the design of management control systems.

Outsourcing is *a phenomenon in which a user organization (client) transfers property or decision rights over information technology infrastructure to an external (vendor) organization* (Levina & Ross, 2003). By using this definition, Levina and Ross direct their research at how vendors can deliver financial and managerial benefits to their clients that outweigh contracting costs and risks. But instead of using traditional economic theories, they apply the concept of complementarity in organizational design as well as the core competency argument in outsourcing and theories of client-vendor relationships. They explain variability in outsourcing outcomes by using relationship factors as predictors.

The term outsourcing can be studied further by using the opposite term of insourcing. Hirschheim and Lacity (2000) define insourcing as the practice of evaluating the outsourcing option but confirming the continued use of internal IT resources to achieve the same objectives of outsourcing. They studied six decision factors: decision scope, decision sponsor, evaluation process, year of decision, size of the organization, and decision outcome. Lacity et al. (1996) define total insourcing as the management and provision of at least 80% of the IT budget internally after evaluating the IT service market. The common element of the two definitions seems to be that customers evaluate the external IT services market before a sourcing decision takes place.

An outsourcing relationship consists of a vendor (supplier) and a client (customer). The vendor is a firm that has the technology. This firm is sometimes called the source firm (Steensma & Coorly, 2001) and sometimes called the outsourcer (Beamount & Costa, 2002). The client is a firm that desires the technology. This firm is sometimes called the sourcing firm and sometimes called the outsourcee. For the purpose of clarity, Figure 8.2 lists some of the key terms used in this chapter.

Figure 8.2. Definitions of some key sourcing terms

Key term	Definition
Insourcing	The practice of evaluating the outsourcing option but confirming the continued use of internal IT resources to achieve the same objectives of outsourcing.
Offshoring	The practice of migrating business process overseas to lower costs without significantly sacrificing quality. This practice is also called global outsourcing.
Outsourcing	A process whereby an organization decides to contract-out or sell the firm's IT assets, people, and/or activities to a third party supplier, who in exchange provides and manages these assets and services for an agreed fee over an agreed time period.
Selective sourcing	Selected IT functions are located with external providers while still providing between 20% and 80% of IT budget.
Source firm	The firm that has the technology. The source firm is sometimes called vendor, supplier, or outsourcer.
Sourcing firm	The firm that desires the technology. The sourcing firm is sometimes called client, customer, or outsourcee.
Transformational outsourcing	Partnering with another company to achieve a rapid, substantial, and sustainable improvement in enterprise-level performance.

IT ORGANIZATIONAL PRINCIPLES TO FACILITATE OUTSOURCING

Outsourcing implies choice of principle and model for organizing the IT function. To understand implicit opportunities and threats involved in such principle and model decision making, we will present all principles and models for organizing the IT function as described by Agarwal and Sambamurthy (2002). Three principles underlie new ways to organize the IT function:

- **Principle 1:** *Organize IT to foster co-evolution between the business and IT function.* Design reporting relationships for key IT executives that focus on strategic business drivers. Engage IT executives in experimenting with new IT-enabled business models and business practices through appropriate incentives.
- **Principle 2:** *Organize IT to nurture relationship networks for visioning, innovation, and sourcing.* Nurture internal coordination mechanisms, including executive councils, IT management councils, divisional steering councils, IT standing teams, account managers, divisional information officers, service level agreements, and informal relationship building. Nurture external partnering tactics, such as multisourcing agreements, strategic alliances, and joint ventures.
- **Principle 3:** *Organize IT to explicitly manage eight value-creating processes.* Adopt a modular approach to selecting optimal organizing options for individual value-creating IT processes. There are eight value-creating processes consisting of three foundation processes (infrastructure management, human capital management, relationship management), three primary processes (value innovation, solutions delivery,

services provisioning), and two secondary processes (strategic planning, financial management).

Outsourcing implies choice of *principle 2* as the dominating principle. According to this principle, sourcing networks are important. Sourcing networks are relationship networks between IT executives and external partners. Their purpose is to foster collaboration between these internal and external parties when they are negotiating and managing efficient, cost-effective, and innovative uses of IT assets and services through sourcing arrangements, joint ventures, and strategic alliances. Three organizational models are typically found in companies:

1. **The partner model** primarily aims to ensure that the IT function is an active and direct participant in collaborating with business executives to make business innovation through IT a reality.
2. **The platform model** primarily aims to ensure that the IT function provides the assets, services, and resources for business innovation across the enterprise. Thus, the IT function acts as an enabler of innovation rather than as a direct catalyst for innovation, as in the partner model.
3. **The scalable model** primarily aims for maximum flexibility in its people resources, so that the IT function can expand and contract in concert with business cycles. A salient aspect of this model, in contrast with the other two models, is that it makes extensive use of sourcing relationships with vendors and systems integrators to achieve flexibility in IT resources.

Outsourcing implies choice of model 3, the scalable model, as the dominating IT function organization. This model seeks to facilitate IT-based business innovation without committing significant organizational investments to in-house IT resources. The scalable model uses sourcing to be flexible. This model emphasizes sourcing networks to leverage external partners, particularly for two IT value-creating processes: solutions delivery and services provisioning. Creative sourcing relationships permit the IT function to control IT costs while changing staff size in response to cyclical business conditions.

Our application of the principles and models suggested by Agarwal and Sambamurthy (2002) to IT outsourcing implies that opportunities and threats can be understood in terms of these principles and models. When outsourcing implies principle 2, then threats are related to lack of co-evolution with the rest of the business (principle 1) and lack of management of all eight value-creating processes (principle 3). When outsourcing implies model 3, then threats are related to lack of participation in collaborating with business executives to make business innovation and lack of proactive partnership in innovation processes.

OUTSOURCING OPPORTUNITIES

An empirical study of information technology sourcing in U.S. and UK organizations identified indicators of success. The objective of the study was to develop indicators of success based on participants' perceptions of whether the outcome of their IT sourcing decisions met their expectations. Participants cited a variety of expectations (anticipated and hoped-for outcomes) and reasons (justifications and explanations) for their sourcing decisions. Fifteen categories of expectations/reasons for sourcing were identified (Lacity & Willcocks, 1998):

1. Reduce IT costs
2. Improve technology or technical service
3. Jump on the bandwagon; outsourcing perceived as a viable, irreversible trend within their industry
4. Focus business on core competencies; IT perceived as non-core
5. Restructure IT budgets from capital budgets to fixed operating budgets
6. Play good corporate citizen; IT managers perceive that an outsourcing evaluation demonstrates their willingness to subordinate the good of the IT department for the good of the overall business
7. Focus internal IT staff on critical IT activities, such as development, while outsourcing more stable and predictable IT activities, such as data center operations
8. Prove efficiency; invite bids to receive a free benchmark
9. Eliminate an IT burden; assume a vendor will solve problematic IT function(s)
10. Downsizing - the entire company is pressured to reduce headcount
11. Preemptive move by IT managers to expose exaggerated claims made to senior executives by consultants or vendors
12. Improve cost controls
13. Forced market testing by the government
14. Justify new IT resources by bundling capital budget requests with a kind of proof that vendors cannot do it cheaper
15. Facilitate mergers and acquisitions - vendors are perceived as experts in merging data centers quickly

Each participant's expectations/reasons were mapped into the 15 chosen categories. In many instances, participants stated more than one expectation/reason. The ranking from 1 to 15 was based on total responses from participants.

Global outsourcing's defenders list a number of arguments in favor of outsourcing. Arguments in favor of outsourcing can be broken down to five areas: concentration on core business development by firms, cost control, access to state of the art technology, market discipline through greater transparency, and added flexibility to respond to demand changes (Clott, 2004). The motivations for outsourcing are evolving from a primary focus on cost reduction to an emerging emphasis on improving business performance. The traditional rationale of vendor economies of scale and specialization is becoming less convincing as companies with well-run, innovative IS departments large enough to accrue the same scale and specialization benefits as a vendor are nevertheless engaged in significant outsourcing deals.

DiRomualdo and Gurbaxani (1998) discovered in their research that while the academic literature and business press discuss IT outsourcing as if it were always driven by a singular focus on reducing the costs and enhancing the efficiency of IT resources; this is in fact only one of three kinds of strategic intent for IT outsourcing. They called this well-established intent IS improvement. The other two have more recently emerged as significant factors in many companies' decision to outsource. Outsourcing for business impact focuses on improving IT's contribution to company performance within the existing lines of business.

The third category of intent, commercial exploitation, focuses on leveraging technology-related assets in the marketplace:

- **IS Improvement.** Companies that want better performance from their core IS resources—the hardware, software, networks, people, and processes involved in managing and operating the technology and supporting users—have the strategic intent of IS improvement. Their objective typically includes cost reduction, service quality improvement, and acquisition of new technical skills and management competencies. They believe that outside specialists who are better able to keep pace with new technologies and skills, and who use superior processes and management methods, should manage some, if not all, of their IT services.
- **Business Impact.** Many IS organizations are struggling to develop the right mix of technical and business skills to exploit technology. As a result, many companies are looking to the IT outsourcing market for help, on the premise that outsourcing vendors' state-of-the-art skills, capabilities, and proficiency at recruiting and managing technologists make them better than internal IS organizations at using IT to improve business results. The strategic intent is deploying IT to significantly improve critical aspects of business performance.
- **Commercial Exploitation.** Outsourcing information technology with the strategic intent of commercial exploitation aims to improve the return on IT investment by generating new revenue and profit or by offsetting costs. The means by which IT assets can be leveraged commercially range from licensing systems and technologies developed initially for internal use, through selling IS products and services to other firms, to launching new IT-based businesses. Our study discovered that companies pursuing commercial exploitation were often those with innovative information systems. Many come from technology-intensive industries, such as air transport and financial services, and have mission-critical systems that are expensive to maintain and enhance.

OUTSOURCING THREATS

While literature on outsourcing has often sought to draw lessons from highly visible companies that have been successful in outsourcing, Barthélemy (2003b) in his article on "The Seven Deadly Sins of Outsourcing" sheds light on failed efforts. Failed outsourcing endeavors are rarely reported because firms are reluctant to publicize them. Firms do not like to report their failures because such information can damage their reputation. His study was based on in-depth analysis of 91 outsourcing efforts carried out by European and North American firms. Through his survey, he found that the same mistakes underlie most failed outsourcing efforts. These mistakes have been termed the seven deadly sins of outsourcing:

1. **Outsourcing activities that should not be outsourced.** Determining which activities can be best performed by outside vendors requires a good understanding of where the firm's competitive advantage comes from. Resources and capabilities that are valuable, rare, difficult to imitate, and difficult to substitute can be employed to create superior performance. Activities that are based on such resources and capabilities

(i.e., core activities) should not be outsourced because firms risk losing competitive advantage and becoming hollow corporations.

2. **Selecting the wrong vendor.** Selecting a good vendor is crucial for successful outsourcing. The literature has identified numerous criteria for successful provider choice. A useful distinction can be made between hard and soft qualifications. Hard qualifications are tangible and can be easily verified by due diligence. They refer to the ability of vendors to provide low-cost and state-of-the-art solutions. Important criteria also include business experience and financial strength. Soft qualifications are attitudinal. They may be unverifiable and may change depending on circumstances. Important soft criteria include a good cultural fit, a commitment to continuous improvement, flexibility, and a commitment to develop long-term relationships.
3. **Writing a poor contract.** Since the 1980s, vendor partnerships have emerged as a model of purchasing excellence. Partnerships replace market competition by close and trust-based relationships with a few selected vendors. The notion that outsourcing vendors are partners and that contracts play a minor role was popularized by early outsourcing deals. However, there are pitfalls in partnership management. A good contract is essential to outsourcing success because the contract helps establish a balance of power between the client and the vendor. Spending too little time negotiating the contract and pretending that the partnership relationship with the vendor will take care of everything is a mistake. Drafting a good contract is always important because it allows partners to set expectations and to commit themselves to short-term goals.
4. **Overlooking personnel issues.** The efficient management of personnel issues is crucial because employees generally view outsourcing as an underestimation of their skills. This may result in a massive exodus even before an actual outsourcing decision has been made. Firms that contemplate outsourcing must face two interrelated personnel issues. First, key employees must be retained and motivated. Second, the commitment of employees transferred to the vendor must also be secured.
5. **Losing control over the outsourced activity.** When the performance quality of an activity is low, managers are often tempted to outsource it. If poor performance is attributable to factors such as insufficient scale economies or a lack of expertise, outsourcing makes sense. If poor performance is attributable to poor management, outsourcing is not necessarily the right solution. For an outsourcing client, it is particularly important to avoid losing control over an outsourced activity. It is critical to keep the outsourced activity in alignment with the overall corporate strategy. While vendor management skills are very important, they must also be complemented with technical skills. If no one in the company is able to assess technological developments, outsourcing is bound to fail.
6. **Overlooking hidden costs of outsourcing.** Outsourcing clients are generally confident that they can assess whether or not outsourcing results in cost savings. However, they often overlook costs that can seriously threaten the viability of outsourcing efforts. Transaction cost economics suggests two main types of outsourcing hidden costs. First, outsourcing vendor search and contracting costs are costs of gathering information to identify and assess suitable vendors and costs of negotiating and writing the outsourcing contract. Second, outsourcing vendor management costs include monitoring the agreement to ensure that vendors fulfill their contractual obligations, bargaining with vendors, sanctioning them when they do not perform according to

Figure 8.3. The seven deadly sins of outsourcing and lessons learned (Barthélemy, 2003b)

Timetable	#	Deadly sin	Lesson learned
Original idea to outsource	1	Outsourcing activities that should not be outsourced	Only non-core business activities
	2	Selecting the wrong vendor	State-of-the art and trustworthy vendors
	3	Writing a poor contract	Precise, complete, balanced, and flexible contract
Beginning of the relationship	4	Overlooking personnel issues	Good communication and ethical behavior towards employees
	5	Losing control over the outsourced activity	Active management of the vendor
	6	Overlooking the hidden costs of outsourcing	Searching, contracting and managing costs
Vendor switch or reintegration of the outsourced activity	7	Failing to plan an exit strategy	Building reversibility clauses into the contract

the contract, and negotiating changes to the contract when unforeseen circumstances arise.

7. **Failing to plan an exit strategy.** Many managers are reluctant to anticipate the end of an outsourcing contract. Therefore, they often fail to plan an exit strategy (i.e., vendor switch or reintegration of an outsourced activity). Outsourcing relationships can be viewed on a continuum. At one end are long-term relationships where one or both partners have made investments specific to the relationship. There is a considerable advantage in recontracting with the same vendor because switching vendors or reintegrating the outsourced activity is very difficult. At the other end are market relationships where the client has a choice of many vendors and the ability to switch vendors with little cost and inconvenience. In this case, there is no real advantage in recontracting with the same vendor.

Today, outsourcing has extended to more crucial activities such as IT, telecommunications, finance, and logistics. Increasingly, complex types of outsourcing have developed. Based on his survey of 91 outsourcing efforts, Barthélemy (2003b) found that there are seven deadly sins of outsourcing, as summarized in Figure 8.3. Historically, outsourcing was restricted to basic support activities such as janitorial services. Some sins were "deadlier" than others. "Writing a poor contract" and "losing control over the outsourced activity" had the largest impact on the outcome of outsourcing efforts. On the other hand, "failing to plan an exit strategy" was not a good differentiator between success and failure, perhaps because planning an exit strategy only becomes necessary in the case of vendor switch or reintegration of an outsourced activity.

Several years before Barthélemy, Earl (1996) identified risks of outsourcing. According to him, there are many risks that, in practice, indicate limits to outsourcing. Those who have outsourced have more regrets than they acknowledge and more anxieties about vendors than they care to confront. Chief information officers in firms that are currently on the cusp of deciding to outsource have confided apparently sound cautionary instincts, but momentum can be difficult to stop. Earl argues that the IT sourcing question should be rephrased to, "Why should we not insource IT services?" instead of, "Why should we outsource IT services?" by considering the following eleven risks of outsourcing:

1. **Possibility of weak management.** If an IT service scores low on operational performance, a company will clearly be tempted to outsource it to a third party. This is true whether poor performance is real or imagined, or whether top management's views are rational or emotional. If the IT activity has been badly managed in the first place, will the IT managers be any better at managing an external provider? Indeed, does executive management want to give the benefits of improving an inefficient management to the marketplace? Once outsourcing has been initiated, managing IT services on the outside is far from easy. If the third party is not necessarily better, a company has to enhance its management of vendor skills and placate users. Hence, to reduce initial risks in outsourcing, a company must first be capable of managing the IT service.
2. **Inexperienced staff.** One argument for outsourcing is that specialist IT companies are likely to have better IT specialists. While this might be true, relatively new IT services businesses do not necessarily have either the best expertise or solid experience. What is worse is that in facilities management contracts with even the most established IT service businesses, the customer's staff may go work with the vendor, transferring internal weak staff and then having to deal with them all over again as contractor staff will not solve the problems. Since some of the largest outsourcing contracts were initiated to transform a resistant and slack IS function, the risk becomes even starker. The biggest risk, however, may occur when a large outsourcing contract is awarded to a major vendor. Headhunters call their network of contacts with a frantic request for someone who can manage a large facility that has just been outsourced or anyone who has experience in managing contracts and can head up a rapidly growing outsourcing division. If the candidate is someone working for the company that has just decided to outsource, the chances are that he or she will be retained by the original company anyway, or will prefer to work for another user company where his or her experience is better suited. Shrewd personnel policies can help mitigate some of the risks at the time an outsourcing contract is signed. However, capable IT staff people are rare, and there is a chance that the customer company will want to keep them or that they will decide to go elsewhere.
3. **Business uncertainty.** If a firm decides to outsource IT services because of costs or focus, it is assuming that its future direction and needs are clear. However, when cost is the driver of outsourcing, or converting fixed costs to variable costs is the declared aim, it is likely that the company will sacrifice crucial competencies or capabilities. The IT marketplace may offer more variety in services and suppliers than any corporation can. Thus, unknown future business needs may, in principle, be satisfied when they arise.
4. **Outdated technology skills.** When a company outsources an IT service to a third party, how can the company be sure that the vendors' skills stay current? If cost reduction is the objective in an outsourcing deal, the hope is that the current cost

case is reduced and that, over time, there are further cost reductions due to learning and technological change. Indeed, a company can force these improvements into the contract at the outset or negotiate them at annual reviews. However, if the vendors' skills do not advance, the cost-reduction potential is lessened, and unless further market testing is done, target setting is suboptimal.

5. **Endemic uncertainty.** IT operations and development have always been inherently uncertain. Users are not sure of their needs, new technology is risky, business requirements change, and implementation is full of surprises. A systems project management regime that demands no changes to specifications and rigid time and budget controls can produce applications that do not achieve their full potential or can create user-specialist conflicts. Companies should avoid outsourcing contracts that are set in concrete. At the same time, contracts should be precise, complete, incentive based, balanced, and flexible, according to Barthélemy (2003a). However, being willing to pay for flexibility may be better than specifying tight performance contracts with penalty clauses, followed by litigation.
6. **Hidden costs.** When cost reduction is the objective of outsourcing, there is typically a promise of early cash flow benefits and long-term cost savings. There are two tendencies, however, that are of concern. First, companies underestimate the setup costs, including redeployment costs, relocation costs, and longer-than-expected hand-off or parallel running costs. Second, companies may underestimate management costs. Some companies never anticipated the management resources and time—and thus cost—that has to be put in. Companies rarely record the costs of management.
7. **Lack of organizational learning.** Much learning about the capability of IT is experiential. Organizations tend to learn to manage IT by doing; they do not appreciate the challenges until they have experienced them. Management tends to learn the value of IT applications (or of infrastructure) by using them and seeing further opportunities for development. Many strategic information systems were discovered in an evolutionary fashion. Thus, the strategic scope of systems often emerges as users learn what is possible and as the business context and needs change. Of course, there is no reason that a third party cannot operate, enhance, or rebuild an application that has been reclassified as strategic. However, in other areas of business, responsibility for strategic assets is not so easily delegated to the marketplace.
8. **Loss of innovative capacity.** In the long run, a company wants to maintain innovative capacity in IT because there will be new ways of providing IT services and of exploiting IT for business. If the company has outsourced IT services and downsized as well, its ability to innovate may be impaired. Innovation needs slack resources, organic and fluid organizational processes, and experimental and entrepreneurial competencies—all attributes that external sourcing does not guarantee.
9. **Dangers of an external triangle.** Some years ago when IT specialists and users could not understand each other, a few companies created a new role for intermediaries or interpreters between the two parties. Often called business analysts, client managers, or systems liaison officers, they sought in theory to understand user needs and convey them to the specialists, while representing the specialists' concerns to the users. Similarly after outsourcing, the remaining IT people may act as conduits or consultants between the line managers and the vendors. In practice, the liaison roles often only succeed in keeping two communities apart and in creating more confusion.

10. **Technological indivisibility.** Much of IT is not divisible or capable of separation. Current information systems are increasingly integrated or interconnected, and problems can occur at the interface of responsibility between different vendors or between the vendor's domains and the customer's domain.
11. **Fuzzy focus.** Outsourcing is essentially concerned with the supply side of IT. The marketplace in principle can provide IT operations, development, service, and training. It is not so able to provide acceptable, innovative application ideas, the challenging effort and commitment required in systems implementation, and the harvesting and delivery of IT benefits. A real problem, then, with outsourcing is that it concentrates on the how of IT, not on the what. It focuses on the supply side, not the demand side. And because it occupies substantial management resources and executive time, it can unwittingly become another form of denominator management rather than revenue creation, not a prescription for long-term success.

Also Bahli and Rivard (2003) identified information technology outsourcing risks. They define risks as factors that influence the occurrence of undesirable outcomes. The degree to which each factor is present in IT outsourcing will contribute to the increased likelihood of a given outcome. Once this list of factors is drawn, risk management methods will consist of devising and using mechanisms that will either diminish the loss related to the outcome or decrease the likelihood of its occurrence by reducing the level of the risk factors. Four undesirable outcomes can be identified in IT outsourcing, and associated risk factors and consequences can be defined as follows:

- *Lock-in* is an undesirable outcome based on risk factors such as high asset specificity, small number of suppliers, and the client's low degree of expertise in outsourcing contracts. Consequences are cost escalation and service debasement. Suggested mitigation mechanisms are mutual hostaging and dual sourcing.
- *Costly contractual amendments* are an undesirable outcome based on risk factors such as high uncertainty and unanticipated changes. Consequences are cost escalation and service debasement. Suggested mitigation mechanisms are sequential contracting and contract flexibility.
- *Unexpected transition and management costs* are an undesirable outcome based on risk factors such as high uncertainty, the client's low degree of expertise in IT operations, and the client's low degree of expertise in outsourcing contracts. Consequences are cost escalation and service debasement. Suggested mitigation mechanisms are clan mechanisms and use of external expertise.
- *Disputes and litigation* are undesirable outcomes based on risk factors such as measurement problems, the supplier's degree of expertise in IT operations, and the supplier's degree of expertise in outsourcing contracts. Consequences are cost escalation and service debasement. Suggested mitigation mechanisms are alternative methods of dispute resolution, clan mechanisms, and use of external expertise.

As global outsourcing or offshoring arises, companies must also be aware of the pitfalls of migrating business process overseas to India, the Philippines, Ireland, and China and elsewhere to lower their costs. Meta Group reports offshoring saves 20% in the first year, and creates a 20% loss in productivity. In other words, actual savings are often misperceived. Other offshoring pitfalls to consider are: security, scope creep, culture, and knowledge transfer. Risks are raised when working internationally and companies must address privacy concerns. Many projects grow during the development cycle. Scoop creep is not only a phenomenon of offshoring but might increase as language and cultural differences increase. Differences in customs must be taken into account, as the differences are often more significant than anticipated. Time and effort to educate and train the vendor is a cost rarely accounted for by the IT client organization (InfoWorld, 2004).

IT SOURCING OPTIONS

IT sourcing is concerned with defining, planning, and managing how an enterprise deploys internal and external resources and services to ensure the continuous fulfillment of its business objectives. A variety of sources have emerged. This variety is illustrated in Figure 8.4. Here we find internal sourcing and external sourcing. Both can be managed either through organizational hierarchy or through market mechanism.

In general, organizations have three basic alternatives for acquiring technological know-how. They can (1) develop the technology independently, (2) acquire another company that already has the technology, or (3) enter into a technology-sourcing arrangement. If a firm lacks the capabilities needed to develop a technology independently and other organizations already have the technology, management can consider external sourcing. There is a continuum of external sourcing methods based on the level of mutual commitment between the firm that has the technology (the source firm) and the firm that desires the know-how (the sourcing firm). These methods range from arms-length licensing contracts, through more tightly coupled codevelopment partnerships and joint ventures, to the outright acquisition of the source firm (Steensma & Corley, 2001).

Steensma and Corley (2001) focused on the two polar extremes in their study of technology sourcing: market contracting through licensing vs. the use of firm hierarchy through acquisition. The polar cases are basic particles from which more elaborate arrangements are constructed. Hierarchy implies that the sourcing firm can hierarchically control the technology, personnel, and other assets of the IT function and apply it to its current needs at its discretion.

Figure 8.4. Sourcing options

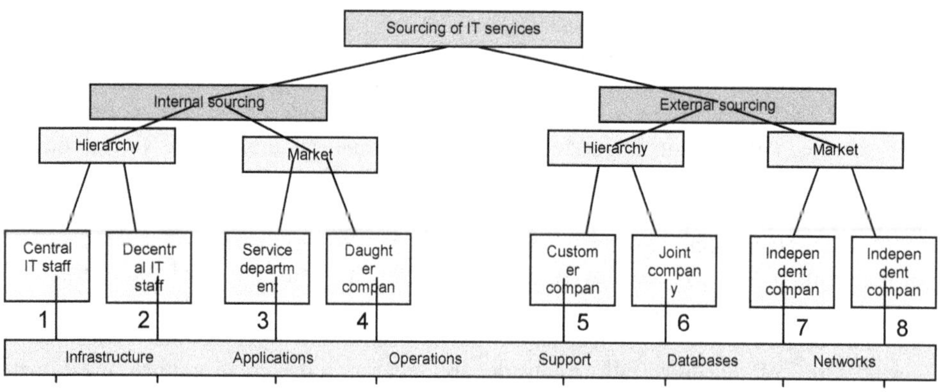

Internal market as illustrated with numbers 3 and 4 in Figure 8.1 has a different sourcing logic. The concept of internal market is not new. The concept was first perceived to have radical implications eliminating superior-subordinate relationships, organizing all activity in terms of self-responsible profit centers, determining compensation objectively, eliminating internal monopolies, allowing freedom of access to information, and establishing a corporate constitution (King & Malhotra, 2000).

These appear to be less radical in today's environment of matrix organizations, self-managed teams, and reengineered business processes. However, the notion of internal markets is not as simple as first suggested. The internal market is a mechanism for unleashing market forces inside the firm. Firms selecting this alternative might be able to retain control of the function while achieving the objectives of cost savings and service-responsiveness that are often ascribed to an external vendor (King & Malhotra, 2000).

Today, the internal market within an organization is characterized by a setup in which internal units are enabled to act autonomously by exerting self-control in conducting transactions with other internal units and with external entities within a framework of an overarching corporate vision, values, and precepts. This notion of internal markets may be best understood in terms of its potential broad applicability in an organizational context (King & Malhotra, 2000).

Implementation of the internal market concept requires the creation of a market economy inside a firm. In this, organizational units buy and sell goods and services among themselves and to others outside the firm at prices established in the open market. In contrast, the transfer prices that are used for internal transactions often represent a simulation of a marketing-clearing mechanism (King & Malhotra, 2000).

In IT sourcing, the term strategic sourcing is often used. Strategic sourcing has the following characteristics (Else, 2002):

- Systematic, ongoing effort to align individual sources and the portfolio of sources with broad high-level corporate strategy.
- Choosing and managing a set of specific sources in ways that advance one or more strategic goals.
- Continuous business process, not a tactical procurement exercise, intended to dynamically map business requirements to service delivery options.
- Methodology to deploy technology strategy and the means, by which a business strategy is optimized.
- Highly multisourced environments will be the norm.
- Enterprises must develop new roles, processes, and governance structures to effectively manage the sourcing spectrum.

The increasing complexity of sourcing options and combinations has lead *Computerworld* (2005, p. 3) to stress qualifications needed by IT leaders: "Today's IT leaders operate in a vast sphere. They are multidimensional business executives, by turns global architects, employee boosters and deal negotiators." The purpose of IT sourcing can best be illustrated by sourcing principles developed for government agencies in the U.S. (Else, 2002, p. 35):

1. Support agency missions, goals, and objectives.
2. Be consistent with human capital practices designed to attract, motivate, retain, and reward a high-performing federal workforce.

Figure 8.5. IT function specialization as 'IS Lite' (Adapted from Nielsen, 2004)

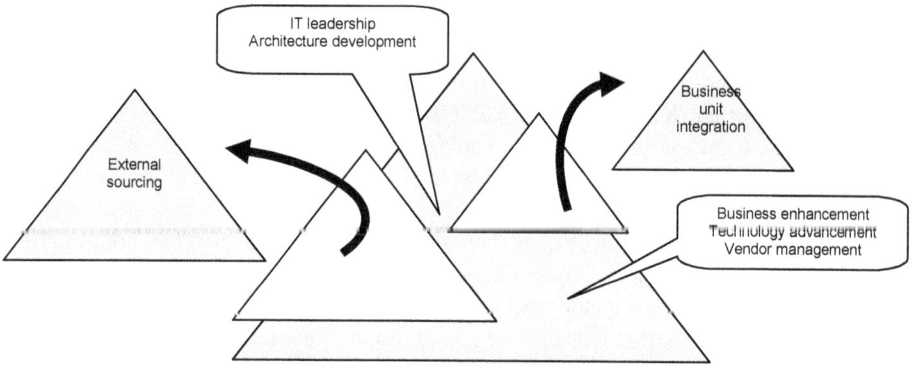

3. Recognize that inherently governmental and certain other functions should be performed by federal workers.
4. Create incentives and processes to foster high-performing, efficient, and effective organizations throughout the federal government.
5. Be based on a clear, transparent, and consistently applied process.
6. Avoid arbitrary full-time equivalent (FTE) or other arbitrary numerical goals.
7. Establish a process that, for activities that may be performed by either the public or the private sector, would permit public and private sources to participate in competitions for work currently performed in-house, work currently contracted to the private sector, and new work, consistent with these guiding principles.
8. Ensure that, when competitions are held, they are conducted as fairly, effectively, and efficiently as possible.
9. Ensure that competitions involve a process that considers both quality and cost factors.
10. Provide for accountability in connections with all sourcing decisions.

Nielsen (2004) tried to study IT sourcing by looking at the IS organization. As illustrated in Figure 8.5, the IS organization can be divided into different parts that may be delegated and integrated into other organizational arrangements.

DISTINCTIVE NATURE OF IT SOURCING

IT is not just another resource that should be managed like any other resource. Before entering outsourcing strategy, there is a need to stand back and carefully consider the specifics of any IT we put forward as an outsourcing candidate. Lacity and Willcocks (2001) identified the following five characteristics that represent the distinctive nature of IT sourcing decisions:

1. **IT is not a homogeneous function, but comprises a wide variety of IT activities.** Some IT applications uniquely enable business operations and management processes.

Other IT activities, such as accounting systems, may appear less critical, but closer scrutiny often reveals that the value of such systems lies in the cross-functional integration of business processes. Outsourcing such activities can hinder business performance because suppliers lack an understanding of the implications IT has on other business processes.

2. **IT capabilities continue to evolve at a dizzying pace; thus, predicting IT needs past a three-year horizon is wrought with uncertainty.** Although companies initially perceive that suppliers will provide access to new technologies, megadeals are usually contracted around current technologies with only vague reference to future technologies. Most companies find that by the third year into an outsourcing deal, the original contract actually hinders their adoption of new technologies.
3. **There is no simple basis for gauging the economics of IT activity.** Although price/performance improvements occur in every industry, in few industries do the underlying economics shift as fast as IT. A unit of processing power that costs $1 million in 1965 costs less than $20,000 today. Today's computer resources may well cost 10% less next year. The rapid change in the underlying economics makes it extremely difficult for senior executives to evaluate the long-term costs of outsourcing. While a 20% reduction of current IT costs for the next 10 years may be appealing to a senior executive today, a few years into the contract he or she may be paying the supplier above-market prices for computer resources. The economics of desktop computing, in particular, change quickly and many managers have been reluctant to lock themselves into a fixed-price outsourcing arrangement.
On the other hand, the price of IT skills will continue to be volatile, and in areas of high demand and shortage, will escalate sometimes quite unpredictably. Staying alive to these switches remains a key skill for client and suppliers alike. Otherwise profit margins for the supplier can erode quickly; and declining service to the client may be a consequence.
4. **Economic efficiency has more to do with IT practices than inherent economies of scale.** Although there are indeed economies of scale in some aspects of IT, they occur at a size achievable by many medium-sized and most large-sized companies. Therefore, supplier bids are based more on improvements in management practices than inherent economies of scale. For example, suppliers may cut costs through charge out mechanisms that motivate business users to manage demand, by consolidating data centers from multiple sites to one site or by standardizing software.
5. **Most distinctively of all, large switching costs are associated with IT sourcing decisions.** In most areas of business operations, management can protect itself against poor sourcing decisions in a number of ways—by dual sourcing of component supply or annual contract reviews of an advertising agency. These techniques are often inapplicable or ineffective for IT outsourcing, particularly when a total outsourcing approach is taken.

And thus, there is a need to make these characteristics of IT visible as sourcing decision has many options. They may not change the decision, but they might play a role deciding what to outsource, for how long, to whom, and how to build the relationship with the vendor.

SOURCING ALTERNATIVES

Companies outsource IT for many reasons, ranging from its high profile and current popularity to cost pressures from competition and economic recession. However, industry watchers attribute the growth of the IT outsourcing market to two main phenomena. First, the interest in IT outsourcing largely results from a shift in business strategy. Many companies have abandoned their diversification strategies—once pursued to mediate risk—to focus on core competencies. As a result, IT has come under scrutiny. Senior executives frequently view the entire IT function as a non-core activity and reason that IT service vendors have the economies of scale and technical expertise to provide services more efficiently than do internal IT departments. Second, uncertainty about IT's value is another reason for the growth of outsourcing. In many companies, senior executives perceive that IT has failed to deliver the promise of competitive advantage propagated in the 1980s and 1990s. Consequently, many senior executives view IT as a necessary cost to be minimized (Lacity et al., 1996).

Three Sourcing Levels

In situations where a firm does not want to tie up some of its capital resources in IT, it can hire the IT tasks to be performed by outside companies or vendors. Schniederjans, Hamaker, and Schniederjans (2004) distinguish between the following three outsourcing strategies:

1. **Subcontracting limited work assignments.** Short-term, overflow work beyond existing capacity is assigned to the subcontractors or vendors. This is just a temporary assignment in much the same way those temporary staffers are hired to fill in for summer vacation assignment of full-time staffers. This strategy is ideal with security issues or when cost prohibits more inclusion from a subcontractor.
2. **Subcontracting project assignments.** Whole IT projects are assigned to subcontractors or vendors. These assignments would entail a complete project where the management of the project would be delegated to the subcontractor and not under the control of the IT management of the hiring firm. This strategy is ideal when a company has unique skill or technology requirements too expensive for them to maintain but affordable for contractors to offer their clients.
3. **Total outsource assignment.** Where part (i.e., staff, IT, facilities) or all of the entire IT function is subcontracted out to a subcontractor or vendor. Here a company may lease all their IT from a subcontractor but run the equipment with their own staff. This strategy is ideal when a company may have a market that requires constant changes in IT or cannot afford to tie up capital in IT.

Schniederjans et al. (2004) discuss IT outsourcing in an investment perspective. They argue that while IT outsourcing is very popular and can be used to avoid many IT investment decision-making pitfall situations that traditionally occur, the most common use of an outsourcing strategy is where the firm partially outsources and partially maintains its own IT resources. This being the case, investment decision-making becomes even more complicated by outsourcing, as both outsourcing investments and in-house investments have to be evaluated. An IT investment can be defined as a decision of allocating resources to an IT activity. Investment methodologies include break-even analysis, payback period, rate of return, net present value, cost-benefit, and cost-effectiveness. In this perspective, IT outsourcing is to be implemented to the extent that such investments are profitable.

Four Sourcing Categories

A survey of IT outsourcing experiences in U.S. and UK organizations revealed a wide spectrum of sourcing decisions, ranging from exclusive use of internal IT functions to large-scale IT outsourcing (Lacity & Willcocks, 2000). This wide spectrum can be classified into the following four sourcing categories (Lacity et al., 1996):

1. **Total outsourcing:** The decision to transfer IT assets, leases, staff, and management responsibility for delivery of IT services from an internal IT function to an external IT provider that represents more than 80% of the IT budget.
2. **Total insourcing:** The decision to retain the management and provision of more than 80% of the IT budget internally after evaluating the IT services market. Included in the definition of insourcing is the buying in of vendor resources to meet a temporary need, such as programmers in the latter stages of a new development project or management consultants to facilitate a strategic planning process. In these cases, the customer retains responsibility for the delivery of IT services; vendor resources are brought in to supplement internally managed teams.
3. **Selective outsourcing:** The decision to source selected IT functions from external provider(s) while still providing between 20% and 80% of the IT budget internally. This strategy may include single or multiple suppliers. The vendor becomes responsible for delivering the result of the selectively outsourced IT activities, while the customer remains responsible for delivering the result of the insourced activities.
4. **De facto insourcing:** The de facto decision to use internal IT departments to provide products and services that arise from historical precedent, rather than from a reasoned evaluation of the IT services market.

With these definitions, Lacity et al. (1996) found 14 cases of total outsourcing, 15 cases of total insourcing, and 33 cases of selective outsourcing in their sample of 62 companies. In a later survey, Lacity and Willcocks (2000) found that 73% of respondents pursued selective outsourcing, while 22% of organizations exclusively use internal IT functions to provide IT services, leaving only 5% to total outsourcing.

Applications service providers (ASPs) deliver and manage applications and computer services from remote computer centers to multiple users via the Internet or a private network. Instead of buying and installing software programs, subscribing companies can rent the same functions from these services. Users pay for the use of this software either on a subscription or per transaction basis. The ASP's solution combines package software applications and all of the related hardware, system software, network, and other infrastructure services that the customer otherwise would have to purchase, integrate, or manage independently. The ASP customer interacts with a single entity instead of an array of technologies and service vendors. Companies are turning to this software service model as an alternative to developing their own software. Some companies will find it much easier to rent software from another firm and avoid the expense and difficulty of installing, operating, and maintaining the hardware and software for complex systems, such as enterprise resource planning (ERP) systems. The ASP contracts guarantee a level of service and support to ensure that the software is available and working at all times. Today's Internet-driven business environment is changing so rapidly that getting a system up and running in three months instead of six could mean the difference between success and failure. Application service providers also enable small and medium-sized companies to use applications that they otherwise could not afford (Laudon & Laudon, 2005).

Barthélemy and Geyer (2004) studied determinants of total IT outsourcing in French and German firms. The total vs. selective IT outsourcing dichotomy is a classic in the literature, and they reported the following findings from their study:

- For firms that outsource IT, the likelihood of total outsourcing is *higher* when the cost reduction motivation is strong.
- For firms that outsource IT, the likelihood of total outsourcing is *lower* when the IT department is large.
- For firms that outsource IT, the likelihood of total outsourcing is *lower* in IT-intensive sectors.
- For firms that outsource IT, the likelihood of total outsourcing is *higher* for French firms than for German firms.

They found no support for the hypothesis that performance improvement motivation is a significant factor nor the hypothesis that non-IT senior executives involvement is a significant factor.

Analysis Framework

A typical analytical framework to aid in decisions concerning outsourcing, developed by Earl (1996), is offered in Figure 8.9. The guiding parameters are the business value of a technology or application and the operational performance of the associated service. The framework suggests, for example, that outsourcing of information systems central to business strategy may be a dangerous diversion, especially if IT operations are already efficient. Insourcing in this situation is preferred. If business value is high but operational performance is weak, then market testing (or benchmarking) might make sense, at least so a company can see what performance improvement might be possible by either internal or external sourcing. However, if operational performance is weak and the business value of the particular technology or application is low, then outsourcing is a more obvious route to improvement. Finally, smart sourcing or selective outsourcing might be a way to simplify the IT domain when elements of it are satisfactory for operational performance but not central to business capability or strategy.

Such arguments are intuitively appealing at an analytical and general level. The trouble is that they can be simplistic in practice. They do not account for the complexities that permeate the management of information resources. Managers should always ask themselves why does outsourcing make sense and why does it not make sense to the company in the current situation.

Figure 8.9. IT sourcing strategies (Earl 1996)

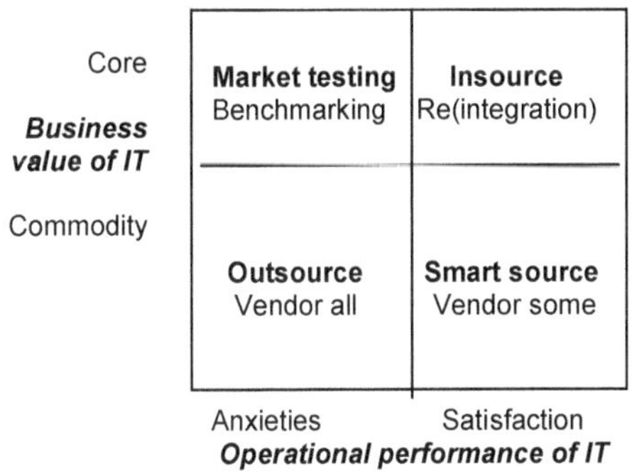

Selective Outsourcing

Lacity et al. (1996) argue that the debate about all-or-nothing outsourcing has obscured the real issue. The question is not, "Should we outsource or insource IT?" but rather "Where and how can we take advantage of the developing market for IT services?" It seems that successful companies carefully select which IT activities to outsource, rigorously evaluate vendors, tailor the terms of the contract, and carefully manage the vendor. IT activities for outsourcing consideration can be classified into different categories. Grover et al. (1996) defined five categories labeled applications development and maintenance, systems operations, telecommunications management and maintenance, end-user support, and systems planning and management:

1. *Applications development and maintenance* include systems analysis, design, and construction of application software and the accompanying software maintenance.
2. *Systems operations* include mainframe and minicomputer operations for daily processing runs, backup and recovery, and systems software maintenance.
3. *Telecommunications management and maintenance* includes hardware and software development for telecommunications, daily management of voice, video, data, and/or image communications, and network operations and maintenance.
4. *End-user support* includes PC procurement, user education and training, and user consulting.
5. *Systems planning and management* includes highly asset-specific activities such as project management, personnel management, financial management, and administrative support.

What should be outsourced successfully? Grover et al. (1996) studied outsourcing success. Outsourcing success was defined as a high score on the following items:

- We have been able to refocus on core business.
- We have enhanced our IT competence.
- We have increased access to skilled personnel.

- We have enhanced economies of scale in human resources.
- We have enhanced economies of scale in technological resources.
- We have increased control of IS expenses.
- We have reduced the risk of technological obsolescence.
- We have increased access to key information technologies.
- We are satisfied with our overall benefits from outsourcing.

Given these items to measure outsourcing success, the researchers looked for relationships between outsourcing categories and outsourcing success. The outsourcing of *systems operations* and *telecommunications management and maintenance* showed a significant relationship with outsourcing success. The outsourcing of applications development and maintenance, end-user support, and systems planning and management did not show a significant relationship with outsourcing success. We have to remind ourselves that this research was conducted a decade ago. Nevertheless, both categorization and empirical results are interesting to note. A statistical test of overall outsourcing reflecting an average effect of the results of all five categories was also conducted. Overall outsourcing showed a positive relationship with success. This indicates that, on average, outsourcing does realize benefits for the service receiver.

We find other categorizations in different research literature. For example, Ang and Straub (1998) define eight categories labeled information systems strategy, information technology planning, capacity management, production scheduling, human resources management, security management, network management, and personal computer management. They found that greatest extent of outsourcing in capacity management, and the least extent in PC management.

Insourcing

Hirschheim and Lacity (2000) argue that the current IT sourcing research covers the motivations and consequences of outsourcing, and has neglected another important option—insourcing. They define insourcing as the practice of evaluating the outsourcing option, but confirming the continued use of internal IT resources to achieve the same objectives of outsourcing. They believe that insourcing must be fully explored to complement the growing body of outsourcing research. Only by understanding the processes and outcomes of both outsourcing and insourcing can a comprehensive understanding of IT sourcing result. This unexplored insourcing option provided the motivation behind Hirschheim and Lacity's research. Can internal IT departments achieve the same results as outsourcing vendors? If so, why have they not done so in the past? Do IT departments actually reduce costs or improve service after winning an insourcing bid? If so, how did IT departments achieve the results? They conducted 14 insourcing case studies to research these issues.

The issues associated with the choice of an IT sourcing strategy are often murky, hidden behind euphemisms, perceived differently by different stakeholder groups, and generally not easily analyzed. Nevertheless, in trying to explain what they found in their research about these issues, Hirschheim and Lacity (2000) noted certain similarities and differences in patterns and these coalesced around four loosely connected alternatives in the way organizations approach IT insourcing. These four alternative approaches are described in terms of archetypes:

- **Archetype 1:** *Senior executives enable internal IT managers to cut costs.* It begins when external pressures threaten the organization causing senior management to search for ways to reduce costs, including IT costs. Under this scrutiny, senior executives question the value of rising IT expenditures and mandate that IT managers cut costs. IT managers counter that costs are high because users resist their cost reduction tactics. Senior management despairs at the gridlock and formally invites outsourcing vendors to submit bids. IT managers rally, requesting they be allowed to compete with vendor bids.
- **Archetype 2:** *IT managers terminate failing outsourcing contracts.* Due to poorly negotiated contracts, IT costs rose and service levels dropped. The senior IT managers assemble a case to terminate the outsourcing contract and rebuilt the internal IT organization. Senior executives and users support the IT managers' proposals. After an initial investment, IT costs drop and service levels improve as a result of insourcing.
- **Archetype 3:** *IT managers defend insourcing.* This archetype is the first time in which insourcing results in a financial failure in that no cost savings occur. IT managers take charge of the outsourcing evaluation for a number of political reasons, such as proving efficiency, justifying new resources, or trying to enhance their reputation as business persons. They used the outsourcing evaluations to confirm to senior management the legitimacy of continued sourcing through the internal IT departments.
- **Archetype 4:** *Senior executives confirm the value of IT.* This archetype indicates the case where the insourcing decisions did not result in significant reduction in IT costs, but the insourcing decisions were still considered a success because companies revalidated and further legitimated internal sourcing. In these companies, organizational structures and processes are implemented to demonstrate the cost effectiveness of their IT departments.

Hirschheim and Lacity (2000) contend that outsourcing evaluations often result from the frustrations caused by different stakeholder expectations and perceptions of IT performance. This belief is based on an analysis of what IT managers can realistically achieve vs. what senior executives and users expect them to achieve. Different stakeholder perspectives set unrealistic performance expectations for IT managers, leading to frustration, loss of faith in internal IT management, and hopes that outsourcing vendors will provide the solutions.

Outsourcing Preparations

The growth of the number and size of outsourcing deals has been paralleled by rising concern with how these deals can be managed, and in particular how the risks they represent can be controlled. Risk here is taken to be a negative outcome that has a known or estimated probability of occurrence based on experience or some theory. Risk is the likelihood of loss as a consequence of uncertainty. Risk has emerged as a key issue in IT outsourcing, not least because of the very mixed picture on success emerging from the trade press and the academic evidence. According to Lacity and Willcocks (2001), the main reasons for failure or negative outcomes in IT outsourcing deals have been various combinations of the following 10 factors:

1. Treating IT as an undifferentiated commodity to be outsourced
2. Incomplete contracting
3. Lack of active management of the supplier on contract and relationship dimensions
4. Failure to build and retain requisite in-house capabilities and skills
5. Power asymmetries developing in favor of the vendor
6. Difficulties in constructing and adapting deals in the face of rapid business and technical change
7. Lack of maturity and experience of contracting for and managing total outsourcing arrangements
8. Outsourcing for short-term financial restructuring or cash injection rather than to levering IT assets for business advantage
9. Unrealistic expectations with multiple objectives for outsourcing
10. Poor sourcing and contracting for development and new technologies

For risk mitigation, all these 10 risk factors have to be managed. Otherwise, the organization is likely to fail when handing over IT without understanding its role in the organization, and what the vendor's capabilities are. One rule of thumb is: never outsource a problem, only an IT activity or set of tasks that a detailed contract and performance measures can be written for.

In addition to risk mitigation, there is another important preparation for outsourcing concerning core IT capabilities. A focus on key capabilities and skills reflects a resource-based approach to how organizations can survive, pursue stakeholder objectives, and compete. Lacity and Willcocks (2001) identified nine emerging key capabilities required for any future high performance IT function: governance, business systems thinking, relationship-building, architecture planning, making technology work, informed buying, contract facilitation, contract monitoring, and supplier development. For IT capabilities management, all these nine key capabilities have to be identified. Otherwise, the organization is likely to fall behind other high performance IT functions.

IT OUTSOURCING DECISIONS

Information technology outsourcing is the practice of transferring responsibility to third-party vendors for the management of IT assets and staff, and for delivery of IT services such as data entry, data center operations, applications development, applications maintenance, and network management. Successful large-scale IT outsourcing can improve firm performance in several respects. By delegating complicated, time-consuming IT tasks to vendors, IT outsourcing customers can focus completely on those core competencies that create competitive advantage and thus firm value (Hall & Liedtka, 2005).

Given the potential headaches of managing IT, it is tempting to hand the job over to someone else. Indeed, outsourcing once appeared to be a simple solution to management frustrations, and senior management teams at many companies negotiated contracts with large service providers to run their entire IT functions. At a minimum, these providers were often able to provide IT capabilities for a lower cost and with fewer hassles than the companies had been able to themselves. But many of these outsourcing arrangements resulted in dissatisfaction, particularly as a company's business needs changed. Service providers, with their standard offerings and detailed contracts, provided IT capabilities that were not flexible enough to meet changing requirements, and they often seemed slow to respond to problems. Furthermore, a relationship with a supplier often required substantial investments of money and time, which entrenched that supplier in the company's strategic planning and business processes. The company then became particularly vulnerable if the supplier failed to meet its contractual obligations (Ross & Weill, 2002).

Problems arose because senior managers, in choosing to outsource the IT function, were also outsourcing responsibility for one or more of the crucial decisions they should have been making themselves. Companies often hired outside providers because they were dissatisfied with the performance of their own IT departments, but that dissatisfaction was primarily the result of their own lack of involvement. In light of this track record, most bigger companies, at least, are deciding to keep their main IT capabilities in-house. But many engage in selective outsourcing. Good candidates for this are commodity services such as telecommunications, in which there are several competing suppliers and specifications are easy to set and services involving technologies with which the company lacks expertise. Unlike decisions to outsource the entire IT function, selective outsourcing decisions are usually best left to the IT unit, assuming that senior management has taken responsibility for overall strategy.

Beaumont and Costa (2002) studied information technology outsourcing in Australia. They found that close to 40% of Australian organizations outsource one or more IT applications. Large organizations tended to outsource more than small ones. The three most important reasons for outsourcing were access to skills, improved quality, and focus on core business. Four factors contributed to successful outsourcing: a tight contract, a partnership, a change process, and the IT manager's role changing from managing projects and operations to acquiring and managing the internal and external resources required to do the organization's IT work.

Successful IT outsourcing relationships enable participants to achieve organizational objectives and to build a competitive advantage that each organization could not easily attain by itself. Outsourcing success can be viewed as the level of fitness between the customer's requirements and the outsourcing outcomes. Outsourcing success can be measured in terms of both business and user perspectives. In a business perspective, outsourcing is motivated by the promise of strategic, economic, and technological benefits. The success of outsourcing, then, should be assessed in terms of attainment of these benefits. In a user perspective, outsourcing success is the level of quality of offered services. A decision to outsource on the basis of saving costs without analysis of the quality of services frequently leads to higher costs and lower user satisfaction. Therefore, it is imperative to conduct a proper analysis of the service quality before building a relationship with a service provider for a successful outsourcing arrangement (Lee & Kim, 1999).

The decision to outsource or insource enterprisewide activities related to the acquisition, deployment, and management of IT represents one of the more complex choices facing a firm's managers. On the one hand, insourcing requires management to commit significant resources to a course of action, the effects of which may be costly to reverse, while foregoing numerous advantages associated with the marketplace. On the other hand, insourcing may be required for a firm to accumulate resources necessary to generate or maintain a competitive advantage.

The complexity of this decision is demonstrated in research conducted by Leiblein, Reuer, and Dalsace (2002). They examined the relationship between governance choice and technological performance. In contrast to popular arguments suggesting that insourcing or outsourcing will lead to superior technological performance, they found that governance decisions per se do not significantly influence technological performance directly. Rather, observed differences in the performance of transactions governed by different organizational forms are driven by factors underlying governance choice. While the increasing rapidity of technological change and the increasing dispersion of knowledge suggest an increased role for outsourcing in the economy, the relationship between governance choice and performance is dependent on the distribution of relevant capabilities and the degree to which performance is driven by autonomous or systemic innovation.

Empirical evidence suggests that carefully crafted outsourcing strategies increase the overall performance of the firm. Outsourcing is generally considered a very powerful tool to cut costs and improve performance. Through outsourcing, firms can take advantage of the best outside vendors and restructure entrenched departments that are reluctant to change. Outsourcing can also help focus on the core business. Since building core competencies and serving customer needs are critical to firm success, anything that detracts from this focus may be considered for outsourcing (Barthélemy, 2003).

The decision to outsource is influenced by a number of factors. They include such factors as production economies, transaction economies, technological uncertainty, functional complexity, transaction specific investments, supplier presence, slack resources, and criticality of IT.

OUTSOURCING PERFORMANCE

The rapidly increasing use of outsourcing for IT services, both in the public and private sectors, has attracted much interest from researchers and practitioners alike. While early studies of IT outsourcing were largely qualitative in nature, more recent studies have attempted to analyze the outcomes achieved in quantitative terms. Domberger, Fernandez, and Fiebig (2000) are consistent with the latter, but goes further by modeling the price, performance, and contract characteristics that are relevant to IT outsourcing. A two-equation recursive regression model was used to analyze 48 contracts for IT support and maintenance. The results did not reveal any quantitatively significant price-performance trade-off, but did suggest that first-term contracts (i.e., the first ever contract awarded by a client for the provision of a particular IT service) were more expensive than repeat contracts. Although competitive tendering did not result in lower prices than directly negotiated contracts, it was associated with comparatively better performance. Well-defined expectations of an organization's IT requirements were also likely to lead to improved performance when the service was outsourced.

Domberger et al. (2000) measured IT outsourcing performance by both desired performance and realized performance. Clients typically have an expectation of service quality prior to awarding a contract. This can be referred to as desired performance. A necessary part of contract management involves an assessment of the realized performance of the contract. The clients responding to the study were asked to rate the desired performance and realized performance of the contracts for each of the following eight service attributes.

1. Service availability and timeliness
2. Out-of-hours availability
3. Response in emergencies

4. Provision at expected cost
5. Delivery to expected quality
6. Accuracy of advice
7. Correctness of error fixes
8. Minimization of system downtime

The original scale for the desired and realized performance ratings was from 1 to 4. A rating of 1 corresponded to not important for the former and unsatisfactory for the latter, while 4 corresponded to very important and excellent, respectively. Ratings which were not reported were filled with zeros to preserve the continuity of the scale on the assumption that they were considered irrelevant or very low in terms of desired or realized performance.

The eight service attributes listed were taken to represent measures of quality. For the purposes of analysis and estimation, a single quality/performance variable was sought. Here there were a number of choices. One possibility was to construct what is called principal components. The first principal component, which explained approximately 50% of the variation in the attributes, is essentially a simple average of the realized ratings. It turned out that the responses were all positively and highly correlated. Thus, the simple average of the ratings attached to the eight attributes represented a simple and readily interpretable choice for a single performance variable.

A second possibility was to consider the realized performance relative to the base, as represented by the desired performance ratings. Constructing a new set of attributes by subtracting the desired from the realized rating for each attribute and contract results in data that have as their first principal component a variable which is essentially the simple average. Once again this accounted for approximately 50% of the variation in the data. Thus, a second possible proxy for the performance variable is the average of the eight realized minus desired attributes. Rather than choose between these alternative proxies, the results for both realized and differences were reported (Domberger et al., 2000). The mean of the eight realized performance ratings was 2.97. This result can be interpreted as satisfactory, but not excellent, indicating that the average response by the 48 firms was that they found realized performance to be satisfactory. The mean of the realized minus desired performance ratings was -0.49. The negative mean for this performance variable indicates a slight tendency to underperform relative to the desired levels of service quality.

TRANSFORMATIONAL OUTSOURCING

The traditional way of thinking in IT outsourcing is to move the current IT function out of the organization and let another organization handle it. There is no strategic thinking behind it, except the idea of solving a problem, saving some money, or improving a function by means of some undefined solutions. The new way of thinking is to make IT outsourcing part of a strategic transformation of the IT function, where new tasks and roles are implemented to replace old tasks and roles. A classic example of this new way of thinking was the transformation of the IT function at British Petroleum (BP) in the 1990s. The IT function went through a fundamental transformation consisting of the following changes (Cross, Earl, & Sampler, 1997):

- **From systems provider to infrastructure planner.** The mission of the IT function shifted from developing systems to overseeing technical integrity and pursuing value creation and cost reduction opportunities through information sharing.
- **From monopoly supplier to mixed sourcing.** In 1991, outsourcing of operations, telecommunications, systems development, and IT maintenance began, as BP recognized that it was not essential that these were carried out in-house. Some local sites already had experience in facilities management, and, as contracts came up for renewal, lessons were recorded and a worldwide outsourcing program implemented.
- **From business standards to industry standards.** IT managers have long been concerned about coordinating various types of computing and communication equipment. However, throughout most of the research on IT infrastructure, the focus has been directed at creating and managing the internal infrastructure. Therefore, BP spearheaded a unique initiative to help create an external software market by being one of the early advocates and founding members of the Petrotechnical Open Software Corporation, which was joined by a number of oil companies such as Elf, Mobil, Statoil, and Texaco.
- **From decentralized bias to centralized top sight.** The senior management team realized that the major benefit of centralized management of IT is not budget authority, but is in setting standards for infrastructure. While some IT resources still remain in the local businesses, it is the job of the top IT management team to provide the global perspective for infrastructure planning and cost control, which is here called top sight.
- **From systems analysts to business consultants.** A new skill set was defined for IT personnel. The new skill set has an equal balance between business, technical, and people skills. Such a radical change in the skill set of IT staff has been supported by a number of human resource initiatives such as skills testing, self-assessment, and personal development planning.
- **From craftsmen to project managers.** IT personnel no longer approach their job as craftsmen, viewing each job as a unique, customized process. Their task has switched to that of project managers, integrating and coordinating stakeholders involved in providing IT applications and operations.
- **From large function to lean teams.** Team orientation was stimulated in different ways. For example, staff was moved around the world to create global not local loyalties. A team building and team-working program was introduced stressing the use of multifunctional teams and diluting the functional focus.

The IT budget was reduced from $360 million in 1989 to $132 million in 1995 after this transformation. IT personnel were reduced from 1400 persons to 150 persons in these six years. Hence, a large portion of the reduced IT budget went to external outsourcing vendors. As this pioneering case of IT outsourcing illustrates, outsourcing can be more than a tool for cutting costs and improving organizational focus. Increasingly, it is a means of acquiring new capabilities and bringing about fundamental strategic and structural change.

According to Linder (2004), the concept of transformational outsourcing is an emerging practice, where companies are looking outside for help for more fundamental reasons—to facilitate rapid organizational change and to launch new strategies and to reshape company boundaries. In doing so, they are engaging in transformational outsourcing: partnering with another company to achieve a rapid, substantial, and sustainable improvement in enterprise-level performance.

Transformational outsourcing places the power to bring new capabilities to the organization squarely in the hands of executives who have and value those capabilities. In other words, the outsourcing partner provides a management team that is experienced in the capability that the organization seeking change needs. And those executives are empowered by the outsourcing process to implement the practices they bring with them.

Not all transformational outsourcing initiatives are alike. Linder (2004) identified four broad categories from her research on 20 companies that have attempted the practice. The four categories are startups (outsource to rapidly scale up a new business), pathway to growth (outsource to fix a key process that stands in the way of growth), change catalyst (outsource to signal broad change and focus on adding value), and radical renewal (outsource to improve core operating capabilities radically).

As executives get more experience with outsourcing, they are learning the tool's potential and beginning to wield it for more strategic purposes. Some will use it to shape and reshape their business models. Instead of massive, sweeping changes, many organizations will master the ability to use outsourcing to make continuous incremental improvements. But while the potential benefits are incontrovertible, the art of joining organizations with unique capabilities is extremely challenging and requires visionary leaders with strong hearts and a large capacity for hard work. By combining the tool's execution effectiveness with their own growing skills in partnering, leaders who display those characteristics will have a practical and realistic roadmap at their disposal for building strategic flexibility.

Transformational outsourcing is an emerging practice, but the track record of companies that have engaged in it is impressive. In a study of 20 companies, 17 of them have been in place long enough to show results. Of that group, 13 have achieved dramatic, organization-level impact. To the extent that other companies can replicate such success, transformational outsourcing may become a more effective way of improving performance than major internal change initiatives, mergers, and acquisitions, or joint ventures (Linder, 2004).

The key issue is new capabilities. In undertaking an internal initiative, a company has concluded that it lacks an important set of skills; otherwise, it would not be seeking transformation. But it often proves too time-consuming to develop the skills internally. In a mergers-and-acquisition scenario, the company acquires the capabilities it lacks, but cultural clashes often interfere with its ability to use them effectively. An acquiring company seldom, for example, puts executives from the acquired company in charge of its own organization in order to learn from them. Similar cultural impediments make it unlikely that a company will transform itself with the expertise it gains in a joint venture. But transformational outsourcing places the power to bring new capabilities to the organization squarely in the hands of executives who have and value those capabilities. The outsourcing partner provides a management team that is experienced in the capability that the organization seeking change needs. And those executives are empowered by the outsourcing process to implement the practices they bring with them.

Transformational outsourcing is concerned with bringing new capabilities to the organization through important sets of skills. These skills can be found in knowledge work, and knowledge management emerges as an important discipline in transformational outsourcing. Executives have to lead a transformational outsourcing initiative much differently from the way they would manage conventional outsourcing.

GLOBAL OUTSOURCING

Global outsourcing is a fast-growing aspect of the world economy. It has been estimated that 3.3 million jobs worldwide will move offshore. Clott (2004) has studied perspectives on global outsourcing and the changing nature of work. The strategic benefits for firms can be portrayed as a means to reduce costs, improve asset efficiency, and increase profits. Criticisms of outsourcing have often been in the areas of changing employment patterns, globalization of labor force, and its effects on individuals and organizations. Outsourcing has been called one of the greatest organizational and industry structure shifts of the century, with the potential to transform the way businesses operate. Some proponents believe it will turn firms from vertically integrated structures into virtual organizations and transform existing fixed structures into variable-cost structures where expenses can move up or down as the business climate dictates. For employees, the trend toward outsourcing has been thought to result in a loss of fixed-employment opportunities as a consequence of firms seeking to use cheaper labor overseas.

Underpinning the move toward outsourcing has been a confluence of structural and theoretical changes in the nature of business and organizations dating back approximately two decades. Theorists have suggested that the changing nature of competition has resulted from two factors: (a) globalization of commerce engendering worldwide competition, and (b) technology developments that have changed basic business processes related to time and distance. Globalization and technology have placed enormous pressure on firms to cut costs and improve efficiency in the interests of self-preservation (Clott, 2004).

The industry most closely associated with outsourcing has been information technology. IT functions have been outsourced to such an extent that the "New Silicon Valley" centered in and around the city of Bangalore in India, which became a major outsourcing provider for IT functions as a result of its lower costs and advanced processing skills. This led to the growth of large Indian outsourcing firms such as Infosys, Tata Consultancy, and Wipro. As of 2003, over 500.000 people were employed in the Indian IT industry. Other countries seeking to replicate India's growth as an IT center for U.S. firms were Ireland, Israel, and the Philippines. As of 2004, among the fastest-growing aspects of global outsourcing is business process outsourcing (BPO). BPO began as back-office process arrangements to run finance and accounting operations such as payroll, accounts payable and receivable, financial, insurance, and property accounting. These services have expanded into new areas such as call centers with staff trained to answer and transact basic service-related areas, including order entry and credit card processing (Clott, 2004).

Wage rate differentials generate cost savings, but the really compelling gains come from pairing savings with top-flight skills. While only a few Asian countries offer enough English-speaking call-center representatives and help-desk functions to deal with foreign customers, many other skills are more abundant in Asia than in Europe and the U.S. According to Hagel (2004), China, for example, produces 350,000 graduate engineers every year, compared to 90,000 for U.S. engineering schools. And most leading Indian IT-outsourcing firms operate at level five, the highest degree of expertise, of the IT service capability maturity model, whereas most internal IT departments in the United States operate at levels two or three. Many skills of Asian companies are distinctive. Product engineers in China and Taiwan, for instance, are more focused on designing for production than are their U.S. counterparts who tend to emphasize features and product performance. The combination of low wages and a plentiful supply of skilled applicants makes it possible for Asian companies to use managerial practices very different from those generally found in developed economies. To begin with, the best offshore companies invest heavily to recruit the right staff because they can afford to be more selective. Furthermore, there are more managers to staff, so that they can spend more time building the skills of employees.

According to Wright and Boschee (2004), workers and managers in the technology field almost certainly have heard of companies like Infosys, Wipro, Cordiant, Tata, MachroTech, and others. These companies are among many technology shops based in India that have taken over a growing share of technical work outsourced by U.S. and other firms, which use Indian IT providers for software engineering, applications development, customer service call centers, and many other high-tech needs. The success of these offshore providers of outsourced IT derives in large part from two economic trends. First, in the wake of the recession, U.S. businesses have focused increasingly on their core skills and outsourced a broad variety of services not integral to their mission, with technology services leading the way. Second, with revenues flat or shrinking, businesses have focused on cutting costs, again with an eye on the high price of technology. The formula of Indian IT companies to capitalize on those trends is simple: excellent technology service at much lower cost. Much of their reduced cost structure is based on their use of highly skilled Indian technology professionals, who are often paid substantially less in India than technology workers in the U.S. With the U.S. employment market in a slump, and the once high-flying technology sector leaving a large trail of laid-off American technical workers, politicians and U.S. workers alike have begun complaining bitterly about the flow of outsourced work to offshore providers.

Such complaints can have consequences for international outsourcing when labor markets are unionized. Skaksen (2004) found that international outsourcing may give rise to an increase in the wage rate, which implies that remaining home-country workers may become economically better off, even though jobs are moved out of the country. Potential, or the threat of, global outsourcing also has important implications for the wage rate and the level of employment. Potential but unrealized international outsourcing can be used as a threat by the firm in the wage negotiations with the trade union. Under these circumstances, a marginal decrease in the cost of international outsourcing implies that there is a decrease in the wage rate and an increase in employment and aggregate social welfare. With respect to the implications of realized global outsourcing, Skaksen (2004) found that a marginal decrease in the cost of such outsourcing, which implies that the firm actually begins to outsource activities, gives rise to an increase in the wage rate and a reduction in employment and aggregate social welfare.

According to Venkatraman (2004), the new hot topic being debated in boardrooms, at meetings, and in Internet discussion groups is offshoring, the practice especially among U.S. and European companies of migrating business processes overseas to India, the Philippines, Ireland, China, and elsewhere to lower costs without significantly sacrificing quality. At first, this would seem like nothing new, but the development of a powerful communication infrastructure is making offshoring an increasingly viable and commonly taken option. Nearly two out of three software companies are already involved, and in a number of industries, IT-enabled back-office business processes are prime candidates for such a shift. The debate about the ethics of offshoring misses the point that it represents the inevitable next generation of business practice. At the heart of the debate is the issue of jobs and wages. As networking technologies have enabled companies to tap into the global marketplace for talent more easily, offshoring has put downward pressure on domestic salaries.

The shifting geography of business processes can be defined as the third wave of geography-related change in the design and operation of corporations. During the first wave, the improving transportation infrastructure of the 20th century enabled corporations to seek effective production capabilities in increasingly far-flung locations that provided access to new markets and tangible resources—land, local factories, mines, and production workers. During the second wave, as capital markets became global and interconnected in the latter half of the 20th century, corporations began to capitalize on vibrant global financial markets for both debt and equity. Now we are in the midst of a third wave in which digitized business processes like order processing, billing, customer service, accounts and payroll processing, and design and development can be carried out without regard to physical location (Venkatraman, 2004).

Business Week (2004) asked: Will outsourcing hurt America's supremacy? For decades, the U.S. has been the world's technology leader, thanks in large part to its dominance of software. The question now is whether the U.S. can continue to lead the industry as programming spreads around the globe from India to Bulgaria. Optimists see the offshore wave as the latest productivity miracle of the Internet. Companies that manage it well—no easy task—can build virtual workforces spread around the world, not only soaking up low-cost talent, but also tapping the biggest brains on earth to collaborate on complex projects. One major challenge then is to organize the work in such a way that knowledge can be exchanged between traditional separation lines and across borders. The line of separation is not only between managers and employees, but also between government and private companies, single companies, and industry networks, and between research and development units and operational units. Global outsourcing might have major implications on future knowledge based product and service production.

Kaiser and Hawk (2004) argue that there is currently an evolution of offshore software development from outsourcing to cosourcing. The Financial Insurance Services Company (FISC) (a pseudonym) is a major U.S. financial services company with thousands of representatives across the country. Offsource (a pseudonym) is a leading India-based company providing consulting and IT services to clients globally. Kaiser and Hawk tell how their eight-year alliance has evolved. The relationship began as a simple pilot of offshore application development outsourcing, aimed at reducing development costs and supplementing in-house IT staff knowledge. It has evolved into a vastly more complex "cosourcing" model, where work is shared. To achieve cosourcing, the two firms had to resolve two major issues. The first was how to keep IT skills and knowledge from draining from FISC. This issue has been resolved by formally linking career development to project assignments and to outsourcer-to-client mentoring. The second issue is how to share work. It has been resolved by creating a dual project management hierarchy, where leadership at each level of a project can be either by FISC or Offsource, depending on the need. Their experiences provide five recommendations for others on structuring offshore outsourcing relationships: (1) understand where cosourcing is applicable, (2) define and develop the appropriate in-house IT competencies, (3) build trust but avoid building a binding relationship, (4) foster mutual understanding of ethnic and corporate cultures, and (5) map out a progression to cosourcing.

Public administration is changing, and new publication management strategies include the globalization of public services production. Inside government agencies bureau-shaping motivations sustain the new public management model approach and create a strong disposition towards embracing radical outsourcing, and residualizing government's implementation roles, a direction reinforced by the marketization of public services. Transnational pressures on nation states to standardize policies will powerfully erode the existing single-country distinctiveness of public service markets. Globalization of public services production is likely for two main reasons (Dunleavy, 1994):

- **Market pressures for globalization.** There are five principal market pressures for globalization of private services production, all of which are likely to have important corollaries or implications for public services production: the contemporary growth of services, changes in technology, new forms of commercial and industrial organization by firms, the development of radical outsourcing, and changes in commodification processes. Radical outsourcing strategies have had far-reaching effects on service growth and the reorganization of corporations by splitting up previously unitary organizational configurations.
- **State pressures for globalization.** Within the public sector, there are analogous pressures for globalization, and some key differentiating features. There are four principal state pressures: the bureau-shaping incentives acting on bureaucrats and public officials, the potential for radical outsourcing in the public sector, the impacts of government procurement rules, and consequent changes affecting the commodification of public services. Radical outsourcing in the public sector entails generalizing best in the world criteria from firms' and corporations' activities to apply also to public service operations.

However, Dunleavy (1994) argues that governments will find it extraordinarily hard to meet the best in the world criterion applied to many or most of their service activities. As large corporations progressively develop and refine their capabilities in current or new implementation areas, they will often be able to acquire extra focus in depth, to make large capital investments, and to reap economies of scale by producing standardized service packages across many different localities, regions or countries. Unlike most governmental units, corporations are able to rapidly change their scope of operations by merging, setting up partnership deals, or franchising, so that scale-escalation in the corporate economy can rather quickly affect public services production. Major corporations are already emerging in key public service areas, and they will be able to take seriously best in world criteria. In this perspective the prospect of trans-European or transglobal firms becoming major players in defining and developing public services production is likely.

The bureau-shaping model also sheds light on the scope for radical outsourcing inside government. Bureau-shaping incentives have emerged as dominant bureaucratic responses to the end of the postwar growth era in public services employment. Rationally self-interested bureaucrats have little stake in maximizing budgets and expanding empires, as older public choice models suggested. The biggest potential for radical outsourcing lies in a large-scale shift to contracting of delivery agencies, where public officials directly organize implementation of public services (Dunleavy, 1994).

DIMENSIONS OF IT OUTSOURCING STRATEGY

IT outsourcing strategy can be defined as the logic underlying a firm's outsourcing decisions. This logic is visible in a firm's portfolio of IT outsourcing decisions. The logic may either have served to guide decisions regarding outsourcing of specific functions or may be revealed in the cumulative pattern visible in individual outsourcing decisions. Thus, strategy need not be a single decision that is consciously made, but rather the manifestation of multiple decisions (Lee, Miranda, & Kim, 2004).

Having defined strategy as such logic, we need to identify the decisions that are salient in constituting or reflecting an IT outsourcing strategy. Firms make decisions on the extent to which transactions will be vertically integrated (degree of integration), the extent to which they will relinquish control of transaction fulfillment (allocation of control), and the duration for which they will commit to a transaction decision (performance period). Lee et al. (2004) defined these decisions as dimensions of IT outsourcing strategy:

- *Degree of integration* has been the focus of much research on IT outsourcing. This focus stems from a recognition that the integration of the IS function is not an all-or-none activity. Outsourcing initiatives may be categorized as comprehensive, selective, and minimal outsourcing. Lacity and Willcocks (2000) found that firms predominantly engage in selective outsourcing, and that such selectivity yielded economies of scale, and resulted in the expected cost savings more often than comprehensive or minimal levels of outsourcing. Therefore, Lee et al. (2004) suggested a hypothesis that selective outsourcing will be more successful than comprehensive or minimal outsourcing. However, in their empirical research, this hypothesis was not supported.
- *Allocation of control* in outsourcing relationships refers to the manner in which compensation or reward structures are set up and the manner in which authority is exercised in the relationship. One control structure is the buy-in contract (Lacity & Willcocks, 2000). This entails the hiring of hourly workers, thereby subjecting them to the day-to-day authority of the client. Here, the client firm retains rights of control because it owns the assets, including labor power, necessary for the completion of work. A second control structure is a fee-for-service contract, which stipulates detailed bases for compensation. Here, rights of control are implicitly allocated to the provider firm that owns resources necessary for work completion. Finally, partnerships rely on complementary resources and voluntary resource allocations so as to benefit the partnership. Authority tends to be internalized within the relationship. Rights of control are therefore shared by client and provider firms. Under ideal conditions, the integrative nature of a partnership orientation minimizes problems stemming from equivocal contracts or uncertainty. However, as the interests of the client and provider diverge, partnerships may prove to be problematic. Therefore, Lee et al. (2004) suggested a hypothesis that buy-in or fee-for-service controls will be more successful than partnerships. However, in their empirical research, this hypothesis was not supported.
- *Performance periods* have been studied in the past. Research indicates that short-term contracts yield cost savings more often than long-term contracts (Lacity & Willcocks, 2000). Short-term contracts motivate providers toward higher performance and allow clients to quickly recover from contractual mistakes. Furthermore, it is difficult for the client to completely anticipate long-term requirements, and client and provider interests are likely to diverge over time. Therefore, Lee et al. (2004) suggested a hypothesis that short-term outsourcing relationships will be more successful than medium- or long-term relationships. However, in their empirical research, the reversed hypothesis was supported, suggesting that medium- and long-term outsourcing relationships will

Figure 8.6. Research model to study dimensions of strategy and success (adapted from Lee et al., 2004)

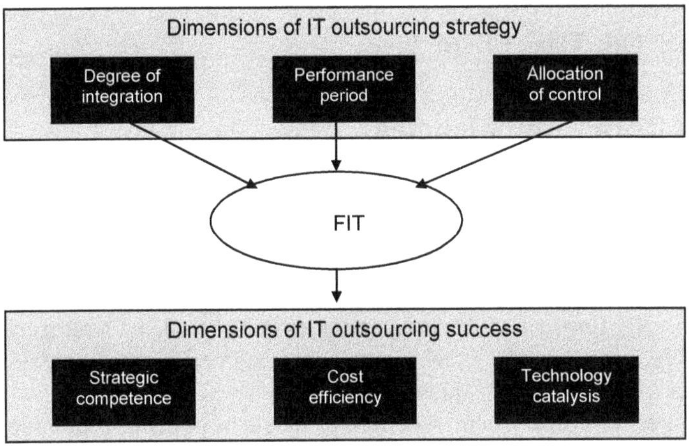

be more successful than short-term relationships. It may not be surprising that their findings contradicted conventional wisdom with respect to performance period of outsourcing relationships. Longer-term contracts are often preferable because they enable initial setup costs to be distributed over a longer period of time. A long-term contract improves financial predictability and reduces the risk and uncertainties associated with important business functions. Time is a critical aspect in the development of relationships. While time introduces an element of risk in relationships, time also facilitates cooperation among self-interested parties and the development of trust. It enables voluntary sharing of resources with anticipation of deferred compensation.

In their empirical study, Lee et al. (2004) defined outsourcing success in terms of three dimensions: strategic competence, cost efficiency, and technology catalysis. Strategic competence refers to a firm's efforts at redirecting the business and IT into core competencies, cost efficiency refers to improving the business' financial position, and technology catalysis refers to strengthening resources and flexibility in technology service to underpin business' strategic direction. Their research model is illustrated in Figure 8.6.

SOURCING THEORIES

In Chapter I, general theories of the firm and value configurations of firms were introduced. Here we return to more theories. We know that many companies choose IT outsourcing based on an analysis of core competencies. As we shall see, there are, however, many other theories that can be applied and that may provide both convergent and divergent answers to an outsourcing question. An example of divergent answer would be the theory of core competencies suggesting that non-core IT can be outsourced, while the resource-based theory suggests that non-core IT should be kept in-house if we have strategic IT resources (valuable, non-imitable, nonsubstitutable, nontransferable, combinable, exploitable, and available).

THEORIES OF THE FIRM

Theory of Core Competencies

Based on the notion of core competency, issues of sourcing should hinge on the degree of criticality of a specific component or business activity to an organization. An extreme case would be for a company to strip itself down to the essentials necessary to deliver to customers the greatest possible value from its core skills and outsource as much of the rest as possible. By limiting or shedding activities that provide no strategic advantage, a company can increase the value it delivers to both customers and shareholders and, in the process, lower its costs and investments (Ang, 1993).

Core competencies theory suggests activities should be performed either in-house or by suppliers. Activities that are not core competencies should be considered for outsourcing with best-in-world suppliers. Some non-core activities may have to be retained in-house if they are part of a defensive posture to protect competitive advantage. Although some authors indicate characteristics of core competencies, most of the literature on this subject seems tautological—core equals key or critical or fundamental. Employees in non-core functions (even if not facing outsourcing) may feel excluded by the organization because they are a nondominant discipline. For example, information technology employees working on Web based legal services in a law firm may feel excluded by lawyers in the firm. In the public sector, there may be particular uncertainty about what is core; and it has been suggested that government may aim to discover its core competencies via a residualization process—outsourcing until and unless the shoe pinches or a political backlash is triggered (Hancox & Hackney, 2000).

An organization may view IT itself as a core competence. It seems that most successful companies have a good understanding of IT's potential. However, some organizations outsource IT even though they see it as core and delivering competitive advantage. This may be because IT can be considered core at the corporate level, but some of its aspects, at lower levels, might be commodities. Thus the complexity of IT, and its (at least in part) core nature, may make the contracting out of IT a particularly challenging exercise. The ability to define IT requirements and to monitor their delivery by third parties may be some of the core IT competencies that any organization must have if it is to outsource IT successfully. It can even be argued that the very acts of specifying and managing supply contracts can themselves give competitive advantage (Hancox & Hackney, 2000).

Resource-Based Theory

The central tenet in resource-based theory is that unique organizational resources of both tangible and intangible nature are the real source of competitive advantage. With resource-based theory, organizations are viewed as a collection of resources that are heterogeneously distributed within and across industries. Accordingly, what makes the performance of an organization distinctive is the unique bland of the resources it possesses. A firm's resources include not only its physical assets such as plant and location but also its competencies. The ability to leverage distinctive internal and external competencies relative to environmental situations ultimately affects the performance of the business (Peppard, Lambert, & Edwards, 2000).

The resource-based theory of the firm holds that, in order to generate sustainable competitive advantage, a resource must provide economic value and must be presently scarce, difficult to imitate, nonsubstitutable, and not readily obtainable in factor markets. This theory rests on two key points: first, that resources are the determinants of firm performance, and second, that resources must be rare, valuable, difficult to imitate, and nonsubstitutable by other rare resources. When the latter occurs, a competitive advantage has been created (Priem & Butler, 2001).

Resources can simultaneously be characterized as valuable, rare, nonsubstitutable, and inimitable. To the extent that an organization's physical assets, infrastructure, and workforce satisfy these criteria, they qualify as resources. A firm's performance depends fundamentally on its ability to have a distinctive, sustainable competitive advantage, which derives from the possession of firm-specific resources (Priem & Butler, 2001).

Investments in IT represent a major approach to asset capitalization in organizations. IT may symbolize firm growth, advancement, and progress. Because investments in IT can promote social prominence and public prestige, managers are induced to utilize slack resources to internalize IS services. Inducements toward investments in in-house IS services are further reinforced by well-publicized case studies that demonstrate the competitive advantage and new business opportunities afforded by IT (Ang, 1993).

The above reasoning suggests that managers may exhibit a penchant for building up internal IT resources such as IS employees, equipment, and computer capacity when organizations possess slack resources. In contrast, when slack resources are low, managers tend to conserve resources in response to the anxiety provoked by loss of financial resources. Anxiety is provoked because the loss of financial resources is often attributed to managerial incompetence and organizational ineffectiveness. As a result, leaders are more likely to be blamed and replaced when financial performance is poor. In response to the anxiety provoked by loss of financial resources, decision makers have been observed to reduce costs through downsizing the company by selling off physical assets and laying off workers (Ang, 1993).

Theory of Firm Boundaries

There has been renewed debate on the determinants of firm boundaries and their implications for performance. According to Schilling and Steensma (2002), the widely accepted framework of transaction cost economics has come under scrutiny as a comprehensive theory for firm scale and scope. At the heart of this debate is whether the underlying mechanism determining firm boundaries is a fear of opportunism (as posited by transaction cost economics), a quest for sustainable advantage (as posed by resource-based view theorists and others), a desire for risk-reducing flexibility (as has recently gained increased attention in work on options), or a combination of factors. Although perspectives on firm boundaries such as transaction costs or the resource-based view are based on fundamentally different motivations for pursuing hierarchical control over market contracts, they rely on common resource or context attributes as antecedents.

Afuah (2003) found that the literature on vertical firm boundaries can be divided into two perspectives. In the first, researchers argue that firms decide to organize activities internally or through markets for efficiency reasons. In the second, researchers argue that firms decide to organize activities internally or through markets for strategic positioning reasons. Since the Internet's largest potential is in reducing costs, Afuah (2003) focused only on the first perspective to keep the arguments traceable. Thus, the decision to outsource or to develop an input internally depends on weighing external component production and transaction costs, on the one hand, and internal component production and transaction costs, on the other hand. If the former are greater than the latter, a firm is better off integrating vertically backward to produce the input internally.

Most studies of firm boundaries emphasize relationships between the division of labor and firms' boundaries. One of the oldest ideas in economics is that returns to specialization increase with market size. In our case of IT outsourcing, firms' boundaries are determined by the extent to which there are large markets for specialization. If there are large markets for IT services available from vendors, then a client company will tend to outsource more of its internal IT function.

ECONOMIC THEORIES

Transaction Cost Theory

In transaction cost analysis, outsourcing decisions are typically framed as determination of firm boundaries. In this perspective, vertical integration can be described as involving a variety of decisions concerning whether corporations, through their business units, should provide certain goods or services in-house or purchase them from outside instead. The study of firm boundaries or vertical integration therefore involves the study of outsourcing, describing which activities are conducted within a firm's hierarchy, and which activities are conducted outside the hierarchy using market mechanisms or other forms of interorganizational relationships (Ang, 1993).

Several studies have used the transaction cost perspective in their study of IT outsourcing (e.g., Ang & Straub, 1998; Grover et al., 1998; Langfield-Smith & Smith, 2003). These studies generally support the thesis of transaction cost economics—that whenever an activity is conducted under conditions of high uncertainty, or whenever an activity requires specific assets, transaction costs, the costs of writing, monitoring, and enforcing contracts are likely to be high. When transaction costs are high, outsourcing is deemed to be relatively inefficient compared with internal, hierarchical administration. Therefore, central to the arguments of transaction cost analysis is the idea of achieving the economic goal of an efficient boundary in organization design (Ang, 1993).

Because production costs are objectively calculated by the accounting system, while transaction costs are assessed subjectively through indirect indicators, functional managers are likely to differ in the importance that they assign to reducing transaction costs. Consequently, the effect transaction costs have on a make-or-buy choice can partly reflect the influence exerted by the purchasing manager. Production cost differences seem more influential in sourcing decisions than transaction cost differences, and experience of the decision maker is related to assessments of technological uncertainty. Profit center managers engage in influence activities that increase the costs of price renegotiations above the level that is observed in comparable external market transactions. Managers sometimes seem more reluctant to outsource when investments in specific assets are necessary; and contrary to theory, managers sometimes consider previous internal investments in specific assets a reason to insource. In certain circumstances decision makers systematically misestimate (or fail to consider) transaction costs (Anderson, Glenn, & Sedatole, 2000).

Neoclassical Economic Theory

Neoclassical economic theory posits that firms outsource IT to attain cost advantages from assumed economies of scale and scope possessed by vendors (Ang & Straub, 1998). This theory has attained more empirical support in studies of outsourcing decisions than transaction cost economics. Neoclassical economic theory regards every business organization as a production function (Williamson, 1991), and where their motivation is driven by profit maximization. This means that companies offer products and services in the market where they have a cost or production advantage. They rely on the marketplace where they have disadvantages.

According to neoclassical economic theory, companies will justify their sourcing strategy based on evaluating possibilities for production cost savings. Thus, the question of whether or not to outsource is a question of whether the marketplace can produce products and services at a lower price than internal production. In the context of IT outsourcing, a company will keep its IT function internally if this has production cost advantages, and it will outsource when the marketplace can offer production cost savings.

However, defining outsourcing simply in terms of procurement activities does not capture the true strategic nature of the issues (Gilley & Rasheed, 2000). IT outsourcing is not only a purchasing decision; all firms purchase elements of their operations. This is done to achieve economic, technological, and strategic advantages. However, the economies of scale and scope argument would predict that outsourcing has little to offer to larger firms because they can generate economies of scale and scope internally by reproducing methods used by vendors. As documented by Levina and Ross (2003), there are other reasons for large firms to move into outsourcing.

In neoclassical economic theory, outsourcing may arise in two ways. First, outsourcing may arise through the substitution of external purchases for internal activities. In this way, it can be viewed as a discontinuation of internal production (whether it be production of goods or services) and an initiation of procurement from outside suppliers. To the extent this type of outsourcing reduces a firm's involvement in successive stages of production, substitution-based outsourcing may be viewed as vertical disintegration. This seems to be the most commonly understood type of outsourcing (Gilley & Rasheed, 2000).

RELATIONAL THEORIES

Contractual Theory

Luo (2002) examined how contract, cooperation, and performance are associated with one another. He argues that contract and cooperation are not substitutes but complements in relation to performance. Contracting and cooperation are two central issues in an IT outsourcing arrangement. A contract alone is insufficient to guide outsourcing evolution and performance. Since outsourcing involves repeated interorganizational exchanges that become socially embedded over time, cooperation is an important safeguard mechanism mitigating external and internal hazards and overcoming adaptive limits of contracts. The simultaneous use of both contractual and cooperative mechanisms is particularly critical to outsourcing arrangements in an uncertain environment.

An outsourcing contract provides a legally bound, institutional framework in which each party's rights, duties, and responsibilities are codified and the goals, policies, and strategies underlying the arrangement are specified. Every outsourcing contract has the purpose of facilitating exchange and preventing opportunism. Appropriate contractual arrangements can attenuate the leeway for opportunism, prohibit moral hazards in a cooperative relationship, and protect each party's proprietary knowledge. A complete contract reduces the uncertainty faced by organizational decision makers and the risks stemming from opportunism on the part of one or more contracting parties. It provides a safeguard against ex post performance problems by restraining each party's ability to pursue private goals at the expense of common benefits. An incomplete contract may bring about ambiguity, which creates a breeding ground for shirking responsibility and shifting blame, raises the likelihood of conflict, and hinders the ability to coordinate activities, utilize resources, and implement strategies (Luo, 2002).

Contractual completeness is not just term specificity (i.e., the extent to which all relevant terms and clauses are specified), nor should every outsourcing contract maintain the same level of completeness. Previous studies that view contractual completeness and term specificity as equivalent have created a controversy about the role of the contract. For instance, it has been suggested that incomplete contracts are optimal in situations where some elements of enforcement are unverifiable. Similarly, it has been argued that economic agents rarely write contracts that are complete because boundedly rational parties may not be able to distinguish certain contingencies. By contrast, others demonstrate that contractual completeness reduces role conflict and role ambiguity for outsourcing managers, which then enhances outsourcing performance. Furthermore, it has been suggested that term specificity protects a partner's strategic resources and reduces operational and financial uncertainties through controlling opportunism and spurring information flow within an outsourcing arrangement.

Agency Theory

Agency theory has broadened the risk-sharing literature to include the agency problem that occurs when cooperating parties have different goals and division of labor (Eisenhardt, 1985). The cooperating parties are engaged in an agency relationship defined as a contract under which one or more persons (the principal(s)) engage another person (agent) to perform some service on their behalf which involves delegating some decision making authority to the agent (Jensen & Meckling, 1976). Agency theory describes the relationship between the two parties using the metaphor of a contract. In an IT outsourcing relationship this is a client-vendor relationship and an outsourcing contract.

The agency theory is applicable when describing client-vendor relationships in IT outsourcing arrangements. Typically, the client organization (principal) transfers property rights to the vendor organization (agent). In the context of IT, assets transferred might be infrastructure, systems and documentation, and employees. For a certain amount of money, the vendor organization provides services to the client organization. This implies a change in legal relationships, and IT services are carried out using a more formal transaction process. The status of personal relationships also changes, from that of a manager and a subordinate, to that of a client-manager and a vendor. According to agency theory, control mechanisms also change, from that of behavioral control, to that of outcome-based control.

The technological and business complexity of IT means that there may be major problems for the principal in choosing a suitable agent and in monitoring the agent's work. Only the agent knows how hard he is working, and that can be especially important in multilateral contracting where one agent acts for several principals. This is often the case in IT outsourcing because of the market dominance of one large firm. Given the difficulties of behavior-based contracts suggested by agency theory, it is reasonable to assume that the overwhelming majority of clients would insist on outcome-based contracts when acquiring IT products and services. Such a strategy can only succeed if the client can confidently specify current and future requirements. But accurate predictions by the client may not always be in the vendor's interests, since vendor account managers often are rewarded according to contract profitability, which is principally achieved through charging the client extra for anything which is not in the contract (Hancox & Hackney, 2000).

Partnership and Alliance Theory

Partnership, often referred to as an alliance, has frequently been noted as a major feature of IT outsourcing. Partnership can reduce the risk of inadequate contractual provision, which may be comforting for clients about to outsource a complex and high-cost activity such as IT. However, in the relationship between vendor and client, the latter may be overdependent on the former, and goals are not necessarily shared. A client may be more comfortable if it knows the vendor already. In partner selection, cultural compatibility is vital and shared values and objectives inform all stages of the partnership development process. This may make a successful relationship especially difficult if the putative partners are from fundamentally different domains and bring fundamentally different perspectives, as might well be argued is the case in a private sector-public sector arrangement. The difficulty may be compounded where, as in the UK government's compulsory competitive tendering policy, the outsourcing can be involuntary (Hancox & Hackney, 2000).

Hancox and Hackney (2000) found that few organizations claim to be in a strategic partnership with their IT suppliers. The contract is more likely to favor the vendor because he has greater experience in negotiation. Clients with loose contracts were more likely to regard outsourcing as a failure; yet, most respondents in a study used the vendor's standard contract as a basis for outsourcing agreement and most did not use external technical or legal advice. It was found that 80% of clients wished that they had more tightly defined contracts. Partly the client's view of IT influences its relationship with the vendor, such that firms regarding IT as a core competence capability are more likely to look upon outsourcing as an alliance. Clients who view IT as a core are also more likely to be satisfied with the outsourcing arrangements because they negotiate from a more knowledgeable position (Hancox & Hackney, 2000).

Hancox and Hackney (2000) interviewed IT managers to find support for the partnership theory in IT outsourcing. Despite assurances found in vendors' marketing literature, most clients were skeptical about partnership. If partnership did exist, it was usually as a collection of some of the intangibles mentioned earlier, rather than as a formalized arrangement. Partnership was more likely to be claimed in the area of systems development, where vendors needed to have a greater understanding of the organization, than in outsourcing of operations and IT infrastructure support. There seemed to be no correlation between those organizations regarding IT as strategic and those regarding relationships with vendors as partnerships.

Relational Exchange Theory

Relational exchange theory is based on relational norms. According to this theory, the key to determining how efficiently contract governance is carried out lies in the relational norms between the transactors. For example, the degree to which transactors engage in joint planning or their extent of interfirm information sharing are process elements that determine the costs associated with periodically renegotiating contracts. Those transactors who have established behavioral norms that can simplify and smooth the renegotiation process can reasonably expect to incur lower ex post bargaining costs than those who have not (Artz & Brush, 2000).

Artz and Brush (2000) examined supplier relationships that were governed by relational contracts, and they found support for the relational exchange theory. By altering the behavioral orientation of the alliance, relational norms lowered exchange costs.

In their measurement of relational norm, Artz and Brush (2000) included collaboration, continuity expectations, and communication strategies. Collaboration refers to the willingness of the client and vendor to work together to create a positive exchange relationship and improve alliance performance. Collaborative actions can act to enhance the client-vendor relationship as a whole and curtail opportunistic behaviors. For example, joint planning and forecasting can allow both the customer and the supplier to participate in determining each firm's roles and responsibilities and foster mutually beneficial expectations.

When one firm attempts to coerce another in order to gain a more favorable negotiation outcome, that firm is likely to be viewed by its alliance partner as exploitative rather than accommodative, and retaliatory behavior often results. In contrast, noncoercive strategies attempt to persuade rather than demand. Noncoercive communications center on beliefs about business issues and involve little direct pressure. Examples include simple requests or recommendations, in which one party stresses the benefits the other party will receive by complying.

Stakeholder Theory

As far as we know, there is no comprehensive use of stakeholder theory in IT outsourcing research. Although Lacity and Willcocks (2000) have used the term identifying four distinct customer stakeholders and three distinct supplier stakeholders, their research has not gotten any further on this path. In an IT outsourcing relationship, a stakeholder theory approach will describe the relationship as a nexus of cooperative and competitive interests possessing intrinsic value.

The term stakeholder is a powerful one. This is due, to a significant degree, to its conceptual breadth. The term means many different things to many different people and hence evokes praise and scorn from a wide variety of scholars and practitioners of myriad academic disciplines and backgrounds. Such breadth of interpretation, though one of stakeholder theory's greatest strengths, is also one of its most prominent theoretical liabilities as a topic of reasoned discourse. Much of the power of stakeholder theory is a direct result of the fact that, when used unreflectively, its managerial prescriptions and implications are merely limitless. When discussed in instrumental variation (i.e., that managers should attend to stakeholders as a means to achieving other organizational goals such as profit or shareholder wealth maximization), stakeholder theory stands virtually unopposed (Phillips, Freeman, & Wicks, 2003).

Stakeholder theory is a theory of organizational management and ethics. Indeed all theories of strategic management have some moral content, though it is often implicit. Moral content in this case means that the subject matter of the theories are inherently moral topics (i.e., they are not amoral). Stakeholder theory is distinct because it addresses morals and values explicitly as a central feature of managing organizations. The ends of cooperative activity and the means of achieving these ends are critically examined in stakeholder theory in a way that they are not in many theories of strategic management (Phillips et al., 2003).

Social Exchange Theory

Typically, an IT outsourcing relationship will be a restricted social exchange. Social exchange theory can be traced to one of the oldest theories of social behavior; any interaction between individuals is an exchange of resources. The resources exchange may be not only tangible, such as goods or money, but also intangible, such as social amenities or friendship. The basic assumption of social exchange theory is that parties enter into and maintain relationships with the expectation that doing so will be rewarding (Lambe, Wittmann, & Spekman, 2001).

Social exchange theory postulates that exchange interactions involve economic and/or social outcomes. Over time, each party in the exchange relationship compares the social and economic outcomes from these interactions to those that are available from exchange alternatives, which determines their dependence on the exchange relationship. Positive economic and social outcomes over time increase the partners' trust of each other and commitment to maintaining the exchange relationship. Positive exchange interactions over time also produce relational exchange norms that govern the exchange partners' interactions (Lambe et al., 2001).

Implicit in these postulates, the four foundational premises of social exchange theory are: (1) exchange interactions result in economic and/or social outcomes, (2) these outcomes are compared over time to other exchange alternatives to determine dependence on the exchange relationship, (3) positive outcomes over time increase firms' trust of their trading partner(s) and their commitment to the exchange relationship, and (4) positive exchange interactions over time produce relational exchange norms that govern the exchange relationship (Lambe et al., 2001).

Commitment is a widely used construct in social exchange research. It has been defined as an exchange partner believing that an ongoing relationship with another is so important as to warrant maximum efforts at maintaining it; that is, the committed party believes the relationship is worth working on to ensure that it endures indefinitely (Lambe et al., 2001).

COMPARISON OF THEORIES

We have introduced eleven theories concerned with outsourcing. In Figure 8.7, these theories are compared in terms of what they recommend for outsourcing. We find that some theories indicate possibilities for outsourcing (theory of core competencies, resource-based theory, transaction cost theory, neoclassical economic theory, and theory of firm boundaries), while others indicate limitations (contractual theory, partnership and alliance theory, relational exchange theory, social exchange theory, agency theory, and stakeholder theory).

Figure 8.8 lists a comparison of the theories when it comes to the next stage. The next stage is when outsourcing has occurred and both client and vendor want the outsourcing arrangement to be successful. What do the theories tell us? As is visible in Figure 8.8, the theories tell us a lot about what to do to be successful. Each theory provides recommendations for actions that will contribute to managing successful IT outsourcing relationships. From different theoretical perspectives, recommendations are made. Taken together, the list in Figure 8.8 represents critical success factors for an outsourcing arrangement.

Armed with these theories of outsourcing, IT managers will now be in a good position to analyze which strategic sourcing options are most suitable for which specific IT activities. Lacity et al. (1996) suggest that managers must carefully select which IT activities to outsource in order to achieve the intended benefits of outsourcing. We review below the key elements of sourcing strategy and management to ensure operational excellence of outsourcing contracts.

CASE EXAMPLES: SOURCING STRATEGIES[1]

Rolls-Royce did a capability study prior to the outsourcing decision. It may be regarded as a strategy process. None of the interviewees were involved in the capability study, as this was done many years ago and before the interviewees entered the companies. The strategic issues considered to be underlying the outsourcing decision were costs, capabilities, and the need for a change agent. Rolls-Royce wanted a 10% reduction in IT costs. The criteria laid out for vendor selection were pretty clear around maximum service levels, around ability to handle large skilled contracts of that size, and also pretty clear around costs. EDS had generally been competitive on costs, and they demonstrated certainly that they could provide capability for large-scale contracts. Rolls-Royce doubted they had necessary in-house capabilities to do the required step change from managing large mainframe systems to graphical user infterface (GUI)-based client-server systems. A change was believed to require both human capabilities and financial capabilities to succeed. Rolls-Royce was looking for a company they might discuss as the *change agent*, a company somewhat different from themselves. They were not looking for a traditional outsourcer, but a very service oriented company. A major transformation seemed to be a part of the plan, a transformation of Rolls-Royce from a manufacturing oriented company to a service oriented company. The culture that EDS was bringing was part of what Rolls-Royce was looking for, a service oriented, global, and people oriented company.

SAS outsourced for three main reasons. First, they wanted to benefit from economies of scale offered by an external service provider and to realize corresponding cost reduction. Compared with other airliners the cost and efficiency of their internal IT group were

Figure 8.7. Possibilities and limitations in IT outsourcing based on theories

Theory	What should be outsourced?
Theory of core competencies	All IT functions which are peripheral to the company's production of goods and services for the market.
Resource-based theory	All IT functions where the company does not have sufficient strategic resources to perform in a competitive way. Strategic resources are unique, valuable, difficult to imitate, exploitable, and difficult to substitute.
Transaction cost theory	All IT functions where benefits for the company are greater than the transaction costs. Benefits include increased revenues and reduced costs.
Contractual theory	Only IT functions where the company can expect and secure that vendor and customer will have the same contractual behavior. Common contract behavioral patterns include role integrity, reciprocity, implementation of planning, effectuation of consent, flexibility, contractual solidarity, reliance, restraint of power, proprietary of means, and harmonization with the social environment.
Neoclassical economic theory	All IT functions which an external vendor can operate at lower costs than the company.
Partnership and alliance theory	Only IT functions where the company can expect and secure a partnership and alliance with the vendor that imply interdependence between the partners based on trust, comfort, understanding, flexibility, cooperation, shared values, goals and problem solving, interpersonal relations, and regular communication.
Relational exchange theory	Only IT functions where the company easily can develop and secure common norms with the vendor. Norms determine behavior in three main dimensions: flexibility, information exchange, and solidarity.
Social exchange theory	Only IT functions where each of the parties can follow their own self-interest when transacting with the other self-interested actor to accomplish individual goals that they cannot achieve alone and without causing hazards to the other party.
Agency theory	Only IT functions where the agent (vendor) and the principal (client) have common goals and the same degree of risk willingness and aversion.
Theory of firm boundaries	All IT functions that satisfy several of the other theories, mainly resource-based theory and transaction cost theory.
Stakeholder theory	Only IT functions where a balance can be achieved between stakeholders. Stakeholders relevant in IT outsourcing include business management, IT management, user management and key IT personnel at the client, and business management, customer account management, and key service providers at the vendor.

Figure 8.8. Recommendations for managing successful IT outsourcing relationships based on theories

Theory	How to succeed in an outsourcing arrangement
Theory of core competencies	Capability to define IT needs and ability to manage IT services from the vendor represent the core competence within IT needed in the client organization to succeed in an IT outsourcing arrangement.
Resource-based theory	Capability to integrate and exploit strategic IT resources from the vendor together with own resources to produce competitive goods and services. An example of such a resource is the vendor's competence in an IT application area where the client has limited experience.
Transaction cost theory	Minimize transaction costs by reducing the need for lasting specific IT assets; increase transaction frequency; reduce complexity and uncertainty in IT tasks; improve performance measurements; and reduce dependence on other transactions.
Contractual theory	A complete IT contract based on information symmetry in a predictable environment with occurrence adoption that prevents opportunistic behavior in an efficient collaborative environment with balance of power between client and vendor, where the contract is a management instrument that grants decision rights and action duties.
Neoclassical economic theory	Capability to integrate and exploit IT services from the vendor together with own services to produce competitive goods and services. An example of such a service is the vendor's operation of the client's communication network.
Partnership and alliance theory	Develop experience with alliances, develop alliance managers, and develop the ability to identify potential partners.
Relational exchange theory	Develop and secure common norms that are relevant to both parties. Norms determine behavior and are mainly concerned with flexibility, information exchange, and solidarity. Norms shall secure integration in the relation, which takes place through involvement. Involvement occurs by coordination of activities, adoption of resources, and interaction between individuals. The degree of involvement in these three dimensions is called activity link, resource link, and actor link.
Social exchange theory	Enable social and economic outcomes in the exchange between client and vendor such that these outcomes outperform those obtainable in alternative exchanges. Positive economic and social outcomes over time increase the partners' trust of each other and commitment to maintaining the exchange relationship. Commitment is important, as it is an exchange partner's belief that an ongoing relationship with another is so important as to warrant maximum efforts at maintaining it.
Agency theory	It must be easy and inexpensive for the principal (client) to find out what the agent (vendor) is actually doing. In addition, both outcome-based and behavior-based incentives can be used to reduce and prevent opportunistic behavior.
Theory of firm boundaries	The supply of IT services from the organization's environment should change firm boundaries between the firm that desires the competence (sourcing firm) and the firm having the technology (source firm) in a clear and unambiguous manner. This can be achieved in a strict and rigid division of labor between client and vendor.
Stakeholder theory	Create efficient and effective communication with and between stakeholders to secure continued support from all stakeholders, to balance their interests, and to make the IT outsourcing arrangement so that all stakeholders achieve their goals.

far too high. Second, they wanted to lift their existing technologies to new platforms and replace their old legacy systems with standard application in order to establish a more cost-effective platform. And third, they wanted to offer the employees in their internal IT group better development opportunities for their professional careers. Information technology is the core competence of CSC, but it is not at the core of an airliner. SIG management group and their chairman of the board took the initiative to start the process.

Global IT management at ABB started to develop a strategy document before the outsourcing, which later were signed up by the management. It was never an outsourcing strategy, but a strategy for how to achieve a number of aims. It was at the time where ABB had strong financial difficulties. Because of this, cost reduction was a significant aim to achieve and provoked outsourcing. One of the things the CIO did was to use a lot of time assuring that the countries in ABB were aligned to the outsourcing project. The starting point was a strategy document, but it ended up as a pure cost case, affected by external environment. During the last few years ABB have been through several organizational changes. Focusing on two core business areas, power and automation technologies, they sold away other business. But, remaining internal functions were huge and inflexible. Simultaneously, the requirements from business unit areas were full transparency regarding IT. ABB's financial difficulties at that time and their restructuring around two core business areas pushed the IT outsourcing.

In all three cases, one important driver of outsourcing was cost reduction. According to neoclassical economic theory, companies will justify their sourcing strategy based on evaluating possibilities for production cost savings. Thus, the question of whether or not to outsource is a question of whether the marketplace can produce product and services at a lower price than internal production. Client companies reported reduction of costs, better cost-performance, and economies of scale, compared to internal IT function. As one senior client manager stated: "We were in financial pressure, and our bankers pushed the outsourcing forward."

But, costs were not the only reasons for none of the client companies. New business strategies and restructuring of client companies was also an important driver. ABB were restructuring around two core business areas, and SAS admitted that information technology was not at the core of an airliner. Core competencies theory suggests that activities, which are not core competencies, should be considered for outsourcing with best-in-the-world suppliers. Their outsourcing vendors, IBM and CSC, respectively, have information technology as their core competence.

The ability to handle technological change was also reported as a major issue for outsourcing. Both Rolls-Royce and SAS had a challenge, handling both cost reduction and new technologies at the same time. According to the resource-based perspective, outsourcing is a strategic decision that can be used to fill gaps in the firm's IS resources and capabilities. In the case of Rolls-Royce and SAS, it was a difference between desired capabilities and actual capabilities. Interesting to notice, the transforming of Rolls-Royce from a manufacturing oriented company to a service oriented company seemed to be a part of the plan. Vendor resources can produce innovation, which might be important for long-term survival of the client. In this specific case, the vendor's ability to perform the change agent role was an important criterion for vendor selection.

SUMMARY

Strategic alignment of IT resources is achieved through CIO aligning IT strategy and the requisite resources to (particularly the core competencies of) business strategy. CIO and IT become enablers of corporate and business strategies when IT resources become a corporate strategic resource. Attainment and sustenance of this status requires ongoing proactive business engagement supported by disciplined application of human resource management best practice.

IT sourcing is concerned with judicious deployment of internal and external IT resources to fulfill business objectives. IT managers must analyze the sourcing opportunities (Lacity & Willcocks, 1998) and threats (Barthelemy, 2003b) from the ways in which the IT functions are organized (Agarwal & Sambamurthy, 2002) and define up-front the desirable performance objectives (Domberger et al, 2000). Sourcing strategy is produced as a result of analysis of business strategy (and, where available, past experience) and attendant requirements for strategic resources. Sourcing strategy serves as the logic underlying the firm's outsourcing decisions such as degree of integration (selective or comprehensive outsourcing), allocation of control (fees for service or partnership), or contract performance periods. Outsourcing success can be measured by strategic competence, cost efficiency, and technology catalysis (Lee et al., 2004). Empirical evidence shows that carefully crafted IT sourcing strategies result in more successful IT outsourcing and increase the overall performance of the firm (Barthélemy, 2003a). Outsourcing success can be measured from business and user perspective (Lee & Kim, 1999). The former is motivated by the promise of strategic, economic, and technological benefits, while the latter is by the quality of offered services.

Underpinning the move toward outsourcing has been a confluence of structural and theoretical changes in the nature of business and organizations dating back approximately two decades. Theorists have suggested that the changing nature of competition has resulted from two factors: (a) globalization of commerce engendering worldwide competition, and (b) technology developments that have changed basic business processes related to time and distance. Globalization and technology have placed enormous pressure on firms to cut costs and improve efficiency in the interests of self-preservation (Clott, 2004).

Kaiser and Hawk (2004) argue that there is currently an evolution of offshore software development from outsourcing to cosourcing. Five recommendations are obtained, from the experience of a financial institution, for others on structuring offshore outsourcing relationships: (1) understand where cosourcing is applicable, (2) define and develop the appropriate in-house IT competencies, (3) build trust but avoid building a binding relationship, (4) foster mutual understanding of ethnic and corporate cultures, and (5) map out a progression to cosourcing.

More and more firms are adopting a new practice known as transformational outsourcing to facilitate rapid organizational change, launch new strategies, and reshape company boundaries—a form of business model innovation (Linder & Cantrell, 2000). While this requires senior executive leadership, dramatic organizational performance improvements have been reported by many firms. To help firms assess what to outsource and how to succeed in an outsourcing arrangement, eleven theories concerned with outsourcing can be used (Gottschalk & Solli-Sæther, 2006): core competencies, resource-based, transactional cost, contractual, neoclassical economic, partnership and alliance, relational exchange, and agency. In developing sourcing strategies, IT managers can leverage from the experiences of several alternatives for sourcing strategies reported by Schniederjans et al. (2004), Lacity and Willcocks (2000), Lacity et al. (1996), Laudon and Laudon (2005), and Barthelemy and Geyer (2004), and from the case studies performed by Gottschalk and Solli-Sæther (2006).

REFERENCES

Afuah, A. (2003). Redefining firm boundaries in the face of the Internet: Are firms really shrinking? *Academy of Management Review, 29*(1), 34-53.

Agarwal, R., & Sambamurthy, V. (2002). Principles and models for organizing the IT function. *MIS Quarterly Executive, 1*(1), 1-16.

Anderson, S. W., Glenn, D., & Sedatole, K. L. (2000). Sourcing parts of complex products: Evidence on transaction costs, high-powered incentives and ex-post opportunism. *Accounting, Organizations and Society, 25*, 723-749.

Ang, S. (1993). *The etiology of information systems outsourcing.* Doctoral dissertation, University of Minnesota.

Ang, S., & Straub, D. W. (1998). Production and transaction economics and IS outsourcing: A study of the U.S. banking industry. *MIS Quarterly, 22*(4), 535-552.

Artz, K. W., & Brush, T. H. (2000). Asset specificity, uncertainty and relational norms: An examination of coordination costs in collaborative strategic alliances. *Journal of Economic Behavior & Organization, 41*, 337-362.

Bahli, B., & Rivard, S. (2003). The information technology outsourcing risk: A transaction cost and agency theory-based perspective. *Journal of Information Technology, 18*, 211-221.

Barney, J. B. (2001). Is the resource-based "view" a useful perspective for strategic management research? Yes. *Academy of Management Review, 26*(1), 41-56.

Barney, J. B. (2002). *Gaining and sustaining competitive advantage.* Prentice Hall.

Barthélemy, J. (2003a). The hard and soft sides of IT outsourcing management. *European Management Journal, 21*(5), 539-548.

Barthélemy, J. (2003b). The seven deadly sins of outsourcing. *Academy of Management Executive, 17*(2), 87-100.

Barthélemy, J., & Geyer, D. (2004). The determinants of total IT outsourcing: An empirical investigation of French and German firms. *Journal of Computer Information Systems, 44*(3), 91-97.

Beamount, N., & Costa, C. (2002). Information technology outsourcing in Australia. *Information Resources Management Journal, 15*(3), 14-31.

Clott, C. B. (2004). Perspectives on global outsourcing and the changing nature of work. *Business and Society Review, 109*(2), 153-170.

Computerworld. (2005, January). Premier 100 IT Leaders 2005.

Cross, J., Earl, M. J., & Sampler, J. L. (1997, December). Transformation of the IT function at British Petroleum. *MIS Quarterly*, pp. 401-423.

Damianides, M. (2005, Winter). Sarbanes-Oxley and IT governance: New guidance on IT control and compliance. *Information Systems Management, 22*(1), 77-85.

DiRomualdo, A., & Gurbaxani, V. (1998, Summer). Strategic intent for IT outsourcing. *Sloan Management Review*, pp. 67-80.

Domberger, S., Fernandez, P., & Fiebig, D. G. (2000). Modelling the price, performance and contract characteristics of IT outsourcing. *Journal of Information Technology, 15*, 107-118.

Dunleavy, P. (1994). The globalization of public services production: Can government be best in world? *Public Policy and Administration, 9*(2), 36-65.

Earl, M. J. (1996). The risks of outsourcing IT. *Sloan Management Review, 37*(3), 26-32.

Eisenhardt, K. M. (1985). Control: Organizational and economic approaches. *Management Science, 31*(2), 134-149.

Else, S. E. (2002). Strategic sourcing and federal government transformation. *Information Knowledge Systems Management, 3*, 31-52.

Gilley, M. K., & Rasheed, A. (2000). Making more by doing less: An analysis of outsourcing and its effects on firm performance. *Journal of Management, 26*(4), 763-790.

Gottschalk, P., & Solli-Sæther, H. (2006). *Managing successful IT outsourcing relationships.* Hershey, PA: Idea Group Publishing.

Grover, V., Cheon, M. J., & Teng, J. T. C. (1996). The effect of service quality and partnership on the outsourcing of information systems functions. *J of Management Information Systems, 12*(4), 89-116.

Grover, V., Teng, T. C., & Cheon, M. J. (1998). Towards a theoretically-based contingency model of information systems outsourcing. In L. P. Willcocks & M. C. Lacity (Eds.), *Strategic sourcing of information systems: Perspectives and practices.* Chichester: John Wiley & Sons.

Haanaes, K. B. (1997). *Managing resource mobilization: Case studies of Dynal, Fiat Auto Poland and Alcatel Tecom Norway* (Ph.D. series 9.97). Copenhagen Business School, Copenhagen, Denmark.

Hagel, J. (2004). Offshore goes on the offensive. *McKinsey Quarterly, 2,* 82-92.

Hall, J. A., & Liedtka, S. L. (2005). Financial performance, CEO compensation, and large-scale information technology outsourcing decisions. *J of Management Information Systems, 22*(1), 193-221.

Håkansson, H. (1982). *International marketing and purchasing of industrial goods: An interaction approach.* Chichester: John Wiley & Sons.

Hancox, M., & Hackney, R. (2000). IT outsourcing: Frameworks for conceptualizing practice and perception. *Information Systems Journal, 10*, 217-237.

Hirschheim, R., & Lacity, M. C. (2000). The myths and realities of information technology insourcing. *Communications of the ACM, 43*(2), 99-107.

Hu, Q., Saunders, C., & Gebelt, M. (1997). Research report: Diffusion of information systems outsourcing: A reevaluation of influence sources. *Information Systems Research, 8*(3), 288-301.

InfoWorld. (2004). *Five risks of outsourcing.* Retrieved September 6, 2008, from www.infoworld.com

Jensen, M. C., & Meckling, W. H. (1976). Theory of the firm: Managerial behavior, agency costs and ownership structures. *Journal of Financial Economics, 3*(4), 305-360.

Johnson, G., & Scholes, K. (2002). *Exploring corporate strategy.* Harlow, Essex, UK: Pearson Education, Prentice Hall.

Kaiser, K. M., & Hawk, S. (2004). Evolution of offshore software development: From outsourcing to cosourcing. *MIS Quarterly Executive, 3*(2), 69-81.

Kern, T., & Willcocks, L. P. (2002). Exploring relationship in information technology outsourcing: The interaction approach. *European Journal of Information Systems, 11*, 3-19.

King, W. R., & Malhotra, Y. (2000). Developing a framework for analyzing IS sourcing. *Information & Management, 37*, 323-334.

Lacity, M. C., & Willcocks, L. P. (1998). An empirical investigation of information technology sourcing practices: Lessons from experience. *MIS Quarterly, 22*(3), 363-408.

Lacity, M. C., & Willcocks, L. P. (2000). Survey of IT outsourcing experiences in US and UK organizations. *Journal of Global Information Management, 8*(2), 5-23.

Lacity, M. C., & Willcocks, L. P. (2001). *Global information technology outsourcing.* Chichester: John Wiley & Sons, Ltd.

Lacity, M. C., Willcocks, L. P., & Feeny, D. F. (1996). The value of selective IT sourcing. *Sloan Management Review, 37*(3), 13-25.

Lambe, C. J., Wittmann, C. M., & Spekman, R. E. (2001). Social exchange theory and research on business-to-business relational exchange. *Journal of Business-to-Business Marketing, 8*(3), 1-36.

Langfield-Smith, K., & Smith, D. (2003). Management control systems and trust in outsourcing relationships. *Management Accounting Research, 14*, 281-307.

Laudon, K. C., & Laudon, J. P. (2005). *Essentials of management information systems: Managing the digital firm* (6th ed.). Upper Saddle River, NJ: Pearson Education.

Lee, J.-N., & Kim, Y.-G. (1999). Effect of partnership quality on IS outsourcing success: Conceptual framework and empirical validation. *Journal of Management Information Systems, 15*(4), 29-61.

Lee, J. N., Miranda, S. M., & Kim, Y. M. (2004). IT outsourcing strategies: Universalistic, contingency, and configurational explanations of success. *Information Systems Research, 15*(2), 110-131.

Leiblein, M. J., Reuer, J. J., & Dalsace, F. (2002). Do make or buy decisions matter? The influence of organizational governance on technological performance. *Strategic Management Journal, 23*, 817-833.

Levina, N., & Ross, J. W. (2003). From the vendor's perspective: Exploring the value proposition in information technology outsourcing. *MIS Quarterly, 27*(3), 331-364.

Linder, J. C. (2004, Winter). Transformational outsourcing. *MIT Sloan Management Review*, pp. 52-58.

Linder, J. C., & Cantrell, S. (2000). Changing business models: Surveying the landscape.

Loh, L., & Venkatraman, N. (1992a). Determinants of information technology outsourcing: A cross-sectional analysis. *Journal of Management Information Systems, 9*(1), 7-24.

Loh, L., & Venkatraman, N. (1992b). Diffusion of information technology outsourcing: Influence sources and the Kodak effect. *Information Systems Research, 3*(4), 334-358.

Luo, Y. (2002). Contract, cooperation, and performance in international joint ventures. *Strategic Management Journal, 23*, 903-911.

Melville, N., Kraemer, K., & Gurbaxani, V. (2004). Information technology and organizational performance: An integrative model of IT business value. *MIS Quarterly, 28* (82), 283-322.

Nielsen, K. B. (2004, October). *Reality of IS Lite and more* (EXP client presentation). Gartner Group. Retrieved September 6, 2008, from www.gartner.com

Peppard, J., Lambert, R., & Edwards, C. (2000). Whose job is it anyway? Organizational information competencies for value creation. *Information Systems Journal, 10*, 291-322.

Pettus, M. L. (2001). The resource-based view as a developmental growth process: Evidence from the deregulated trucking industry. *Academy of Management Journal, 44*(4), 878-896.

Phillips, R., Freeman, R. E., & Wicks, A. C. (2003). What stakeholder theory is not. *Business Ethics Quarterly, 13*(4), 479-502.

Priem, R. L., & Butler, J. E. (2001). Is the resource-based "view" a useful perspective for strategic management research? *Academy of Management Review, 26*(1), 22-40.

Ravichandran, T., & Lertwongsatien, C. (2005). Effect of information systems resources and capabilities on firm performance: A resource-based perspective. *Journal of Management Information Systems, 21*(4), 237-276.

Ross, J. W., & Weill, P. (2002, November). Six IT decisions your IT people shouldn't make. *Harvard Business Review*, pp. 84-91.

Santhanam, R., & Hartono, E. (2003). Issues in linking information technology capability to firm performance. *MIS Quarterly, 27*(19), 125-153.

Schilling, M. A., & Steensma, H. K. (2002). Disentangling the theories of firm boundaries: A path model and empirical test. *Organization Science, 13*(4), 387-401.

Schniederjans, M. J., Hamaker, J. L., & Schniederjans, A. M. (2004). *Information technology investment: Decision-making methodology*. World Scientific.

Skaksen, J. R. (2004). International outsourcing when labour markets are unionized. *Canadian Journal of Economics, 37*(1), 78-94.

Steensma, H. K., & Corley, K. G. (2001). Organizational context as moderator of theories on firm boundaries for technology sourcing. *Academy of Management Journal, 44*(2), 271-291.

Venkatraman, N. V. (2004, Spring). Offshoring without guilt. *MIS Sloan Management Review*, pp. 14-16.

Wade, M., & Hulland, J. (2004). The resource-based view and information systems research: Review, extension, and suggestions for future research. *MIS Quarterly, 28*(1), 107-142.

Williamson, O. E. (1991). Comparative economic organization: The analysis of discrete structural alternatives. *Administrative Science Quarterly, 36*.

Wright, S., & Boschee, K. (2004). The offshore IT provider is under fire: Will the US company be next? *Employee Relations Law Journal, 30*(1), 60-64.

ENDNOTE

1 Source: Gottschalk, P., & Solli-Saether, H. (2006). *Managing successful IT outsourcing relationships*. Hershey, PA: Idea Group.

Chapter IX
The CIO Enabling IT Governance

INTRODUCTION

In many organizations, information technology has become crucial in the support, sustainability, and growth of the business. This pervasive use of technology has created a critical dependency on IT that calls for a specific focus on IT governance. IT governance consists of the leadership and organizational structures and processes that ensure that the organization's IT sustains and extends the organization's strategy and objectives (Grembergen, Haes, & Guldentops, 2004).

IT governance matters because it influences the benefits received from IT investments. Through a combination of practices (such as redesigning business processes and well-designed governance mechanisms) and appropriately matched IT investments, top-performing enterprises generate superior returns on their IT investments (Weill, 2004).

WHAT IS IT GOVERNANCE?

IT governance can be defined as specifying decision rights and accountability framework to encourage desirable behavior in the use of IT (Weill & Ross, 2004). This is the definition we will use here.

Other definitions are, for example: (i) IT governance is the structures and processes that ensure that IT supports the organization's mission. The purpose is to align IT with the enterprise, maximize the benefits of IT, use IT resources responsibly, and manage IT risks; (ii) A structure of relationships and processes to direct and control the enterprise in order to achieve the enterprise's goals by adding value while balancing risk vs. return over IT and its processes; (iii) IT governance is the responsibility of the board of directors and executive management. It is an integral part of enterprise governance and consists of the leadership and organizational structures and processes that ensure that the organization's IT sustains and extends the organization's strategies and objectives; and (iv) IT governance is the system by which an organization's IT portfolio is directed and controlled. IT governance describes (a) the distribution of decision-making rights and responsibilities among different stakeholders in the organization, and (b) the rules and procedures for making and monitoring decisions on strategic IT concerns (Peterson, 2004).

An extensive definition was presented by the IT Governance Institute (2004) as follows. It is a board or senior management responsibility in relation to IT to ensure that:

- IT is aligned with the business strategy, or in other words, IT delivers the functionality and services in line with the organization's needs, so the organization can do what it wants to do.
- IT and new technologies enable the organization to do new things that were never possible before.
- IT-related services and functionality are delivered at the maximum economic value or in the most efficient manner. In other words, resources are used responsibly.
- All risks related to IT are known and managed and IT resources are secured.

A distinction has to be made between IT management as discussed previously in this book and IT governance that we introduce here. IT management is focused on the internal effective supply of IT services and products and the management of present IT operations (Grembergen et al., 2004). IT governance in turn is much broader and concentrates on performing and transforming IT to meet present and future demands of the business (internal focus) and the business' customers (external focus).

The difference between IT management and IT governance is illustrated in Figure 9.1. While IT management is concerned with implementing IT services at the present, IT governance is concerned with making decisions for the future.

Figure 9.1. Distinction between IT management and IT governance (Grembergen et al., 2004)

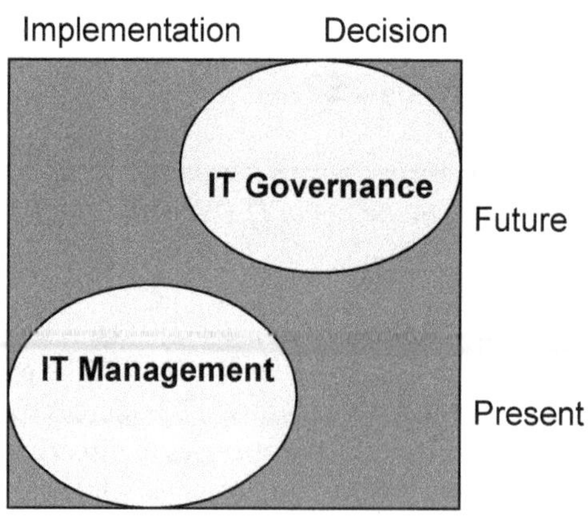

Whereas the domain of IT management focuses on the efficient and effective supply of IT services and products, and the management of IT operations, IT governance faces the dual demand of (1) contributing to present business operations and performance, and (2) transforming and positioning IT for meeting future business challenges. This does not undermine the importance or complexity of IT management but indicates that IT governance is both internally and externally oriented, spanning both present and future time frames. One of the key challenges in IT governance is therefore how to simultaneously perform and transform IT in order to meet the present and future demands of the business and the business' customers in a satisfying manner (Peterson, 2004).

IT governance is concerned with decision rights. In a survey by Gartner (2005) on how IT spending is controlled, it was found that 62% of IT spending was centrally controlled by the IT organization in the U.S.; 35% was blended controlled by IT and business units or functions, while 3% was directly controlled by business units or function.

IT governance encourages desirable behavior in the use of IT. A desirable behavior is one that is consistent with the organization's mission, strategy, values, norms, and culture, such as behavior promoting entrepreneurship, sharing, and reuse or relentless cost reduction. IT governance is not about what specific decisions are made. That is management. Rather, governance is about systematically determining who makes each type of decision (a decision right), who has input to a decision (an input right), and how these people (or groups) are held accountable for their roles (Weill, 2004).

Good IT governance draws on corporate governance principles to manage and use IT to achieve corporate performance goals. Effective IT governance encourages and leverages the ingenuity of all enterprise personnel in using IT, while ensuring compliance with the enterprise's overall vision and principles. As a result, good IT governance can achieve a management paradox: simultaneously empowering and controlling (Weill, 2004).

All enterprises have IT governance. The difference is that enterprises with effective governance have actively designed a set of IT governance mechanisms (e.g., committees, budgeting processes, approvals, IT organizational structure, chargeback, etc.) that encourage behaviors consistent with the organization's mission, strategy, values, norms, and culture. In these enterprises, when the "desirable behaviors" change, IT governance also changes (Weill, 2004).

IT governance cannot be considered in isolation because it links to the governance of other key enterprise assets (such as financial, human, intellectual property, etc.). Governance of the key assets, in turn, links to corporate governance and desirable behaviors (Weill, 2004).

In the models of *corporate governance* one can organize the variety of variables and concepts used to describe the complexity of corporate governance mechanisms into two main categories: capital-related and labor-related. The capital-related aspects contain, among others, variables like ownership structure, corporate voting, the identity of owners, and the role of institutional owners. The labor-related aspects refer mainly to the stakeholding position of labor in corporate governance. Here one could mention employee involvement schemes, participatory management, codetermination, and so forth (Cernat, 2004).

CORPORATE GOVERNANCE

Before we dive into IT outsourcing governance, we must look at the broader issue of corporate governance in enterprises. Corporate governance is concerned with governing key assets such as (Weill & Ross, 2004):

- **Human assets:** People, skills, career paths, training, reporting, mentoring, competencies, and so on.
- **Financial assets:** Cash, investments, liabilities, cash flow, receivables, and so on.
- **Physical assets:** Buildings, plant, equipment, maintenance, security, utilization, and so on.
- **IP assets:** Intellectual property (IP), including products, services, and processes know-how formally patented, copyrighted, or embedded in the enterprises' people and systems.
- **Information and IT assets:** Digitized data, information, and knowledge about customers, processes performance, finances, information systems, and so on.
- **Relationship assets:** Relationships within the enterprise as well as relationships, brand, and reputation with customers, suppliers, business units, regulators, competitors, channel partners, and so on.

As we can see from this list, IT outsourcing governance includes not only information and IT assets. IT outsourcing governance is concerned with several of these assets, sometimes even all of these assets. In this perspective, IT outsourcing governance may be as comprehensive in scope as corporate governance.

In governing IT outsourcing, we can learn from good financial and corporate governance. For example, the CFO (chief financial officer) does not sign every check or authorize every payment. Instead, he or she sets up financial governance specifying who can make the decisions and how. The CFO then oversees the enterprise's portfolio of investments and manages the required cash flow and risk exposure. The CFO tracks a series of financial metrics to manage the enterprise's financial assets, intervening only if there are problems or unforeseen opportunities. Similar principles apply to those who can commit the enterprise to a contract or a partnership. Exactly the same approach should be applied to IT governance (Weill & Ross, 2004).

The dichotomy market or hierarchy has exercised a dominant influence on the study of forms of governance and their operation for some time. However, in the past two decades there have been large numbers of investigations of intermediate forms of governance. Subsequently, it has been recognized that the behavior that occurs within exchanges is not necessarily determined by the forms of governance used, and this points to a need to understand behavior within a variety of exchanges (Blois, 2002).

CONTRACTS IN GOVERNANCE

Blois (2002) defines governance as the institutional framework in which contracts are initiated, monitored, adapted, and terminated. An exchange occurs between two organizations when resources are transferred from one party to the other in return for resources controlled by the other party.

The organization of interfirm exchanges has become of critical importance in today's business environment. Many scholars have criticized the inadequacies of legal contracts as mechanisms for governing exchange, especially in the face of uncertainty and dependence.

Other scholars argue that it is not the contracts per se but the social contexts in which they are embedded that determine their effectiveness. Cannon, Achrol, and Gundlach (2000) investigated the performance implications of governance structures involving contractual agreements and relational social norms, individually and in combination (plural form) under varying conditions and forms of transactional uncertainty and relationship-specific adaptation. Hypotheses were developed and tested on a sample of buyer-seller relationships. The results provide support for the plural form thesis, increasing the relational content of a governance structure containing contractual agreements that enhanced performance when transactional uncertainty was high, but not when it was low.

Cannon et al. (2000) applied the term *legal bonds* to refer to the extent to which detailed and binding contractual agreements were used to specify the roles and obligations of the parties. To the extent contracts were characterized in this way, they were less flexible and therefore more constrained in their adaptive properties. Highly detailed contracts were also less likely to possess the kinds of general safeguards that are more effective in thwarting self-interest-seeking behavior under circumstances of ambiguity.

Various perspectives on the nature of contracts as a mechanism of governance may be found in the literature. According to the original transaction cost framework (Williamson, 1979), formal contingent claims contracts (i.e., classical contracts) are inefficient mechanisms of governance in the face of uncertainty because organizations are bounded in their rationality and find it impossible to contemplate all possible future contingencies. For exchanges involving high levels of idiosyncratic investments and characterized by uncertainty, internal organization or hierarchy is predicted to be a more efficient form of governance than the market (Cannon et al., 2000).

However, neoclassical contract law argues that contracts can provide useful governance in exchange relationships even in the face of uncertainty and risk. This tradition of contract law is marked by doctrine and rules that attempt to overcome the difficulties posed by the classical tradition's emphasis on discreteness and presentation of exchange. The new doctrines enable parties to respond to unforeseen contingencies by making adjustments to ongoing exchange and ensuring continuity in their relationships. For example, concepts such as "good faith" and "reasonable commercial standards of fair dealing in the trade" are recognized under the Uniform Commercial Code (UCC) of 1978 in the U.S. as general provisions for contracting behavior that also helps to ensure continuity in exchange relationships. Similarly, "gap filler" provisions of the UCC rely on "prior dealings" between parties and "customary practices" across an industry or trading area for completing contract terms intentionally left open or omitted, thus allowing for adjustments to contingencies (Cannon et al., 2000).

However, neoclassical contracts are not indefinitely elastic (Williamson, 1991). Many scholars remain skeptical of how effective even the most carefully crafted contracts can be. It is argued that the scope for drafting rules in contracts to address changing or ambiguous conditions, or the ability to rely on general legal safeguards for controlling commercial conduct, is limited by both practicality and the law itself.

Drawing on these views, Cannon et al. (2000) argue that when a transaction involves relationship-specific adaptations and is (1) subject to dynamic forces and future contingencies that cannot be foreseen or (2) involves ambiguous circumstances where tasks are ill-defined and prone to exploitation, the difficulty of writing, monitoring, and enforcing contracts is increased, and their overall governance effectiveness is weakened. In each case, efforts to govern the relationship on the basis of detailed and formal contracts without the benefit of some additional apparatus are not likely to enhance performance.

Social or relational norms are defined generally as shared expectations regarding behavior. The norms reflect expectations about attitudes and behaviors parties have in working cooperatively together to achieve mutual and individual goals. The spirit of such sentiments is captured by many overlapping types of relational contracting norms. These can be reduced to a core set of five (Cannon et al., 2000):

- **Flexibility.** The attitude among parties that an agreement is but a starting point to be modified as the market, the exchange relationship, and the fortunes of the parties evolve.
- **Solidarity.** The extent to which parties believe that success comes from working cooperatively together vs. competing against one another. It dictates that parties stand by one another in the face of adversity and the ups and downs of marketplace competition.
- **Mutuality.** The attitude that each party's success is a function of everyone's success and that one cannot prosper at the expense of one's partner. It expresses the sentiment of joint responsibility.
- **Harmonization of conflict.** The extent to which a spirit of mutual accommodation toward cooperative ends exists.
- **Restraint in the use of power.** Forbearance from taking advantage of one's bargaining position in an exchange. It reflects the view that the use of power not only exacerbates conflict over time but also undermines mutuality and solidarity, opening the door to opportunism.

Together, these cooperative norms define relational properties that are important in affecting adaptations to dynamic market conditions and safeguarding the continuity of exchanges subject to task ambiguity (Cannon et al., 2000).

Norms represent important social and organizational vehicles of control in exchange, where goals are ill-defined or involve open-ended performance. They provide a general frame of reference, order, and standards against which to guide and assess appropriate behavior in uncertain and ambiguous situations. In such situations contracts are often incomplete, and legal remedies can undermine relationship continuity. In contrast, norms motivate performance through focusing attention on the shared values of the partners to safeguard and rely on peer pressure and social sanctions to mitigate the risk of shirking and opportunistic expropriation. Because they involve expectations rather than rigid requirements of behavior, they create a cooperative as opposed to a confrontational environment for negotiating adaptations, thus promoting continuity in exchange (Cannon et al., 2000).

The plural form thesis contends that exchange is best understood as embedded in a complex matrix of economic, social, and political structures and that the governance of exchange relations more often relies on combinations of market-, social-, or authority-based mechanisms than on any one category exclusively. While the plural form thesis is that the various mechanisms in fact work together to reinforce or complement one another in some way, little attention has focused on exactly how these mechanisms actually complement one another (Cannon et al., 2000).

Academic literature and business practice are directing increased attention to the importance of creating value in buyer-supplier relationships. One method for creating value is to

Figure 9.2. Model explaining how supplier affects customer costs (adapted from Cannon & Homburg, 2001)

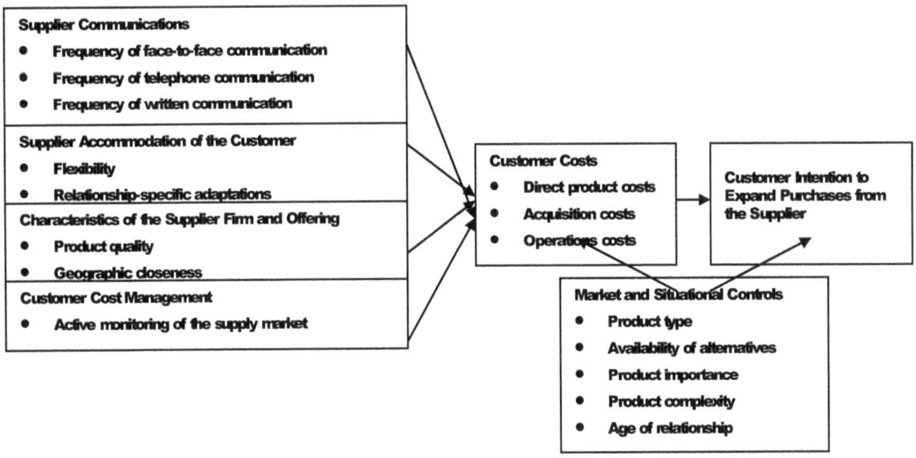

reduce costs in commercial exchange. Cannon and Homburg (2001) developed a model that explains how supplier behaviors and the management of suppliers affect a customer firm's direct product, acquisition, and operations costs. The model proposes that these costs mediate the relationship between buyer-supplier relationship behaviors and the customer firm's intentions to expand future purchases from the supplier, as illustrated in Figure 9.2.

Cannon and Homburg (2001) empirically tested all relationships in their model in Figure 9.2. Their findings provide support for the expectation that more complex operational issues at times may require the richer interaction provided in face-to-face communications, but at other times may benefit from simpler written exchanges. As expected, the more standardized issues typical of product acquisition benefit from more efficient written/electronic communication.

In contrast, open information sharing by suppliers was not found to be related to a customer firm's costs. The lack of support for these hypotheses may be caused by buying firms' failure to use the information received from suppliers effectively. For example, customer firms may suffer from information overload and be unable to process and act on such information effectively.

Further hypotheses in Figure 9.2 predict the effects supplier accommodation would have on customer costs. The empirical results support the prediction that greater supplier flexibility results in lower acquisition and operations costs. Contrary to the researchers' predictions, higher levels of relationship-specific adaptation did not lead to lower acquisition or operations costs. This may be because many of these adaptations are targeted at enhancing value through increasing the benefits a customer receives, not through cost reduction.

Whereas Cannon and Homburg (2001) developed a hypothesis that higher direct product costs would be associated with greater supplier adaptation, the result was statistically significant in the opposite direction. Several factors may explain this unanticipated finding. First, relationship-specific adaptations may evolve into regular business practices with all customers, which may subsequently lower the cost of accommodation. Second, buying organizations may effectively bargain away the premium prices a supplier must initially charge for customized products. Finally, at a more general level, buyers may compensate suppliers through long-term commitments and/or promises of higher sales volume. Typically, such agreements also involve lower prices over time.

As predicted in the model in Figure 9.2, geographic proximity of the supplier's facilities helped lower acquisition costs. The expected effects of quality in lowering the customer's acquisition costs and operations costs were found, but Cannon and Homburg (2001) were surprised to find that higher quality products had lower direct product costs. Possible explanations for the unexpected finding for the product quality-direct product costs relationship can be drawn from the quality literature. It may be that quality operates as an order qualifier and high quality is necessary just to be considered as a supplier but does not allow a supplier to charge higher prices.

Another hypothesis in Figure 9.2 predicts the effects of actively monitoring the supply market on each cost. More active monitoring of the supply market was found to be associated with higher operations costs but not with higher acquisition costs.

A final hypothesis in Figure 9.2 was supported in the empirical data. It predicts that lowering the customer firm's direct product, acquisition, and operations costs leads the customer to expand its business with the supplier. These findings suggest that a supplier's efforts to lower a customer firm's costs can have long-term benefits to suppliers as well.

As IT outsourcing becomes more commonplace, new organizational forms are emerging to facilitate these relationships. Chase Bank has created "shared services" units that compete with outside vendors to furnish services to the bank's own operating units. Delta Airlines has established a "business partners" unit to oversee its relations with vendors. Microsoft outsources almost everything from the manufacturing of its computer software to the distribution of its software products, thereby focusing the organization on its primary area of competitive advantage: the writing of software code. Still other firms are creating "strategic services" divisions in which activities formerly decentralized into autonomous business units are now being recentralized for outside contracting. As these various approaches suggest, the best ways to structure outsourcing remain the subject of ongoing management debate and media coverage (Useem & Harder, 2000).

As companies devise new forms of organization to assure that outsourcing works as intended, those responsible require a new blend of talents. Rather than issuing orders, managers must concentrate on negotiating results, replacing a skill for sending work downward with a talent for arranging work outward. Thus, the outsourcing of services necessitates lateral leadership, according to Useem and Harder (2000).

Useem and Harder (2000) reached this conclusion about leadership capabilities required for outsourcing through interviews conducted with several companies. What emerged from the interviews and a broader survey was a picture of a more demanding leadership environment, even as day-to-day management tasks are streamlined by outsourcing. They found that four individual capabilities encompass much of what is required of managers as outsourcing becomes commonplace:

- **Strategic thinking.** Within the outsourcing framework, managers must understand whether and how to outsource in ways that improve competitive advantage.
- **Deal making.** Outsource process managers must broker deals in two directions simultaneously, securing the right services from external providers and ensuring their use by internal managers.

Figure 9.3. Management roles for the CIO

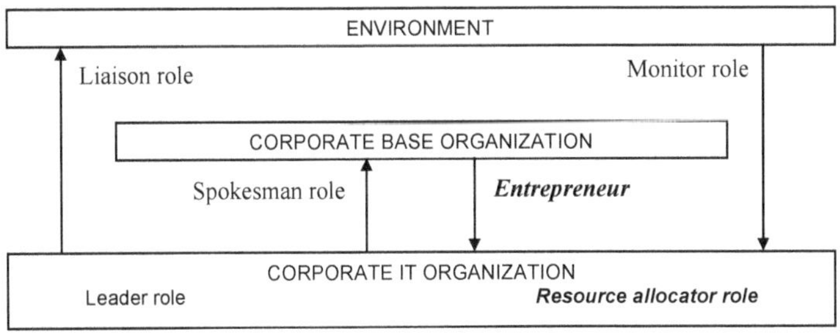

- **Partnership governing.** After identifying areas suitable for outsourcing through strategic assessment and upon clinching a deal, effectively overseeing the relationship is essential.
- **Managing change.** Forcefully spearheading change is critical because companies are certain to encounter employee resistance.

These four capabilities emerged repeatedly when Useem and Harder (2000) were discussing the essential skills of those responsible for outsourcing decisions, contracting, and oversight. None of these qualities taken singly were found to be unique to outsourcing, but their combination is critical to leading laterally.

GOVERNANCE AND MANAGEMENT ROLES

Managers undertake activities to achieve the objectives of the organization. In the context of IT management, the relevance of six management roles has been identified—leader, resource allocator, spokesman, entrepreneur, liaison, and monitor.

The six roles are again illustrated in Figure 9.3. Leader and resource allocator are roles internal to the IT function. Spokesman and entrepreneur are roles internal to the organization. Monitor and liaison are roles external to the organization.

In terms of decision-making for IT governance, two management roles are visible. First, the resource allocator role is mainly concerned with decisions. The manager must decide how to allocate human, financial, and information resources to the activities of the IT function. Second, the entrepreneur role is mainly concerned with decisions. The manager identifies the users' needs and management expectations and makes decisions concerning solutions that change business situations. Hence, IT governance affects the two CIO leadership roles of resource allocator and entrepreneur.

WHY IS *IT* GOVERNANCE IMPORTANT?

IT governance matters because it influences the benefits received from IT investments. Through a combination of practices (such as redesigned business processes and well-designed governance mechanisms) and appropriately matched IT investments, top-performing enterprises generate superior returns on their IT investments (Weill, 2004).

Weill and Ross (2004, p. 22) list the following reasons why IT governance is important:

- **Good IT Governance Pays Off.** Among the for-profit firms we studied, the ones pursuing a specific strategy (for example, customer intimacy or operational excellence) with above-average IT governance performance had superior profits as measured by a three-year industry adjusted return on assets.
- **IT Is Expensive.** The average enterprise's IT investment is now greater than 4.2 percent of annual revenues and still rising. This investment results in IT exceeding 50 percent of the annual total capital investment of many enterprises. As IT has become more important and pervasive, senior management teams are increasingly challenged to manage and control IT to ensure that value is created. To address this issue, many enterprises are creating or refining IT governance structures to better focus IT spending on strategic priorities.
- **IT Is Pervasive.** In many enterprises, centrally managed IT is no longer possible or desirable. There was a time when requests for IT spending came only from the IT group. Now IT spending originates all over the enterprise. Some estimates suggest that only 20 percent of IT spending is visible in the IT budget. The rest of the spending occurs in business process budgets, product development budgets, and every other type of budget. Well-designed IT governance arrangements distribute IT decision making to those responsible for outcomes.
- **New Information Technologies Bombard Enterprises with New Business Opportunities.** Foresight is more likely if an enterprise has formalized governance processes for harmonizing desirable behaviors and IT principles.
- **IT Governance Is Critical to Organizational Learning About IT Value.** Effective governance creates mechanisms through which enterprises can debate potential value and formalize their learning. Governance also facilitates learning by formalizing exception processes. Enterprises often learn through exceptions—where a different approach from standard practice is used for good reasons. Effective governance makes learning via exceptions explicit and shares any new practices across the enterprise if appropriate.
- **IT Value Depends on More Than Good Technology.** In recent years there have been spectacular failures of large IT investments—major enterprise resource planning (ERP) systems initiatives that were never completed, e-business initiatives that were ill-conceived or poorly executed, and data-mining experiments that generated plenty of data but few valuable leads. Successful firms not only make better IT decisions, they also have better IT decision-making processes. Specifically, successful firms involve the right people in the process. Having the right people involved in IT decision making yields both more strategic applications and greater buy-in.
- **Senior Management Has Limited Bandwidth.** Senior management does not have the bandwidth to consider all the requests for IT investments that occur in a large enterprise let alone get involved in many other IT-related decisions. If senior managers attempt to make too many decisions, they become a bottleneck. But decisions throughout the enterprise should be consistent with the direction in which senior management is taking the organization. Carefully designed IT governance provides a

clear, transparent IT decision-making process that leads to consistent behavior linked back to the senior management vision while empowering everyone's creativity.

- **Leading Enterprises Govern IT Differently.** Top performing firms balancing multiple performance goals had governance models that blended centralized and decentralized decision making. All top performers' governance had one aspect in common. Their governance made transparent the tensions around IT decisions such as standardization versus innovation.

THE OUTSOURCING GOVERNANCE MODEL

IT outsourcing governance can be defined as specifying the decision rights and accountability framework to encourage desirable behavior in the IT outsourcing arrangement, where resources are transferred from one party to the other in return for resources controlled by the other party. Governance is not about making specific decisions—management does that—but rather determines who systematically makes and contributes to those decisions. Governance reflects broader principles while focusing on the management of the outsourcing relationship to achieve performance goals for both client and vendor. Governance is the institutional framework in which contracts are monitored, adapted, and renewed. Effective outsourcing governance encourages and leverages the ingenuity of the vendor's and client's people in IT usage and ensures compliance with both enterprises' overall vision and values (Gottschalk & Solli-Sæther, 2006).

Our governance model is illustrated in Figure 9.4. It consists of five elements (contracts, principles, resources, activities, and managers), two main links (terms-exchanges link between contracts and resources, and norms-relationships link between principles

Figure 9.4. Governance model for outsourcing relationships (Gottschalk & Solli-Sæther, 2006)

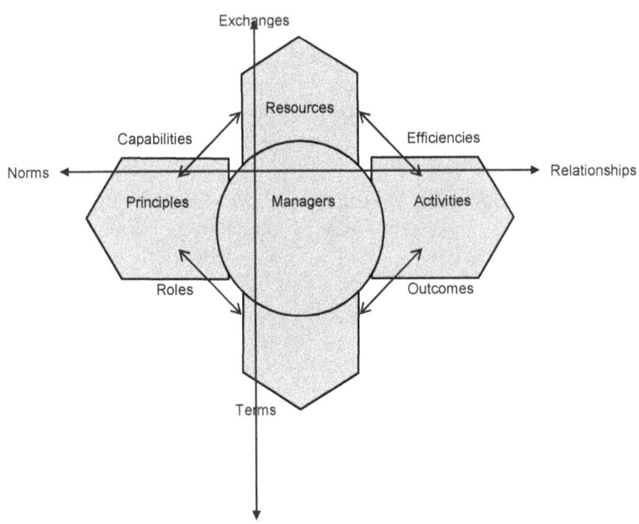

and activities), and four local links (roles between contracts and principles, capabilities between principles and resources, efficiencies between resources and activities, and outcomes between activities and contracts).

Contracts provide a legally bound, institutional framework in which each party's rights, duties, and responsibilities are codified and the goals, policies, and strategies underlying the arrangement are specified. *Principles* define decision rights concerning general IT principles, IT infrastructure, IT architecture, business application needs, and IT investments. *Resources* define decision rights concerning human assets, financial assets, physical assets, IP assets, information and IT assets, and relationship assets. *Activities* define decision rights concerning transactions, projects, problem solving, and reporting. *Managers* are classified into stakeholder groups of client business management, client IT management, vendor business management, and vendor account management.

Exchanges of resources occur through transactions based on contracts. *Terms* for use of resources are defined in contracts. *Norms* create expectations of behavior and imply a certain action and are shared by the actors. Norms are based on principles and they occur in activities. Norms are concerned with flexibility, solidarity, mutuality, harmonization, and power. *Relationships* frame activities based on principles and norms.

Roles are defined by contracts and carried out when making decisions about principles. Management roles include spokesperson, entrepreneur, personnel leader, resource allocator, monitor, and liaison roles. *Capabilities* enable the use of resources based on principles. *Efficiencies* are determined by the use of resources in activities. *Outcomes* occur in activities that are performance results from contracts.

Figure 9.5 illustrates how managers and principles are related through decision rights. *General principles* are high-level statements about how IT is used in the business. *IT infrastructure* are strategies for the base foundation of budgeted-for IT capability (technical

Figure 9.5. The governance model defines decision rights concerning principles (Weill & Ross, 2004)

Principles Stakeholders	General principles	IT infrastructure	IT architecture	Business application needs	IT investments
Client business management	Strategic information systems planning decisions	Infrastructure capabilities decisions	Architecture performance decisions	Strategic information systems planning decisions	Financial investments decisions
Client IT management	Technology business alignment decisions	Infrastructure functions decisions	Architecture structure decisions	Information systems decisions	Investment analysis contents decisions
Vendor business management	Service level decisions	Service organization decisions	Service organization decisions	Information systems organization decisions	Financial investments decisions
Vendor account management	Technology decisions	Infrastructure integration decisions	Architecture integration decisions	Technology decisions for information systems	Investment analysis contents decisions

Figure 9.6. The governance model defines decision rights concerning resources (Weill & Ross, 2004)

Resources Stakeholders	**Human assets**	**Financial assets**	**Physical assets**	**IP assets**	**Information and IT assets**	**Relationship assets**
Client business management	Knowledge management decisions	User investment decisions	Tangible assets policy	Intangible assets policy	Strategic information systems planning decisions	Information sharing policy
Client IT management	Internal IT personnel decisions	User tehnology investment decision	Tangible assets management	Intangible assets management	Technology business alignment decision	Project sharing policy
Vendor business management	Knowledge management decisions	Vendor investment decisions	Tangible assets governance	Intangible assets governance	Service level decisions	Competence sharing policy
Vendor account management	Internal IT personnel decisions	Vendor technology investment decisions	Tangible assets governance	Intangible assets governance	Technology decisions	Knowledge transfer policy

Figure 9.7. Stages of growth in IT outsourcing

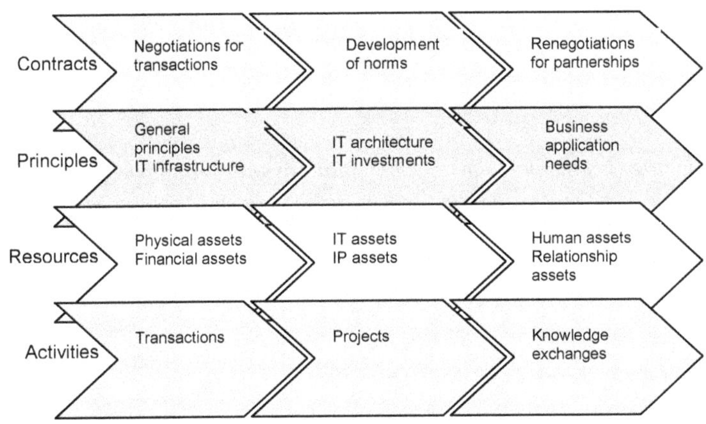

and human), shared throughout the firm as reliable services, and centrally coordinated such as network, help desk, and shared data. *IT architecture* is an integrated set of technical choices to guide the organization in satisfying business needs. The architecture is a set of policies and rules that govern the use of IT and plot a migration path to the way business will be done (includes data, technology, and applications). *Business application needs* are concerned with business applications to be acquired and built. *IT investment* and prioritization are decisions about how much and where to invest in IT, including project approvals and justification techniques (Weill & Ross, 2004).

Figure 9.6 illustrates how managers and resources are related through decision rights. *Human assets* are people, skills, career paths, training, reporting, mentoring, competencies, and so on. *Financial assets* are cash, investments, liabilities, cash flow, receivables, and so on. *Physical assets* are buildings, plant, equipment, maintenance, security, utilization, and so on. *IP assets* are intellectual property (IP), including product, services, and process know-how formally patented, copyrighted, or embedded in the enterprises' people and systems. *Information and IT assets* are digitized data, information, and knowledge about customers, processes performance, finances, information systems, and so on. *Relationship assets* are relationships within the enterprises as well as relationships between client and vendor at all levels (Weill & Ross, 2004).

IT outsourcing governance consists of five elements as illustrated in Figure 9.4. Four of these elements are really dimensions of governance, while the remaining element is management, which integrates the four dimensions of governance. In Figure 9.7, the four dimensions of governance are illustrated along the time dimension, defined as the formation stage (vision, evaluation, negotiation), the operation stage (transition, improvement), and the outcome stage (performance, results, goals, objectives).

In the formation stage, contracts are concerned with transactions in the outsourcing arrangement. Later, as relationships and norms develop between vendor and client, contracts will be renegotiated, shifting focus from transactions to relationships and partnerships. While the first contracts will be transactional contracts, later contracts will be relational contracts. Contract work is characterized by progressive contractual work, where focus slowly shifts from transactions to relationships as contract outcomes start to materialize.

It is important to design effective IT outsourcing governance. We defined governance as specifying the decision rights and accountability framework to encourage desirable behavior in an IT outsourcing relationship. Governance performance must then be how

Figure 9.8. Managing successful IT outsourcing relationships through the governance model based on IT outsourcing theories (Gottschalk & Solli-Sæther, 2006)

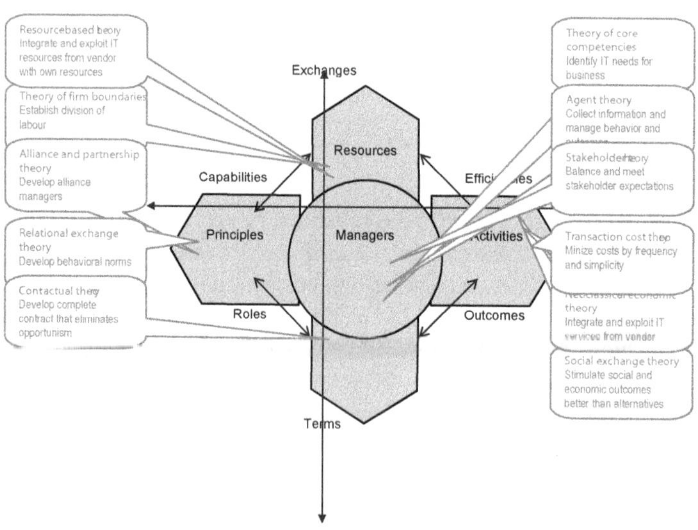

well the governance arrangements encourage desirable behaviors and ultimately how well both firms achieve their desired performance goals as vendor and client.

There are many IT outsourcing theories (Gottschalk & Solli-Sæther, 2006). Each theory implies suggestions for managing successful IT outsourcing relationships. As a total set of suggestions and ideas from all theories, these guidelines represent critical success factors after outsourcing. The guidelines can be implemented in the governance model as illustrated in Figure 9.8. We see that resource-based theory and theory of firm boundaries both provide guidelines for resource management. Alliance and partnership theory and relational exchange theory both provide guidelines for principles management. Transaction cost theory, neoclassical economic theory, and social exchange theory all provide guidelines for activity management, while contractual theory provide guidelines for contract management. Theory of core competencies, agency theory, and stakeholder theory provide guidelines directly to managers in charge of the outsourcing arrangement.

HOW TO SUCCEED AS A CLIENT

Based on outsourcing theories and practice, we are able to list the following key success factors for a sourcing firm as listed in Figure 9.9.

HOW TO SUCCEED AS A VENDOR

Based on outsourcing theories and practice, we are able to list the following key success factors for a source firm as listed in Figure 9.10.

CIO LEADERSHIP AND IT GOVERNANCE

Monnoyer and Willmott (2005) are skeptical of IT governance. They argue that something has gone very wrong with the structures, processes, and policies that govern how a business makes IT decisions and who within the organization makes them. They find that IT governance arrangements have become a substitute for real leadership. Companies are relying on tightly scripted meetings, analyses, and decision frameworks to unite CIOs and business executives around a common vision for IT. But committee meetings and processes are poor stand-ins for executives who can forge a clear agreement among their peers about IT investment choices and drive the senior-level conversations needed to make tough trade-offs.

Monnoyer and Willmott (2005) find that in companies with strong IT leaders, governance constitutes a much more flexible set of managerial activities, involves fewer people and fewer meetings, and is typically tailored to fit the IT leader's style, much as executive committee activities often reflect a CEO's leadership approach.

The CIO can be defined as the highest-ranking IT executive who typically exhibits managerial roles requiring effective communication with top management, a broad corporate perspective in managing information resources, influence on organizational strategy, and responsibility for the planning of IT. This definition is in line with research that applied

Figure 9.9. Key success factors for the client in managing successful IT outsourcing relationships based on theories

Theory	How to succeed as a client company in an outsourcing arrangement
Theory of core competencies	We have to define our IT needs and manage IT services from the vendor.
Resource-based theory	We have to integrate and exploit strategic IT resources from the vendor together with our own resources to produce competitive goods and services.
Transaction cost theory	We have to minimize transaction costs by reducing the need for lasting specific IT assets; increase transaction frequency; reduce complexity and uncertainty in IT tasks; improve performance measurements; and reduce dependence on other transactions.
Contractual theory	We must have a complete IT contract based on information symmetry in a predictable environment with occurrence adoption that prevents opportunistic behavior in an efficient collaborative environment with balance of power between client and vendor, where the contract is a management instrument that grants decision rights and action duties.
Neoclassical economic theory	We have to integrate and exploit IT services from the vendor together with our own services to produce competitive goods and services.
Partnership and alliance theory	We have to develop experience with alliances, develop alliance managers, and develop the ability to identify potential vendors.
Relational exchange theory	We have to develop and secure common norms that are relevant to both parties.
Social exchange theory	We have to enable social and economic outcomes in the exchange between the vendor and us such that these outcomes outperform those obtainable in alternative exchanges.
Agency theory	We have to make it easy and inexpensive for ourself to find out what the vendor is actually doing. In addition, both outcome-based and behavior-based incentives can be used to reduce and prevent opportunistic vendor behavior.
Theory of firm boundaries	We have to implement a strict and rigid division of labor between the vendor and us.
Stakeholder theory	We must create efficient and effective communication with and between stakeholders to secure continued support from all stakeholders, to balance their interests, and to make the IT outsourcing arrangement so that all stakeholders achieve their goals.

Figure 9.10. Key success factors for the vendor in managing successful IT outsourcing relationships based on theories

Theory	How to succeed as a vendor company in an outsourcing arrangement
Theory of core competencies	We have to provide complementary core competencies, such as personnel, methodologies, and services, to the client.
Resource-based theory	We have to enable the client to integrate and exploit strategic IT resources from us together with the clients' own resources to produce competitive goods and services.
Transaction cost theory	We have to minimize transaction costs by reducing the need for lasting specific IT assets; increase transaction frequency; reduce complexity and uncertainty in IT tasks; improve performance measurements; and reduce dependence on other transactions.
Contractual theory	We must have a complete IT contract based on information symmetry in a predictable environment with occurrence adoption that prevents opportunistic behavior in an efficient collaborative environment with balance of power between client and vendor, where the contract is a management instrument that grants decision rights and action duties.
Neoclassical economic theory	We have to enable the client to integrate and exploit IT services from us together with our own services to produce competitive goods and services.
Partnership and alliance theory	We have to develop experience with alliances, develop alliance managers, and develop the ability to identify potential clients.
Relational exchange theory	We have to develop and secure common norms that are relevant to both parties.
Social exchange theory	We have to enable social and economic outcomes in the exchange between the client and us such that these outcomes outperform those obtainable in alternative exchanges.
Agency theory	It must be easy and inexpensive for the principal (client) to find out what the agent (vendor) is actually doing. In addition, both outcome-based and behavior-based incentives can be used to reduce and prevent opportunistic behavior.
Theory of firm boundaries	We have to implement a strict and rigid division of labor between the client and us.
Stakeholder theory	We have to create efficient and effective communication with and between stakeholders to secure continued support from all stakeholders, to balance their interests, and to make the IT outsourcing arrangement so that all stakeholders achieve their goals.

the following criteria when selecting CIOs for empirical observation: (i) highest-ranking information technology executive; (ii) reports no more than two levels from the CEO, that is, either reports to the CEO or reports to one of the CEOs direct reports; (iii) areas of responsibility include information systems, computer operations, telecommunications and networks, office automation, end-user computing, help desks, computer software, and applications; and (iv) responsibility for strategic IS/IT planning.

According to Gartner (2005), only a few CEOs view CIOs as boardroom peers. Most CEOs view their CIOs as effective operational leaders. Yet only a few view them as full business leaders. There is an opportunity for CIOs to build their relationship with their CEOs and other stakeholders to increase their influence and to enhance the contribution of information systems and information technology.

THE CIO POSITION

The CIO position emerged in the 1970s as a result of increased importance placed on IT. In the early 1980s, the CIO was often portrayed as the corporate savior who was to align the worlds of business and technology. CIOs were described as the new breed of information managers who were businessmen first, managers second, and technologists third (Grover, Jeong, Kettinger, & Lee, 1993). It was even postulated that in the 1990s, as information became a firm's critical resource, the CIO would become the logical choice for the chief executive officer (CEO) position.

Job advertisements for information systems positions from 1970 to 1990 were reviewed by Todd, McKeen, and Gallupe (1995). They investigated specific positions related to programmers, systems analysts, and information systems managers. It is the latter position that is of interest here. At the time of the research, it was considered that successful information systems managers should have a blend of technical knowledge and sound business related skills. Further, in general, they should possess effective interpersonal skills. Over the 20-year period, Todd et al. determined that there had not been much change in the required skills indicated in job advertisements.

Benjamin, Dickinson, and Rockart (1985) suggested that the emergence of the CIO role represented the recognition of the importance of the role to be played within the organization. Kaarst-Brown (2005), however, suggests it is unfortunate that 20 years later, in 2005, the CIO is still held in lower regard than those senior managers of other more traditional business units. Kaarst-Brown suggests the reasons for this gap may be attributed to some of the items on the following list:

- Personality conflicts
- Lack of corporate technology vision
- Poorly aligned IT goals
- Lack of business knowledge
- Lack of IT awareness among the business executives
- Incorrect formal structure and reporting relationships

However, Kolbasuk (2005) reported that the perception of CIOs within organizations may be evolving. She suggests they may finally be getting the respect they deserve as they become members of the board of directors of large companies. This movement to the board level in the organization indicates the perception of the CIO role is evolving from a manager primarily focused on regulations, back office operations, and administrative duties to applying information technology at a strategic level to facilitate competitive advantage through an understanding of how business processes function and may be adapted to a changing corporate environment.

As a manager of people, the CIO faces the usual human resource roles of recruiting, staff training, and retention, and the financial roles of budget determination, forecasting, and authorization. As the provider of technological services to user departments, there remains a significant amount of work in publicity, promotion, and internal relations with user management. As a manager of an often-virtual information organization, the CIO has to coordinate sources of information services spread throughout and beyond the boundaries of the firm. The CIO is thus concerned with a wider group of issues than are most managers.

While information systems executives share several similarities with the general manager, notable differences are apparent. The CIO is not only concerned with a wider group of issues than most managers, but also, as the chief information systems strategist, has a set of responsibilities that must constantly evolve with the corporate information needs and with information technology itself. It has been suggested that the IT director's ability to add value is the biggest single factor in determining whether the organization views information technology as an asset or a liability.

According to Earl and Feeny (1994, p. 11), chief information officers have a difficult job:

Chief information officers have the difficult job of running a function that uses a lot of resources but that offers little measurable evidence of its value. To make the information systems department an asset to their companies—and to keep their jobs—CIOs should think of their work as adding value in certain key areas.

Creation of the CIO role was driven in part by two organizational needs. First, accountability is increased when a single executive is responsible for the organization's processing needs. Second, creation of the CIO position facilitates the closing of the gap between organizational and IT strategies which has long been cited as a primary business concern.

Alignment of business and IT objectives is not only a matter of achieving competitive advantage but is essential for the firm's very survival. Though the importance of IT in creating competitive advantage has been widely noted, achieving these gains has proven elusive. Sustained competitive advantage requires not only the development of a single system, but the ability to consistently deploy IT faster, cheaper, and more strategically than one's competitors. IT departments play a critical role in realizing the potential of IT. The performance of IT functions, in turn, often centers on the quality of leadership, that is, the CIO.

As early as 1984, some surveys suggested that one third of U.S. corporations had a CIO function, if not in title. While exact percentages differ, ranging from 40% to 70%, Grover et al. (1993) found that the number of senior-level information systems executive positions created over the past 10 years had grown tremendously. Early research conducted on the CIO position examined 43 of 50 top ranked Fortune 500 service organizations in the U.S., and noted that 23 (58%) of these organizations had the CIO position. In 1990, the 200 largest Fortune 500 industrial and service organizations were examined, and it was found that 77% of the industrials had a CIO position as compared with 64% of the service organizations. It is very likely that these numbers have increased in recent years.

Few studies have examined the reasons behind the creation of the CIO position in firms. Creation of the position effectively increases accountability by making a single executive responsible for corporate information processing needs. In a sample of Fortune 500 firms, that is, appearing on the list for four consecutive years, 287 firms with CIOs were compared in 1995 to firms without CIOs on a number of variables hypothesized to predict creation of the position. It was observed that a number of characteristics of the corporate board, including the number of outside directors and equity ownership of the directors, predicted the existence of the CIO position. A firm's information intensity was also found to be positively related to the creation of the CIO position. Furthermore, the CIO position was more likely to exist when the CEO appreciated the strategic value and importance of IT.

The CIO title itself has become a source of confusion. The term CIO has been somewhat loosely defined and is often used interchangeably with various titles such as IT director, vice president of IS, director of information resources, director of information services, and director of MIS, to describe a senior executive responsible for establishing policy and controlling information resources. Sometimes, the CIO label denotes a function rather than a title. Studies relating to the CIO have focused on the evolution of the position and the similarities between the CIO and other senior-level executives.

The CIO label itself has been met with resistance, and some firms have replaced the title with alternative labels such as knowledge manager, chief knowledge officer (CKO), or chief technology officer (CTO). It has been found that the CKO has to discover and develop the CEO's implicit vision of how knowledge management would make a difference, and how IT can support this difference.

There are differences between the tasks of a CTO, CIO, and CKO. While the CTO is focused on technology, the CIO focuses on information, and the CKO focuses on knowledge. When companies replace a CIO with a CKO, it should not only be a change of title. Rather, it should be a change of focus. Alternatively, as we shall see later in this book, the CIO might expand his or her powerbase by including the roles of the CTO and the CKO in the position of the CIO.

Applegate, McFarlan, and McKenney (1996) indicate that the CIO is becoming a member of the top management team and participates in organizational strategy development. Similarly, it has been stated that CIOs see themselves as corporate officers and general business managers. This suggests that CIOs must be politically savvy and that their high profile places them in contention for top line management jobs. The results of these studies indicate that today's CIO is more a managerially oriented executive than a technical manager. Some provide a profile of the ideal CIO as an open communicator with a business perspective, capable of leading and motivating staff, and as an innovative corporate team player. Karimi, Somers, and Gupta (2001) found that successful CIOs characterized themselves in the following way:

- I see myself to be a corporate officer
- In my organization I am seen by others as a corporate officer
- I am a general business manager, not an IT specialist
- I am a candidate for top line management positions
- I have a high profile image in the organization
- I have political as well as rational perspectives of my firm
- I spend most of my time outside the IT department focusing on the strategic and organizational aspects of IT

Business strategist is likely to be among the most significant roles that CIOs will fulfill in the digital era, according to Sambamurthy, Straub, and Watson (2001). As a business strategist, the CIO must understand and visualize the economic, competitive, and industry forces impacting the business and the factors that sustain competitive advantage. Further, the CIO must be capable of plotting strategy with executive peers, including the chief executive officer (CEO), chief operating officer (COO), and other senior business executives (Sambamurthy et al., 2001, p. 285):

Business strategist is likely to be among the most significant roles that CIOs will fulfill in the digital era. As a business strategist, the CIO must understand and visualize the economic, competitive, and industry forces impacting the business and the factors that sustain competitive advantage. Further, the CIO must be capable of plotting strategy with executive peers, including the chief executive officer (CEO), chief operating officer (COO), and other senior business executives. Not only are CIOs drawn into the mainstream of business strategy, but also their compensation is being linked with the effectiveness of competitive Internet actions in many firms. With an understanding of current and emergent information technologies and an ability to foresee breakthrough strategic opportunities as well as disruptive threats, CIOs must play a lead role in educating their business peers about how IT can raise the competitive agility of the firm. Obviously, to be effective business strategists, the CIOs must be members of an executive leadership team and part of the dominant coalition that manages the firm.

Blair (2005) cautions, however, that while there is a movement toward more of an emphasis for the CIO to understand the business, the CIO must still be the information technology champion within the organization. The CIO needs to know both the business and the information technology. Thus, while the CIOs of the future will be involved in strategy, they must understand information technology and how it can be applied to positively impact the business.

With an understanding of current and emergent information technologies and an ability to foresee breakthrough strategic opportunities as well as disruptive threats, CIOs must play a lead role in educating their business peers about how IT can raise the competitive agility of the firm. To be effective business strategists, the CIOs must be members of an executive leadership team and part of the dominant coalition that manages the firm.

Reporting Levels

Although it was originally expected that the CIO would have high levels of influence within the firm, as the definition of job responsibilities would suggest, recent surveys indicate that this may not be the case. CIOs may not actually possess strategic influence with top management, and they may lack operational and tactical influence with users. Some specific problems include higher-than-average corporate dismissal rates compared with other top executives, diminished power with belt tightening and budget cuts, high expectations of new strategic systems that CIOs may not be able to deliver, lack of secure power bases due to the fact that CIOs are viewed as outsiders by top management, and the fact that few CIOs take part in strategic planning, and many do not report to the CEO.

Over time, the number of CIOs reporting to CEOs seems to increase. In 1992, only 27% of surveyed CIOs in the U.S. reported to CEOs, while this number had increased to 43% five years later, as listed in Figure 9.11. In 2005, Gartner (2005) found that 40% of the surveyed CIOs reported to the CEO, 18% to the CFO, 21% to the COO, and 21% to other executives.

Figure 9.11. CIO reporting in the U.S. and Norway over time

Chief Information Officer (CIO) reporting to:	USA 1992	USA 1997	USA 2000	USA 2005	Norway 1997	Norway 1999	Norway 2000
Chief Executive Officer (CEO)	27 %	43 %	33 %	40 %	48 %	44 %	41 %
Chief Financial Officer (CFO)	44 %	32 %	20 %	18 %	21 %	23 %	16 %
Other top executive in the company	29 %	25 %	47 %	42 %	31 %	33 %	43 %

In Norway, the numbers in Figure 9.11 seem to indicate a stable level above 40% or maybe an insignificant decline in the fraction of CIOs reporting to the CEO. An interesting development is indirect reports moving from CFOs to other top executives.

It has to be noted that the difference in size of the business community between the USA and Norway makes the comparison weak. Also, European companies tend to have a very different executive reporting structure compared to companies based in the USA.

In a survey in the USA in 2000 cited by Schubert (2004), 33% of the CIOs reported to the CEO, while 20% reported to the CFO; 47% reported to another top executive in the company, as listed in Figure 9.11. It is interesting to note that among those CIOs not reporting to the CEO in 2000 in the U.S., most of them reported to the chief operating officer (COO).

In most countries surveyed by Gartner (2005), CIOs tended to report to an executive other than the CEO. Not so in Japan and South Korea, where more than two thirds of IT executives had the CEO for a boss. Regardless of whom they reported to, CIOs in the U.S., Canada, South Korea, and Singapore said they spent the most time interacting with other business executives.

In a Gartner (2005) CIO 100 survey in the U.S., 40% of the respondents held the title of CIO, 7% were both CIO and executive vice presidents (EVP), 16% were both CIOs and senior vice presidents (SVP), 22% were chief technology officers (CTO), and 15% had other titles such as director.

The CIO's pivotal responsibility of aligning business and technology direction presents a number of problems. Moreover, rapid changes in business and information environments have resulted in corresponding changes at the IT function helm. This role has become increasingly complex, causing many firms to look outside the organization for the right qualifications. Characteristics such as professional background, educational background, and current length of tenure have been examined in previous research. CIO problems seem to indicate that, when compared with other senior executives, CIOs do not have the authority or ability to achieve the kind of changes that were promised when the position was initially proposed. A second and possibly related explanation is that CIOs are experiencing managerial role conflicts that prevent them from meeting those expectations as originally envisioned in the CIO position.

HYBRID MANAGER

Robson (1997) has suggested that CIOs have to be hybrid managers to be successful. Hybrid managers require business literacy and technical competency plus a third dimension. This third item is the organizational astuteness that allows a manager to make business-appropriate IS use and management decisions that enhance or set business directions as well as follow them. It is fairly well recognized that *hybrid manager* is problematic, perhaps requiring in-built talent and personal qualities, but can be encouraged or discouraged. For this reason undergraduate study can generally produce only hybrid users while postgraduate and post-experience study can support the development of hybrid managers.

Hybrid users are the people involved in user-controlled computing; they combine a degree of technical competence with business literacy required to fulfill their primary role (Robson, 1997, p. 367):

This management description is not just another term to describe the users engaged in the user-controlled computing. A clear distinction exists between hybrid users and hybrid managers and this distinction is one of emphases and purposes. Hybrid users are the people involved in user-controlled computing; they combine a degree of technical competence (perhaps defined by notions such as the end-user continuum) with, of course, the business literacy required to fulfill their primary role. Hybrid managers, as opposed to managers who are hybrid users, require this business literacy and technical competency plus a third dimension. This third item is the organisational astuteness that allows a manager to make business-appropriate IS use and management decisions that enhance or set business directions as well as follow them. It is fairly well recognised that hybrid users can be trained whereas the more sophisticated development of hybrid managers is problematic, perhaps requiring inbuilt talent and personal qualities, but can be encouraged or discouraged. For this reason undergraduate study can generally produce only hybrid users whilst postgraduate and post-experience study can support the development of hybrid managers.

The notion of hybrid management is an essentially British one and a significant amount of work on the concept of hybrid management has been done. Earl provided the initial working definition of hybrid managers that has been subsequently adopted by other works. Hybrid managers are a high risk, high cost, people infrastructure that enables the organisational integration of IS and business. This integration ensures both business-consistent IS and IS-exploitative business and so hybrid managers straddle two, previously disparate, disciplines. No amount of communication, or translation bridges, between the two separate disciplines can achieve the same degree of integration. Whilst there is no theoretical reason why hybrid managers cannot be drawn from any discipline, experience seems to show that it proves easier to add IS "technical" knowledge to a base of business awareness than to inculcate IS technicians with a broader, organisational vision. The primary benefits of hybrid managers are that they create "islands" of true business/IS understanding; these islands then provide the catalyst that leads to an organisational hybridisation. Even from the earliest stages of hybridisation programmes, organisational gains in flexibility and effectiveness are reported.

Since developing hybrid managers (or any form of management development) is a costly and uncertain exercise it can be a problem notion in recessionary times. The long-term benefits, rather than short-term gains, of such a development programme can look easy to "trim" out of recession-hit budgets. And yet, paradoxically, it is precisely this type of people infrastructure that supports the cross-boundary, radical re-works typically associated with business process redesign to enable significant future cost savings. The business redesign focus of the 1990s demands the hybrid manager who is, not narrowly specialist, but capable of seeing the broad picture and the opportunities present in this total view. Hybrid managers will be critical to the survival of the IS function into the next decade. The continuing devolution of many IS areas requires a hybrid manager to manage the "new" IS and indeed even the act of assessing the relative merits of different paths to devolution, and judging what not to devolve requires the skills as defined to be of a hybrid manager.

According to Robson (1997), hybrid managers will be critical to the survival of the IT function in the future. The continuing devolution of many IS areas requires a hybrid manager to manage the new IS and indeed even the act of assessing the relative merits of different paths to devolution, and judging what not to devolve requires the skills as defined to be of a hybrid manager.

This is certainly true if the company is to succeed in knowledge management. Knowledge management requires not only business literacy and technical competency; it requires first and foremost an ability to combine the two. Sometimes information technology is (part of) the solution to knowledge management challenges, sometimes it is not. Only business literacy combined with technical competency can enable a CIO to make an optimal judgment.

Announcements of CIO Positions

What most differentiates those firms able and not able to build strong IT management skills? A very likely answer lies with the quality of IT leadership, as evidenced in the capabilities and character of the IT function's most senior executive, popularly referred to as the chief information officer (CIO). The CIO position has gained increased prominence over the past decade. Not only has the CIO role become increasingly common in all types of firms, CIOs are also beginning to contend for CEO openings, especially with technology- and information-based businesses searching for a chief executive possessing a strong combination of technology and business skills (Chatterjee, Richardson, & Zmud, 2001).

In the U.S., Chatterjee et al. (2001) conducted an investigation to study if newly created CIO positions have any impact. The study's findings provide strong support for the proposition that announcements of newly created CIO positions do indeed provoke positive reactions from the marketplace, but primarily for firms competing in industries with high levels of IT-driven transformation. Within such industries, IT is being applied in innovative ways for competitive purposes. For firms to engage in such strategic behaviors, they must first develop and then effectively exploit an appropriate set of IT capabilities. Strong executive leadership, as reflected in the CIO role, is likely to play a crucial enabling role in the effective deployment of these IT capabilities, and hence be highly valued by a firm's shareholders. Just how valuable is a newly created CIO role? One way to consider the magnitude of the stock market reaction is to compute the impact on each firm's market valuation of common equity.

Even with the trend in escalated executive salaries, the expected return from such an investment in IT capability appears quite reasonable (Chatterjee et al., 2001, p. 59):

This study's findings provide strong support for the proposition that announcements of newly created CIO positions do indeed provoke positive reactions from the marketplace, but primarily for firms competing in industries with high levels of IT-driven transformation. Within such industries, IT is being applied in innovative ways for competitive purposes. For firms to engage in such strategic behaviors, they must first develop and then effectively exploit an appropriate set of IT capabilities. Strong executive leadership, as reflected in the CIO role, is likely to play a crucial enabling role in the effective deployment of these IT capabilities, and hence be highly valued by a firm's shareholders.

Just how valuable is a newly created CIO role? One way to consider the magnitude of the stock market reaction is to compute the impact on each firm's market valuation of common equity. A conservative approach would calculate this effect through the median statistic (multiplying the median stock market reaction by the median market valuation of common equity); a less conservative approach would use the mean statistic (multiplying the mean stock market reaction by the mean market valuation of common equity). For our entire sample of firms, the net impact per firm of a newly created CIO position is in a range from \$7.5 million (median approach) to \$76 million (mean approach). If only the IT-driven transformation subgroup is considered, the net impact is in a range from \$8 million (median approach) to \$297 million (mean approach). Even with the trend in escalated executive salaries, the expected return from such an investment in IT capability appears quite reasonable!

CIO Wisdom

In the book *CIO Wisdom: Best Practices from Silicon Valley's Leading IT Experts*, Lane (2004) discusses the extended enterprise CIO, background of the CIO, and reporting relationships, as briefly described below.

The extended enterprise CIO. One of the many transformations in our business institutions during the past decade has been the growing importance of the extended enterprise. As our businesses changed, so have the information systems that support them. The changing roles of those systems and of the executives responsible for them become a map for the broader transformations in our commerce, in our culture, and in our socioeconomic relationships. By better understanding the changing role of the CIOs in these institutions, we can better understand the institutions themselves.

The extended enterprise CIO is a partner in a networked community designed to deliver systems and services with and between customers, vendors, and partners, a matrixed role in a network of associations for which some executives are suited and others are not. More and more, CIOs are the executives who are foreging alliances and ensuring alignment with critical owners of business relationships, both within and outside the corporate boundary.

Background of the CIO. The role of the CIO has become as varied as the business models in place today. Expectations of the CIO role often include the following:

- The Technology Leader: This role incorporates the various engineering and information technology functions within a common functional area.
- The Business Leader: This role takes ownership of some IT-based tools and systems to satisfy their business requirements, which require that they become more knowledgeable about these tools and systems.
- The Strategist and Mentor: This role operates in a high-tech environment.

- The Corporate Influencer: This role is directly shaped by the type of business environment he or she must support, and his or her influence is driven by the characteristics of the business, including their relative maturity levels.

Reporting relationships. The CIO who reports to a CFO is typically part of the administrative side of the business and is always expected to focus on cost reduction as a key strategy for the IT organization. The CIO who reports to the CEO possesses a higher degree of freedom and responsibility than a comparable CIO who reports to the CFO.

CIO challenges. The CIO role is inherently challenged because it is constantly beset by conflicts and problems. A CIO has to wear many hats: service provider, business enabler, business partner, strategic visionary, and company executive.

ROLES AND RESPONSIBILITIES

According to Schubert (2004), the state of the information technology leadership profession is no different from any other profession in its earliest stages: It is evolving. From an organizational context, because all companies work at a unique level of IT management maturity, the responsibilities of the person at the top of the IT organization follow those same idiosyncratic centralization cycles and respond to influences that the prevailing business climate has from the standpoint of overall organizational maturity. Amidst all this flux, CIOs can count on one consistency from organization to organization at all levels of IT maturity: the horizontal reach of and expectations put on the CIO are significantly greater than they were 10 years ago. Whether the CIO reports to the chief executive officer (CEO), the CIO is expected to be more businessperson than technologist; he or she is expected to lead and manage directly, by means of influence, or through a combination of both. Within this same context of greater horizontal reach, the organization may or may not expect the CIO to perform as a key member of the senior executive team directly participating in the development of key company strategies, tactics, and initiatives. Depending on the company, the culture, and the CEO in particular, the CIO either holds a key executive position with all its obligate leadership responsibilities or works as the head manager of the company's IT utility.

In the context of the significant economic and technological growth periods and significant economic downturns, more enlightened senior executive teams look to the CIO in times of growth to help them maximize the opportunities for the company and its employees to benefit from that growth: to gain significant competitive advantage. Similarly, those same enlightened senior executive teams look to the CIO in times of downturn to help them make the most of what they have, find ways to leverage any advantage against the competition, provide the technology to get the greatest productivity from their workforce, and to find ways to get more for less throughout the company (Schubert, 2004).

Looking at the CIO in the context of organizational authority, it is interesting to look at the range of the CIO reporting responsibilities. In a survey cited in Schubert (2004), 26% of 500 of the Fortune 1000 had CIOs who reported to the CEO, chairperson, or president, with the remainder reporting to lower-level executives. In the same survey, 30% of the 100 CIOs in the top-ranked companies reported directly to the highest executive.

Focus and prioritization always challenge people who work in senior executive positions, especially the CIO. By the very nature of the job, he or she has a strategic as well as a tactical role. Although the CIO's role is supposed to be primarily strategic, CIOs are forever associated with the IT group. Consequently, the CIO must be prepared to handle any number of tactical issues, and even projects, whether the position involves direct IT group management responsibilities. As such, the CIO is continually challenged to stay focused on achieving strategic objectives while prioritizing key personal work activities and IT organizational work activities to meet enabling commitments to peers and partners (Schubert, 2004).

Specifically, the CIO works in partnership with peers to ensure that the company's organizational strategies are translated into actionable plans that the IT team can execute. The CIO demonstrates an enabling partnership relationship by visibly aligning and prioritizing IT resources with commitments made to peers (Schubert, 2004).

A special challenge might emerge for the current CIO when the new CEO has IT background. Nortel Networks Corp. named former Motorola Inc. executive Mike Zafirovski president and CEO in 2005. Before he started his new job, Zafirovski announced at a press conference that he plans to build support systems for customers and have a sharper focus on corporate IT (Computerworld, 2005a, 2005b).

According to Gartner (2005), CIOs face increasing demands on their time and attention. Time robs CIOs of management capacity. CIOs can expand their management capacity by leveraging an "office of the CIO." CIOs have big jobs with diverse business, technical, and organizational responsibilities. The complex issues surrounding these responsibilities require coordination and thought to resolve properly. The result is often long days, and sometimes even longer nights for the CIO. CIOs need a way to get more management capacity without increasing overhead and bureaucracy. Making time involves extending the management capacity of the CIO and the IS leadership team. Leading CIOs create an office of the CIO in response to these challenges.

The office of the CIO provides an organizational structure for extending management capacity without building overhead and bureaucracy. An office of the CIO leverages management capacity and builds the next generation of leaders in the IS organization. The office of the CIO is an organizational structure for the CIO, IS, and the business. CIOs define the scope and roles of the office to fit their needs. CIOs use the office to strengthen IS. Roles within an office of the CIO reflect its enterprise wide focus and specialized position. Gartner suggests four alternative office models:

1. A semiformal office of the CIO provides a flexible tool for responding to IT issues. TRW Automotive's semiformal office is integrated into the IS leadership.
2. A collaborative office of the CIO provides agility to address issues and resources to follow them through.
3. A coordinating office of the CIO connects IS across business units. Tyco Fire & Security uses the office to help run IS like a business.
4. A directional office of the CIO extends the CIO's leadership reach. Landsbond der Christelijke Mutualiteiten uses the office to direct IS and business change.

The office of the CIO is an enhancement to existing management and governance structures. CIOs choose a model most relevant to business needs, thereby avoiding to create an administrative function that would be seen as management overhead or bureaucracy (Gartner, 2005).

LEADERSHIP BEHAVIOR

Gartner (2005) has studied the changing role of the CIO. The study showed that critical issues for IT leaders include:

- Driving infrastructure management at a time when industries are colliding and technology is becoming a commodity
- Innovating at a time when corporate intellect appears to be the only thing that can be differentiated
- Prioritizing at a time when market opportunities are temporary and fleeting
- Increasing the perception of information about transactions becomes more important than the transactions themselves

Leaders have to lead transforming while performing. Leaders are required to bridge the gap between moving toward a bright new future and ensuring required performance levels. The process requires CEO competencies in CIOs. Based on talents, skills, supporting processes, and desire to get the right things done right, the CIO will develop vision, plan, and achieve current performance and future transformation. In doing so, the CIO will demonstrate a leadership behavior characterized by (Gartner, 2005):

- **Researching.** The ability to quickly gather information from a broad variety of sources, analyze it, and synthesize a method or model that solves a problem or various problems in a creative or innovative manner.
- **Interviewing.** The ability to formulate questions used in conversation to elicit facts or statements from another individual, and a willingness to listen to what the individual has to say.
- **Engineering.** The ability to apply principles of logic, science, and mathematics to the understanding of systems and processes to improve them.
- **Lecturing.** The ability to expound on an important subject delivered before audience members to inform/instruct them and convince or persuade them to further action.
- **Arbitrating.** The ability to reconcile the differences in components of networked resources or assets to achieve a common objective.
- **Coaching.** The ability and willingness to transfer knowledge about a subject to individuals, enabling them to succeed at a given task, and (if necessary) to identify their weaknesses and aid them in correcting those weaknesses.
- **Organizing.** The ability to put things together in an orderly, functioning, and structured whole.

Gartner (2005) argues that what is required in CIO leadership is intellect, passion, and courage. The convergence of technology and business trends will require business and technology intellect. Passion is needed to create a common and cohesive vision. Courage is needed to take personal and professional risk, to make quick decisions in light of ambiguity, to be true to core values and the necessary values of future organization, and to recognize this is not an altruistic endeavor.

It is sometimes argued that there are differences in leadership behavior between public sector CIOs and private sector CIOs. Private sector leadership is generally regarded as superior to that of the public sector, and efforts are often made to transfer private sector leadership strategies to the public sector (Dargie, 1998). However, it is not clear that the contexts are sufficiently similar. Political scientists view the political nature of public management as a unique social context where the citizens and elected officials, not the individual executive, are the principal actors. This puts the public sector CIO in the role of balancing between the series of tensions that are intrinsic to the duality of the public domain.

Existing studies predict more formalized contact and external contact for public sector managers. In a survey by Dargie (1998), it was found that public sector chief executives spent nearly three quarters of their time in meetings, and most meetings are also planned. Contact is formalized. Chief executives meet groups rather than individuals. They do not work alone. Work is office based, and the public CIO meets predominantly contacts from within his or her own organization. Chief executives in the public sector spend most time in review sessions, with less time on strategy. Review describes the majority of meetings in which the public chief executive is involved: issue based, engendered, multipurpose, lengthy, and internal (Dargie, 1998).

In a later study, Dargie (2000) draws on case studies of chief executives from the public, private, and voluntary sectors, which looked at what chief executives do and how their role relates to the context in which they work. The private sector chief executives did not work with groups nor were they involved in decision-making committees; they preferred to meet people on a one-to-one basis. The voluntary sector chief executives acted in a supportive role for trustees, members, and volunteers.

CIO'S INFLUENCE BEHAVIOR

In their roles as senior managers, CIOs are often responsible for the initiation and implementation of information systems that are vital to the success, and even survival of the firm. In doing so, CIOs must exercise influence successfully in order to attain these objectives (Enns, Huff, & Golden, 2003a).

The potential for the CIO, the company's senior information systems executive, to play a critical role in the strategy and change process of firms is arguably greater today than ever before. CIOs spend much of their time attempting to convince other top managers to commit to strategic IS initiatives, share in a vision for IS, and allocate resources to IS projects.

CIO Lateral Influence Behaviors

In order to develop and bring to fruition strategic information systems projects, chief information officers must be able to effectively influence their peers. Enns, Huff, and Higgins' (2003b) study examined the relationship between CIO influence behaviors and the successfulness of influence outcomes, and their research is presented in the following.

Since no idea is intrinsically strategic or important, the give-and-take of senior managers about what matters largely determines which initiatives are implemented. Within the give-and-take context, a critical part of the CIO's strategic role is to provide thought leadership to other top executives, making them aware of the potential for information systems to support and enhance the strategy of the firm. One way CIOs do this is to effect proactive influence behaviors to convince other top managers to allocate attention and resources to strategic information systems projects.

Indeed, CIOs have an inherent responsibility to do so. A CIO's hesitance to exert influence may increase the risks that the agenda for IS will be shaped by other, less knowledgeable sources.

Effective organizations recognize that having line managers take ownership of critical IS projects increases the likelihood of appropriate IS deployment and organization success. If a CIO wants a strategic application proposal implemented, he or she requires the commitment of the top management team, without which the project would stand a lesser chance of success. Similarly, the practitioner literature suggests that effective CIOs must skillfully apply their powers of influence to encourage other functional heads to become partners with them and embrace ownership of these initiatives.

In the past, when most CIOs were not part of the top management team, they often needed to apply different forms of upward influence to convince top management to seriously consider strategic information systems projects, with varying degrees of success. More recently, as they have gained acceptance on their firms' top management teams, CIOS require skills at applying lateral influence, in order to convince their peers in other functional areas to commit to IS initiatives. There is evidence that CIOs may be less effective than their executive counterparts in proactively exerting peer-level influence. For example, CIOs may attempt to use "hard" tactics such as edicts, which do not work as well as "softer" tactics like persuasion and participation.

In order to clarify the CIO-peer influence context, it is important to distinguish between influence and authority. Authority can be viewed as the legitimate exercise of decision-making that affects the behavior of individuals. Thus, subordinates agree without question to the decisions of a superior and are willing to set aside any judgments about the suitability of a superior's request or behave as if they agreed with the superior. Similarly, authority can be viewed as designated across hierarchical management positions.

It is also commonly recognized that a superior relies on advice or information from others, including subordinates. This advice or information comprises influence. Thus, a person exerts influence by offering information, providing advice, persuading, and the like. Importantly, in contrast with authority that flows downward, influence can be multidirectional. Thus, individuals have the capacity to influence superiors or colleagues. The dispersion of influence permits actors from all levels in the organization to make their expertise felt in specific decision areas. The distinction between authority and influence is important in situations where CIOs do not possess formal authority. Specifically, CIOs must rely primarily on influence to affect the thinking and behavior of their peers.

Good working relationships with peers are a necessary condition for the success of IT executives. The CIO requires integrity and interpersonal skills in order to develop these important relationships. These effective working relationships set the stage for CIOs to successfully approach peers in a "personal informal" style, to make causal contact with peers to discuss these initiatives and build support before a formal proposal is discussed. CIO influence behaviors comprise an important part of the CIO-peer communications that lead to the development of shared vision and IS project success.

Coalition and consultation tactics have been effectively used to convince executives of the potential strategic impact of IS, to gain acceptance of other executives, to achieve a shared vision of IS's role in the organization, and to create a positive impression of the IS department. Rational persuasion has been used to identify new uses of IT, create a positive view of IS, and to convince top managers of the need for greater central IT coordination. Also, CIO tactics used to overcome resistance to IS implementation include bargaining with IS resources (i.e., exchange), and co-opting opposition (i.e., consultation).

Influence tactics can be studied in terms of an agent (i.e., initiator) influencing attempt trying to gain something from the target (i.e., recipient). Here are some examples of such influence behaviors:

- **Rational Persuasion.** The agent uses logical arguments and factual evidence to persuade the target that a proposal or request is viable and likely to result in the attainment of task objectives.
- **Consultation.** The agent seeks target participation in planning a strategy, activity, or change for which target support and assistance are desired, or is willing to modify a proposal to deal with target concerns and suggestions.
- **Ingratiation.** The agent uses praise, flattery, friendly behavior, or helpful behavior to get the target in a good mood or to think favorably of him or her when asking for something.
- **Personal Appeals.** The agent appeals to target feelings of loyalty and friendship toward him or her when asking for something.
- **Exchange.** The agent offers an exchange of favors, indicates willingness to reciprocate at a later time, or promises a share of the benefits if the target helps accomplish a task.
- **Coalition Tactics.** The agent seeks the aid of others to persuade the target to do something, or uses the support of others as a reason for the target to agree also.
- **Pressure.** The agent uses demands, threats, frequent checking, or persistent reminders to influence the target to do what he or she wants.

Influence behaviors, and their effectiveness, vary depending on whether the target is a subordinate, peer, or superior. For instance, rational persuasion is often linked with effective upward influence, while pressure behaviors are more commonly associated with downward influence and are most effective under these conditions.

Influence leads to a number of possible outcomes. Influence outcome might include commitment, compliance, and resistance. Commitment is evident when the target displays strong enthusiasm and special effort beyond what is expected. Compliance occurs when the target completes the request but is apathetic and makes minimal effort. Resistance is displayed when the target avoids performing the requested actions by arguing, delaying, and so forth.

Socialization Theory

Enns et al. (2003a) framed their analysis of CIO influence behavior around socialization theory, and the following description is adopted from their work. Socialization, broadly speaking, is the process by which an individual learns and adopts the norms, value systems, and behavior patterns of a group. For example, new organizational members learn how to act in their different surroundings by observation of and interaction with long-term members. Socialization is also formally accomplished via orientation programs, for example. Of particular importance are behaviors and norms that are learned through early organizational experiences, such as a first job or university experience, since they lead to relatively stable patterns of behavior. Thus, socialization theorists contend that a newly promoted manager will continue to engage in behaviors that were acceptable and reinforced in the manager's prior work environment. This is consistent with the concepts of manifest and latent roles. Manifest roles focus on the way group norms produce prescribed similarities in the behavior of those in equivalent roles. Latent roles are relatively stable and are acquired via different degrees of commitment to professional skills, reference group orientations, and loyalty to the organization.

The concept of latent roles suggests that people playing different manifest roles may be performing similar latent roles and conversely, that those performing the same manifest role may be playing different latent roles. The concept of latent role may then aid in accounting for some of the differences (in behavior or belief) among those in the same manifest role.

The concept of latent roles is important in understanding CIOs since latent roles may impact the behavior of CIOs who have greater technical backgrounds. Despite the fact that they function in the manifest role of the CIO, with expectations that they behave in prescribed ways, CIOs may continue to act out their latent role, and behave more like their technologist colleagues.

Socialization theory also suggests that the work and educational experience of individuals has a bearing on their use of influence behaviors. It has been argued that individuals with greater technical backgrounds, in contrast to those who have limited technical backgrounds, tend to have different experiences that affect their use of influence behaviors. Technically oriented people, according to advocates of this perspective, tend to deal with objects and things, are more task focused, and are less relationship centered. In addition, the socialization of technically trained individuals differs from that of nontechnically trained managers. For instance, technically oriented individuals are often focused on contributions to their profession, as opposed to their organizations.

A survey instrument was developed by Enns et al. (2003a), and the survey targeted CIOs working in U.S. and Canadian companies. Surprisingly, survey results provided no support for stereotypical accounts of CIOs or socialization theory as applied to CIOs.

WORK EXPERIENCE

According to McCall (2004), the primary source of learning to lead, to the extent that leadership can be learned, is experience. He argues that the role played by training and other formal programs is relatively modest in comparison to other kinds of experiences. The implication of this belief is rather profound, because it suggests that experiences (mostly assignments) rather than programs should form the core of executive development.

Work experience of CIOs can be captured using three measures: quantitative, qualitative, and interaction (Dawson & Watson, 2005). Quantitative measures are time-based and amount measures. Time-based measures are the traditional measurement of the length of time spent work in a task, job, or organization and are operational in terms of tenure. Amount measures are the number of times that a task has been performed and reflect the opportunity to practice and perfect the task. However, quantitative measures provide little insight into the value of experience since learning from experience is not automatic. Some people come away with nothing, the wrong lessons, or only some of what they might have learned (McCall, 2004).

The second measure is qualitative. Work experiences are associated with learning when they challenge the individual, and challenge is mostly likely to occur when there is a lack of congruence between the individual's knowledge, skills, and abilities and the demands of the assignment. Two individuals with equal job, organizational, and position tenure can vary widely in the amount of challenges encountered in their work experience and resulting job performance. Qualitative measures capture this challenge and allow a more full analysis of its value of the work experience. They best represent by the specific nature of work situations that contribute to the richness of the experience construct, such as the variety and breadth of tasks and responsibilities performed in a job, the types of challenges encountered in an assignment, or the complexity of the task. Qualitative measures may be best represented by the specific nature of work situations that contribute to the richness of the experience construct, such as the variety and breadth of tasks and responsibilities performed in the job, the types of challenges encountered in an assignment, or the complexity of a task (Tesluk & Jacobs, 1998). Qualitative measures might include: (1) unfamiliar responsibilities, (2) new direction, (3) inherited problems, (4) problems with employees, (5) high stakes, (6) scope and scale, (7) external pressure, (8) influence without authority, (9) work across cultures, and (10) work group diversity (Dawson & Watson, 2005).

The third measure is the interaction between the qualitative and quantitative dimensions and includes the experience's density, placement within the career, and criticality of the work experience. Density is intended to capture the intensity of experiences (Tesluk & Jacobs, 1998). High-density experiences have a greater number of challenges within a short time period and are associated with the developmental punch of the experience. They are particularly important because they have a disproportional influence on learning and the individual's career trajectory. They are career-making assignments (Quinones, Ford, & Teachout, 1995).

According to Quinones et al. (1995), work experience refers to events that are experienced by an individual that relate to the performance of some job. They created a framework specifying two dimensions along which work experience measures can vary. The dimensions of measurement mode (amount, time, and type) and level of specificity (task, job, organizational) formed nine separate categories of measures of work experience, as illustrated in Figure 9.12.

When applying the framework in Figure 9.12 to CIO experience, it can be argued that the closer positions and tasks match positions and tasks of a top executive, the more relevant the CIO is as a candidate for the CEO position. For example, an indication of job complexity might be the kinds of people that are involved in the same issues as the CIO.

According to Dawson and Watson (2005), the goal of work experience is to build the knowledge necessary to be successful. This is often referred to as tacit knowledge (Hed-

Figure 9.12. Framework of work experience measures (adapted from Quinones et al., 1995)

	Amount	**Time**	**Type**
Organization	Number of organizations	Organizational tenure	Organization maturity
Position	Number of tasks	Job tenure	Job complexity
Task	Number of times performing a task	Time on task	Task difficulty

Figure 9.13. Work experience influences CIO effectiveness through tacit knowledge (adapted from Dawson & Watson, 2005)

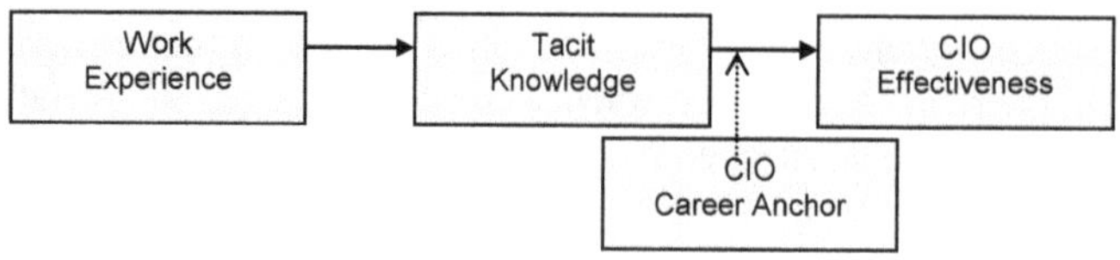

lund et al., 2003). Tacit knowledge is a factor of practical intelligence and is expressed in everyday phrases such as common sense. Tacit knowledge results from understanding work experiences and represents an individual's ability to learn from everyday problems.

Dawson and Watson (2005) suggest a causal relationship between work experience and tacit knowledge, and between tacit knowledge and CIO effectiveness, as illustrated in Figure 9.13. It is assumed that quantitative measures of work experience, qualitative measures of work experience, as well as interaction measures of work experience will all be correlated with a CIO's tacit knowledge. Furthermore, a CIO's tacit business knowledge, tacit IS knowledge, tacit political knowledge, tacit power knowledge, and tacit operations knowledge will all be correlated with CIO effectiveness.

Most CIO leadership studies use a role-based perspective. Dawson and Watson (2005) present six distinct CIO roles:

1. *IT educator* concerned with ensuring that the human foundations for innovation are in place. In this role the CIO is a champion for computer literacy.
2. *IT contract oversight* concerned with ensuring that strategic partnerships with external vendors are optimized. In this role the CIO negotiates and accomplishes contracts.
3. *IT support/utility provider* focuses on classic IT support ensuring that the IT unit is operationally efficient and effective. In this role the CIO ensures that the IT unit is responsive to customer needs.
4. *Integrator* concerned with developing value-added integration among and between business units as well as with external partners. In this role the CIO directs efforts to build an integrated delivery system.
5. *Informaticist/IT strategist* concerned with developing sound data management and IT plans and processes. In this role the CIO ensures that organizational data is secure and confidential.
6. *Business partner/strategist* concerned with issues relating to the greater organization outside of the IT unit. In this role the CIO helps to shape the organization's overall mission and vision.

CIO career anchor might have a moderating effect on the relationship between tacit knowledge and CIO effectiveness, as illustrated in Figure 9.13. Career anchor is a concept focusing on the pattern of self-perceived talents, motives, and values, which serve to guide, constrain, stabilize, and integrate a CIO's career. According to Feldman and Bolino (1996), the career anchor concept suggests that individuals develop "careers within careers" after their true abilities, needs, and values become crystallized through a variety of real-world work experiences. Moreover, once formed, these stable identities (career anchors) have significant consequences for individuals' career satisfaction and job stability.

The career anchor concept provides four key contributions. First, it proposes that a stable career identity evolves through concrete real world work experiences. Second, it highlights the variety of careers within an occupation. Third, the differences within these career tracks can be as distinct as between those people in entirely different occupations. Finally, as an individual makes choices about jobs, the career anchor functions as a constraining force (Dawson & Watson, 2005).

THE NEW CIO LEADER

According to Broadbent and Kitzis (2005), CIOs are at a crossroads and must choose for themselves which path to follow: to become new CIO leaders or chief technology mechanics. Simply maintaining status is impossible, since focusing on managing request queues, keeping as large an IS organization as possible, being wowed by emerging technology, and operating IS divorced from business goals and specific business benefits is itself a choice to follow the path to enterprise irrelevance.

For those CIOs who aspire to more, to being integral parts of their enterprise leadership team, to having a valued and respected seat at the enterprise strategy table, there is an alternative. This alternative is built on the 10 areas of focus:

1. Understand the fundamentals of your environment
2. Create your vision
3. Shape expectations for an IT-enabled enterprise
4. Inform expectations for an IT-enabled enterprise
5. Create clear and appropriate IT governance
6. Weave business and IT strategies together
7. Build a new IS organization
8. Develop a high-performing IS team
9. Manage enterprise and IT risks
10. Communicate your performance

The McKinsey consulting firm argues that the next-generation CIO must step up to the new responsibilities of an IT leader (Mark & Monnoyer, 2004). CIOs must delegate or shed some operational duties and spend more time helping business leaders identify and use technologies that will help companies innovate. Next-generation CIOs will (i) ensure that IT is efficient and then make the transition to effectiveness, (ii) reengineer relationships with business leaders, and (iii) invest in a business committee with technology oversight. A few leading companies have disbanded their technology committees, typically staffed by business managers and IT staff, and are asking senior-executive committees to take responsibility for IT-investment decisions.

According to Gartner (2005), the keys to being a successful CIO are the same around the world. Like CIOs in the U.S., IT executives in Singapore, Sweden, and Germany cite good communication skills, ability to think strategically, and understanding business processes and operations as the skills that are most pivotal for success. Swedish CIOs add "being a good leader" to their list. Like CIOs in the U.S. and Germany, IT executives in Southeast

Asia give strategic planning a high priority. But getting it done is less of a struggle for Southeast Asians. They rank finding time for strategic thinking and planning near the bottom in a list of 10 barriers to their effectiveness.

CIOs in Canada surveyed by Gartner (2005) spent the bulk of their time meeting with their company's executives and business partners. Their U.S. counterparts said they spend a good portion of their time with company executives and IT providers.

To be successful, most of the respondents (78%) in the survey by Gartner (2005) responded that aggressive leadership is most important. Also, good communication of goals throughout the organization (59%) and agility (59%) are important CIO skills.

Thompson (2005, p. 59), himself a CIO at the Shaw Group, noted the following characteristics of a successful CIO:

To be a successful CIO, you have to be a businessperson first, not an IT person. You have to sit amongst your peers at the executive committee level and stand toe to toe with them on business issues and talk the business, and walk your talk. That's the first characteristic that CIOs need to have—an understanding of the business and being able to make sure that you can communicate at the executive level.

The second thing is you need to understand good talent, and be able to hire good people and to surround yourself with good talent... . The third characteristic is to walk amongst the people. You can't expect your staff to do things you're not willing to do, to go that extra mile.

CIO BACKGROUNDS

Enns et al. (2003a) studied the extent of technical background that CIOs have. Technical background can be conceptualized in a variety of ways, normally centering on the length and type of a CIO's education and work experience. In the study, CIO technical background was measured via four survey items about the technical component of the individual's work experience and formal education. Respondents in the survey rated thier previous education, overall work history, and detailed work history on a scale (1 = nontechnical, 7 = highly technical). The mean score of these ratings was used to produce an overall CIO technical score. Then, out of 69 responses, 42 CIOs were classified as technical, while 27 CIOs were classified as nontechnical.

In another survey by CIO Research Reports (2003) on work experience, survey respondents reported that they have been the CIO or have held an equivalent head of IT title for an average of four years and nine months. When asked how long they have been in their current job, the average length of time was four years.

In the same survey, 82% of the IT heads surveyed listed IT as a functional area that they worked in previously and that had an impact on their career path to CIO. Other areas most frequently listed included consulting (34%), administration (25%), engineering (20%), customer service (17%), and research and development (17%). Eighty-seven percent of the IT heads in the survey were male and 13% were female.

On average, CIOs earned in 2003 a total annual compensation, including base salary, bonus, and stock options, of $186,000. The highest paying industries for CIOs were insurance, where the average compensation was $223,000, followed by finance ($220,000) and computer-related business ($209,000). CIOs in manufacturing earned an average of $176,000 annually while CIOs in education and government (federal, state, and local) earned the lowest compensation at $126,000 and $120,000, respectively (CIO Research Reports, 2003).

THE CEO-CIO RELATIONSHIP

Building strong social networks and coalitions within a firm is an essential task for those who aspire to be the CEO. When they are promoted to a firm's CEO position, inside successors not only have the approval of outside directors, but also have support within the top management group (Shen & Cannella, 2002). For a CIO who aspires to become the next CEO, he or she needs to manage relationships, develop coalitions, and understand power dynamics in top management.

The quality of the CEO-CIO relationship influences the CIO's effectiveness and success as a business leader, and the value gained from information technology. CEOs are demanding and not always clear about their expectations. That can create a situation where their views are radically different from the CIO's perceptions, a situation fraught with risk for both. CEOs and CIOs often see the relationship between business and information differently. CIOs tend to view their role and contribution optimistically. CEOs, by contrast, are more critical (Gartner, 2005).

The difference between how the CEO views the CEO-CIO relationship, and how the CIO views this relationship creates the potential for a dangerous disconnect, limiting the value generated by information technology and the power of the executive team. Understanding the CEO's expectations and view of the CIO helps create the right relationship based on personal style and enterprise need.

In the survey conducted by Gartner (2005), CIOs believed they are trusted and respected business leaders, and to a great extent they are right. But few CEOs share the same unqualified view. This is partly because CEOs have a broad span of control, with IT just one of many priorities. It is also because of CIOs' technology and operations focus, which does not always allow them to show traditional business leadership styles and behaviors.

In the survey by Gartner (2005), responding CEOs found that healthy relationships with other executives (CXOs) are very important for the CIO. Furthermore, the CIO must oversee that IT objectives are aligned with the CEOs objectives and overall business strategy. Survey results indicate that CIOs and CEOs are in agreement on the most important skills for the CIO's success. They stress strategic thinking and planning, and understanding business processes and operations.

CEOs hire CIOs to fit with enterprise needs and the changing context. CIOs must understand the type of relationship they are in and the actions required to reach the right relationship type. Four relationship types describe how CIOs relate to CEOs: at-risk, transactional, partnering, and trusted-ally. These relationships are not set in stone. Sudden events, a change of CEO or a strategic IT initiative, can change the balance. And if both CEO and CIO are open to the possibility, they can change the relationship.

The first step for the CIO is to understand where his or her relationship is now, through self-assessment and dialog with the CEO. Then the CIO uses that information to decide the next step, and then move one step at a time, cementing credibility and the enterprise's appetite for change at each level.

According to Gartner (2005), CIO success stems from a four-step cycle—leading, shaping demand, setting expectations, and delivering. The CIO is recommended to build an action plan based on this cycle, tailored to personal relationship type. The plan might have tangible, time-bounded goals. Embedded in the plan might be six powerful and proven practices: Get coaching and mentoring, make time for relationship building, take on non-IT responsibilities, build the strength of deputies, educate personally, and educate shareholders. This will increase the chances of achieving the right CEO-CIO relationship.

Gartner (2005) has the following note to CEOs:

The age of the operational CIO is almost over

Your relationship with your CIO matters. The CIO can be a powerful and positive member of your executive team. A recent study by Burson and Marsteller shows that 5 percent of Fortune Global 500 companies have CIO skills on their board. And these companies' stocks have outperformed the industry index by 6.4 percent per year since the CIO-skilled member was elected.

You set the tone of the relationship with your CIO. Successful CEOs are getting more from IT by building their CIO relationship. Getting CIO input into enterprise strategy has proved much more powerful than getting the CIO to execute a fixed strategy.

This trend is increasing, not decreasing, as enterprises become more reliant on IT to implement efficient processes and to drive sources of competitive advantage.

For an enterprise to be effective in using IT to drive innovation and growth, a good working relationship between the CEO and CIO is crucial. But there is still a lot of misunderstanding and suspicion among CEOs of CIOs and IT. To succeed, CIOs need to understand the CEO's perspective on them, and on IT's role in the enterprise.

SUMMARY

Judicious resource allocation to strategic programs and initiatives is the key to successful strategy execution. A sound IT governance lead by a disciplined CIO is a necessary condition for successful IT strategy execution. IT governance defines the firm's decision rights and accountability framework to encourage the desirable behaviors in the management and use of IT (Weill & Ross, 2004). Distinct from IT management which focuses on effective management of IT operations to deliver quality IT services, IT governance focuses on performing and transforming IT to meet present and future demands of the business and external customers (Grembergen et al., 2004). IT governance includes enterprise architecture governance and IT portfolio management governance and outsourcing governance. Research has shown that IT governance has enabled top-performing firms to generate superior returns on their IT investments (Weill & Ross, 2004). Outsourcing governance model consists of four elements: contracts, principles, resources, and activities. Governance issues for each element evolve with outsourcing life cycle which comprises three stages: formation, operation, and outcome. For instance, contracts are concerned with transactions at the formation stage but evolve to relationships and partnerships at the outcome stage.

The eleven outsourcing theories can also help both the client company and the outsource vendor analyze how to be successful in the relationship (Gottschalk & Solli-Sæther, 2006). IT governance demands strong IT leadership to ensure success. From an IT governance standpoint, CIO plays an astute resource allocator and entrepreneurial roles (Useem & Harder, 2000). Both roles require strong understanding of business and competitive markets to excel. Strong leadership also renders governance process more efficient and effective. From an outsourcing standpoint, CIO needs to be skilled in strategic thinking, deal making, partnership governing, and managing change (Useem & Harder, 2000). In hypercompetitive markets, the "new" CIO must excel in both business and technology capabilities, as well as being organizationally (some say politically) savvy. These capabilities allow the CIO to lead IT organizations towards a high level of maturity in all core practices: business/IT strategic alignment, strategic integration, enterprise architecture, IT portfolio management, service management, knowledge management, and business innovation. When IT organization becomes a highly recognized key contributor to business success, CIO's leadership standing will be such that business will be seeking his/her input for future growth strategy (Broadbent & Kitzis, 2005). Influencing, shaping business expectations, conceiving, and implementing business model innovation may become the new CIO's core focus. It may even pave the way for possible growth into becoming a future CEO!

REFERENCES

Applegate, L. M., McFarlan, F. W., & McKenney, J. L. (1996). *Corporate information systems management* (4th ed). Irwin.

Austin, R. D. (2001). The effects of time pressure on quality in software development: An agency model. *Information Systems Research, 12*(2), 195-207.

Benjamin, R. I., Dickinson, C., & Rockart, J. F. (1985). Changing role of the corporate information systems officer. *MIS Quarterly, 9*(3), 177-197.

Blair, R. (2005). The future of CIOs. *Health Management Technology, 26*(2), 58-59.

Blois, K. (2002). Business to business exchanges: A rich descriptive apparatus derived from MacNeil's and Menger's analysis. *Journal of Management Studies, 39*(4), 523-551.

Broadbent, M., & Kitzis, E. (2005). *The new CIO leader: Setting the agenda and delivering results.* Cambridge, MA: Harvard Business School Press.

Cannon, J. P., Achrol, R. S., & Gundlach, G. T. (2000). Contracts, norms, and plural form governance. *Journal of the Academy of Marketing Science, 28*(2), 180-194.

Cannon, J. P., & Homburg, C. (2001). Buyer-supplier relationships and customer firm costs. *Journal of Marketing, 65*, 29-43.

Cernat, L. (2004). The emerging European corporate governance model: Anglo-Saxon, continental, or still the century of diversity? *Journal of European Public Policy, 11*(1), 147-166.

Chatterjee, D., Richardson, V. J., & Zmud, R. W. (2001). Examining the shareholder wealth effects of announcements of newly created CIO positions. *MIS Quarterly, 25*(1), 43-70.

CIO Research Reports. (2003). *The state of the CIO 2003.* Retrieved September 6, 2008, from www.cio.com

Computerworld. (2005a, January). *Premier 100 IT leaders 2005*. Retrieved September 6, 2008, from www.computerworld.com

Computerworld. (2005b, October). *Nortel hires CEO*. Retrieved September 6, 2008, from www.computerworld.com

Dargie, C. (1998). The role of public sector chief executives. *Public Administration, 76*, 161-177.

Dargie, C. (2000, July-September). Observing chief executives: Analysing behaviour to explore cross-sectoral differences. *Public Money & Management*, pp. 39-44.

Dawson, G., & Watson, R. (2005). *An empirical analysis of the career paths of effective CIOs* (Working Paper). University of Georgia.

Earl, M. J., & Feeny, D. F. (1994). Is your CIO adding value? *Sloan Management Review, 35*(3), 11-20.

Enns, H. G., Huff, S. L., & Golden, B. R. (2003a). CIO influence behaviors: The impact of technical background. *Information & Management, 40*, 467-485.

Enns, H. G., Huff, S. L., & Higgins, C. A. (2003b). CIO lateral influence behaviors: Gaining peers' commitment to strategic information systems. *MIS Quarterly, 27*(1), 155-176.

Gartner. (2005). The changing role of the CIO: The state of the CIO around the world. Retrieved September 6, 2008, from www.gartner.com

Gottschalk, P., & Solli-Sæther, H. (2006). *Managing successful IT outsourcing relationships*. Hershey, PA: Idea Group Publishing.

Grembergen, W. V., Haes, S. D., & Guldentops, E. (2004). Structures, processes and relational mechanisms for IT governance. In W. V. Grembergen (Ed.), *Strategies for information technology governance* (pp. 1-36). Hershey, PA: Idea Group Publishing.

Grover, V., Jeong, S. R., Kettinger, W. J., & Lee, C. C. (1993). The chief information officer: A study of managerial roles. *Journal of Management Information Systems, 10*(2), 107-130.

IT Governance Institute. (2004). IT governance global status report. Retrieved September 6, 2008, from www.itgi.org

Kaarst-Brown, M. (2005). Understanding an organization's view of the CIO: The role of assumptions about IT. *MIS Quarterly Executive, 4*(2), 287-301.

Karimi, J., Somers, T. M., & Gupta, Y. P. (2001). Impact of information technology management practices on customer service. *Journal of Management Information Systems, 17*(4), 125-158.

Kolbasuk, M. (2005). CIOs get respect. *Insurance and Technology*, 30 (9), 18.

Lane, D. (2004). *CIO wisdom: Best practices from Silicon Valley's leading IT experts*. Upper Saddle River, NJ: Prentice Hall.

Mark, D., & Monnoyer, E. (2004, July). Next-generation CIOs. *McKinsey on IT*.

McCall, M. W. (2004). Leadership development through experience. *Academy of Management Executive, 18*(3), 127-130.

Monnoyer, E., & Willmott, P. (2005, August). What IT leaders do. *McKinsey Quarterly*. Retrieved September 6, 2008, from www.mckinseyquarterly

Peterson, R. R. (2004). Integration strategies and tactics for information technology governance. In

W. V. Grembergen (Ed.), *Strategies for information technology governance* (pp. 37-80). Hershey, PA: Idea Group Publishing.

Quinones, M. A., Ford, J. K., & Teachout, M. S. (1995). The relationship between work experience and job performance: A conceptual and meta-analytic review. *Personnel Psychology, 48*, 887-910.

Robson, W. (1997). *Strategic management and information systems* (2nd ed). Prentice Hall.

Sambamurthy, V., Straub, D. W., & Watson, R. T. (2001). Managing IT in the digital era. In G.W. Dickson & G. DeSanctis (Eds.), *Information technology and the future enterprise: New models for managers* (pp. 282-305). Prentice Hall.

Schubert, K. D. (2004). *CIO survival guide: The roles and responsibilities of the chief information officer*. Hoboken, NJ: John Wiley & Sons.

Shen, W., & Cannella, A. A. (2002). Power dynamics within top management and their impacts on CEO dismissal followed by inside succession. *Academy of Management Journal, 45*(6), 1195-1206.

Tesluk, P. E., & Jacobs, R. R. (1998). Toward an integrated model of work experience. *Personnel Psychology, 51*, 321-355.

Thompson, P. (2005). Where business and IT meet. In *CIO leadership strategies*. Aspatore Books. Retrieved September 6, 2008, from www.aspatore.com

Todd, P. A., McKeen, J. D., & Gallupe, R. B. (1995). The evolution of IS job skills: A content analysis of IS job advertisements from 1970 to 1990. *MIS Quarterly, 19*(1), 1-27.

Useem, M., & Harder, J. (2000, Winter). Leading laterally in company outsourcing. *Sloan Management Review*, pp. 25-36.

Weill, P. (2004). *Don't just lead, govern: How top-performing firms govern IT* (Research article, CISR WP No. 341). Center for Information Systems Research, Sloan School of Management, Massachusetts Institute of Technology (MIT).

Weill, P., & Ross, J. W. (2004). *IT governance*. Boston: Harvard Business School Press.

Williamson, O. E. (1979). Transaction-cost economics: The governance of contractual relations. *The Journal of Law and Economics, 22*, 233-261.

Williamson, O. E. (1991). Comparative economic organization: The analysis of discrete structural alternatives. *Administrative Science Quarterly, 36*.

Chapter X
Business Innovation and Information Management

INTRODUCTION

The Global CEO Survey by IBM (2006) shows that two thirds of the CEOs anticipate significant change to their companies over the next two years. The inevitable change is attributed to changing market forces caused by intensifying competition and increasing customer expectations, which are further compounded by globalization, technological advances, regulatory changes, and workforce changes. The CEOs see innovation as the only way to survive and thrive in this rapidly changing industry landscape. Firms can no longer be satisfied with their current market performance, however superior they may be. They must constantly challenge the status quo and reinvent themselves to stay ahead of the curve to avoid being made obsolete by the competition.

The 2005 McKensey Survey of Global Business Executives (Marwaha, Seth, & Tanner, 2005) also "identifies the increasing pace of technological innovation, the growing affluence of emerging economies and the low-cost offshore manufacturing (and now services) as the most important trends of global business." Both the business and technology executives see innovation as the number one driver for growth.

The Gartner (2007) Survey of Global CIOs show that 63% of enterprises expect to grow at a faster rate than the market, twice the percentage from 2006. Innovation is also rated as the key driver for growth.

All these global surveys highlight the critical importance of innovation for companies worldwide to remain competitive. Moreover, disruptive innovation (Christensen & Overdorf 2000), business concept or management innovation (Hamel, 2000, 2006), strategy innovation

(Johnson & Bates, 2003), and value innovation (Kim & Mauborgne, 2005) show various approaches to business model innovation to create significant new market growths and profitability. These authors show how companies have successfully reshaped their strategic frontiers from the prevailing competitive landscapes to establish a new set of ground rules which leave competition in their wake. Corporate and business strategies invariably will seek growth through innovation to sustain their competitive positioning. CIOs and IT organizations must therefore proactively redefine their roles and develop the requisite capabilities to effectively contribute to business innovation pursued by their enterprises. How can IT contribute to such dramatic shift in business models and corporate strategies? IT organizations are increasingly expected to not only run IT efficiently and effectively to save costs, but also to contribute to innovation for business growths. Research has shown that highly effective and fast growing enterprises in majority of cases have highly effective and innovative IT organizations (Ross, Weill, & Robertson, 2006). Indeed, today's successful IT organizations must not only be innovative in managing IT but particularly innovative in exploring and exploiting information technology to create new business capabilities to increase revenues and achieve differentiation for the enterprise, so much so that there are some in the industry who suggest that moving forward, CIO should be called chief innovation officer instead of chief information officer. This new title reflects more accurately the emerging new role of CIO globally being responsible for innovation (through leveraging information). Hamel (2000) argues that "to turn IT into a secret weapon" CIO must possess the skills to conceive new business models that will transform their company's business. To quote Hamel (p. 17): *"If technology is going to become anything other than a great leveler, CIOs will have to become Chief Imagination Officers."* It behooves CIOs and IT organizations, therefore, to understand the principles of innovation and in what ways information, knowledge, and information technology management can contribute to business innovation. This chapter discusses the principles of innovation and the ways information and information technology management contribute to business innovation. Knowledge management is a relatively new discipline whose close relationship with innovation is rapidly gaining international attention. The next chapter is devoted to understanding the principles, theories, and practices of knowledge management from the business innovation perspective.

So what is innovation? What do organizations need to become innovative? How does innovation get done in an enterprise? What are the critical success factors? What does it mean to CIO and IT? How do IT and CIO create and deliver business innovation? These are some of the contemporary research questions relating to IT organizations. We will describe some well known innovation principles and practices to provide a balanced perspective to the broader IT management challenges.

In this chapter we review the various classes and types of innovation, and how IT contributes to innovation in organizations. We will describe the organizational resources required to engender innovation, as well as the framework, process, and infrastructure for business innovation.

BUSINESS INNOVATION TYPES

Innovation is commonly defined as the process of converting a new idea into a new product, service, or process (Popadiuk & Choo, 2006, p. 303), or a new business model (Christensen

& Overdorf, 2000; Hamel, 2000; Johnson & Bates, 2003; Kim & Maugorgne, 2005), resulting in new *value* being created that will benefit the company and its customers. Sawhney, Wolcott, and Arroniz (2006) define business innovation as the creation of substantial new value for customers and the firm by creatively changing one or more dimensions of the firm's business system. Further, they assert that business innovation is not just about product or service innovation, but also about business model innovation. According to Sawhney et al. (2006), business innovation is *systemic* and comes in many different flavors. Business innovation must be studied holistically across all dimensions of the business system. Central to all innovations is the ability of the company to change and adapt its capabilities and products or services in response to or take strategic advantage of the constant changes in the external competitive market and regulatory environments. The company's ability to change depends critically on its competencies, knowledge management, and information systems. Before we examine the roles of IT and knowledge management, we first describe the various types of innovation below.

Innovation is central to all business strategies. All business strategies will seek to achieve cost efficiency and/or differentiation (Porter, 1985). Both strategic imperatives will depend on the firm's ability to innovate. For example, cost efficiency will seek to achieve operational process efficiency to produce the goods or services at the lowest cost possible. Similarly, differentiation will seek to create product or service features (value propositions) that are unique and appeal to the taste of the customers. Both strategic imperatives are increasingly dependent on the firm's ability to exploit technology (and integrate it into its core competencies and processes) to achieve the cost efficiency and differentiation objectives. To understand the various types of innovation commonly found in companies and how these innovations are brought to bear by technologies we turn to the concept of *value disciplines* (Treacy & Weirsema, 1995). Value discipline defines the discipline or strategic approach by which unique customer value propositions can be created. The value discipline will influence the organizational competencies, culture, and structure, and the way the business systems and infrastructure are organized. They will drive the innovation focus of the company. There are three value disciplines that companies commonly use to achieve strategic competitive advantage, namely:

- **Product leadership:** The firm can strive to be the product leader being the first to market with new innovative products with features and value propositions that delight the customers and sometime even influence the customer and market behaviors. Product leaders excel in exploiting new technologies to disrupt the market competition. They are focused on product innovation and continuous improvement to retain their leadership position. Examples are Apple (e.g., with iPod) and Sony (e.g., with Walkman and Playstation).
- **Customer intimacy:** The firm can gain advantage by having an intimate knowledge of their customers—their needs and service experience—such that customized products and services can be delivered to the customers to increase customer loyalty. Firms with this strategy are also proactive in engaging their customers to solicit the customer's input to further improve service innovation. Examples are Wal-Mart and McKinsey.
- **Operational excellence:** The firm can gain advantage by having the most cost-efficient, effective, and reliable operational processes in serving their customers. Customers

benefit from the speed and reliability of service delivery with the most competitive price in the industry. Examples are Dell and Southwest Airlines.

These value disciplines in turn give rise to three innovation types: product innovation to achieve product leadership, service innovation to achieve customer intimacy, and process innovation to achieve operational excellence.

Process Innovation

Process innovation is focused on operational excellence (Hammer, 2004). In particular, companies are seeking innovative ways to achieve process agility which allows business processes to be readily reconfigured in response to, or more importantly, in anticipation of changes in the competitive market conditions.

Process excellence could be achieved from a specific core strategic process standpoint. For instance the company may choose the supply chain as the core process as the key focus for differentiation, therefore supply chain is the focus of process innovation to achieve sustainable competitive advantage.

A more challenging context is when the enterprise seeks to achieve process excellence across the whole enterprise process network which interlinks all core processes to give the best customer service. This is akin to the *integration operating model* defined by Ross et al. (2006).

Product Innovation

Product innovation is focused on product leadership. IT roles in product innovation are twofold. The first and the most common role concerns the creative use of disruptive information technology to create better product capabilities of value to the customers. The second is in the context of product development process—how IT support environment can speed up the product development activities. This is a kind of process innovation and is part of the innovation process. We will return to this in the innovation process section.

Service Innovation

Service innovation aims to achieve customer intimacy. It aims to deliver superior customer experience that differentiates the company from its competitors. It addresses brand innovation and executes the brand value propositions through service excellence. It is related to process innovation in that process innovation addresses part of the issues: the process dimension. Service innovation relies significantly on the data dimension as well. It is the integrated data that gives the customer insights required for customer intimacy to achieve service excellence. This covers both of Ross et al.'s (2006) operating models for integration and unification. The product offerings of services industries such as finance, telecommunications, and airlines are services. For these industries seeking product leadership becomes synonymous with service leadership, and thus customer intimacy more often than not becomes the second pillar of their twin strategies.

Berry, Shankar, Parish, Cadwallader, and Dotzel (2006) identify four types of market-creating service innovations in accordance with two service dimensions: (1) the type of benefit offered by creating a valuable new core benefit or a new delivery benefit that radically changes the ways in which services are delivered to customers; (2) the degree of service "separability"—whether the service must be produced and consumed simultaneously (e.g., health care is an "inseparable" service, and telemedicine allows "separable" delivery of health care service). The four types of service innovations (Berry et al., 2006) are:

1. **Flexible solutions:** They offer new core benefit that can be consumed separately from where and when they are produced, for example, FedEx, CNN, and eBay.
2. **Controllable convenience:** They offer a new delivery benefit of controllable convenience to a separable service, for example, Google with free information access and Skype with free phone service between Skype members.
3. **Comfortable gains:** They offer new core benefit of comfortable gains—customers experiencing new emotional or physical comfort—at the time and place of production, for example, Starbucks and Cirque du Soleil.
4. **Respectful access:** They offer a new delivery benefit to an inseparable service that grants respectful access for their customers—that is, respect for the customer's time and physical presence in using the service, resulting in a stress-free customer experience, for example, Walgreens and Hertz #1 Club Gold.

Through their case study research, Berry et al. (2006) discover nine drivers of successful service innovations:

1. A scalable business model (of a business which is people intensive)
2. Comprehensive customer-experience management
3. Investment in employee performance
4. Continuous operational innovation
5. Brand differentiation
6. An innovation champion
7. A superior customer benefit
8. Affordability
9. Continuous strategic innovation

Berry et al. (2006) find that the successful service innovators leverage all nine drivers; they "take a holistic approach to market leadership."

Business Innovation

There is a fourth innovation type called business innovation, which dramatically and completely transforms the company and the ways it conducts business. Hamel (2000) argues that companies should shift their thinking from innovating a single *component* (e.g., a product) of the business to innovating the whole business—that is, the whole *system* of all business components. Further, he argues that to be a market or industry leader, the company should seek to *radically change—that is, to revolutionize*—the complete business system. Hamel (2000) terms the radical innovation of the business system *business concept innovation.* It involves a major paradigm shift to the firm's product, process, and service across the entire business system that will transform— "revolutionize"—the industry. This radical innovation will redefine the existing business models and create significant value for both the customer and the innovative firm. The IBM (2006) Global CEO Survey finds that business model innovation (in addition to product and service innovations) has gain greater prominence as a means of firms' competitive differentiation. High performing firms tend to use a portfolio mix of innovation types (IBM 2006). Hamel (2000) posits that business concept (or model) innovation is the only strategy for new entrants to unseat the incumbents. Business concept innovation will change the rules for conducting business and renders the incumbents' resource advantage powerless, for example, Dell vs. Compaq in the 1990s. The concept is similar to Christensen and Overdorf's (2000) disruptive innovation and Kim and Maugorne's (2005) blue ocean strategy.

According to Hamel (2000, p. 66), the building blocks of business concept and business model are the same. (See Chapter I for the definition of business model.) A business model is the result of implementing the business concept. In Hamel's (2000) view competition is about contest of business concept (or business model), and firms should seek differentiation in their business concepts and resulting business models. Business concept innovation goes beyond product or technology innovation. It creates a new business model for doing business, introducing holistically the new way of doing things from product creation, delivery, sales, marketing, and customer service to human resource and financial management to partnership with suppliers and customers. For example, Wal-Mart has a unique business model that many other retailers are trying to emulate with little success. New business models inject *new variety* to the industry that the customers value. So the new business models will gradually displace old business models by creating new markets as well as capturing market shares from the old models.

Hamel (2000, p. 70) defines a business concept or business model to comprise four *integrated* key components (Figure 10.1):

- **Core strategy:** Comprising business mission, product/market scope, and basis for differentiation. The business mission defines the "*what*" of the business—the objective of the strategy. The business model is designed to accomplish that mission, which includes the value propositions, the strategic intent/goals, purpose, and overall financial performance objectives. Products and market scope defines "*where*" the company competes. The basis of differentiation defines "*how*" the firm competes *differently*.

Figure 10.1. Hamel's business concept model (Hamel, 2000)

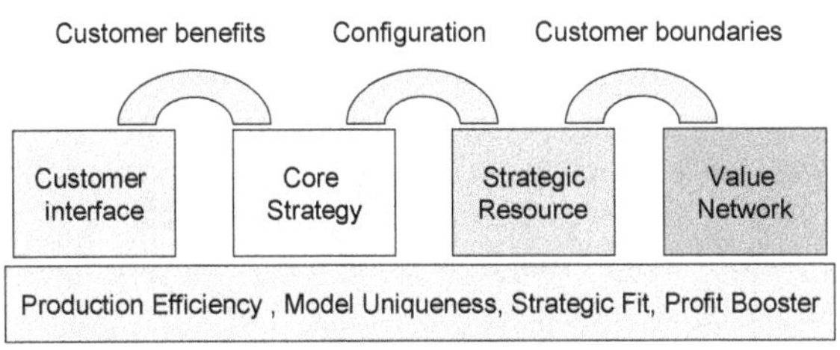

- **Strategic resources:** Comprising core competencies, strategic assets, and core processes.
- **Customer interface:** Comprising the service fulfillment and support infrastructure required to deliver value to the customers; customer information and insight to understand customer experience and needs in order to serve them better; and customer relationship (interaction) dynamics and pricing structure.
- **Value network:** Comprising suppliers, partners, and coalitions.

The four components are *integrated* by three *"bridge"* components:

- **Customer benefits:** This "bridge" connects core strategy to customer interface. It refers to the bundle of benefits (value propositions) being offered by the core strategy to the customers.
- **Configuration:** This "bridge" links the strategic resources to the core strategy. It refers to the unique configuration of the strategic resources (core competencies, processes, and other strategic assets) in support of the core strategy, which is valuable and inimitable.
- **Company boundaries:** This "bridge" links the value network to the strategic resources. It refers to the extension of the firm's strategic resources to include those of its selected partners, for example, via an outsourced contract for a specific external resource which when combined with the firm's core competencies will create a unique configuration to deliver highly valued services to the customers.

The four components of the business concept/model when combined together to offer services to the customers must be capable of generating value to the customers and profits to the firm. Thus, the profit potential of the business model is underpinned by four key factors:

- **Efficiency:** It refers to the rate of customer value generated vs. the costs of production. The more efficient the business model is in generating customer value the more profits it can generate.
- **Uniqueness:** It refers to the unique way that the business model's four components and three bridges interact with one other, dynamically, to deliver value to the customers.
- **Fit:** It refers to the degree to which the business model's components and bridges align with and reinforce each other to deliver superior service to the customers.
- **Profit boosters:** It refers to the business model's "self-reinforcing" ability to generate substantial and sustainable profit. Hamel (2000) identifies four types of profit boosters:
  - *Increasing returns:* Increasing the rate of returns perpetually through network effects, positive feedback effects, or learning effects;
  - *Competitor lock-out:* Through pre-emption by first-mover, controlling the choke points, or customer lock-in;
  - *Strategic economies:* Via economies of scale, economies of focus (specialization), or economies of scope (leveraging unique strategic resources across a broad array of opportunities);

- *Strategic flexibility:* Ability to change with the market through: breadth of portfolio (of countries, products, businesses, customer types, or competencies), operating agility, or lower breakeven point to make profit.

The four business model components together with the three bridges and the four wealth generation factors are the "levers," which a business concept innovator can use creatively to invent a new business model, one that could totally change an industry.

Hamel (2006) extends the business concept innovation to *management innovation.* He calls management innovation a revolutionary way of managing the business to create long-lasting advantage. He cites Procter & Gamble's conception of brand management and Visa's conception of a new organizational model for a consortium of financial institutions to serve global cardholders as examples of management innovations. Hamel (2006) stipulates that management innovation satisfies three criteria:

- It creates a new principle that challenges management orthodoxy
- It is systemic, encompassing the complete business model and the attendant processes and methods
- It is part of an ongoing innovation that improves nonlinearly

CHARACTERISTICS AND SCALE OF INNOVATION

Popadiuk and Choo (2006) note that Afuah (1998) classifies innovations in terms of the new knowledge incorporated into products, services, and processes. Afuah (1998) classifies innovations in terms of three characteristics:

- **Technological:** This characteristic defines the knowledge of components, linkages between components, methods, processes, and techniques that constitute a product, service, or process. Product or service innovations are defined as new products or services that meet some market needs. Process innovation is the result of introducing new elements into the company's operations, processes, and systems used to produce a product or deliver a service.
- **Market :** This characteristic defines the knowledge embedded in the company's distribution channels, products, customer expectations, needs, wants, and preferences, that is, the four P's of marketing: product, price, place, and promotion (Popadiuk & Choo, 2006).
- **Administrative/organizational:** This characteristic defines the knowledge of the firm's strategies, organizational structure, systems, and people.

Popadiuk and Choo (2006) summarize several innovation theoretical models, proposed by various authors, using the technology and market perspectives, as follows. Abernathy and Clark (1985) classify innovations according to their preservation or destruction of the firm's technological and market knowledge/capabilities. For example, regular (or incremental) innovation is one that builds on the firm's existing technological capabilities and market knowledge; and architectural (or radical) innovation is one that makes both the firm's technological and market capabilities obsolete. Henderson and Clark (1990) classify product innovations according to their impacts on the knowledge of the firm's product components and the architecture that links these components into a product. For example, an incremental innovation is one that enhances both the product components and product architecture; a radical innovation is one that both types of knowledge are destroyed. Tushman, Anderson, and O'Reilly (1997) define incremental product, service, or process innovation as one that has an incremental improvement in technology but serves the same market and major (or radical) product or service innovation as one that has a radical technology change and creates a new market. Chandy and Tellis (1998) classify incremental innovation as one where the technology improvement is small and the customer fulfillment per dollar is also low; and radical innovation where the technology is new and the fulfillment dollar is high.

Sawhney et al. (2006) define business innovation as comprising 12 business system dimensions or characteristics, which when considered together constitute the firm's innovation radar:

- **Offerings:** The firm's products and services.
- **Platform:** A set of common components, assembly methods, or technologies that serve as building blocks for a portfolio of products and services. Platform innovation allows a firm to create a derivative set of offerings quickly by using modularity (common components), for example, Nissan Motor Co.
- **Solutions:** A customized integrated combination of products, services, and information that solve a customer problem.
- **Customers:** Individuals or organizations that consume the firm's offerings to satisfy certain needs.
- **Customer experience:** Everything that the customer experiences when interacting with the firm. Innovation will involve redesign the interface between customers and the company.
- **Value capture:** The mechanism that the firm uses to recapture the value it creates, for example, to create new pricing models to capture untapped revenue streams.
- **Processes:** Configurations of business processes used to conduct internal operation and to serve customers.
- **Organization:** The way in which the firm is structured as well as the partnerships and employee roles and responsibilities.
- **Supply chain:** Supply chain innovation involves streamlining the flow of information, changing the structure, and enhancing collaborations with partners to give flexibility and speed to market.
- **Presence:** This is concerned with distribution channel innovation to maximize presence and reach.
- **Networking:** The network through which the firm's products and services are connected to its customers can be redefined to add value to the customers, for example, CEMEX.
- **Brand:** Brand innovation involves extending the brand in a creative way, for example, Virgin music, train, airlines, and mobile companies.

According to Sawhney et al. (2006), a firm can develop its innovation strategy along these 12 dimensions to change the basis of competition. As these dimensions interact with each other in some ways, the firm will need to ensure value propositions are balanced and consistent across all related dimensions such that a portfolio of dimensions is resulted.

For instance, brand innovation is related to offering, customer experience, and presence dimensions.

The ***scale of innovation*** can thus range from *incremental innovation* (or continuous improvement) of an existing product or process or service at one end, to *disruptive* (Christensen & Overdorf, 2000) *or radical* (Hall & Baghi-Sen, 2007) innovation at the other end. Von Stamm (2003) (as quoted in Popadiuk & Choo, 2006) defines nine dimensions for comparing incremental and radical innovations:

1. Time frame: short term (months) vs. long term (years)
2. Development trajectory: step by step per standard linear product development process vs. discontinuous, iterative with high level of uncertainty
3. Idea generation and opportunity recognition: continuous incremental improvement vs. unpredictable sources of ideas
4. Process: formal with stages and gates vs. less structured and opportunistic
5. Business case: clear-cut as customer needs can be anticipated vs. iterative throughout development as customer needs less predictable.
6. Players: doers with formal roles and responsibilities vs. diverse skills with informal network, tolerant of ambiguity, and willingness and perseverance to experiment.
7. Development structure: cross-functional team with a business unit vs. research and development (R&D).
8. Resource and skill requirements: project team allocation per standard development process vs. eclectic and emergent skills, flexibility, and openness to new skills from external organizations.
9. Operating unit involvement: from inception vs. when idea proves feasible.

These nine dimensions must be managed judiciously to support the different types and scale of innovations within the company.

Radical Innovations

Disruptive innovation makes a paradigm change to the firm's process, product, service, or business model, thus rendering competition irrelevant. Incremental innovation is a day-to-day business as usual improvement of the business environment (such as its products, services, and processes in servicing the customers), necessary to sustain incremental business growth. On the other hand, disruptive or radical innovations occur less frequently but the scale of their business is dramatic; they will change business model and indeed the industry. Most product and service improvements in any industry are incremental innovations. IT operating as an enabler to business tends to facilitate more incremental than disruptive innovations. Disruptive and radical innovations are generally high risk as they will involve invention or exploitation of new technologies, new processes and procedures, and new markets. However, they can generate extremely high profit if successful. Thus they tend to have transformative impacts to business and are synonymous with IT operating as a business transformer. An example of a disruptive innovation is MP3 and the iPod which created a new digital music industry and a totally new personal portable and flexible entertainment system. A disruptive innovation will confer the innovator enormous market power and strategic competitive advantage. However, this power and advantage must be leveraged and extended through further innovative application of the disruptive technology for a sustainable period. Once introduced, however, a disruptive innovation will henceforth be improved incrementally.

Disruptive innovations are commonly deployed to serve two opposite types of market—existing and unserved markets. One on hand, the disruptive innovation could bring about a superior product or service to serve the current market and customer base with better features, customer experience, and much better value proposition overall compared to the previous generation product or service. For example, ADSL or other broadband network technology in replacing the dial-up telephony network for Internet access has given the millions of Internet users vastly superior services and customer experience.

Disruptive innovations often have many promising new capabilities, but many of which have yet to be fully developed to even match the prevailing commercial quality experienced by existing customer base of the incumbent technology. This nascent innovation will therefore be unattractive to the current customer base. However, as Christensen and Overdorf (2000) pointed out, there are other customers who currently have not been served by the incumbent technology because of costs of the higher quality offering, but who will accept a lower quality with a much lower cost structure. This unserved market could be ripe for exploitation by the new disruptive innovation. Voice over Internet protocol (VoIP) is an example of a disruptive innovation which can displace the public switched telephone network (PSTN) plain old telephone (POT) service. However, at its inception VoIP voice quality and reliability was well below that of POT service. VoIP's low cost value proposition was introduced to substitute the long distance POT (particularly international traffic) which is still very costly for most consumers. Its success is a good example of a disruptive innovation with "good enough" quality serving the unmet market demand of low cost long distance telephone service with variable quality. Once gaining a foothold on this new unserved market, the innovator may improve the service quality of the disruptive innovation and over time could reach a level to begin to usurp the market share of the incumbent technology. According to Christensen this has proved to be an extremely successful strategy for innovators to change the industry competitive landscape. Another example is exemplified by Amazon which started from online book store to general online retail store with much wider selection of merchandise. Other examples are digital photography replacing film and inkjet printers replacing laser printers. Business concept innovation (Hamel, 2000) is also a disruptive innovation. It transforms completely the ways the company conducts it business in every aspect.

According to Dewar and Dutton (1986) (as quoted in Popadiuk & Choo, 2006), a theoretical model of a firm's innovation capabilities should address three variables and their interactions:

1. The distribution of knowledge in the firm: the depth and diversity of knowledge and the extent of exposure to information from external sources (that is the external market and regulatory environments)
2. Attitudes of the firm's management: the value they place on change
3. The firm's organizational structure: effects of centralization upon adoption behavior

Later in this chapter we will focus specifically on the first variable concerned with knowledge management's (and hence IT's) relationship to innovation, since this is within the realm of responsibility of the firm's IT organization. We first review in the following the direct role that IT organizations can contribute to the value creation of business enterprises.

VALUE OF IT: LEVELS OF BUSINESS TRANSFORMATION CAPABILITIES

To understand how IT can contribute to business innovation, we first review the different ways IT add value to the business from a business support role to a business transformation role. IT organizations will improve their business capabilities over time. The transformation role can only be attained after the IT organization has reliably and successfully support business year after year. Thus, in addition to describing the different business transformation capability levels that IT organizations can attain at the macrolevel, we also examine the most fundamental capabilities, known as *information capabilities* by Marchand, Kettinger, and Rollins (2001) which are critical for the company to possess in order for IT to be able to transform the business. Information capabilities are integral to knowledge management capabilities. Both capabilities are critical for business innovation.

IT delivers value to business in three increasingly sophisticated ways (Marchand et al., 2001):

- **IT *supports* the business:** IT, as a utility, serves to improve the productivity of the business; it automates tedious manual work. Examples are order taking and point of sales. In this mode, IT is perceived as a commodity, and the focus is to do IT at the lowest cost possible; cost efficient IT is the mission. IT is important and necessary but not critical for business.
- **IT *enables* the business:** IT, as an enabler, creates new business capabilities that cannot be done otherwise without IT. For example, IT, through enterprise resource planning (ERP) software, enables cross-functional integration of business processes to deliver superior customer services; or, using data mining and data warehouse, business is able to mine customer information to improve service and increase customer loyalty. In this mode, IT becomes a critical business function. IT provides the basic capabilities to allow a business to find creative ways to differentiate its services and products. IT is a basic necessity for competition, and often is used creatively for competitive differentiation.
- **IT *transforms* the business:** IT, as a transforming agent, redefines the ways the company does business, or creates new products and services that change the ways the business offers value to customers, that is, creates a new business model to compete. This is the most advance way of exploiting IT for business. In this mode IT is the (core of the) business. Examples are Amazon, FedEx, UPS, eBay, and Google.

These three modes of IT value delivery relate to the maturity of IT organization. As IT organization's service delivery capability matures, the business impacts of IT value delivery improve from basic necessity to strategic differentiation. IT organizations generally evolve from a business support level to business enabler and finally to business transformation level. Clearly the three stages are a continuum. Research (Gartner, 2006; Marchand et al., 2001) shows that IT organizations must achieve competency in business support level before

Figure 10.2. Level of IT-enabled transformation capabilities (Venkatraman, 1994)

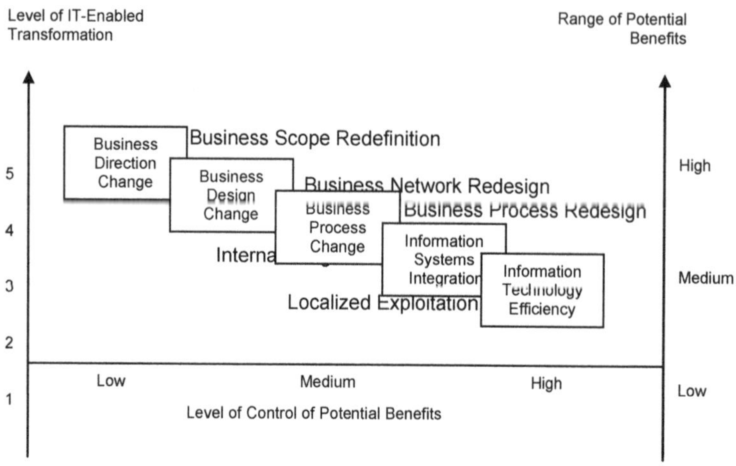

they can become competent in the business enabler level. Thus, IT organizations that have attained the business transformation level are competent in all three levels.

Venkatraman (1994) develops a finer grain framework for defining IT capabilities in business transformation. The Venkatraman (1994) framework breaks IS/IT-enabled business transformation into five levels. It provides a description of each level's characteristics and offers guidelines for deriving maximal benefits. He suggests that each organization first determine the level at which the benefits are in line with the costs or efforts of the needed changes and then proceeds to higher levels as the demands of competition and the need to deliver greater value to the customer increases as illustrated in Figure 10.2

Level One: *Information Technology Efficiency.* The first level is the basic one for leveraging IS/IT functionality within a business through localized exploitation. The expression "localized exploitation" is chosen to indicate that, in many cases, decisions to deploy isolated systems (e.g., a customer order-entry system, inventory control system, internal electronic mail system) are decentralized to the appropriate functional, operational managers. Typically, managers initiate and deploy these systems to respond to operational problems or challenges. This level one is best viewed as the deployment of standard IS/IT applications with minimal changes to the business processes.

This underutilizes IS/IT's potential capabilities and fails to provide organizations with as many possible advantages if the company attempted to change the business processes to leverage the technical functionality. The main weakness is that competitors can easily imitate standard technical applications with minimal changes to the underlying business processes to neutralize sources of strategic advantage.

Level Two: *Information Systems Integration.* The second level is a logical extension of the first, reflecting a more systematic attempt to leverage IS/IT capabilities throughout the entire business process. This level involves two types of internal systems integration: technical interconnectivity (dealing with the interconnectivity and interoperability of the different systems and applications throughout a common IT platform) and business process interdependence (dealing with the interdependence of organizational roles and responsibilities across distinct functional lines). Neither type alone is sufficient. Often, firms allocate more attention to technical interconnectivity than to business process interdependence. Efforts at technical interconnectivity have been enhanced by significant developments in connectivity capabilities during the past decade, such as increased availability of integrated technological solutions and favorable cost-performance trends.

Efforts at business process interdependence should first emphasize the view that the firm should develop its own vision for internal integration after assessing the benefits of integrating current business processes. If a company deems the current processes to be effective, then it is important to articulate the specific objectives of internal integration: for instance, some firms may seek to create cross-functional, horizontal business processes that are parallel to the traditional organization. Alternatively, the logic for internal integration may reflect a transition toward fundamentally redesigning the business processes over a period of time.

Efforts at business processes interdependence should then emphasize the need to ensure that marketplace considerations guide internal integration efforts. Simply fine-tuning existing outmoded processes through current technological capabilities does not create the required organizational capabilities.

Level Three: *Business Process Change*. The third level reflects a strong view that the benefits from IS/IT functionality are not fully realized if superimposed on the current business processes, however integrated they might be. This is because the current business processes subscribe to a set of organizational principles that responded to the industrial revolution. Organizational concepts such as centralization vs. decentralization, span of control, line vs. staff, functional specialization, authority–responsibility balance, and administrative mechanisms for coordination and control are all derived from the general principles. Although these concepts are still valid, IS/IT functionality can significantly alter some of these old principles. Some modes of organizing may be rendered relatively inefficient. In the opinion of professionals and academics, the new logic of organization should be predicated on current and emerging IS/IT capabilities. IS/IT functionality should not be simply overlaid on existing business processes but should be used as a lever for designing the new organization and associated business processes.

Three critical questions for exploiting IS/IT-related benefits at the level of business process redesign are: (i) what is the rationale for the current organizational design? (what are its strengths and limitations?), (ii) what significant changes in business processes are occurring in the marketplace? (what are the likely impacts?), (iii) what are the costs of continuing with the status quo? (when should we redesign the business process? what should be our pace of redesign?).

A company should initiate business process redesign after ascertaining the significant changes in its key competitors' business processes, especially those of new entrants, so that it can formulate appropriate responses beforehand.

Benefits from business process redesign are limited in scope if the processes are not extended outside the focal organizational boundary to identify options for redesigning relationships with the other organizations that participate in ultimately delivering value to the customer.

Level Four: *Business Design Change*. The three levels discussed thus far have focused on IS/IT-enabled business transformation within a single organization. These levels, either implicitly or explicitly, assumed that the boundary of the focal organization is fixed or given. Even when there are interconnections with external businesses, such as suppliers, buyers, and other intermediaries, the distribution of business activities across the different firms is not altered. In contrast, this level represents the redesign of the nature of exchange among multiple participants in a business network through effective deployment of IS/IT capabilities.

If this is the current IS/IT level in the company, then we should see evidence of a strategic logic influencing related participants in the business network to provide products and services in the marketplace, exploiting IS/IT functionality for learning from the extended network as well as for coordination and control. We should further see evidence of elimination of activities where our organization may not have the required level of competence, streamlining business scope to remain flexible as well as responsive to fast-changing and diverse customer needs, and ability to exploit sources of competence in the larger business network (beyond what is available in our organization).

Level Five: *Business Direction Change.* Strategy analysis typically starts with the mission and vision. When the mission describes the business we are in, then the vision describes what we want to achieve in that business. At the fifth level, IS/IT will play a role in influencing mission and vision.

If this is the current IS/IT level in the company, then we should see evidence of a business scope redefinition that is enabled and facilitated by IS/IT functionality. We should see evidence of opportunities and actions to take advantage of IS/IT capabilities to create a more flexible and effective business entity. We should see substitution of interfirm business relationships as an effective alternative to vertical integration. This is the level in which business transformation through IT capabilities will become evident.

INFORMATION CAPABILITIES FOR INNOVATION

A related concept to knowledge distribution in firms (Dewar & Dutton, 1986) is a concept studied by Marchand et al. (2001) called *information capability.* Research by Marchand et al. show that a company's business performance is directly linked to its *information capabilities.* Firms with stronger information capabilities will outperform firms with less capability. Thus to be in Level 5 (business direction change) of the Venkatraman (1994) framework, where IT is able to transform the business, the company must possess a high level of competence in information capabilities.

Businesses of all types are inherently information- (and knowledge-) based and often information or knowledge intensive. Information when applied (or acted on) correctly by business to a business task or situation within the context of the firm's value network will create value. Davenport and Prusak (1998) define knowledge as a fluid mix of framed experience, values, contextual information, and expert insights that provides a framework for evaluating and incorporating new experiences and information. It originates and is applied in the minds of the knower. The judicious application information to a business situation will also create knowledge as a byproduct. Specialist knowledge, unique to the firm's business operation, accrued by knowledge workers in performing their daily tasks gives rise to the firm's core competencies. Studies have shown that not only is innovation related to knowledge management (Popadiuk & Choo, 2006), but also effective knowledge management will enhance greatly the firm's innovation capabilities (Metaxiotis & Psarras, 2006). Effective knowledge management is contingent to the firm's information capabilities. Business innovation through IT is therefore predicated on the firm's mastery of all aspects of information practice. Thus, we argue that the three information capabilities as defined by Marchand et al. (2001) are prerequisite for firms to excel in business innovation. Furthermore, the firm must be proficient in knowledge management to maximize its innovation capability. We first review the Marchand et al. constructs for each of the information capabilities, and then the knowledge management principles and practice required for enhancing the firm's innovation capabilities.

Marchand et al. (2001) introduce a new measurement framework, known as *information orientation*, for linking business performance to information capabilities. Marchand et al. define three information capabilities for assessing the *information orientation* of a firm:

- **Information behaviors and values (IBV):** The capability of a firm to instill and promote behaviors and values in its staff for effective use of information and IT;
- **Information management practice (IMP):** The capability of a firm to manage information effectively over its life cycle
- **Information technology practice (ITP):** The capability of a firm to effectively manage appropriate IT infrastructure and applications to support, enable, or transform the business. This capability is largely defined by the different levels of IT value delivery described in the previous section.

An important finding by Marchand et al. (2001) is that a firm must *concurrently* possess and manage the *interaction* of all three information capabilities to achieve superior business performance. We know in practice that having an excellent set of IT infrastructure and applications will not necessarily deliver superior business performance if the business users do not diligently and purposefully (*i.e., exhibit the requisite behaviors and values to effectively*) use these applications and the information available from them to perform their business functions.

Marchand et al. find that it is the *interaction* of these three information capabilities, which defines what they call the *information orientation* (IO) of the firm that directly influences business performance. Thus, a firm must excel in managing all three capabilities *integratively* and *holistically* (that is, *high IO*) to deliver high business performance. People, processes, and systems must be unified holistically and aligned with business strategy to achieve competitive differentiation, reinforcing Dewar and Dutton's (1986) theory that the attitudes of the firm's management and people and the firm's organizational structure must be supportive of innovation and knowledge sharing.

Information Behaviors and Values

Information behaviors and values (Marchand et al., 2001) of a firm are related to the attitudes of the firm to knowledge behaviors and values (Dewar & Dutton, 1986), and comprise the following attributes (with an increasing level of maturity):

- **Integrity:** Information integrity is about information that tells the business truth; it is manifested by a behavioral characteristic that is absent of information manipulation for personal or political gain, or any other unethical purposes. It will support information formality and information transparency (defined below) and result in effective sharing of sensitive information.

- **Formality:** The degree to which members of an organization use and trust the formal source of the information. It will support information control.
- **Control:** The disclosure of information about business performance to all employees to influence and direct individual, and subsequently, company performance. It depends on existence of information formality and will support information transparency.
- **Information transparency:** Refers to the level of trust and readiness of members to talk about (and learn from) failures and mistakes openly and constructively without fear and repercussion. It depends on information integrity and information control and will support information sharing.
- **Sharing:** The free exchange of nonsensitive and sensitive information between individual in teams within organizations and between organizations (with customers and suppliers or partners). It depends on information transparency and information control, and will enable information proactiveness (defined next).
- **Proactiveness:** Refers to the ability of members of an organization to proactively seek out emerging changes in its competitive environment and analyze and proactively use the information to create new products or services to enhance its competitive positioning in response to the changes. This proactive information behavior is fundamental to the firm's innovation ability using IT. It is directly dependent on the firm's capability to share information and to provide accurate business performance feedback or direction (information control). According to Marchand et al.'s (2001) study of the firm's information behaviors and values maturity level, information proactiveness is regarded as the most mature level. It is only attainable with the culmination of the firm's competencies in all the aforementioned information attributes.

Information Management Practice

As discussed in Chapter II, environmental analysis is an important competence for innovation (Robson, 1997). According to resource-based theory of the firm (Chapter I), "outside-in" resources (Wade & Hulland, 2004) allow firms the ability to manage linkages between the IT function and stakeholders (e.g., customers) outside the firm and ability to sense external market changes and respond to them speedily and flexibly. Information management practice is the key to environmental analysis and leveraging the "outside-in" resources to innovate and achieve competitive advantage.

Information management practice capability (Marchand et al., 2001) consists of the following attributes which constitute the management life cycle:

- **Sensing:** Refers to the ability of members of an organization to detect and identify information concerning emerging changes to the firm's environment such as economic, social, and political changes; competitors, market, and customer changes; suppliers, partners, and channels changes. This capability directly links with and is a *prerequisite* for the information proactive behavioral capability described previously. Thus, it is a critical skill for business innovation, as it is the sensing of emerging changes in customer interface and value network (Hamel, 2000) that stimulates the drive to innovate and compete.
- **Collecting:** Refers to the practice of systematically collecting *relevant* information pertaining to the changing competitive environment of the firm to create knowledge and intelligence that can be used for developing the requisite strategic and tactical

responses to sustain the firm's competitive advantage. This must be founded on sound knowledge management practice, which requires:

- o Managers to understand the information responsibilities and needs of other managers and of employees at various levels and for various tasks;
- o The right type and amount of information to be collected to prevent information overload when the information is synthesized into pertinent knowledge for use by the right people (knowledge workers);
- o Identification of existing employee knowledge and information sources to prevent duplication (and thus waste) of efforts;
- o Clear role and responsibility definition for information collection task, backed by appropriate training, reward, and recognition programs to ensure effective performance of task.

- **Organizing:** Refers to the classification, linkage, and overall organization of information and databases (and knowledge bases) to provide timely and controlled access within and across business units and functions, as well as between organizations[1] where appropriate (customers, suppliers, and partners). As it involves both structured and unstructured data, this phase is closely linked to and depends on the definition of information architecture (described in Chapter V). The information architecture will define the standard language, terminology, and classification schemes for organizing the information entities and sources. As with information collecting, this task also involves people, so to make organizing an effective practice, it requires clear definition of role and responsibility and attendant training, reward, and recognition programs.
- **Processing:** Refers to the analysis and conversion of information sources and databases into pertinent knowledge that individuals can use for decision making in line with corporate strategy and values. Together with sensing, information processing are the most critical capabilities[2] that a firm must possess to be able to proactively innovate its strategy, products or solutions in anticipation of an emerging change in the competitive landscape. They are *fundamental business innovation capabilities*. Information processing creates codified explicit knowledge for use by knowledge workers in accordance with *knowledge management principles* and practice (to be described later). Use and sharing of the knowledge among collaborating knowledge workers will allow domain experts to conceive and develop innovative ideas for strategic competitive advantage.
- **Maintaining:** Refers to the task of keeping information databases (and knowledge bases) current and without duplication to ensure the best information possible is available for knowledge workers use and reuse.

Information Technology Practice

Information technology practice capability (Marchand et al., 2001) addresses the three ways IT organizations deliver value to firms described earlier. Marchand et al (2001) dissect the enabler role into two finer and distinct roles: enabling business processes and enabling management decision making. Thus, according to Marchand et al. (2001), IT practice consists of four dimensions (Figure 10.3):

Figure 10.3. Information technology practices maturity model (Marchand et al., 2001)

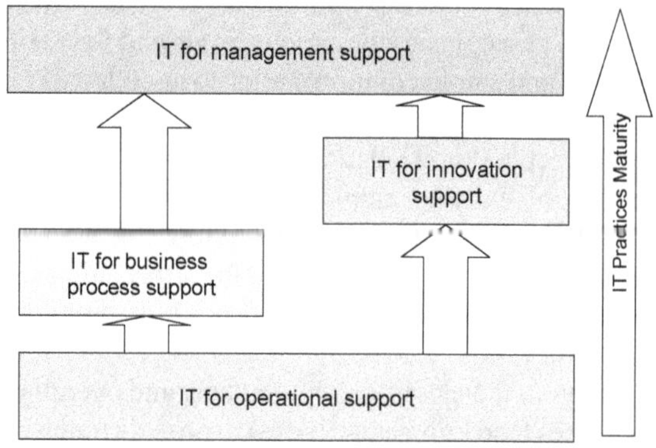

- **IT for operational support:** Refers to using IT hardware, software, telecommunications, and technical expertise to control and automate business transactions, such as order processing and payment, so as to improve the efficiency and effectiveness of semiskilled workers. This is the most basic mode of IT services—the utility support function.
- **IT for business process support:** Refers to using IT hardware, software, telecommunications, and technical expertise to support the management of business processes *across* functions within a company and with suppliers, partners, distributors, and customers. It focuses on data or information integration between business processes across functional domains from supplier chain (from suppliers) to customer service delivery (to customer management). Through effective use of IT, it provides a platform for operational excellence and risk management.
- **IT for innovation support:** Refers to the effective use of IT to facilitate the innovation capabilities of employees by allowing employees to collaboratively explore, develop, share, and implement creative ideas to improve business performance.
- **IT for management support:** Refers to the effective use of IT to enable strategic and managerial decision making in a company, which supports the positive *interactions* of the three information capabilities. Marchand et al. (2001) considers this mode the most mature and advanced use of IT in firms because it allows firms to *anticipate* market trends, *evaluate* new business opportunities (and solution ideas), and *exploit* their market position. In other words, firms are leveraging IT to increase its "predictive analytics" power. Davenport (2006) finds that high performance companies (such as UPS, Procter & Gamble, and Capital One) have, through their information-based strategy, successfully empowered all parts of their business with the appropriate analytics power (or *business intelligence*) to act decisively on emerging opportunities or challenges to create significant value for their customers and stakeholders. The capability to anticipate and evaluate new market opportunities requires strong information sensing and processing, and *hence knowledge management*, capabilities. We will return to knowledge management in Chapter XI. IT applications for management (analytics or business intelligence) support include:

- o Data mining and online analytical processing for customer understanding and possibly other knowledge management systems;
- o Executive information management systems for business performance monitoring and external industry environment tracking;
- o Risk management system for risk analysis; and
- o Group decision support systems for analysis of multivariate business factors (from inputs from the above applications) to produce optimized decisions to act on intelligence collected from market changes.

Marchand et al. (2001) find that IT for operational support is a prerequisite IT capability for all other IT capabilities. Firms must excel in this capability before they can master IT for business process support and IT for innovation support. Moreover, Marchand et al. find that firms must possess both the IT capabilities for business process support and for innovation support in order to be effective in their IT for management (analytics) support. Similar to Venkatraman (1994), they conclude that the natural evolution of IT practice maturity is from operational support to business process support to innovation support and finally to management support. Likewise, business innovation through IT will go through a similar evolutionary path.

In summary, firms with high information orientation will invest in IT to enable them to proactively sense and act on market trends to sustain their competitive positioning. Firms will invest appropriately across a portfolio of applications for operations, business processes, innovation, and management supports to achieve the best return in business performance.

IT-DRIVEN BUSINESS INNOVATION

At a given level of business value delivery capability, what kinds of innovation can we expect IT organizations be able to contribute? As a utility to support the efficient operation of the enterprise, focus for IT is primarily on cost efficiency: do the task effectively at the lowest possible cost. Thus, operating in a utility-centric business environment, requirements for IT innovation are most basic; it is centered on the enterprise's ability to adopt and leverage proven technology in a timely manner to control and lower the total cost of ownership in running IT. For instance, a firm needs the ability to understand the power of technology and may consider adopting utility computing for IT service to pay-as-you-go to control IT costs in line with (not ahead of) business growth and to minimize or avoid the costs of technology obsolescence. As an IT organization matures evolving from a utility to an enabler or transformational modes of operation, the focus for IT also moves from being purely cost-focus to increasingly value-focus. Thus, in these modes, the business will expect IT to be, not only cost-efficient, but also innovation oriented to create increasing levels of business capability for competitive differentiation, and to deliver greater value to customers. IT innovation becomes more sophisticated and complex as business and IT capabilities become closely intertwined when the IT organization is operating at the enabler and particularly transformer roles. This chapter concentrates on innovation concepts with respect to these latter two modes of IT use in enterprises.

Generally, IT value delivery in firms will change with time in line with the evolution of their business strategies and propensity to grow, either organically or inorganically by

Table 10.1. Technology adoption in value chain (adapted from Bharati & Chaudhury, 2006)

Value Activity	IT
Inbound Logistics	Supply Chain Management Supplier Management
Operations	Materials Management Production Planning Computer Aided Manufacturing
Outbound Logistics	Supply Chain Management Order Management
Marketing and Sales	Market and Competitive Analysis Customer Needs Understanding Point of Sales and Merchandise Management Customer Relationship Management
Customer Service	Customer Relationship Management
Firm Infrastructure	Accounting and Finance
Human Resource Management	Innovation and Core Competency (development and reward) Management; Knowledge Management
Technology Development or Exploitation	Customer-centric innovation, disruptive technology absorption and diffusion; innovation infrastructure support
Procurement	Electronic Procurement

merger and acquisition. The increasing business demand for growth will correspondingly demand IT organizations to improve their innovation capabilities and performance. This means IT deployment in these firms must evolve from being a (basic necessity) commodity service to a competitively differentiated service. In the following we study the ways IT contribute to business innovations.

IT support for business innovation (especially operational and business process support) can be studied by using the *Porter's value chain model to map out how IT is being used to create both tangible and intangible business values in an enterprise.* This is illustrated in Table 10.1.

IT VALUE IN DISRUPTIVE INNOVATIONS

From an IT management point of view, it is important to understand the characteristics of disruptive innovation. It is through this understanding that IT will be able to exploit disruptive technologies to transform the business. According to Christensen and Overdorf (2000), disruptive innovations possess the following characteristics: (1) They create systemic industry change through scaling and replication; (2) They meet a need that is either overserved (because the existing solution is more complex than many people require) or not served at all; (3) They offer products and services that are simpler and less costly than existing alternatives and may be perceived as having a lower level of performance, but users consider them good enough; (4) They generate resources in ways that are initially unattractive to incumbent competitors; and (5) They are often ignored or even encouraged by existing players for whom the business model is unprofitable or other unattractive and who therefore avoid or retreat from the market segment." Technology will also enable management innovation (Hamel, 2006). Hamel stipulates three reasons (Barsh, 2008) technology will innovate the ways business is managed in the future: (1) "the availability of powerful new tools for coordinating human efforts will profoundly change the work of management"; (2) "there is the increasing demand for companies to be adaptable, innovative, and exciting places to work"; (3) "a revolution in the Web," where Generation Y expects that one's "contribution should be judged simply on the merits of what you do rather than on the basis of your title or your credentials." Lowell Bryan of McKinsey (Barsh, 2008) further adds that "new organizational models are needed" to leverage the combined power of technology and globalization. The new organizational models will extend the traditional hierarchical model *horizontally* to empower "self-directed professionals to collaborate with their peers continuously" by "creating mechanisms to enable such collaboration to be efficient and effective." Hierarchical decision making will be restricted to activities that require authority such as resource allocation. Bryan (Barsh, 2008) asserts that "the leading companies today are combining talent and technology and organizational design to generate much higher profits per employee than was possible in the past."

Business innovation requires creative skills and various organizational supports throughout the company to sustain the generation and commercialization of ideas. IT organizations will need to transform themselves to enable and nurture the innovation ecosystem. IT will need to build an innovation-oriented workforce, improve their interaction with the business and governance for decision making to speed up time-to-market of innovation. The IT governance will clearly measure and communicate IT value as part of IT contribution to innovation. In particular, IT governance must evolve to incorporate any emerging new business models resulting from strategy or disruptive innovation. The importance and business expectations of IT in enabling business innovation will be exceptionally high. To fulfill the business expectations, IT organizations must first be reliable and credible in delivering traditional IT services (that is already renowned for operational excellence in providing the basic IT utility service to business), second be effective in contributing to new idea generation and commercialization. On the latter, IT will be become a strategic weapon for points of differentiation. IT leaders must therefore think and act like a business executive, with an eye for stable and reliable IT services and another for exploiting IT to create new business capabilities for growth. IT leaders must become a business innovator, ready to challenge the conventional business model and push the strategic frontiers from the angle of creating new values for customers by exploiting technologies (Hamel, 2000). Similarly, the IT workforce must also be equally strong in both technology and business knowledge. They must also possess strong collaborative skills and project execution discipline to convert good ideas into commercial realities quickly and effectively, and the IT organizations must be adaptive for reconfiguration to align with new business strategies and to execute any new business models. The IT service management paradigm will expand to measure both the values of traditional infrastructural and project delivery services and innovation contributions (from idea creation right through to commercial implementation and customer value delivered). The innovation contributions will depend on IT acting like a business and closely involved in shaping new corporate strategy and reshaping business models with the business. At times IT through its knowledge of emerging disruptive technologies will be able to articulate new ways of introducing new products and services or new products and services to create more value to customers for less cost. At this level of business maturity, IT strategic alignment will readily be adaptive to change, and IT value measurement will add a new more significant dimension from the basic cost efficiency dimension to include a new business growth (revenue or profit) dimension. We will look at the characteristics of innovative IT organizations in the next section.

INNOVATIVE IT MANAGEMENT

Watts and Henderson (2006) explore the concept of IT management climate through qualitative analysis of interviews with 36 CIOs with the view to understand the basic characteristics of innovative IT management. According to Boynton, Zmud, and Jacobs (1994, p. 303) (as quoted in Watts & Henderson, 2006), IT management climate is defined as *"shared, enduring perceptions of salient aspects of the IT work environment, that is the organizational practices, procedures and forms associated with IT-related activities."* They found IT management climate, comprising clear mission, planning commitment, information sharing, and delegation of power, was highly correlated with managerial IT knowledge and consequent *absorptive capacity*. Watts and Henderson (2006) argue that absorptive capacity is a necessary but not sufficient condition for innovation, and they set out to investigate: what are *the dimensions and characteristics of innovative IT climates?*

Watts and Henderson (2006) find seven dimensions of innovative IT climates from the CIO's perspective:

1. **Peer relations and networking:** CIOs must be seen to be "playing in the same sandbox" as the business peers. CIOs must be viewed as colleagues of business in order to gather business information and knowledge to accomplish conflict resolution, influence senior executives, and promote their IT organizations;
2. **Support:** CIOs must support their subordinates and IT users acting as "the archer not the arrow." CIO supports subordinates by leading and empowering them, spurring creativity, motivating them to excel, building strong human resources, and leveraging on teaming. CIO supports IT users by improving communication with users to understand their business needs, and educating and empowering them to influence IT directions and solutions.
3. **Motivation to achieve towards a common organizational goal:** CIO shares a common organizational vision with the business, communicates the vision with their subordinates, translates the business vision into technology vision, and motivates them to achieve the visions. The CIO influences the organizational vision by motivating and educating the business executives to understand the technology vision and their power to transform the business.
4. **Institutional motivation to achieve:** The CIO uses institutional resources such as strategic planning processes, portfolio management, and program management processes and governance processes to engage and motivate business executives and IT subordinates to link long term objectives with short term IT plans so as to execute and deliver the innovations conceived by the company.
5. **Innovation:** The CIO creates a learning organization which promotes and demonstrates active learning, able to synthesize new ideas from diverse perspectives from diverse sources and willing to try new things.

6. **Reality checking:** The CIO has the ability to identify and quickly, without fear, kill off failing "bad" projects among the portfolio of projects to be experimented, while delicately managing the emotional attachments that IT subordinates or business executives may have on that project. Realty-checking weeds out bad ideas quickly while focusing resources on the promising projects to maximize the chances of innovation hit-rate.
7. **Promoting credibility:** The CIO and IT organization need to be perceived to be credible by the business in order to win their trust and respect. Credibility depends on CIO ability to deliver results reliably and consistently. However, CIO and IT organization must proactively promote these delivery successes to gain credibility and respect. Only then will the CIO be able to influence others in the company to undertake the effort to change work practices and behaviors required by the new innovations introduced by IT.

CONDITIONS FOR INNOVATION

Amabile, Conti, et al. (1996) find that an organizational culture that strongly promotes, encourages, and recognizes innovation, supported by a committed leader with a clear strategic direction for innovation, is a necessary condition for innovation to thrive. The other necessary conditions are challenges of new opportunities; individual freedom to decide how to do work; sufficient resources allocated to experimenting with new ideas. Implicit in the definition of innovation, that of turning a creative idea into a commercial reality that will benefit the customers and the company, is the need for a streamlined innovation process, supported by a sound IT infrastructure.

Diversity often promotes innovativeness. Florida (2005), and Sethi, Smith, and Park (2002) find that loosely coupled collaborators with strong level of information and knowledge sharing, particularly those with an open culture of readily accepting newcomers with different ideas into the social network, strongly promote innovation. Conversely, strong social ties that promote conformity often undermine innovation. Another important ingredient for innovation is the organization's tolerance of risk-taking and rigorous discipline of learning from failures (without a blame culture). Most importantly is the organization's ability to sense and take advantage of the emerging change in the external market, technologies, and regulatory environments. Market or customer needs are the source of innovation ideas, so being able to anticipate their changing needs and respond quickly with new innovations will give the company distinct market advantage. Equally important is the company's ability to marshal the right mix of resources both internal and external to produce the innovations in response to market changes (Brown, 2005). The company's core competencies and the knowledge management system to support the learning process to grow the core competencies are also basic requirements.

Innovation is a process and an outcome. It produces a set of values that customers are willing to pay (a high) price for. Innovations are produced by collaborative and diverse talents that may spread across diverse geographical regions, within and outside the company. They are facilitated by an enterprise comprising a well balanced combination of people, processes, and systems, which together constitute the enterprise's innovation ecosystem. According to Sivasubramanian (2008), the enterprise innovation ecosystem (Figure 10.4) comprises four critical parts: driver, enabler, infrastructure, and catalyst.

Figure 10.4. Innovation ecosystem (Adapted from Sivasubramanian, 2008)

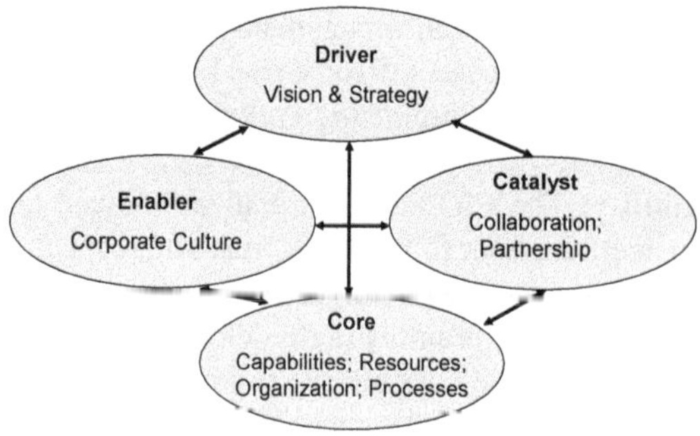

Drivers constitute the corporate strategy which defines the enterprise direction. Drivers are the prime movers of innovation in two ways. One major way can be as described by Christensen (1995), Hamel (2000), Johnson and Bates (2003), and Kim and Maugorgne (2005), where a company can transform itself through strategy innovation into a new business model. Strategy innovation changes everything the company does in a fundamental way. Another way can be that the strategy articulates the importance of innovation and allocates resources required to undertake innovation throughout the company. In both cases, drivers create the impetus, direction, and necessary resources for innovation.

Corporate culture underpins the innovative behaviors of the people in the organization. It is strongly shaped by the leadership (and their behaviors) of the organization (Raju, 2007). Corporate culture influences and is informed by the human and organizational assets of the organization. The leader is expected to "orchestrate" the organization resources to create the "right" work environment and climate which "liberates" idea/information flows and maximizes collaboration between knowledge workers both within the organization and (particularly) with external partners to promote innovation (IBM, 2006).

Human and organizational assets constitute the enabler (Sivasubramanian, 2008). In a strategically aligned organization, the human and organization assets will be structured to enable the innovation-centric corporate strategy to be executed effectively. Human asset will acquire, develop, and accumulate the competencies necessary to achieve the desired innovation articulated in the corporate strategy. Organizational asset will provide the "soft" infrastructure conducive for innovation, which includes the networked organizational model (without hierarchical control) to facilitate an open trusting environment for ideas to flourish, the reward and recognition programs to celebrate innovation achievements and encourage learning from failures, the collegiate and collaborative environment for intra and interorganizational collaboration to source innovative ideas from within and outside, and the professional discipline for intellectual property protection.

The infrastructure provides the process and support systems for innovation. The support systems include the IT environment to enable open collaboration and to manage knowledge base and protect intellectual property rights. IBM (2006) finds that innovation outperformers have leveraged greater number of externally collaborated innovative ideas than the low-performers. In this regard, IT plays an enabler role which enables innovation to flourish within an enterprise and in conjunction with other organizations. We will examine this role further in the next section.

The catalysts (Sivasubramanian, 2008) are the external environment comprising the market, technologies, government regulation, customers, partners, suppliers, and third party organizations that will create discontinuities in the company's business environment and can accelerate the overall process of innovation. As described in the previous Information Capabilities for Innovation section, how the catalysts could be leveraged to trigger off innovation activities depends on the organization's information behaviors and values (Marchand et al., 2001).

DRIVERS OF INNOVATION

According to Engel, Thompson, Nunes, and Linder (2006), there are seven drivers, or philosophies of innovation, which can be categorized by *organization-based drivers* and *value chain-based drivers*. The *organization-based innovation drivers* are attributed to:

- **Top management-led:** Innovation occurs as a result of CEO and leadership team taking responsibility to lead and fund innovation initiatives;
- **Internally networked:** Innovation occurs because teams and parts of the organization have better linkages to allow greater access to organizational resources, such as expert knowledge, funding, processes, and distribution channel;
- **Distributed:** Innovation occurs when everyone is responsible for innovation, and decision making power is delegated accordingly to local manager responsible.

The *value chain-based innovation drivers,* also known as open innovation, are externally sourced innovations which include the following:

- **Supplier-driven:** Innovations are sourced from the firm's suppliers, which is a low cost approach to innovation;
- **Partner-driven:** Innovation occurs by leveraging ideas, expertise, talent, and resources of the firm's partner, such as an outsourcing partner;
- **Competitor-driven:** Innovations are "copied" from the first-to-market competitor by providing distinctive features from the competitor's offering;
- **Customer-driven:** Innovation occurs from customer insights with deep understanding of their changing needs.

Firms can use a portfolio of these drivers to enhance their innovation capabilities depending on their state of innovation maturity. All these innovation drivers will need supports of the appropriate innovation process and infrastructure, and hence information technology.

McKinsey (Barsh, Capozzi, & Davidson, 2007) finds from their survey of senior executives across the globe that the following processes would have the greatest impact on *innovation performance* (order in decreasing level of importance):

- Making innovation a core part of the leadership agenda,
- Modeling behavior that encourages innovation such as taking risks,
- Improving tools and processes for managing innovation risk and making sound innovation decisions,
- Gaining alignment among senior leadership team on correct role of innovation in driving growth,
- Creating and communicating compelling story and sense of urgency about innovation,
- Carifying accountability for innovation,
- Creating dedicated team or group outside core business to carry out innovation activities.

Thus, McKinsey (Barsh et al., 2008) recommends that: (1) firms should formally integrate innovation into the strategic-management agenda of senior leaders. This will allow firms to not only encourage but also manage, track, and measure innovation as a core element in a company's growth strategy; (2) firms should create the conditions that allow dynamic innovation networks to emerge and flourish within the firms and with partners, so as to leverage the existing internal talent for innovation, without implementing disruptive change programs; (3) firms should foster an innovation culture centered on trust where ideas are valued and where it is safe to express (radical) ideas and manage risk proactively in conjunction or consultation with their managers. Further IBM (2006) finds that innovative companies are excellent in integrating business with technology. It is thus prudent for CIOs and IT organizations to find ways in which they can contribute to the above innovation value chain and key processes that drive innovation performance.

INNOVATION PROCESS AND INFRASTRUCTURE

As described above, innovation flourishes in organizations where there is a culture conducive to innovation and where there are organizational policy, process support, access to knowledge, and technology support for collaborating communities—both internal and external communities. The importance of communities in innovation has been described in Nahapiet and Ghoshal (1998). They stress the importance of encouraging behavior that fosters innovation and distinguishes between creating and exploiting new intellectual capital. They also emphasize the link to knowledge management and ways to convert the tacit knowledge and explicit knowledge defined by Nonaka into "social" tacit and explicit knowledge through social interactions between people. They identify four conditions for community support, namely, providing the opportunity to make knowledge combination possible, encouraging people to avail themselves of these opportunities, motivation, and, finally, providing the combination capability. Earlier research has also shown that distributed groups often result in improved team performance and creative abilities when compared to local groups (Kratzer, Leenders, & Van Engelen, 2006; Szulanski, 1996). The business innovation framework must support collaboration between geographically diverse knowledge workers and integrate collaboration with knowledge management into a business innovation process to facilitate the emergence of groups and communities (Adenfelt & Lagenstrom, 2006; Biehl, 2007).

We define the innovation process and infrastructure framework as shown in Figure 10.5. The framework defines the relationship of process, knowledge, and community, *integratively.* According to Gartner (2007), based on their research of numerous innovative forms, the most critical success factor of business innovation is the existence of a clear innovation process. Innovation successes from using the process will cultivate the requisite innovation culture, as innovation culture cannot be created from promises and vacuums. Innovation process generally (Engel et al., 2006) consists of five phases:

- **Ideation:** This phase defines the idea its scope and business benefits
- **Selection:** This phase develops the idea into a (low cost low risk) experiment to test its feasibility; go/no go decision is made quickly to speed up the chance of identifying a feasible idea
- **Development:** This phase takes the feasible idea through a rigorous product development life cycle
- **Commercialization:** This phase launches the product
- **Review:** This phase reviews the results of the innovation to improve current performance and as a feedback for future process improvement

From their interview of 30 firms in U.S. and Europe, Desouza, Dombrowski, Kim, Papagari, and Sanjeev (2007) identify a similar innovation process model comprising five stages: (1) idea generation, (2) advocacy and screening, (3) experimentation, (4) commercialization, and (5) diffusion and implementation. The innovation process is akin to the traditional strategic planning process described in Chapters IV and VII. It has been adopted by many companies as their product development process. The process aims to take advantage of IT to enhance the speed-to-market of product development. They form an integral part of the innovation infrastructure and process.

Hansen and Birkinshaw (2007) define the innovation process as an innovation value chain that consists of idea generation which feeds conversion and which in turn feeds diffusion. In particular, they assert that to maximize innovation performance, the firm must

Figure 10.5. Business innovation framework

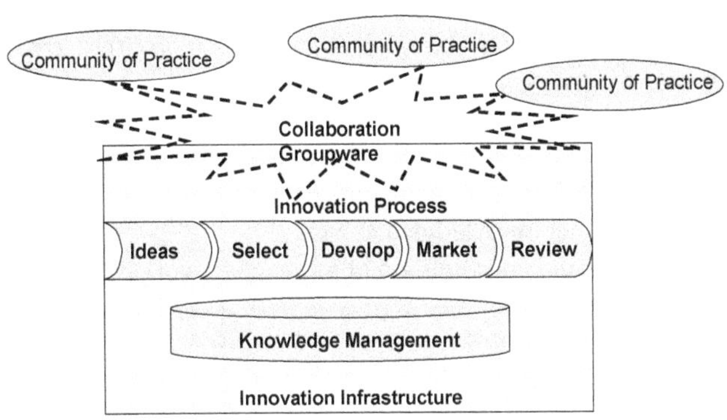

understand which part of its innovation value chain is broken or weakest. This insight will help find the right innovation practice to remedy the weakness and improve the firm's innovation capabilities. We review below the stages of the innovation value chain and where IT could provide support:

- **Idea Generation:** Ideas can be generated from either "in-house" within a business unit, "cross-pollination" via collaboration across business units, or "external" via collaboration with parties outside the firm. All three approaches will require IT support for knowledge management and collaboration.
- **Idea Conversion:** This involves "selection," screening, and funding of selected promising ideas, and "development," implementing the idea into reality. IT support will facilitate portfolio and program management.
- **Idea Diffusion:** This involves selling the end-product of the idea to the customers and other constituencies within the firm to maximize its acceptance and diffusion.

According to Govindarajan and Trimble (2004), the above waterfall innovation process model is not apt for strategic innovation. Strategic innovation is business concept innovation (Hamel 2000). According to Govindarajan and Trimble (2004) strategic innovation is different from traditional product or service innovation in at least three areas: (a) design of end-to-end supply chain architecture (e.g., Dell's direct-sales model); (b) conceptualization of delivered customer value (e.g., IBM's shift to services); and (c) identification of potential customers (Cannon's copiers focusing on small businesses rather than large corporations). Most importantly, strategic innovation has many uncertainties. It requires strategic experiment to explore the unknown and create new knowledge to identify new possibilities. The traditional strategic planning model does not support these requirements. Therefore, Govindarajan and Trimble (2004) propose that a new theory-focused planning process model is required to manage strategic innovation. This model support testing of the strategic innovation through experimentation. The emphasis is on learning (and hence knowledge creation and sharing), not on accountability of execution as in the conventional model.

IT provides the infrastructure for process automation. This includes:

- The workflow process automation of the "gate process" of product development value chain, which requires each development stage to be reviewed and approved by the product stakeholders at each nominated "gate" (separating one development stage to the next advance stage) before the product project can progress to the next stage;
- The repositories for online storage and retrieval of product "artifacts" by the knowledge workers as an integral part of their specific, predefined, and preassigned product development activities in the overall product development value chain workflow, for example, product development documents (such as product requirements or design documents) and product knowledge database;
- Online collaboration and coordination of knowledge workers to create a lean development process.

In line with IT strategy execution, the innovation process should also include the fifth stage, outcome validation, to make sure that the business benefits of the idea are accrued after a reasonable period postlaunch of the product.

There is now an increased emphasis on aligning the innovation process to strategy to meet innovation goals by creating environments that allow people to focus on innovation goals (Henderson & Venkatraman, 1999). Thus, it is important to integrate innovation process into the overall business processes. Popadiuk and Choo (2006) describe the alignment of innovation process to the Nonaka and Takeuchi knowledge creation process (Nonaka, 1994). The Nonaka model is based on the manufacturing industry. It consists of socialization, externalization, combination, and internalization of knowledge (see more details in Chapter XI). Chudoba, Wynn, Lu, and Watson-Manheim (2006) also emphasize process aspects by outlining the importance of continuity of work in virtual enterprises using factors such as geography, time zone, culture, work practice, organization, and technology to measure distance. The goal here will be to provide technologies that will seamlessly integrate business processes, collaboration, and knowledge management to improve enterprise innovation.

In this framework, technology can contribute to innovation in two ways. One is to reduce activity times using collaborative tools to accomplish individual tasks in a business process. What is more important is that technology can also support the critical dependencies of innovation capabilities on knowledge management (Popadiuk & Choo, 2006), collaboration (Kratzer et al., 2006), or enterprise's processes (Christensen & Overdorf, 2000) by presenting such dependencies through flexible workspaces.

The way technology is used will depend on innovation goals. Innovation goals can take a variety of forms (for example, "to reach the market quickly," "to develop technology leadership," or "to achieve operational excellence"), but all should ultimately deliver financial gain. According to Beardsley, Johnson, and Manyika (2006), a quarter to a half of knowledge workers within a company such as managers, salespeople, marketers, and product developers collaborate continually and with others outside the company such as partners and customers to develop new products and services to remain competitive in the marketplace. Beardsley et al. (2006) further states that "few companies understand how to manage intra-company networks in which collaboration typically occurs" and that "successful interventions (in encouraging collaboration) help companies reduce complexity, redefine roles, and allocate financial, physical, and human resources more efficiently." IBM (2006) also finds that innovative companies are better in integrating business with technology. Technology will be exploited to improve collaboration capabilities of communities of knowledge workers within and outside the enterprise. Technology will also be exploited to improve the productivity of knowledge workers through better knowledge management facilities for both explicit and tacit knowledge. In this context, technology is the enabler of innovation in that it is designed to support the management of innovation which facilitates and monitors the idea experimentation process, and if feasible, the production and launch stages. The technology also provides the infrastructure and applications for collaboration and knowledge management. To understand the requirements for the technology infrastructure, we discuss in detail the principles and practice of knowledge management in the Chapter XI.

INNOVATION MANAGEMENT MEASUREMENT

Driving business performance innovation must be managed with appropriate performance metrics supported by a practical measurement framework. In addition to supporting the innovation management process (and attendant governance model), there is a need to find ways by which IT can be leveraged to enable and simplify the task of measuring the organization's innovation capabilities and performance. Adams, Bessant, and Phelps (2006) find that despite its importance to business performance, the practice of innovation management measurement is not well understood with often confusing and contradicting approaches. From their extensive literature review, Adams et al. (2006) propose a framework for measuring firm's innovation management process, which consists of the following seven categories:

Inputs management. This refers to the resourcing of innovation activities which includes financial, human, and physical resources, as well as the generation of new ideas. Adams et al. (2006) find that there has been greater concentration on financial measurement of inputs but much less on the "softer" inputs of skills and knowledge (especially tacit knowledge) which have much greater impacts on the organization's innovation capabilities. Also, there is a greater emphasis on measuring R&D and new product development and less on other forms of innovation, such as service, process, and business model.

Knowledge management. Three areas of knowledge management are critical for innovation management: idea generation, knowledge repository (including the management of explicit and implicit knowledge), and information flows (including information gathering and networking). Measurement of ideas can be quantitative and simple at the initial idea generation and screening stage. Adams et al. (2006) find that it becomes increasingly qualitative, time consuming, and costly to measure when the ideas progress to feasibility and business case stages. With respect to knowledge repository, Adams et al. (2006) discuss the importance of measuring the knowledge "absorptive capacity" of the organization, since it has a direct positive correlation to the innovation performance of a firm. They note that while patents, as codified knowledge, are a useful measure, it is equally important to measure the tacit knowledge of the organization, since tacit knowledge is rare and a sustainable competitive advantage that cannot be imitated by competitors. However, simple and effective methods of measuring tacit knowledge are not yet available. Adams et al. (2006) identifies three approaches to measuring information flows: (1) measures of linkages maintained by the innovation group with external organizations or sources; (2) measures of internal information gathering processes; and (3) measures of customer information contacts. Information flows relate directly to the organization's information capabilities (Marchand et al., 2001) described in the previous section. The successful organizations will be able to leverage information flows to create powerful analytics (business intelligence) to create greater value for the customers and win the competition (Davenport, 2006). External organizations or partners and customers are often good sources of innovation ideas. Thus, it pays for firms to network and collaborate with external partners and customers to maximize their innovation capabilities.

Innovation strategy. It refers to aligning an organization's internally consistent and conditional resource allocation decisions to its innovation objectives. Anthony, Johnson, and Sinfield (2008) support the importance of innovation strategy and argue that "companies that create blueprints for growth, construct the innovation engines and support that engines with the right systems and mindsets can establish favourable conditions for substantial innovation." Measures from strategic management research can be adopted to explore the existence, nature, and extent of innovation strategy. Some key components identified by Adams et al. (2006) include, for example, measure of the degree by which innovation strategy is embedded in the culture, behaviors, and actions of organizations such as risk-taking, proactive behaviors and persistent commitment to innovation; commitment to differentiated funding to innovation; fitness of innovation goals with corporate strategic objectives; and leadership vision and action, or proactiveness in creating the right climate to implement innovation and effect organizational change. IBM (2006) finds that "innovation requires orchestration from the top (CEO)." The direct influence of leadership practice on innovation performance is well known (Raju, 2007) but not well understood, which requires further research. Indeed, Tellis, Prabhu, and Chandy (2007) find from their research on 759 companies that the most important factor (more than the number of patents created) that drives innovation is the internal culture of the company. Three critical elements of innovative culture identified are (Tellis et al., 2007): a future-market orientation, willingness to cannibalize successful products or services, and tolerance for risk. They argue that these elements should be measured in evaluating a firm's innovation capabilities.

Organizational culture and structure. It concerns the way staff are groups and the organizational culture within which they work. It is well known that work environment does make a difference to the level of innovation (it can either enhance or hamper innovation) in organization (Amabile et al., 1996). Some measures considered include, for example, degree of freedom to allow for the exploration of creative possibilities; sufficient control to manage innovation process efficiently and effectively; multidisciplinary team and interfunctional communication; flexible or agile organizational model to respond to change; organizational complexity and climate; participative safety; tolerance to failure; freedom to experiment; propensity to take risks; and interaction frequency.

Portfolio management. It refers to making strategic technological and resource choices that govern R&D project selection to arrive at a portfolio which will optimize trade-off between returns and risks. More details can be found in Chapters IV and V.

Project management. It is concerned with the process of converting the inputs into a marketable innovation—the implementation of innovative idea into a new product or service—using the project management discipline described in Chapters IV and V. Examples of measures include formal processes and methodologies; use of tools; internal and external communications (timeliness and frequency); and collaboration with suppliers and customers.

Commercialization. It refers to taking an innovation to market, which includes marketing, sales, distribution, and joint ventures.

Opportunities exist for IT to be leveraged to support inputs management, knowledge management, and portfolio and project management. We focus on the role of IT in innovation-driven knowledge management in the Chapter XI.

SUMMARY

Business innovation is an increasingly important discipline in which the CIO must become skillful. To contribute to company growth, CIOs must be skillful in product, service, and process innovation. To help transform the business, CIOs must be capable of conceiving business concept/model innovation (Hamel, 2000; IBM, 2006) through creative use of disruptive technologies. IT organizations must be capable of investing resources in a portfolio of incremental innovations (product and service improvement) for incremental revenue growth, and higher risk radical or disruptive innovations (business model transformation) for dramatic profit growth. IT organizations must grasp the characteristics and scale of innovation. To become an innovator, IT must first win business trust and respect by becoming an excellent IT service provider with high quality and reliable service 7 days per week, 24 hours per day, and 365 days per year. Then, IT must improve its maturity to level 5 of IT-enabled transformation—business direction change (Venkatraman, 1994). At this level, IT must have simultaneously attained level 5 of strategic alignment process—optimized process (Luftman et al., 2004), where strategic integration is the norm (King & Teo, 1997), and level 4 of IT portfolio management—synchronized process (Jeffery & Leliveld, 2004). At this level, too, IT and the firm must possess all three information capabilities of information behaviors and values, information management practice, and information technology practice (Marchand et al., 2001); and, more importantly, be able to concurrently manage their interactions. For example, at this level of maturity, firm's knowledge workers will be proactive in sensing dynamic external market and technology environmental changes, and taking timely action on the new "intelligence" to create an innovative response, whether a new product idea or strategy repositioning, which will strengthen the firm's competitive position. IT will add value in two ways: provide the IT infrastructure to streamline the innovation process (with environmental sensors, collaborative and knowledge management tools, and customer feedback loops) and provide the IT solution for new product idea and create the innovative idea as a result of detection of emerging market or technology environmental changes. This is the ultimate level of IT management excellence. To prepare for the journey of business innovation excellence, IT organizations must understand the conditions for and drivers of innovation, and investigate the issues surrounding innovation process, infrastructure, and management measurement. An organization's innovation capability is shaped by the leadership agenda (Barsh, Capozzi, & Mendonca, 2007). CIOs must lead by example and actively create and sustain an innovative IT climate (Watts & Henderson, 2006) and the associated culture that encourages and promotes innovation across the whole IT organization.

REFERENCES

Abernathy, W., & Clark, K. B. (1985). Mapping the winds of destruction. *Research Policy, 14*, 3–22.

Adams, R., Bessant, J., & Phelps, R. (2006). Innovation management measurement: A review. *International Journal of Management Reviews, 8*(1), 21–47.

Adenfelt, M., & Lagenstrom, K. (2006). Enabling knowledge creation and sharing in transnational projects. *International Journal of Project Management, 24*, 191–198. Elsevier Press.

Afuah, A. (1998). *Innovation management: Strategic implementation andprofits*. New York: Oxford University Press

Amabile, T., Conti, R., et. al (1996). Assessing work environment for creativity. *Academy of Management Journal, 39*(5), 1154–1184.

Anthony, S. D., Johnson, M. W., & Sinfield, J. V. (2008, Winter). Institutionalizing innovation. *MIT Sloan Management Review*, pp. 45–53.

Barsh, J. (2008). Innovation management: A conversation with Gary Hamel and Lowell Bryan. *The McKinsey Quarterly, 1*.

Barsh, J., Capozzi, M., & Davidson, J. (2008). Leadership and innovation. *The McKinsey Quarterly, 1*.

Barsh, J., Capozzi, M., & Mendonca, L. (2007). How companies approach innovation: The McKinsey survey. *The McKinsey Quarterly.*

Beardsley, S., Johnson, B., & Manyika, J. (2006). Competitive advantage from better interactions. *The McKinsey Quarterly, 2*.

Berry, L. L., Shankar, V., Parish, J. T., Cadwallader, S., & Dotzel, T. (2006, Winter). Creating new markets through service innovation. *MIT Sloan Management Review, 47*(2), 56–63.

Bharati, P., & Chaudhury, A. (2006, October). Studying the current status of technology adoption. *Communication of ACM, 49*(10), 88–93.

Biehl, M. (2007, January). Success factors for implementing global information systems. *Communications of the ACM, 50*(1), 53–58.

Bower, J. L., & Christensen, C. (1995, January–February). Disruptive technologies: Catching the wave. *Harvard Business Review*, pp. 43–53.

Boynton, A. C., Zmud, R. W., & Jacobs, G. C. (1994). The influence of IT management practice on IT use in large organizations. *MIS Quarterly, 18*(3), 299–318.

Brown, J. S. (2005). The next frontier of innovation. *The McKinsey Quarterly, 3*.

Chandy, R. K., & Tellis G. J. (1998). Organizing for radical product innovation: The overlooked role of willingness to cannibalize. *Journal of Marketing Research, 35*(4).

Christensen, C., & Overdorf, M. (2000, March–April). Meeting the challenge of disruptive change. *Harvard Business Review*, pp. 67–76.

Chudoba, K. M., Wynn, E., Lu, M., & Watson-Manheim, M. B. (2006, October). How virtual are we? Measuring virtuality and understanding its impact in an global organization. *Information Systems Journal, 15*(4), 279–319.

Davenport, T. (2006, January). Competing on analytics. *Harvard Business Review.*

Davenport, T., & Prusak, L. (1998). *Working knowledge*. Boston: Harvard Business School Press.

Desouza, K., Dombrowski, C., Kim, J. Y., Papagari, S., & Sanjeev, J. (2007, Spring). The five stages of successful innovation. *MIT Sloan Management Review*, pp. 8–9.

Dewar, R., & Dutton, J. E. (1986). The adoption of radical and incremental innovations: An empirical analysis. *Management Science, 32*(11).

Engel, J. F., Thompson, A. M., Nunes, P. F., & Linder, J. C. (2006). Innovation unbound. *Outlook, 1*, 28–37. Accenture Publication.

Florida, R. (2005). Managing for creativity. *Harvard Business Review, 83*(7/8), 124–131.

Gartner. (2007, January). *2007 global CIO survey.* Gartner Executive Program Publication.

Govindarajan, V., & Trimble, C. (2004, Winter). Strategic innovation and the science of learning. *MIT Sloan Management Review, 45*(2), 67–75.

Hall, L. A., & Bagchi-Sen, S. (2007). An analysis of firm-level innovation strategies in the U.S. biotechnology industry. *Technovation, 27*, 4–14. Elsevier Press.

Hamel, G. (2000). *Leading the revolution.* Boston: Harvard Business School Press.

Hamel, G. (2006, February). The why, what, and how of management innovation. *Harvard Business Review*, pp. 72–84.

Hammer, M. (2004, April). How operational innovation can transform your company. *Harvard Business Review.*

Hansen, M. T., & Birkinshaw, J. (2007, June). The innovation value chain. *Harvard Business Review,* pp. 121–130.

Henderson, R. M., & Clark, K. B. (1990). Architectural innovation: The reconfiguration of existing product technologies and the failure of established firms. *Administrative Science Quarterly, 35*(1), 9–22.

Henderson, J. C., & Venkatraman, N. (1999). Strategic alignment: Leveraging information technology for transforming organizations. *IBM Systems Journal, 38*(2/3).

IBM. (2006). *The global CEO study 2006: Expanding the innovation horizon.* IBM Global Business Services.

Johnson, R., & Bates, D. (2003). *The power of strategy innovation: A new way of linking creativity and strategic planning to discover great business opportunities.* AMACOM Books.

Kim, W. C., & Mauborgne, R. (2005). *Blue Ocean Strategy: How to create uncontested market space and make the competition irrelevant.* HBS Publishing.

Kratzer, J., Leenders, A., Th., r., & Van Engelen, J. (2006). Managing creative team performance in virtual environments: An emprirical study in 44 R&D teams. *Technovation, 26*, 42–49. Elsevier Press.

Marchand, D., Kettinger, W., & Rollins, J. (2001). *Making the invisible visible: How companies win with the right information, people and IT.* Wiley England.

Marwaha, S., Seth, P., & Tanner, D. W. (2005, Fall). What global executives think of technology and innovation. *The McKinsey Quarterly, 5*, 18–21.

Metaxiotis, K., & Psarras, J. (2006). Analysing the value of knowledge management leading to innovation. *International Journal of Knowledge Management Studies, 1*(1/2), 79–88.

Nahapiet, J., & Ghoshal, S. (1998, April). Social capital, intellectual capital, and the organizational advantage. *The Academy of Management Review,* pp. 242–266.

Nonaka, I. (1994, February). A dynamic theory of organizational knowledge creation. *Organization Science, 5*(1), 14–37.

Popadiuk, S., & Choo, C. W. (2006). Innovation and knowledge creation: How are these concepts related? *International Journal of Information Management, 26*, 302–312.

Porter, M. E. (1985). *Competitive strategy*. New York: The Free Press.

Raju, R. P. (2007, September). Spurring value creation in IT companies: An interview with chairman of India's satyam computers. *The McKinsey Quarterly*.

Robson, W. (1997). *Strategic management & information systems* (2nd ed.). London: Prentice Hall.

Ross, J., Weill, P., & Robertson, D. C. (2006). *Enterprise architecture as strategy*. Boston: Harvard Business School Press.

Sawhney, M., Wolcott, R. C., & Arroniz, I. (2006, Spring). The 12 different ways for companies to innovate. *MIT Sloan Management Review, 47*(3), 75–81.

Sethi, R., Smith, D. C., & Park, W. (2002, August). How to kill a team's creativity. *Harvard Business Review*.

Sivasubramanian, S. (2008, February). *Promoting innovation through strategies, management and investment* (Doctoral Assessment Briefing Paper). University of Technology, Sydney, Faculty of Information Technology.

Szulanski, G. (1996, Winter). Exploring internal stickiness: Impediments to the transfer of best practice within the firm [Special issue]. *Strategic Management Journal, 17*, 27–43

Tellis, G. J., Prabhu, J. C., & Chandy, R. K. (2007, Summer). Measuring the culture of innovation. *MIT Sloan Management Review*, p. 7.

Treacy, M., & Wiersema, F. (1995). *The discipline of market leaders*. Cambridge, MA: Perseus Books.

Tushman, M. L., Anderson, P. C., & O'Reilly, C. (1997). Technological cycles, innovation streams, and ambidextrous organizations: Organizational renewal through innovation streams and strategic change. In M. L. Tushman & P. Anderson (Eds.), *Managing strategic innovation and change: A collective readings*. New York: Oxford University Press.

Venkatraman, N. V. (1994, Winter). IT-enabled business transformation: From automation to business scope redefinition. *Sloan Management Review*, pp 74–86.

Von Stamm, B. (2003). *Managing innovation, design & creativity*. London Business School, Wiley.

Wade, M., & Hulland, J. (2004). The resource-based view and information systems research: Review, extension, and suggestions for future research. *MIS Quarterly, 28*(1), 107–142.

Watts, S., & Henderson, J. C. (2006). Innovative IT climates: CIO perspectives. *Journal of Strategic Information Systems, 15*, 125–151.

ENDNOTES

1 This will enable the "country boundaries" factor of the Hamel (2000) business model innovation, described earlier in this chapter.

2 The core competencies with the strategic resources of the Hamel (2000) business model innovation.

Chapter XI
Innovation Driven Knowledge Management

INTRODUCTION: KNOWLEDGE DRIVES INNOVATION

As described in Chapter X, fundamental to the company's innovation capabilities is the level of collaboration and knowledge management capabilities available to support the innovation process. The ability of an organization to identify, acquire, and utilize external knowledge, known as knowledge absorption, can be critical to the firm's operational success (Adams, Bessant, & Phelps, 2006). A survey by Adams et al. (2006) shows that three areas of knowledge management are critical for innovation management: idea generation, knowledge repository (including the management of tacit and explicit knowledge), and information flows (including information gathering and networking). Further they note that several researchers have found that the firm's ability to "absorb and put to use new knowledge," known as knowledge "*absorptive capacity,*" has direct impact on the firm's innovation and performance (Chen, 2004; Tsai, 2001). Popadiuk and Choo (2006) have further shown that innovation and knowledge creation are related. Innovation is a result of knowledge creation. Innovation is related to the firm's ability to combine new knowledge with existing knowledge to create new knowledge that is unique to the firm. It is also related to the firm's ability to diffuse knowledge throughout the organization so that the organization as a whole increases its absorptive capacity. Knowledge diffusion can be facilitated by IT infrastructure and knowledge management system. Knowledge management is aimed at leveraging internal and external knowledge to create value from the firm's intangible assets. According to Metaxiotis and Psarras (2006), knowledge management contributes to value creation by enhancing: intellectual asset management, operational efficiency, customer and competitor intelligence, continuous improvement, organizational learning, innovation in products and services, and time to market. They report of findings from American Productivity and Quality Center that greater emphasis should be made by firms on "using knowledge management to become more efficient innovators."

To leverage knowledge management for business innovation, IT managers must first understand the basic principles, theories, and practices of knowledge management. Next, they must understand how knowledge management will contribute to innovation. This chapter aims to address both topics to help make IT managers become the IT innovators.

KNOWLEDGE AS A STRATEGIC RESOURCE

The knowledge-based view of the firm stems from the resource-based theory of firm. The resource-based theory asserts that long-run superior performance is associated with the possession of scarce, valuable, and inimitable firm-specific resources. The tenet is that knowledge as a focal resource creates unique advantages for governing economic activities through a logic that is very different from a market. The knowledge-based view argues that the success of firms is not only based on the economics of the contracts it implements (property rights, incentives), but also on its heterogeneous stocks and flows of knowledge. Further work from this perspective has examined different models of organizational design and development of organizational capabilities. The latter view conceptualizes the firm as an institution for integrating knowledge and examines how the mechanisms for integration establish flexible response capabilities in hypercompetitive markets (Grover & Davenport, 2001).

The knowledge-based view of the firm argues that the products and services produced by tangible resources depend on how they are combined and applied, which is a function of the firm's know-how. This knowledge is embedded in and carried through individual employees as well as entities such as organization culture and identity, routines, policies, systems, and documents. The knowledge-based view of the firm posits that these knowledge assets may produce long-term sustainable competitive advantage for the organization because knowledge-based resources are socially complex to understand and difficult to imitate by another organization (Alavi & Leidner, 2001).

According to Alavi and Leidner (2001), it is less the knowledge existing at any given time per se than the firm's ability to effectively apply the existing knowledge to create new knowledge and to take action that forms the basis for achieving competitive advantage from knowledge-based assets. It is here that information technologies may play an important role in effectuating the knowledge-based view of the firm. Advanced information technologies (e.g., the Internet, intranets, extranets, browsers, data warehouses, data mining techniques, and software agents) can be used to systematize, enhance, and expedite large-scale intra and interfirm knowledge management. While having unique access to valuable resources is one way to create competitive advantage, in some cases either this may not be possible, or competitors may imitate or develop substitutes for those resources. Companies having superior knowledge, however, are able to coordinate and combine their traditional resources and capabilities in new and distinctive ways, providing more value for their customers than can their competitors. That is, by having superior intellectual resources, an organization can understand how to exploit and develop their traditional resources better than competitors, even if some or all of those traditional resources are not unique. Therefore, knowledge can be considered the most important strategic resource, and the ability to acquire, integrate, store, share, and apply it the most important capability for building and sustaining competitive advantage. The broadest value proposition, then, for engaging in knowledge management is that it can enhance the organization's fundamental ability to compete (Zack, 1999).

Knowledge, especially context-specific, tacit knowledge embedded in complex organizational routines and developed from experience, tends to be unique and difficult to imitate. Unlike many traditional resources, it is not easily purchased in the marketplace in a ready-to-use form (Zack, 1999). Knowledge-based competitive advantage is also sustainable because the more a firm already knows, the more it can learn. Sustainability may also come from an organization already knowing something that uniquely complements newly acquired knowledge, which provides an opportunity for knowledge synergy not available to its competitors. New knowledge is integrated with existing knowledge to develop unique insights and create even more valuable knowledge. Organizations should therefore seek areas of learning and experimentation that can potentially add value to their existing knowledge via synergistic combination (Zack, 1999).

Information sensing, collection, organization, communication, and use with a high information orientation (Marchand et al., 2001) are critical to the knowledge-based organization. As described in Chapter 10, Marchand et al. (2001) has shown that companies with high information orientation have consistently achieved superior business performance. According to Kettinger and Grover (1995), information can be a source of power to justify ideologically based decisions as well as symbolize adherence to norms. Knowledge, the combination of experience and information, applied to a context, has a dynamic quality and is defined by individuals in shared and coordinated interaction. The strength and characteristics of individual and group ties impact knowledge transmission. Knowledge-sharing capability can determine an organization's processes and structural form. The capability of an organization to share and leverage knowledge as a whole facilitates its ability to change.

Organizations should strive to use their learning experiences to build on or complement knowledge positions that provide a current or future competitive advantage. Systematically mapping, categorizing, and benchmarking organizational knowledge not only can help make knowledge more accessible throughout an organization, but by using a knowledge map to prioritize and focus its learning experiences, an organization can create greater leverage for its learning efforts. It can combine its learning experiences into a critical learning mass around particular strategic areas of knowledge (Zack, 1999).

While a knowledge advantage may be sustainable, building a defensible competitive knowledge position internally is a long-term effort, requiring foresight and planning as well as luck. Long lead-time explains the attraction of strategic alliances and other forms of external ventures as potentially quicker means for gaining access to knowledge. It also explains why the strategic threat from technological discontinuity tends to come from firms outside of or peripheral to an industry. New entrants often enjoy a knowledge base different than that of incumbents (see, for example, Christensen & Overdorf, 2000), one that can be applied to the products and services of the industry under attack. This has been especially evident in industries where analog products are giving way to digital equivalents (Zack, 1999).

Knowledge has a strategic role if unique firm knowledge can successfully be applied to value-creating tasks and if it can be used to capitalize on existing business opportunities. Since competitors in developing their own survival strategies are likely to benchmark themselves against the industry leader to level out performance, knowledge must be difficult to imitate (Krogh, Ichijo, & Nonaka, 2000).

CHARACTERISTICS OF KNOWLEDGE

Knowledge is a renewable, reusable, and accumulating resource of value to the firm when applied in the production of products and services. Knowledge cannot be stored in computers; it can only be stored in the human brain. According to Fahey and Prusak (1998, p. 267), knowledge is what a knower knows; there is no knowledge without someone knowing it: Knowledge is information combined with experience, context, interpretation, reflection, intuition, and creativity. Information becomes knowledge once it is processed in the mind of an individual. This knowledge then becomes information again once it is articulated or communicated to others in the form of text, computer output, spoken, or written words or other means. Six characteristics of knowledge can distinguish it from information: knowledge is a human act, knowledge is the residue of thinking, knowledge is created in the present moment, knowledge belongs to communities, knowledge circulates through communities in many ways, and new knowledge is created at the boundaries of old.

According to Grover and Davenport (2001), knowledge processes lie somewhere between information and the firm's source of revenue, its products, and services. This process can be generically represented in three subprocesses: knowledge generation, knowledge codification, and knowledge transfer/realization. Knowledge generation includes all processes involved in the acquisition and development of knowledge. Knowledge codification involves the conversion of knowledge into accessible and applicable formats. Knowledge transfer includes the movement of knowledge from its point of generation or codified form to the point of use.

Knowledge is commonly distinguished by explicit and tacit knowledge. *Explicit knowledge* can be expressed in words and numbers and shared in the form of data, scientific formulae, specifications, manuals, and the like. This kind of knowledge can be readily transmitted between individuals both formally and systematically. *Tacit knowledge* is on the other hand highly personal and hard to formalize, making it difficult to communicate or share with others. Subjective insights, intuitions, and hunches fall into this category of knowledge. Tacit knowledge is deeply rooted in an individual's actions and experience as well as in the ideals, values, or emotions he or she embraces. Tacit knowledge is embedded in the human brain and cannot be expressed easily, while explicit knowledge can be easily codified. Both types of knowledge are important, but Western firms have focused largely on managing explicit knowledge (Grover & Davenport, 2001).

Distinctions can also be made between *core, advanced,* and *innovative* knowledge. These knowledge categories indicate different levels of knowledge sophistication.

Core knowledge is the basic knowledge required to stay in business (Tiwana, 2002). Core knowledge can create efficiency barriers for entry of new companies, as new competitors are not up to speed in basic business processes. Since core knowledge is present at all existing competitors, the firm must have this knowledge even though it will provide the firm with no advantage that distinguishes it from its competitors (Zack, 1999).

Advanced knowledge is what makes the firm competitively viable and active (Tiwana, 2002). Such knowledge allows the firm to differentiate its products and services from that of a competitor through the application of superior knowledge in certain areas. The firm may

Figure 11.1. Strategic knowledge framework (Zack, 1999)

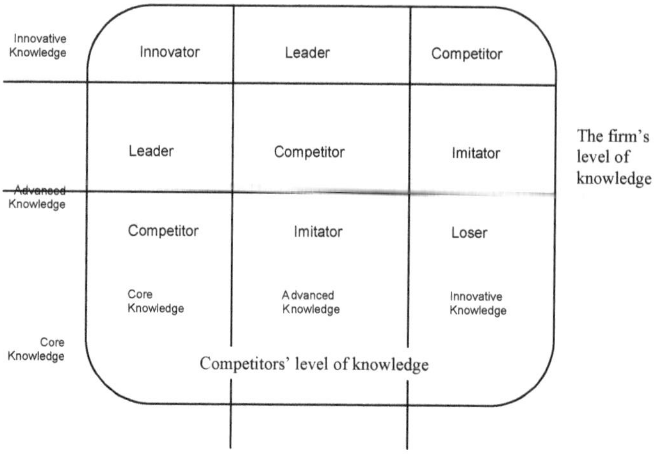

have generally the same level, scope, or quality of knowledge as its competitors although the specific knowledge content will often vary among competitors, enabling knowledge differentiation. The firm may compete for the strategic position by differentiating their knowledge (Zack, 1999). Firms, hence, must least possess advanced knowledge to become innovative.

Innovative knowledge allows a firm to lead its entire industry to an extent that clearly differentiates it from competition (Tiwana, 2002). Such knowledge allows a firm to change the rules of the game by introducing new business practices. It derives from the firm's new business concept innovation (Hamel, 2000) or disruptive innovation (Christensen & Overdorf, 2000). Such knowledge enables a firm to expand its market share by winning new customers and by increasing service levels to existing customers. Innovative knowledge is knowledge that enables a firm to lead its industry and competitors and to significantly differentiate itself from its competitors. Innovative knowledge often enables a firm to change the rules of the game itself (Zack, 1999).

THE KNOWLEDGE-STRATEGY LINK

To align knowledge to business strategy, a firm must articulate its strategic intent, identify the knowledge required to execute its intended strategy, and compare that to its actual knowledge, thus revealing its strategic knowledge gaps (Zack, 1999). The firm needs to perform a knowledge-based SWOT analysis, mapping their knowledge resources and capabilities against their strategic opportunities and threats to better understand their points of advantage and weakness. They can use this map to strategically guide their knowledge management efforts, bolstering their knowledge advantages and reducing their knowledge weaknesses. Knowledge strategy, then, can be thought of as balancing knowledge-based resources and capabilities to the knowledge required for providing products or services in ways that are unique and superior to those of competitors (Zack, 1999). This is part of assessing the strategic gap of the learning and growth perspective (which includes the human, organizational, and information capitals) of an organization (Kaplan & Norton, 2004) in developing the firm's strategy map, as described in detail in Chapter V.

The ability of an organization to learn, accumulate knowledge from its experiences, and reapply that knowledge is itself a skill or competence that—beyond the core competencies directly related to delivering its product or service—may provide strategic advantage (Zack, 1999). Zack (1999) defines a strategic knowledge framework, as shown in Figure 11.1, to help firm identify where its current position is, in terms of core, advanced, and innovative knowledge, vis-à-vis its desired strategic knowledge profile (to assess its external knowledge gaps). The framework can be used as a strategic knowledge map to plot the historical path and future trajectory of the firm's knowledge. It may be applied by area of competency or, taking a more traditional strategic perspective, by strategic business unit, division, product line, function, or market position (Zack, 1999).

Based on a strategic knowledge and capabilities map, an organization can identify the extent to which its various categories of existing knowledge are in alignment with its strategic requirements. The result is a set of potential knowledge gaps. In some cases, an organization might even know more than needed to support its competitive position. Nevertheless, a knowledge strategy must address any possible misalignments. The greater the number, variety, or size of the current and future knowledge gaps, and the more volatile the knowledge base because of a dynamic or uncertain competitive environment, the more aggressive the knowledge strategy required. A firm not capable of executing its intended or required strategy must either align its strategy with its capabilities or acquire the capabilities to execute its strategy (Zack, 1999). To give knowledge management a strategic focus, the firm's knowledge management initiatives should be directed toward closing this strategic knowledge gap. The important issue is that the knowledge gap is directly derived from and aligned with the strategic gap, as illustrated in Figure 11.2 (Tiwana, 2002). This simultaneous alignment of strategy and knowledge is a crucial element of a firm's knowledge strategy. In many firms, knowledge management efforts are divorced from strategic planning and execution. However, having an appropriate knowledge strategy in place is essential for assuring that knowledge management efforts are being driven by and are supporting the firm's competitive strategy (Zack, 1999).

Figure 11.2. Knowledge gap derived from and aligned with strategic business gap (Tiwana, 2002)

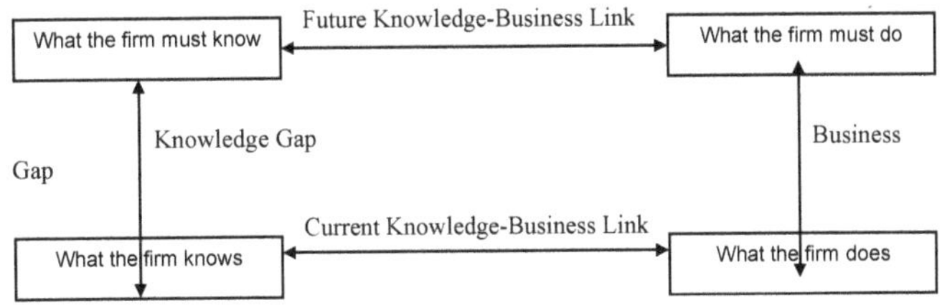

APPROACHES TO KNOWLEDGE MANAGEMENT

Knowledge management is concerned with identifying and leveraging the collective knowledge in a company to help the company compete. Knowledge management is a method for achieving corporate goals by collecting, creating, and synthesizing and sharing information, insights, reflections, thoughts, and experience. Knowledge management is a discipline focused on systematic and innovative methods, practices, and tools for managing the generation, acquisition, exchange, protection, distribution, and utilization ofknowledge, intellectual capital, and intangible assets (Montana, 2000). Knowledge management is purported *to increase both innovation* and responsiveness.

Earl (2001) develops taxonomy for knowledge management in terms of three schools of knowledge management: *the economic school, the organizational school,* and *the strategic school.* The economic school has a focus of income, where the aim is to exploit knowledge assets. The organizational school has a focus of networks, where the aim is knowledge pooling. The strategic school has a focus of competitive advantage, where the aim is to identify, exploit, and explore knowledge capabilities. Firms may choose a combination of principles from these schools to guide their knowledge management strategies.

THE ECONOMIC SCHOOL

According to Earl (2001), the economic school is explicitly concerned with both protecting and exploiting a firm's knowledge or intellectual assets to produce revenue streams (or rent). It is concerned with managing knowledge as an asset, where knowledge or intellectual assets include patents, trademarks, copyrights, and know-how. Intellectual property could be another means of describing the object being managed. This school is more concerned with *exploitation* of knowledge, that is, *incremental innovation,* and less concerned with exploration. One critical success factor in this school appears to be the development of a specialist team or function to aggressively manage knowledge property through *intellectual capital accounting, intellectual capital management,* and *creation of effective and efficient knowledge marketplaces.*

Intellectual Capital Accounting

According to Roslender and Fincham (2001), intellectual capital is a resource that requires careful management if it is to fulfill its maximum potential. Appropriate performance measurement is required to effectively manage intellectual capital. Three components of intellectual capital can be identified, namely:

- **Human capital:** Consisting of the know-how, capabilities, skills, and expertise of human members of an organization.
- **Relational capital:** Consisting of any connection that people outside the organization have with it, together with customer loyalty, market share, the level of backorders, and so forth.
- **Structural capital:** Consisting of the remaining component of intellectual capital, including both systems and networks, and cultures and values, together with elements of intellectual property such as patents, copyrights, trademarks, and so forth.

A number of approaches to valuing knowledge assets exist. Reliable approaches require a common language to discuss the underlying value of an organization's knowledge assets. The knowledge-value-added (KVA) methodology as described by Housel and Bell (2001) addresses a need long recognized by executives and managers by showing how to leverage and measure the knowledge resident in employees, information technology, and core processes. KVA analysis produces a return-on-knowledge (ROK) ratio to estimate the value added by given knowledge assets regardless of where they are located.

Intellectual Capital Management

Sveiby (2001) distinguishes between three families of intangible assets. The *external structure* family consists of relationships with customers and suppliers and the reputation (image) of the firm. Some of these relationships can be converted into legal property such as trademarks and brand names. The value of such assets is primarily influenced by how well the company solves its customers' problems, and there is always an element of uncertainty here. The *internal structure* family consists of patents, concepts, models, and computer and administrative systems. These are created by the employees and are thus generally owned by the organization. The structure is partly independent of individuals and some of it remains even if a large number of the employees leave. *The individual competence* family consists of the competence of the professional staff, the experts, the research and development people, the factory workers, sales and marketing—in short, all those that have a direct contact with customers and whose work are within the business idea. Competence can be defined as the sum of knowledge, skills, and abilities at the individual level. With this definition, we say that knowledge is part of competence, and competence is part of intellectual capital.

These three families of intangible resources have slightly different definitions when compared to the capital elements. The external structure seems similar to relational capital; the internal structure seems similar to structural capital, while the individual competence seems similar to human capital. To appreciate why a knowledge-based theory of the firm can be useful for strategy formulation, Sveiby (2001) considers some of the features that differentiate knowledge transfers from tangible goods transfers. In contrast to tangible goods, which tend to depreciate in value when they are used, knowledge grows when used and depreciates when not used. Competence in a language or a sport requires huge investments in training to build up; managerial competence takes a long time on-the-job to learn. If one stops speaking the language, it gradually dissipates. Given three families of intangible assets, it is possible to identify nine knowledge transfers. These knowledge transfers can occur within a family and between families as illustrated in Figure 11.3.

Each of the nine knowledge transfers in Figure 11.3 can be explained as follows (Sveiby, 2001):

- *Knowledge transfers between individuals* concern how to best enable the communication between employees within the organization. The strategic question is: how can we improve the transfer of competence between people in the organization? Activities for intellectual capital management focus on trust building, enabling team activities, induction programs, job rotation, and master/apprentice scheme.
- *Knowledge transfers from individuals to external structure* concern how the organization's employees transfer their knowledge to the outer world. The strategic question

Figure 11.3. Knowledge transfer within and between families of intangible assets (Sveiby, 2001)

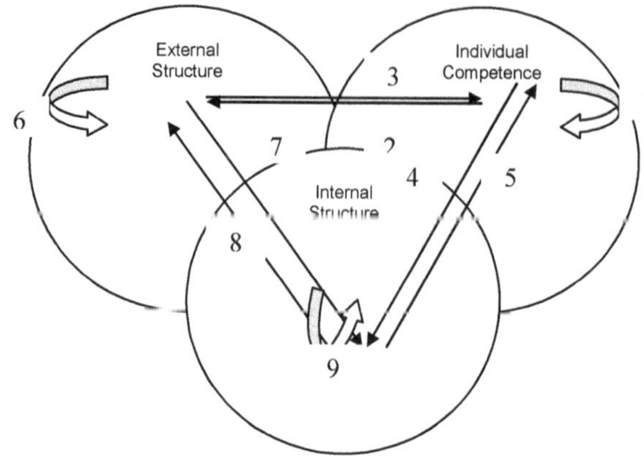

is: how can the organization's employees improve the competence of customers, suppliers, and other stakeholders? Activities for intellectual capital management focus on enabling the employees to help customers learn about the products, getting rid of red tape, enabling job rotation with customers, holding product seminars, and providing customer education.

- *Knowledge transfers from external structure to individuals* occur when employees learn from customers, suppliers, and community feedback through ideas, new experiences, and new technical knowledge. The strategic question is: how can the organization's customers, suppliers, and other stakeholders improve the competence of the employees and the firm's innovation capabilities? Activities for intellectual capital management focus on creating and maintaining good personal relationships between the organization's own people and the people outside the organization.
- *Knowledge transfers from competence to internal structure* concern the transformation of human capital into more permanent structural capital through documented work routines, intranets, and data repositories. The strategic question is: how can we improve the conversion individually held competence to systems, tools and templates? Activities for intellectual capital management focus on tools, templates, process, and systems so they can be shared more easily and efficiently.
- *Knowledge transfers from internal structure to individual competence* is the counterpart of the above. Once competence is captured in a system it needs to be made available to other individuals in such a way that they improve their capacity to act. The strategic question is: how can we improve individuals' competence by using systems, tools, and templates? Activities for intellectual capital management focus on improving human-computer interface of systems, action-based learning processes, simulations, and interactive e-learning environments.
- *Knowledge transfers within the external structure* concern what customers and others tell each other about the services of an organization. This is related to brand innovation. The strategic question is: how can we enable the conversations among the customers, suppliers, and other stakeholders so they improve their competence?

Activities for intellectual capital management focus on partnering and alliances, improving the image of the organization and the brand equity of its products and services, improving the quality of the offering, and conducting product seminars and alumni programs.

- *Knowledge transfers from external to internal structure* concern what knowledge the organization can gain from the external world and how the learning can be converted into action. The strategic question is: how can competence from the customers, suppliers, and other stakeholders improve the organization's systems, tools, processes, and products? Activities for intellectual capital management focus on empowering call centers to interpret customer complaints, creating alliances to generate ideas for new products and research and development alliances.
- *Knowledge transfers from internal to external structure* is the counterpart of the above. The strategic question is: how can the organization's systems, tools, and processes and products improve the competence of the customers, suppliers, and other stakeholders? Activities for intellectual capital management focus on making the organization's systems, tools, and processes effective in servicing the customer, extranets, product tracking, help desks, and e-business.
- *Knowledge transfers within the internal structure* where the internal structure is the backbone of the organization. The strategic question is: how can the organization's systems, tools, processes, and products be effectively integrated? Activities for intellectual capital management focus on streamlining databases, building integrated information technology systems, and improving the office layout.

According to Earl and Scott (1999, p. 30), knowledge management activities need not be solely, or even mainly, intraorganizational. There is usually potential for improving knowledge capabilities, both within and between units of an organization. But external or interorganizational possibilities may be at least as attractive and ultimately more important. These include, for example, mutual sharing of knowledge with partners, allies, intermediaries, suppliers, and customers. Equally, protecting external leakage of some knowledge can be a vital concern to companies that have focused on intellectual capital formation. Earl and Scott (1999) find that current movements such as intellectual asset (or capital) management and organizational intelligence are closely related to knowledge management.

The push for greater collaboration within and between organizations to maximize the firm's innovation capabilities, described in Chapter X, is very dependent on the above knowledge sharing capabilities to succeed.

Knowledge Market Framework

Within the economic school, knowledge transfers occur in knowledge markets. This is a transactional perspective, where knowledge exchanges occur in a marketplace. In defining any market, one must be clear as to who the buyers and sellers are, and what pricing system exists to determine what the consumer pays for a product or service. Knowledge markets exist within every organization. These markets include not only knowledge that has been codified or synthesized (realized) into a company's processes, structure, technology, or strategy, but also include all dynamic exchanges of knowledge between buyers and suppliers.

According to Grover and Davenport (2001), organizations can be viewed to have two categories of buyers of knowledge, local buyers, and global buyers. The local buyers are people who are searching for knowledge assets to address an issue that they need to resolve. They require more than information. Expertise, experience, insight, and judgment are needed to bring to bear on the issue. They could pay for knowledge in hard currency via for example a consultant from outside the firm or buy the knowledge from internal suppliers. The global knowledge buyer is the firm, which has a vested interest in realizing knowledge assets into valuable products and services. The global knowledge buyer, represented by organizational stakeholders whose benefits are tied to organizational level outcomes, has a strong interest in transferring local knowledge to global knowledge. Doing so reduces dependency on knowledge sellers in case they choose to leave the firm. Knowledge sellers are people who have knowledge (usually tacit) to sell. The quality of this knowledge might be high or low depending on the credibility of the source.

The concept of knowledge markets recognizes the interest that individuals have in holding onto the knowledge they possess. In order to part with it, they need to receive something in exchange. Any organization is a knowledge market in which knowledge is exchanged for other things of value—money, respect, promotions, or other knowledge (Grover & Davenport, 2001).

All markets have a price system so that value exchanges can be efficiently rendered and recorded. The price system of a knowledge market includes *reciprocity, repute,* and *altruism* (Davenport & Prusak, 1998). *Reciprocity* implies payment in terms of knowledge. A knowledge seller will spend the time and effort needed to share knowledge effectively if the person expects the buyer to be willing seller when he is in the market for knowledge. *Repute* implies being known as a knowledge source. A knowledge seller usually wants others to know him as a knowledgeable person with valuable expertise that he is willing to share with others in the company. Having a reputation for knowledge sharing makes achieving reciprocity more likely: being known as a knowledge seller makes one a more effective knowledge buyer. *Altruism* implies that a knowledge seller may be so passionate about his knowledge that he is happy to share it whenever he gets a chance. This seems to be the case with many university professors. Many knowledge sharers are motivated in part by a love of their subject and to some degree by altruism, whether for the good of the organization or based on a natural impulse to help others.

Knowledge markets are dependent on *market signals* that indicate where knowledge actually resides in the organization and how to gain access to it. Title and position are the most common formal signals indicating who has or should have valuable knowledge. Another knowledge market signal flows through informal networks of practice that develop in organizations. Within such networks, people ask each other who knows what.

Davenport and Prusak (1998) argue that to develop effective knowledge markets, information technology has to be used wisely, marketplaces have to be built, and knowledge market value has to be created and defined: Networks and desktops computers, with their ability to connect people and store and retrieve virtually unlimited amounts of content, can dramatically improve knowledge market efficiency. Information technology can provide an infrastructure for moving knowledge and information about knowledge as well as for building virtual knowledge marketplaces. Electronic knowledge markets such as the Internet, intranet discussion groups, and groupware discussion databases provide convenience and choice with desktop access to a vast variety of material.

THE ORGANIZATIONAL SCHOOL

According to Earl (2001), the organizational school describes the use of organizational structures, or networks, to share or pool knowledge. Often described as knowledge communities, the archetypal arrangement is a group of people with a common interest, problem, or experience. These communities are designed and maintained for a business purpose, and they can be intra or interorganizational. Two approaches to knowledge management belonging to the organizational school are defined by Earl (2001). The first approach is managing common knowledge; the second is the socialization-externalization-combination-internalization (SECI) process.

Managing Common Knowledge

Dixon (2000) defines common knowledge as the knowledge that employees learn from doing the organization's tasks. Common knowledge is managed through knowledge transfer mechanisms. Knowledge transfer in an organization can be defined as the process by which one unit (e.g., a group, department, or division) is affected by experiences. Another definition suggests that knowledge transfer at the individual level is how knowledge acquired in one situation applies to another. Both of these definitions describe knowledge transfer as something that manifests itself through changes in knowledge or performance of the recipient units.

Markus (2001) has identified *four different types* of knowledge *reuse* situations. The first reuse situation is called "shared knowledge producers," where knowledge reusers may be close to or distant from those who produced the knowledge. A second type of knowledge reusers is "shared work practitioners," people who share a practice community, including specialists who occupy the same roles in different locations, work units, or organizations, such as consultants in a practice. The third reuse situation is called "expertise-seeking novices" and involves people who differ substantially from the knowledge creators, where novices seek access to experts and expertise. The fourth knowledge reuse situation is "secondary knowledge miners" and is perhaps the most extreme case of reuse as it involves data mining, in which analysts attempt to extract knowledge from records that were collected by others, possibly unknown to the reuser, for very different purposes.

Dixon's (2000) defines *five knowledge transfer mechanisms*. The criteria that Dixon uses to define these knowledge transfer mechanisms are the following: who is the intended receiver, what is the nature of the task, and what is the type of knowledge to be transferred? The five transfer mechanisms for sharing knowledge in the organization are serial, explicit, tacit, strategic, and expert transfers.

- *Serial transfer* takes place when the same group of knowledge workers performs the same work one more time by applying their own knowledge. The nature of the task is frequent and nonroutine, and the type of knowledge that is transferred can be both tacit and explicit.
- *Explicit transfer* takes place when a group of knowledge workers performs the same work as another group has done before by applying knowledge from the other group. The knowledge from the other group is transferred explicitly as words and numbers

and shared in the form of data, scientific formulae, specifications, manuals, and the like. The nature of the task performed by the team is frequent and routine.

- *Tacit transfer* takes place when a group of knowledge workers performs the same work as another group by applying knowledge from the other group, but in a different context. The knowledge from the other group is transferred through social activity as tacit knowledge. The nature of the task that the group is engaged in is frequent and nonroutine. This is also called near transfer not because of the geography involved but because of the similarity between the source team and the receiving team.
- *Strategic transfer* takes place when a team has taken on a task that happens only infrequently, a one-off project, and wants to benefit from the experience of others, within the same organization that has achieved a similar task. Typical of this transfer mechanism is that the senior-level managers are often involved and define what kind of knowledge is needed to solve the task. The type of knowledge that is transferred can be both tacit and explicit.
- *Expert transfer* takes place when generic and explicit knowledge is transferred from an expert source inside or outside the organization to enable the team to solve new problems with new methods and knowledge. This knowledge transfer is applicable when the team is performing a task that is infrequent and routine, and faces an unusual technical problem beyond the scope of their own knowledge. Typically, the knowledge that is requested is not found in a manual or in standard documentation.

Management has to emphasize all five mechanisms for successful sharing and creation of common knowledge. For serial transfer, management has to stimulate meetings and contacts between group members, while for explicit transfer documentation of work by the previous group needs to be stimulated. For tacit transfer, management has to stimulate contacts between the two groups, while for strategic transfer, strategic knowledge, and knowledge gaps have to be identified. For expert transfer, management has to create networks where experts can transfer their knowledge.

Socialization-Externalization-Combination-Internalization Process

Organizations create and define problems, develop and apply knowledge to solve the problems, and then further develop new knowledge through the action of problem solving. In many organizations, developing new knowledge is even more important than keeping track of existing knowledge. The organization is not merely an information processing machine, but an entity that creates knowledge through action and interaction. It interacts with its environment and reshapes the environment and even itself through the process of knowledge creation. Hence, Nonaka, Toyama, and Konno (2000) argue that the most important aspect of understanding a firm's capability concerning knowledge is the dynamic capability to continuously create new knowledge out of existing firm-specific capabilities, rather than the stock of knowledge that a firm possesses at any one point in time.

Knowledge creation is a continuous, self-transcending process through which one transcends the boundary of the old self into a new self by acquiring new context, a new view of the world, and new knowledge. One also transcends the boundary between self and other, as knowledge is created through the interactions among individuals or between individuals and their environment.

To understand how organizations create knowledge dynamically, Nonaka et al. (2000) proposed a model of knowledge creation consisting of three elements: (i) *the SECI process*, the process of knowledge creation through conversion between tacit and explicit knowledge, where SECI captures socialization, externalization, combination, and internalization; (ii) *ba*, the shared context for knowledge creation and the place to create knowledge; and (iii) *knowledge assets*, the resources required to enable knowledge creation, such as inputs, outputs, and moderator of the knowledge creating process.

The three elements of knowledge creation have to interact with each other to form the knowledge spiral that creates knowledge. An organization creates knowledge through interactions between explicit and tacit knowledge. This interaction is called knowledge conversion. Through the conversion process, tacit and explicit knowledge expands in both quality and quantity. There are four steps in knowledge conversion: from tacit to tacit, from tacit to explicit, from explicit to explicit, and from explicit to tacit. These four steps are called socialization, externalization, combination, and internalization, and they cover the SECI process (see Figure 11.4).

Socialization is the conversion of tacit knowledge to tacit knowledge. New tacit knowledge is converted through shared experiences. Socialization takes place through social processes when new skills are acquired by spending time with others who have those skills. Socialization is the sharing of tacit knowledge between individuals, usually through joint activities rather than written or verbal instructions. For example, by transferring ideas and images, apprenticeships allow newcomers to see the way others think. Knowledge is produced in a group setting not only through mere acquisition of the individuals' knowledge, but also through the sharing of common understanding.

Externalization is the conversion of tacit knowledge to explicit knowledge. Tacit knowledge is articulated into explicit knowledge. Explicit knowledge can be expressed in words and numbers and shared in the form of data, scientific formulae, specifications, manuals and the like. This kind of knowledge can be readily transmitted between individuals both formally and systematically. The successful conversion of tacit knowledge into explicit knowledge depends on the common knowledge space as well as use of means such as metaphors, analogies, and mental models. Conventional learning methodologies require the externalization of the professor's knowledge as the initial step in the students' learning process.

Combination is the conversion of explicit knowledge to explicit knowledge. Explicit knowledge is converted into more complex and systematic sets of explicit knowledge. Explicit knowledge is collected from inside and outside the organization and then combined, edited, and processed to form new explicit knowledge, for example, corporate financial report synthesized from financial information collected from all parts of the firm. The new knowledge is then disseminated among the members of the organization. Focusing on communication, diffusion, integration, and systemization of knowledge in combination contributes to knowledge at the group level as well as at the organizational level. Innovative organizations seek to develop new concepts that are created, justified, and modeled at the organizational, and sometimes interorganizational, level. Complex organizational processes require the cooperation of various groups within the organization, and combination supports these processes by aggregating technologies and knowledge.

Internalization is the conversion of explicit knowledge to tacit knowledge. Individuals convert explicit knowledge into tacit knowledge. By reading documents or manuals about their jobs and the organization, new employees can internalize this explicit knowledge in such documents to start doing their jobs. When internalization has occurred, the new knowledge becomes part of existing mental models and know-how. This tacit knowledge accumulated at the individual level can stimulate a new spiral of knowledge creation when it is shared with others through socialization. Internalization requires the individual to identify the knowledge relevant to oneself within the organization's explicit knowledge. In internalization processes, the explicit knowledge may be embodied in action and practice, so that the individual acquiring the knowledge can re-experience what others go through.

Knowledge creation is a continuous process of dynamic interactions between tacit and explicit knowledge as illustrated in Figure 11.4. Such interactions are shaped by shifts between different modes of knowledge conversion, not just through one mode of interaction. Knowledge created through each of the four modes of knowledge conversion interacts in the spiral of knowledge creation. Nonaka et al. (2000) emphasize that it is important to note that the movement through the four modes of knowledge conversion forms a spiral, not a circle.

The first element of the Nonaka et al. (2000) model for knowledge creation is the SECI process. The second element is ba which is the name given the location or context where knowledge creation takes place. Knowledge needs a context to be created. The context is defined in terms of who participates and how they participate. Knowledge needs a physical context to be created; there is no creation without a place. Ba, which can be translated to place, offers such a context. Ba is the real cultural, social, and historic context which is of importance to each knowledge worker, and which enables each knowledge worker to understand and appreciate information. Ba is the place where information is understood so that it becomes knowledge. The key concept in understanding ba is interaction. Knowledge creation is a dynamic human process that transcends existing boundaries. Knowledge is created through the interactions among individuals or between individuals and their environments, rather than by an individual operating alone. Ba is the context shared by those who interact with each other, and through such interactions, those who participate in ba and the context itself evolve through self-transcendence to create knowledge. Participants

Figure 11.4. SECI process of knowledge creation (Nonaka et al., 2000)

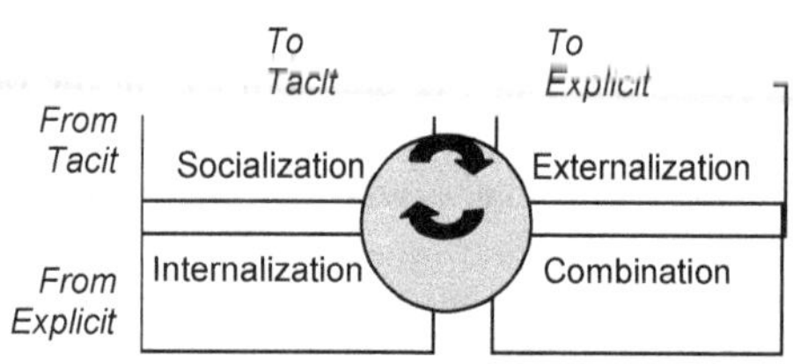

of ba cannot be mere onlookers. Instead, they are committed to ba through action and interaction.

The third and final element of the knowledge creation model is knowledge assets. Assets are firm-specific resources that are used to create value for the firm. Knowledge assets are resources required to support the knowledge-creating process. Important knowledge assets are trust, roles, and routines. Trust is required to stimulate knowledge workers to share knowledge and to enter into a social knowledge creation process. Roles have to be defined so that knowledge workers are familiar with how the knowledge creation process is to take place. Routines are important to know, so that different knowledge workers in different roles handle time and place and frequencies for knowledge creation equally. Knowledge assets must be built and used internally in order to be valuable to the firm, as they cannot be acquired externally.

To understand how knowledge assets are created, acquired, and exploited, Nonaka et al. (2000) proposed to categorize knowledge assets into four types: experiential knowledge assets, conceptual knowledge assets, systemic knowledge assets, and routine knowledge assets. Experiential knowledge assets consist of the shared tacit knowledge that is built through shared hands-on experience among the members of the organization, and between the members of the organization and its customers, suppliers, and affiliated firms. Skills and know-how that are acquired and accumulated by individuals through experiences at work are examples of experiential knowledge assets. Conceptual knowledge assets consist of explicit knowledge articulated through images, symbols, and language. They are the assets based on the concepts held by customers and members of the organization. Systemic knowledge assets consist of systematized and packaged explicit knowledge, such as explicitly stated technologies, product specifications, manuals, and documented and packaged information about customers and suppliers. Routine knowledge assets consist of the tacit knowledge that is routinized and embedded in the actions and practices of the organization. Know-how, organizational culture, and organizational routines for carrying out the day-to-day business of the organization are examples of routine knowledge assets. These four types of knowledge assets form the basis of the knowledge-creating process. To manage knowledge creation and exploitation effectively, a company has to map its stocks of knowledge assets. However, cataloging the existing knowledge is not enough. As stated above, knowledge assets are dynamic, and new knowledge assets can be created from existing knowledge assets.

The three elements of the knowledge creation model—SECI, ba, and assets—represent requirements which all have to be taken care of by management to achieve successful knowledge creation. The SECI process takes care of the interaction between tacit and explicit knowledge, while ba is the place for this interaction, and knowledge assets are the resources for this interaction. When moving through the SECI process in a spiral, the organization develops new knowledge. This spiral is dependent on ba and is stimulated by conditions of growth based on available knowledge assets. Management is important in all three elements. Executive management is responsible for articulating corporate knowledge ambitions. Middle management is responsible for creating and sustaining ba. Both executive and middle management are responsible for the availability of knowledge assets. The knowledge-creating process cannot be managed in the traditional sense of management, which centers on controlling the flow of information. Managers can, however, lead the organization to actively and dynamically create knowledge by providing certain conditions.

Nonaka et al. (2000) argue that fostering love, care, trust, and commitment among organizational members is important as it forms the foundation of knowledge creation. For example, trust among organizational members is produced as an output of the knowledge-creating process, and at the same time trust moderates how ba functions as a platform for the knowledge-creating process. This definition of knowledge assets focuses on resources for knowledge creation.

Managing Knowledge Workers

Knowledge is closely linked to knowledge workers in the company. A knowledge worker can be defined as an employee, for example, a lawyer or engineer, who is able to find, understand, and use knowledge in the organization on his or her own. A knowledge worker is able to use such information in daily knowledge work to solve problems for customers.

People who are knowledgeable not only have information, but also have the ability to integrate and frame the information within the context of their experience, expertise, and judgment. In doing so, they can create new information and innovative ideas that expand the state of possibilities and in turn allow for further interaction with experience, expertise, and judgment. Therefore, in an organizational context, all new knowledge stems from people (Grover & Davenport, 2001). According to Gartner Group (2001), knowledge work represents the ultimate free market. People manage themselves as assets, have the freedom to diversify their professional portfolios and seek sources of social and knowledge capital to stimulate and enrich them. And, unlike the case with traditional capital assets, which remain on the books for years, people involved in knowledge work can depart. Mobility becomes much more an issue of satisfaction: Knowledge work professionals will work with a company as long as the company works for them.

A central lesson emerging is that if knowledge management is going to be successful, then organizations must concentrate on people. The importance of people as creators and carriers of knowledge is forcing organizations to realize that knowledge lies less in its databases than in its people. Research shows that people most freely share experiences in informal, self-organizing networks (Ward & Peppard, 2002). Consequently, it becomes necessary for organizations to create and promote those environments. Often labeled *communities of practice*, these are groups of people informally bound together by shared expertise and passion for a joint enterprise. Communities of practice are groups of people who are informally bound to one another by exposure to a common class of problem. Communities of practice exist to build and exchange knowledge, and, in the process, develop the capabilities of members. They differ from project teams composed of employees assigned by management, in that they select themselves. The glue that holds the community together is the passion, commitment, and identity with the group's expertise, while for a team it is the goals and project milestones.

Advances in information technology have increased the potential for greater dissemination of information and knowledge beyond its creator. IT has increased both technical and social connectivity in organizations, facilitating information and knowledge sharing.

THE STRATEGIC SCHOOL

According to Earl (2001), the strategic school sees knowledge management as a dimension of competitive strategy. Indeed, it may be seen as the essence of a firm's strategy. Approaches to knowledge management are dependent on management perspective. Distinctions can be made between the information-based perspective, the technology-based perspective, and the culture-based perspective: *Information-based perspective* is concerned with access to information. I have a problem, and I am looking for someone in the organization who has knowledge that can solve my problem. *Technology-based perspective* is concerned with applications of information technology. We have all this hardware and software in the firm; how can we use this technology to systematize, store, and distribute information to knowledge workers? *Culture-based perspective* is concerned with knowledge sharing. We are an organization because division of labor makes us more efficient and because we can draw on each other's expertise.

All three perspectives need to be addressed in order for a knowledge management project to be successful. However, the main focus may vary depending on corporate situation. If reinventing the wheel all the time is the big problem, then the information-based perspective should dominate project focus. If the technology in the firm is unable to provide even basic services to knowledge users, then the technology-based perspective should dominate project focus. If knowledge workers are isolated and reluctant to share knowledge, then the culture-based perspective should dominate project focus.

Codification and Personalization Strategy

Some companies automate knowledge management, while others rely on their people to share knowledge through more traditional means. In some companies, the strategy centers on the computer. Knowledge is carefully codified and stored in databases, where it can be accessed and used easily by anyone in the company. These companies have developed elaborate ways to codify, store, and reuse knowledge. Knowledge is codified using a people-to-documents approach: it is extracted from the person who developed it, made independent of that person, and reused for various purposes. Knowledge objects are developed by pulling key pieces of knowledge such as interview guides, work schedules, benchmark data, and market segmentation analysis out of documents and storing them in the electronic repository for people to use. This approach allows many people to search for and retrieve codified knowledge without having to contact the person who originally developed it. That opens up the possibility of achieving scale in knowledge reuse and thus of growing the business. Hansen, Nohria, and Tierny (1999) call this the *codification strategy* for managing knowledge. By codification, the company invests heavily in IT, where the goal is to connect people with reusable codified knowledge.

In other companies, knowledge is closely tied to the person who developed it and is shared mainly through direct person-to-person contacts. The chief purpose of computers at such companies is to help people communicate knowledge, not to store it. These companies focus on dialog between individuals, not knowledge objects in a database. Knowledge that has not been codified is transferred in brainstorming sessions and one-on-one conversations. Knowledge workers collectively arrive at deeper insights by going back and forth on problems they need to solve. These companies invest heavily in building networks of people. Knowledge is shared not only face-to-face, but also over the telephone, by e-mail, and via video conferences. Networks can be fostered in many ways: by transferring people between offices, by supporting a culture in which knowledge workers are expected to return phone calls from colleagues promptly, by creating directories of experts, and by using knowledge managers within the firm to assist project teams. These firms may also have developed electronic document systems, but the purpose of the systems is not to provide knowledge objects. Instead, knowledge workers scan documents to get up to speed in a particular area and to find out who has done work on a topic. They then approach those people directly. Hansen et al. (1999) call this the *personalization strategy* for managing knowledge. By personalization, the company invests moderately in IT, where the goal is to facilitate conversations and exchange of tacit knowledge.

Codification and personalization strategy can be contrasted with each other using criteria such as competitive strategy, economic model, knowledge management strategy, information technology, and human resources. The competitive strategy by codification is to provide high quality, reliable, and fast information-systems implementation by reusing codified knowledge. The competitive strategy by personalization is to provide creative, analytically rigorous advice on high-level strategic problems by channeling individual expertise. The economic model for codification strategy can be labeled reuse economics, while the economic model for personalization can be labeled expert economics. Reuse economics implies investing once in a knowledge asset, and then reuse it many times. Expert economics implies charging high fees for highly customized solutions to unique problems.

Hansen et al. (1999) found that companies that use knowledge effectively pursue one strategy predominantly and use the second strategy to support the first. This can be thought of as an 80-20 split: 80% of their knowledge sharing follows one strategy, 20% the other. Executives who try to excel in both strategies of codification and personalization risk failing both.

Knowledge Management Strategy to Create Value

How do companies choose the right strategy for managing knowledge? Competitive strategy must drive knowledge management strategy. Executives must be able to articulate why customers buy a company's products or services rather than those of its competitors. What value do customers expect from the company? How does knowledge that resides in the company add value for customers? Assuming the competitive strategy is clear, managers will want to consider three further questions that can help them choose a primary knowledge management strategy. The three questions developed by Hansen et al. (1999) are concerned with standardized vs. customized products, mature or innovative products, and explicit vs. tacit knowledge.

The first question is: do you offer standardized or customized products? Companies that offer standardized products will fit the codification strategy, while companies that offer customized products will fit the personalization strategy. The second question is: do you have mature or innovative products? Companies that offer mature products will fit the codification strategy, while companies that offer innovative products will fit the personalization strategy. The final question is: do your people rely on explicit or tacit knowledge to solve problems? Explicit knowledge is knowledge that can be codified, such as simple software code and market data. When a company's employees rely on explicit knowledge to do their work, the people-to-documents approach makes the most sense. Tacit knowledge, by contrast, is difficult to articulate in writing and is acquired through personal experience. It includes scientific expertise, operational know-how, and insights about an industry, business judgment, and technological expertise. When people use tacit knowledge most often to solve problems, the person-to-person approach works best.

Hansen et al. (1999) stress that people need incentives to participate in the knowledge sharing process. The two knowledge management strategies call for different incentive systems. In the codification model, managers need to develop a system that encourages people to write down what they know and to get those documents into the electronic repository. And real incentives, not small enticements, are required to get people to take those steps. The level and quality of employees' contributions to the document database should be part of their annual performance review. Incentives to stimulate knowledge sharing should be very different at companies that are following the personalization approach. Managers need to reward people for sharing knowledge directly with other people.

Stock, Flow, and Growth Strategy

Approaches to knowledge management are dependent on knowledge focus in the organization. Distinctions can be made between expert-driven business, experience-driven business, and efficiency-driven business:

- *Expert-driven business* solves large, complex, risky, new, and unusual problems for customers. Competitive advantage is achieved through continuous improvization and innovation. Knowledge workers apply general high-level knowledge to understand, solve, and learn. Learning from problem solving is important to be able to solve the next new and unknown problem for customers. An expert-driven business is characterized by both new problems and new methods for solution. This model is more conducive to discovering radical innovations.
- *Experience-driven business* solves large and complicated problems for customers. The problems are new, but they can be solved with existing methods in a specific context every time. Competitive advantage is achieved through effective adaptation of existing problem solving methodologies and techniques. Continuous improvement in effectiveness is important to be able to solve the next problem for customers. An experience-based business is characterized by new problems and existing methods for solution. The model is typically used in incremental innovations, particularly product and service innovations.
- *Efficiency-driven business solves* known problems. The quality of the solution is found in fast and inexpensive application to meet customer needs. Competitive advantage is achieved in the ability to make small adjustments in existing goods and services at a low price. An efficiency-driven business is characterized by known problems and known methods for solution. This model is typically used in incremental innovations, particularly process innovation.

Few knowledge-intensive firms are only active in one of these businesses. Most firms are active in several of these businesses. For example, medical doctors in a hospital are mainly in the experience-driven business of solving new problems with known methods. Sometimes, they are in the expert-driven business of solving new problems with new methods. Similarly, lawyers in a law firm are often in the expert-driven business, but most of the time in the experience-driven business. In some engineering firms, engineers are often in the efficiency-driven business, but most of the time in the experience-based business.

Knowledge focus will be different in expert-driven, experience-driven, and efficiency-driven businesses. In the expert-driven business, learning is important, while previous knowledge becomes obsolete. In the experience-driven business, know-how concerning problem solutions is important, while knowledge of previous problems becomes obsolete. In the efficiency-based business, all knowledge concerning both problems and solutions is important in an accumulation of knowledge to improve efficiency. These differences lead us to make distinctions between the following three knowledge management strategies of stock strategy, flow strategy, and growth strategy:

- *Stock strategy* is focused on collecting and storing all knowledge in information bases in the organization. Information is stored in databases and made available to knowledge workers in the organization and in knowledge networks. Knowledge workers use databases to keep updated on relevant problems, relevant methods, news, and opinions. Information on problems and methods accumulate over time in databases. This strategy can also be called person-to-knowledge strategy.
- *Flow strategy* is focused on collecting and storing knowledge in information bases in the organization as long as the information is used in knowledge work processes. If certain kinds of knowledge work disappear, then information for those work processes become obsolete and can be deleted from databases. This is a yellow-pages strategy where information on knowledge areas covered by individuals in the firm is registered. The link to knowledge sources in the form of individuals is made specific in the databases, so that the person source can be easily identified. This strategy can also be called person-to-person strategy.
- *Growth strategy* is focused on developing new knowledge. New knowledge is developed in *innovative* work processes taking place when knowledge workers have to solve new problems with new methods for customers. Often, several persons are involved in the innovation, and together they have gone through a learning process. When a knowledge worker starts on a new project, the person will use the intraorganizational and interorganizational network to find information on work processes and learning environments, which colleagues have used successfully in previous innovation processes.

There is a strong link between these three knowledge management strategies and the three alternatives of expert-driven, experience-driven and efficiency-driven business as shown in Figure 11.5. Typically, efficiency-driven businesses will apply the stock strategy, while experience-driven businesses will apply the flow strategy, and expert-driven businesses will apply the growth strategy.

CHIEF KNOWLEDGE OFFICER

One action for knowledge management is to establish support functions dedicated to knowledge management in the organization. The person leading this function is typically called knowledge manager or chief knowledge officer (CKO). A CKO is responsible for

Figure 11.5. Characteristics of knowledge management strategies (Hansen et al., 1999)

Characteristics	***Stock strategy***	***Flow strategy***	***Growth strategy***
Knowledge focus	Efficiency-driven business	Experience-driven business	Expert-driven business
Important persons	Chief knowledge officer Chief information officer Database engineers	Chief knowledge officer Experienced knowledge workers	Management experts
Knowledge base	Databases and information systems	Information networks	Networks of experts, work processes, and learning environments
Important elements	Access to databases and information systems	Access to knowledge space	Access to networks of experts and learning environments
Management task	Collecting information and making it available	Connecting persons to experienced knowledge workers	Providing access to networks
Learning	Efficiency training applying existing knowledge	Experience accumulation applying existing knowledge	Growth training developing new knowledge

knowledge-based innovations in the firm. While the chief information officer (CIO) is concerned with applications of information technology in the firm, the CKO is only interested in information technology to the extent that it enables knowledge-based innovations in the firm. In addition to the CKO, we find knowledge engineers, librarians, project managers, and database experts in knowledge management support functions.

The CKO role is an important one for both operational and symbolic reasons, according to Grover and Davenport (2001). Operationally, CKOs perform a variety of key roles, including serving as the chief designer of the knowledge architecture, the top of the reporting relationship for knowledge professionals, the head technologist for knowledge technologies, and the primary procurement officer for external knowledge content. Symbolically, the presence of a CKO serves as an important indicator that a firm views knowledge and its management as critical to its success. If the CKO is a member of the senior executive team, it becomes obvious to employees that knowledge is a critical business resource on the level of labor and capital.

Davenport and Prusak (1998) suggest the following main tasks for a CKO:

- Advocate or "evangelize" knowledge and learning from it. Long-term changes are necessary in organizational cultures and individual behaviors relative to knowledge. These changes will require sustained and powerful advocacy.
- Design, implement, and oversee a firm's knowledge infrastructure, including its libraries, knowledge bases, human and computer knowledge networks, research centers, and knowledge-oriented organizational structure.

- Manage relationships with external providers of information and knowledge (for example, academic partners or database companies), and negotiate contracts with them. This is already a major expense item for many companies, and efficient and effective management of it is important.
- Provide critical input to the process of knowledge creation and use around the firm (for example, new product development, market research, and business strategy development), and facilitate efforts to improve such processes if necessary.
- Design and implement a firm's knowledge codification approaches. Such approaches specify key categories of information or knowledge that the organization would address, and entail mapping both the current knowledge inventory and future knowledge models.
- Measure and manage the value of knowledge, either by conventional financial analysis or by anecdote management. If the organization has no sense of the value of knowledge and its management, the function will not last long.
- Manage the organization's professional knowledge managers, giving them the sense of community, establishing professional standards, and managing their careers. These workers may be reporting in a matrix between the CKO and managers of the domains where the company focuses knowledge management efforts (for example, a particular market, product set, or type of customer).
- Lead the development of knowledge strategy, focusing the firm's resources on the type of knowledge it needs to manage most, and the knowledge processes with the largest gaps between need and current capability.

CKO is expected to initiate, drive, and coordinate knowledge management programs. Earl and Scott (1999) study 20 CKOs in North America and Europe both to understand their roles and to gain insight on evolving knowledge management practice. They find that CEOs expect CKOs to correct the following perceived corporate deficiencies:

- Inattention to the explicit or formal management of knowledge in ongoing operations.
- Failure to leverage the hidden value of corporate knowledge in business development.
- Inability to learn from past failures and successes in strategic decision making.
- Not creating value or "making money" from knowledge embedded in products or held by employees.

And, CKOs are expected to evangelize the nature and value potential of knowledge and knowledge management. They must sell the value to both corporate and line or local management. It is the CKO's job to proactively interact with four types of business managers (Earl & Scott, 1999): the *knowledge champions* who seek improvement in knowledge management; the *knowledge sponsors* who are enthused about and will invest in knowledge management projects; *knowledge skeptics* who are doubtful of the value of KM; and the *knowledge partners* who will support the implementation of the KM projects, such as IT and HR professionals.

Earl and Scott (1999) also find that CKOs are designers of knowledge directories, knowledge-based systems, knowledge-intensive business and management processes, knowledge exchange events, knowledge-sharing physical spaces, and knowledge protection policies.

Mostly, their design is conceptual. In other words, they work on an idea with a champion and contribute design suggestions and inject thinking from emerging knowledge management practice, as a consultant or systems analyst would. They then enlist the help of relevant partners.

Applehans, Globe, and Laugero (1999) define the CKO as part of the knowledge architecture. The knowledge architecture identifies the scope of the investment that will be made in managing knowledge. More than a technical solution, it encompasses three components: people, content, and technology. A knowledge architecture brings these components together into a powerful working relationship. In this architecture, the CKO or the CLO (chief learning officer) is the change agent who markets the importance of knowledge inside the company and enables a global audience to take advantage of it. The CKO ensures that the knowledge architecture is funded, designed, built, and administered.

The value that senior managers hope to create from managing knowledge generally lies at one of three levels (Foote, Matson, & Rudd, 2001). At the lowest level, the managers aim to help their organization become better at what it already does. At the second level, knowledge can be used to underpin new forms of commercial activity, such as customer-focused teams and cross-unit coordination. At level three, knowledge management can go even further by generating an entirely new value proposition for customers (Foote et al., 2001, p. 3).

The knowledge management agenda is implemented through a cadre of managers who understand knowledge and its uses in various aspects of the business, the motivational and attitudinal factors necessary to get people to create, share, and use knowledge effectively, and the ways to use technology to enhance knowledge activities. Each individual, at the *personal knowledge management* level, will need to exhibit the right "knowledge behavior"—akin to Marchand et al.'s (2001) information orientation (Chapter 10)—in applying KM practice (sensing, using, creating, storing, and sharing knowledge) as an integral part of their daily job to create business value. On a daily basis, knowledge managers perform a broad collection of tasks, including (Grover & Davenport, 2001):

- Facilitation of knowledge sharing networks and communities of practice
- Creation, editing, and pruning of "knowledge objects" in a repository
- Building and maintaining technology-based knowledge applications
- Incorporating knowledge-oriented job descriptions, motivational approaches, and evaluation and reward systems into the human resource management processes of the organization
- Redesigning knowledge work processes and incorporating knowledge tasks and activities into them

To develop and execute a knowledge management agenda, the CKO should develop skills in intrapreneurship (defined as entrepreneurship within existing organizations). Intrapreneurship is viewed as being beneficial for revitalization and performance of corporations (Antoncic & Hisrich, 2001). Knowledge management will never be the sole responsibility of a CKO. Line managers have responsibilities as well. Hansen and Oetinger (2001) argue that there is a need for T-shaped managers. They call the approach *T-shaped management*. It relies on a new kind of executive (Hansen & Oetinger, 2001, p. 108): "one who breaks out of the traditional corporate hierarchy to share knowledge freely across the organization (the horizontal part of the 'T') while remaining fiercely committed to individual business unit performance (the vertical part)."

IT REQUIREMENTS OF KNOWLEDGE MANAGEMENT

The critical role of information technology and information systems lies in the ability to support communication, collaboration, and those searching for knowledge, and the ability to enable collaborative learning. From discussions in the preceding sections we summarize the following requirements:

- **Interaction between information and knowledge.** Information becomes knowledge when it is combined with experience, interpretation, and reflection. Knowledge becomes information when assigned an explicit representation. One important implication of this two-way direction between knowledge and information is that information systems designed to support knowledge in organizations may not appear radically different from other forms of IT support, but will be geared toward enabling users to assign meaning to information and to capture some of their knowledge in information (Alavi & Leidner, 2001).
- **Interaction between tacit and explicit knowledge.** Tacit and explicit knowledge depend on each other, and they influence each other. The linkage of tacit and explicit knowledge suggests that only individuals with a requisite level of shared knowledge are able to exchange knowledge (Alavi & Leidner, 2001). IT is both dependent on the shared knowledge space and an important part of the shared knowledge space. One important implication of this two-way relationship between knowledge space and information systems is that a minimum knowledge space has to be present, while IT can contribute to growth in the knowledge space (Alavi & Leidner, 2001).
- **Knowledge management strategy.** Efficiency-driven businesses may apply the stock strategy where databases and information systems are important. Effectiveness-driven businesses may apply the flow strategy where information networks are important. Expert-driven businesses may apply the growth strategy where networks of experts, work processes, and learning environments are important (Hansen et al., 1999).
- **Combination in SECI process.** The SECI process consists of four knowledge conversion modes. Not all of these modes are suited for IT support. According to Nonaka et al. (2000), only the combination (C) mode of knowledge conversion will benefit most from creative use of computerized communication networks and large-scale databases.
- **Explicit transfer of common knowledge.** Common knowledge is shared in the organization using five mechanisms: serial transfer, explicit transfer, tacit transfer, strategic transfer, and expert transfer (Dixon, 2000). Of the five mechanisms, explicit transfer seems very well suited for IT support as the explicit knowledge in the form of data, scientific formulae, specifications, manuals, and the like can be easily transferred electronically. Expert transfer also seems suited for IT support when generic knowledge is transferred from one individual to another person to enable the person to solve new problems with new methods.
- **Link knowledge to its uses.** One of the mistakes in knowledge management is disentangling knowledge from its uses (Fahey & Prusak, 1998). A major manifestation

of this error is that knowledge management initiatives become ends in themselves. For example, data warehousing can easily degenerate into technological challenges. The relevance of a data warehouse for decisions and actions gets lost in the turmoil spawned by debates about appropriate data structures.

- **Treat knowledge as an intellectual asset in the economic school.** In this case, intellectual capital accounting should be part of the knowledge management system. The knowledge management system should support knowledge markets where knowledge buyers, knowledge sellers, and knowledge brokers can use the system.
- **Treat knowledge as a mutual resource in the organizational school.** The potential contribution of IT is linked to the combination of intranets and groupware to connect members and pool their knowledge, both explicit and tacit.
- **Treat knowledge as a strategy in the strategy school.** The potential contribution of IT is manifold once knowledge as a strategy is the impetus behind knowledge management initiatives. One can expect quite an eclectic mix of networks, systems, tools, and knowledge repositories.
- *Value configuration determines knowledge needs in primary activities.* Knowledge needs can be structured according to primary and secondary activities in the value configuration. Depending on the firm being a value chain, a value shop or a value network, the knowledge management system must support more efficient production in the value chain, adding value to the knowledge work in the value shop, and more value by use of IT infrastructure in the value network.
- **Incentive Alignment.** Incentive alignment includes incentives influencing user behavior and the user's interaction with the system, deterrence of use for personal gain, use consistent with organizational goals, and robustness against information misrepresentation (Ba, Stallaert, & Whinston, 2001).

IS/IT IN KNOWLEDGE MANAGEMENT

Information technology can play an important role in successful knowledge management initiatives. Modern information technology such as the Internet, intranets, extranets, browsers, data warehouses, data filters, software agents, and expert systems can effectively support knowledge creation, sharing, and exchange in an organization and between organizations. Modern information technology can collect, systematize, structure, store, combine, distribute, and present information of value to knowledge workers (Nahapiet & Ghoshal, 1998). According to Davenport and Prusak (1998), more and more companies have instituted knowledge repositories, supporting such diverse types of knowledge as best practices, lessons learned, product development knowledge, customer knowledge, human resource management knowledge, and methods-based knowledge. Groupware and intranet-based technologies have become standard knowledge infrastructures. The low cost of computers and networks has created a potential infrastructure for knowledge sharing and opened up important knowledge management opportunities. The computational power as such has little relevance to knowledge work, but the communication and storage capabilities of networked computers make it an important enabler of effective knowledge work. Through e-mail, groupware, the Internet, and intranets, computers and networks can point to people with knowledge and connect people who need to share knowledge independent of time and place.

According to Grover and Davenport (2001), most knowledge management projects in organizations involve the use of information technology. Such projects fall into relatively few categories and types, each of which has a key objective. Although it is possible, and even desirable, to combine multiple objectives in a single project, this was not normally observed in a study of 31 knowledge management projects in 1997 (Davenport & Prusak, 1998). Since that time, it is possible that projects have matured and have taken on more ambitious collections of objectives.

Ward and Peppard (2002) find that there are two dominant and contrasting views of IS/IT in knowledge management: the engineering perspective and the social process perspective. The engineering perspective views knowledge management as a technology process. Many organizations have taken this approach in managing knowledge, believing that it is concerned with managing pieces of intellectual capital. Driving this view is the view that knowledge can be codified and stored; in essence that knowledge is explicit knowledge and therefore is little more than information.

The alternative view is that knowledge is a social process. As such, it asserts that knowledge resides in people's heads and that it is tacit. As such, it cannot be easily codified and only revealed through its application. As tacit knowledge cannot be directly transferred from person to person, its acquisition occurs only through practice. Consequently, its transfer between people is slow, costly, and uncertain. Technology, within this perspective, can only support the context of knowledge work. It has been argued that IT-based systems used to support knowledge management can only be of benefit if used to support the development and communication of human meaning. One reason for the failure of IT in some knowledge management initiatives is that the designers of the knowledge management systems fail to understand the situation and work practices of the users and the complex human processes involved in work.

While technology can be used with knowledge management initiatives, Ward and Peppard (2002) argue that it should never be the first step. Knowledge management is to them primarily a human and process issue. Once these two aspects have been addressed, then the created processes are usually very amenable to being supported and enhanced by the use of technology.

What, then, is knowledge management technology? A key focus here, however, should be on technology that captures, stores, and distributes structured knowledge for use by people. The goal of these technologies is to take knowledge that exists in human heads and partly in paper documents, and make it widely available throughout an organization. Similarly, Alavi and Leidner (2001) argue that information systems designed to support knowledge in organizations may not appear radically different from other forms of IT support, but will be geared toward enabling users to assign meaning to information and to capture some of their knowledge in information. Therefore, the concept of knowledge management technology in our view is less concerned with any degree of technology sophistication and more concerned with the usefulness in performing knowledge work in organizations and between organizations. Moffett and McAdam (2003) illustrate the variety of knowledge management technology tools by distinguishing between collaborative tools, content management, and business intelligence. Collaborative tools include groupware technology, meeting support systems, knowledge directories, and intranets/extranets. Content management includes the Internet, agents and filters, electronic publishing systems, document management systems, and office automation systems. Business intelligence includes data warehousing, decision support systems, knowledge-based systems, and workflow systems.

KNOWLEDGE MANAGEMENT PROCESSES

We now use the Alavi and Leidner (2001) framework to review the potential role of information technology in knowledge management. According to this framework, organizations consist of four sets of socially enacted knowledge processes: (1) creation (also referred to as construction), (2) storage and retrieval, (3) transfer, and (4) application. The knowledge-based view of the firm represents the cognitive and social nature of organizational knowledge and its embodiment in the individual's cognition and practices, as well as the collective (i.e., organizational) practices and culture. These processes do not represent a monolithic set of activities, but an interconnected and intertwined set of activities.

Knowledge Creation

Organizational knowledge creation involves developing new content or replacing existing content within the organization's tacit and explicit knowledge. Through social and collaborative processes as well as individual's cognitive processes (e.g., reflection), knowledge is created. The model developed by Nonaka et al. (2001) involving SECI, ba, and knowledge assets, views organizational knowledge creation as involving a continual interplay between the tacit and explicit dimensions of knowledge and a growing spiral flow as knowledge moves through individual, group, and organizational levels. Nonaka et al. (2001) suggest that the essential question of knowledge creation is establishing an organization's ba, defined as a common place or space for creating knowledge. Four types of ba corresponding to the four modes of knowledge creation are identified: (1) originating ba, (2) interacting ba, (3) cyber ba, and (4) exercising ba. Originating ba entails the socialization mode of knowledge creation and is the ba from which the organizational knowledge creation process begins. Originating ba is a common place in which individuals share experiences primarily through face-to-face interactions and by being at the same place at the same time. Interacting ba is associated with the externalization mode of knowledge creation and refers to a space where tacit knowledge is converted to explicit knowledge and shared among individuals through the process of dialogue and collaboration. Cyber ba refers to a virtual space of interaction and corresponds to the combination mode of knowledge creation. Finally, exercising ba involves the conversion of explicit to tacit knowledge through the internalization process. Thus, exercising ba involves the conversion of explicit to tacit knowledge through the internalization process.

Understanding the characteristics of various ba and the relationship with the modes of knowledge creation is important to enhancing organizational knowledge creation. For example, the use of IT capabilities in cyber ba is advocated to enhance the efficiency of the combination mode of knowledge creation. Data warehousing and data mining, document management systems, software agents, and intranets may be of great value in cyber ba. Considering the flexibility of modern IT, other forms of organizational ba and the corresponding modes of knowledge creation can be enhanced through the use of various forms of information systems. For example, information systems designed for support or collaboration, coordination, and communication processes, as a component of the interacting ba, can facilitate teamwork and thereby increase an individual's contact with other individuals.

Electronic mail and group support systems have the potential of increasing the number of weak ties in organizations. This in turn can accelerate the growth of knowledge creation. Intranets enable exposure to greater amounts of online organizational information, both horizontally and vertically, than may previously have been the case. As the level of information exposure increases, the internalization mode of knowledge creation, wherein individuals make observations and interpretations of information that result in new individual tacit knowledge, may increase. In this role, an intranet can support individual learning (conversion of explicit knowledge to personal tacit knowledge) through provision of capabilities such as computer simulation (to support learning by-doing) and smart software tutors.

Computer-mediated communication may increase the quality of knowledge creation by enabling a forum for constructing and sharing beliefs, for confirming consensual interpretation, and for allowing expression of new ideas. By providing an extended field of interaction among organizational members for sharing ideas and perspectives, and for establishing dialog, information systems may enable individuals to arrive at new insights and/or more accurate interpretations than if left to decipher information on their own.

Although most information repositories serve a single function, it is increasingly common for companies to construct an internal "portal" so that employees can access multiple different repositories and sources from one screen. It is also possible and increasingly popular for repositories to contain not only information, but also pointers to experts within the organization on key knowledge topics. It is also feasible to combine stored information with lists of the individuals who contributed the knowledge and could provide more detail or background on it (Grover & Davenport, 2001).

According to Grover and Davenport (2001), firms increasingly view attempts to transform raw data into usable knowledge as part of their knowledge management initiatives. These approaches typically involve isolating data in a separate "warehouse" for easier access and the use of statistical analysis or data mining and visualization tools. Since their goal is to create data-derived knowledge, they are increasingly addressed as a part of knowledge management. Some vendors have already begun to introduce e-commerce tools. They serve to customize the menu of available knowledge to individual customers, allowing sampling of information before buying and carrying out sales transactions for knowledge purchases. Online legal services are typical examples where clients can sample legal information before buying lawyer's time.

Knowledge Storage and Retrieval

According to Alavi and Leidner (2001), empirical studies have shown that while organizations create knowledge and learn, they also forget (i.e., do not remember or lose track of the acquired knowledge). Thus, the storage, organization, and retrieval of organizational knowledge, also referred to as organizational memory, constitute an important aspect of effective organizational knowledge management. Organizational memory includes knowledge residing in various component forms, including written documentation, structured information stored in electronic databases, codified human knowledge stored in expert systems, documented organizational procedures and processes, and tacit knowledge acquired by individuals and networks of individuals.

Advanced computer storage technology and sophisticated retrieval techniques, such as query languages, multimedia databases, and database management systems, can be effective tools in enhancing organizational memory. These tools increase the speed at which organizational memory can be accessed. Groupware enables organizations to create intraorganizational memory in the form of both structured and unstructured information and to share this memory across time and space. IT can play an important role in the enhancement and expansion of both semantic and episodic organizational memory. Semantic memory refers to general, explicit, and articulated knowledge, whereas episodic memory refers to context-specific and situated knowledge. Document management technology allows knowledge of an organization's past, often dispersed among a variety of retention facilities, to be effectively stored and made accessible. Drawing on these technologies, most consulting firms have created semantic memories by developing vast repositories of knowledge about customers, projects, competition, and the industries they serve.

Grover and Davenport (2001) found that in Western organizations, by far the most common objective of knowledge management projects involves some sort of knowledge repository. The objective of this type of project is to capture knowledge for later and broader access by others within the same organization. Common repository technologies include Lotus Notes, Web-based intranets, and Microsoft's Exchange, supplemented by search engines, document management tools, and other tools that allow editing and access. The repositories typically contain a specific type of information to represent knowledge for a particular business function or process, such as:

- "Best practices" information within a quality or business process management function
- Information for sales purposes involving products, markets, and customers
- Lessons learned in projects or product development efforts
- Information around implementation of information systems
- Competitive intelligence for strategy and planning functions
- "Learning histories" or records of experience with a new corporate direction or approach

The mechanical generation of databases, Web sites, and systems that process data are good and have the potential to take us to a higher plane in the organization, help us understand work flows better, and help us deal with organizational pathologies and problems. The data-to-information transition often involves a low level mechanical process that is well within the domain of contemporary information technologies, though humans are helpful in this transition as well. This information could exist in different forms throughout the organization and could even form the basis of competitive advantage or information products. For example, provision of information to customers about their order or shipment status is something that companies like Baxter and FedEx have been doing for years. But unlike knowledge, mechanically supplied information cannot be the source of sustained competitive advantage, particularly when the architectures on which it is based are becoming more open and omnipresent (Grover & Davenport, 2001).

IT in knowledge management can be used to store various kinds of information. For example, information about processes, procedures, forecasts, cases, and patents in the form of working documents, descriptions, and reports can be stored in knowledge management systems. TietoEnator, a Scandinavian consulting firm, has a knowledge base where they store methods, techniques, notes, concepts, best practices, presentations, components, references, guidelines, quality instructions, process descriptions, routines, strategies, and CVs for all consultants in the firm (Halvorsen & Nguyen, 1999). Knowledge retrieval can find support in content management and information extraction technology, which represents a group of techniques for managing and extracting information from documents, ultimately delivering a semantic meaning for decision makers or learners alike. This type of computer applications is targeted at capturing and extracting the content of free-text documents.

A group of computational techniques are available to alleviate the burden of these tasks. They include fuzzy technology, neural networks, and expert systems. On a more application-oriented level there are several approaches that apply one or more of the general techniques. The field is currently very dynamic, and new advances are made continuously.

Knowledge Transfer

Knowledge transfer occurs at various levels in an organization: transfer of knowledge between individuals, from individuals to explicit sources, from individuals to groups, between groups, across groups, and from the group to the organization. Considering the distributed nature of organizational cognition, an important process of knowledge management in organizational settings is the transfer of knowledge to locations where it is needed and can be used. However, this is not a simple process in that organizations often do not know what they know and have weak systems for locating and retrieving knowledge that resides in them. Communication processes and information flows drive knowledge transfer in organizations.

Knowledge transfer channels can be informal or formal, personal or impersonal. IT can support all four forms of knowledge transfer, but has mostly been applied to informal, impersonal means (such as discussion databases) and formal, impersonal means (such as corporate directories). An innovative use of technology for transfer is use of intelligent agent software to develop interest profiles of organizational members in order to determine which members might be interested recipients of point-to-point electronic messages exchanged among other members. Employing video technologies can also enhance transfer.

IT can increase knowledge transfer by extending the individual's reach beyond the formal communication lines. The search for knowledge sources is usually limited to immediate coworkers in regular and routine contact with the individual. However, individuals are unlikely to encounter new knowledge through their close-knit work networks because individuals in the same clique tend to possess similar information. Moreover, individuals are often unaware of what their cohorts are doing. Thus, expanding the individual's network to more extended, although perhaps weaker, connections is central to the knowledge diffusion process because such networks expose individuals to more new ideas.

Computer networks and electronic bulletin boards and discussion groups create a forum that facilitates contact between the person seeking knowledge and those who may have access to the knowledge. Corporate directories may enable individuals to rapidly locate the individual who has the knowledge that might help them solve a current problem. For example, the primary content of such a system can be a set of expert profiles containing information about the backgrounds, skills, and expertise of individuals who are knowledgeable on various topics. Often such metadata (knowledge about where knowledge resides) proves to be as important as the original knowledge itself. Providing taxonomies or organizational knowledge maps enables individuals to rapidly locate either the knowledge or the individual who has the needed knowledge, more rapidly than would be possible without such IT-based support.

Knowledge Application

An important aspect of the knowledge-based view of the firm is that the source of competitive advantage resides in the application of the knowledge rather than in the knowledge itself. Information technology can support knowledge application by embedding knowledge into organizational routines. Procedures that are culture-bound can be embedded into IT so that the systems themselves become examples of organizational norms. An example according to Alavi and Leidner (2001) is Mrs. Field's use of systems designed to assist in every decision from hiring personnel to when to put free samples of cookies out on the table. The system transmits the norms and beliefs held by the head of the company to organizational members.

Technology enforced knowledge application raises a concern that knowledge will continue to be applied after its real usefulness has declined. While the institutionalization of best practices by embedding them into IT might facilitate efficient handling of routine, linear, and predictable situations during stable or incrementally changing environments, when change is radical and discontinuous, there is a persistent need for continual renewal of the basic premises underlying the practices archived in the knowledge repositories. This underscores the need for organizational members to remain attuned to contextual factors and explicitly consider the specific circumstances of the current environment. Although there are challenges with applying existing knowledge, IT can have a positive influence on knowledge application. IT can enhance knowledge integration and application by facilitating the capture, updating, and accessibility of organizational directives. For example, many organizations are enhancing the ease of access and maintenance of their directives (repair manuals, policies, and standards) by making them available on corporate intranets. This increases the speed at which changes can be applied. Also, organizational units can follow a faster learning curve by accessing the knowledge of other units having gone through similar experiences. Moreover, by increasing the size of individuals' internal social networks and by increasing the amount of organizational memory available, information technologies allow for organizational knowledge to be applied across time and space.

IT can also enhance the speed of knowledge integration and application by codifying and automating organizational routines. Workflow automation systems are examples of IT applications that reduce the need for communication and coordination and enable more efficient use of organizational routines through timely and automatic routing of work-related documents, information, rules, and activities. Rule based expert systems are another means of capturing and enforcing well specified organizational procedures.

To summarize, Alavi and Leidner (2001) has developed a framework to understand IS/IT in knowledge management processes through the knowledge-based view of the firm. One important implication of this framework is that each of the four knowledge processes of creation, storage and retrieval, transfer, and application can be facilitated by IT:

- **Knowledge creation:** Examples of supporting information technologies are data mining and learning tools, which enable combining new sources of knowledge and just in time learning.
- **Knowledge storage and retrieval:** Examples of supporting information technologies are electronic bulletin boards, knowledge repositories, and databases, which provide support of individual and organizational memory as well as intergroup knowledge access.

- **Knowledge transfer:** Examples of supporting information technologies are electronic bulletin boards, discussion forums, and knowledge directories, which enable more extensive internal network, more available communication channels, and faster access to knowledge sources.
- **Knowledge application:** Examples of supporting information technologies are expert systems and workflow systems, which enable knowledge application in many locations and more rapid application of new knowledge through workflow automation.

SUMMARY

A firm's innovation capabilities are underpinned by its knowledge and knowledge management capabilities—that is, "ability to absorb and put to use new knowledge" (Adams et al., 2006). Knowledge management contributes to value creation by enhancing: intellectual asset management, operational efficiency, customer and competitor intelligence, continuous improvement, organizational learning, product and service innovation, and time to market (Metaxiotis & Psarras, 2006). To leverage knowledge management for business innovation, IT leaders must understand the basic principles, theories, and practices of knowledge management. Extending resource-based theory of firm to knowledge-based, the success of firms is not only based on the economics of the contracts it implements, but also on its heterogeneous stocks and flows of knowledge (Grover & Davenport, 2001). Companies having superior knowledge are able to coordinate and combine their traditional resources and capabilities in new and distinctive ways, providing more value to their customers than can their competitors (Zack, 1999). Knowledge, especially context-specific, tacit knowledge embedded in complex organizational routines and developed from experience, tends to be unique and difficult to imitate (Zack, 1999). To gain a knowledge-based strategic advantage, firms need to understand the characteristics of knowledge. Knowledge is information combined with experience, context, interpretation, reflection, intuition, and creativity. There are three categories of knowledge, with increasing level of sophistication: core (to stay in business), advanced (to remain competitively viable), and innovative (to lead entire industry) knowledge (Zack, 1999). This strategic knowledge framework helps firms conduct strategic knowledge gap analysis to define their business and knowledge strategies. Knowledge management is a discipline focused on systematic and innovative methods, practices, and tools for managing the generation, acquisition, exchange, protection, distribution, and utilization of knowledge, intellectual capital, and intangible assets (Montana, 2000). There are three schools of knowledge management: the economic school, the organizational school, and the strategic school (Earl, 2001). The economic school has a focus of income, where the aim is to exploit knowledge assets (i.e., incremental innovation). The organizational school has a focus of networks, where the aim is knowledge pooling (e.g., socialization, externalization, combination, and internalization SECI process). The strategic school has a focus of competitive advantage, where the aim is to identify, exploit, and explore knowledge capabilities (as the essence of the firm's strategy). Firms may choose a combination of principles from these schools to guide their knowledge management strategies. Commonly, from IT-enabling perspective, firms adopt a dual codification (automation) and personalization (people network) strategy, with one being more dominant than the other (typically 80/20 ratio) (Hansen et al., 1999). Three variant strategies are identified for three different types of businesses: stock strategy for efficiency-driven business, flow strategy for experience-driven business, and growth strategy for expert-driven business (Hansen, 1999). A chief knowledge officer is often appointed to lead corporatewide knowledge management initiative in the organization. The CKO role is an important one for both operational and symbolic reasons (Grover & Davenport, 2001). CKO is responsible for knowledge-based innovations in the firm. CKO evangelizes the business valuc of knowledge management to get the whole organization to embrace sound knowledge management practice both operationally and behaviorally. CKO leads the development and implementation the organization's knowledge management strategy (to close the strategic knowledge gap) in line with business strategy. CKO needs to be an intrapreneur (Antoncic & Hisrich, 2001), skillful in knowledge design (Davenport & Prusak, 1998; Earl & Scott, 1999), and knowledge architecture (Applehans et al., 1999).

Eleven distinct IT requirements of knowledge management emerge: interaction between information and knowledge; interaction between tacit and explicit knowledge; knowledge management strategy; combination of SECI process; explicit transfer of common knowledge; link knowledge to uses; treat knowledge as an intellectual asset in the economic school; treat knowledge as mutual resource in the organizational school, treat knowledge as a strategy in the strategy school; value configuration determines knowledge needs in primary activities; incentive alignment (Alavi & Leidner, 2001; Ba et al., 2001; Hansen et al., 1999).

The source of strategic advantage lies with the application of knowledge. IT can enhance the speed of knowledge integration and application by codifying and automating organizational routines. Workflow automation and rule based expert systems are example applications. IT can also facilitate each of the four knowledge processes of creation, storage and retrieval, transfer, and application (Alavi & Leidner, 2001). In short, IT can improve knowledge management to support business innovation for competitive advantage.

REFERENCES

Adams, R., Bessant, J., & Phelps, R. (2006). Innovation management measurement: A review. *International Journal of Management Reviews, 8*(1), 21-47.

Alavi, M., & Leidner, D. E. (2001). Knowledge management and knowledge management systems: Conceptual foundations and research issues. *MIS Quarterly, 25*(1), 107-136

Antoncic, B., & Hisrich, R. D. (2001). Intrapreneurship: Construct refinement and cross-cultural validation. *Journal of Business Venturing, 16*, 495-527.

Applehans, W., Globe, A., & Laugero, G. (1999). *Managing knowledge: A practical Web-based approach.* Addison-Wesley.

Ba, S., Stallaert, J., & Whinston, A. B. (2001). Research commentary: Introducing a third dimension in information systems design: The case of incentive alignment. *Information Systems Research, 12*(3), 225-239.

Chen, C. J. (2004). The effects of knowledge attribute, alliance characteristics, and absorptive capacity on knowledge transfer performance. *R&D Management, 34*, 311-321.

Christensen, C., & Overdorf, M. (2000, March-April). Meeting the challenge of disruptive change. *Harvard Business Review*, pp. 67-76.

Davenport, T. H., & Prusak, L. (1998). *Working knowledge*. Boston: Harvard Business School Press.

Dixon, N. M. (2000). *Common knowledge*. Boston: Harvard Business School Press.

Earl, M. J. (2001). Knowledge management strategies: Toward a taxonomy. *Journal of Management Information Systems, 18*(1), 215-233.

Earl, M. J., & Scott, I. A. (1999, Winter). What is a chief knowledge officer? *Sloan Management Review*, pp. 29-38.

Fahey, L., & Prusak, L. (1998). The eleven deadliest sins of knowledge management. *California Management Review, 40*(3), 265-276.

Foote, N. W., Matson, E., & Rudd, N. (2001). Managing the knowledge manager. *The McKinsey Quarterly, 3*. Retrieved September 7, 2008, from www.mckinseyquarterly.com

Gartner Group. (2001). *The disruptive impact of knowledge work: Retention*. Retrieved September 7, 2008, from www.gartner.com

Grover, V., & Davenport, T. H. (2001). General perspectives on knowledge management: Fostering a research agenda. *Journal of Management Information Systems, 18*(1), 5-21.

Hamel, G. (2000). *Leading the revolution*. Boston: Harvard Business School Press.

Hansen, M. T., Nohria, N., & Tierny, T. (1999, March-April). What's your strategy for managing knowledge? *Harvard Business Review*, pp. 106-116.

Hansen, M. T., & Oetinger, B. (2001, March). Introducing t-shaped managers: Knowledge management's next generation. *Harvard Business Review*, pp. 107-116.

Housel, T., & Bell, A. H. (2001). *Measuring and managing knowledge*. New York: McGraw-Hill Irwin.

Kaplan, R. S., & Norton, D. P. (2004). *Strategy maps*. Boston: Harvard Business School Press.

Kettinger, W. J., & Grover, V. (1995). Special section: Toward a theory of business process change management. *Journal of Management Information Systems, 12*(1), 9-30.

Krogh, G., Ichijo, K., & Nonaka, I. (2000). *Enabling knowledge creation*. Oxford, UK: Oxford University Press

Marchand, D., Kettinger, W., & Rollins, J. (2001). *Making the invisible visible: How companies win with the right information, people and IT.* Wiley England.

Markus, M. L. (2001). Toward a theory of knowledge reuse: Types of knowledge reuse situations and factors in reuse success. *Journal of Management Information Systems, 18*(1), 57-93.

Metaxiotis, K., & Psarras, J. (2006). Analysing the value of knowledge management leading to innovation. *International Journal of Knowledge Management Studies, 1*(1/2), 79-88.

Moffett, S., & McAdam, R. (2003). Contributing and enabling technologies for knowledge management. *International Journal of Information Technology and Management, 2*(1/2), 31-49.

Montana, J. C. (2000, July). The legal system and knowledge management. *The Information Management Journal*, pp. 54-57.

Nahapiet, J., & Ghoshal, S. (1998). Social capital, intellectual capital, and the organizational advantage. *Academy of Management Review, 23*(2), 242-266.

Nonaka, I., Toyama, R., & Konno, N. (2000). SECI, Ba and leadership: A unified model of dynamic knowledge creation. *Long Range Planning, 33*(1), 5-34.

Popadiuk, S., & Choo, C. W. (2006). Innovation and knowledge creation: How are these concepts related? *International Journal of Information Management, 26*, 302-312.

Roslender, R., & Ficham, R. (2001). Thinking critically about intellectual capital accounting. *Accounting, Auditing & Accountability Journal, 14*(4), 383-398.

Sveiby, K. E. (2001). A knowledge-based theory of the firm to guide in strategy formulation. *Journal of Intellectual Capital, 2*(4), 344-358.

Tiwana, A. (2002). *The knowledge management toolkit: Practical techniques for building a knowledge management system* (2nd ed.). Upper Saddle River, NJ: Prentice Hall.

Tsai, W. (2001). Knowledge transfer in intraorganizational networks: Effects of network position and absorptive capacity on business unit innovation and performance. *Academy of Management Journal, 44*, 996-1004.

Ward, J., & Peppard, J. (2002). *Strategic planning for information systems.* Wiley England.

Zack, M. H. (1999). Developing a knowledge strategy. *California Management Review, 41*(3), 125-145.

Chapter XII
Business-Aligned IT Strategy Case Example: CLP Group, Hong Kong

INTRODUCTION

Motivation

This chapter is about the "*know-how*" part of IT strategy and management best practices. This case example aims to illustrate a successful practical application of IT strategy principles and concepts by using a proven best practice from the industry. It can therefore be used as a guiding example of how to effectively develop and execute a business-aligned IT strategy.

Kaplan and Norton's (2004) strategy maps approach (described in Chapter V) has been chosen as the methodology for formulating the business–IT alignment strategy. To that end, the case study requires an in-depth study of the selected company's business and IT strategies, from which a strategy map of the espoused business and IT strategies are "reconstructed" using the strategy maps principles. The reconstruction process follows the strategy maps methodology (Kaplan & Norton, 2004). The readers can thus adopt a similar approach to help them formulate or "reconstruct" their company's business–IT alignment process and the resulting business-aligned IT strategy.

Methodology

IT strategies from several companies have been considered as candidates for this case example. The selection criteria for this case study are that the nominated companies must have:

1. Clear and successful application of key IT strategy and management principles and concepts
2. Evidence of formulation and execution of the IT strategy with at least two years track record to demonstrate alignment with the business strategy and where true business value has been delivered by the IT strategy
3. Tangible business value delivered by the IT strategy under study validated by the company's IT governance process
4. Consent given by the company's CIO[1]:
    - To make available the firm's documentation of IT strategy and implementation results
    - To partake in in-depth interview by the author to validate the contents and rationale of the IT strategy, its explicit alignment with the business strategy, and the business value resulted from its implementation

The methodology for constructing this case example is as follows:

a. Nomination of a company's IT strategy from peer recognition within a country
b. Critical review by the author (Chew) of the nominated company's business and IT strategies documentations
c. Interview by the author and discussion with the CIO of the nominated company
d. Synthesis[2] of the case example by the author (Chew) in collaboration with the CIO (using the knowledge and documentations gained from above) using basic principles described in this book
e. The case example produced is reviewed and validated by the CIO and approved by the company for publication

The company selected for the case example in this edition of the book is CLP Group,[3] Hong Kong.

CLP GROUP COMPANY PROFILE

CLP is a fortune global 1000 company, listed on the Hong Kong Stock Exchange. It has been an electricity supplier since 1901. An Asia Pacific leading power utility supplier, CLP was voted Asia's Best Utility in the 2006 Euromoney Awards. CLP is the largest foreign power investor in China. It is the owner and operator of the largest vertically integrated electricity supply business in Hong Kong. According to the CLP Annual Report 2007, CLP achieved, in 2007, HK$50.8 billion in revenue and HK$10.6 billion in earnings. It achieves supply reliability of 99.99%, the best in its class. It generates over 17,000MW of total generating capacity in Asia. In Hong Kong, CLP has 19,880 km of transmission and distribution lines, with 2.26 million customers with a supply area of approximately 1,000 sq. km. covering 80% of Hong Kong's population and supplying 73% of the electricity demand (CLP Annual Report, 2006).

According to the CLP chairman, "since the mid 1990s, the CLP Group has steadily widened its activities beyond its original Hong Kong base. CLP has become one of the leading external investors in the electricity sectors of the Chinese mainland, Australia, India, Thailand, and Taiwan. During 2007, these investments contributed HK$3.4 billion to overall CLP Group earnings" (CLP Chairman's Statement, Annual Report 2007).

CLP GROUP VISION/MISSION

CLP mission is "to deliver outstanding quality of electricity supply which is world-class in terms of reliability, cost-effectiveness, affordability, customer service and *environmental performance*" (CLP Holdings Annual Report 2006, Chairman's Statement)

CLP aims to maintain its cost leadership with the industry's best cost efficiency and to achieve sustainable profitable growth by regional expansion in Asia Pacific (CLP Annual Report, 2006)

STRATEGIC POSITIONING

In line with its corporate core values, CLP positions itself as an environmentally and socially responsible energy supplier. CLP regards environmental performance together with its community initiatives as critical part of CLP's commitment to be a responsible energy supplier who adds value to the communities to which CLP belong. "Environmental issues, including the risks associated with climate change, will continue to have a growing impact on CLP's activities beyond Hong Kong. They offer challenges and opportunities." (CLP Annual Report, 2006)

CLP issued the CLP Climate Vision 2050 in December 2007, which "commits CLP to a 75% reduction in the carbon intensity of CLP's generating portfolio by 2050, backed by a range of immediate and intermediate initiatives" (Chairman's Statement, CLP Annual Report, 2007). The vision calls for a new approach to CLP's electricity generating business.

CLP Renewables Group was established to manage and develop CLP's portfolio of renewable energy assets. CLP's efforts in this area have received international recognition, as evidenced by CLP being named as 'Corporate Developer of the Year' in the Euromoney and Ernst & Young Global Renewable Energy Awards 2006 (CLP Annual Report, 2006).

According to the CEO, CLP's long term success and credibility depend on the effective management, operation, and maintenance of its assets. Looking ahead, CLP is well positioned to meet the challenge of growing electricity demand in an affordable yet environmentally sustainable manner to maintain its competitive edge (CLP Annual Report, 2006). Thus the central theme of CLP strategy is operational excellence which will deliver CLP the sustainable cost leadership position.

The CLP Group derives its strategic advantage from having the following strengths and points of differentiation (CLP Annual Report, 2006):

- Expertise in a variety of technologies and fuel sources
- A good track record in the promotion and adoption of new technology
- The geographical range of its operations
- Strong, preserved financial position
- High standards of corporate governance, including internal financial and operating controls
- Proactive culture in addressing the environmental implications of CLP business

- The capacity to exploit the group synergies present in a business which operates on a large scale with a wealth of experience throughout the region

However, the CLP Group is facing a dynamic environment in sustaining its competitive position (Locandro, 2006):

- Modification of HK (Regulatory) Scheme of Control post-2008
- Growth
- Regional business transformation
- Environmental issues
- Compliance pressures

All these strategic issues are influencing the shape of CLP Group's corporate goals and strategy and, consequently, IT goals and strategy.

CLP GROUP STRATEGY

CLP group strategy is focused on *operational excellence* and supported, to a large extent, by customer intimacy values.

CLP IT STRATEGY

Since the formulation of IT Strategy in 2004, CLP has undergone significant business change. The ability of IT to adapt to changing business requirements over the years has required effective execution of the IT strategy supported by a strong IT governance process to instill discipline in IT investment prioritization and program management to deliver value.

The IT governance process initiated in 2005 has enabled the business to understand the value of IT and have greater ownership of IT projects. Significant business value has been delivered by the disciplined execution of the 2004 CLP IT Strategy (described at the end of this chapter). However, the changing business requirements and a new regional model are challenging the way IT operates in CLP.

Therefore a refinement of the IT Strategy has become necessary. The remainder of this chapter describes the emergent (renewed) business-aligned CLP IT Strategy as a result of the need for readjustment to respond to business changes. It also describes the business benefits delivered by the previous CLP IT Strategy (Locandro 2006).

The business-aligned CLP IT strategy is developed in collaboration with the business. It starts from in-depth understanding of the CLP group mission, vision, and strategy. The CLP IT strategy development process, using the Kaplan & Norton (2004) strategy maps approach, is synthesized and described below.

CLP STRATEGY MAP

Strategy map is a graphical representation of the alignment of the CLP IT strategy to the business strategy. The alignment process is in accordance with the strategy maps principles espoused by Kaplan and Norton (2004), described in Chapter V. The resultant business–IT alignment ensures that effective execution of the IT strategy will lead to CLP achieving the financial performance objectives articulated in the financial perspective.

The CLP strategy map synthesized by the case study is shown in Figure 12.1, and explained in the remainder of this chapter. It is intended to be used as a guiding example of how to formulate and execute a business-aligned IT strategy.

Table 12.1. CLP customer service performance pledges[6] (CLP © used with permission)

Delivering Our Pledges to You

Performance Pledges	2007 Results	2008 Targets
Reliability of electricity supply	Target met	99.99%
Notify customers 3 working days in advance of planned outage	Target met	99.00%
Arrive at site for loss of supply inspection within 1 hour of notification	Target met	99.67%
Restore supply within 4 hours of fault outage	Target met	97.30%
Provide appointments for installation inspections within 3 working days	Target met	96.25%
Keep appointments to visit customers for supply applications within a 1.5-hour time slot	Target met	96.00%
Connect and supply electricity within the same day after satisfactory installation inspection	Target met	99.95%
Reconnect supply within the same day of payment of outstanding charges	Target met	95.00%
Answer Emergency Service Hotline in less than 9 seconds	Target met	90% of answering time
Answer Enquiries Hotline in less than 9 seconds	Target met	80% of answering time
Average queuing time for payment at Customer Service Centres during peak hours*	Target met	Within 4 minutes
Average queuing time for customer service enquiries at Customer Service Centres	Target met	Within 10 minutes
Carry out site investigations on consumption enquiries within 3 working days	Target met	97.75%

*All CLP Customer Service Centres will discontinue payment service from July 2008.

Strategy map consists of four interrelated perspectives: financial, customers, (internal) core processes, and (internal) learning and growth perspectives (Kaplan & Norton, 2004). The map shows the firm's strategic alignment by means of the explicit linkages of the externally focused financial and customer perspectives to the internal core processes and learning and growth perspectives of the organization. Specifically, strategic alignment in the strategy map is "validated" by explicitly linking (or tracing) the strategic statements of one perspective to the correspondences in the adjacent perspectives, in terms of a causal relationship. For example, the financial perspective of productivity and growth will link to the CLP group strategy. The CLP customer value propositions in the customer perspective are designed to deliver great value to customers so as to achieve (and thus link directly to) the twin financial goals of cost-efficiency and profitable growth. The customer value propositions will also, in turn, shape the ways in which the core processes in the CLP internal perspective will be configured to create and deliver the "promised" customer values. Finally, the CLP information, human, and organizational capitals of the learning and growth perspective are defined, in line with the process requirements and corresponding customer value propositions, to support, work with, and enable the core business processes.

Explaining the step by step "reconstruction" of CLP strategy map and the attendant IT strategy below will be instructive to students who want to learn the strategy maps "know-how" for crafting their own IT strategy. A commentary remark *(in italic)* will appear next to each strategic statement to indicate the casual relationship with another strategic statement in the adjacent perspectives. Readers are encouraged to view the CLP strategy map diagram (Figure 12.1) in conjunction with reading the explanatory text.

CLP FINANCIAL PERSPECTIVE

CLP aims to maximize return on asset via (CLP Annual Report, 2006):

- Best-in-industry cost efficiency
- Profitable growth by regional expansion in Asia Pacific

This will be achieved through the operational excellence (primary) and customer intimacy (supporting) strategies, to be detailed by the strategy map below.

CLP CUSTOMER PERSPECTIVE

CLP provides world-class quality of electricity supply which is manifested by: best-in-class service reliability and customer service with affordable price and sustainable environmental performance (Chairman's Statement, CLP Annual Report, 2006) through the customer value propositions (CVP-a to CVP-e) below:

a. Reliable electricity supply (99.99%), supported by fast and efficient restoration of power interruption to premises (supports operational excellence)
b. Personalized and responsive customer service to enhance customers' lifestyle quality through world-class service excellence practice with stringent service KPIs published

as performance pledges to customers (see Table 12.1) (supports operational excellence and customer intimacy)

c. Efficient deployment of electricity services and maintenance to customer premises to enhance customer's lifestyle quality with reliability KPIs as stipulated in the service performance pledges of Table 12.1 (supports operational excellence and customer intimacy)

d. Globally competitive price tariffs on electricity (supports operational excellence)

e. Environmentally and socially responsible: (Renewable and clean) energy sources[4] are increasingly being deployed to improve customer's quality of life as they become

Figure 12.1. CLP strategy map

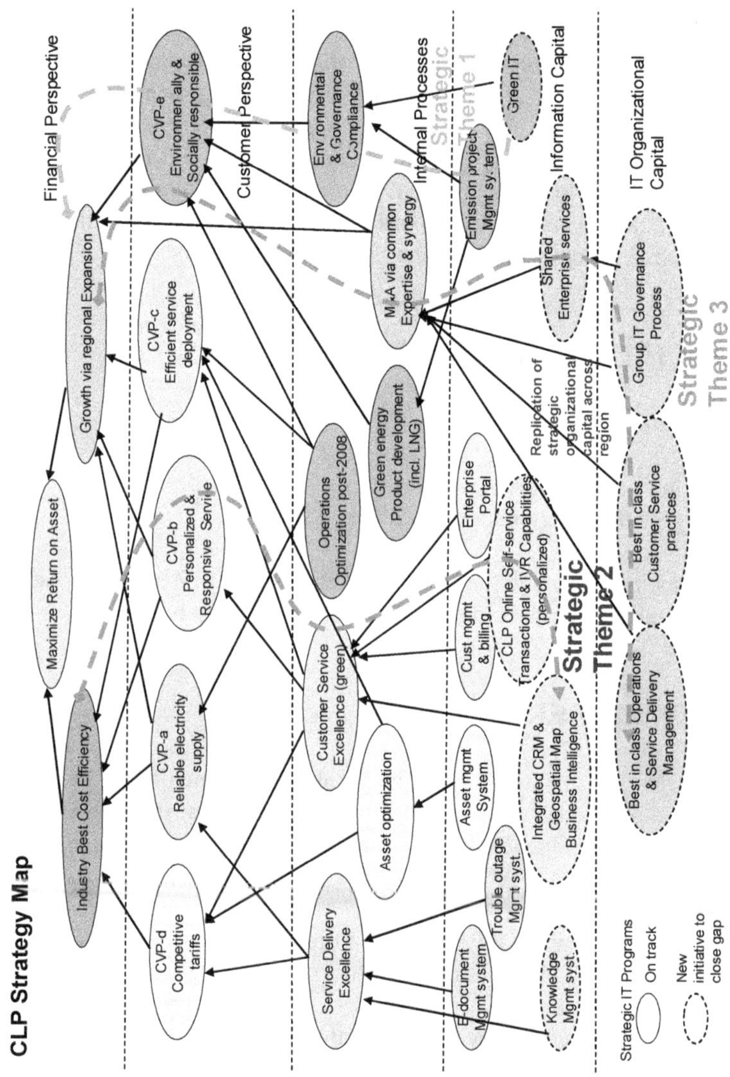

technically and economically feasible[5] (supports operational excellence and customer intimacy)

CLP INTERNAL PERSPECTIVE (CORE PROCESSES)

The purpose of the internal core processes perspective is to make a strategic choice on which particular processes with each core process group are fundamental to delivering the above differentiated customer value propositions. The selected processes are ones that the firm must excel in to ensure it will achieve a sustainable competitive advantage (Kaplan & Norton, 2004). Below we list and explain the strategic choices that CLP has made within each core process group, in the context of alignment with the business strategy and fulfilling the customer value propositions.

Operation Management

To achieve the business strategy and deliver on the value propositions committed to the customers, CLP has selected two key operations management processes to distinguish itself from the competition:

- **Service delivery (operational) excellence**
  Continue to enhance supply reliability (99.99%) and power quality; to ensure stable generation and distribution. This process deliver the customer value propositions of reliable electricity supply CVP-a, and competitive tariffs CVP-d, and supports operational excellence strategy.
- **Asset optimization**[7]

Deliver high financial performance (maximum profit at minimum total costs of ownership) and flexible operations from generating assets through: Excellent management, operation, and maintenance of core assets (such as generation power plants, transmission lines, distribution substations, underground cables, switch gears, and customer service centers) to achieve flexible operations, reduce total costs of ownerships, and maximize profits. *This process delivers the customer value propositions of efficient deployment of service CVP-c and competitive tariffs CVP-d, and supports operational excellence strategy.*

Operations Process Optimization Initiative

Additionally a new strategic operations process optimization initiative has been identified for investment, which will strengthen and optimize the current operations management core processes, to meet the "post-2008 Hong Kong Regulatory Scheme of Control" requirements. *This initiative will ensure that electricity supply reliability CVP-a, service deployment efficiency CVP-c, and the environmental and social responsibility CVP-e will continue to be satisfied upon enforcement of the new 2008 Hong Kong Regulatory Scheme of Control. It fulfills CLP mission and values, and contributes to strengthening CLP brand value proposition.*

Customer Management

CLP chooses to excel in the core customer process that focuses on serving as customers' trusted partner. As a trusted partner, CLP provides neutral and professional advice on efficient energy strategies and solutions. The objectives of this advice are to enhance consumer quality lifestyle or increase business competitive advantages and to create a better environment for the community. *This process delivers the customer value propositions of personalized and responsive customer service CVP-b, efficient service deployment CVP-c, and competitive tariffs CVP-d, and supports customer intimacy strategy.*

The key process selected aims to provide customer service excellence through:

- Offer greater convenience and flexibility to customers in managing different aspects of their electricity accounts. *(It supports customer intimacy and operational excellence strategy.)*
- Commit to customer service excellence KPIs as stipulated in publicly announced service performance pledges (Table 12.1). *This process delivers the customer value propositions of personalized and responsive customer service CVP-b, efficient service deployment CVP-c, and competitive tariffs CVP-d, and it supports customer intimacy and operational excellence strategy.*
- Green customer service, through community education and innovative use of technology, to help create a sustainable environment for present and future generations. *This process delivers the customer value proposition of personalized and responsive customer service CVP-b. It supports customer intimacy strategy.*

Innovation Management

To achieve CLP mission of being an environmentally and socially responsible electricity supplier, and its vision of profitable growth via expansion in the Asia Pacific region, CLP focuses on two core innovation management processes:

- **Green energy product development process**
  Efficient process for developing green energy products such as liquid natural gas is a critical innovation initiative. *This process supports the operational excellence strategy and fulfills CLP mission (and customer value proposition CVP-e) of being an environmentally and socially responsible energy supplier. Improvement of speed-to-market of green product development process will contribute to meeting CLP financial growth objective.*
- **Merger and acquisition regional synergy process**
  Streamlining and systematizing the due diligence process of pre-M&A activities and the regional expertise synergy process of post-M&A are enabling CLP growth via M&A. They improve CLP's competitive position in the M&A bid process and speed up CLP Group value accretion post-M&A. *This process supports the operational excellence strategy, delivers the customer value proposition of environmentally and socially responsible energy supplier CVP-e, and contributes to meeting CLP financial growth objective.*

Regulatory Management

Sustainable environmental management is a key CLP strategy, fundamental to strengthening the CLP brand which enables growth. It sets responsible environmental policies and implements internationally certified environmental management systems such as ISO 14001. CLP voluntarily reports its environmental performance by publishing the Sustainability Report (previously known as *CLP Social and Environmental Report*). Over the years, CLP has received accolades for its efforts in environmental performance, innovation, and reporting.

Thus the regulatory management core process, known as environmental and governance compliance process, which is subject to external audit by independent authorities, is to ensure CLP maintain its world class and industry leadership in:

- Power station emission reduction
- Environmental requirement compliance
- Corporate governance compliance

The process delivers the customer value propositions of efficient service deployment CVP-c and of environmentally and socially responsible energy supplier CVP-e, and supports customer intimacy and operational excellence strategies. Regulatory management process enhances CLP brand values and promotes growth.

The information capital requirements of CLP core processes are next analyzed below to determine the core of CLP IT strategy. The strategy defines the business applications development (i.e., capital investment) required to support or enable the core processes and to attain CLP twin financial goals of industry-best cost efficiency and growth via regional expansion.

CLP LEARNING AND GROWTH PERSPECTIVE INFORMATION CAPITAL (IT STRATEGY)

Information capital requirements[8] analysis of the CLP strategic core processes has identified the following business applications required for achieving the CLP corporate strategy and financial goals. They are shown in Table 12.2 in terms of four application classes (Weill & Broadbent, 1998) previously described in Chapter VII. Gap analysis of the information capital requirements against CLP current business applications environment (part of architecture gap analysis) has revealed which existing applications need to be enhanced and which totally new applications will need to be developed to meet the "target state" future business requirements.

Gap Analysis

Gap analysis is the assessment of the strategic readiness of existing applications or programs (Kaplan & Norton, 2004). This is often color-coded to facilitate visual recognition, which is particularly helpful for an enterprise with numerous applications and programs. The color code has three colors: green denotes the application of program is ready strategically (i.e., little or no gap), yellow denotes partial readiness (i.e., there is a small gap of 20–25% or

Table 12.2. Aligning business applications to the CLP strategic core processes

Core Strategic Processes	Service delivery excellence	Asset optimization	Customer service excellence; CLP Online	Green energy product development	M&A Due Diligence and Expertise Synergy	Environment and governance compliance
Strategic Applications		Asset management system	Integrated CRM	Emission project management system	Shared enterprise services	Emission project management system; SOX 404 compliance
Informational Applications	E-document management system		Geospatial map business intelligence integrated with CRM above; Knowledge management system			External management and reporting system; Records management system
Transactional Applications	Trouble outage management system		E-commerce; Customer management and billing			
Infrastructure Applications			Enterprise portal		Internet security (Group)	Holistic green IT
Application Gap: Enhance/New	Enhance	Enhance	Enhance & New	New	New	Enhance & New

less of the target set of capabilities for the required business application, or of the target completion date for the required business program) and red denotes unreadiness (i.e., the target application or program does not yet exist and needs to be developed).

To be fully aligned with the business strategy, yellow (which usually requires enhancement to an existing application) and red (which requires a new application) programs or applications will require resource allocation. They need to be prioritized via IT governance process (Chapter IX), and IT project portfolio process (Chapter VII), aided by the enterprise architecture roadmap (Chapter VI). Balanced investment will be decided by the relative priorities of the portfolio of applications: from infrastructure to transactional, informational (or analytics) to strategic (or transformational) applications. The relative priorities depend on the IT maturity of the enterprise (see Chapter VII for more detailed discussion).

From the result of the application gap analysis, it is identified that several in-flight programs remain relevant for the emergent IT strategy and are on-track to deliver on the requisite business capabilities for competitive advantage (Locandro, 2006). The application development programs (yellow) that require enhancements to satisfy the information requirements of the core processes are as follows:

- **Customer relationship management (CRM) capabilities.** Enhancement of the CRM application will close the partial functionality gap identified, and *will meet the customer service excellence process requirements and contribute to service deployment efficiency CVP-c, personalized and responsive customer service CVP-b, and competitive tariffs CVP-d of the operational excellence and customer intimacy strategies.*

- **E-Commerce (e-procurement, e-channel, revamp group Web site).** Enhancement of the e-commerce platform will close the partial functionality gap identified, and *will meet the customer service excellence process requirements and contribute to service deployment efficiency CVP-c, personalized and responsive customer service CVP-b, and competitive tariffs CVP-d of the operational excellence and customer intimacy strategies.*
- **Enterprise portal** increases employee productivity and efficiency by creating a single interface into the company's information systems and news broadcasts. Employees who interact with customers are aware of all company announcements and press releases. They have easy access to customer and other related systems that sit within the portal. *This will meet the customer service excellence process requirements and contribute to personalized and responsive customer service CVP-b.*
- **Asset management system** *is the strategic application that will satisfy the asset optimization core process which optimizes CLP asset deployment to deliver maximum return on asset. It will enable the customer value propositions of efficient (CVP-c) and reliable (CVP-a) provision, transmission, and distribution of electricity.*
- **Electronic document management system** *satisfies the requirements of electricity service delivery excellence process, and contributes to the customer value propositions of reliable electricity supply CVP-a, and competitive tariffs CVP-d.*
- **Customer management and billing** *application satisfies the requirements of customer service excellence core process, and contributes to the customer value propositions of service deployment efficiency CVP-c, and personalized and responsive customer service CVP-b.*
- **Trouble call outage management system** *application satisfies the requirements of electricity service delivery excellence process, and contributes to the customer value propositions of reliable electricity supply CVP-a, and competitive tariffs CVP-d.*

These business programs are on-track and being managed by the program management office as business-as-usual programs. Other in-flight business as usual programs are:

- **New best practices from the latest enterprise resource planning (ERP) releases:** *To satisfy the requirements of electricity service delivery excellence process, and contribute to the customer value propositions of reliable electricity supply CVP-a.*
- **Mobile solutions for field workforce:** *To satisfy the requirements of electricity service delivery excellence process, and contribute to the customer value propositions of reliable electricity supply CVP-a.*
- **Enhanced group information security policies:** *To meet corporate governance compliance requirements.*
- **Plant automation and infrastructure upgrades:** *To meet corporate governance compliance requirements.*
- **Sarbanes-Oxley (SOX) 404 Compliance:** *To meet corporate governance compliance requirements.*

Analysis of the remaining strategic gap reveals three major strategic areas which CLP must close to achieve the corporate strategy. This is the core of the emergent CLP Group IT strategy. The CLP IT strategy stipulates that in order to help execute the corporate strategy and contribute to delivering the twin financial goals of industry-best cost efficiency and growth via regional expansion, IT must excel in executing the following three strategic areas:

1. **Mandatory regulatory and corporate governance compliance:** *To reinforce CLP mission and brand value of being an environmentally and socially responsible energy supplier.*
2. **Customer service differentiation:** *To improve CLP position as the industry-best cost leadership (and therefore customer acquisition and retention performance),* through innovative online capability and business intelligence through integrated customer relationship management.
3. **IT organizational capital alignment:** *To support CLP growth by regional expansion strategy,* via leveraging of IT resource or capability synergy and replication of common expertise across the region to increase speed to market and maximize growth.

The new business programs required to meet the business requirements of these three strategic themes are reviewed below.

Theme 1: Regulatory and Corporate Governance Compliance

This theme has four core programs. The first program institutionalizes a new IT work practice throughout the group—Green IT, as part of *CLP social responsibility business strategy.* Not only will Green IT support CLP brand, but also it will save energy consumption and costs. The Green IT initiative involves a spectrum of activities:

- **Green Recycle**
  - 100% of printer toners are recyclable
  - 100% batteries for PC peripherals such as keyboard and mouse are rechargeable
  - Recycle by donating 300+ aged PC to nine charity organizations
- **Green Printing**
  - 20% reduction of printer paper in corp units
  - 100% increase in recycled paper in last 18 months
  - Increase the efficiency of printer to user ratio from 1:4 to 1:8
- **Energy Efficiency**
  - Power off idle PC during and after work saves between 71–97% power usage per hour
  - Data center cooling and lighting initiatives save approximately 15% energy usage
- **Technology Green**
  - Video conference to substitute travels to offset and reduce carbon-mile
  - Real time site monitoring

The other three new business programs for regulatory and corporate governance compliance strategic theme are:

- **Project management system for emission control and liquid natural gas construction sites** *meet the environmental and governance compliance process and green energy product development process requirements.*
- **External management and reporting systems to meet the government requirements for generation business and the group environmental affairs requirement for a Web-based sustainability report.** *It meets the environmental and governance compliance process requirements.*
- **Records management system to electronically capture, record, maintain, and dispose of all information (including safety, legal, customer performance pledges, and operational regulatory performance records) required to meet legal and customer obligations of the company.** *It meets the environmental and governance compliance process requirements.*

Theme 2: Customer Service Differentiation

There are three major strategic thrusts to achieving customer service differentiation: CLP Online, business intelligence, and knowledge management. These strategic programs will deliver on two principal CLP commitments to customers: personalized and responsive customer service CVP-a, and efficient service deployment CVP-c, both of which are CLP differentiation from competition.

CLP Online

CLP Online increases service responsiveness to customers by allowing them online access to do enquiries and some transactions 24/7. It allows CLP to fulfill the customer service performance pledges stated in Table 12.1. The e-channel also allows CLP to send electricity bills and conduct marketing campaigns via e-mail. For example, it also allows CLP to educate consumers on the benefits of all electric home and induction cooking. CLP Online offers customers the flexibility to contact CLP via *their* preferred method. It will ease the pressure on the call center without deteriorating customer service (Locandro, 2007c).

CLP Online enables customer self-service such as electricity account application, billing, and payment. It also enables customer e-mail marketing, which "leverages the green bill message" targeted to Green Bill customers. It provides customized hyperlinks, for example, by rate category, segment, trade class, and so forth. And it directs traffic to www.clpgroup.com. It is relatively passive, sent according to the billing cycle. It allows large customer bills to be "grouped" to enhance user friendliness and increase efficiency. It also provides enhanced bill download format to suit customer needs, for example, text, Excel, PDF (Locandro, 2007c).

CLP Online further enhances appointment time slots. Ten time slots are now available to customers instead of three, previously. And it extends to 10 time slots of 10 working days. It provides self-meter reading. About 5% (5000) of CLP Online customers live in village housing. CLP Online facilitates village customers whose premises may not be accessible for meter reading. Customers can also submit online requests to arrange for timely move-in (connect) and move-out (disconnect) when relocating premises. There are simple to use guidelines to show customers how to input meter readings online (Locandro, 2007c).

CLP Online enables personalization. It provides targeted messages according to customer types (Locandro, 2007c) such as overdue bill reminders. Promote autopay (direct debit) and credit card autopay for targeted customers. It also offer customized and call-for-action promotion banners.

CLP Online is supported by customer service hotline and customer service centers. CLP IT provides improved customer service through creative use of technology such as the CRM Interaction Center. It also provides an interactive voice response system (IVRS) with major functions such as account status, change of billing options, copy bill request, report payment, and so on, and the IVRS provides optimized call center resource scheduling. In short, CLP IT provides a fully integrated customer-serving platform in support of customer intimacy and operational excellence strategies (Locandro, 2007c).

Business Intelligence

Enhanced customer experience can also be achieved by migrating from data paradigm to business intelligence paradigm, through strategic use of geospatial technology. As the CLP Group CIO states, *"The value of data is not what information it displays, but rather what perceptions and insights of the business you gain"* (Locandro, 2007c).

Indeed, despite improvements at the higher-end of the value chain, the business has highlighted a need to extract greater value from enterprise information (Locandro, 2006). It calls for CLP IT to improve *business information* and *process* capabilities, which require business intelligence to enable or support:

- **Operational excellence:** By selecting appropriate tools that can interrogate the transactional ERP systems to assist in giving new insights to improve operational efficiency. For example, CLP use BI tools to give predictive monitoring of maintenance wear and tear of power plants and transmission equipment to proactively replace wearing parts *before* they fail. *It contributes to reliable electricity supply value proposition CVP-a.*
- **Business growth:** By conducting effective data mining on customer segments to identify trends for each segment and develop innovative products to meet the trends for each segment. For example, marketing campaign to influence Chinese restaurants to switch to induction cooking. .

Geospatial data and operational data can be integrated (mashed up) as part of business intelligence to create new customer and market insights and gain competitive advantage. The following data sources are available for gaining the business insights and creating the CLP advantage (Locandro, 2007b, 2007c):

- Market data - CRM
- Network capacity – supply points
- Customer profile – customer billing
- Census data – government
- Geospatial map – location data

Data mashing from these sources gives CLP business insights. For example, by choosing an area from the geospatial map, CLP can identify the highest consumption per customer;

the biggest bad debt; the competitors with highest market share; and the highest income per customer (Locandro, 2007b, 2007c).

Knowledge Management

Knowledge management is focused on sharpening CLP competency in reliable electricity supply. For example, knowledge management tools are used to capture experiential learning and record all tacit and explicit knowledge from engineers to improve worker knowledge on problem resolution and improve maintenance processes. It allows CLP to harness its world class expertise built over many years through skilful engineers and employees. As a result many faults that can cause a disruption to electricity supply can be rectified very quickly. CLP knowledge base also helps other employees to access the accumulated experience and knowledge to tackle power supply reliability issues efficiently and effectively to match CLP customer service performance pledges (Table 12.1). It contributes to reliable electricity supply value proposition CVP-a.

Theme 3: IT Organization Capital Alignment

CLP's *growth strategy through regional expansion* poses a number of challenges to the business (Locandro, 2006; Locandro 2007a, 2007b, 2007c). The expansion into China, Thailand, India, and Australia has resulted in geographically and culturally disperse operations with diverse regulatory schemes. The CLP subsidiaries and affiliates have diverse and growing portfolio with different levels of management control and varying degree of IS management maturity. They demand decentralized decisions and disintegrated solutions to maintain local market responsiveness. However, at the same time, there is the strategic advantage to increase group synergy and gain economies of scale. The IT organizational capital strategy therefore needs *to support the group synergy and local market responsiveness strategic objectives of the regional expansion strategy. And it supports the M&A due diligence and expertise synergy process to enable CLP to grow by further regional expansion.* Specifically, CLP IT organization needs to achieve (Locandro, 2006):

a. Culture shift to deal with new business dynamics
b. Business oriented IT service delivery model
c. Regional synergy and leverage
d. Develop group enterprise architecture
e. Extending IT governance for the group

The strategic objective of each element of the IT organizational capital is discussed in turn below.

A: Cultural Shift

IT cultural shift is instituted by the IT leadership team along three paths:

- Develop a commercial-minded culture across IT regionally through a human capital management program. The program focuses on improving IT responsiveness and orientation to business needs, and on experience sharing between regulated and deregulated markets.

- Improve inter and intrateams planning and communication through continue focus of cross-pollination through engagements with representatives across the group (e.g., biannual regional IT managers meeting), and knowledge sharing of business processes and application templates.
- Enhance staff mobility through staff rotation to achieve a truly regional mobile workforce. For example, 30% of staff are available for postings of 6 months or less. Staff have also been seconded to various projects around the region on projects.

To support this cultural shift, several programs have been instituted as part of IT human resource management practice (Locandro, 2007), including:

- **Recognition program:** Staff commendation at monthly team meetings
- **Two-way, cross-team communication and business exposure** to increase business operation and knowledge sharing and IT group orientation to business
- **Sharing best practices program** via monthly cross team gathering and sharing
- **Measurement and monitoring program** through linkage of core values to individual performance objectives
- **Skill enhancement program** through professional development and skills competency training in progress

B: Business-Oriented Service Delivery Model

IT alignment to regional business expansion is executed through a business oriented IT service delivery model, as illustrated in Figure 12.2. It stresses enhancing IT culture toward stronger *service orientation*, and transforming its service delivery model from an "internal service company" model to a more commercially and customer focused "group shared services," acting like an external service provider (albeit not-for-profit). *This is in response to the business need for regional synergy and leverage.*

For example, the current strengths in applications and infrastructure development and operations support (Operations and Service Management Excellence) capabilities of Hong Kong business are being shared across the region. CLP has a world class data center and IT infrastructure operations in Hong Kong. CLP leverages these strengths to host systems such as back-office financials and e-mail for their businesses in China, India, and Thailand. CLP Hong Kong also has excellent capability in development and support of key applications that are standard across the CLP Group such as ERP, document management, and plant information systems. This strength allows CLP to effectively deploy its intellectual properties and expertise across the region.

Thus, the modus operandi is to leverage group IT skills and capabilities to create a federated model of regional IT departments that exploits group synergies and yet is aligned with the local business. For example, groupwide Internet security is strengthened by leveraging the group IT skills. This federated model must leverage and implement the regional synergy strategy as described below. *It supports M&A expertise synergy process to enable growth via regional expansion.*

Figure 12.2. CLP IT service delivery model (CLP © used with permission)

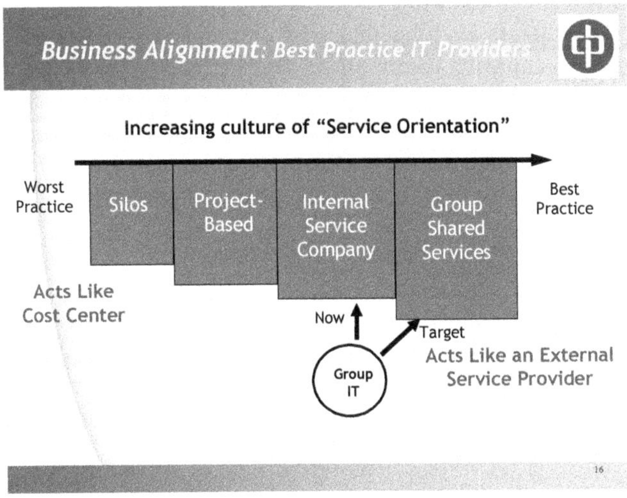

C: Regional Synergy

Regional synergy is achieved through four phases (Locandro, 2006):

- **Phase 1:** *Leverage regional agreements* – Use economies of scale to negotiate the most commercially advantageous agreements for the region in hardware, software (such as desktop, ERP), and communications vendors.
- **Phase 2:** *Ad hoc consulting* – Leverage Hong Kong's expertise in IT planning, product selection, system integration evaluation, and infrastructure architecture to speed up roll out of IT services to the newly acquired or joint-ventured regional utility and enhance IT management maturity in the region.
- **Phase 3:** *Cross sharing on standard platforms* – Institute the culture of knowledge sharing across the region, which includes: intellectual properties (templates, documentation), knowledge base, and implementation support from internal selected centers of excellence (COE). For example, the initial COEs include: enterprise COE, customer COE, engineering COE, and decision support COE.

For example, regional cross sharing of IT strategy and project management professionals, certified ERP consultants, certified security professionals, certified office systems and networking specialists, certified ITIL specialists, and certified BS7799 security implementer and auditor. The COE also provides regional support and coordination in IT strategy and planning, application, and architecture development, operational and project implementation and quality assurance, as well as regional procurement frameworks, IT governance and best practices, and construction of greenfield site IT to operations and maintenance phase. *M&A expertise synergy process is used to share and replicate CLP best-in-class operations and service management (and other) practices across the regions, where ap-*

propriate. This will ramp up the operational capabilities of new acquisitions and speed up their ability to contribute value to CLP Group.

To achieve a rapid integration capability, CLP developed the concept of *"IT in a box."* It applies a *"template"* approach to new sites. This approach allows CLP IT to design a solution once and roll out many times, which improves speed of implementation. It also allows a new site to leverage experience from other sites using, where appropriate, packaged policies and architectural standards. To that end, "IT in a box" provides an agile "technology platform" and provides opportunities to leverage regional procurement agreements to gain economies of scale.

- **Phase 4:** *Centralized environment* – Implement the full complement of the regional shared services model, in which a centralized environment will provide shared infrastructure, central/regional hosting, and single instance of common applications (e.g., e-mail, SAP).

D: Enterprise Architecture

The enterprise architecture references the CLP business context (business strategy and external environments) to set the direction for: business architecture, information architecture, and technology architecture. See Chapter VI for details on enterprise architecture.

CLP enterprise architecture is founded on the business function reference model. The business function reference model is a high level representation of the key business components of CLP Power's utility business based on a standard industry model.

Figure 12.3. CLP business function reference model (CLP © used with permission)

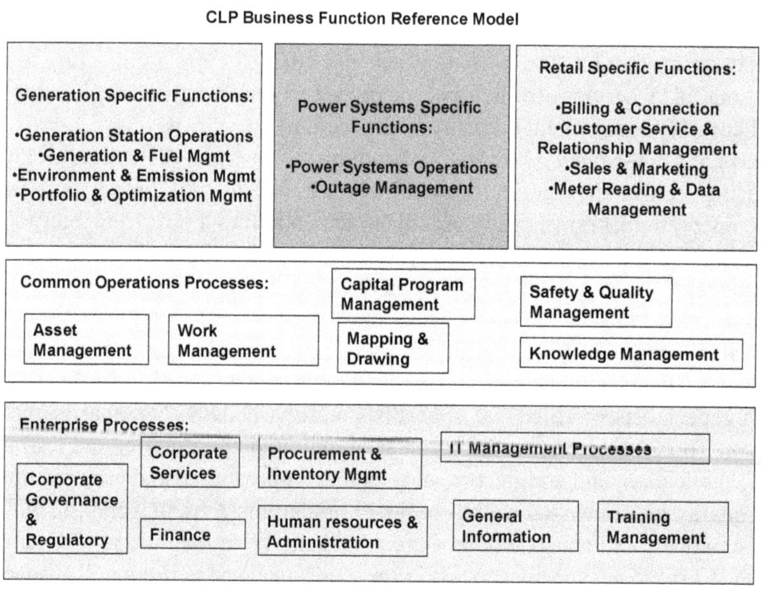

The three layers of the business function reference model (see Figure 12.3) are as follows:

- **Business group-specific functions**: Business processes that are specific and unique to the individual lines of business (or business groups), for example, generation business, power systems business, or retail business specific functions.
- **Common operational processes:** Business processes that are common in nature (but not necessarily in content) across the core lines of business (or business groups), for example, asset management, work management, and safety and quality management.
- **Enterprise processes:** Business processes that operate across the enterprise and that are common across all business units (front-office, back-office, support, enabling, etc.), for example, corporate governance and regulatory functions, procurement and inventory management, and human resource management functions.

In addition, the common operational process layer will provide a view of the business components that are often enabled by similar or same application solutions, for example, asset management system to efficient and effective management of core electricity generation assets.

Enterprise information is managed through business-lead data governance by the central IT project office (see Figure 12.6). Data governance defines the decision rights for data standards, models, repositories, and access control. Business intelligence program described above is guided by enterprise information management principles and control.

The enterprise technology architecture (Figure 12.4) links CLP strategy to the requisite IT solutions. In essence it defines the framework of for assessing what platforms will be

Figure 12.4. CLP enterprise technology architecture (CLP © used with permission)

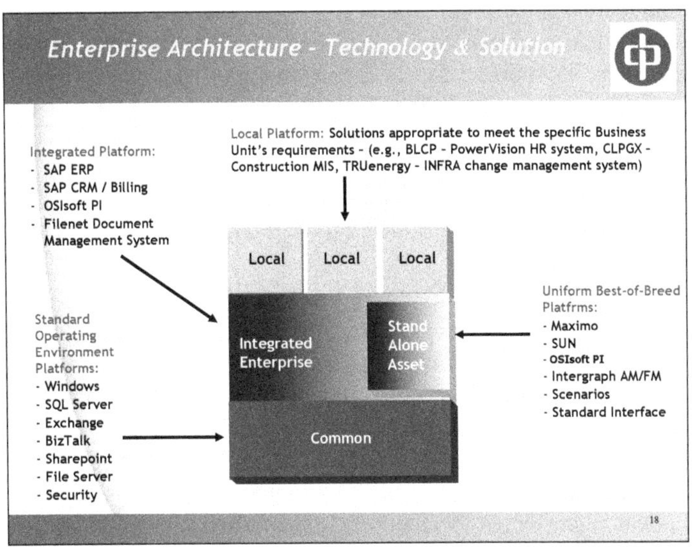

Figure 12.5. CLP group technology management process (CLP © used with permission)

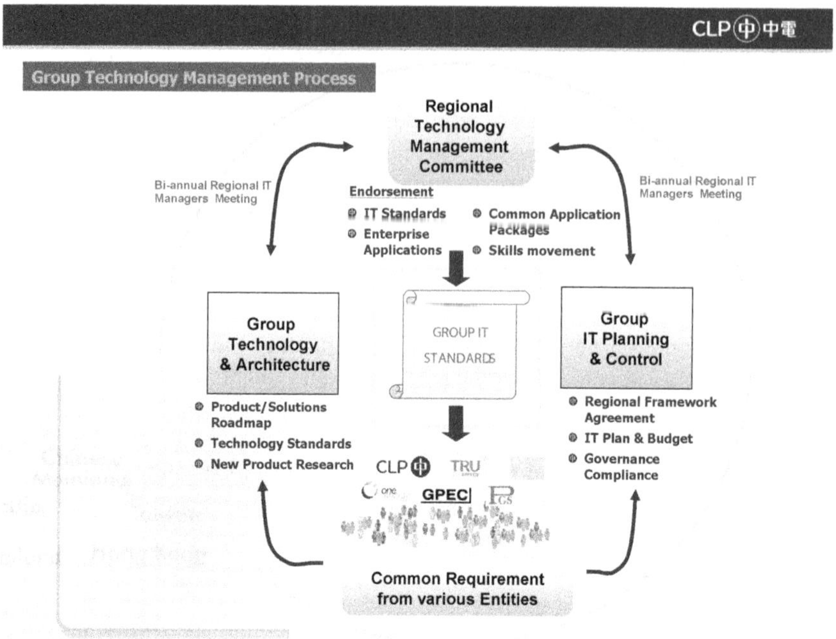

common across the whole of CLP Group of companies (the bottom layer) and what will be allowed to be specific for the unique local business purpose (the top layer). The middle layer illustrates a two-tier strategy which mandates that large companies and affiliates with more complex and greater scale business will adopt a common ERP platform, while the smaller subsidiaries or affiliates with standalone assets (e.g., power stations) without distribution and retail channels will standardize on a select set of best-of-breed prescribed software products. The enterprise technology architecture defines the common principles and standards, where appropriate, for the region and improves the end-to-end integration of information which will result in (Locandro, 2006):

- Improved speed-to-market (e.g., up to 30% improvement due to reuse of predefined platforms with standardized configurations and test plans)
- Sharing of best practices and improved cost control due to adoption of common standards
- Enabling group interoperability through standardization
- Real-time capability for enterprise performance management (*i.e., business intelligence for operational excellence in Theme 2*). Real time information flows cover operational power plant performance, transmission, and distribution flows to certain areas as well as near real time power consumption for large customers through smart meters. In each of these lines of business speed of information is essential so that predictive or remedial action can be taken to improve performance of the power assets or potential customer consumption in the future.

Enterprise Architecture Governance

A key component of CLP's IT governance (described later) is enterprise architecture governance, which is related to enterprise architecture principles and standards (see Figure 12.4). These standards dictate what will be common across the group of companies in terms operating and environment and applications and what type of applications and policies can be used locally. As mentioned above, CLP has defined a standard for applications set for large companies and subsidiaries to adopt an ERP solution, while it permits smaller standalone businesses to adopt a best of breed approach. This is known as a two-tier architecture strategy that allows flexibility and cost effectiveness for smaller assets while enforcing standards to leverage economies of scale for larger enterprises.

CLP architecture governance operates as follows (Figure 12.5). For local business-specific applications, solution decision rests with local head of IT. This is because while the group preferred solutions may exist, they might not fit all utilities. This is in line with the prevailing global IT strategy management practice described in Chapter V.

For integrated enterprises with cross-business applications, the strategic direction is for the existing legacy to move to CLP standards. All new projects should conform to CLP Group IT standards. Deviation requires approval from the IT steering committee (which oversees the end-to-end IT management life cycle, Figure 12.6) with business case. This

Figure 12.6. CLP IT governance framework (CLP © used with permission)

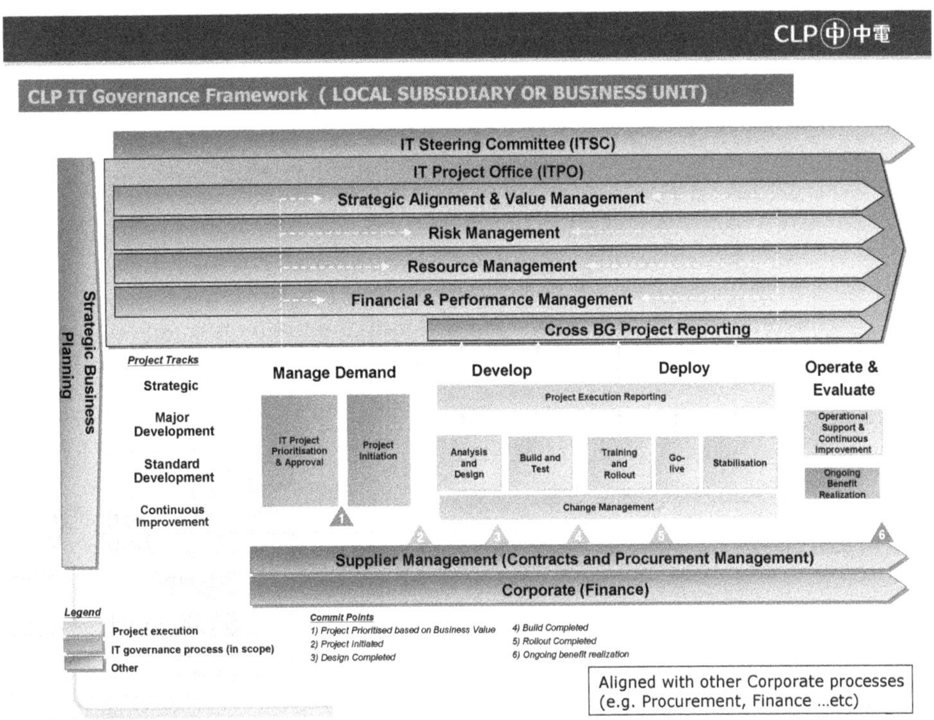

is handled by the "Exception to the IT Architecture and Standards" decision area of the IT governance matrix (Figure 12.7). For the CLP Group, sign-off approval from the group CIO is required. For smaller affiliate companies, the decision right rests with the country manager, while the group CIO provides a review input.

Standard operating environment (SOE) platforms are mandated for common infrastructure system across the CLP group. SOE is the core architecture component of the group IT strategy. All new projects must conform to CLP Group IT standards, and nonconforming systems must have replacement plan or approval to remain as-is. All common products have defined upgrade points and desired versions.

While it is important to have the group IT standards and architecture, there needs to be a process to allow it to continually evolve and also allow all stakeholders to effectively participate in the formulation of new standards, and so forth. Within CLP this is done via a *collaborative* approach between group IT and the IT management in each of the subsidiaries. This process is highlighted in Figure 12.5. In essence, common requirements are gathered from companies, subsidiaries, and JV partners in terms of systems or technology. These requirements are submitted to CLP Group IT Technology and Architecture for review (left-hand-side process). They are then endorsed at a regional technology management committee meeting which meets twice a year. The regional technology management committee consists of group IT management as well as regional IT managers from all companies

Figure 12.7. CLP IT governance matrix (CLP © used with permission)

CLP 中電

Group IT Governance Mat

wholly-owned subsidiaries | subsidiaries | majority own/ jointly control | joint control, Intend to exercise | joint control, not intend to exercise | associated companies

	Subsidiary Companies							Affiliated Companies*					
	Business Unit				Functional*			Business Unit			Functional*		
Key Decision Area	Head of BU / ITSC	Director Group IT	Group IT Functional Review	Local Head of IT	Local HR	FIN**	O&C**	Head of BU	Director Group IT	Local Head of IT	Local HR	FIN**	O&C**
Alignment to IT Vision and Strategy	E	A	R	R			R	A	R	R			R
Annual IT Plan and Budget	A	E		R		R	R	A		R		R	R
Exception to IT Architecture & Standards	E	A	R	R			R	A	R	R			
IT Project Initiation													
Major Development Projects	A	E		R			R	A		R			
Strategic Projects	A	E		R			R	A		R			
IT Organisation													
Major Restructuring	A	E		R	R			A		R	R		
IT Governance and Compliance													
IT Security Standards	E	A	R	R						R			
SOX Compliance Process	A	E		R		R				R			
IT Due Diligence	A	R							R	R			

Note: After approval of budget, only exception need functional review

ITSC – IT Steering Committee

A – Final Approval
E – Written Endorsement required
R – Review Required

* - Other Group Functional Heads to be involved as required
** – Group Functional Head or Delegate
BU – Business Unit

and subsidiaries. Once approved by the regional technology management committee, the standards are published to all CLP companies and affiliates to enforce compliance through the middle process of the diagram. Annual IT plan and budget submission and governance compliance are managed by the group IT planning and control (the right-hand-side process) for approval by the regional technology management committee.

E: IT Governance

IT governance is deployed throughout the regional offices. The CLP IT governance framework is illustrated in Figure 12.6. The federated IT model is preferred based on CLP's operating strategy (Locandro, 2007a). The federated model supports groupwide functional IT leadership. It allows business unit ownership and users control priorities to ensure responsiveness to local market needs. At the same time, the federated model leverages the regional synergy of pooled experience to create a critical mass of skills. These skills and experience allow CLP to set and control the business-appropriate standards to guide and ensure regional operational excellence and achieve economies of scale advantage for the group.

The IT governance framework builds on organization, process, and technology, as follows (Locandro, 2007a):

- **People/organization:**
  - Reporting structure and governance matrix:
  - Implement a *group IT governance matrix* – to balance accountabilities with decision rights, so as to speed up decision making process
  - Formalize the *functional reporting structure* – in line with the IT governance process.
- **Process**
  - IT planning and project governance:
  - Formalize the *annual IT planning process* – to "do the right things"
  - Enhance *project governance* – to "do the thing right"
- **Infrastructure and application architecture standards:**
  - Formalize the definition and application of *Group IT standards* – to improve speed to market and reduce total costs of ownership.
- **Technology**
  - Increasing business capabilities

CLP Group governance process has several main constructs. The first construct is the principle of IT decision making authority between head office and the subsidiaries or JV partners. The governance matrix illustrated in Figure 12.7 gives clarity and accountability for IT related decisions in the CLP environment.

CLP works in a federated environment whereby some key policies or decisions are made at the group level and others made at a local level. The matrix ensures that both parties have input into key decisions to allow group synergy to be maintained and exploited while at the same time allowing the local management the capability to manage costs and the business. The other main advantage is that there is no ambiguity in who has decision rights and hence decisions are streamlined.

The IT governance matrix offers many benefits. From the CLP Group level perspective, the governance matrix: (1) reduces bureaucracy and improve decision making due to clear accountabilities, (2) leverages intellectual property in *due diligence for M&A,* (3) continues to support business growth through IT synergy, and (4) provides better talent development and retention—regional employer branding. From the business-unit level perspective, the governance matrix reduces: (a) risk for execution of IT projects using group IT resources and methods, (b) *IT risk in M&A bids*, (c) development and support costs using group standards and systems, and (d) enables rapid deployment of IT projects by leveraging group knowledge and experience (Locandro, 2007a).

IT Project Governance

Table 12.3 represents the approval process for IT projects within CLP. The most important aspects of this process are that there are clear guidelines and approval criteria on how projects are approved, which require escalation for endorsement. For example standard projects that do not meet the required return in investment (ROI) percentage hurdle rate and have insufficient percent of tangible benefits require escalation of approval by both the sponsoring business unit director and the IT director. Examples are IT infrastructure projects for a business unit or projects which are increasing brand image of a marketing initiative via the Web site.

Projects and business cases are a joint effort between IT and the business. The business initiates the request highlighting the business needs for such a project and the relevant tangible and intangible benefits of the proposed project. The relevant IT delivery team estimate costs and solutions to meet the business need. They are then submitted to a central project office for review. In practice those projects which have a high ROI and a high tangible benefit get approved very quickly with no escalation. This then allows management to focus on review of strategic IT projects or those that need escalation due to low ROI or high intangible benefits.

The information from the business case is used to monitor and report, upon project completion, on the business benefits derived from the project, the Corporate KPIs that the project supports. This monitoring of project outcomes will determine how closely strategic IT projects and hence the IT strategy are aligning to business needs. (See Chapter IV for detailed description of business benefits monitoring.)

Financial criteria refer to the estimated total capital project cost for full implementation. It ensures appropriate level of investment is spent in line with corporate KPI (Locandro, 2007a).

Portfolio management practice is instituted which enables project prioritization, facilitates judicious resource scheduling, and provides overall view of IT investment to ensure that all projects are aligned with CLP strategy. Portfolio management ensures business benefit realization is monitored, which:

- Enables project prioritization/ranking
- Aids tracking on IT investment
- Compares the realized benefits against planned ROI to justify fulfillment of the governance-approved project business case
- Ensures IT delivery transparency

By measuring business benefits realization, CLP assures IT investment stands on ROI, and the realized benefits meet the business need as stipulated in the IT strategy.

Table 12.3. CLP IT governance project approval framework (CLP © used with permission)

Project Track	Financial Criteria	Structural Representation	Reporting	Approval Criteria
Strategic	Investment $ varies; Require endorsement from IT Director & BU Director	Project Steering Committee formed with BU Sponsor, BU Director, IT Director, and key stakeholders	• Monthly IT Steering Committee meeting • Monthly report to IT Project Office	ROI >= x % and % of tangible benefits >= y %
Major Development	➢ HK$xM Large expenditure	Project Steering Committee formed with BU Sponsor, BU Director, IT Director, and key stakeholders	• Monthly IT Steering Committee meeting • Monthly report to IT Project Office	ROI >= a % and % of tangible benefits >= b %
Standard Development	> HK$xM and <= HK$yM Range $ between small and medium expenditure	Project Management Office with COE[9] Manager, BU Sponsor, and Business Improvement Manager	• Monthly report to IT Project Office	ROI >= m % and % of tangible benefits >= n %
Continuous Improvement	Support and minor enhancement <= HK$xM Minor expenditure		• Monthly report to BU Sponsor	No threshold on ROI or % of tangible benefits

Project Track	Normal Level of Approval	Escalation Level of Approval
Strategic	IT Director & BU Director	IT Steering Committee to have visibility of all strategic projects
Major Development	IT Director & BU Director	IT Steering Committee
Standard Development	IT Project Office and BU Sponsor	IT Director and BU Director
Continuous Improvement	BU's Business Improvement Manager, COE Manager, and BU Sponsor	N/A

Portfolio management practice has ensured that IT investments are aligned with the business strategy to create the desired business capabilities. To that end, as a result of executing the business-aligned IT strategy, CLP has shifted its IT application (capital spend) portfolio mix from heavily weighted on infrastructure (10%) and transactional (82%) applications in 2004, when the focus was to create the IT platforms for operational

Table 12.4. Business value delivered by IT strategy implementation (CLP © used with permission)

Business Improvement		Achievement
New web site	: Move in/out per month	▪ **Increased usage by 100%**
	Internet-bills request	▪ **number of customers**
Call Answering System	: Average call wait time	▪ **over 80% reduction**
	Customer usage rate	▪ **Increased by 10%**
	Customer Satisfaction Level	▪ **Increased to 95%**
Postman Beat Code for HK Post		▪ **Postage savings of $x per year**

excellence, to heavily weighted on informational (40%) and strategic (27%) applications in 2007. This is explained by the shift in focus from internal (2004) to external market (2007) where new business capabilities to greatly differentiate CLP services are required via greater business analytics (*business intelligence*) power and new online business model (*CLP Online*). This new strategic focus builds on the earlier IT platforms and *reinforces the CLP operational excellence strategy*. In the same period, investments in infrastructure and transaction applications are maintained (albeit at slower rates) reaching a mix in 2007 of 22% and 12% respectively. (See Chapter VII for details in IT portfolio management and portfolio mix for high performance organizations.)

Rigorous execution of CLP IT governance has resulted in: (a) maximizing of business benefits with greater returns on investment, (b) better management of project portfolio, (c) maximizing the value and improving the transparency of IT spending, (d) enabling benefit tracking and realization, (e) highlighting contribution of IT to corporate KPIs, and (f) alignment of strategic investment with business strategy and priorities (Locandro, 2006).

COMMERCIAL BENEFITS DELIVERED BY CLP GROUP IT STRATEGY

The business benefits are shown for illustration purposes only. For commercial reasons, some results are desensitized while preserving the context within which they are being measured.

(1) IT-enabled business benefits were measured diligently for the period 2005–2007, as shown in Table 12.4.

(2) Benefits/costs curve – The cumulative 2005–2007 NPV project benefits to costs ratio is monitored on an annual basis, as shown in Figure 12.7. It shows that through rigorous

IT governance practice and its attendant IT project portfolio management practices, CLP has been consistently achieving cumulative business benefits of greater than twice its total expenditure over the last few years.

(3) Improving IT operational performance (2004–2006)

CLP's IT spending is *lower* than the industrial average in the past three years. For example (Locandro 2007a, 2007b, and 2007c):

- **IT spend as percent of revenue:**
  - Industry average 3% (2004) to 1.9% (2006)
  - CLP: 1.7% (2004) to 1.4% (2006)
- **IT spend per customer:**
  - Industry average: 76 to 56
  - CLP: 28 to 23

IT Service Level Achievement 2006

CLP has achieved a *higher* service level of IT help desk support than the industry average. For example (Locandro 2007a, 2007b, and 2007c):

- Queue time of IT help desk calls
  - Industry average is 23.1 seconds
  - CLP is 9 seconds

Figure 12.8. CLP IT benefits/costs performance (CLP © used with permission)

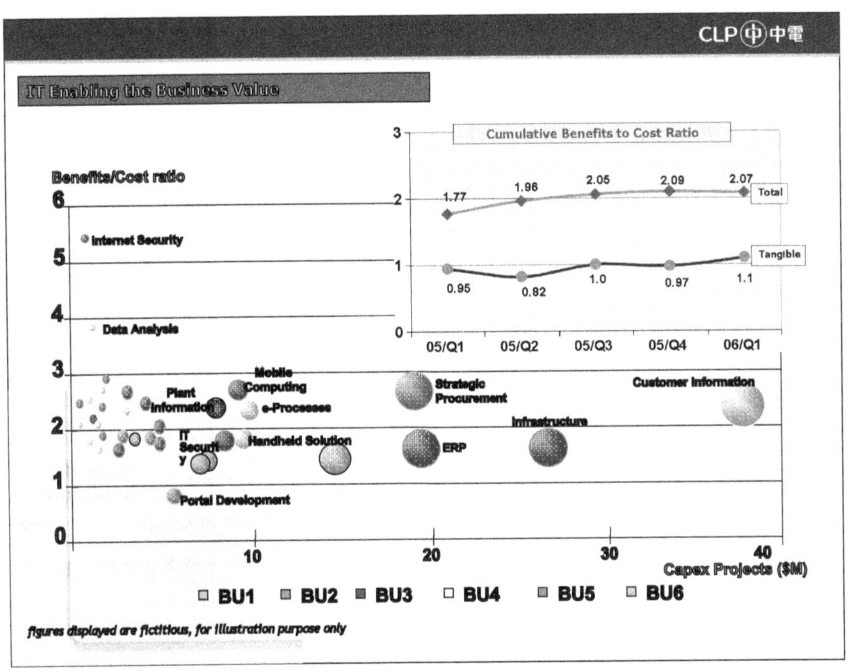

- Calls resolved with 24 hours by IT help desk
  - Industry average is 72.7%
  - CLP is 97.3%
- Resolution rate for application-specific problem by IT help desk
  - Industry average is 57.2%
  - CLP is 64.4%
- User account and security profile administration request handles within one working day
  - Industry average is 69.5%
  - CLP is 97.6%

The dedication to customer service excellence has gained widespread recognition for CLP from the community, winning many prestigious awards including:

- "The Hong Kong Award for Services: Customer Service"
- "The Customer Service Excellence Awards" organized by the Hong Kong Association for Customer Service Excellence

Furthermore, as a result of this industry leading IT service performance, business investment in IT has been increasing to gain operational efficiencies. With significant increase in asset base, operational expense has been contained in real terms despite pressure of natural increases. It has reduced from over 5% to 4% and sustaining. Sustainable productivity and efficiency initiatives deliver a low maintenance to asset ratio (Locandro, 2007).

Driving IT group synergy has resulted in cost optimization. Regional IT support and procurement contract has leveraged economies of scale to the benefit of the CLP Group. For example, an aggregate cost savings of over US$7 million was achieved across the Group in 2005–2006, through acceleration of IT project implementation, and discount for software and hardware purchase. Further, nearly US$1.5 million was recovered from support services provided to group business through offering such services as infrastructure and hosting services (e-mail, storage, etc.), project implementation guidance, and consultancy to overseas IT operations (Locandro, 2007a, 2007b, 2007c).

This has helped drive the CLP Operational Excellence business strategy and resulted in the reduction in operations costs with an increase in customer service (Locandro, 2007c).

SUMMARY

Over the last four years, CLP's business-aligned IT has consistently delivered measurable business value (as seen in the last section), in line with the business strategy, through diligent IT management practices of enterprise architecture, project portfolio management, and IT governance.

Recent business climates change has necessitated a thorough gap analysis of CLP IT environment resulting in a refinement of the IT strategy. The emergent CLP IT strategy will ensure: (Locandro 2007a, 2007b, 2007c):

- Continued drive towards operational excellence – particularly in the areas of asset management, operational reliability, and environmental regulatory compliance.

- Heightened focus on superior customer service through online service innovation and various technology channels, allowing real time customer interaction with CLP.
- Development of IT organizational capital focused on economies of scale through standardization and synergy to support regional growth through a clear framework of accountability between IT and the business and group IT and local IT subsidiaries and JV partners.

REFERENCES

CLP Annual Report. (2006). Retrieved September 7, 2008, from https://www.clpgroup.com/Inv/FinInfo/FinRpt/FinRpt2007/Pages/FinancialReport2007.aspx

CLP Annual Report. (2007). Retrieved September 7, 2008, from www.clpgroup.com, https://www.clpgroup.com/Inv/FinInfo/FinRpt/FinRpt2007/Pages/FinancialReport2007.aspx

CLP CEO Report. (2006). Retrieved September 7, 2008, from www.clpgroup.com, https://www.clpgroup.com/Inv/FinInfo/FinRpt/FinRpt2007/Pages/FinancialReport2007.aspx

CLP Chairman's Statement. (2007). Retrieved September 7, 2008, from www.clpgroup.com, https://www.clpgroup.com/Inv/FinInfo/FinRpt/FinRpt2007/Pages/FinancialReport2007.aspx

Kaplan, R. S., & Norton, D. P. (2004). *Strategy maps: Converting intangible assets into tangible outcomes*. Boston: Harvard Business School Press.

Locandro, J. (2006). *CLP Group IT vision and strategy*. CLP Internal Publication.

Locandro, J. (2007a, September). *CLP's experience: IT governance*. CLP Internal Publication.

Locandro, J. (2007b, August). *Chairman office update*. CLP Internal Publication.

Locandro, J. (2007c, June). *Innovation for delivering operational excellence to customers*. CLP Internal Publication.

Weill, P., & Broadbent, M. (1998). *Leveraging the new infrastructure: How market leaders capitalize on information technology*. Boston: Harvard Business School Press.

ENDNOTES

1. Written consent (via e-mail) from both the CIO and the corporation are sought before the study can begin.
2. This is by means of 'reconstructing' the company's business-aligned IT strategy into a strategy map model, using Kaplan & Norton (2004) principles.
3. Permission has been granted by CLP Group to publish the case example including their tables, graphs and diagrams.
4. CLP's renewable energy portfolio now includes solar (Victoria, Australia), small hydro (Huaiji, Guangdong Province), wind (Changdao, Shangdong Province), and biomass energy (Boxing, Shangdong Province) sources, in addition to the traditional coal and nuclear powered generators.
5. As of the end of 2007, 5.1% of CLP generating capacity is supplied by renewable sources three years ahead of target set in 2004.

6 CLP's service strategy is to publicly commit to delivering a reliable, safe, and adequate power supply and provide excellent customer service, with explicit service targets as defined in Table 12.1, at a reasonable cost, to its more than two million customers. CLP pledges to continuously improve both its productivity and efficiency for the benefit of their customers.

7 Asset management process is process that CLP uses to manage the construction, maintenance, and operation of a comprehensive set of fixed assets it owns to ensure maximum return on asset—assets operating efficiently and generating maximum revenues and profit at minimum total cost of ownership.

8 Requirements engineering method is used to define the information requirements of the core processes. This usually involves IT experts holding workshops or interviews with the business owners of the core processes.

9 COE=Center of Excellence

About the Authors

Eng Chew is professor of business and IT strategy at the University of Technology, Sydney (UTS), and part-time Gartner advisor. From 2005–2008, he held the UTS-Gartner chair of business and IT strategy at UTS. He is a former chief information officer of SingTel Optus, and has over 25 years of industry experience in IT and telecommunications in Australia. His achievements include delivery of several hundreds of million Australian dollars of business value through business process reengineering and organizational transformation. Under the Gartner chair, he has produced insightful research papers for Gartner on China's ICT telecommunications industry market trends, China's ICT R&D and education institutions, and China's CIO leadership maturity. Prior to Optus, Professor Chew has held senior roles with Telstra Research Laboratories, Australian Centre for Unisys Software, and Digital Equipment Corporation. He had also held the chair of the joint International Standards Organization-International Telecommunications Union (ISO/ITU) Standards Committee on Open Distributed Processing (1992–1997). Professor Chew's research interest is on information and technology management and leadership, particularly in the context of service innovation. With his PhD research students, current research investigations include: leadership and innovation, business-IT alignment, business process management, service architecture, and organizational factors of information security and enterprise architecture. He also leads a UTS research unit on business intelligence and information management for commercial applications. He teaches graduate class to IT and business professionals in IT strategy and management within the IT Management Program of UTS, on which this book is based. Professor Chew also serves as consultant to industry. He has advised companies in Australia and Asia Pacific region. He is a non-executive board director of an IT firm. Professor Chew received his BE from the University of Melbourne, MEngSc and PhD from the University of Sydney, all in electrical engineering. His PhD research was on telecommunications software controlled switching systems.

Petter Gottschalk completed his MBA in Germany (Technische Universität Berlin), MSc in the U.S. (Dartmouth College), and DBA in the UK (Brunel University). Dr. Gottschalk is professor of information strategy and knowledge management in the Department of Leadership and Organization at the Norwegian School of Management. He has been the CEO of ABB Datacable and the CIO of ABB Norway. His current research is focused on IT strategy and knowledge management systems.

Index

D

E

F

G

H

I

S

T

U

V

W

X

Y

www.ingramcontent.com/pod-product-compliance
Lightning Source LLC
LaVergne TN
LVHW062244200926
848484LV00006B/1610
* 9 7 8 1 5 9 9 0 4 8 0 2 4 *